A WAMPUM DENIED

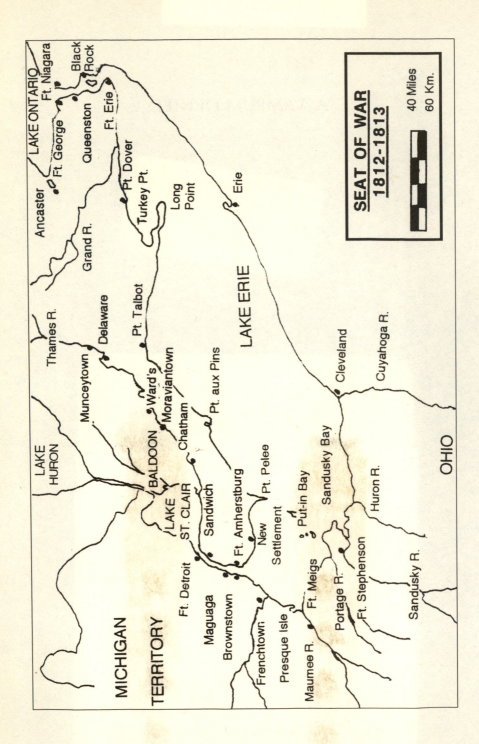

SEAT OF WAR
1812-1813

40 Miles
60 Km.

LAKE ONTARIO
Ft. Niagara
Black Rock
Ft. George
Queenston
Ft. Erie
Ancaster
Pt. Dover
Grand R.
Turkey Pt.
Long Point
Erie

LAKE ERIE

Thames R.
Delaware
Pt. Talbot
Munceytown
Pt. aux Pins
Cleveland
Cuyahoga R.

LAKE HURON
Ward's
Moraviantown
BALDOON
Chatham

LAKE ST. CLAIR
Sandwich
Ft. Amherstburg
New Settlement
Pt. Pelee
Put-in Bay
Sandusky Bay

MICHIGAN
TERRITORY
Ft. Detroit
Maguaga
Brownstown
Frenchtown
Presque Isle
Maumee R.
Ft. Meigs
Portage R.
Ft. Stephenson
Huron R.
Sandusky R.

OHIO

A WAMPUM DENIED
PROCTER'S WAR OF 1812

Second Edition

Sandy Antal

CARLETON LIBRARY SERIES 191

McGill-Queen's University Press
Montreal & Kingston • London • Ithaca

© Sandy Antal and McGill-Queen's University Press 2011

ISBN 978-0-7735-3937-2

Legal deposit fourth quarter 2011
Bibliothèque nationale du Québec

First edition, 1998

Printed in Canada on acid-free paper that is 100% ancient forest free
(100% post-consumer recycled), processed chlorine free

This book was first published with the help of a grant from the Canadian
Federation for the Humanities and Social Sciences, through the Aid
to Scholarly Publications Program, using funds provided by the Social
Sciences and Humanities Research Council of Canada.

McGill-Queen's University Press acknowledges the support of the Canada
Council for the Arts for our publishing program. We also acknowledge the
financial support of the Government of Canada through the Canada Book
Fund for our publishing activities.

Library and Archives Canada Cataloguing in Publication Data

Antal, Sandy, 1950–
    A wampum denied: Procter's War of 1812

(The Carleton library; 191)
Includes bibliographical references and index.
ISBN 978-0-7735-3937-2

    1. Procter, Henry, d. 1822. Canada – History –
War of 1812. I. Title. II. Series.

FC443.P76A58 1997   971.034   C97-900272-9
E353.1P76A58 1997

Captions for part title page illustrations:
Page 1: The old windmill at Sandwich, one of several that dotted the
Detroit River in 1812 (from *Canadian Achievement: The Detroit River
District* by Hugh Cowan). Page 65: The Battle of Frenchtown; page 189:
The attack on Ft. Stephenson; page 313: The Detroit River and vicinity
(from *The War of 1812* by Benjamin Lossing).

To Jane, Kathy, and Peter
for faith and patience
beyond the call ...

CARLETON LIBRARY SERIES

The Carleton Library Series publishes books about Canadian economics, geography, history, politics, public policy, society and culture, and related topics, in the form of leading new scholarship and reprints of classics in these fields. The series is funded by Carleton University, published by McGill-Queen's University Press, and is under the guidance of the Carleton Library Series Editorial Board, which consists of faculty members of Carleton University. Suggestions and proposals for manuscripts and new editions of classic works are welcome and may be directed to the Carleton Library Series Editorial Board c/o the Library, Carleton University, Ottawa K1S 5B6, at cls@carleton.ca, or on the web at www.carleton.ca/cls.

CONTENTS

ILLUSTRATIONS

After the Seven Years' War of 1756-63, the British government presented the Natives of the "Old Northwest" with the Great Wampum Belt. One end of the symmetrical bead arrangement was white, the other darker, each end featuring a black hand. The belt was joined in the centre by the figure of a heart, signifying the common interests of the two sides. During the following decades, the Natives engaged in a losing struggle against relentless American encroachment onto their lands.

In 1811, the Shawnee war chief, Tecumseh, produced the Great Wampum in council as an invitation to rejuvinate the alliance in his forthcoming struggle with the United States. British officials accepted the offer, repeatedly assuring their allies that there would be no peace without the recognition of a Native state south of the Great Lakes. Despite a string of stunning military successes, British-Native fortunes waned, as did the notion of a Native state, and by September 1813, Tecumseh threatened to cut the Great Wampum in two.

This is the story of the War of 1812 on the Detroit frontier.

PREFACE

"The major issues will be recognizable because they are basically with us today: the conflicts between coloured and mixed races; self determination and colonialism; local leadership and centralized government; individual "natural" rights and general welfare; private contract and national policy; casual and efficient use of land; the old order and the new; primitivism and progress; savagery and spirituality in our natures; cool discussion and open warfare; cruelty and humanity in the treatment of enemies; propaganda and respect for truth."

Carl F. Klinck, in his Preface to
Tecumseh: Fact and Fiction in Early Records

THE WAR OF 1812 was a strange and complex conflict. Although historians attribute its principal causes to maritime issues, the majority of combatants on the distant Detroit frontier were backwoods settlers and Native warriors, few of whom had ever seen an ocean-going vessel. While U.S. expansionists hoped to establish a new border along the Ottawa River, their British counterparts envisioned the Ohio River as the new American boundary. Loyalist myth-makers credited British success that first year to "the bold Canadian" militiamen, while military historians focussed on the contributions of the regular troops. These Eurocentric views barely acknowledge the critical players on the British side, the Native warriors, who cared little for "free trade and sailors rights." Ironically, while neither the British nor American belligerents achieved their anticipated territorial gains, it was the Natives who lost lands to both parties during the conflict and as a result of it.

Just as British officials justified the Native alliance as a means by which to augment their shortage of troops, the warriors' involvement was also driven by self-interest. The partnership was based on the mutual benefits to be derived from the creation of a Native homeland, a British protectorate in "the Old Northwest." Britain had passed this vast territory (consisting of the modern states of Michigan, Ohio, Indiana, Illinois, and Wisconsin), to the U.S. after the Revolutionary War but considered it Native territory. Given the pattern of American encroachment into this region, the declaration of war in 1812 provided leading colonial élites with an opportunity to join with Native zealots in the common quest of its reconstitution as a Native state. To the tribesmen, this allied goal was signified by the "Great Wampum."

The military members of this allied camp drew their plans well before the outbtreak of hostilities. With war declared, British diplomats struggled to achieve a negotiated settlement but found themselves working at cross-purposes with Maj. Gen. Isaac Brock, who had pledged that there would be no peace until Native lands were restored. To this end, he promptly "ceded" Michigan Territory to the Crown, thus assuring continuation of the American war effort now aimed at its recovery. To the allied expansionists (the British, "Canadian," and Native leaders), an extended contest provided opportunities for further conquest in Ohio and the territories of Indiana and Illinois. With Brock's untimely death a few weeks after the cession, military leadership of this ambitious undertaking fell to Col. Henry Procter, commander of the British forces on the Detroit frontier (styled the Right Division).

Although Brock and Procter wrote of pre-emptive strikes and acts of "offensive defense," their actions constituted much more than imaginative military thrusts. Brock revealed his purpose, after ceding Michigan to Britain, by convincing his government to embrace the issue of a Native homeland as a mandatory condition in peace talks. Procter's thesis on the northwest and his subsequent actions were fully consistent with this aim, even when it jeopardized his military judgment. Through spirited operations in Michigan, Indiana, and Ohio, he almost realized the allied expansionist goal, one that would significantly have altered the course of North American history. Indeed, at war's end, the opening British position at the peace talks featured an unconditional demand for recognition of a Native state south of the Great Lakes.

As the central wartime figure on the Detroit frontier, Procter squared off successively and successfully against generals William Hull, James Winchester, and William Harrison during the first year of the conflict.

The logistic and strategic failures that led to his ultimate defeat at Moraviantown have largely been ignored as posterity attributed the disaster to his mishandling. Of all the British generals, only Procter was thoroughly disgraced, leaving a murky legacy of his actual role.

Procter's critics can be grouped into four distinct categories. First, the commander-in-chief in North America, Sir George Prevost, found it politically expedient to blame him for the British defeat in the west, even though London made it clear that a sacrifice was unnecessary. Second, two of Procter's teenaged subalterns chose to abuse him in postwar accounts. The writings of John Richardson, Canada's first novelist, were particularly bitter, driven by a grudge against his commander over promotion issues. Nor was the other, James Cochrane, a brother to the prosecutor at Procter's trial, entirely objective in his assessment. Nonetheless, their biased and simplistic criticisms have exerted a tremendous impact on subsequent interpretations, leading military historian J. McKay Hitsman to conclude, "Of the British officers, only Procter managed to blunder consistently." Third, in a bizarre misplacement of responsibilities, American accounts have extolled Tecumseh's humanity while depicting Procter as a diabolical brute for the atrocities perpetrated by his allied "demons from hell." Finally, romantic sympathies for the expropriated Natives have led writers to attribute the demise of Tecumseh and his cause to Procter's shortcomings. In this vein, John Sugden declared in his work, *Tecumseh's Last Stand*, "Procter was deficient in one of the most important ingredients of a commander—leadership," a revelation that does little to reflect on his previous wartime record and an unblemished military career that spanned three decades. Focussed blame remains a fashionable method by which to explain away unhappy and complicated events.

Other writers have sensed that military failure is seldom attributable to a solo performance and have judged Procter's actions with increasing circumspection. Pierre Berton viewed him overwhelmed by difficulties, while George Stanley emphasized the insurmountable logistical challenges he faced. Jack Hyatt added further perspective to the argument, in his biographical sketch, by pointing out that generalized condemnations seldom acknowledge Procter's significant contributions early in the war that were "beyond reproach." While Procter has been more frequently condemned than defended, a comprehensive assessment of his role remains missing. The opinion parade has muddied such rudimentary points as Procter's age and birthplace. Even the spelling of his name varies by account. It seems that the very memories

of this man have been "salted." The cameo image of Procter's abandonment of Tecumseh on the field of battle remains a popular one.

Although failure is easier to condemn than explain, Procter's record
on the Detroit frontier deserves at least a hearing, particularly in view
of the far-reaching implications of his defeat. British control of
Michigan Territory and the Western District of Upper Canada was
broken, as Americans occupied these areas until war's end. The mighty
Native confederacy was shattered, Tecumseh, the very embodiment of
its aspirations, killed. Furthermore, the British flanks at Michilimackinac and the Niagara frontier became exposed to attack in the face
of a determined American general offensive. To add to these calamities,
a celebrated regiment became prisoner as had a naval squadron, major
embarrassments in British military and naval annals. On learning of
Procter's defeat and fearing total disaster, Prevost repeatedly directed
the wholesale evacuation of Upper Canada.

Given the geographic implications of the western theatre, it
remains for the reader to appreciate travelling time in communications,
a critical consideration during periods of rapidly unfolding events.
Amherstburg was over two hundred miles from the Niagara frontier,
while the closest American centre to Detroit was 150 miles distant.
This isolation left water transport as the critical vehicle for both correspondence and resupply. A schooner could average 60 miles per day
under typical conditions. Adverse winds could keep it windbound for
weeks, while a good tail wind could drive a trim vessel the length of
Lake Erie in one day. Travel by horseback averaged 30 to 40 miles a
day, although express riders were capable of covering 60 miles by
nightfall. While troop movements were more complicated, a disciplined, unencumbered corps could travel 40 miles a day in an exhausting forced march, but seldom averaged more than half that in practice.
The state of roads and weather conditions could severely hamper
movements by land. Sad indeed were the soldiers at day's end after
struggling through the mud with their 60-pound packs. Overland conveyance of heavy stores (suggestively termed impedimenta) was even
more nightmarish and sometimes impossible. The principal strategic
lesson of the War of 1812 was to avoid such situations through the
maintenance of naval superiority.

In attempting to avoid a purely "drums and bugles" history, I found
it necessary, nonetheless, to devote considerable attention to the military engagements as these were closely linked to allied relations. Given
the isolation of the Detroit country, strategy and logistics, facilitated

by naval support, determined the outcomes. Commanders aimed to engage the enemy under favourable tactical conditions, or at least in a manner that offered prospects of gaining those advantages. As no commander willingly engaged in battle to lose, his worst fear was to be placed into a circumstance whereby he had no chance of gaining the advantage. Although "victory or death" made for rousing rhetoric, most commanders and soldiers alike were quick to consider other alternatives when victory became unattainable. They were only human.

A word on the Natives is also in order. Although frequently lumped together as "the Indians," they were never homogeneous in organization or unanimous in conduct during the war. Some were neutral. Others were pro-American of necessity. While those allied to the British side were formed into a loose confederacy, it would be simplistic to overlook the fact that they spoke diverse languages and suspended bitter inter-tribal feuds only to confront a common threat. These tribes were, in fact, distinct nations. Even the warriors of a given tribe seldom projected unified views and actions. As a consequence, the greatest of their leaders, Tecumseh, was not commander (in a military sense) of the Native confederacy or even of the Shawnee nation. He was a war chief whose vision and strong character made him leader of and spokesman for confederated interests. Individual warriors were free to subscribe to any school of thought they deemed appropriate and equally free to cancel their subscriptions at any time. Owing allegiance to no one, they fought in their traditional individualistic manner and, when it served their interests, grudgingly observed the White man's rules of war.

In reconstructing events, I have utilized wide-ranging archival and printed primary sources. Many of the records of the Right Division were pilfered during the retreat of 1813, while the official documents of the 41st Regiment were "lost," probably to fire, in the spring of that year. Thus a meaningful study of events called for a lengthy search for surviving records that have become badly scattered. The Procter Court Martial transcripts were highly useful in tracing the events of the Thames campaign, while the seldom used transcripts of Lt. Benoit Bender's trial provided a detailed insight into the engagements at Frenchtown and Fort Meigs, as well as the internal politics of the 41st Regiment. The *Narrative* and *Notes* of Ensign James Cochrane included helpful details on British actions in the summer of 1813. The virtually unknown documents captured at the battle of Moraviantown, Procter's *Miscellaneous Intercepted Correspondence*, now held by the U.S.

National Archives, articulate clearly his thinking on the contemplated Native state and include the only documented British explanation for the controversial "massacre" at Frenchtown. Procter's views further emerged in two obscure and anonymous writings, *Lucubrations of Humphrey Ravelin* and the *Quarterly Review* article, "Campaigns in the Canadas." The seldom consulted but authoritative *Journal of Major John Norton* showed Tecumseh's allied relations in a different light than has been generally represented. In addition, the little-known *Letters of Veritas* served to expose contemporary views of Procter and Prevost. To further gauge contemporary perceptions, I have also utilized British, "Canadian," and American newspaper entries.

I remain grateful to Dr. W.A.B. Douglas (former Director of History, National Defence Headquarters, Ottawa), for his assistance in bringing to Canada the Procter Court Martial transcripts, previously available only in the Public Records Office, Kew, England. In past years, the scholarly insights of Professors Syd Wise of Carleton University and Jack Hyatt of the University of Western Ontario helped "shape my tools" for this work. I must thank Donald E. Graves for his useful suggestions to part of my first draft. Likewise, I am indebted to Larry Nelson, Director of Fort Meigs State Memorial for his observations on a later draft and for rushing source materials to me with complimentary confidence. The staff of Fort Malden National Historical Site (past and present), Tim Dubé of the National Archives of Canada, Dennis Carter Edwards of Parks Canada, and Lt. Bryn Owen of the Welch Regimental Museum, Cardiff Castle, Wales, were most helpful in locating and furnishing specific primary materials. Stewart Sutherland graciously shared items of biographical detail from his files on British officers. The other readers, Robert Allen, Robert Malcomson, and Jane Antal were of help in making apparent the transparent in my writing. It is with regret that I mention the passing of Robert Allen just months before the printing of this book. Finally, I am extremely grateful to Peter Rindlisbacher for the use of his excellent paintings. In attempting to fill a void in this remarkable period of North American history, I hope to have done justice to the facts.

PREFACE to the 2011 Edition

IT IS FITTING that this third printing of *A Wampum Denied* should appear for the bicentennial anniversary of the War of 1812. Aside from minor corrections, the text is essentially unchanged from its original form.

All told, the preparation of this book spanned a period of three decades. Given the scant attention previously devoted to allied (meaning Anglo-Native) operations on the Detroit frontier, it was no small task to gather the scattered materials, reconstruct the events, and present them in a focused and comprehensive narrative. As the first in-depth examination of those operations, the findings diverge substantially from those contained in most writings of the last hundred years.

Previous works overwhelmingly attribute the allied defeat in the west to the alleged incompetence of the local commander, Henry Procter. This single issue analysis falls egregiously short in a number of ways. First, it tends to substitute ill-substantiated opinion for research. Second, the persistent negative emphasis on Procter's role has overshadowed major issues such as Isaac Brock's cession of Michigan and his pledge to the Native chiefs that their lands lost to the Americans south of the Great Lakes would be restored. Third, this approach fails to reconcile the repeated allied thrusts into Ohio, Michigan, and Indiana with Governor-General George Prevost's official position that this was to be a "defensive war." Instead, these incursions into the U.S. are often represented as a series of isolated events, devoid of any meaningful pattern. Last, the personality-based approach neglects those considerations associated with any serious military study, namely the elements and principles of war.

One does not have to be of a military bent to appreciate the disparity of the contending sides on the Detroit River frontier. Fort Meigs was the largest wooden fortification built in North America to that time, while Harrison's invasion of the Western District in 1813 featured the largest amphibious operation conducted by U.S. forces to that time. Indeed, after Brock's cession of Michigan, the Madison administration committed virtually unlimited funds for its recovery. Commanding a small force of British regulars, augmented by Native and militia auxiliaries of intermittent utility, Procter's prospects of ultimate success were hardly assured.

When this book first appeared in print, accounts with a prominent negative focus on Procter were alive and well, so much so that I deliberately kept my distance from adherents of that simplistic school of thought in order to avoid any chance of contamination. It was time to point out that "the emperor had no clothes." Responses were predictable. To keep attention focused on Procter, some have represented this work as revisionist, aimed at defending him. As the writers who suggest this are anything but disinterested, I can only treat their comments with the attention they deserve. My aim (as declared at the outset and implicit in the title) is to provide an account of the war on the Detroit River frontier. While Procter is certainly the central and continuous figure, the broader issues are of far greater importance.

A number of recurring questions have been raised by both readers and presentation audiences on both sides of the border and I address them here.

BROCK'S PROMISE TO THE NATIVE LEADERS

Brock's commitment to the Native chiefs is crucial to understanding allied operations. It explains his unilateral cession of Michigan Territory, the subsequent allied thrusts deep into the U.S, the active resettlement of displaced tribes along the Detroit River, and Procter's threat to deport those American residents of Michigan who refused to take the oath of allegiance to King George III. Furthermore, the Anglo-Native crisis of late 1813 emerges in an entirely new light when viewed within the context of Brock's promise.

An example of Brock's promises came to light recently during the Caldwell settlement. For almost two centuries the Caldwells, a small Native band of southwestern Ontario, had been petitioning the

Canadian government for a tract of land as promised to them in return for their participation in the War of 1812. The offer had been made to them by Matthew Elliott of the Indian Department but it had originated with Brock, the administrator of Upper Canada. As Brock died early in the war, leaving no written record of his commitment, the Caldwells were left with nothing but their oral traditions with which to argue their case. After almost two hundred years, their persistence paid off and in 2010, the federal government agreed to fund a community centre for the band in the vicinity of Leamington and Point Pelee.

The greatest difficulty with the Caldwell claim was its lack of supporting documentation. However, when viewed within the pattern of Brock's other promises, the Caldwell contention appears credible. Indeed, Brock was so desperate for manpower at the outbreak of war that he offered inducements to anyone who would listen. For instance, he led the Six Nations of the Grand River to believe that their demand for sovereign status would receive a favourable hearing if they took up arms. Also, he assured the Essex and Kent militia that, in return for their early participation in the war, the Fort Amherstburg garrison would be increased tenfold to sixteen hundred regular troops, so that the local militia would be excused of further military service and free to tend their farms. But Brock's most ambitious promise was extended to the Native tribes on American soil – that he would recover their lands that had been lost to American encroachment.

Although Brock's death early in the war precluded fulfillment of these promises, the Natives kept their part of the agreement, consistently forming the largest element of the allied combatants in the west, outnumbering the redcoats by as much as six to one. Indeed, without their participation, Upper Canada would have been overrun early in the war, a point that Eurocentric interpretations tend to ignore or minimize.

THE ROOT CAUSE OF THE ALLIED DEFEAT

In hindsight, it is evident that the outcome of the war in the west was the result of the Americans committing superior human and material resources that the British simply failed to match, making the allied effort a case of strategic over-reach, doomed to failure. Traditional accounts, if they mention the notably weak British presence at all, point to the primacy of the Napoleonic struggle in Europe. But this explanation falls short. By early 1813, Prevost had overcome his initial doubts about the possibility of a successful stand in the west and actually committed substantial resources to that front; however, these materialized either "too little, too late" or not at all. Facing a determined American offensive while handicapped on both land and sea, Procter was left to sustain himself largely on Prevost's unfulfilled promises and his bizarre exhortation that Procter ought to remedy his pressing shortages at the expense of the enemy!

But if Prevost had indeed allocated resources for the west in early 1813, why did they not arrive? The answer is found far to the east, at the principal American naval base on the lakes, Sacket's Harbour. Had Prevost eliminated that facility in a timely fashion, results might have been very different. But the governor delayed that assault until the spring of 1813, by which time the Americans had strengthened their defences and he was repulsed with heavy losses. Worse yet, by the time he attacked, the U.S. Navy had already emerged from port to support the capture of Forts York, George, and Erie. During these assaults, vital armaments, marine stores, and other necessities intended for the west were either captured or destroyed. Moreover, the destruction of an almost finished frigate in the weakly defended York dockyard deprived the British of their anticipated mastery on Lake Ontario, meaning that minimal resources would become available for Lake Erie. Similarly, the troops intended for Procter were detained as they were required to deal with the Americans on the Niagara River frontier. Thus Proctor was left to face the American 1813 offensive without the resources that had been specifically allotted to him.

The British failure at Sacket's Harbour had dramatic results on the western frontier, beginning with their loss of mastery on Lake Erie. That defeat, in turn, made allied positions untenable, strategically, tactically, and logistically. Procter's diminished options then boiled down to a timely allied retreat. But at this critical juncture, an enraged Tecumseh reminded the allied council of Brock's unfulfilled promise to help the Natives recover their lost lands. Refusing to accompany the British retreat, he threatened to dissolve the alliance. Indian Department officials feared that the furious warriors would ravage the Detroit River communities and perhaps fall on the British troops. With the Americans massing for invasion, Procter picked the best of his bad options, resorting to a fateful compromise. He agreed to limit his retreat to the Thames River, a decision that culminated in the allied defeat at Moraviantown. Subsequently, southwestern Ontario remained occupied territory until the end of the war.

It is generally recognized that loss of mastery on the Great Lakes was the single greatest mistake made by the British during the war. Nowhere did the adverse effects of that error figure more prominently than in the western theatre.

BLAME AND THE PERSONALITY-BASED INTERPRETATION

One must bear in mind that Procter's court martial was initiated and managed by the same Prevost whose command decisions had impacted heavily on allied operations in the west. Even before receiving Procter's official report on the Thames campaign, the governor, on the basis of unreliable information, publicly denounced Procter's role. Yet, when required to articulate formal charges, it took him a full year to do so. The singular wording of those charges, that Procter "did not take the best measures conceivable," raises self-evident questions about their fairness. Held against such impossible standards, who of the British commanders, Prevost included, would not be found guilty? For their part, senior officials in London recognized that the western frontier had been overwhelmed. As if anticipating Prevost's reaction, the minister for war and colonies advised him that a scapegoat was not necessary but that trans-Atlantic direction arrived too late to have effect and Procter's promising army career was ruined.

Prevost's dealings with Procter might have been less than commendable but they were not the primary vehicle of Procter's historical condemnation. That distinction falls to *Richardson's War of 1812*, a thrilling account authored by John Richardson, destined to gain posthumous fame as Canada's first novelist. Although a delightful read, it is also error-ridden, self-serving, and highly opinionated. By definition a primary account, it was written more than three decades after the fact, based on impressions from his teen-aged years. Richardson's grudge against Procter over promotion issues permeates his entire book, making it less than objective. While uncritically incorporating Richardson's strictures, later writers have consistently failed to mention that even he attributes the "destitution" and "physical disorganization" of Procter's command to Prevost's "imbecility," placing Prevost "at the head of calumny" for the allied defeat in the west.

THE EVOLVING HISTORIOGRAPHY

To understand how the negative personality-based interpretation came about, a chronological sampling of the principal relevant works is useful.

Only a handful of writers have actually examined the court martial transcripts and, through inattention to the findings, many have found Procter guilty of the very charges of which he was acquitted! That pattern is rooted in *Richardson's War of 1812*, which received wide circulation through several editions. As there was no comparable work to contest Richardson's opinions, his book emerged as the most widely consulted source on the war in the west. It established the trend toward a negative personality-based approach, one that has been readily embraced by generations of writers as an easy alternative to serious research.

Interestingly, the earliest Canadian writers on the war, Robert Christie, James Hannay, and Robert Lucas, ignore Richardson's account and consider Procter's defeat inevitable, the result of Prevost's neglect. They represent Procter's overall record as creditable and acknowledge his valuable services in holding the line against superior numbers for the first year of the conflict. This view was shared even by Alexander Casselman, editor of the popular 1902 edition of *Richardson's War of 1812*. Casselman added that in light of the neglect that Procter endured, he was "disgracefully used." Overwhelmingly, though, subsequent general works deferred to Richardson's views. The detailed works of Pierre Berton, Victor Lauriston, and Paul Morgan Couture, which reinforced the earliest interpretations, were noteworthy exceptions.

Negative interpretations of Procter's role gained such currency that they influenced the works of even fair-minded writers. Berton's otherwise balanced and factual account in *Flames Across the Border* (1981) has Procter putting the blame for his defeat on his own troops. Actually, the harsh words that Berton quotes were not Procter's but were taken from Prevost's public general orders which smeared Procter, as well. Given Berton's overall even-handedness, the error was undoubtedly an honest one but it inadvertently promoted an unjustified criticism that has been repeated by others.

Berton's error is minor compared to those contained in other works such as J. Mackay Hitsman's *The Incredible War of 1812* (1965). Hitsman's book provides a good overview of the war, but when it comes to the western theatre, he not only incorporates Richardson's opinions at face value but introduces new criticisms. He blames Procter for delaying his attack on Fort Meigs when it was Prevost who would not allow it, declaring it "too hazardous." He is also in error in blaming Procter for forcing the Lake Erie Squadron into battle against a superior enemy as that pressure came, again, from Prevost. For his part, Procter held back his approval until the last moment, at which time Robert Barclay, the naval commander, expressed his full agreement. Hitsman also represents Tecumseh's warriors as lazy and the Western District militia as cowardly, ungenerous assessments in light of their significant contributions throughout the struggle. Hitsman's bias can be easily identified by following his index entries on Procter, each of which reveals a barb aimed at supporting his assessment that "Procter managed to bungle continuously." Nowhere does Hitsman credit Procter's vital contribution to the Detroit campaign or his widely acclaimed role in annihilating the fighting wing of the second Northwest Army at Frenchtown. Nor does he recognize the handicaps under which Procter laboured throughout 1813 or Prevost's central role in the deteriorating situation in the west. Hitsman provides neither proof nor citations in his book but his bias can be traced through his bibliography to *Richardson's War of 1812* as his primary, if not exclusive, source on the war in the west, illustrating the hazards of excessive reliance on a single source.

In 1999, Donald Graves undertook to provide citations to Hitsman's book, but he did nothing to correct the errors and omissions. On the contrary, he attempted to justify Hitsman's assertions through selective use of references. In some cases, Graves's statements are factually incorrect. For example, he credits Edward Brenton's book on Prevost's civil administration as "refuting point by point" Procter's criticisms of Prevost's management of the war in his *Quarterly Review* article "Campaigns in the Canadas." In fact, Brenton's book does nothing of the sort; it is entirely civil in its focus, devoid of any commentary on the war.

More recently, in *For Honour's Sake: The War of 1812 and the Brokering of an Uneasy Peace* (2006), Mark Zuelke puts a noteworthy emphasis on the diplomatic implications of the war. But, like George Stanley in *The War of 1812, Land Operations* (1983), Zuelke attributes Procter's alleged incompetence to his being a twenty-six-year-old general. This seemingly logical explanation holds no water at all since Procter was fifty years of age, having spent over thirty years in the army, ten of them in the Canadas! Far from being an upstart, Procter earned most of his promotions through merit, unlike many of his peers (such as Brock and Gordon Drummond) who acquired them through purchase. Such

erroneous explanations are indicative of the ease with which the negative mind-set of traditional accounts continues to thrive.

Finally, I must mention John Sugden's *Tecumseh, A Life* (1997), published the same year as the first edition of this book. Sugden's is the
most exhaustive research on Tecumseh and he is one of the few to have
actually examined the voluminous transcripts of Procter's court martial.
During and after our presentations at a symposium in Ohio, he and I
tangled in stimulating discussions about Tecumseh, Procter, and their
struggles. But, given our different approaches, our assessments differed
as well. In fairness to Sugden, his work recognizes the prevailing bad
press associated with Procter, asserting "commentators on the war enjoy
abusing him." Moreover, he debunks as fantasy American allegations of
Procter's brutality. (Indeed, even Richardson, the arch-critic, admitted
that Procter had tried "every means" to soften the ferocity of the warriors.) But Sugden systematically sets Procter up as a foil for Tecumseh. At first mention, he depicts Procter as a shadowy figure, asserting
that not much is known about him. In fact, with effort, Sugden could
have uncovered the same biographical information as is contained in
this book.

Like others before him, Sugden blames Procter for many of the allied
misfortunes, even for matters on which his court martial acquitted him,
revealing, once again, Richardson's far-reaching influence. In Sugden's
view, Tecumseh looms large in allied victories at Detroit and Fort Meigs
but is less prominent in allied reverses. He plays down the significance
of the battle of Frenchtown since Tecumseh was absent from the alliance at the time. (Nor does he mention that Tecumseh was absent for
seven months, half the time of the struggle in the west.) Sugden barely
acknowledges that it was Tecumseh who insisted on the second siege of
Fort Meigs, where his subterfuge scheme failed. He extols Tecumseh's
argument at the allied council prior to the Thames campaign that urged
Procter to stand and fight but fails to examine the illogic of the argument itself. Considering the conditions of the day, Tecumseh's proposal
had little prospect of success. Sugden might also have pointed out that
the Natives, by delaying the retreat and impeding its progress, contributed to the allies being overtaken in an unprepared state by a superior
force of the enemy. All this is not to diminish Tecumseh's positive contributions or to suggest that Procter was infallible. It is only to point
out that, being human, both men were susceptible to error. It is entirely
possible to depict the war chief in his full colours without tarnishing his
overall place in history and it is equally possible to present each man

in a fair light without detriment to the other. A balanced assessment would recognize that while Tecumseh and his followers were largely responsible for allied successes, they also contributed to allied failures.

ON THE OCCASION OF THE BICENTENNIAL

For the critical first half of the war, the Anglo-Native alliance achieved Brock's strategic objective of diverting substantial enemy resources from the urban centres to the east. By holding firm in Michigan and threatening American positions beyond, the allied defenders contributed greatly to the protection of Upper Canada until significant reinforcements arrived from Britain. That they were able to hold the line as long as they did under deteriorating conditions is a credit to them and to their leaders. Tecumseh and Procter emerge from this conflict as tragic figures since both were victimized by unfulfilled promises. But perhaps the most miserable outcome of the war in the west occurred well after the struggle ended, in the form of the historical amnesia regarding Brock's unfulfilled promise to the tribesmen – *a wampum denied*. On the bicentennial anniversary of the War of 1812, this account is a reminder of a forgotten theatre of what has been called "the forgotten war."

Sandy Antal
Cameron, Ontario
2011

ABBREVIATIONS

BCM	*Barclay Court Martial* (Transcripts)
Bender CM	*Bender Court Martial* (Transcripts)
CHR	*Canadian Historical Review*
DAB	*Dictionary of American Biography*
DCB	*Dictionary of Canadian Biography*
DHCNF	*Documentary History of the Campaign upon the Niagara Frontier* (E. Cruikshank, ed.)
DICSD	*Documents Relating to the Invasion of Canada and the Surrender of Detroit* (E. Cruikshank, ed.)
DPCUS	*Debates and Proceedings in the Congress of the United States*
HCM	*Hull Court Martial* (Transcripts, James Forbes)
JAP	*John Askin Papers* (M. Quaife, ed.)
JES	*Journal of Erie Studies*
MIC	*Miscellaneous Intercepted Correspondence* (16 Jul. 1812-10 Sept. 1813), U.S. National Archives
MLWHH	*Messages and Letters of William Henry Harrison* (L. Esarey, ed.)
MPHC	*Michigan Pioneer and Historical Collections*
NAC	National Archives of Canada (Ottawa)
NAUS	National Archives of the United States (Washington, D.C.)
NOW	*Notices of the War* (John Armstrong)
OH	*Ontario History*
OA	Ontario Archives (Toronto)
PCM	*Procter Court Martial* (Transcripts)
PRO	Public Record Office (Kew, U.K.)
SBD	*Select British Documents of the War of 1812* (W. Wood, ed.)
SLB	*Sheaffe Letter Book*
TP	*Talbot Papers*
TPUS	*Territorial Papers of the United States*
TRSC	*Transactions of the Royal Society of Canada*
WAMB	*Webster's American Military Biographies*
WCHS	Women's Canadian Historical Society of Toronto (*Transactions*)
WHC	*Wisconsin Historical Collections*
WRHS	Western Reserve Historical Society (Annual Reports)

I

FORWARD MARCH

I

AN EARTHLY PARADISE

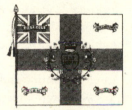

"I have been as far as Detroit, a delightful country, far exceeding anything I had seen on this continent." [1]

Brock to his brothers, 13 September 1810

THE DETROIT COUNTRY had been successively Native, French and British territory. The Treaty of Paris (1783) divided this region into American and British spheres. By 1812, it consisted of the American territory of Michigan and the Western District of the British colony of Upper Canada, the two separated by the porous international boundary of the Detroit River.

Largely surrounded by water, the Western District (now the counties of Essex, Kent, and Lambton, Ontario) formed the peninsula unofficially known as "Uppermost Canada." Except for minor undulations, the district was generally low, level, and marshy. The rich loam soil combined with a temperate climate to produce excellent prospects for farming grains, corn, and garden crops. Nonetheless, in 1812, other than the farms and small communities that huddled along the waterways, the country remained in its pristine state.

Although four of five settlers in Upper Canada were born in what had become the New England area of the United States, the residents of the Western District did not reflect this mix. The district had a population of between three and four thousand white persons, predominantly *Canadiens*, descendants of the original French settlers who occupied the area in the days of the *ancien régime*. The rest were

Loyalists, late-Loyalists (those Americans who immigrated for cheap land rather than political scruples), and immigrants from the British Isles. With the Amerind, Black and mixed-race residents, the population on both sides of the Detroit River was highly multicultural.[2]

The indigenous population of the vicinity consisted mainly of the descendants of those who survived the seventeenth century Iroquois forays. These Neutral (Attiwandaronk) and Tobacco (Petun) joined with the remainder of the Huron dispersion to form a collective nation, the Wyandot (Wendat), respected among the other nations as ancient and wise. The Christian Wyandot were concentrated along the Detroit River at Brownstown, Maguaga, and the Huron Reserve, where they cultivated crops of Indian corn, wheat, beans, peas, squashes, and melons. A large satellite group of Wyandot was also situated on the Sandusky River of Ohio. Scattered hunting and fishing bands of Ojibwa (Chippewa), pitched their bark lodges in present-day Kent County and among the cedar stands of Point Pelée, while pockets of Delaware and Muncey tribesmen encamped on the Upper Thames. Roving bands of Ottawa, Ojibwa, and Potawatomi nations occupied the margins of Michigan as the surface of the interior was largely covered by marshy lagoons.[3]

White settlement in the Western District was grouped in four distinct areas: Sandwich/Petite Côte, the New Settlement, Amherstburg, and the Lower Thames. Sandwich was the oldest non-Native farming community of Upper Canada with three hundred residents. The village contained a string of some 35 frame houses with large farms lying back plus a school, court house, jail, two churches, a small shipyard, trading warehouses, and several windmills. Although planned as the administrative centre for the Western District, Sandwich was a small community in 1812, populated mainly by *habitant* families who also occupied areas as far east as the Thames River.[4]

Between Sandwich and the Canards River (known to the Natives as the Ta-ron-tee), the scenic *Canadien* settlement of Petite Côte nestled along the river, its narrow ribbons of farmland laid out in traditional seigneurial form, crowned by quaint dwellings roofed with bark or thatched straw. Visitors invariably commented on the scenic beauty of this neat settlement. The estates abounded with fruit, vegetables, and grains while the extensive roses, lilacs, hollyhocks, and aromatic herbs gave the appearance and fragrance of one continuous garden along the river. A number of windmills broke the contour of the level shoreline to give the scene a serene and rustic charm.[5]

The New Settlement (as opposed to the old settlements of Sandwich and Petite Côte) was located on the south shore of Essex County. This area was settled after 1787 by discharged soldiers of the Revolutionary War (Butler's Rangers and Hessian mercenaries), Loyalists from Detroit, and pacifist Germans from Pennsylvania. From Marsh Creek, the New Settlement stretched east to Point Pelée, with a grist mill located on Mill Creek (now Kingsville).[6]

Amherstburg was the principal community of the Western District, with 150 dwellings plus a few taverns, smiths, and other commercial activities. Its residents were mainly Loyalists who migrated there in 1796 after U.S. ownership of Michigan was confirmed. A number of Black runaway slaves also settled in the area to join those already brought there by their immigrant masters. As regional headquarters for the British Indian Department, Amherstburg contained a lofty council house. The town was 250 road miles from Fort Erie and 310 miles from York (known as Muddy York or Little York), a town of eight hundred residents and the seat of colonial government.

Amherstburg was the centre for the British defence establishment west of the Niagara frontier. Its commodious and sheltered harbour was home station of the Provincial Marine Squadron and Dockyard for the Upper Lakes. A small field work, Fort Amherstburg, stood four hundred yards north of the town. Two blockhouses protected the harbour. These facilities, along with a third blockhouse on Bois Blanc Island (literally White Wood, corrupted through usage as Bob-lo), were strategically located to control shipping at the entrance to the deep water channel of the Detroit River. Fort Amherstburg also served as the support base for the distant post of Fort St. Joseph on Lake Huron.[7]

The Thames River (known to the *Canadiens* as La Tranchée, variously corrupted as Tranche, Trench, and French) was indifferently settled. Its banks were sprinkled with a few Loyalist farms, some rude squatters' hovels, and the occasional cluster of Native wigwams. The river was navigable by sailing vessels for 19 miles to Chatham, but a sand bar at its mouth limited passage to vessels of a six-foot draft. Lieutenant-Governor John Graves Simcoe had hoped to found an administrative and defense centre at Chatham 20 years previously, building a blockhouse and two gunboats. These plans did not mature, and by 1812, officials had removed the blockhouse to Sandwich for a jail and courthouse while the unfinished gunboats rotted on the Thames shore. Aside from occasional farm dwellings and a few taverns and mills, there were no sizable communities upriver until one reached the prosperous Moravian mission of Fairfield (Moraviantown, also known as Moravianstädt, Schönfeldt, and Nassau), comprised of 60 homes, a church, and a school. Established in 1792, the village was self-sustaining and developed a thriving economy based on the manufacture of copper utensils, pottery, fur clothing, canoes, and woven mats. In addition, the residents of this Native mission annually marketed two thousand bushels of Indian corn and five thousand pounds of maple sugar.[8]

The small Scottish settlement of Baldoon was situated on the marshy, lower reaches of the Chenail Ecarté (Bear Creek). Thomas Douglas, Earl of Selkirk, founded this isolated colony in 1804 as an experiment in immigration. By 1812, the struggling settlement of several dozen families had made little progress in converting the soggy wetlands into arable farmland. Nonetheless, the colonists persisted in their efforts, contending with immense swarms of malarial mosquitoes that proliferated in the marshy wastes. In an effort to boost the community's fledgling economy, Selkirk imported some nine hundred rugged Merino sheep as breeding stock.[9]

There was only one road (if one could call it that) to connect the settlements of the Western District to the head of Lake Ontario. Travellers agreed that it was "shockingly bad." Originally an ancient Native trail, it was obstructed by huge potholes, fallen trees, and stumps. Washouts were frequent and coarse, makeshift corduroy bridges spanned the dozens of intersecting creeks and rivers. Winter provided the best travelling conditions; in wet seasons, this mud-soaked road was virtually impassable. Known as the King's Road (or Detroit Road), it started at the New Settlement and ran along the shoreline through Amherstburg, Petite Côte, and Sandwich. Passing over a number of rivers and creeks along the south shore of Lake St. Clair, it crossed the Thames near its mouth and wound its way along the river's north side to Fairfield. From that point, the road left the Western District and passed through the infamous Longwoods Wilderness, a thickly wooded wasteland of 40 miles. Emerging from this thicket, the traveller would encounter the Native villages of Muncey-town and Delaware before coming upon Dundas Street (this road and Yonge Street being the only proper roads in the province), which led to the Grand River, Ancaster, and Burlington.[10]

Michigan Territory came into existence in 1805, when the American government sub-divided the immense Northwest Territory into Ohio state and the new territories of Michigan, Indiana, and Illinois.

The road near Chatham, c.1840. The tree (18 feet in diameter) was adjacent to the corduroyed road. Passing through several such forests, the King's Road connected the Western District to Lake Ontario. Since it was "shockingly bad" much of the year, water conveyance was preferred.

Michigan's boundaries were unofficially defined by the Maumee and St. Joseph rivers to the south and the Great Lakes waterways on the other perimeters. The 1810 census counted 4762 inhabitants of European descent, four-fifths of them *Canadiens.* North of Detroit, the only sizable community was a cluster of homes adjacent to Fort Michilimackinac, with an aggregate population of 615, mainly fur traders. White settlements occupied a tiny fraction of the land, most of which legally belonged to the Natives. Michigan was not self-sufficient in foodstuffs as drivers took in hundreds of livestock from Ohio annually.[11]

Founded by the French in 1701, Detroit was an established town, laid out with regular streets and alleys. In 1812, it consisted of seven hundred residents, mainly *Canadiens,* occupying 160 homes, all newly rebuilt after the great fire of 1805. The community contained the territorial council house, a church, several taverns, smiths, hatmakers, butchers, distillers, and weavers. It was stockaded in 1811 in response to fears of a Native rising. Fort Detroit, the only proper fortification within the region, stood adjacent to the town. Detroit was the largest settlement west of Kingston or north of the Ohio River.[12]

Frenchtown (now Monroe) was the unofficial name ascribed to the village that straddled the Raisin River at its intersection with the connecting road, about four miles from Lake Erie. This was a satellite community of Detroit, populated mainly by the families of *Canadien* settlers who founded homesteads here in the 1780s. About 120 families occupied a 12 mile stretch along the river, their homes laid out on ribbon farms that stretched back a mile and a half from the riverbank. With a stockade, grist mill, and chapel, the village of Frenchtown was home to 33 families and was the local centre for several tiny hamlets of the immediate area. The residents were closely associated with the neighbouring Natives, with whom they gathered regularly for footraces and lacrosse matches.[13]

About 50 American settlers sited their scattered farms on the lower Maumee (Miami) River, mainly at the hamlets of Presque Isle (now Toledo) and the Maumee Rapids (now Perrysburg), the head of river navigation. South of the rapids, an uninhabited wilderness known as the Black Swamp reached some 140 miles in all directions. This gloomy wasteland effectively separated the Detroit country from the populated parts of Ohio just as the Longwoods Wilderness isolated the Canadian side.[14]

A very poor road known as Hull's Trace (named after William Hull, appointed Michigan's first governor in 1805) ran from Detroit along the Detroit River through the Wyandot villages of Maguaga (now Trenton) and Brownstown (now Gibraltar) to Frenchtown. Here it connected to another coarse road that hugged the north shore of Ohio to the villages of Cleveland, Erie, and Buffalo. As on the Canadian side, water travel was faster, cheaper, and more comfortable than land conveyance.[15]

Some 20 small commercial sailing vessels operated on the Upper Lakes (frequently called by the collective term, the "St. Lawrence") hauling furs, salt, produce, livestock, manufactured goods, and passengers. U.S. government vessels consisted of a single army transport brig which resupplied the distant posts on the Upper Lakes. Its counterpart, the British Provincial Marine, was a transport service of the British Army, boasting two armed vessels, with a third under construction at Amherstburg. The sailing craft on the Canadian side plied the waters between forts St. Joseph, Amherstburg, and Erie, while the American routes connected forts Dearborn (Chicago), Michilimackinac, and Detroit, plus the villages of Erie and Buffalo. A virtually unguarded border accommodated considerable cross-border traffic, and it was common for residents to be related to folks on the opposite bank. The Detroit River was 18 miles long and averaged two miles in width with a 14-foot draft in the main channel between Amherstburg and Bois Blanc Island.[16]

Lake Erie was three hundred miles long, and unlike the other Great Lakes it was shallow, averaging only 70 feet deep. Its shallowness made navigation treacherous, as a sudden storm could churn the waters into a terrifying cauldron that dashed ships against the shore like match sticks, especially in early spring and late fall. Travellers reported the awesome phenomenon of waterspouts, enormous pillars of water lifted up by powerful whirlwinds. Crossing the lake in an open boat was possible but extremely hazardous. Water navigation ceased between November and March because of freeze-ups.[17]

A few miles inland from the shoreside communities, the interior was uninterrupted and impenetrable bush, a soggy hinterland of virgin hardwood forests where trees actually stood in water for part of the year. This wilderness abounded with a variety of animals ranging from cougars to rattlesnakes. In one year, four hundred bears were killed at Point Pelée alone. The lakes, marshes, rivers, and creeks teemed with amphibious creatures, aquatic fowl, and numerous species of fish.[18]

In this isolated frontier setting, individuals on both sides of the river encountered minimal state influences. The majority were poor, illiterate, and politically apathetic, more concerned with fighting off wolves from their livestock, grasshoppers from their gardens, and even passenger pigeons from the branches of their fruit trees, which broke under the sheer weight of itinerant flocks. Neighbours often took recess from their tedium to gather for logging, threshing, and barnraising; however, these occasions were not always images of stoic industry and co-operative enterprise. Diversions and social activities being few, bees provided the opportunity for "noisy, riotous drunken meetings, often terminating in drunken quarrels, sometimes even in bloodshed." The settlers engaged in the manufacture and consumption of alcohol, especially whiskey. One visitor described the New Settlement as "the most wicked and dissipated part of North America," while the overseer of Baldoon called its settlers "the most drunken, quarrelsome, spunging [sic], indolent of any people in Upper Canada." Isolated spots were notoriously sinister. One traveller described the tavern at Ward's Station in the infamous Longwoods Wilderness as a place of strange goings-on, a den of "thieves, murderers, villains and scape gallows."[19]

Detroit, the regional centre, was little better, condemned by one pious pilgrim as "a sink of iniquity, a wicked and accursed place" characterized by "idleness, drunkenness and gaming." Observing the vices of its fleshpot taverns on the river front, a principal resident concluded, "I do not think there is any place on the continent of America of the size of Detroit and the number of its inhabitants that has produced so many drunkards." The *Canadiens* typified the frontier way of life, the result of cultural and geographical isolation on both sides of the border. Inured to hardship, their lives engendered independence and assertiveness. One visitor described them as "generally intermarried among the Indians ... dressy, obliging and tractable ... a thoughtless and wicked, a cheerful and good-natured people." Governor William Hull considered the settlers "miserable farmers" who "depended on hunting, fishing and trading with the Indians" for their livelihood.[20]

Commercial activity in the region revolved around fur trading activity and government contracts. Currency consisted of hard coin in gold and silver, circulated by commercial interests and government agencies. The scarcity of money left barter as the primary method of doing business for common folks.

As the countryside was generally marshy from a lack of drainage, the populace suffered greatly from the ravages of bilious fever (lake or intermittent fever, a kind of malaria), typhoid, typhus, and a host of other diseases spread by vermin, animal contact, and lack of sanitation. In addition, residents had to contend with the relentless swarms of mosquitoes, which, with black flies, proliferated in the extensive wetlands.

Compounding the settlers' difficulties, the long drought and premature frost of 1811 greatly diminished the harvest. The poor yield barely satisfied local demand. Although the settlers could survive one such lean year, they could not sustain repeated failures in the harvest without facing starvation. The winter of 1811-12 was the coldest in living memory, temperatures remaining below -15° F. and frequently dipping as low as -35° F. Given these adverse conditions, people on both sides of the Detroit River looked forward to the summer of 1812 with high hopes that their lot would improve.[21]

It was against this harsh but peaceful wilderness backdrop that Washington and London let loose their opening volleys in an extended struggle over "Free Trade and Sailors' Rights." Given the circumstances of the Detroit country, one would not expect these residents to become wildly excited over the news that the people across the river were suddenly the enemy. Yet this unlikely frontier was to become the scene for some of the most bitter fighting in the first year of hostilities during the War of 1812.

NOTES

1. Ferdinand Brock Tupper, *The Life and Correspondence of Sir Isaac Brock*, 82.

2. Michael Smith, *A Geographic View of the Province of Upper Canada*, 62-70.

3. William C. Sturtevant, *Handbook of North American Indians* 15: 404; Helen Tanner, *Atlas of Great Lakes Indian History*, 99. The Wyandot settled in the Detroit River area in about 1730. They became the keepers of Native archives for the loose confederation of the Four Nations, the others being the Ottawa, Ojibwa, and Potawatomi. In 1812, their population of 2700 was distributed as follows: 1300 in Ohio; 1200 in Michigan and 200 in Canada. Their strategic location, leadership role, and sheer numbers made them a force with which to be reckoned. Peter Dooyentate Clarke, *Origin and Traditional History of the Wyandotts*, 37, 80.

4. Capt. James Sympson diary, cited in Anderson C. Quisenberry, *Kentucky in the War of 1812*, 101. A detailed examination of the early settlement of Detroit and Essex County is contained in Hugh Cowan, *Canadian Achievement in the Province of Ontario, The Detroit River District.*

5. Isaac Weld, *Travels Through the States of North America*, 181; William McCormick, *A Sketch of the Western District*, 21-33.

6. Francis Cleary, "Notes on the Early History of the County of Essex," 5-15; George MacDonald, "The New Settlement On Lake Erie," 1-10; Thomas Verchères de Boucherville, *The Journal of Thomas Verchères de Boucherville*, 131.

7. Lt. Gen. Peter Hunter to Duke of Kent, undated 1800, *MPHC* 15: 14; Lt. Col. Bruyères Report, 24 Aug. 1812, *MPHC* 15: 54; Tupper, *Brock*, 181-82.

8. MacDonnell, Miles, "Captain Miles MacDonnell's Jaunt to Amherstburg in 1801," 171; Diary of Brothers David Zeisberger and Benjamin Mortimer, cited in "From Fairfield to Schonbrun, 1798," 67.

9. Fred Coyne Hamil, *The Valley of the Lower Thames*, 46-56.

10. Charles Aikins [Askin], "Journal of a Journey From Sandwich to York in the Summer of 1806," 15-20.

11. Woodward to Procter, 20 Aug. 1812, *TPUS* 10: 405-09; William Hull, *Memoirs of the Campaign of the Northwest Army of the United States, A.D. 1812*, 76.

12. C.M. Burton, *The City of Detroit* 1, 984-85; Robert Breckenbridge McAfee, *History of the Late War in the Western Country*, 59.

13. Calvin Goodrich, *The First Michigan Frontier*, 72.

14. Marylin Van Voorhis Wendler, *The Foot of the Rapids*, 36.

15. *Trump of Fame*, 22 Dec. 1812, cited in WRHS, Tract No. 92: 91.

16. "From Fairfield to Schonbrun, 1978," 71.

17. The first Europeans to visit the Detroit country found a painted stone idol at the Detroit River. The area Natives held the spot in great veneration, offering homage and sacrifices to this figure, supplicating the deity for fair sailing weather on Lake Erie's turbulent waters. Dollier de Casson and de Bréhant de Gallinée, "Exploration of the Great Lakes, 1660-1670," 67.

18. McCormick, *Western District*, 32-33; *Pierre Charlevoix Journal*, 8 June, 1721, cited in Ernest J. Lajeunesse, *The Windsor Border Region*, 26; Samuel White, *History Of The American Troops During The Late War*, 79.

19. Edwin C. Guillet, *Early Life in Upper Canada*, 280; Reverend William Case narrative, cited in Hamil, *Valley of the Thames*, 53, 76; *The John Hunt Memoirs*, 58-59.

20. Elijah Brush to John Askin, 31 Dec. 1812, *JAP* 1: 744; *The Robert Lucas Journal of the War of 1812*, 90; Zeisberger and Mortimer, "From Fairfield to Schonbrun,1798," 71-73; Hull, *Memoirs*, 76.

21. John McGregor, *British America* 2, 373; Lt. Col. St. George to Brock, 9 Mar. 1812, *MPHC* 15: 81; Col. Edward Baynes to Brock, 23 Jan. 1812, Tupper, *Brock*, 141.

2

CLOUDS OF WAR

"Cunning began to take the place of wisdom; professions answered instead of deeds, and duplicity stalked forth with the boldness of integrity." [1]

ON 18 JUNE 1812, President James Madison approved the declaration of war against Great Britain, a country already locked in a deadly struggle with Napoleonic France. While contemptuous of the fledgling American republic, the British government was anxious to avoid a costly war across the Atlantic, and pressed through diplomatic channels for a suspension of hostilities for some months to come. Ironically, it was the very maritime measures that Britain viewed as essential for a successful prosecution of the European war that generated a new and unwanted conflict in North America. "Never before in the history of enlightened nations," declared an early American historian, "did such ... an absurd issue result in war." [2]

Since the U.S. salt water navy was minuscule in comparison to its British counterpart, American strategists (perhaps reminiscing on Sparta's success against Athens) postulated that Britain was best attacked through her North American colonies. A New York weekly, *The War*, expounded:

With the loss of Canada, England must lose her supplies of naval stores, timber, pitch, etc., so necessary to her gigantic navy. She now employs 300 ships annually in taking timber to England, for the repair of her navy. As these inestimable resources would cease with our occupation of the

Canadas, so would Britain lose a market for her manufactured goods; the savages would lose an instigator that offers gold for innocent scalps; and we should be relieved on our borders from a brace of enemies, savage and British, the one excelling in cruelty the other in perfidy. We should also acquire a considerable addition to revenue, by duties and imports. Until the northern provinces be ours then, let Americans never sheath their swords.[3]

American means for prosecuting war were as dubious as the rationale for its declaration. Some sober congressmen, notably John Randolph, questioned the wisdom of attacking British power "in the frozen depths of Labrador," especially when the republic was wholly unfit to go to war. He viewed the scheme as a perilous and irresponsible adventure. Indeed, the standing American army barely exceeded the British forces in the Canadas. Congress hastily addressed this deficiency by authorizing an increase of twenty-six thousand men, plus fifty thousand volunteers for a "provisional army," to be further augmented by a hundred thousand militiamen. American leaders considered these measures adequate to compensate for the virtual absence of a naval facility on the Great Lakes, the military frontier with Upper Canada.[4]

Significantly, the most vocal demands for war came not from the eastern seaboard states (which presumably suffered most directly from British maritime intransigence) but from landlocked frontier states. Henry Clay of Kentucky, foremost leader of the congressional War Hawks, hoped that war would create an opportunity for the consolidation of aboriginal lands in the Northwest by smashing Upper Canada, the perceived source of Native discontent. The U.S. government was not adverse to expansionism, as revenues at this time were limited to customs duties and the proceeds arising from the sale of public lands. Nonetheless, Congress remained divided about the question of war. The views of Representative Samuel Taggart typified common reservations: "The conquest of Canada has been represented as so easy as to be little more than a party of pleasure.... It has been suggested that they are a debased race of poltroons, incapable of making anything like a stand in their own defence, that the mere sight of an army of the United States would immediately put an end to all thoughts of resistance, that we had little more to do than march and that in the course of a few weeks, one of our valiant commanders ... might adopt the phraseology of Julius Caesar: *Veni, Vedi, Vici.*"[5]

Although the thorny maritime issues were close to diplomatic resolution, the War Hawks persisted in their uncompromising demands for war. With Britain occupied in Europe, they competed with each other in defining the ease by which her colonies would be overwhelmed. "We can take the Canadas without soldiers; we have only to send officers," announced Secretary of War William Eustis. Henry Clay, that fiery patriot, declared, "Strike wherever we can reach the enemy, at sea or on land, and negotiate the terms of peace at Quebec or Halifax." Despite such talk, the American government viewed the conquest of the Canadas not as an end in itself but a means by which to compel Britain to respect American sovereign rights on land and sea.[6]

Of all the states, Kentucky was most eager for war. Kentuckians had had a strong tradition of Indian fighting since Daniel Boone first led homesteaders across the Appalachians into Shawnee country. Kentuckians were prominent in all subsequent campaigns against the Natives. By 1812, they widely believed that British influence at Amherstburg was the root cause of continued Native unrest on the frontier. Their bellicosity was also driven by the depressed economy of their state caused by a plummeting demand for cotton and tobacco. As in other periods, military service was preferable to abject poverty.[7]

Kentuckians were not entirely without justification in their conviction that British instigation lay behind Native hostilities. This belief was based on a long tradition of very real British-Native collaboration dating back to the Revolutionary War. Since that time, Britain had been slow to evacuate American territory even though the Treaty of Paris (1783) had clearly established the international boundary along the Great Lakes chain. British-Native collusion was suspected at the American defeats of Brig. Gen. Josiah Harmar (1790) and Maj. Gen. Arthur St. Clair (1791) in Ohio. Furthermore, in 1794, Lieutenant-Governor John Graves Simcoe had established the British post of Fort Miamis in Ohio in open defiance of American sovereignty. This international slight almost erupted into a shooting war when American forces under Maj. Gen. Anthony Wayne came within sight of this British post after defeating the Natives at the battle of Fallen Timbers that year.[8]

Even after Britain evacuated U.S. territory in 1796, her activities continued to rouse resentment in the republic: "I cannot believe our government will neglect to authorize us to take immediately the British side of the strait [the Detroit River], from the lowest settlement to the River Thames ... which puts down forever Indian apprehensions," wrote Michigan's Governor Hull to the secretary of war on assuming office. "A thousand militia from Kentucky or Ohio would be necessary to secure the acquisition." In 1807, American newspapers learned that two thousand warriors had been armed and provisioned at Amherstburg and accused the British government of a "nefarious" frontier conspiracy. When Lieutenant Governor Francis Gore visited Amherstburg the following year, his very presence created a stir at Detroit as one resident wrote, "Report says that he has invited them to war against the United States, stating to them that now was the proper time to reclaim their lands making the Ohio their boundary." 9

In 1811, Native unrest verged on all-out war. In response, Governor William H. Harrison of Indiana advanced against a concentration of warriors on the Tippecanoe River, dispersing them on 7 November. This latest effort by the tribes to resist American encroachment through concerted action revived suspicions of British complicity, even though British officials only learned of the engagement after it occurred. Americans perceived Fort Amherstburg (commonly but erroneously known as Fort Malden, its later designation) as the "nest" in which were "hatched" all manner of "machiavellian machinations" and "diabolical intrigues." They were suspicious of the annual pilgrimage of Natives who crossed the international border to Amherstburg, that "emporium of the King's bounty," viewing the British custom of bestowing annual presents (knives, ammunition, blankets, hatchets, trinkets, and other goods) on the Natives as a means of exciting their animosity against the republic. Maj. Gen. Andrew Jackson typified Americans' impatience with the troublesome Natives, writing to Harrison, "That banditti ought to be swept from the face of the earth." 10

By 1812, many Americans were convinced that British associations with the Natives included active incitement. Frontier hostilities flared up once more in April of that year, and the War Hawks immediately pointed to British collusion. A subsequent congressional statement summarized the cumulative frustrations with British Native policy, "Whatever may have been the disposition of the British government, the conduct of its subordinate agents had tended to excite the hostility of the Indian tribes.... Her [Britain's] invisible arm was felt in the defeats of General Harmar, and General St. Clair, and even the victory of General Wayne [at the battle of Fallen Timbers] was achieved in the presence of a fort which she had erected, far within the territory of the United States to stimulate and countenance the barbarities of the Indian warrior." 11

If British agents were not openly urging the Natives to take up the hatchet in 1812, they certainly courted the favour of the tribes.

Harrison, ever anxious to promote the notion of a British-Native conspiracy, took each opportunity to elevate frontier anxieties into a broader threat to national security. As a principal agent of land "treaties" (between 1802 and 1809, he personally "negotiated" much of Indiana and Illinois away from the Natives), the governor undoubtedly contributed to frontier tensions. Yet there was some truth to his concerns. In July 1811, a Miami chief reported to Harrison that Matthew Elliott, head of the Indian Department at Amherstburg, was indeed restraining the warriors, but only till the right moment. "My son keep your eyes fixed on me," Elliott instructed the trigger-happy Sac and Fox warriors, "My tomahawk is now up but do not strike until I give the signal." [12]

For his part, Maj. Gen. Isaac Brock, military commander in Upper Canada, was aware of Elliott's selective interpretation of official policy. In 1811, he chastised the commander at Fort Amherstburg for his failure to restrain Elliott and the warriors from hostile acts. He repeated the official British position *verbatim*: "Upon every principal of policy our interest should lead us to see all our endeavours prevent a rupture between the Indians and the subjects of the United States. Upon these considerations, I think it would be expedient to instruct the officers of the Indian Department to use all their influence to dissuade the Indians from their projected plan of hostility, giving them to clearly understand that they must not expect any assistance from us." [13]

While British Native policy had softened, the difficulty was that it still existed. On 16 June 1812, two days before the declaration of war, Superintendent of Indian Affairs William Claus personally examined affairs at Amherstburg. He reported that the warriors had received only 1211 pounds of gunpowder over the previous six months, less than half the previous allocations over similar periods, and no lead at all. As a result, they were reduced to "constantly making bows and arrows, not having any ammunition." Despite this reduction in support, American statesmen viewed any British collaborations with the tribesmen residing on American soil as too much. [14]

To compound this tangled mess, British North America boasted its own version of expansionists among its colonial leaders. For them, the impending struggle was to be not one of defence but of reconquest of the Ohio lands to which the United States was not truly entitled. They hoped to reconstitute that region as a Native state that would be harmonized with British fur trading interests as a defence buffer against the U.S. The leaders of the North West Company (James McGill, John

Richardson, and William McGuillivray); its surrogate, the Southwest Company (Robert Dickson, John Lawe, James Aird, Joseph Rolette, and Thomas Anderson), and their London counterparts (Inglis, Ellice and Company, and McTavish, Fraser, and Company), were foremost in demands for a restoration of these lost lands. The élite of the fur trading community of Montreal put its views forcefully to their governor general:

Posterity will hardly believe, although history must attest the melancholy and mortifying truth, that in acceding to the Independence of the Thirteen Colonies as States, their territory was not merely allowed to them, but an extent of Country, then a portion of the Province of Quebec, nearly of equal magnitude to the said Thirteen Colonies or States, was ceded, notwithstanding not a foot of the Country so ceded, was at the time occupied by an American in Arms, nor could have been had the war continued.[15]

A second component to this expansionist camp consisted of the Loyalists at Amherstburg. During the Revolutionary War, these men were prominent in leading Native warriors in irregular operations against the rebels as far south as Kentucky. Noteworthy among these were Matthew Elliott, Simon Girty, Alexander McKee, and William Caldwell. Americans identified them as "renegades" and "malignant tories." Forced to remove to the Canadian side in 1795-96, they had maintained close associations with the American warriors as members of the British Indian Department. By 1812, however, McKee was dead, Girty was virtually blind, Elliott was almost 80 years old, and Caldwell was relatively inactive in Native affairs. Nonetheless, Elliott remained head of the Indian Department at Amherstburg, while Alexander McKee's son, Thomas, followed in his father's footsteps as an interpreter. Although *bona fide* agents of the British Crown, Elliott and McKee took great liberties in translating official policy to suit Native aspirations, maintaining influence with the warriors by distributing annual presents to them on behalf of the king, a long-established tradition.[16]

The third element of this consortium of interests consisted of the foremost military commanders in Upper Canada, namely Maj. Gen. Isaac Brock, and his senior lieutenant, Col. Henry Procter. These officers had been rubbing elbows with the commercial élite of the colonies for over a decade and came to sympathize with their views. Since an open declaration of expansionist designs would have been contrary to official policy, their writings merely alluded to the Natives as potential manpower in case of impending conflict. However, their immediate commitment to the recovery of Native lands at the outbreak of war reveals their willingness to engage in expansionist designs. They were following the example of John Graves Simcoe, who had resisted American expansion and even took active steps towards rolling back the international boundary to the Ohio River.[17]

Thus, the combination of commercial, Indian Department, and military interests united in a common objective that was to be achieved through force of arms. Indeed, by declaring war, "the United States had presented Great Britain with an opportunity of recovering the lost provinces, of redeeming *Canada Irredenta* for the natives and the commercial conglomerates."[18]

Through the British Indian Department, the colonial expansionists were further linked to the leaders of a Native movement on U.S. soil. For years, the chiefs of the Ohio country had tried to secure official recognition of their remaining lands through peaceful means; however, talks broke down in 1793. In council, American officials declared that "it was now impossible to make the river Ohio the boundary between your lands and the lands of the United States." The collapsed talks precipitated the engagement of Fallen Timbers (1794), leading to an even more calamitous event, the Treaty of Greenville (8 August 1795). Through the terms of this "agreement," representatives of the Wyandot, Ojibwa, Ottawa, Potawatomi, Shawnee, Miami, Delaware, Wea, Piankashaw, Kickapoo, and Kaskaskia nations formally surrendered to the republic another enormous stretch of land (about two-thirds of Ohio) for settlement. The subsequent British evacuation of the posts at Detroit, Michilimackinac, Niagara, and Oswego in 1796 prompted the foremost Native chiefs to conclude that their cause was lost and that British diplomats had again abandoned their interests, just as they had after the Revolutionary War.[19]

Despite these distressing reverses to Native aspirations, a core of leaders persisted in their dream of a Native state. Foremost among these zealots were the Shawnee brothers Tenskwatawa (the Prophet) and Tecumseh. Tenskwatawa had been an annoying drunk until a mystic experience with the "Master of Life" altered his outlook and he became a holy man. He preached collective resistance to the White advance and a return to traditional Native values and ways of life. His brother complemented this movement by organizing the diverse indigenous tribes into an armed confederacy aimed at forcibly halting the relentless American encroachments. Tecumseh was first mentioned in British records in 1808 at a council with senior officials of the Indian Department at Amherstburg. The war chief proposed a military pact with British officials, asserting, "If ... the king should be in earnest and appear in sufficient force they [the warriors of his movement] would hold fast by him." British representatives could only respond by urging restraint until the right moment. Since that time, Tecumseh had demonstrated indefatigable energy in molding his followers into an armed confederacy. In 1811, while the war chief was recruiting followers in the southern United States, Harrison scattered this potentially dangerous concentration at Tippecanoe. Having led the warriors into this defeat, the Prophet suffered a loss of influence and Tecumseh assumed the leadership of the virtually dissolved Native movement.[20]

Convinced that his only chance of succeeding against the Americans lay in a British alliance, Tecumseh again held council with Matthew Elliott on 15 November 1811. The war chief produced the Great Wampum, which British officials had presented to the tribes after the Seven Years War. He had discovered it in 1805 and formally presented it to Elliott, offering a revitalization of the traditional partnership in the impending hostilities:

We have a belt to show you, which was given to our kings [chiefs] when you laid the French on their back. Here it is, Father. On the one end is your hand, on the other, that of the red people (both hands in black wampum, but the Indian end of the white belt darker than the other) and in the middle the hearts of both. This belt, Father, our great chiefs have been sitting upon ever since, keeping it concealed, and ruining our country. Now the warriors have taken all the chiefs and turned their faces towards you and never again look towards the Americans; and we, the warriors, now manage the affairs of our nation; and we sit at or near the borders where the contest will begin.[21]

Anticipating the outbreak of war, Elliott hastened to advise his superiors of these developments. He introduced Tecumseh as "brother of the Shawanese [sic] Prophet" and requested "ample and explicit instructions" on the proposed alliance. Some weeks later, Elliott outlined the basic ingredients for what became the defence strategy for Upper Canada. "My plan would be to have a respectable body of troops here [Fort Amherstburg] to give the Indians confidence in our sincerity and with five hundred of the former and the same number of the latter, who could soon be collected, seize Detroit in the first instance," he wrote. "That once done, the Indians, with some regular troops, would keep the Americans at bay until all the nations were assembled; which they would do immediately. All the Indians may be depended upon."[22]

Brock, desperate to augment the few regulars available for the defence of Upper Canada, eagerly embraced Elliott's proposal. He immediately drew up comprehensive plans, outlining its essential elements in his memorandum of February 1812, entitled "Plans for the Defence of Canada." He identified the warriors on the Detroit frontier as germane to his strategy. On the outbreak of war, he intended to seize the American post of Michilimackinac in order to sway the mass of warriors to the British side. Then, anticipating the arrival of a battalion of regulars from Lower Canada, he would send the entire 41st Regiment of Foot under Col. Henry Procter with artillery support to Amherstburg to assume offensive operations against Fort Detroit.[23]

With the critical western posts in British hands, Brock anticipated a general uprising of the Natives in the west that would paralyze American offensive operations. To support the sustained co-operation of the Native allies, he emphasized naval preparations as vital to success, planning for the construction of seven gunboats on Lake Erie with a protective battery at Long Point. He intended to augment the Provincial Marine squadron on Lake Erie with one hundred seamen and two companies of the Royal Newfoundland Regiment to serve as gunners. He also stressed the need to sustain Native co-operation in material terms, declaring, "The measure will, however, be attended with a heavy expense, especially in the article of provision for not only the Indians who take the field, but their families must be maintained." What Brock did not say (but certainly knew) was that he would knowingly commit himself to the cause of a homeland for that "much wronged people."[24]

Predictably, the fur barons were delighted with Brock's plans, readily tendering their enthusiastic support in the upcoming hostilities. Not only did they offer their vessels, agents, merchandise, and facilities for military use but they prepared to rouse Natives in distant regions. In response to a confidential letter from Brock, Robert Dickson of the Southwest Company wrote on 18 June 1812 (the very day war was declared) that hundreds of warriors were on the way to Michilimackinac and Detroit to co-operate in offensive operations.[25]

The commander-in-chief and governor-general of British North America was Lt. Gen. Sir George Prevost, a recent arrival to the

Although this lithograph shows a martial-looking Lt. Gen. Sir George Prevost in ceremonial dress, his wartime record has attracted widespread criticism. His military and marine policy on the Detroit frontier proved to be "too little, too late."

Canadas. He stepped ashore at Quebec on 14 September 1811 to take charge of military and civil matters of an immense territory that included Bermuda, Newfoundland, Nova Scotia, New Brunswick, Upper Canada, and Lower Canada. Forty-five years of age, Prevost had been born in New Jersey, the son of a British general. Joining the army as an ensign in 1779, he served in the West Indies and rose rapidly in rank to become lieutenant governor of Dominica in 1798. His successful repulse of a French attack on that island in 1801 earned him a knighthood, followed by a promotion to lieutenant general and governorship of Nova Scotia in 1808. He was further rewarded for three years of popular administration of that province with his latest appointment.[26]

As Prevost's combat experience was based on the command of nothing larger than a regiment, his grasp of strategic operations was limited. Furthermore, he was largely unacquainted with the lands for which he had charge. Consequently, he responded cautiously to Brock's plans, which he received shortly after assuming office. Prevost was correct in anticipating minimal support from England. Furthermore, Brock's strategy for aggressive action in the west ran contrary to the views of the previous governor, Sir James Craig, who advocated a stout defence from Quebec City. Prevost was understandably reluctant to commit himself to a radical departure from established defence plans. He became further convinced of the advisability of a defensive posture by the recommendation of his acting deputy quartermaster general, Capt. Andrew Gray. Gray inspected affairs in the west and recommended the immediate evacuation of the Western District in the event of war, advising his chief, "The route by Detroit and the River Sinclair [sic] must be abandoned and that by York adopted."[27]

From a purely military point of view, Upper Canada was extremely vulnerable to attack. Its defence fell to only one regiment, the 41st, augmented by a smattering of other units, the whole amounting to 1658 regular soldiers (including colonial fencible troops who were trained, paid, and equipped as regulars). These were spread over a dozen posts along the exposed frontier waterways from Montreal to upper Lake Huron. The eleven thousand Upper Canadian militiamen were ill equipped, untrained, and poorly motivated. Moreover, four-fifths of them had been born in what became the United States and some openly espoused American sympathies. "It might not be prudent to arm more than 4,000" of them, Prevost observed. The matter of arming the militiamen was greatly simplified by the fact that there were few muskets on hand. Furthermore, the primitive economy of Upper Canada limited most settlers to subsistence living, precluding their active participation in defence, even if driven by patriotic fervour. "It is impossible for them to remain long from home without subjecting their families to utter ruin," wrote Rector John Strachan of York.[28]

Prevost's reluctance to support Brock's plan was not limited to practical considerations. He was aware that employment of the warriors would outrage U.S. public opinion and strengthen the war party there. Yet contemporary British observers in Upper Canada were overwhelming in their agreement with the view expressed by Rector Strachan, who wrote, "The matter of employing the Indians is not a question of policy but one of absolute necessity." Thus Prevost's strategic options boiled down to two approaches. He could either abandon much of Upper Canada or join the Natives in an alliance to hold the invaders on all fronts.[29]

Convinced that Brock's strategy could not be sustained in a prolonged conflict, Prevost scoffed at his lieutenant's scheme. "If the Americans are determined to attack Canada, it would be in vain the General [Brock] would flatter himself with the hopes of making an effectual defence of the open country, unless powerfully assisted at home," he reported to the colonial office. In his view, the precious regulars must be conserved as a strategic reserve within Lower Canada to hold the fortified port of Quebec until Britain could afford reinforcements to recover what had been lost. Prevost sent off his plans to London, enclosing Brock's proposals as well. Strangely, the minister for war and colonies accepted both strategies, holding up Prevost's "defence of Quebec [as] paramount to every consideration." Thus London endorsed two strategies as a confused *mélange*.[30]

Naval superiority on the waterways was a critical consideration for British defence planners. One of the peculiarities of this war was that the extended military frontier of Upper Canada also constituted the principal British logistics pipeline, exposed in its length to enemy attack. The maintenance of Native loyalties would call for the generous supply of presents, food, and war materiel. Most of these would have to be shipped west by water, coming ultimately from England. In addition, control of the waterways would facilitate the strategic flexibility of shifting scarce regular troops to threatened areas. Britain already possessed superiority on the Upper Lakes through three armed vessels: the ship *Queen Charlotte*, the brig *General Hunter*, and the nearly finished schooner *Lady Prevost*. Brock anticipated the need to retain this superiority through further preparations. Navy men were also required to take charge of this undermanned, ill-equipped colonial transport service.

American planners were also aware of the importance of controlling the waterways to assure success. William Hull, the 59-year-old governor of Michigan Territory, was a Revolutionary War hero who spent his subsequent years in federal service on the frontier. When summoned to Washington for consultation in the summer of 1811, he stressed the paramount need for naval superiority as the single American

vessel on the Upper Lakes was the 14-gun brig, *Adams*. Hull's advice
fell on deaf ears, lost in the morass of financial constraints and political ineptitude, precluding timely naval preparations. By March 1812,
Hull altered his position and urged the secretary of war to send an adequate force to Detroit to awe the Natives and effect the evacuation of
the Western District, whereby "the British naval force would fall into
American hands without the expense of building a fleet." Washington
seized on Hull's proposal, commissioning the white-haired governor
a brigadier general in the U.S. Army, charged with command of the
Northwest Army which he was to march to Detroit in anticipation of
war.[31]

Hull's command was only the vanguard of several planned assaults.
Secretary of War Eustis hoped to overrun Upper Canada in the fall of
1812 by driving three massive wedges into the colony from Detroit,
Niagara, and Lake Champlain. With the communications lifeline of
the waterways severed, he expected to mop up the isolated pockets of
defenders, after which Upper Canada would fall like a ripe plum.[32]

Although the frontier inhabitants of the Detroit country were
unconcerned with the diplomatic squabbles of Britain and the United
States, they sensed that the rising tensions would inevitably break out
in war. One Detroit resident correctly interpreted events and lobbied
Congress in February, 1812, to assure the security of this frontier:

From a careful perusal of the proceedings of Congress, I am led to believe
that war with England is probable. Our situation exposes us in a peculiar
manner to the calamity of war. But sir, a war with England has no terrors
compared with those arising from their savage allies. Our melancholy fate ...
need not be pointed out.... Several officers of distinction have lately visited
Amherstburg.... The British are greatly enlarging their works, building
extensive barracks, and apparently under the expectation of a much larger
force than has ever been stationed in the upper country.... It is evident that
they will make a firm and formidable stand in this upper country.... Great
calculations are made from the aid which they expect to derive from the
Indians. Should Detroit fall, it is evident it would cost the United States
much blood and treasure to regain what they had lost.[33]

NOTES

1. Charles A. Goodrich, *History of the United States of America*, 285.
2. Rufus Blanchard, *The Discovery and Conquest of the Northwest*, 257.
3. *The War*, 25 July 1812.
4. Representsative John Randolph, cited in J.T. Headley, *The Second War With England* 1: 46.
5. Speech of Congressman Samuel Taggart, *PDCUS*, 1811-1812, Vol. 1, Part 2: 1663-64.
6. Historians agree that the causes of the war were maritime issues. Reginald Horsman, *The Causes of the War of 1812*; Julius Pratt, *Expansionists of 1812*. Henry Clay (1777-1852) was a prominent Kentucky congressman between 1806 and 1852. He was a vocal proponent for war and was largely responsible, as speaker of the House of Representatives, for its stubborn prosecution, asserting that the Kentucky militia were adequate to take the Canadas. He became one of the American commissioners at the subsequent peace talks. After the war, the impetuous Clay was thrice an unsuccessful candidate for the presidency and became secretary of state 1825-29. *DAB* 2: 173-79.
7. Kentucky's role in the war is examined in James Wallace Hammack, Jr., *Kentucky and the Second American Revolution*.
8. Gov.-Gen. Sir James Craig to Lt. Gov. Francis Gore, 10 Feb. 1808, Lord Castlereigh to Craig, 8 Apr. 1809, *MPHC* 25: 238, 259.
9. Hull to Secretary of War James Madison, 3 Aug. 1805, *MPHC* 31: 225; J.R. Williams to Mssrs. I. and T. Schieffen, 22 July 1808, *MPHC* 32: 516.
10. Andrew Jackson to Harrison, 28 Nov. 1811, *MLWHH* 2: 665. Although usually called Fort Malden, the correct name of the post at this time was Fort Amherstburg, so named from 1797, when it was built, until 1813, when it was occupied by the Americans. The confusion seems to have existed in 1812. Prevost wrote to Brock, "The possession of Malden, which I consider means Amherstburg, appears a favourite object with the government of the United States." Francis Cleary, "Fort Malden or Amherstburg," 5-19; Prevost to Brock, 31 July 1812, Tupper, *Brock*, 228.
11. *DPCUS 1814-1815* Vol. 3: 1466. Secretary of War Alexander J. Dallas was the supposed author of "An Exposition on the Causes and Character of the War" (10 Feb. 1815).
12. William C. Sturtevant, *Handbook of North American Indians* 5: 37; Harrison to secretary of war, July 11, 1807, *MLWHH* 1: 223; Harrison to secretary of war, 18 July 1810, *DPCUS 1811-1812* Vol. 2: 1858. Harrison did not corrupt the sense of Elliott's speech. It is found in almost identical wording in British records. NAC, CO 42, 14: 269.
13. Brock to Maj. Taylor, 4 Mar. 1811, Tupper, *Brock*, 97.

14. William Claus to Brock, 16 June 1812, NAC, C 676:144.

15. Memorial of merchants of Upper and Lower Canada to Prevost, 24 Oct. 1812, cited in Donald Creighton, *Empire of the St. Lawrence*, 176. The British diplomats' indifference about North America is illustrated in their handling of the border settlement at the conclusion of the Revolutionary War. Their initial proposal to the Americans included not only the Ohio country but all lands south of the Ottawa-Nipissing chain! The Americans refused this offer as it would have included the headwaters of the Mississippi in the British sphere. William Kingsford, *The History of Canada* 6: 151.

George Prevost (1767-1816) was born in New Jersey, the eldest son of Maj. Gen. Augustus Prevost, who served in America during the Revolutionary War. The younger Prevost was commissioned in his father's regiment in 1779 and purchased his promotions rapidly. He became lieutenant colonel of the 60th Foot in 1794 and was twice wounded in action against the French on the island of St. Vincent in 1796. He earned a reputation as a conciliatory governor in the West Indies and Nova Scotia. *DCB* 5: 693-98.

16. Blanchard, *Northwest*, 195.

Matthew Elliott (c.1739-1814) was born in Ireland and grew up in Pennsylvania. During the Revolutionary War, he was prominent in leading the Shawnee at the battles of Sandusky and Blue Licks. He established himself on a four thousand acre estate at Amherstburg where dozens of Black and Native slaves worked his extensive plantation. Elliott's first wife (a Shawnee or Wyandot woman) bore him two sons, Matthew and Alexander, both active in the War of 1812. Alexander, a promising lawyer, was killed in Ohio in the fall of 1812. The elder Elliott remarried a young woman named Sarah Donovan who produced three more offspring. During the war, Elliott continued in his post in the Indian Department, and despite his advanced years, remained colonel of the First Essex Regiment. *DCB* 5: 301-03.

Simon Girty (1741-1818) was born in Pennsylvania and grew up in Iroquois captivity. He fled Pennsylvania in 1778 with McKee and Elliott to begin a notorious career as a loyalist renegade. Americans reviled him as a sadistic spectator at the Natives' torture of Col. William Crawford after the battle of Sandusky in 1782. For an eye-witness account of this gruesome event, see Dr. [John] Knight, *A Narrative of a Late Expedition Against the Indians, with an Account of the Barbarous Execution of Col. Crawford and the Wonderful Escape of Dr. Knight and John Slover from Captivity in 1782.* His role in the battle of Fallen Timbers (1794) served to enflame suspicions of British complicity in native raids. He settled near Amherstburg in 1796, dying there in 1818. *DCB* 5: 345-46.

William Caldwell, Sr. (c.1750-1820) was born in Ireland and emigrated to Pennsylvania in 1773. A captain in Butler's Rangers, 1776-84, he achieved some success (and notoriety) in 1782 at the battles of Sandusky and Blue Licks. In 1793, he became a principal founder of the New Settlement. The next year, Caldwell was present at the battle of Fallen Timbers as an "advisor." During the War of 1812, he resumed his work with the Natives, being particularly influential with the Wyandot. *DCB* VI, 101-03.

Alexander McKee (1720-1799) was Irish by birth. He settled in Pennsylvania in about 1740 and became closely associated with the tribes of the northwest, marrying several Native women. An ardent Loyalist, he abandoned his extensive property at Pittsburg and maintained a bitter enmity for the Americans. He was particularly active in collaborating with Lieutenant-Governor Simcoe in promoting a Native buffer state north of the Ohio River. In 1794, he became deputy superintendent of the Indian Affairs and moved to Upper Canada from Detroit. He urged British-Native resistance to U.S. expansion until his death on the Thames River. *DCB* 4: 499-500.

His son, Thomas McKee (1770-1815) was married to Therese Askin, daughter of fur trader, John Askin, Sr. He served in the 60th Foot before replacing Matthew Elliott as deputy superintendent of Indian Affairs from 1797 till 1808 but was superseded, in turn, by Elliott. Before the war, he represented Essex and Kent in the legislature. McKee's influence among the Natives was legendary, and he led a party of warriors at the capture of Detroit. Unfortunately, inebriation and "rheumatism of the head" precluded his meaningful participation during much of the war. He was despised by the Americans as a "notorious, bloodthirsty reactionary." *DCB* 5: 499-500.

17. J.A. MacDonnell, "Major-General Sir Isaac Brock, K.B.," 10. As part of his military preparations, Brock gathered intelligence from British fur traders in Indian country through secret communications. In 1811, at Fort George, Procter assisted traders in conducting a clandestine operation aimed at forcibly recovering from the U.S. their merchandise seized by American customs officials. Boucherville, *Journal*, 68. A concise summary of Simcoe's aggressive military designs is contained in Malcolm McLeod, "Fortress Ontario or Forlorn Hope? Simcoe and the Defence of Upper Canada," 150-78.

18. Creighton, *Empire*, 176.

19. American Commissioners to Native chiefs, 30 July 1793, cited in Blanchard, *Northwest*, 205.

20. Sturtevant, *Handbook of North American Indians* 4: 15, 37; Proceedings of Council at Amherstburg, 11 and 13 July 1808, cited in Robert Allen, *His Majesty's Indian Allies*, 114. A summary of the Native movement is contained in R. David Edmunds, "The Thin Red Line:

Tecumseh, the Prophet and Shawnee Resistance," 2-19. Detailed
works on Tecumseh and the Prophet are contained in Alvin Josephy,
The Patriot Chiefs; Glenn Tucker, *Tecumseh, Vision of Glory*; R. David
Edmunds, *The Shawnee Prophet*, and *Tecumseh and the Quest for Indian
Leadership*. Tenskwatawa or "the Open Door" (formerly known as
Elkswatawa and Laulawathika or Olliwochica) was frequently called
"the Prophet." He accompanied his older brother to Amherstburg in
the War of 1812 but exerted no significant role. *DCB* 7: 847-900.

Tecumseh or Shooting Star (1768-1813) was born in Ohio, the son
of a Shawnee, Puckashinwa, and a Creek woman. With his nation
dislocated and decimated, Tecumseh's mission was greatly influenced by
the deaths of his father and older brother at the hands of encroaching
Americans. As a young warrior, he was probably present at St. Clair's
defeat (1791) and the battle of Fallen Timbers (1794). After 1805, he
assisted his brother in the creation of a Native confederacy and assumed
leadership of the movement after the battle of Tippecanoe. Although
Tecumseh and Harrison met several times, their irreconcilable positions
regarding American settlement of the Northwest made them inveterate
foes. *DCB* 5: 795-600. A fine collection of accounts relating to Tecumseh
is contained in Carl F. Klinck, *Tecumseh, Fact and Fiction in Early Records*.

Tecumseh's legacy is surrounded by so much mythology that his
genuine greatness is often obscured. Often depicted as a Canadian
hero, his association with the British side during the War of 1812 was
a matter of necessity as he was totally dedicated to the welfare of his
own people. Although considered the Napoleon of the Native warriors,
he was a war chief, whose sheer forceful nature made him the most
prominent of Native leaders. His control over the warriors has been
much exaggerated as he was unable to direct them in a uniform aim
(on the Maumee and Thames campaigns). Tecumseh's lofty vision of
collective Native resistance to white encroachment followed the example
established by the Ottawa chief, Pontiac and the Miami chief, Little
Turtle. Even without the mythology, Tecumseh was an exceptionally
intelligent, energetic, dedicated, and eloquent Native leader who
demonstrated humanity and vision. He gave his all courageously for
his people.

21. Speech of Tecumseh, 15 Nov. 1810, *MPHC* 25: 275-76.
22. Elliott to Claus, 9 Dec. 1811, *MLWHH* 1: 661. Elliott estimated 4400
    warriors would join the British side in a war. In 1768, the Native popu-
    lation in the Great Lakes area was some 60,000. Warriors, who consti-
    tuted one-fifth of this number, had diminished to some 9000 by 1812.
    Tanner, *Atlas of Great Lakes Indian History*, 65-66.
23. Brock's Defence memorandum, nd. Feb. 1812, *SBD* 1: 288-89; Brock
    to Prevost, 2 Dec. 1811, Tupper, *Brock*, 126.

24. Brock's Defence memorandum, nd. Feb. 1812, *SBD* 1: 288-89; Brock to Prevost, 2 Dec. 1811, Tupper, *Brock*, 125-26.

25. Robert Dickson to Brock, 18 June 1812. NAC, C 256: 211; Gray to Prevost, 13 Jan. 1812, *SBD* 1: 285-87; Capt. Roberts to Brock, 12 July, 1812, NAC, C 676: 156.

26. *DCB* 5: 693-94.

27. Capt. Gray to Prevost, 13 Jan. 1812, *SBD* 1: 284.

28. Prevost to Liverpool, May 18, 1812, *DHCNF* 1812, Vol. 3: 63; Strachan to John Richardson (NW Co.) 30 Sept. 1812, George W. Spragge, *The John Strachan Letter Book*: 1812-1834, 7. Distribution of regular troops in Upper Canada at the outbreak of war was:

Royal Artillery	80
10th Royal Veteran Battalion	386
41st Foot	1014
Royal Newfoundland Regiment	369
Total	1658

    By comparison, Lower Canada was defended by 5489 troops. The 49th Foot would shortly be sent up by Prevost. General Return of Troops in Upper and Lower Canada, 4 July 1812. *DHCNF* 1812, Vol. 3: 98-99.

29. Strachan to Hon. Wilberforce, 1 Nov. 1812, Spragge, *Strachan Letter Book*, 23.

30. Prevost to Liverpool, 18 May 1812, NAC, CO 42: 146. This letter contains a concise summary of Prevost's defence plans. The British government's desire to contain the war with the U. S. is detailed in Bathurst to Prevost, 10 Aug. 1812, NAC, CO 42: 23.

31. Hull to Eustis, 15 June 1811, Hull, *Memoirs*, 19; Hull to Eustis, 6 Mar. 1812, *MPHC* 40: 362-68. William Hull (1753-1825) was born in Connecticut. His distinguished services during the Revolutionary War at the engagements of Trenton, Saratoga, Morrissania, and Stony Point, raised him to the rank of colonel. He was a Yale graduate, teacher, lawyer, congressman and, from 1805 till 1812, Governor of Michigan Territory. Closely associated with border issues, Hull was considered by Washington as knowledgeable on matters relating to the frontier. As a result, he was made commander of the Northwest Army on 8 April 1812, specifically to lead an invasion of Canada, his first independent command. Maria Campbell, *Revolutionary Services and Civil Life of General William Hull*, 254; *WAMB*, 188. By 1812, Hull had been "demilitarized" for almost 30 years. He was married and had five daughters and a son, Capt. Abraham Fuller Hull of the 13th U.S. Infantry. This son served as his aide at Detroit and was later killed at the battle of Lundy's Lane. A brother, Isaac Hull, was living on the Lower Thames during the American invasion. Isaac Hull's son, militia Capt. David Hull, (1781-1837) settled at the Maumee Rapids in 1807

and commanded a small militia party at the Maumee blockhouse until the surrender of Michigan. After the war, he returned to the Maumee Rapids to open a tavern, dying in 1837 in an asylum. The naval war hero, Isaac Hull, was another nephew to the general. *DAB*, 188; *DISCSD*, 117n.

32. James Freeman Clarke, *History of the Campaign of 1812 and the Surrender of the Post of Detroit*, 352.

33. Solomon Sibley to Senator Thomas Worthington, 26 Feb. 1812, H.S. Knopff, *Document Transcripts of the War of 1812 in the Northwest 3 (Thomas Worthington and The War of 1812)*: 66.

3

DUELS ON THE SEWERS

"The powerful army under my command is now in possession of Canada." [1]
Hull to the Six Nations, 8 July 1812

BORED DURING MOST of his decade in the colonies, Maj. Gen. Isaac
Brock preferred Europe to the backward province of Upper Canada.
Although promotions had come readily enough, he thirsted for active
service on the continent. Then, in 1811, his luck changed. The
escalating tensions convinced him that war with the United States
was inevitable. Furthermore, when Lieutenant-Governor Francis Gore
returned to England for health reasons, Brock, on 8 October, assumed
the duties of civil administrator, in addition to his responsibilities as
military commander of Upper Canada. A sense of duty (and one of
opportunity) tempered his desire to serve under Wellington in Spain,
and he cancelled his request for a transfer.

Forty-one years of age, Brock had been born on the Channel Island
of Guernsey. Although he was an intelligent, energetic, and ambitious
officer, few of his rapid promotions had come through merit. He
purchased all his commissions up to the rank of colonel and was
appointed lieutenant-colonel of the 49th Regiment of Foot at 28 years
of age! Nonetheless, Brock was experienced. A soldier since the age of
15, he had served in the low countries, at Copenhagen with Nelson,
and in the West Indies. Since his arrival in the Canadas in 1802, Brock
had been actively improving the defences of Upper and Lower Canada.
A large man of six feet, three inches, he was affable in disposition,

Lossing, *The Pictorial Fieldbook of the War of 1812*

While unfairly criticized for the the surrender of Detroit, Brig. Gen. William Hull certainly contributed to the outcome. His lethargic operations were partially attributable to the inept preparations of the War Office.

mingling easily within colonial social circles. During his many years in the Canadas he came into close contact with the privileged élites of the family compact.[2]

Although his proposals for aggressive action in the west met with a cool reception from the governor-general, Brock still believed in the possibilities of a vigorous defence of Upper Canada. In a letter to Prevost, he designated Amherstburg as "the first and most important point," emphasizing that weakness there would revive Native suspicions of past British abandonments. On the other hand, he predicted that a show of strength would neutralize the warriors as potential enemies and win them over as formidable allies. In his view, security in the Detroit sector "must deter any offensive movement on the province from the Niagara westward." Brock complained of the "inert and neutral proceedings" of withholding ammunition from the Natives while assuring them of "common interests." Prevost remained unmoved, and through Adjutant-General Edward Baynes wrote Brock that without reinforcements from England, little could be expected from the lower province to support aggressive measures, and that he was to exercise "cautious forbearance" in dealings with the Natives. Prevost was anxious not to aggravate relations with the republic by appearing to collaborate with the Native confederacy. Although his indifference to

Brock's plan did not expressly forbid offensive plans, it left Brock to his own slender resources.[3]

Undeterred, Brock boarded *Queen Charlotte* and conducted a flying visit to Fort Amherstburg on 14-17 June 1812, to bolster the garrison with a hundred regulars from the Niagara frontier. Brock met with the Native leaders, and through Matthew Elliott pledged British commitment to their cause of a homeland, adding, "You must abstain from scalping the dead and ill-treating your prisoners. Promise me that and you shall have all you want."[4]

Meanwhile, the Americans had already taken steps toward the invasion of Upper Canada. On 25 May 1812, Brig. Gen. Hull arrived in Dayton, Ohio to assume command of three regiments of state militia raised by Governor Return Meigs. To these he would shortly add some three hundred regulars of the 4th U.S. Infantry plus elements of the 1st. In anticipation of war, the American commander commenced his march on Detroit. Arriving there, Hull's troops would join 118 regulars in garrison, plus three local companies of the First Michigan Regiment, bringing the aggregate strength of the Northwest Army to about 2500 men.[5]

Hull's two hundred mile march to Detroit was a difficult one. Although the Natives granted him permission to pass through their lands, the movement through the Black Swamp was tough and slow, as the army had to literally blaze a road through the wilderness, building bridges and causeways. It rained incessantly, and the horse teams were often "belly-deep" in the morass. To secure his communications to Ohio, Hull built and garrisoned five blockhouses prior to reaching the Maumee Rapids. Arriving there on 1 July, he decided to ease the strain on his men by hiring two schooners to transport the convalescents, medical staff, army wives, bandsmen, baggage, and impedimenta to Detroit. Through some error, Hull's aides also stowed his official papers in the hold of *Cuyahoga Packet*, the larger vessel. Her master, Capt. Cyrenius Chapin, had been at Amherstburg the day before, and since there was no word of war, Hull did not fear for the safety of the vessels.[6]

On 2 July, the American commander pushed his main force on to Frenchtown. Prior to his arrival, Lt. Col. John Anderson, commander of the local Michigan militiamen, read a speech from the general to Native leaders of the area, which threatened reprisals if they interfered with the American advance. Anderson directed Capt. Hubert Lacroix and 80 volunteers of the 2nd Michigan Regiment to improve Hull's

The Capture of *Cuyahoga Packet*, 2 July 1812. Lt. Rolette's daring action provided the British with invaluable intelligence relating to Hull's army. *General Hunter* and Fort Amherstburg are shown in the background.

Courtesy of artist Peter Rindlisbacher

road and build blockhouses in the vicinity of Frenchtown. While Hull paraded his troops there to impress the Natives with U.S. might, he received Eustis's letter of 18 June, by regular mail, announcing that war was declared and that he was to hasten to Detroit and await further orders. Hull immediately sent horsemen to overtake the schooners, but they were already beyond recall.[7]

Unfortunately for Hull, the British garrison at Fort Amherstburg received word of war on 1 July, the very day his vessels set sail. Next day, as *Cuyahoga Packet* entered the deep-water channel of the Detroit River, a bateau containing six British soldiers from Fort Amherstburg intercepted her. Their commander, Lt. Charles Frederick Rolette, was a veteran of the battles of Trafalgar and the Nile, now master of the Provincial Marine brig, *General Hunter*. With weapons drawn, he boarded the American vessel and directed her captain to sail into Amherstburg harbour. The 30 American soldiers on board, who had no reason to suspect danger, had secured their weapons in the hold. They found themselves prisoners of war before they knew that hostilities had broken out.[8]

To add chagrin to the Americans' misfortune, Rolette ordered the bandsmen to play a rousing rendition of "God Save the King" as the vessel came into port. In the hold, the captors found entrenching tools, hospital stores, and officers' baggage. Of greater importance were two trunks containing Hull's instructions from the secretary of war as well as the complete muster rolls of the Northwest Army, invaluable intelligence. Capt. Matthew Dixon, the engineer officer, and Lt. Edward Dewar, deputy assistant quartermaster-general at Fort Amherstburg, examined the documents that furnished not only the rare luxury of knowledge of the enemy's objective but of the resources dedicated to its attainment. The smaller schooner carrying the medical staff, invalids, and miscellaneous stores avoided capture by sailing unobserved up the west side of Bois Blanc Island, and bore tidings of her consort's capture to Detroit.[9]

The commander at Fort Amherstburg was Lt. Col. Thomas Bligh St. George, inspecting field officer of the militia in the Western District. Almost 60 years old, St. George had last seen action at Corsica and Toulon against the French some 20 years previously. In April 1812, the certainty of war prompted Brock to assign him command at Fort Amherstburg. St. George was skeptical of his commander's ability to realize his plans in the west and complained loudly about his assignment. According to Brock, the colonel went "in such a state of mind that forbids my placing any dependence on his exertions ... his conduct in the presence of some officers was so improper and otherwise so childish that I have since written to say that if he continued in the same disposition, he was at liberty to return to Niagara." Despite such inauspicious beginnings, St. George took up his duties to the best of his abilities. As early as 7 May 1812, he reported large milita concentrations in Ohio, prompting Brock's flying visit with reinforcements within days of the declaration of war.[10]

Fort Amherstburg was a small "temporary field work in a ruinous state," located about 14 miles south of Detroit and 30 yards from the Detroit River. It was bounded with earthen bastions connected by mounds of dirt, the whole surrounded by a line of palisades perforated for musketry, flanked by a dry ditch. Its artillery consisted of 20 pieces, ranging from 3- to 18-pdr. guns. The wooden buildings within the fort were susceptible to combustion by hotshot, especially from the north side which was commanded by high ground some five hundred yards upriver. Given the rising tensions, Brock undertook hurried efforts to improve the condition of this fort, the only established defensive position in the Western District.[11]

The regular forces at St. George's disposal consisted of three part-companies of the 41st Regiment under the command of Capt. Adam Muir, a corporal's command of artillerymen under Lt. Felix Troughton,

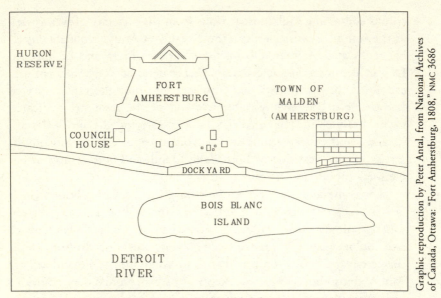

Graphic reproduction by Peter Antal, from National Archives of Canada, Ottawa: "Fort Amherstburg, 1808," NMC 3686

Fort Amherstburg, 1808, was the only established defensive position in the Western District. Richardson described this strategically located fort at the mouth of the Detroit River as "quadrangular."

and a handful of support staff, the whole totaling about 250 regular soldiers. Also available to him were the vessels of the Provincial Marine anchored off the King's Dockyard: the ship, *Queen Charlotte* of 18 guns; the small brig, *General Hunter* of six guns; and the almost finished schooner, *Lady Prevost*, pierced for 12 guns. In addition, he commanded (nominally) seven hundred militiamen of the Essex and Kent regiments. Although the area Natives were overwhelmingly noncommittal, Tecumseh arrived at Amherstburg on 1 July 1812 with two hundred pro-British followers.[12]

On learning of the state of war and the fate of *Cuyahoga Packet*, Hull accelerated the march, though with heightened vigilance, fortifying his encampments with timber breastworks. On 4 July, Independence Day, he halted at Brownstown to await the construction of a bridge strong enough to bear his wagons over the Huron River, while the crew of *Queen Charlotte* observed from a distance. Finally, on 6 July, after an exhausting 35-day march, the Northwest Army arrived at Detroit, and Hull's armourers set to work repairing the militiamen's flintlocks, most of which were in poor repair.[13]

Designed and built by Britain (as Fort Lernoult) during the Revolutionary War, Fort Detroit stood on a rise behind the town, 750

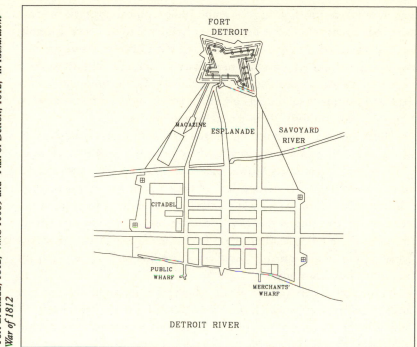

Graphic reproduction by Peter Antal, from National Archives of Canada, Ottawa: "Fort L'Arnaud, 1812," NMC 10069 and "Plan of Detroit, 1812," in *Richardson's War of 1812*

Fort Detroit, 1812. Although the features of the fort are accurately depicted, the town would have changed considerably after the fire of 1805.

feet from the river. It was a quadrangular structure with corner bastions and barracks built into its walls, occupying about two acres of land. The parapets or walls were 22 feet high and 12 feet thick at the top. A dry moat or ditch, 12 feet wide and 8 feet deep, surrounded the walls with a row of 11-foot cedar pickets embedded in the trough. The main gate was double-doored with a long portcullis (a covered bridge) extending over the moat. The fort walls boasted 26 guns, in addition to a field train stored in the compound. Immediately adjacent to the south wall, the citadel occupied an additional two acres, encompassed by a row of 16-foot pickets. It contained the officers' quarters, public stores, and miscellaneous military buildings. Having undergone major repairs in 1811, the fort was in good repair. Toward the river and connected to fort and citadel was the town of Detroit, entirely enclosed by a wall of stout posts containing loop holes for musketry.[14]

Fort Detroit was garrisoned by 108 American regulars. The immediate vicinity also produced several militia companies comprising the 1st Michigan Regiment. Like their Canadian counterparts, these militiamen had little interest in fighting for grand philosophical abstractions and were indifferent soldiers, at best. Prior to Hull's arrival, "a considerable mutiny" occurred among their number and some of the *Canadien* members openly advocated resistance to military service and even urged their comrades to desert to Amherstburg. Hull's Ohio militiamen also expressed mutinous sentiments over their commander's refusal to attack Upper Canada without Washington's express approval.[15]

Hull's greatest apprehensions related to the loyalties of the Natives of the area. On 7 July, he held a neutrality council with the principal chiefs of the Wyandot, Ojibwa, Shawnee, Seneca, Potawatomi, and Mohawk nations, who assured him of their friendship and neutrality. The American commander was particularly happy that he secured the goodwill of the influential Wyandot. Tecumseh was conspicuously absent at these talks, sending word from the Canadian side that "his bones would bleach on the Canadian shore before he would join in any council of neutrality."[16]

Prior to Hull's arrival at Detroit, Michigan militiamen fired several artillery rounds at Sandwich on 5 July 1812, from the sand dunes at Spring Wells, in retaliation for the capture of *Cuyahoga Packet*. Hull halted the cannonading as the needless destruction of private property. The following day, he sent one of his Ohio militia commanders, Col. Lewis Cass, with a letter for St. George in which he apologized for the artillery discharges. The American general asked if the officers' baggage (which included his splendid new uniform) taken on *Cuyahoga Packet* might be considered private property. St. George replied politely that although he was "honoured" with Hull's letter, "in justice to the captors," he must be "guided by the rules of war."[17]

After these niceties were concluded, Hull received authority to undertake offensive operations on 9 July and prepared boats for the crossing of the Detroit River. He had doubts, though. "The British command the water and the savages," he wrote to the secretary of war, "I do not think the force equal to the reduction of Amherstburg. You therefore must not be too sanguine." Hull also issued a general order for the garrisons of forts Detroit, Wayne, Michilimackinac, and Dearborn (Chicago), announcing the declaration of war; strangely, he failed to transmit it to the last two isolated posts.[18]

St. George was also busy, updating Brock by letter on 8 July about his defence measures. He assigned Col. James Baby, commander of the Kent Regiment, the task of defending Sandwich with four hundred militiamen, bolstering these with a small detachment of regulars and two 6-pdr. guns. Nonetheless, when the Americans cannonaded Sandwich, the militiamen became so alarmed that Baby withdrew them toward Amherstburg the next day. St. George reinforced the edgy militiamen with 50 more regulars under Capt. Adam Muir of the 41st and additional light field pieces, sending the entire detail back to Sandwich. Given the shortage of provisions, weapons, and manpower, St. George reported using everything "that falls in my way." He ordered the North West Company schooner, *Nancy*, down from Sandwich to the shelter of Amherstburg. In addition, he intercepted a fleet of 11 Northwest Company bateaux en route to Lake Huron. St. George commandeered their cargoes of arms, ammunition, and blankets for the ill-equipped militiamen and armed the bateaux as small gunboats with the 3-pdr. guns from *Nancy*, manning the craft with the 70 voyageurs.[19]

St. George experienced enormous difficulties in his feverish efforts to mobilize auxiliary fighters. At the grand council of Native chiefs on 7 July, he hoped to recruit the area warriors to the British side. Despite the influence of Tecumseh, the chiefs remained overwhelmingly neutral. The militiamen also presented difficulties, lacking strength returns, weapons, uniforms, equipment, pay, training, discipline, spirit, and leadership; in short, everything. The three militia units (the 1st Essex, 2nd Essex, and Kent regiments) were formations in name only, being little more than administrative pools of untrained men. Moreover, it was harvest time for the best crop in years. Concern for their distressed families prompted some of the citizen-soldiers to avoid military service. To feed his own combined force, St. George directed his quartermaster staff to gather the cattle of the Sandwich area and drive them down to the fort. On 10 July, he reported the militiamen still alarmed. Anticipating an American crossing, he planned to concentrate them at Amherstburg where the example of the regulars could better animate them.[20]

Meanwhile, at far-off Quebec City, Prevost had received the first intelligence of war and transmitted it to his commanders on 25 June. Brock had already received word through commercial sources and hurried to Fort George to join Col. Henry Procter. He wrote to Prevost, "I have been anxiously expecting for some days to receive the honour of your excellency's commands in regard to the measures the most proper to be pursued in the present emergency." For the first few weeks of the war, he would receive no directions except to restrain the Natives and not provoke the Americans by offensive action. Prevost conveyed his "best wishes" but refused to send aid to Upper Canada until he received a "considerable reinforcement" from England.[21]

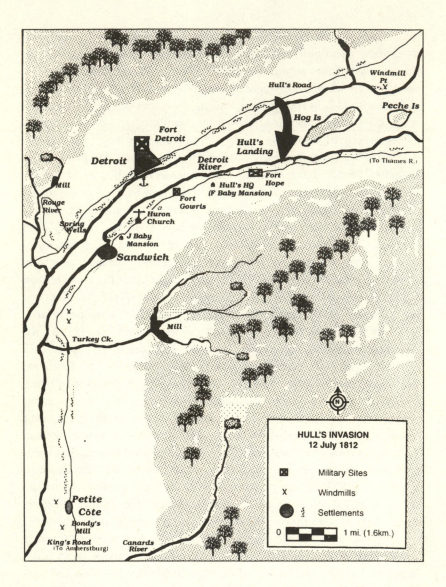

Given Prevost's retiscence and the uncertain state of affairs, Brock could do little more than call out the militiamen, issue a proclamation to the province to cease communications with the enemy, and deal with treasonable activity. Like St. George, he experienced immediate problems with the militiamen of the Niagara frontier regarding equipment and the harvest. Their reluctance to step forward for king and country was aggravated by a shortage of weapons in the colony. Six thousand stand of arms had been sent from England in late 1811 via the transport, *Cambo*, but that vessel foundered in a heavy gale, a mishap that Prevost termed "a serious inconvenience."[22]

Back at Detroit, Hull designated the evening of Friday, 10 July, for the crossing of the Detroit River. He delayed the invasion because of the accidental discharge of a musket which badly wounded an officer and threw the entire camp into an uproar. The following day, 180 men of Col. Duncan McArthur's regiment refused to enter Canada, as by state law they were required to serve only on U.S. soil. In order to conceal his design and provide meaningful employment for the insubordinate militiamen, Hull ordered McArthur's regiment to Spring Wells as a diversion, while the main body crossed the river from Bloody Ridge, below Hog Island (Belle Isle). On Sunday, 12 July, the Northwest Army rowed across the three-quarter mile river, landing unopposed above Sandwich. The invasion of Upper Canada had begun.[23]

John Hunt, a Detroit resident, described the spectacular appearance of the crossing, "My blood thrilled with delight when I saw from Detroit that beautiful morning the march of that fine army, with drums beating and colours flying, with the gleaming of bright muskets." Col. Lewis Cass blustered ashore, the first to set foot on the enemy beachhead, anxious to attach to himself the historic import of being at the forefront of the invasion. Amid loud huzzahs to the unfurling of the stars and stripes, Hull waded onto the shore, pronouncing, "The critical moment draws near!" *The War* reported that two thousand men made the unopposed crossing into Upper Canada, while Hull subsequently estimated half that number.[24]

Col. Baby had observed McArthur's feigned flanking movement from Sandwich and wrote to St. George on 11 July that he could no longer hold the jittery militiamen at their post. St. George rushed to the scene and learned that if he did not withdraw them to Amherstburg, they would disperse to their homes. As a result, he marched them to the fort that night, ripping up the bridge over Turkey Creek on the way. Even at Amherstburg, the militiamen deserted rapidly, and by 15 July, he counted only 471 of the 700 in the district. Meanwhile, the dockyard men launched *Lady Prevost* on 13 July.[25]

At Sandwich, Hull established his invasion headquarters at the unfinished brick home of Capt. François Baby (quartmaster-general of the district militia and brother to James Baby) and threw up entrenchments for a fortified camp he called Fort Hope. The next day, 13 July, he prepared two hundred copies of a bombastic proclamation in English and French. Offering Upper Canadians liberty or the less pleasant alternative of destruction, he threatened to execute any White man found fighting beside a Native warrior. On 14 July, he sent 250 men under Col. McArthur to pursue some two hundred Mississauga Ojibwa tribesmen who, with their families, fled toward the Thames River. Unable to overtake the fugitives who had dispersed on the Ruscom River, McArthur received orders from Hull to proceed to the Thames settlements in order to secure provisions, as American stocks were running low.[26]

Hull's invasion showed promise, since his proclamation visibly intimidated the enemy. In addition to the Native defections, up to 60 militiamen daily approached the American camp seeking protection. A total of 367 eventually offered their paroles to the Americans, promising not to fight during the war. Furthermore, the Brownstown neutrality council assured Hull that the majority of warriors would not take sides in the conflict. The principal chiefs, Crane of the Ohio Wyandot, Walk-in-the-Water of the Michigan Wyandot, and Logan Blue Jacket of the Detroit River Shawnee, all favoured neutrality. The number of pro-British warriors under Tecumseh and the Pottawatomi war chief, Main Pock, fluctuated at some two hundred. Even Tecumseh's supporters, such as the Wyandot brothers Roundhead, Splitlog, and Warrow were awed by American might. Although Roundhead had recently relocated some three hundred of the Ohio Wyandot to the Detroit River, the limited British preparations prompted him to remain uncommitted. Most important, Walk-in-the-Water, head chief of the 1200 Michigan Wyandot, was decidedly noncommital, effectively neutralizing the potential of this important nation. Even Warrow and his two hundred Canadian Wyandot of the Huron Reserve remained aloof.[27]

St. George tried to win over the local Natives. He summoned their principal leaders and pressed them to take up arms, censuring Roundhead for his reluctance to remove his followers to the Canadian side of the river. The council became stormy as St. George angrily seized his sword hilt, threatening to cut off all supplies and presents. Roundhead calmed him down and urged that discussions be undertaken in a "friendly spirit." He affirmed his nation's past loyalties and finally agreed to take hold of the tomahawk offered by the British commander. Splitlog and Warrow followed suit. Nonetheless, Walk-in-the-Water still refused to co-operate, having committed himself to inaction at the Brownstown council. He withdrew the greater part of his nation into the interior of Michigan.[28]

Matthew Elliott's letter of 15 July to the superintendent of Indian Affairs was the report of a passive observer rather than that of a principal official of the region. He lamented that supplies for the warriors had not arrived in quantity, and concluded haplessly, "If more Indians come, I really don't know how to act." Through omission, St. George commented on Elliott's inaction, observing to Brock that he seemed "preoccupied with his papers."[29]

During this time, Hull consolidated his hold, building batteries on both banks of the river at Detroit to control access to Lake Huron. With the refitted brig, *Adams,* launched at the River Rouge shipyard on 4 July, he moved that vessel to Detroit to be rigged and armed. With *Adams* finished, the American general triumphantly predicted, "We shall then command the Upper Lakes!"[30]

Despite Hull's success to date, all was not well within his camp. The refusal of some militiamen to cross U.S. boundaries dampened his confidence in the raw troops. When a court martial examined the case of one officer and found him unfit to serve, his men promptly re-elected him to his post. As state law did not require balloted soldiers to serve outside the United States, Hull could not press the issue without alienating the rank and file. In a council of war on 5 July, the Ohio colonels flatly declared that they could not answer for their men in an assault on Fort Amherstburg. Only Lt. Col. James Miller expressed confidence in his regulars.[31]

Chief Justice Augustus Woodward constituted another impediment to Hull's authority. Contemptuous of all arbitrary powers (except his own), the judge was only too willing to intervene in military affairs by placing a British deserter of Hull's army under his protection while complaining to the secretary of war that Hull was not showing adequate respect to the civil power. Woodward and Hull had arrived in Michigan in 1805 to establish federal authority in the new territory. The independent-minded inhabitants had little respect for the pair, viewing them as corrupt and self-serving. An 1807 petition presented an unflattering description of the first men of Michigan:

The history of William Hull and Augustus B. Woodward since they took upon themselves the government of this territory, is a history of repeated injuries, abuses and deceptions, all having a direct tendency to harass, distress, and impoverish, if not absolutely expel the present inhabitants, and to accomplish their private schemes ... they have been guilty of unfeeling cruelty and barbarity ... through their systematic speculation.... They have by their intrigues and ridiculous manoeuvres, sunk themselves into the deepest contempt and they are ... a reproach and bye-word among the people.[32]

On 17 July, Col. McArthur returned from his foraging expedition on the Thames. Bearing two hundred barrels of flour and a large sail boat from John McGregor's Mill, four hundred three-point blankets from John Dolsen's, and assorted guns, ammunition, salt, and whiskey, he provided useless receipts to the bilked owners. Three malcontents, Ebenezer Allan, Andrew Westbrook, and Simon Zealotus Watson, accompanied McArthur back to Sandwich and readily offered their services to Hull. Ten days later, another detachment under Capt. Thomas Forsyth returned from Baldoon, having plundered eight or nine hundred Merino sheep, and their aged Scottish keeper, as well as the settlement's large boat and ten smaller ones, all loaded with grain, flour, and other booty. His looting expedition devastated this struggling settlement.[33]

By this time, Brock was anxious. On receiving word of war, he hoped to implement his plan by seizing the isolated Fort Michilimackinac. Perched on a high bluff of rock two hundred feet above the churning waters, this wind-swept post was virtually impregnable to attack from the seaward side. Situated at the confluence of three of the Great Lakes, it controlled commercial traffic in the area and had great symbolic value to the Natives of the region. On 26 June, Brock ordered Capt. Charles Roberts, commander of nearby Fort St. Joseph, to attack that post. Uncertain of the state of diplomatic affairs, he countermanded his orders the next day, suspending the attack. The following day, 28 June, Brock wrote Roberts again, this time leaving an assault to the garrison commander's discretion. Roberts must have been perplexed at receiving yet another letter from Prevost who, circumventing the chain of command, directed him to adopt a defensive posture or retreat if necessary.[34]

Roberts assessed the situation and decided to act. He had at his disposal 30 old soldiers of the 10th Veteran Battalion, two hundred *Canadien voyageurs* of the North West Company under Robert Crawford, 113 Menominee, Sioux, and Winnebago warriors under the direction of South West Company agent Robert Dickson, and 280 Ottawa and Ojibwa warriors under John Askin, Jr., of the Indian Department. Accompanied by the North West Company brig, *Caledonia*, Roberts led this motley force (armed with muskets, blunderbusses, and fowling pieces) against Michilimackinac's garrison of 61 regulars of all ranks. The expedition sailed the 40 miles to Michilimackinac Island, arriving before dawn on 17 July. Surrounding the American post on the landward side, Roberts mounted two rusty old iron 6-pdr. guns (used to fire salutes on appropriate occasions) on the high ground overlooking the fort and promptly received its bloodless surrender. The American commander, Lt. Porter Hanks, had not received word of war and capitulated to avert a "general massacre." Among the captured goods were seven pieces of ordnance, 10 tons of flour, 13 tons of salted pork, and miscellaneous other stores. Roberts also took charge of two merchant vessels, *Salina* and *Mary*, in the harbour and later apprehended two others, *Erie* and *Friendsgoodwill,* coming up from Lake Michigan. Roberts's decisive action swayed the area Natives to the British side. Significantly, the signed capitulation went beyond a military occupation. Its terms included a requirement for all U.S. citizens to either take the oath of allegiance to Britain or leave the island within one month.[35]

Unaware of the capture of Michilimackinac, Hull initiated movements toward Amherstburg. About three miles north of this post lay the marshy Canards River, 30 yards wide and unfordable for several miles upstream. The north bank was bordered by an open plain, while the opposite side was heavily timbered about a hundred yards from the river margin. St. George recognized this natural barrier as a strong defensive position from which to protect Amherstburg. It was here that he hoped to hold the Americans.[36]

On 16 July, Hull sent Col. Cass with 280 Ohio men of his regiment to scout the approaches to Amherstburg. Thirty years of age, Cass was a huge, strong man of coarse, unflattering features. Nonetheless, the blunt, uncomplicated manner of the ambitious frontier lawyer suited his followers. Cass was unimpressed with Hull from their first meeting in Ohio, writing to his brother-in-law, "Instead of having an energetic commander, we have a weak old man." An observer recalled that after a stormy two hour session with Hull on the 16th, Cass declared, "If God lets me live, I will have Malden before I return."[37]

Perceiving the American advance on the Canards, Lt. John Clemow of the 41st withdrew his observation detachment to the south side of the river; however, two soldiers, privates John Dean and James Hancock, remained cut off on the opposite bank, refusing to surrender to the impossible odds. The Americans killed Hancock and took Dean prisoner; they were the first British casualties of the war. The incident was later held up by Brock in general orders as an example of "heroism, self-devotion, firmness and intrepidity" for others to emulate. Ensign James Cochran presents a less inspiring version of the affair: "Hancock and Dean, a double sentry from the advanced picket, were both drunk and asleep when the advancing enemy drove in the picket and in their stupid surprise, offered useless resistence when roused by the Americans. The first was killed and the last made prisoner." [38]

Leaving a 40-man detachment near the bridge, Cass led his men five miles upstream, forded the Canards, and managed to drive off the 50 British defenders, commanded by Captain Joseph Tallon of the 41st, before darkness halted the pursuit. He left a guard at the bridge and spent the night with his main force in the homes and barns of Petite Côte. Anxious to advance on Fort Amherstburg, that "nest of vultures," Cass sought provisions and reinforcements from Hull, who replied next day that, despite the importance of the bridge, it could be flanked by circumvention upstream, as Cass had done. Since the American artillery carriages would not be repaired for a week, he favoured abandoning the site but left that decision to Cass's discretion. The chagrined colonel returned to Sandwich. [39]

During the shooting of 16 July, Hull sent another emissary to Fort Amherstburg with a letter for St. George. In it, the American commander again raised the subject of the *Cuyahoga Packet* capture and made an awkward attempt to recover his official papers, "which it is presumed will be of no service to the British Government." Hull also sought the return of the officers' baggage, threatening retaliation were his demand not met. St. George rejected both requests, adding that "retaliation can be carried out to a great degree by both sides." Hull responded with the general order of 18 July, in which he decreed that "all personal property of officers now serving in the British Army at the aforementioned post [Fort Amherstburg], shall be taken." His ill-advised edict was little more than a license for the unruly soldiers to pilfer the militia officers' homes at Sandwich, prompting one of the Ohio volunteers to label Hull's motives as indicative of "dwarfishness of soul." [40]

On 17 July, in response to a report that *Queen Charlotte* was sailing upriver, Hull sent a detachment under Col. James Findlay to investigate. Findlay went down as far as the Canards River and observed that the British detachment ripped up the sills of the bridge and constructed a breastwork from its timbers on the south bank. He located *Queen Charlotte* stationed at the river's mouth, commanding the bridge area with her 24-pdr. guns. Findlay also found the body of the slain British soldier, Hancock; he had been scalped by the Natives. [41]

Two days later, 19 July, Hull sent Col. McArthur with two hundred men to the Canards. His mission was to reconnoiter *Queen Charlotte*,

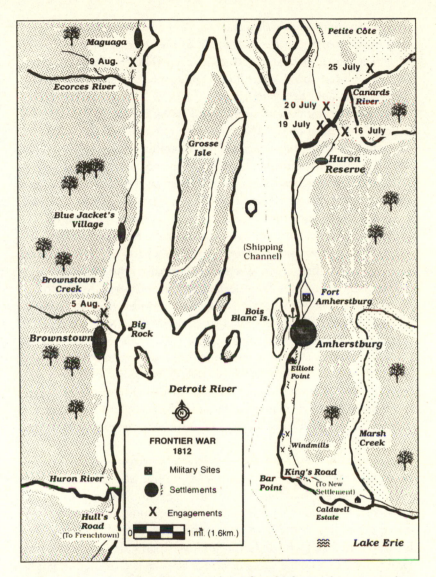

with a view to boarding her at night. After deploying his men in line against the breastwork on the opposite bank, McArthur went down-river for a close look at the vessel. Skulking with his spyglass among the bulrushes, he came under fire from a previously unperceived gunboat, which drove off his party. After some desultory shooting across the river, he withdrew his men to Petite Côte, where he was joined by Cass and 150 men of his regiment with a 6-pdr. gun. Tecumseh and Main Pock (noted for his deformed hand and drunken, lecherous lifestyle), were conspicuous in this skirmish. An American participant reported the British strength on the south side of the river as 50 warriors, 25 horsemen, 60 regulars and 150 militiamen. The following morning, 20 July, Cass convinced McArthur to conduct an artillery duel with the enemy for an hour before retiring.[42]

Yet another skirmish occurred near Petite Côte on 25 July. As Hull returned to Detroit on the 21st, (where he remained till the 26th) Col. McArthur ordered Maj. James Denny to ambush some warriors who were reported in the thickets near the Canards. Early that morning, Denny led off his detachment of 117 men and apprehended a local resident, Capt. Laurent Bondy of the 1st Essex Regiment, on well-grounded suspicions of provisioning hostile warriors. Denny's detachment went on to the forks of the Canards where his men laid down for a rest. Their repose was rudely interrupted by a party of 22 Menominee warriors led by their chief, Weenusate (Tomah), who stumbled upon the sleeping men. The soldiers leaped to arms but were driven off and pursued several miles to Turkey Creek. Six were killed and two captured. At least one warrior was also killed, as Capt. William McCulloch, commander of Hull's rangers, took a warrior's scalp. *The New York Gazette* printed an account of this three-hour running engagement, reporting that the Ohio militiamen had misbehaved. When the officers threatened to shoot them if they did not fight, the men replied, "It's better to be killed by them than those d—d Indians." McArthur's court of inquiry examining Denny's role concluded that "no imputation rests on him."[43]

Aside from disturbing the inoffensive waterfowl of the Canards River, the result of these misbegotten adventures was immaterial. Both sides sustained a handful of casualties for no visible gain to the invaders. On the contrary, the pointless skirmishing and inactivity produced grumbling in the American camp. Cass, recently designated by his troops as "the Hero of Ta-ron-tee," was particularly incensed that Hull refused to hold the Canards bridge after he had secured it. For his part, Hull had little reason to reassess his opinion of the undisciplined Ohio militiamen. In his view, offensive operations could succeed only with artillery support; however, the wet ground precluded movement of the heavy cannon by land, and *Queen Charlotte* effectively blocked any American advance beyond the Canards. He awaited the construction of rafts for his artillery with which to drive off the enemy vessel.[44]

By lingering at Sandwich, Hull missed opportunities that worked to the advantage of his enemy. Cass's initial attack of the 16th created considerable panic at Amherstburg. As the British force fell back on the fort, the garrison prepared for evacuation. One of the *Cuyahoga Packet* prisoners observed *Queen Charlotte* taking on baggage and women, "her topsails loose, ready to sail." Another reported that the townspeople had virtually deserted Amherstburg. Matthew Elliott fully expected the fort to be attacked that day. St. George and Brock agreed that if the Americans breached the Canards, the weak defences of the fort would leave no alternative for the garrison but to board the King's vessels and proceed to Fort Erie.[45]

Had Hull moved quickly upon Amherstburg after the capture of the Canards bridge, circumstances would have favoured his advance. The overwhelming majority of Natives remained neutral. Moreover, their principal chiefs (Crane, Walk-in-the-Water, Blackhoof, Colonel Lewis, and Wolf) undertook deliberate efforts to detach those who had joined the British standard. For his part, Hull insisted on waiting to repair his artillery carriages, assigning other artificers to finish *Adams* and yet others to make boarding pikes and artillery barges. Thus the carriages were not ready until 7 August. Hull would say in his defence, "My opinion was that an attempt on Malden should never be made until there was an absolute certainty of success." Nonetheless, the democratic inclination of Hull's citizen-army favoured an advance on Amherstburg. Hull and the Northwest Army each reflected a mutual contempt.[46]

At Fort George, Brock was also unhappy with his commander at Amherstburg. His assessment of St. George seemed confirmed as he noted that three days elapsed before the latter reported the American invasion. He complained that the Americans would not hesitate to attack an enemy that allowed him to cross the river without a shot in resistance. To salvage the situation, Brock sent his commander on the Niagara frontier, Col. Henry Procter, expecting his arrival at Amherstburg on 21 July. To support Procter and counteract American activities on the Thames, he forwarded a detachment of 50 regulars to Moraviantown to rally the Long Point militiamen and the Grand River Mohawk for a descent on Detroit. On hearing of Hull's "insidious proclamation," he responded with a spirited one of his own on 22 July.[47]

While Brock paced impatiently, awaiting the opening of the legislature on 27 July, he became gravely concerned with the "critical" events on the Detroit frontier. Indeed, his grand scheme for Amherstburg was seemingly derailed. The commander's frustration was self-evident in his letter to Prevost of 20 July: "I should have derived much consolation in the midst of my present difficulties had I been honoured, previously to the meeting of the Legislature with your excellency's determination in regard to this province." Having sent Procter to Amherstburg, he wrote, "I have great dependence on that officer's judgment but I fear he will arrive too late to be of much service." Brock directed the 1st and 2nd Norfolk Regiments, as well as the Oxford militiamen to assemble at Moraviantown, but to his mortification, malcontents and renegades, notably Ebenezer Allan, Andrew Westbrook, and Simon Zealotus Watson (members of the "Canadian Volunteers"), had boldly circulated Hull's proclamation on the Thames, paralyzing efforts to mobilize the militiamen. The American-born residents of the Long Point and upper Thames areas were reluctant to rally under the British banner, partly because of republican leanings and partly out of festering resentments against the arbitrary methods of land allocation in the colony. Col. Thomas Talbot, the principal militia officer of the region (and prominent land baron) wrote to Brock that he expected two hundred volunteers to step forward but only 60 mustered and even these refused to march. Talbot virtually conceded defeat, asking Brock to consider his settlers in any "conditions" arranged with Hull.[48]

Worse yet, the Six Nations of the Grand River, prompted by Hull's emissaries, adopted a noncommittal position. As a consequence, even the few loyal militiamen of the region became reluctant to leave their families to the mercy of the Natives. An exasperated Brock wrote, "I shall think it my bounden duty at some future day to call your lordship's attention to the absolute necessity of removing this infatuated people from their present situation." Furthermore, Brock learned that large numbers of Delaware and Westminster residents of the Upper Thames followed the example of those at Sandwich, Baldoon, and the Lower Thames by offering their paroles to Hull's agents. A despondent Talbot summed up the situation, writing, "In fact, my dear General, the prospect is dismal." Almost beside himself, Brock reported the deteriorating situation to Prevost, saying that the militiamen had "ruined all my plans." He conceded that the province could not be held with its small regular force, adding, "Unless the enemy be driven from Sandwich, it will be impossible to avert much longer the impending ruin of the country."[49]

At this point, Brock lost contact with both Procter and Amherstburg. On 25 July, he wrote to Prevost, "I have not heard from Lt. Colonel St. George, nor from any individual at Amherstburg since I last had the honour of addressing your excellency, which makes me apprehensive that Colonel Procter has been detained on his journey too long for the good of the service." Brock had received word from Col. James Baby (on his way to York for the legislative session), that Procter was windbound on the 23rd in a small boat a few miles above Port Talbot. On 28 July, Brock wrote that each day the situation became more critical, that the population was worse than expected, and with Procter stranded, "I almost despair of succeeding." The following day he was somewhat heartened by news of the capture of Michilimackinac but still apprehensive about Amherstburg. Although he put on a bold front, writing to Baynes, "I talk loud and look big," his letters verged on frantic as he declared to Prevost, "Never was an officer placed in a more awkward predicament!... I entreat the advice of your excellency." This was Brock's darkest hour.[50]

In contrast to Brock's desperate letters, Prevost, who had previously declared his lieutenant's plans futile, reviewed reports on recent repairs to Fort Amherstburg, and with bizarre logic confidently reassured Brock, "The result of General Hull's attempt upon that fort will terminate honourably to our arms." Brushing aside Brock's alarmed warnings, the commander-in-chief still insisted on defensive measures, arguing that according to his diplomatic contacts, Hull's invasion was some kind of mistake, as the American secretary of state had assured British diplomats in Washington that Amherstburg would not be attacked. In his ponderous language, Prevost explained the grand scheme of things to Brock: "The King's government having most unequivocally expressed to me their desire to preserve peace with the United States, that they might, uninterrupted, pursue with the whole disposable force of the country, the great interest in Europe." Indeed, the British government was so confident of a peaceful resolution that the minister for war and colonies assured Prevost on 4 July, "Suspend with perfect safety all extraordinary measures for defence."[51]

By 4 August, Brock was as confounded by Prevost's passivity as he was ignorant about developments in the west, writing, "I cannot hear what is going on at Amherstburg. I begin to be uneasy for Procter. Should anything befall him, I shall begin to despond for the fate of Amherstburg.... What can be done with such a vile population?" Brock received little more than sympathy from Prevost's office, Baynes writing that 150 soldiers had been forwarded in place of the two regiments Brock requested, adding, "I regret to find your militia at Sandwich so lukewarm, to call it by no harsher name; but I fear little can be expected from those recently settled or of American extraction and with our Canadians [meaning the French-speaking inhabitants of Lower Canada] we have found a very reluctant compliance."[52]

Finally, Brock's apprehensions were relieved. He heard that Elizabeth Procter at Newark had received a letter from her husband at Amherstburg. Then, just as Brock was preparing to convene the provincial legislature at York, he received two highly reassuring letters from Procter. Reinforced in the belief that all was not lost, after all, he delivered a powerful address to the Legislative Council and House of Assembly: "We are engaged in an awful and eventful contest. By unanimity and dispatch in our councils and by vigour in our operations, we may teach the enemy this lesson, that a country defended by free men, enthusiastically devoted to the cause of their King and constitution, can never be conquered!"[53]

NOTES

1. Hull to Six Nations, 8 July, 1812, *DICSD*, 72.
2. Brock to Prevost, 12 Feb. 1812, *SBD* 1: 294; *DCB* 5: 109-16.
   Richardson described Brock as "tall, stout, inclining to corpulency ... of fair and florid complexion ... a large forehead, full face ... rather small greyish-blue eyes ... exceedingly affable and gentlemanly, of a cheerful and sociable habit, partial to dancing and although never married, extremely devoted to female company." John Richardson, *Richardson's War of 1812*, 116.
3. Brock to Prevost, 2 Dec. 1811, Brock to Prevost, 25 Feb. 1812, Baynes to Brock, 21 May 1812, Tupper, *Brock*, 124, 154, 161.
4. Tupper, *Brock*, 191; Hull to Eustis, 24 June 1812, *MPHC* 40: 398; Brock to Prevost, 18 Sept. 1812, *SBD* 1: 593; William Coffin, *1812: The War and Its Moral*, 198.
5. Hull to Eustis, 24 June, 1812, *MPHC* 40: 398. The 4th U.S. Infantry was raised at Boston in April, 1808 and manned by New Englanders. The regiment gained national fame as "the Heroes of Tippecanoe" in 1811 when, under Governor Harrison's command, it scattered the Native confederacy. Its members constituted the disciplined element of Hull's hastily assembled Northwest Army. Lt. Col. James Miller joined the regiment at its inception and commanded it after April 1812.
   Hull subsequently maintained that he took command of only 1200 Ohio militiamen and three hundred regulars. Yet, he reported his strength at Urbana, Ohio as two thousand men plus officers. Ernest Cruikshank extracted the following figures (exclusive of the Detroit garrison and Michigan militia) from documents presented at General Dearborn's court martial:

4th U.S. Infantry (Lt. Col Miller)	483
1st Ohio Regiment (Col. Findlay)	509
2nd Ohio Regiment (Col. Cass)	483
3rd Ohio Regiment (Col. McArthur)	552
Troop of Cincinnati Light Dragoons	48
Total	2075

Hull, *Memoirs*, 8; Hull to Eustis, 11 June 1813, *MPHC* 40: 389; Extract from Return of Hull's Brigade, *DICSD*, 39.

6. Parish, *The Robert Lucas Journal*, 10; Hull to Eustis, 24 June 1812, *MPHC* 40: 398; Lt. Aaron Forbush, *HCM*, 145.

7. Dennis Au, *War on the Raisin*, 8. Hull received a letter from Eustis on 26 June at the Maumee Rapids dated 18 June (the day war was declared) but it contained no intimation of war. Eight days transpired before Hull learned of the state of hostilities. Hull to Eustis, 26 June 1812, *MPHC* 40: 399.

8. Return of Prizes by HM Vessels on Lake Erie, *DICSD*, 232. Charles Frederick Rolette (1783-1831) was born at Quebec City. Entering the Royal Navy at a young age, he served under Nelson at the battle of the Nile and at Trafalgar. Returning to Canada in 1807 as a second lieutenant in the Provincial Marine, he was made lieutenant five years later to command *General Hunter*. Rolette's daring capture of *Cuyahoga Packet* was an event of great importance for the vital intelligence it secured. He later shared credit for the capture of 12 boats and bateaux in the Detroit River after the battle of Maguaga. Rolette's biographers seldom mention that he commanded the brig, *Detroit I* (ex-*Adams*) when she was surprised and surrendered to an American boarding party off Fort Erie on 9 Oct. 1812. Biographical note on Frederick Rolette, cited in *DHCNF* 1812, Vol. 2: 57-59.

9. G.M. Fairchild Jr., *Journal of an American Prisoner at Ft. Malden and Quebec in the War of 1812*, cited in Francis Cleary, "Defence of Essex in the War of 1812," 73; Adam Walker, *A Journal of Two Campaigns of the Fourth Regiment of U.S. Infantry*, 48; Capt. Piatt to Eustis, 17 July 1812, *MPHC* 40: 416; Gooding, *HCM*, 100; Lucas, *Journal*, 19; Capt. Dixon to Lt. Col. Bruyères, 8 July 1812, *SBD* 2: 351. Edward Dewar (100th Foot) was deputy assistant quartermaster general at Fort Amherstburg. He supervised the crossing of Brock's troops to Michigan for the capture of Detroit. His detailed reports provide valuable insight into British activities in the region. Dewar perceived the impending food shortages of the Right Division and was active in organizing foraging operations at Frenchtown and the Maumee Rapids. An enterprising officer, he died suddenly in December 1812 from a burst blood vessel, the first of a string of logisticians in Upper Canada to be overwhelmed by sheer stress. *DICSD*, 44n.

10. Brock to Baynes, 12 Feb. 1812, Tupper, *Brock*, 149; St. George to
    Brock, 7 May 1812, *DICSD*, 23-24.
    Thomas Bligh St. George, of the 63rd Foot joined the British Army
    in 1771 as an ensign in the 27th Foot. After serving against the French
    in the Mediterranean, he was promoted to captain and major in 1794.
    Although Brock had few good things to say about him, Procter
    appointed him brevet colonel on 6 September 1812. *DICSD*, 24n.
11. Descriptions of Fort Amherstburg are found in Dalliba, *HCM*, 19;
    Prevost to Liverpool, 18 May 1812, *SBD* 1: 304; Richardson, *War of
    1812*, 20. The emergency repairs conducted in 1812 are detailed in
    Capt. Dixon to Lt. Col. Bruyères, 8 July 1812, *SBD* 1: 350-51;
    St. George to Brock, 8 July 1812, *DICSD*, 23-24.
12. Brock's Defence Memorandum, Feb. 1811, *SBD* 1, 288-89. Provincial
    Marine affairs are examined in W.A.B. Douglas, "The Anatomy of
    Naval Incompetence: the Provincial Marine in Defence of Upper
    Canada before 1813," and *Gunfire on the Lakes*.
    Adam Charles Muir (c.1776-1829) was born in Scotland. He joined
    the army as a common private of the 41st Foot in 1788 and rose to
    sergeant-major within five years. In 1793, he was appointed regimental
    adjutant and promoted to ensign. The next year, he served in San
    Domingo, earning a promotion to lieutenant. Muir accompanied the
    41st to Canada in 1799 and advanced to captain in 1804 at Fort
    Amherstburg. He commanded Fort St. Joseph before returning to Fort
    Amherstburg, remaining there until the American occupation of 1813.
    DCB 6: 529-30.
    Felix Troughton was in charge of the artillery detachment at Fort
    Amherstburg during the war. He was wounded at Frenchtown but
    recovered to participate in all subsequent operations of the Right
    Division. He survived the war, only to die of natural causes on 26 June
    1815 during his homeward voyage to England. *DICSD*, 149n.
13. Lucas, *Journal*, 20-27; Hunt, *Memoirs*, 13. Brock had directed St.
    George to attack Fort Detroit on the outbreak of war and he prepared
    to do so on 2 July 1812, but the false alarm created by the approach of
    a fleet of Northwest Company boats caused the plan to be aborted. The
    arrival of Hull's army at Detroit placed St. George on the defensive.
    Robert Reynolds narrative, cited in Coffin, *The War and Its Moral*, 200;
    Lucas, *Journal*, 20-21; Merritt, *Journal*, *SBD* 3: 548-49.
14. Dalliba, *HCM*, 81-82; Richardson, *War of 1812*, 84n.; Stanley Hatch,
    A Chapter in the History of the War of 1812 in the Northwest, 79; [James
    Foster], *The Capitulation or A History of the Expedition Conducted by
    William Hull*, 221. Fort Detroit is not to be confused with the original
    French post, Fort Ponchartrain, which had been torn down long before
    the war. The new fort was renamed Fort Shelby when the Americans
    reoccupied it in 1813.

15. Lucas, *Journal*, 90; Hull, *Memoirs*, 10. One of the Michigan militia companies was manned exclusively by 36 "renegade Negroes," former slaves who had escaped to Michigan from their British owner, Matthew Elliott. Although slavery was illegal on both sides of the border, those Loyalist immigrants who brought slaves with them to Upper Canada were allowed to keep them. Thus, Black slaves actually escaped to the freedom of Michigan from the future terminus of the "underground railroad." Lt. Col. Grant to Secretary Green, 17 Aug. 1807, *MPHC* 15: 42.

16. [Foster], *Capitulation*, 220; Anthony Shane records, cited in Benjamin Drake, *The Life of Tecumseh*, 163.

17. Hull to St. George, 16 July 1812, and St. George to Hull, 16 July 1812, *DICSD*, 69-70; McAfee, *History of the Late War*, 58. Lewis Cass (1782-1866), native of New Hampshire, moved to Ohio at the age of 17. He studied law and gained prominence as a vigorous prosecutor in the Aaron Burr trial. He was a U.S. marshall in 1807 but resigned in May 1812, to enlist as colonel of the 3rd Ohio Regiment of Volunteers. *DAB* 2: 562.

18. Hull to Eustis, 9 July 1812, *MPHC* 40: 406.

19. St. George to Brock, 8 July 1812, *DICSD*, 44-48; Boucherville, *Journal*, 84. James (Jacques) Baby (1762-1833) was colonel of the Kent Regiment and long-time member of the provincial legislature. He was captured at the battle of Moraviantown but released by Harrison. Baby (pronounced Bawby) suffered extensive damage to his property during the war, after which he became president of the Legislative Council. His brother Jean-Baptiste Baby was lieutenant colonel of the 2nd Essex Regiment. A third brother, Capt. François Baby, assistant quartermaster general for the Western District, was at the battle of Frenchtown and kidnapped by American raiders in 1814. His property was also greatly damaged in the war. *DCB* 6: 21-22.

20. John Askin, Sr., to James McGill, 17 July 1812, *JAP* 2: 710; St. George to Brock, 8 July 1812, *DICSD* 46-48; St. George to Brock, 10 July 1812, *SBD* 1: 368. Robert Lucas (1781-1853) was born in Virginia and moved to Ohio in 1800. He joined the 19th U.S. Infantry just before the war began, and accompanied Hull's march to Detroit as a scout. He escaped capture at Detroit in 1812 by hiding among noncombatants. After the war, he became a state senator and governor of Ohio. His published journal remains one of the best American accounts of the Detroit campaign. *DAB* 6: 487-88.

21. Baynes to Brock, 25 June 1812, Brock to Prevost, 3 July 1812, Tupper, *Brock*, 194, 195.

22. Brock's Proclamation of 6 July 1812, Brock to Prevost, 12 July 1812, Tupper, *Brock*, 197-98, 202-04; Prevost to Brock, 27 July 1812, *SBD* 2: 381.

23. Lucas, *Journal*, 26-28; Hull, *Memoirs*, 56; Hull to Eustis, 13 July 1812, *DICSD*, 57-58. Duncan McArthur (1772-1839) was a frontier scout for generals Harmar and Wayne before being elected colonel of the 1st Ohio Regiment during Hull's Detroit campaign. *DAB* 6: 549.

24. Hunt, *Memoirs*, 13; McAfee, *History of the Late War*, 60; William T. Young, *Sketch of the Life and Public Services of General Lewis Cass*, 24; *The War*, 8 Aug. 1812; Hull, *Memoirs*, 57.

25. St. George to Brock, 15 July 1812, *MPHC* 15: 103-04; Dyson, *HCM*, 133.

26. Taylor, *HCM*, 143; Hull to Eustis, 14 July 1812, *MPHC* 40: 413-14.

27. Hull to Eustis, 19 July 1812, *MPHC* 40: 418-19; Joseph Watson, *HCM*, 151; Clarke, *Wyandotts*, 77-102. Walk-in-the-Water or Mière was head chief of the Michigan Wyandot. Little is known of him. Although an unwilling participant in the war, he was prominent in the battle of Maguaga and the capture of Detroit. He also accompanied the Fort Wayne expedition and took part in the battle of Frenchtown. Walk-in-the-Water died about 1817. *DCB* 5: 619-20.

Roundhead or Stayegtha (c.1773-1813) was a principal chief of the Sandusky Wyandot. Although a participant at the battle of Fallen Timbers (1794), he was signatory to the Treaty of Greenville (1795). An early supporter of Tecumseh and the Prophet, he removed about three hundred of his tribesmen to Brownstown shortly before the war. With his brothers, Splitlog and Warrow he set the example for the Michigan Wyandot to join the British side, participating in the engagement of Maguaga and the capture of Detroit. Legend has Tecumseh presenting Brock's gift of a sash to Roundhead as "older and abler." The Wyandot chief accompanied the Fort Wayne expedition but is best remembered for his critical role in the battle of Raisin River (22 Jan. 1813). He led Native contingents on both invasions of Ohio. Subsequent to Procter's reverses in the summer of 1813, it was Roundhead (not Tecumseh) who rejected Harrison's proposals at the Brownstown parley of August 1813. The American commander considered him "entirely in the British interest." Roundhead's death of natural causes that same month was, in Procter's words, "a serious loss." *DCB* 5: 774-75; Clarke, *Wyandotts*, 80-102, 117, 136; Procter to Rottenberg, 23 Oct. 1813, NAC, C 680: 273; [Henry Procter and George Procter], *Lucubrations of Humphrey Ravelin*, 335.

Thomas Splitlog or Tharoutorea (c.1775-1838) was two or three years younger than his brother, Roundhead. He was an inveterate enemy of American encroachment in Ohio, participating in the battle of Fallen Timbers (1794). With his brother, he led about 70 Wyandot warriors at the battle of Maguaga (6 Aug. 1812) and accompanied Muir's Fort Wayne expedition. Splitlog was prominent in resisting the American winter advance at the Maumee Rapids (14 Nov. 1812) and at Frenchtown (22 Jan. 1813). After the defection of Walk-in-the-Water and the death of Roundhead, Splitlog and Warrow led the remnant of the loyal Wyandot at the battle of Moraviantown. Clarke, *Wyandotts*, 117, 143; *DCB* 7: 821-22.

Warrow was chief of the Canadian Wyandot on the Huron Reserve. The younger brother of Roundhead and Splitlog, he played an important role in the first weeks of the war as Procter's special envoy to the Michigan Wyandot, helping to sway them to the British side. Although seldom mentioned, Warrow undoubtedly took part in subsequent engagements. He joined Matthew Elliott at Burlington to continue the struggle after the allied defeat at Moraviantown. Ernest Cruikshank, "General Hull's Invasion of Canada in 1812," 253; Clarke, *Wyandotts*, 88, 102, 118; *DCB* 7: 821.

28. Clarke, *Wyandotts*, 102-03.
29. Lucas, *Journal*, 29-30; Elliott to Claus, 15 July 1812, *MPHC* 15: 105; St. George to Brock, 10 July 1812, *SBD* 1: 368.
30. Hull to Eustis, 19 July, *MPHC* 40: 418-19.
31. Dyson, *HCM*, 133; Hull, *Memoirs*, 54.
32. Alec R. Gilpin, *The War of 1812 in the Old Northwest*, 75; Michigan inhabitants' petition, 9 Dec. 1807, cited in Frank B. Woodford, *Mr. Jefferson's Disciple, A Life of Justice Woodward*, 46. Augustus Elias Brevoort Woodward (1774-1827) was born in Virginia. He started his public service career as a minor official in the Treasury Department mentored by Thomas Jefferson. In 1805, Woodward became chief justice of the newly formed Michigan Territory. Arriving at Detroit, he found it completely destroyed by fire and laid out a far-sighted plan for the rebuilding of the city. Brilliant and eccentric, Woodward was noted for his strong egalitarian principles. *DAB* 10: 506-07.
33. Lucas, *Journal*, 35; [Foster], *Capitulation*, 234-39; John Askin, "John Askin Diary," 17 July 1812, *MPHC* 15: 469. The American raid on Baldoon was essentially a plundering expedition that devastated the settlers and contributed to the eventual failure of the settlement. The sheep, kept as breeding stock, were removed to the common behind Fort Detroit; most of them were returned to Baldoon after Hull's capitulation. Whistler, *HCM*, 151; Hatch, *Chapter*, 31.
34. J. Mackay Hitsman, *The Incredible War of 1812*, 67. Fort Michilimackinac, was built by the British in 1780. It was transferred to the United States in 1796 when the British garrison removed to St. Joseph Island.
35. For the first-hand details of this important event, see Roberts to Brock, 12 July 1812, Roberts to Baynes, 17 July 1812, Roberts to Brock, 17 July 1812, Capitulation of Michilimackinac, 17 July 1812 and John Askin to Col. Claus, 18 July 1812 , *SBD* 1: 429-37; Hanks to Hull, 4 Aug. 1812, *HCM*, Appendix 2: 21-22. Despite the significance of his

action, Capt. Roberts received little official recognition, Prevost viewing it as verging on insubordination. Roberts was to remain at this dreary post unrewarded until his health failed. Procter sent Capt. Richard Bullock to relieve him in September 1813.

36. [Foster], *Capitulation*, 247.

37. Willis Stillman, *HCM*, 136; Hunt, *Memoirs*, 14; Lucas, *Journal*, 30-33; Cass to Hull, 17 July 1812, cited in [Foster], *Capitulation*, 240-42.

38. Procter to Brock, 26 July 1812, *MPHC* 15: 119-20. After the capture of Detroit, Brock personally released Dean from confinement. By Richardson's account, "While his voice betrayed strong emotion, he warmly approved his conduct and declared that he was indeed an honour to the profession of a soldier." According to Ensign Cochran, "Deane [*sic*] was again captured in October 1813 and eventually deserted the service." Brock to Prevost, 29 July 1812, *SBD* 1: 399; Richardson, *War of 1812*, 58; James Cochran, *Notes to Richardson's War of 1812*, NAC, MG 40, G4, File 1: 45.

    James Cochran (1791-1845) joined the Right Division on 3 August 1813, the day after the battle of Fort Stephenson, and was captured at the battle of Moraviantown. He remained with the 41st Foot after the war, serving in India, Afghanistan, and Burma, retiring from the army in 1845 as a major. In 1814, he wrote an account of the war. While useful in its minute observations, much of this account was based on the statements of second-hand observers, the narrative abounding in material inaccuracies. Like Richardson's work, Cochran's observations were written from a highly focussed "worm's eye" point of view, oblivious to the broad considerations that drove events. Cochran also annotated a copy of Richardson's work in which he contested some of the latter's observations. His brother, Ensign Andrew William Cochran, was Prevost's acting civil secretary and prosecutor at Procter's trial.

39. Miller, *HCM*, 105; Cass to Hull, 17 Aug. 1812, [Foster], *Capitulation*, 240-42; Hull to Cass, 17 July 1812, *HCM*, Appendix 1: 76.

40. Hull to St. George, 16 July 1812, *DICSD*, 69; St. George to Hull, 16 July 1812, *DICSD*, 70; [Foster], *Capitulation*, 246.

41. [Foster], *Capitulation*, 244; Lucas, *Journal*, 35-36. James Findlay (1770-1835) was born in Pennsylvania and became U.S. marshall for Ohio and mayor of Cincinatti before the war. With the other Ohio colonels of Hull's campaign, he was promoted brigadier general in the U.S. Army after the Detroit campaign. *DAB* 3: 385.

    Joseph Tallon (1773-1821) joined the 41st in 1796 and was promoted to captain 10 years later. Although present at Amherstburg from the outbreak of war and senior captain of the 41st, his name was seldom mentioned in despatches as he suffered from "debility of constitution." Nonetheless, he commanded the defenders at the Canards fighting

and was present at the battles of Maguaga and Frenchtown (when he
was badly wounded). He also fought at the battles of Fort Meigs and
Moraviantown, where he was captured. Tallon remained with the 41st
after the war, selling his commission in 1821. D.A.N. Lomax, *A
History of the Services of the 41st (the Welch) Regiment*, 60.

42. James Baby to Captain Glegg, 27 July 1812, *MPHC* 15: 120-21;
Hatch, *Chapter*, 32; [Foster], *Capitulation*, 246-51; Lucas, *Journal*,
36-40. Lucas's narrative of Hancock's scalping was confirmed by Robert
Reynolds, who stated that Main Pock took the scalp to gain favour with
the British. Recognizing the scalp, Hancock's colleagues gave Main
Pock a "good thrashing for his pains." The matter of the first scalping
was a major point with contemporary accounts. According to Capt.
Merritt, the warriors had solemnly promised in council not to conduct
scalping; however, after McCulloch's precedent, they "retracted all
former promises." Reynolds narrative, cited in Coffin, *The War and
Its Moral*, 200; Merritt, *Journal*, 549-50.

Main Pock (Mai Pock, Marpot, Withered Hand, or Crafty One)
(?-1816) was a Pottawatomi chief, a convert to the Prophet's teachings
after 1807. He was one of the first chiefs to join Tecumseh at Amherstburg.
Wounded in the fighting on the Canards River, he also participated in
the battles of Brownstown and Maguaga. A drunken, violent lecher,
Main Pock was notorious for his barbaric outrages during the war and
was considered responsible for directing the Fort Dearborn massacre.
Although a signatory to the Harrison's armistice of 14 October 1813,
his pacific professions were short-lived. He continued a postwar struggle with the Americans west of Lake Michigan until his death. R. David
Edmunds, *The Potawatomis*, 188, 199; Glenn Tucker, *Tecmseh: Vision
of Glory*, 246.

43. John Askin, "John Askin Diary," 25 July, 1812, *MPHC* 15: 469;
Robert Allan, *His Majesty's Indian Allies*, 128; Lucas, *Journal*, 43-44;
[Foster], *Capitulation*, 255-62; *New York Gazette*, 12 Aug. 1812. The
Menominee came from the western shore of Lake Michigan. They
arrived through the influence of fur trader Robert Dickson who had
been conducting secret communications with Brock in cloaked language
for months. Correspondence between Brock and Dickson, 27 Feb. and
18 June 1812, *SBD* 3: 423-24.

Laurent Bondy was an active officer of the First Essex Regiment. He
owned a mill at Petite Côte from which he provisioned the warriors
during Hull's attempts on the Canards. He was captured by the
Americans and probably released with the surrender of Detroit. The
British were unaware of his captivity as the muster roll of 26 July 1812
listed him as absent without leave. He was killed on 5 May 1813
during the siege of Fort Meigs. Return of First Essex Regiment,
26 July 1812, *MPHC* 32: 525-26.

44. Cass, Dyson, *HCM*, 20, 133.
45. Hull to Eustis 19, 21, 22 July 1812, *MPHC* 40: 418-22; Forbush, *HCM*, 146; Taylor to Eustis, 14 July 1812, *MPHC* 40: 412; Fairchild, *Journal*, 74; Elliott to Claus, 15 July 1812, *SBD* 1: 357-58; Brock to Prevost, 20 July 1812, Tupper, *Brock*, 213.
46. Hull to Eustis, 21 July 1812, *MPHC* 40: 420; Lucas, *Journal*, 41; Foster, *Capitulation*, 254.
47. Brock's General Order, 27 June 1812, in WCHS, *Transactions* 19 (1920):5; Brock to Prevost, 20, 25 July 1812, Tupper, *Brock*, 212-13, 216-19. Peter Latouche Chambers (1788-1827) joined the 41st as an ensign in 1803 and advanced to lieutenant in 1806, purchasing a captain's commission two years later. Although possessing only half the years of experience of the senior captains of the regiment, he was eager for promotion, so eager that he became embroiled in disputes with Matthew Elliott, Capt. Adam Muir, Lt. Benoit Bender, and Procter himself. In 1813, Chambers distinguished himself at the battle of Fort Meigs and participated in the battles of Fort George, Stoney Creek, and Fort Stephenson before being captured at Moraviantown. Lomax, *The 41st*, 372; *DICSD*, 84n.

    Although well written, Brock's counter-proclamation was not entirely bare of wartime "gasconading." His calling the American declaration of war "unprovoked" was not entirely true in light of the long-standing American grievances. His reference to the "unequalled growth of prosperity" in Upper Canada did little to reflect the poor and backward state of the province, a condition that precipitated the Rebellion of 1837 against an arbitrary colonial élite. Futhermore, the hint that if conquered, Canada would be ceded to France, has little basis in fact. As for the faith of the British government never being violated, the Native chiefs certainly knew otherwise. Brock's Proclamation, 22 July 1812, *SBD* 1, 371-74.
48. Talbot to Brock, 27 July 1812, *TP*, 151; Brock to Prevost, 20, 25 July 1812, Tupper, *Brock*, 212, 217; Brock's General Order of 22 July 1812, *SBD* 1: 374; Brock to Prevost, 26 July 1812, *SBD* 1: 379; Capt. Daniel Springer to Brock, 23 July 1812, *DICSD*, 86; Joseph Watson, *HCM*, 148. Ebenezer Allan (1771-1835) earned a reputation as a bloodthirsty tory during the American Revolution. He settled in Delaware Township on the Thames where he rectified his financial difficulties through counterfeiting activities for which he served time in the Vittoria Jail, Long Point. He was arrested again in early July 1812 for his treasonable activities in spreading Hull's proclamation with accomplices, Andrew Westbrook and Simon Zealotus Watson. Allan's personal life was equally eventful as he surrounded himself with an assortment of wives, White, Native, and Black. He survived the war to die of natural causes

in Delaware Township in 1816. *JAP* 2: 157-58n.

Andrew Westbrook (1771-1848) was born in Massachusetts and moved to Delaware, where he became a blacksmith. An archenemy of patronage, he preferred the republican principles he had abandoned as a "late Loyalist." Westbrook offered his services to Hull and circulated the latter's proclamation as far as the Grand River. In 1814, he led groups of like-minded partisans against Loyalist settlers in the Upper Thames area, burning, looting, and kidnapping militia officers, notably Mahlon Burwell and François Baby. Westbrook torched his own estate at Delaware to prevent its use by the British army. Although indicted for treason in 1814, he was never caught. After the war, he retired to Fort Gratiot, Michigan, where he became well-known for his eccentricites as "Baron Steuben." He appears in John Richardson's novels, *Westbrook The Outlaw* and *The Canadian Brothers*. *DCB* 6: 808-09.

Simon Zealotus Watson, had been a justice of the peace in Montreal before settling in Delaware where, as a land surveyor he engaged in bitter quarrels over Thomas Talbot's high-handed real estate dealings. Watson circulated Hull's proclamation on the Upper Thames and among the Grand River Natives. Brock described him as "a desperate character ... [who] has been allowed to parade with about 20 men of the same description as far as Westminster ... vowing all along the way the most bitter vengeance against the first characters of the province." In the summer of 1813, Harrison appointed him to the post of topo-graphical engineer in the Northwest Army. Accounts frequently confuse him with Joseph Watson, customs officer at Detroit, lieutenant colonel in the Michigan militia and aide to Hull. *DICSD*, 86n; Harrison to Eustis, 11 June, 1813, *MLWHH* 2: 472.

Thomas Talbot (1771-1853) was born in Ireland. Appointed ensign in the 66th Foot in 1783, he arrived in Canada seven years later and became secretary to Lieutenant-Governor Simcoe from 1791 till 1794. After serving in Holland as a lieutenant colonel, he returned to Canada in 1801 to settle in Elgin County. Talbot received an enormous grant of 6200 acres from the Crown for his services and became active in settling the Long Point region. Elected to the legislature in 1809, he was recognized as a leading figure of the "Family Compact." During the war, he was colonel of the 1st Middlesex Regiment but saw no action. Much of the treasonable activity of the Long Point and Upper Thames areas was attributable to the arbitrary dealings of this privileged land tycoon. *DCB* 8: 857-61.

49. Brock to Liverpool, 29 Aug. 1812, *DICSD*, 191; Merritt, *Journal*, 351; Brock to Prevost, 26 July 1812, *SBD* 1: 377-81. Prevost also encoun-tered problems in mobilizing Native warriors, scolding the chiefs of the Seven Nations of Lower Canada for being "like old women and that if

they would not fight willingly where and when they were ordered, they should be considered unworthy of receiving provisions and presents from their Great Father's Government." Cited in George Stanley, "The Indians in the War of 1812," *CHR* 31: 149.

50. Brock to Prevost, 25 July 1812, Tupper, *Brock*, 216-18; James Baby to Capt. Glegg, 27 July 1812, Brock to Prevost, 28 July 1812, Brock to Baynes, 4 Aug. 1812, *SBD* 1: 386-88, 408.

51. Prevost to Brock, 2 Aug. 1812, Prevost to Brock, 31 July 1812, Bathurst to Prevost, 4 July 1812, cited in Prevost to Brock, 14 Sept. 1812, Tupper, *Brock*, 226, 232, 309.

52. Brock to Baynes, 4 Aug. 1812, *DICSD*, 119; Baynes to Brock, 1 Aug. 1812, Tupper, *Brock*, 229.

53. Brock to Prevost, 4 Aug. 1812, Glegg to Baynes, 5 Aug. 1812, *DICSD*, 121-22; Prevost to Brock, 12 Aug. 1812, Tupper, *Brock*, 229-33; *The War*, 22 Aug. 1812; Brock's Address to the Legislature, Tupper, *Brock*, 219-22.

II

INVADERS INVADED

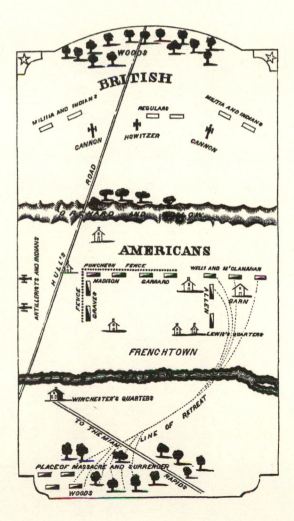

4

PROCTER ARRIVES

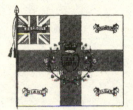

"Five hundred of the 41st would, I am confident, soon decide matters."[1]
Procter to Brock, 26 July 1812

AT DAYBREAK, 26 July, Col. Henry Procter arrived at Amherstburg in an open boat, accompanied by his aide Lt. Allan MacLean and about ten soldiers, after a "much vexatious delay" resulting from adverse winds. Procter was not surprised by his sudden assignment to this distant frontier. As early as December 1811, Brock had prepared him to proceed to Amherstburg on short notice to take charge of offensive operations on the outbreak of war. He arrived with the understanding that Brock would send the whole of the 41st Foot, 970 strong, once he was reinforced with an additional battalion.[2]

Henry Procter was 49 years of age, a career soldier of 31 years experience. He was "a stout, thick-set, fine-looking man" with "a red face set in its half circle of a beard." A *Canadien* resident of the Amherstburg area provided the following colourful description: "He was a very stout built man, so stout that he did not like to ride on horseback. I guess his horse not like it pretty well neither [*sic*]. His face was very full and very red like the moon when she come up in a fog. He had a big bush of brown whiskers."[3]

Procter was born in 1763 in the British Isles. In 1781, while his father Richard Procter, a British army surgeon, was on service in New England, Henry enlisted as an ensign in the 43rd Foot. He was 18 years old. Returning to England after the Revolutionary War, he accompanied

Courtesy of the Department of Canadian Heritage: Fort Malden Historic Site, artist C.H.J. Forster

Although much misunderstood, the actions of Col. Henry Procter are consistent and logical when viewed from the alliance point of view. That alliance facilitated his successes as well as his eventual failure. This is a modern portrait; no contemporary one exists.

his regiment to Ireland (1788-93) where he started a family. His unit spent the next seven years in the West Indies before returning to England. As was common at the time, Procter purchased his first promotions to lieutenant (1781), captain (1792), and major (1795). On 9 October 1800, Procter was promoted to lieutenant colonel and transferred to the 41st (Welch) Regiment of Foot, marking the beginning of his long association with that corps. He arrived in Canada in 1802 with another lieutenant colonel, Isaac Brock of the 49th, with whom he developed a close association over the next 10 years. On joining his regiment Procter worked relentlessly to convert this unit of garrison invalids into a well-ordered unit fit for field operations. His success in this regard was a matter of record. In the inspection return of 1809, Maj. Gen. Gordon Drummond attributed the favourable transformation of the 41st to his "zeal and attention." Procter was promoted to colonel in 1810 but remained in command of the 41st. Again in 1811, Drummond praised Procter's "indefatigable industry" in attending to the men's discipline and needs. That same year, Maj. Gen. Brock reported, "Colonel Procter may justly claim the merit of having ... brought the corps to its present high state of discipline."[4]

Procter's prominence as regimental commander of the 41st was enhanced by his popularity in the various garrison towns where he served. On the regiment's departure from Quebec City in 1805, the *Quebec Gazette* expressed gratitude for the "zeal of the commanding officer and good discipline of the 41st Regiment." That same year, provincial administrator Alexander Grant wrote from York, "Lt. Col. Procter and the gentlemen of the 41st Regiment are pleasant men, on a good footing with everybody." In 1811, Montreal newspapers expressed indebtedness to Procter and the 41st for "politeness" and "meritorious conduct."[5]

When war broke out, Colonel Procter was in command of Fort George, and Brock placed him in charge of the entire Niagara frontier on 27 June. During their decade in the Canadas, the two officers mingled with the élite of colonial society. They became aware of the expansionist impulses aimed at rolling back the boundary to the Ohio River and appreciated the wretched condition of American military organization. In sending Procter to Amherstburg, Brock hoped to realize his prewar plans.[6]

Procter, in turn, had great confidence in the regiment he had nurtured into a combat-ready unit. The soldiers of the 41st had spent much of their time in isolated detachments in Upper Canada. Although some of the officers and men were accompanied by their wives, the majority had not seen their families since 1799, when the regiment first arrived in Canada. Marriage was discouraged in all units since it competed with the soldiers' loyalty and attention. As desertions from the British army were frequent, Procter became adept at maintaining the men's loyalties through a combination of regimental welfare and appropriate discipline. He paid particular attention to important details such as accoutrements and winter clothing. Nonetheless, some of the soldiers went to extreme lengths to "beat the system." One apprehended deserter from Fort Amherstburg cut off both his ears while in confinement. Procter fumed over this "most extraordinary instance of depravity" and recommended "such an incorrigible individual be turned out of the service." The regiment was slated to return to England just when war broke out and Prevost cancelled its long awaited homecoming.[7]

As early as 1807, Brock made an ominous warning about the 41st. He wrote to Adjutant General Edward Baynes, "[Given] its dispersed state and the many evils by which it is surrounded, however great the zeal and intelligence of Lieutenant-Colonel Procter and the other officers ... the discipline and morals of the men ... will suffer progressively as the regiment remains situated in the Upper Province." In 1812, Brock observed to his brothers, "The 41st is an uncommonly fine regiment but with few exceptions wretchedly officered," a reference to the critical shortage of experienced officers.[8]

On arrival at Fort Amherstburg, Procter assumed command, and after an update from St. George, wrote a report to Brock that very morning. He summarized the Canards fighting and confirmed the absence of half the militiamen, expressing the hope that many would return after the harvest. In this first impression report, he reassured his chief: "Five hundred of the 41st would, I am confident, soon decide matters.... I do not apprehend this post is in any immediate danger." Unfortunately, Procter's first express turned back on the path at Point aux Pins, narrowly missing an enemy patrol there. On 30 July, he sent a second letter along with the first via *Lady Prevost*. These dispatches arrived at Fort Erie and were immediately forwarded to Brock at York, arriving just before his address to the legislature, the first news on affairs at Fort Amherstburg since St. George's initial report of Hull's invasion. Timely communications with this distant post would continue to be a problem.[9]

Procter wasted no time in assessing his resources. He agreed with St. George's observations on the lack of ability and cordiality among the Indian Department officials, clearly referring to Matthew Elliott, who at almost 80 years of age, he considered too old for actual service. The role of the top official of the Indian Department for the region had been less than prominent since the American invasion. Procter wrote, "You will be surprised to know that the greatest number of Indians, among whom were several boys that the utmost exertion of the Indian Department could collect did not exceed two hundred and thirty. This was on the 18th instant and they have rather decreased since." Although Brock tolerated Elliott, he harboured reservations about the old frontiersman, considering his judgment "biased and prejudiced ... in everything that regards the Indians."[10]

Within days, Procter focussed on offensive measures, ignoring the enemy beyond the Canards. He understood Brock's plan and was committed fully to its realization. By Brock's strategy, "Unless Detroit and Michilimackinac be both in our possession immediately at the commencement of hostilities, not only the district of Amherstburg but most probably the whole country as far as Kingston must be evacuated." Procter knew the stakes were high. Before he could achieve anything, though, he had to augment his manpower.[11]

The British commander first tried to round up the wayward militiamen, particularly in the Thames and New Settlement areas. He mustered their ranks, recorded the disposition of all officers, and issued a proclamation of conciliation, offering to pardon all militiamen who returned to duty immediately. His efforts had some effect, as Hull observed on the day of Procter's arrival: "The desertions of the militia ceased." To further bolster his numbers, Procter sent the schooner, *Nancy*, to Fort Erie to convey any available regulars to Amherstburg.[12]

Next, Procter tried to increase the influence of the Indian Department by hiring "active interpreters" to sway the wavering Wyandot to the British side. Given their leading role among the tribes of the region, Procter hoped that their commitment would not only serve to threaten Hull's communications but that other tribes would follow their example. The Wyandot were the holders of the great calumet, the kindlers of the northwestern council fire, and keepers of the wampum archives. This nation exerted considerable influence on the "Lake Indians" (the Ojibwa, Ottawa, and Potawatomi), the Wabash nations (the Miami, Shawnee, Delaware, and Kickapoo), and the western tribes (Sac, Fox, Menominee, Winnebago, and Sioux). Despite their proximity to White settlers, the Wyandot were relatively uncorrupted. According to Chief John Norton, a leader of the Grand River

Mohawk, "The Wyandot were the principal exception in that neighbourhood. Their morality had been more firmly established by the precepts of Christianity and they were not therefore so suddenly changed [by white traders' rum]."[13]

Procter met the Wyandot chiefs in council. He reaffirmed the British commitment to Native interests and announced the fall of Michilimackinac. Walk-in-the-Water, the principal elder chief, continued to maintain an uncompromising neutral stance during these talks and reproached Procter for past British abandonments. His influence was counterbalanced by Tecumseh, McKee, Roundhead, Splitlog, and Warrow, who spoke out strongly in favour of their traditional allies. After four days of talks, the majority of Wyandot chiefs declared for the British side. This shift of opinion overruled the reluctance of Walk-in-the-Water. Procter acknowledged the critical players in these talks: "We are indebted to McKee and much more to the chief Tecumshe [sic] for our Indian arm. He [Tecumseh] convinced the Indians that our cause was theirs and his influence by example determined and fixed the Wyandots whose selection determined every tribe."[14]

During this time, Tecumseh remained unswervingly pro-British, strongly seconding Procter's efforts and rapidly emerging as the principal spokesman for the warriors. "I have more confidence of a British than a Big Knife," he declared. "Here is a chance presented to us; yes such as will never occur again for us Indians of North America to form ourselves into one great combination and cast our lot with the British in this war. Should they conquer and again get mastery of the whole of North America, our rights, at least a portion of the land of our fathers would be respected by the King." Tecumseh had barely received passing mention in prior dispatches, Brock referring to him as "a Shawnese [sic] of no particular note." Now he assumed a new prominence in British accounts. Procter described him in the following manner:

Tecmuthé [sic] had raised himself to the situation of a chief by his tried hardihood, and that natural superiority of genius which, sometimes in civilized communities and almost always in a rude society challenge deference from common minds.... While he swayed the whole Indian body, Tecmuthé could scarcely number a score of immediate followers of his own people [the Shawnee].

... His habits and deportment were perfectly free from whatever could give offence to the most delicate female. He readily and cheerfully accommodated himself to all novelties of his situation and seemed amused

Considered the most reliable portrait of Tecumseh, this rendition agrees with descriptions given by British officers. Many "larger than life" myths have grown up around this Native patriot.

without being embarrassed by them. He could never be induced to drink
spirituous liquors of any sort, though in other respects, he fed like every
one else at the table. He said that in his early youth, he had been greatly
addicted to drunkenness, the common vice of the Indian, but that he had
found its detrimental effects and had resolved never again to taste any
liquid but water.... He had probably anticipated the period when he was
to appear as the first man of his nation.

In battle, Tecmuthé was painted and equipped like the rest of his
brethren but otherwise, his common dress was a leathern frock descending
to his knees and confined to his waist by a belt, leggings and moccasins for
the feet, of the same material completed his clothing. He was above the
middle stature, the general expressions of his features pleasing and his eyes
full of fire and intelligence.[15]

Before the Wyandot changed their minds, Procter directed their
removal to the Canadian side of the river. Under the guidance of
Tecumseh and Roundhead, they gathered at the Big Rock crossing
place near Brownstown. The British commander sent Capt. Muir and
a hundred men of the 41st to assist (and perhaps encourage) the crossing of the warriors, and their families, cattle, and effects on 2 and 3
August.[16]

While this movement was underway, Hull's water battery at Detroit
apprehended a schooner flying British colours. She proved to be *Salina*,
one of the vessels captured at Michilimackinac, carrying Capt. Hanks
and other paroled American prisoners, who notified Hull that
Michilimackinac had fallen. Another bit of unwelcome news was that
on 1 August, one of his labouriously constructed floating artillery batteries had broken away from its moorings and drifted downriver, where
the Provincial Marine secured it as a prize.[17]

News of the Wyandot defection, coming on the heels of the capture of Michilimackinac, made Hull "much agitated." Fearing encir-
clement by hordes of warriors, Hull abandoned Fort Hope for a
smaller work directly across the river from Detroit. This new post, Fort
Gowie (or Gowris), was built for a garrison of three hundred men. To
further consolidate his army, Hull ordered Capt. Nathan Heald at the
isolated outpost of Fort Dearborn (Chicago) to evacuate his small garrison and fall back on Fort Wayne, Indiana. Hull also wrote to Eustis
and the governors of Kentucky and Ohio, stating that his flour would
last only another two weeks, and urgently seeking provisions and
another two thousand troops.[18]

Hull had good reasons for being concerned with his logistics. As governor of Michigan, he knew that the territory was seldom self-sufficient in foodstuffs, relying on the annual delivery of up to 1500 hogs and two hundred cattle from Ohio. The exceptionally fine wheat crop in the territory remained largely unharvested, as the men were called out for military service. To augment rapidly depleting food stocks, Hull had already conducted foraging expeditions in the Western District. Fearful for his supply line to Ohio, he proposed to establish outposts at Brownstown, the Raisin River, and the Maumee Rapids, having already begun construction on a blockhouse at the Ecorces River, near Detroit. The rations contractor, Augustus Porter, wrote that he could not deliver by water the foodstuffs purchased on the south shore of Lake Erie because of the British vessels. Even transporting goods by land was hazardous, he noted, because the woods were infested with hostile warriors.[19]

Governor Meigs of Ohio, anticipating Hull's needs, had already fowarded aid. He sent a detatchment of Ohio volunteers under Capt. Henry Brush toward Detroit with a drove of three hundred beef cattle and 70 packhorses, each carrying two hundred pounds of flour lashed to the saddle. Brush arrived at the Raisin River on 4 August and took post in the Wayne Stockade. This small fort was surrounded by a picket of 12-inch posts, eight feet high, with two log blockhouses at opposite diagonals, each 18 feet square. Two detached blockhouses were situated outside the pickets to enfilade the fort walls. With only 160 men, mostly Ohio volunteers, as his escort, Brush was fearful of proceeding further. He notified Hull of his arrival and awaited instructions. Lt. Col. John Anderson of the 2nd Michigan Regiment wrote to Hull from Frenchtown that hostile warriors had killed some of the area settlers, adding, "It appears that we are invaded on all sides." He assembled all the local militiamen within the stockade.[20]

In far-off Washington, Eustis, made a desperate bid to relieve the pressure on Hull, directing Maj. Gen. Henry Dearborn, commander-in-chief of the U.S. Army, "You will make a diversion in his favour at Niagara and Kingston as soon as practicable." This direction came as a surprise to the American commander, as just weeks previously, Eustis had led him to believe that Hull would be advancing "in a direction for Niagara, Kingston and Montreal." Despite Eustis's orders, Dearborn was unprepared for serious offensive activity. He could do nothing to help his harried colleague. Hull was not only strategically isolated but quite alone in his struggle.[21]

Indeed, the ring was closing on the Northwest Army. A band of Shawnee and Ottawa braves under Tecumseh discovered Brush's arrival at the Raisin River and reported it to Procter. To intercept Brush's anticipated advance, the British commander directed his favourite captain, Adam Muir of the 41st, to establish an outpost on Hull's Road. Muir occupied the Wyandot village of Brownstown while native warriors scouted the approaches. Forty-six years of age, the white-haired Muir enlisted in the 41st as a private in 1788 and rose to become a sergeant major within five years. He was commissioned in 1794 and promoted to captain 10 years later. Muir was an experienced officer, with 12 years' service in the Canadas, mostly at Amherstburg.[22]

In sending most of his regulars across the river, with the Americans still beyond the Canards, Procter took a considerable risk. One of the *Cuyahoga Packet* prisoners secreted information to Hull's camp, reporting the British garrison as only a sergeant and 12 soldiers.[23]

By this time, Hull was rapidly losing interest in his fruitless designs on Fort Amherstburg as he became preoccupied with communications. On 4 August, the warriors captured the regular mail from Ohio, the first intimation to Hull that his communications to the south were interrupted. He detailed Maj. Thomas Van Horne and 150 Ohio riflemen, plus those militiamen who had refused to cross to Canada as an escort for the public mail, some two hundred men in all. He was to return to Detroit with Brush's supply train. The expedition crossed the Detroit River on 4 August 1812 and spent the night at the Ecorces River.[24]

The next day, in an eerie fog, the Americans resumed the march. At a fork in the road known as Big Apple Tree, stealthy warriors ambushed Capt. William McCulloch and Van Horne's Black servant, scalping McCulloch. The Americans reformed in two columns with horsemen as point and rear guards and continued the advance. After another five miles, Van Horne's men arrived at the ford of Brownstown Creek, three miles north of the Wyandot village. The marshy stream lay immediately to the right of the road, cornfields and a thicket on the left. Van Horne did not send scouts ahead to examine this narrow defile, and as the head of his column reached the creek, the point men suspected nothing amiss. Suddenly, from a range of 25 yards, Tecumseh's warriors, painted and naked except for loin cloths, sprang a well-laid ambush. Arrows hissed through the air, accompanied by loud war whoops. The Americans' surprise was complete, as terrified horses reared and lunged, pitching their mounts and throwing the entire column into utter confusion. In the words of an observer, "The horses of our officers were drinking when the Indians raised from behind their ambush and fired. The men became panick [sic] struck and turned their faces to Detroit and could not be stoped [sic] by the orders or perswasion [sic] of their officers."[25]

Ranger Robert Lucas (a future Ohio governor), witnessing the "dastardly conduct" of the militiamen and the "precipitate retreat" of the entire column, described their escape as "marvelous," estimating the enemy strength as triple that of Van Horne's and the warriors' loss as "much greater than that of the Americans." Seventeen Americans were killed (seven of them officers) and scalped, their hair impaled on long poles along the road, their corpses staked into the ground to terrify future expeditions. Twelve more were wounded. Although 70 members of Van Horne's party were declared as missing, 68 of them eventually emerged from the thickets and returned to camp. The single Native casualty was Logan Blue Jacket, a popular interpreter and village chief of a displaced band of Shawnee located on the Detroit River.[26]

There was wide disagreement on the number of warriors engaged in this short action. According to a 15-year-old volunteer with the 41st, John Richardson, they numbered only 25, though he did not witness the fighting. Other sources put the figure at a more likely 70 braves.[27]

One of the two Americans captured in the engagement was taken to the council house at Brownstown. Tecumseh selected Alexander Elliott (Matthew Elliott's lawyer son and party to the Brownstown ambush) to join the 24 warriors who would decide his fate. The unhappy American was brought in, fed to divert his attention, and silently but deliberately tomahawked from behind. By Native custom, prisoners were often executed in honour of slain braves. At other times, the prisoners were adopted by the dead warrior's family as a replacement for the lost member. Thus when warriors died in an action, the chiefs relinquished American prisoners to British officials with great reluctance. In this case, the execution by Tecumseh's war party was in honour of Logan Blue Jacket.[28]

Arriving at the scene of the recent action, Capt. Muir noticed the second American prisoner and bargained for his release. His captor, Main Pock, agreed to surrender the captive for a barrel of rum and clothing for his entire family. Just as the deal was concluded, the body of Logan Blue Jacket was brought in and placed at the feet of the young American. A number of squaws, relatives of the dead warrior, immedi-

ately fell upon the prisoner with butcher knives and Main Pock ended
his sufferings with a tomahawk stroke. A Detroit resident confirmed
the principle details, "Capt. [Robert] Gilchrist of Dayton, Ohio was
taken prisoner and killed by an old sqaw [sic]. He was sitting in the
boat to be taken across to Malden when the sqaw came up behind him
and struck him with a tommyhauk [sic] to revenge the death of a son
she lose [sic] in a fight." While British observers were shocked by such
acts, they independently affirmed that any attempt at intervention
would have caused their allies to defect. In the view of Thomas
Verchères de Boucherville, an entrepreneur who volunteered with
Muir's party, "Our garrison was weak and these warriors were numerous enough to impose their will on us." 29

Although the battle of Brownstown confirmed the isolation of the
Northwest Army, it produced another highly important result. Van
Horne's men rushed off in such haste that they abandoned the mail-
bags. From their contents, Procter learned of the widespread dissatisfaction within Hull's undisciplined army. An American prisoner who
had escaped from Amherstburg to Frenchtown reported "much sport
... in consequence of arresting the public papers which were examined
by the enemy." 30

Most significantly, Hull's letter to Eustis of 4 August fell into
Procter's hands. In it, the American general wrote, "Circumstances
have occurred which seem materially to change our future prospects."
He listed his woes: the tardy operations on the Niagara frontier, the
surrender of Michilimackinac, three thousand northern warriors mobilized against Detroit, 55 redcoats and four pieces of brass artillery having "penetrated" as far as Delaware on the Upper Thames, the Wyandot
having been made "prisoner," his shortage of provisions, and his inability
to secure more. Although Hull still wrote of storming Fort Amherstburg, he hinted at the possible need to concentrate his army at Detroit
in order to reopen his communications to Ohio. Procter fully appreciated the importance of this intelligence, forwarding copies to Brock, in
whose absence Lt. Col. Christopher Myers (100th Foot) concluded,
"The contents ... lead to the certain hope of the overthrow of the
enemy's force in that quarter." 31

On hearing of Van Horne's defeat, Hull was "divested of all self
possession or control over his fears." The seriousness of his situation
was not reflected in American newspapers. On the day of the battle of
Brownstown, a writer for the New York Gazette announced, "The
General has promised us a trip to Malden ... to Michilimackinac ... and

down Lake Erie through some pleasing settlements...., I already declare the peninsula of the lakes as a state."[32]

Meanwhile, Brush and his detachment remained at the Raisin River in expectation of attack. A small reinforcement of 21 rangers arrived from Ohio, whose leader, Jessup N. Couch wrote, "Our army is in a precarious situation. It is possible the whole corps may dissolve." He reported the local residents flocking into the Wayne Stockade but that the Americans were suspicious of the *Canadiens'* friendly relations with the Natives. Five successive expresses were sent to Detroit; all vanished on Hull's road.[33]

On 7 August, after three weeks of exertion, Hull's artificers completed the carriages for two 24-pdr. guns and three howitzers. That morning, Hull issued a general order in preparation for an attack on Fort Amherstburg. He directed three days' provisions to be cooked and entrenching tools prepared. One day's whiskey was to be drawn, with 12 more barrels loaded on wagons. The floating batteries were to be moved downriver. The convalescents would remain at Fort Gowris. Having mobilized his camp, Hull received reports that British troops were moving up the lake from Fort Erie. He abruptly countermanded his previous orders that night, directing the army to recross the Detroit River, an act that ranger Robert Lucas termed the "dastardly evacuation of Sandwich ... contrary to the general wish of all his troops."[34]

The crossing continued on the morning of 8 August, leaving only 130 convalescents and a small corps of artillerists under Maj. Denny at Fort Gowris. Their purpose was to signify non-abandonment to those residents of Upper Canada who had collaborated with the American invasion. Hull gave this rear party the dubious directions "to hold possession of this part of Upper Canada and afford all possible protection to the well-disposed inhabitants and to defend this post to the last extremity against musquetry [*sic*]; but if overpowered by artillery, to retreat. I am satisfied you will defend your post in a manner honourable to yourself and your country." The American commander reported the situation somewhat differently to Eustis, saying he left 230 infantrymen and 25 artillerists, while he focussed on reopening communications.[35]

At this time, Hull intercepted a disturbing letter. It was from one "K. McKenzie" (Alexander McKenzie), factor of the distant Northwest Company post of Fort William on Lake Superior to Duncan McIntosh (son the Sandwich factor, Angus McIntosh), dated 19 July. McKenzie declared that in 10 days, five thousand Indians would be gathered, ready to descend on Fort St. Joseph. The fantastic (and nonexistent) numbers greatly unnerved Hull.[36]

On 8 August, with most of his army concentrated at Detroit, Hull resolved to break through to Frenchtown. This time, he detailed six hundred troops and placed them under the command of his most competent commander, Lt. Col. James Miller. These included 280 regulars, a company from each of the three Ohio regiments, 60 Michigan militiamen, a troop of dragoons, and a detachment of artillerists with a 6-pdr. gun and a howitzer. A large man, the 37-year-old Miller was a no-nonsense professional, unlike the Ohio colonels who outranked him. Miller paraded his detachment, and alluding to the militiamen's previous misbehaviour, told them with characteristic bluntness, "You shall not disgrace yourself or me. Every man who shall leave the ranks or fall back without orders shall be instantly put to death. I charge the officers to execute this order. Any man who fears to meet the enemy, fall out!"[37]

While Miller's column left Detroit, Muir was at his post at Browns-town with 90 regulars, two companies of Essex militiamen, and Tecumseh's braves, still awaiting Brush's convoy. Procter wrote, "Saturday [the 8th of August] being the usual day of the post's arrival at Detroit, every road and Indian path was occupied on the 7th, 8th, and 9th, instant, in the hopes of intercepting the mail for Detroit as well as expected supplies."[38]

After waiting for two fruitless days at Brownstown for Brush's convoy, Muir was re-embarking the soldiers in the boats under Lt. Benoit Bender of the 41st when Native scouts reported Miller's advance "like the mosquitoes of the swamp in number." Muir immediately marched the troops upriver toward the enemy, sending a messenger by canoe to advise Procter of developments, seeking any available reinforcements. The British commander had that very morning received 60 men (20 grenadiers, 20 light infantry, and 20 battalion men) of the 41st under Lt. Richard Bullock from Fort Erie via *Nancy*, and promptly forwarded them to Muir.[39]

Muir's detachment marched through ankle-deep mud, past the grisly site of the Brownstown battle to the deserted 20-cabin Wyandot village of Maguaga. Tecumseh had selected an oak thicket a quarter mile above Maguaga for his ambush. The warriors and soldiers were already concealed behind trees and logs when Lt. Bullock's reinforcement arrived. The new arrivals were hastily positioned in the centre of the allied position, manned by 150 regulars, 50 militiamen, and 200 warriors. In addition to Tecumseh, the Natives were led by Round-head, Walk-in-the-Water, Splitlog, Billy Caldwell (the mixed-blood son of William Caldwell), and Main Pock.[40]

At 4:00 PM on the afternoon of 9 August, Miller's advance guard drew the first fire of the allied party laying in ambush, the warriors concealed on the right of the road while Muir's troops faced the American left. Miller calmly deployed his force against the enemy. After the opening volleys, Muir directed his bugler to sound the charge, but Bullock's newly arrived troops misunderstood the signal and retreated instead, leaving the British centre exposed. The American commander opened with musket and cannon fire on the British positions, followed by a determined bayonet charge, flushing his enemy from their concealment. The action became general, and with Muir and his principal officer wounded, the British flank recoiled from the force of the charge. At this point, the British troops mistook a body of braves on the far right for the enemy and fired upon them, the warriors returning the fire with spirit. Given the deteriorating situation, Muir, now twice wounded, ordered a retreat. Back at the road, the American right wing encountered stiff opposition from Tecumseh's followers. Miller, not wishing to divide his troops, called off the pursuit of Muir to deal with them. On learning that the Natives had also retreated, he resumed the pursuit of the British troops to Brownstown, only to see them hastening to Amherstburg in Bender's boats. The Americans spent the night at the battle site.[41]

The battle of Maguaga was a clear-cut tactical victory for the Americans, although they sustained heavier casualties than the allies. Procter's official report readily conceded, "In this affair, we have not entirely succeeded ... some mistake was made ... the ground was not as it ought to have been occupied. The party retreated, the 41st lost three dead, thirteen wounded, and two missing. Militia, one killed and two wounded. Indians, two killed and six wounded." According to Capt. William Merritt, a Canadian dragoon officer who arrived at Amherstburg some days after the action, the British soldiers were somewhat depressed over the battle, attributing its result to Muir's acceding to Tecumseh's choice of the ambush site. Procter particularly regretted Muir's injuries, calling him a "brave, good officer." Twenty-two-year-old Lt. Charles Sutherland, a promising Newfoundland native, who had spent a decade in the Royal Newfoundland Regiment before transferring to the 41st, was also wounded, in the mouth. Sutherland showed every sign of recovery until he disturbed the scab while brushing his teeth and bled to death. Tecumseh also sustained a buckshot wound in the action. American contemporary accounts place the loss among the warriors at possibly 40, all scalped. Miller's casualties in the two-hour engagement were 10 soldiers killed and 45 wounded in the 4th U.S. Infantry alone. Of his militiamen, eight were killed and 13 wounded, six of them officers. Miller was seriously injured when thrown from his horse during the confused fighting.[42]

Miller wrote Hull for provisions since the warriors managed to abscond with the Americans' knapsacks during the engagement. Accordingly, on the morning of 10 August 1812, Hull sent Col. McArthur with a convoy of nine boats bearing one day's rations. McArthur managed to elude the British vessels under the cover of a tremendous downpour of rain to deliver the foodstuffs. Taking on the wounded soldiers and British prisoners, he started his return to Detroit. British spotters observed his convoy and as *General Hunter* approached, the boatmen ran off, abandoning their charges on the shore. McArthur enticed them back with a keg of whiskey, and they resumed their journey, only to encounter *General Hunter* again, this time, blocking their passage. The Americans removed the wounded to wagons on Hull's Road and proceeded to Detroit under harassing fire from *General Hunter*'s 6-pdr. guns. A party of warriors emerged from the bush to take possession of the abandoned boats containing two British prisoners. These craft were handed over to the crews of *Queen Charlotte* and *General Hunter*, who secured them as prizes.[43]

Miller's detachment remained at Maguaga until 11 August, delayed by heavy rains, lack of provisions, and fear of another ambush. That day, Hull ordered Miller's expedition back to Detroit, writing to Brush that an escort was not possible and that his convoy should remain at the Raisin River. Miller's men returned to Detroit at noon on 12 August "covered with mud from head to toe, their clothes not having dried in two and a half days." Thus Hull's hard-earned tactical victory at Maguaga became Procter's strategic success by default. Hull subsequently wrote, "Nothing but honour was gained by this victory ... the blood of seventy-five gallant men could only open the communication as far as the points of their bayonets extended." The beleaguered American commander planned to send another large force to secure Brush's convoy by way of an inland back route known as Wayne's Trace.[44]

Thoroughly alarmed at the growing isolation of his army, Hull ordered Maj. Denny to evacuate and destroy Fort Gowris on 11

August. One American newspaper carried a story that five hundred Canadians had claimed American protection since the invasion, adding, "It was a heart rending sight to see these poor fellows flocking down to the river and begging General Hull to remain and protect them or take them with him. When they could not get into the boats, numbers of them jumped into the river and swam over. Some few were drowned in the attempt." The army that Hull boasted would "look down all opposition" had conducted an ignomious retreat. On the day of Denny's withdrawal, Procter was able to report, "The militia are coming in and the Indians also."[45]

The Northwest Army was clearly on the defensive. Wasting no time, Procter repaired the Canards bridge and occupied Sandwich the day after the American evacuation was completed. He directed his engineer officer, Capt. Matthew Dixon, to construct two artillery batteries on the François Baby estate, half a mile above Fort Gowris. One of these was screened by a number of oak trees that could be chopped down for action, while the other was sheltered in the cellar of an unfinished house. The construction of these batteries was accelerated with the help of a recently arrived company of Long Point militiamen under Lt. George Ryerson. Procter also ordered up *Queen Charlotte* and *General Hunter* to cover the preparations and deliver munitions for the artillery. These activities progressed under the cover of night, unhindered by the guns at Detroit. Having hemmed in the Northwest Army, Procter was preparing to threaten his adversary in his very stronghold.[46]

By this time, the Ohio militiamen were expressing openly mutinous sentiments. According to one participant, they addressed a "Round Robin" letter (so termed for the circular form of the signatures that left none to be identified as the initiator) to their colonels, requesting Hull's arrest or displacement. Nor was the discontent confined to the ranks. On 12 August, Cass wrote to Governor Meigs, stating that (contrary to his subsequent assertions) the condition of the army was "reduced to critical and alarming," and that only an immediate resupply and additional force of two thousand men could save the situation. He also reported that Hull was considering capitulation and asked the governor to come in person to assume command.[47]

Within a few days of his arrival, Procter had totally reversed the military situation on the Detroit frontier. Brock would shortly acknowledge his role:

I found the judicious arrangement which had been adopted immediately upon the arrival of Colonel Procter, had compelled the enemy to retreat and take shelter under the guns of his Fort. That officer commenced operations by sending strong detachments across the river with a view of cutting off the enemy's communication with his resources. This produced two smart skirmishes on the 5th and 9th instant, in both of which the enemy's loss was very considerable, while ours amounted to three killed and thirteen wounded.... Batteries had likewise been commenced opposite Fort Detroit for one 18 pounder, two 12, and two 5 and 1/2 inch mortars.[48]

At this time, a large reinforcement was being mobilized for Hull's relief. On 6 August, three militia regiments assembled in Kentucky, drawing arms and equipment in preparation for the march to Detroit. Few could anticipate that only a remnant of these would cross the Detroit River — and not until 1813, as prisoners of war.[49]

NOTES

1. Procter to Brock, 26 July 1812, *SBD* 1: 415.
2. Brock to Prevost 10 Nov. 1811, Tupper, *Brock*, 126, Gooding, *HCM*, 101; Brock to Prevost, 2 Dec. 1811, *SBD* 1: 271-78; Brock's defence memorandum, nd. Feb. 1812, *SBD* 1: 288-89. Allan Henry MacLean, became a lieutenant in the 41st Foot in 1811 and Procter's acting aide on 29 June 1812, remaining with him until late 1813. MacLean was the son of Donald MacLean, clerk of the legislative assembly, killed at the battle of York in 1813. The younger MacLean served in all the engagements of the Right Division. Procter tried to promote him by sending MacLean eastward with news of the British victory at French-town, but unsuccessfully. After the war, McLean accompanied the 41st to Europe and India before retiring on half pay in 1831 at Scarborough, Upper Canada. Lomax, *The 41st*, 70; Richardson, *War of 1812*, 142n.
3. Father Gabriel Richard to Bishop Pleissis, 24 Sept. 1813, cited in George Paré, *The Catholic Church in Detroit, 1701-1888*, 317; reminiscences of Jean Baptiste Bertrand, cited in George Catlin, *The Story of Detroit*, 180.
4. Carl F. Klink, "Some Anonymous Literature of the War of 1812," 49, Brock to Prevost, 22 Oct. 1811, *PCM*, 392; Inspection Returns of the 41st, cited in A.C. Whitehorne, *History of the Welch Regiment*, 64-65. Although inspection returns indicate that Henry Procter was native to Ireland, as does the *Dictionary of Canadian Biography*, this point is in dispute. Clarence Burton asserts that he lived on the Isle of Man for a time and may have been born there, while John Sugden and William

Wood identify Procter as a Welshman. *DCB* 6: 616; Clarence Burton, "Biography of Henry Procter," *MPHC* 15: vii; John Sugden, *Tecumseh's Last Stand*, 14; *SBD* 3, Pt. 2: 1009. In 1792, Procter married Elizabeth Cockburn, daughter of Archdeacon Cockburn of St. Mary's Parish at Kilkenny, Ireland. By 1812, the couple had at least four daughters and one son (Sarah Anne born at Leominster in 1794; Henry, born at Orleton, England in 1795; Charlotte Elizabeth Frances, born at Leominster in 1802; Frances Sarah, born at Quebec City in 1803; Augusta Margaret Firth, born at Niagara in 1808. One Richard Procter, baptized at Niagara in 1807, may have been a second son. *DCB* 6: 616-18; *JAP* 2: 487n.; Klinck, "Some Anonymous Literature of the War of 1812," 49-60.

5. *Quebec Gazette*, 25 July 1805 and 8 Aug. 1811; *Quebec Mercury*, 8 Aug. 1811.

6. Brock to Prevost 2 Dec. 1811, *SBD* 1: 271-78; Brock's Defence memorandum, nd. Feb. 1812, *SBD* 1: 288-89.

7. Procter to Maj. Green, 12 Jan. 1810, NAC, C 909: 62; Lomax, *The 41st*, 369. During the transatlantic voyage of the 41st to Canada in 1799, 20 men died of typhus. Within three months, an additional 85 soldiers (including two officers) were carried off by the disease, along with their doctors and attendants. Finally, a strange country doctor appeared and peremptorily ordered all the doors and windows of the hospital flung open to admit the brisk winter air. The next day, there were no patients to treat, only corpses to bury. "Some of the men of the 41st, hearing of this extraordinary treatment resolved that could they find the doctor, his victims should not go unaccompanied into the next world. They consequently repaired to the hospital, but their enemy fled from a vengeance which most assuredly would have cost him his life." Whitehorne, *Welch Regiment*, 87.

8. Brock to Baynes, 1 July 1807, Brock to his brothers, 3 Sept. 1812, Brock to Savery Brock, 18 Sept. 1812, Tupper, *Brock*, 60, 286, 316. The sensitive John Richardson took offence to Brock's comments on the 41st as well as Tupper's failure to suppress them, prompting a spirited public defence of his regiment. The context of Brock's statement becomes clear in another letter in which he again wrote, "The 41st is an uncommonly fine regiment but wretchedly officered," but then went on to describe how his own 49th was also deficient in experienced officers. John Richardson, *Major General Isaac Brock and the 41st Regiment*, 3-13; Tupper, *Brock*, 316.

9. Procter to Brock, July 26 1812, *SBD* 1: 415; Procter to Brock, 30 July 1812, *MPHC* 15: 125.

10. Procter to Brock, 26 July 1812, *SBD* 1: 415; Brock to Maj. Taylor, 4 Mar. 1811, Tupper, *Brock*, 97.

11. Brock to Baynes, 12 Feb. 1812, Tupper, *Brock*, 150.

12. Procter to Brock, 30 July 1812, *SBD* 1: 415-16; Return of 1st Essex Regiment, 26 July 1812, *MPHC* 32: 525-26; Hull, *Memoirs*, 60, 115; Hull to Eustis, 26 Aug. 1812, *MPHC* 15: 462.

13. John Norton, *The Journal of Major John Norton*, 315; Harrison to Secretary of War, 22 Mar. 1814, *MLWHH* 2: 636; Consul W. Butterfield, *An Historical Account of the Expedition Against Sandusky Under the Command of Col. William Crawford*, 163.

14. Procter to Sheaffe, 20 Nov. 1812, NAUS, *MIC*, 19-21.

15. Clarke, *Wyandotts*, 93; Brock to Prevost, 2 Dec. 1812, Tupper, *Brock*, 125; [Procter and Procter], *Lucubrations*, 338-43. The term "big-knife" or "long knife" originated during the Revolutionary War when a Virginian, Col. John Gibson, decapitated a distinguished Mingo chief called Little Eagle in combat. The Natives used the term initially for Virginians and subsequently for Americans in general. Butterfield, *Expedition Against Sandusky*, 32-33.

16. Procter to Brock, 11 Aug. 1812, *SBD* 1: 455-56; E.A. Cruikshank, "General Hull's Invasion of Canada in 1812," 253.

17. Matthew Irwin to Gen. John Mason, 16 Oct. 1812, *TPUS* 10: 414; "John Askin Diary," *MPHC* 32: 469-70; Return of Prizes made by HM vessels on Lake Erie, *DICSD*, 232. The schooners, *Mary* and *Salina*, were respected as private property at the surrender of Michilimackinac and sent down on cartel service with the American prisoners on board when Hull intercepted them. Recaptured as American public property with the fall of Detroit, they were taken into British service as prizes of war. For the chequered history of *Salina*, see S. Antal, "The *Salina*, a Stubborn Patriot."

18. Van Horne, Taylor, *HCM*, 66, 141; Hull to Eustis, 29 July 1812; Hull to Scott, 29 July 1812, Hull to Meigs, 29 July 1812, *MPHC* 40: 424-28.

19. Maxwell, *HCM*, 128; Porter to Meigs, 28 July 1812; Horace Knapp, *History of the Maumee Valley*, 129.

20. Samuel Williams, *Two Western Campaigns*, 17, 25; Anderson to Hull, 4 Aug. 1812, *HCM*, Appendix 2, 19-20.

21. Eustis to Dearborn, 27 June 1812, *DICSD*, 40; Eustis to Dearborn, 1 Aug. 1812, *MPHC* 40: 429.

22. *DCB* 6: 529-30; Boucherville, *Journal*, 88. Boucherville confirmed that most of the garrison moved across the river under Muir and five officers, accompanied by a number of volunteers that included John Richardson and himself. He estimated the allied crossing to consist of three hundred canoes plus the British boats. The British waited at Brownstown for Brush's approach for over a day before the warriors attacked Van Hornes' column some miles away. Muir's detachment moved forward too late to participate in the engagement. Boucherville, *Journal*, 85-90. Brownstown faced Amherstburg across the Detroit River. Midway between Detroit and Frenchtown, it was the principal

village of the Wyandot, containing their newly built council house and a hundred huts, including that of Walk-in-the-Water. Samuel R. Brown, *Views of the Campaigns of the Northwest Army*, 151.

23. Forbush, *HCM*, 146

24. Walker, *Journal*, 56. Maj. Thomas B. Van Horne (1783-1841) was born in New Jersey. On the Detroit campaign, he commanded a company of the Second Ohio Volunteers while a state senator. He was promoted to lieutenant colonel in the 26th U.S. Infantry on 9 Apr. 1813 and transferred to the 19th the following year. Discharged on 15 June 1815, he resumed his career as a politician and public servant of Ohio. *DICSD*, 117n.

25. Lucas, *Journal*, 46-49; Hull to Eustis, 11 Aug. 1812, *DICSD*, 125; Procter to Brock, 11 Aug. 1812, 129, *MPHC* 15: 129; Richardson, *War of 1812*, 27-34; Hunt, *Memoirs*, 18.

26. Lucas, *Journal*, 47-51; Richardson, *War of 1812*, 27; Boucherville, *Journal*, 89; Hull to Eustis, 7 Aug. 1812, *DICSD*, 125; Procter to Brock, 11 Aug. 1812, *MPHC* 15: 129. Native strength and casualty figures were seldom documented; hence, warrior casualties were possibly higher. By custom, the Natives did not disclose their losses, quietly carrying off their dead from the battlefield.

27. Robert Livingstone of the Indian Department was certainly present at the battle of Brownstown since he was captured there. He notes that he was one of 42 persons commanded by Tecumseh in the action. Interpreter Andrew Clark asserted he was in the Brownstown action, as did Pte. Thomas Neil of the 41st. As the battle of Maguaga was frequently called the battle of Brownstown, these men may have referred to the former engagement. Petition of Robert Livingstone, 24 July 1815, *MPHC* 16: 168; Petition of Robert Livingstone, 6 Jan. 1827; *DHCNF* 1813, Vol. 3: 42; Tupper to Meigs, 9 Nov. 1812, Knapp, *Maumee*, 147; Private Neil, *Proceedings of a Court Martial Holden at Quebec for the Trial of Lieutenant Benoit Bender*, 104.

28. Richardson, *War of 1812*, 27-29; Lucas, *Journal*, 19. Despite the popular mythology surrounding Tecumseh, some early American accounts depict the Shawnee war chief in a very different light. Thomson described Tecumseh's "dexterity with the scalping knife," his "undeviating practice never to make a prisoner," and also that "he would never yield the privilege of destroying the victim." A contemporary participant, Samuel Brown, confirmed that Tecumseh never took prisoners but was attentive and humane to those taken by others. The war chief was clearly responsible for the execution of the first prisoner, a fact that his admirers have overlooked. John Lewis Thomson, *Historical Sketches of the Late War*, 13; 170-71; Brown, *Campaigns*, 104.

29. Richardson, *War of 1812*, 29-31; Boucherville, *Journal*, 90-93; Hunt, *Memoirs*, 18.

30. Jessup N. Couch to Meigs, 11 Aug. 1812, Knapp, *Maumee*, 136.

31. Richardson, *War of 1812*, 29; Hull to Eustis 4 Aug. 1812, *MPHC* 40: 433-35; Myers to Prevost, 17 Aug. 1812, *MPHC* 15: 133-34.

32. Hatch, *Chapter*, 34; *DICSD*, 76.

33. Williams, *Two Campaigns*, 30; Couch to Meigs, 11 Aug. 1812, Knopf, *Documentary Transcripts* 2: 211.

34. Hull's General Order of 7 Aug. 1812, McAfee, *Late War*, 76. Hull received an express from generals Porter and Hall that they could not support him by undertaking offensive operations on the Niagara frontier. Hull to Eustis, 26 Aug. 1812, *HCM*, Appendix 2: 13-14; Lucas, *Journal*, 52.

35. Hull to Denny, 8 Aug. 1812, [Foster], *Capitulation*, 278; Hull to Eustis, 8 Aug. 1812, *MPHC* 40: 437-38.

36. K. McKenzie to Duncan McIntosh, 19 July 1812, cited in *HCM*, Appendix 1, 47; Hull, *Memoirs*, 59; McKenzie to McIntosh, 19 July 1812, *DICSD*, 72. Several histories assert that Procter wrote the letter and deliberately allowed it to fall into Hull's hands. Although doubtful, the mention of five thousand warriors is so fantastic that Procter may well have engineered the scheme to feed Hull's fears. Nonetheless, no definitive proof exists to support the theory. The same McKenzie resurfaced in October 1812 to alarm Procter with the false report of a total British defeat at Queenston Heights. Procter to Sheaffe, 30 Oct. 1812, *MPHC* 15: 174.

37. Lucas, *Journal*, 53; Dalliba's Narrative, cited in Richardson, *War of 1812*, 38; Hull to Eustis, 13 Aug. 1812, *DICSD*, 139-41; Benjamin Witherall memoir, cited in Burton, *The City of Detroit* 2: 1006. Even before the Northwest Army left Ohio, it was apparent to Hull that his real strength rested in Miller's regulars. When the Ohio men threatened to mutiny at Urbana, Hull called on Miller's regiment to inspire them, saying to their commander, "By God, Sir, your regiment is a powerful argument. Without it, I could not march these volunteers to Detroit." Bacon, *HCM*, 125.

  James Russel Miller (1776-1851) was born in New Hampshire and became a lawyer in 1803. Five years later, he was commissioned major in the 4th U.S. Infantry and promoted to lieutenant colonel in 1810, serving that unit under Harrison at the battle of Tippecanoe. He was rewarded with a brevet colonelcy after the battle of Maguaga. *WAMB*, 283; *DAB* 6: 628.

38. Procter to Brock, 11 Aug. 1812, *SBD* 1: 456.

39. Richardson, *War of 1812*, 35; Charles Askin, "Charles Askin Journal," *JAP* 2: 714. Benoit Bender became lieutenant in the 41st in 1810. Procter placed him in charge of the auxiliary vessels supporting British operations in Michigan and Ohio. As Capt. Adam Muir's brother-in-law, he became subject to accusations of cowardice at the battles of

Frenchtown and Fort Stephenson from Muir's competitor, Capt.
Peter Chambers. The mounting slights led to a major feud within the
regiment, resulting in Bender's court martial in 1815 in which he was
honourably acquitted of all charges. The published transcripts of the
trial provide valuable details on the engagements and internal politics of
the Right Division. Bender retired on half pay in 1817 and later served
in the 70th and 82nd Foot, retiring in London on full pay in 1846 as a
lieutenant colonel. Lomax, *The 41st*, 92; Bender, *Bender CM*, 50.

Richard Bullock appears in the records of the 41st as a lieutenant in
1808. He participated in the engagements of Maguaga, Detroit,
Queenston Heights, Fort Erie (28 Nov. 1812), Fort Meigs (5 May
1813), Fort Stephenson, Moraviantown, Fort Niagara, (9 Dec. 1813),
Black Rock and Buffalo (30 Dec. 1813), and Fort Erie (15 Aug. 1814).
He transferred to the 88th Foot in 1823 before selling his commission
five years later. He returned to Upper Canada, where he married a
woman of the Niagara region and became adjutant-general of the
Upper Canadian militia. His father, Capt. Richard Bullock, was also of
the 41st, serving under Procter. Lomax, *The 41st*, 92.

40. Brown, *Campaigns*, 151; Boucherville, *Journal*, 95-98; Richardson, *War
of 1812*, 34-35, 44; Walker, *Journal*, 61; Norton, *Journal*, 300. Accurate
returns for the number of warriors engaged in the action of Maguaga
are non-existent; however, Richardson's figure of two hundred is probably too low while Dalliba's estimate of 450 is certainly inflated. Dalliba
Narrative, cited in Richardson, *War of 1812*, 39.

Billy Caldwell or Saugaunash (1780-1841) was the son of William
Caldwell and his first wife, a Shawnee or Mohawk woman. An agent of
the Indian Department from 1810, he worked closely with the Pottawatomi, Ottawa, and Chippewa during the war, participating in the
engagements of Maguaga, Frenchtown, Fort Meigs and Moraviantown.
After the war, he plotted to succeed his father as deputy superintendent
of the Indian Department and later moved to Chicago, dying in Iowa.
DCB 7: 132-33.

41. Dalliba Narrative, cited in Richardson, *War of 1812*, 39-43;
Boucherville, *Journal*, 97-98.

42. Dalliba Narrative, cited in Richardson, *War of 1812*, 39-43;
Boucherville, *Journal*, 97-98; Procter to Brock, 11 Aug. 1812, *SBD* 1:
455-57; Merritt, *Journal*, *SBD* 3, Part 2: 553; *The War*, 12 Sept. 1812;
Hull to Eustis, 13 Aug. 1812, *DICSD*, 139-41; Walker, *Journal*, 61.

43. [Foster], *Capitulation*, 283-86; Lucas, *Journal*, 55-57; Richardson, *War
of 1812*, 45. Commodore Hall listed 12 boats taken after the battle of
Maguaga. Return of prizes made by HM vessels on Lake Erie, *DICSD*,
232.

44. Hull to Brush, 10 Aug. 1812, cited in Thomson, *Sketches of the Late
War*, 18; Dalliba Narrative, cited in Richardson, *The War of 1812*, 43;

Hull to Eustis, 26 Aug. 1812, *HCM*, Appendix 2: 13; Au, *War on the Raisin*, 14; Robert Wallace (aide-de-camp to Hull) to R.C. Langton, nd., cited in Clarke, *History of the Campaign of 1812*, 448.

45. Lucas, *Journal*, 57; *Columbian Centinel*, 9 Sept. 1812; Procter to Brock, 11 Aug. 1812, *DICSD*, 136.

46. Richardson, *War of 1812*, 49-51; Walker, *Journal*, 63; Egerton Ryerson, *The Loyalists of America and Their Times* 2: 353; Lt. George Ryerson narrative, cited in D.B. Read, *Life and Times of Major General Sir Isaac Brock, K.B.*, 156.

47. Hatch, *Chapter*, 40; Cass to Meigs, 12 Aug. 1812, *DICSD*, 137-38.

48. Brock to Prevost, 17 Aug. 1812, *SBD* 1: 467. The foremost British writers on these events, Tupper (Brock's kinsman) and Richardson, have gone to great lengths to minimize or obscure Procter's achievements. Subsequent writings have perpetuated their oversights and omissions. Richardson's impact extends to modern works such as Dennis Carter Edwards's, "The War along the Detroit Frontier: A Canadian Perspective," 25-50. Yet Maj. Gen. John Armstrong (secretary of war from Jan. 1813 till Sept. 1814), readily acknowledged Procter's actions in the manner of Brock, "This officer who arrived at Malden on the 29th of July, brought with him no important accession to the number of the garrison but what was justly considered as even more necessary, a competent knowledge of his profession, a thorough acquaintance with the views and a ready submission to the authority of his chief. He determined to not merely recall him [Hull] from Canada but literally compel him to fight for his daily bread or surrender at discretion." John Armstrong, *Notices of the War of 1812*, vol. 1: 24.

49. *The War*, 29 Aug. 1812.

5

THE CESSION OF MICHIGAN

"I have already been asked to pledge my word that England would enter no negotiations in which their interests were not consulted."[1]
                    Brock to Prevost, 18 September 1812

"The Indians conceive our government pledged to their interest. Indeed, General Brock made the chiefs every assurance of it."[2]
                    Procter to Sheaffe, 28 November 1812

"When the war was declared, our father stood up and gave us the tomahawk and told us he ... would certainly get us our lands back which the Americans had taken from us."[3]
                    Tecumseh in council, 15 September 1813

BROCK WAS READY to act. Concluding his official duties with the legislature on 5 August but unaware of Procter's recent successes, he hastened to Fort Amherstburg, hoping that it was not too late.

Before his departure, Brock had sent two small detachments of the 41st to Procter's aid. The first was 60 men under Capt. Peter Chambers. It was to proceed down the Thames, rallying the militiamen and Grand River Mohawk. Although this detachment created great alarm in Hull's mind, the project failed completely, advancing no further than Delaware since the Natives and militiamen refused to move. Another 60-man detachment under Lt. Richard Bullock arrived by water at Amherstburg in time to participate in the battle of Maguaga.[4]

Brock now rushed to the seat of war. Prevost had alerted him to British diplomatic efforts aimed at "a suspension of hostilities as a preliminary to negotiations for peace," having sent Col. Edward Baynes to negotiate an armistice with Maj. Gen. Dearborn. Ignoring the weak American presence on the Niagara frontier, Brock took advantage of the interlude to deal with the invaders in the west.[5]

Moving rapidly via the Grand River, Brock arrived at Long Point on 8 August, where he mustered more than 350 flank company militiamen of the York, Norfolk, Lincoln, and Oxford regiments and 20 Grand River warriors. (The men of the militia flank companies were the best trained and otherwise most efficient of the militia units.) One of his aides, Capt. John Glegg wrote, "Such is his popularity that I feel confident in saying that provided Amherstburg is not overwhelmed our troops will give a good account of his army." In "twelve sail of all kinds," the expedition left Dover on the 8th and made Port Talbot two days later.[6]

On 12 August, an additional 40 men of the 41st from Fort Erie joined Brock's expedition at Point aux Pins. Next day, the little army pressed on through stormy weather past the high clay shoreline. The men landed on the sandy beach of Point Pelée, dried their clothes and bivouacked for the night. Then at 8 PM, on 14 August they arrived at Amherstburg. It was there that Brock learned that Hull's invasion had not only collapsed, but that the Northwest Army had withdrawn and was actually isolated at Fort Detroit.[7]

While Procter briefed his chief at Matthew Elliott's home, Tecumseh arrived to meet Brock for the first time. The two aggressive-minded leaders formed an immediate friendship that served to cement the alliance. Capt. Glegg described the war chief:

Tecumseh's appearance was very prepossessing; his figure light and finely proportioned; his age I imagined to be about five and thirty [he was in his early forties]; in height, five feet nine or ten inches; his complexion, light copper, countenance, oval, with bright hazle [sic] eyes, beaming cheerfulness, energy and decision. Three small silver crowns or coronets were suspended from the lower cartilage of his aquiline nose and a large silver medallion of George the Third, which I believe his ancestor had received from Lord Dorchester, when Governor-General of Canada, was attached to a mixed coloured wampum string and hung round his neck. His dress consisted of a plain, neat uniform, tanned deer-skin jacket, with long trousers of the same material, the seams of both being covered with neatly cut fringe and he had on his feet leather moccasins.[8]

The next morning, Brock addressed the Native multitude whose numbers had swollen by this time to about a thousand Wyandot, Ottawa, Pottawatomi, Ojibwa, Shawnee, Sac, Winnebego, and Menominee. Brock told them that the "great father" had sent him to drive away the Americans from Fort Detroit. At the unanimous request of the assembled warriors, Tecumseh replied in his customary metaphoric language, expressing pleasure that the King had awakened from "his long sleep" and confirmed that the tribesmen were ready to fight in his service. Brock then met separately with Tecumseh and the principal chiefs to propose offensive plans against Detroit. They responded with unqualified support. Although there was no shortage of White men to describe the environs of Detroit, Brock waited patiently as Tecumseh outlined the features of the area on a map he drew on a roll of elm bark with his hunting knife. When the British general asked for assurances that the Natives would refrain from consuming liquor, Tecumseh could only answer for his war party from the Wabash, saying that they had pledged not to drink until they had humbled the "big knives."[9]

Aware of Hull's irresolution and the widespread dissatisfaction within his army, and encouraged by the Native support, Brock decided to accelerate Procter's work. He wrote afterward that he crossed the river intending to force the Americans out of the fort to meet him in the field. Procter's batteries at Sandwich and the Provincial Marine vessels were already in place for the bombardment of Fort Detroit. Nonetheless, Brock's proposal for a direct assault on the American fortification was initially opposed by all the senior officers except Lt. Col. Robert Nichol, quartermaster general of the provincial militia. Brock offered no explanation for their reluctance, writing to his brothers, "I crossed the river contrary to the opinion of Cols. Procter, St. George, etc. The state of the province admitted of nothing but desperate remedies." Brock pressed forward with his plan.[10]

Through his general order of 14 August, Brock called for returns for the troops in the district, congratulated Procter and the garrison for the "judicious measures" that prompted a "disgraceful" American retreat, expressed "surprise" at the numerous militia desertions, and called on absentees to report immediately or be subject to the penalties of the new Militia Act. He appointed captains Adam Muir, Joseph Tallon, Peter Chambers (all of the 41st), John Glegg (49th), Robert Mockler (Royal Newfoundland Regiment), and Matthew Dixon (Royal Engineers) brevet majors (local and temporary appointments). Brock organized the troops within the Western District into three tiny brigades. The

first, under St. George, consisted of the three local militia units augmented by soldiers of the Royal Newfoundland Regiment. Chambers'
brigade was comprised of 50 men of the 41st and the flank companies
of the York, Lincoln, Oxford, and Norfolk militia. The third brigade,
commanded by Tallon, was made up of the remainder of the 41st.
Procter commanded the whole under Brock's immediate direction.[11]

On 14 August, while Brock drew his plans, his adversary was
organizing yet another expedition to open his communications to
Frenchtown. This third attempt was led by Col. McArthur, assisted by
Col. Cass, the detachment consisting of 350 picked men of their regiments. They were to advance by the inland route to meet Brush at
Godfroy's trading house on the upper Huron River. In one of those
curious oddities that occur in war, Hull was unaware of Brock's arrival
with reinforcements, just as Brock remained uninformed of the departure of the party under McArthur and Cass.[12]

The next day, 15 August, Brock marched his little army to Sandwich.
From there, he sent his aides to Hull with an ultimatum:

The force at my disposal authorises me to require of you the immediate
surrender of fort Detroit. It is far from my intention to join in a war of
extermination, but you must be aware of that the numerous body of Indians
who have attached themselves to my troops, will be beyond controul [sic]
the moment the contest commences. You will find me disposed to enter into
such conditions as will satisfy the most scrupulous sense of honour. Lieut.-
Colonel M'Donnell and Major Glegg are fully authorised to conclude any
arrangement that may lead to any unnecessary effusion of blood.[13]

After delaying the British aides for five hours (an attempt to buy
time as he urgently recalled McArthur and Cass), Hull replied: "I have
received your letter of this date. I have no other reply to make, than to
inform you, that I am prepared to meet any force which may be at your
disposal, and any consequences which may result from any exertion of
it you may think proper to make."[14]

Receiving Hull's response, Brock ordered Commodore George
Benson Hall of the Provincial Marine, commanding the Sandwich
batteries, to open fire on Fort Detroit. Joined by the guns of *Queen
Charlotte* and *General Hunter*, the bombardment continued well into
the night. Although the Americans returned fire from their detached
batteries of 24-pdr. guns, the exchange inflicted little material damage
on either side, and only one soldier within Fort Detroit was injured.[15]

That night, the warriors assembled on Bois Blanc Island and prepared themselves physically and psychologically for battle. They painted their tatooed bodies in vermilion, blue, black, and white. Their charcoal-streaked faces grimaced into grotesque expressions as they tossed their streaming scalp locks to the rhythm of the drum and gourd rattle. They performed the war dance around their campfires well into the early morning, their wolf-dogs yelping wildly. Thomas Verchères de Boucherville witnessed the fierce spectacle, describing it as "frightful, horrifying beyond expression," imagining himself "standing at the entrance to Hell, with the gates thrown open to let the damned out for an hour's recreation on earth." [16]

Before sunrise of 16 August, the Native warriors crossed silently from McKee's Point to Spring Wells, three miles south of Detroit. After they secured the landing site, the British brigades followed at dawn. These movements were covered by the Provincial Marine vessels. The British force (including regulars, militiamen, provincial marine, the Sandwich gun detachment, commissariat, and skeleton garrison of Fort Amherstburg) consisted of 1460 men. With the six hundred Native warriors, the total allied force corresponded closely with Brock's orders for two thousand rations. To magnify the effect of his regulars, the British general clothed the militiamen in the cast-off tunics of the 41st. As he led the troops toward the fort, the warriors, mainly Ojibwa, Wyandot, and Potawatomi, screened the British flank on the landward side, "running after horses in all directions." [17]

Brock hoped that a heavy artillery bombardment would force the Americans into the field. Thus far, his enemy had refused to cooperate. Suddenly he learned of a new ingredient to the equation. He subsequently wrote, "Receiving information upon landing that Col. McArthur, an officer of high reputation, had left three days before with five hundred men, and hearing soon afterwards that his cavalry had been seen three miles in our rear, I decided on an immediate attack." In tactical terms, Brock's decision was astonishing. He had taken no scaling ladders with him. Even if he possessed ladders, his few and puny artillery pieces were no match for Hull's fort guns. Brock took a shrewd psychological gamble. He reckoned that his Native threat would prompt the jittery Hull to avoid bloodshed. In his words, the bluff came "from a cool calculation of the *pours* and the *contres*." Brock knew his enemy. [18]

While the column marched on Detroit, two American 24-pdr. guns at the town gate faced the British front. The artillerymen stood by with fuses burning, ready to fire their pieces loaded with grapeshot and an additional 6-pdr. gun loaded with canister. The red coats advanced to within a mile of the artillery before deploying into line, taking cover in an orchard behind a low ridge. The American artillerists could have raked the length of the enemy column but just as they were preparing to fire, Capt. Samuel Dyson, senior American artillery officer, rode up with sword drawn and "swore that the first man who would attempt to fire on the enemy, should be cut to pieces." On Hull's orders, Dyson also silenced the river batteries. The American general had sent an officer under a white flag to Sandwich to discuss terms of surrender![19]

From a purely tactical point of view, the fort of Detroit was strong, mounting 26 pieces of artillery (plus the field train) and well stocked with ammunition. Hull had about a thousand armed combatants in the immediate area. The adjacent town of Detroit was totally palisaded on three sides, the fourth being common with the fort. Even if the town's defences had to be abandoned, the fort could hold all the soldiers and civilians within the two-acre enclosure. Foodstuffs were adequate to feed the aggregate occupants for at least a week, during which time the British might have abandoned the siege upon the advance of McArthur and Cass. As Native warriors were of limited value in assaults on fortified positions, Brock's little army with his five small guns would certainly have been repulsed in an assault.

Hull's fears were magnified by the increasing accuracy of the British guns. These pieces, an 18-pdr. gun, two twelves and two 5-in. mortars, resumed the bombardment at dawn on the morning of 16 August and found the correct range. In the next three hours, one round shot killed a man outside the fort. Another bounced inside, killing an ensign and a soldier. Another 18-pdr. round shot found its way through an embrasure and deflected into the officers' mess, killing Dr. James Reynolds. The ball bounced again, killing Lt. Porter Hanks, who had survived the capture of Michilimackinac and was taking a recess from the court martial that investigated his surrender. Still not spent, the round shot severely wounded a surgeon's mate with the unlikely name of Dr. Hosea Blood. Robert Livingstone, a British prisoner captured at the battle of Maguaga, petitioned Judge Woodward to be removed to the schooner, *Mary*, as several round shot had passed through his prison walls.[20]

Everything seemed to go wrong for Hull. About 9 AM, his son and aide, Capt. Abraham Hull, engaged in unseemly conduct with some

Ohio militiamen loitering about the fort, pursuing them on horseback, sword in hand, to their posts. Their commanding officer, Col. Findlay demanded that the general place his son under arrest. The younger Hull responded by challenging his antagonist to a duel; the episode greatly upset the general. Then he received word of the havoc in the officers' mess. About the same time, he learned that the Michigan militiamen were deserting their posts and that two of their companies had surrendered. At this point, Hull seems to have completely lost his composure. "His lips quivering, the tobacco juice running from the sides of his mouth upon the frills of his shirt," said one observer of his agitated condition, "I do not think it was over twenty minutes (after the round hit the officers in the mess) when he hoisted the white flag for a parley with Genl. Brock." In his apologia, Hull would write, "The fort at this time was filled with women, children and the old and decrepit people of the town and country. They were unsafe in the town, as it was entirely open and exposed to the enemy's batteries. Back of the fort, or above it, there was no safety for them on account of the Indians."[21]

At this critical time, two of Hull's colonels were absent on duty and his most capable senior officer, Lt. Col. Miller, was bedridden, sick with the ague. Uninformed of the movements of McArthur and Cass, Hull sent an officer with a white flag at 10 AM to Sandwich to propose a truce for surrender discussions. At Sandwich, the envoy learned that Brock was on the American side and recrossed the river to find him. During this interval, both sides suspended their artillery fire. Brock's aides met Hull's messenger, and on determining his purpose, entered Fort Detroit to conclude the terms of capitulation.[22]

Hull's fears of Native savagery induced him to include in the surrender not only the detachment under McArthur and Cass but that of Brush at Frenchtown, as well as the garrison in the blockhouse at the Maumee Rapids. The surrender document contained an attempt to add a provision for the American troops to march out with the honours of war, but this was crossed over, apparently rejected by Brock. Hull subsequently argued that the capture of Michilimackinac had roused the "hive" of hostile warriors from the north. Although the Lake Indians, had indeed declared themselves to the British side, their numbers were hardly as menacing as the American general implied. Subsequent to the fall of Michilimackinac, they were incapacitated, "drunk as ten thousand devils." It was only on the day of Detroit's surrender that a mere 270 warriors, led by chief Big Gun, departed for Detroit.[23]

With the surrender, Fort Detroit reverted to British control. A 40-man honour guard commanded by Lt. Bullock marched into the fort with fife and drums playing "The British Grenadiers." It included elements of the flank companies of the 41st (the grenadiers and light company) and some of the volunteers. Brock's selection of loyal colonials was aimed at glamourizing the "Canadian" dimension of the war. One volunteer, Charles Askin, recorded in his journal, "I must say that I never felt so proud as I did just then." Another colonial, 15-year-old John Richardson, shorter than his musket, was also present, recalling, "I was not a little elated, I must confess, at the very enviable position in which, as a young warrior, I conceived myself to be placed on this occasion, strutting to and fro on my post." Pte. Shadrach Byfield of the 41st entered the officers' apartments to save the colours of the 4th U.S Infantry from being destroyed by their custodians. So unprepared were the victors for the outcome that they lacked an ensign of their own to hoist over Detroit until "a stray bluejacket," a member of the Provincial Marine, produced one that he had wrapped around his waist. Hull's son suddenly awoke from a sound sleep (some called it a drunken stupour), burst though a window and confronted Brock, demanding his business and that of his "red-coated rascals." Brock drew his sword to cut down the intruder, but another of Hull's aides intervened, explaining that the general's son was "partially deranged."[24]

On the day of the surrender, Brock issued a proclamation to the inhabitants of Michigan guaranteeing freedom of religion and protection for their persons and private property and directing the surrender of all public property to British officials. The militiamen of Ohio and Michigan were to return home on parole while the regulars were detained as prisoners of war. The exultant British commander wrote a hasty report to Prevost, declaring, "I have been admirably supported by Colonel Procter, the whole staff and I must justly say every individual under my command." That same day, he issued a general order thanking all departments for their part in the successful endeavour, noting, "The Major-General requests Colonel Procter will accept his best thanks for the assistance he derived from his experience and intelligence." The next day he wrote his official report, crediting all concerned parties. In both his general order and official report, he praised the Natives for their restrained conduct.[25]

The capture of Detroit produced unrestrained jubilation in the Canadas. The newly acquired public property included a major fort, 35 brass and iron cannon (including nine 24-pdr. guns), about ten thousand units of grape, round, and case shot, three thousand muskets and rifles, tons of lead, gunpowder, and small arms ammunition, and assorted ordnance stores, in addition to large quantities of wagons, camp equipment, and other stores. The refitted brig, *Adams*, plus the commercial schooners, *Salina* and *Mary*, joined the Provincial Marine establishment. Brock estimated the value of captured public property at between £30,000 and £40,000. British soldiers had personal reasons to rejoice, as even a private was entitled to almost half a year's pay in prize money.[26]

Hull's capitulation generated harsh recriminations on the grounds that he surrendered to an inferior enemy. Indeed, his combined force outnumbered Brock's. Gross figures, though, are deceptive. Hull pointed out that no less than 1182 of his men were non-effectives, unable to assist in the defence of Detroit. These included the McArthur-Cass expedition, paroled soldiers, convalescents, wagoners, mariners, and artificers. By deducting these non-effectives, Hull calculated his remaining force as 976 men. His contention that "I could not have carried into the field more than 600 men and left an adequate force in the fort" is not so impossible as his critics would assert. Admittedly, one could argue that the wagoners, mariners, and artificers attached to the American army could handle a musket on the walls. Furthermore, Hull did not count the four hundred Michigan militiamen he admitted were under arms on the 16th.[27]

Had Hull deployed his effectives in the open field, he would have faced an enemy on the Detroit side consisting of 330 regulars, four hundred militiamen and six hundred warriors for an aggregate total of 1330. By deducting the two hundred boatmen, Brock's 1130 combatants still outnumbered the effective American force. Although Hull would have had an overwhelming advantage in artillery, his troops were few and of questionable quality. The mysterious movements of McArthur and Cass did little to encourage him to count on their support but his contention that Brock had brought with him "all the forces of his province from Montreal to Malden" is certainly exaggerated.[28]

Sheer numbers do not provide a realistic assessment of Hull's strength. As governor of Michigan, Hull was also concerned with the safety of the noncombatants, including his own family. With over a hundred wounded men, his hospital was crowded with sick men. Furthermore, even the effectives were in a bad condition. British participants described them as "unhealthy," and "dirty and ragged." Not only had the Americans lost their hospital stores on *Cuyahoga Packet* but

Lossing, *The Pictorial Field Book of the War of 1812*

Despite Lewis Cass's vicious denunciations of Hull's actions during the Detroit campaign, his own conduct was not entirely praiseworthy. Nonetheless, he was promoted and gained further prominence as governor of Michigan.

poor camp sanitation and hygiene made the static concentrations in the mosquito-infested Detroit area a fertile breeding ground for disease.[29]

In short, Hull believed he could not fight effectively from the fort or on the field. Aside from the tactical considerations of the day, Hull also had to consider the serious provisioning challenges of the future. Although Michigan contained some cattle and crops of grain, Detroit was hemmed in and three successive efforts could not facilitate a resupply. Despite the subsequent outrage emanating from his Ohio colonels, Hull considered his options simple. He could either capitulate or sustain casualties and then capitulate, running the risk of a general slaughter. Sounding more like the governor of Michigan than the commander of the Northwest Army, he was heard to declare on the day of the surrender, "I have done what my conscience directed. I have saved Detroit and the Territory from the horrors of an Indian massacre."[30]

Although Hull's critics discredited the Native threat, British observers agreed with the American commander. Capt. William Merritt wrote, "It would have been impossible to restrain the Indians." At Michilimackinac, John Askin, Jr., was of a similar opinion, "It was a fortunate circumstance that the Ft. [Michilimackinac] capitulated without firing a gun, for had they done so, I firmly believe not a soul of them would have been saved." Brock's bluff was daring, but the threat of Native horrors was very real.[31]

Duncan McArthur was promoted after the Detroit campaign. Succeeding Harrison as commander of the Northwest Army, his predatory raid into Upper Canada in 1814 discouraged a British resurgence in the Detroit country.

While the shocked Americans observed white flags hoisted from the walls of Fort Detroit, McArthur and Cass were encamped near Spring Wells, seven miles from the fort. It will be recalled that on 14 August, they had taken a back route to rendezvous with Brush, guided by a local militiaman, Gabriel Godfroy. The plan, as proposed by Brush, was to meet the expedition in the backwoods. Strangely, the detachment left without rations, subsisting on corn and pumpkins. Cass and McArthur travelled 24 miles the first day, sending some dragoons forward to Godfroy's trading house on the Huron River to seek Brush's column. These found no sign of Brush and returned the following day. Then Hull's messengers arrived to report Brock's surrender demand, that they hasten to Detroit immediately. On the 16th, McArthur and Cass advanced within a mile of the fort, heard the cannonading, and received another order from Hull to return forthwith. Instead of advancing, they withdrew to the River Rouge, sending scouts to reconnoiter Detroit while the hungry men feasted on a roasted ox. As they were enjoying their repast, Capt. William Elliott, an officer of the Essex militia (no relation to Matthew Elliott, despite frequent assertions to the contrary), arrived with yet another message from Hull, directing the expedition to march to Detroit and surrender.[32]

Outraged at the news, Cass refused to surrender his sword, breaking it in two. Not to be outdone in theatrics, McArthur broke his into

Lossing, *The Pictorial Field Book of the War of 1812*

three pieces and wept, for good measure. Robert Lucas expressed the sentiments of many Americans: "My feelings were affected beyond expression. My God, who could bare [sic] the sight without vowing eternal vengeance against the nation that would employ such detestable savage allies, to see our colours prostitute, to see and hear the firing from our own battery and the huzzahs of the British troops, the yells of the savages and the discharge of small arms, as the signals of joy over our disgrace was scenes too horrid to meditate upon with any other view than to seek revenge."[33]

Four days after the surrender, it occurred to the secretary of war that coded correspondence with the Northwest Army might be advisable. "Occasions may arise in which you may find it convenient to make use of a cipher," he wrote Hull, "I enclose one with explanations." Also, it should have occurred to both Eustis and Hull to employ express riders which would have reduced by half the mail time of 15 days between Washington and Detroit.[34]

First news of Hull's lamentable failure generated mingled feelings of disbelief and outrage in the U.S. The first instance of the surrender of American soil to a foreign power plunged Washington into political turmoil. The principal documents, Hull's capitulation, Brock's proclamation, and Cass's denunciations of Hull's actions became public, appearing in the leading American newspapers. The *Niles Weekly Register* openly condemned Hull for having "treacherously surrendered" Detroit, and a strong sense of public outrage demanded an accounting. In Kentucky, the news was received with undiminished resolve as "an immense number of volunteers immediately came forward, among whom were several members of Congress."[35]

Cass's damning account of 12 September 1812 was held up as the principal vehicle for Hull's condemnation (though it was generously laced with opinion and assumption). Some observers considered the blame for the debacle misplaced, *The War* asserting, "That suspicion of dishonor or perfidy should attach to his character, we will not allow." The Boston *Columbian Centinel* went further and laid the blame on the government's inept preparations:

General Hull may not have conducted the expedition with as much skill as a more experienced General would have done; but it is evident to any person of reflection that no general however brave he might have been could have conducted an expedition planned as this one has been to a favorable conclusion. The thing was impossible and if Ft. Malden had been taken when Hull first made the descent into Canada, it would have been retaken by General Brock. It must have been starved out as no supplies could have been sent to it while the British commanded the lake and the Indians the roads through the wilderness. We must have a naval force on the lakes as well as on the ocean or we may expect many such a disaster as this of general Hull before we get possession of Canada. [36]

The defeat of the Northwest Army was more complete than Brock or Hull knew, as Fort Dearborn had fallen the day before Detroit did. The capture of Michilimackinac had isolated this outpost, and Hull had ordered its commander, Capt. Nathan Heald, to evacuate his garrison to Fort Wayne. Heald complied but delayed his withdrawal six days. Furthermore, he enraged local warriors by destroying the ammunition and liquor stocks. By the time he initiated his retreat on 15 August, hundreds of Potatawatomi, Kickapoo, Sac, and Fox warriors had gathered under the leadership of chiefs Mad Sturgeon and Blackbird. As the 54 regulars, 12 militiamen, and 27 dependents withdrew from the fort, some five hundred braves overwhelmed the column. Fifty-three Americans were killed, most of the remainder wounded.[37]

The allied victories in the west completely altered the military situation for Upper Canada. With the capture of the principal fortress of the Detroit country, the Western District was secure, the closest American forces of any consequence being beyond the Black Swamp. Brock returned to the Niagara line, intent on "sweeping it of the American garrisons." Through concentrated thrusts at strategic points, he hoped to eject the Americans from the frontier before they could mobilize superior resources against the colony. Brock's success thus far attested to his ability to do so. The Detroit ordnance could be advantageously employed in other critical areas. For the colonials, the prevailing sense of impending doom was displaced by one of elation. The militiamen could be armed not only with captured flintlocks but with the conviction that the invaders were not invincible. In Procter's words, the capture of Detroit "inspired the timid, fixed the wavering and awed the disaffected." Equally important, the Northwest and Grand River Natives committed themselves to the British side. The British-Native alliance was consummated.[38]

Before returning to the Niagara frontier, Brock ordered a court of inquiry with Col. James Baby as president and colonels Matthew Elliott and William Caldwell as members, to investigate the militiamen's deser-

Isaac Brock

Capable and energetic, Maj. Gen. Isaac Brock promised the Natives restoration of their lands, ceded Michigan, and convinced the British government to represent Native demands at peace talks.

National Archives of Canada, Ottawa: C-36181

tions and defections. Then, on 19 August, he boarded *Chippawa* and hurried to Fort Erie, intent on his pre-emptive strikes. During his voyage, he learned that Prevost had concluded his truce, halting all offensive activity.[39]

The far-reaching effects of the capture of Detroit have obscured the connection between Brock's proclamation and the allied expansionist design. In his declaration, the British commander unilaterally "ceded Michigan to the arms of his Britannic Majesty," prompting American newspapers to challenge its legitimacy. *The War* of 12 September 1812 declared the cession a "nullity," asserting that not even the president had the authority to "convey a single inch of the country ... to a foreign government." Learning of Brock's success, Admiral Sir John Borlase Warren, commander of the North American Naval Station, urged the British government to go further, to reconquer all lands (north of the Ohio River) surrendered by the Native tribes at the Treaty of Greenville in 1795. He advocated the creation of a Native state that would guarantee the security of Upper Canada via the buffer. Brock had already taken steps toward this end, directing Procter to reduce Fort Wayne, deep in Indiana Territory.[40]

The British general followed up his military success by pressing the expansionist goal on the political front, writing directly to Prime Minister Robert Jenkinson, Lord Liverpool (who was also minister for war and colonies). Although Brock had previously represented the Native alliance as a "diversion," useful for the defence of Upper Canada, his carefully worded letter revealed the political dimension of his relations with the tribesmen, while introducing Tecumseh as their leader:

He who most attracted my attention was a Shawnee chief, Tecumset, brother to the Prophet.... He was the admiration of everyone who conversed with him.... A more sagacious or a more gallant warrior does not I believe exist.... From a life of dissipation, he is become ... abstemious. They appear determined to continue the contest until they obtain the Ohio for a boundary.... The armistice ... has suspended all offensive operations.... The Indians ... will naturally feel disheartened and suspicious of our intentions.... No effort ... of mine shall be wanting in keeping them attached to our cause. If the condition of this people could be considered in any future negotiations for peace, it would attach them to us for ever.[41]

Brock's victory produced another long-term result. His act of detaching Michigan Territory from the United States virtually guaranteed a continuation of the war at the very time when Britain was seeking a peaceful settlement. Brock's action dashed any efforts by the diplomats to resolve the differences. If he could clear the frontier of growing American defences, he might be able to consolidate his gains. On the other hand, if he failed to dislodge the Americans on the Lakes, the republic would certainly mobilize vast untapped resources for the war effort. In fact, within weeks, the U.S. government adopted a policy of unlimited expenditure for the recovery of Michigan, earmarking ten thousand troops for the task. Despite the overall restrained conduct of the Native warriors, President Madison declared to Congress that the British-Native alliance was an "outrage" against the "benevolent policy" of the republic, calling forth the "patriotic zeal and invigorated efforts" of his countrymen to deal with the "blood-thirsty savages ... let loose by the enemy." Admitting that the land campaign from Detroit was "disappointed," Madison undertook to construct "a naval force superior to that of the enemy."[42]

On the day of Detroit's surrender, Napoleon invaded Russia, his marshals driving the enemy rearguard before them. That same day, Henry Clay addressed two thousand Kentucky volunteers prior to their march on the Detroit frontier. On opposite sides of the world, two armies were marching off on fall campaigns. Given the Napoleonic threat and the hazards of seasonal navigation, England would not soon be able to afford reinforcements to meet the renewed American war effort.[43]

NOTES

1. Brock to Prevost, 18 Sept. 1812, *SBD* 1: 593.
2. Procter to Sheaffe, 28 Nov. 1812, NAUS, *MIC*, 22-26.
3. Tecumseh in Council, 15 Sept. 1813, cited in Richardson, *War of 1812*, 204.
4. Tupper, *Brock*, 238.
5. Prevost to Brock, 2 Aug. 1812, Tupper, *Brock*, 231. The armistice with the commander of the U.S. Army excluded the Detroit frontier as Hull acted directly under war department orders.
6. Glegg to Baynes, 5 Aug. 1812, *SBD* 1: 413; Lt. Col. John MacDonald to Duncan Cameron, 10 Aug. 1812, *DICSD*, 130-31; Charles Askin, "Charles Askin Journal," *JAP* 2: 714-16.
7. Brock to Evans, 17 Aug. 1812, *DHCNF* 1812, Vol. 3: 186; Charles Askin, "Charles Askin Journal," *JAP* 2: 716; Richardson, *War of 1812*, 47-49; Tupper, *Brock*, 238-42; Fairchild, *Journal*, 75; William McKay, *Journal, SBD* 1: 548.
8. Capt. J.B. Glegg, cited in Tupper, *Brock*, 243. Early American accounts assert that Tecumseh was a general in the British army. There is no evidence to support this notion although several contemporary witnesses reported Tecumseh wearing a scarlet jacket on formal occasions. He often dined with the British officers, who called him the "general of the Indians" and "the Wellington of the Indians." Tupper, *Brock*, 262.
9. Boucherville, *Journal*, 108. There is no documented transcript of these meetings with the Native chiefs; however, Brock's aide, Capt. Glegg, witnessed the events and subsequently recorded his recollections. Glegg, cited in Tupper, *Brock*, 243-45; William James, *Military Occurrences of the Late War* 1: 291-92.

10. Brock to Prevost, 17 Aug. 1812, *SBD* 1: 468; Brock to his brothers, 3 Sept. 1812, *DHCNF* 1812, Vol. 3: 233. Robert Nichol (c.1780-1824) was commander of the 2nd Norfolk Regiment but spent most of the war years as staff advisor to Brock, Procter, Sheaffe, Rottenberg, and Drummond in his capacity of quartermaster general of the Upper Canadian militia. Nichol possessed extensive knowledge of the Lake Erie country. He organized boats for the Detroit campaign and was said to be the only white officer to support Brock's proposal of storming Detroit. After the battle of Moraviantown, Nichol supported Procter's urgings that Upper Canada not be abandoned. He fought at Fort Erie and advised Drummond on the feasibility of rebuilding a naval presence on the Upper Lakes. In May 1814, American raiders destroyed his extensive holdings in the Long Point area, losses for which Nichol received little or no compensation. He represented Norfolk Country in the provincial assembly between 1813 and 1820. Nichol died under peculiar circumstances when his carriage went over the Niagara River embankment on a stormy evening while he was working on the erection of Brock's monument. *DCB* 6: 539-45.

11. Brock's General Order, 14 Aug. 1812, *SBD* 1: 459-60.

12. Lucas, *Journal*, 61; Hull to Brush, 11 Aug. 1812, cited in *Columbia Centinel*, 9 Sept. 1812.

13. Brock to Hull, 15 Aug. 1812, *SBD* 1: 461. By using the passive voice in his letter to Hull, Brock cleverly concealed his active role in seeking the support of the Natives. Although Brock had never seen the warriors in a shooting action, he certainly knew from reputation that they could seldom be restrained during and after the heat of battle.

14. Lucas, *Journal*, 63; Snelling, *HCM*, 35; Hull to Brock, 15 Aug. 1812, *SBD* 1: 461-62.

15. Lucas, *Journal*, 62; [Foster], *Capitulation*, 295; L.W. Claypool Journal, cited in Blanchard, *Northwest*, 268.

16. Boucherville, *Journal*, 107-08.

17. Brock's General Order, 15 Aug. 1812, *SBD* 1: 462; Prize List, Surrender of Fort Detroit, *SBD* 1: 474; Charles Askin, "Charles Askin Journal," *JAP* 2: 717.

18. Brock to Prevost, 17 Aug. 1812, *SBD* 1: 468.

19. [Foster], *Capitulation*, 298; Richardson, *War of 1812*, 54; Dalliba, *HCM*, 83.

20. Claypool Journal, cited in Blanchard, *Northwest*, 268; Lucas, *Journal*, 63-64; Livingstone to Woodward, 16 Aug. 1812, *MPHC* 8: 636.

21. James Miller, *HCM*, 109; Robert Wallace to R.C. Langton, nd., cited in Clarke, *Campaign of 1812*, 450; Snelling, *HCM*, 40; Hull to Eustis, 26 Aug. 1812, *HCM*, Appendix 2: 15.

22. Lucas, *Journal*, 64.

23. John Askin to Charles Askin, 16 Sept. 1812, *JAP* 2: 731.

24. Charles Askin, "Charles Askin Journal," *JAP* 2: 719; Richardson, *War of 1812*, 58; Shadrach Byfield, *A Common Soldier's Account*, 6; Robert Wallace to R.C. Langdon, nd., cited in Clarke, *Campaign of 1812*, 453.

25. The Capitulation of Detroit, *SBD* 1: 470-72; Hull to the officer at the blockhouse on the Maumee, 17 Aug. 1812, *MPHC* 40: 454; Brock's Proclamation, 16 Aug. 1812, *DICSD*, 155-56; Brock to Prevost, 16 Aug. 1812, Brock's General Order, 16 Aug. 1812, *SBD* 1: 463-65.

26. Brock to Prevost, 17 Aug. 1812, *SBD* 1: 465-70; Return of Ordnance Stores Taken at Detroit, *SBD* 1: 495-96; [Procter and Procter], "Campaigns in the Canadas," 409-10; Brock to his brothers, 3 Sept. 1812, Tupper, *Brock*, 284.

27. General Return of Prisoners of War Surrendered by Capitulation at Detroit, 26 Aug. 1812, *SBD* 1, 497; Hull's notations to General Return of Prisoners, cited in Burton, *City of Detroit* 2: 1020; Monthly Return of Garrison of Fort Michilimackinac, June 1812, *MPHC* 15: 114; Hull to Eustis, 26 Aug. 1812, *MPHC* 40: 466; Hull, *Memoirs*, 123.

28. Brock to Prevost, 17 Aug. 1812, Tupper, *Brock*, 271; Richardson, *War of 1812*, 52; Hull, *Memoirs*, 83.

29. William McKay Diary, *SBD* 1: 550; Charles Askin, "Charles Askin Journal," *JAP* 2: 720.

30. Manson, *HCM*, 103.

31. Merritt, *Journal*, *SBD* 3, Pt. 2: 555; John Askin, Jr., to Claus, 18 July 1812, *SBD* 1: 436-37. John Askin, Jr., was interpreter for the Indian Department at Fort St. Joseph. He led about three hundred Ottawa and Chippewa at the capture of Michilimackinac, working closely with Robert Dickson in sending warriors to Amherstburg during the first year of the war. He became Deputy Superintendent of Indian Affairs at Amherstburg in 1820 and died there the same year. Richardson, *War of 1812*, 25n.

32. Cass, McArthur, *HCM*, 24-25, 59-61; Capt. Elliott to Procter, 22 Aug. 1812, *DICSD*, 172. William Elliott commanded a flank company of the 1st Essex Regiment. Having served in the American army, he was one of the few militia officers of the Western District to posess military training. Elliott participated in the Detroit campaign, both battles of Frenchtown and the siege of Fort Meigs. In 1837, he was dismissed from his position of colonel in the militia for denouncing the execution of patriot prisoners by Col. John Prince. Accounts frequently confuse him with Matthew Elliott or his sons. *JAP* 2: 503n.

33. *Niles Weekly Register*, 15 Sept. 1812; Lucas, *Journal*, 67.

34. Eustis to Hull, 20 Aug. 1812, *MPHC* 40: 454.

35. Cass to Eustis, 10 Sept. 1812, Forbes, *HCM*, Appendix 2: 25; *Columbia Centinel*, 9 Sept. 1812; *Niles Weekly Register*, 15 Sept. 1812; *The War*, 6, 19 Sept. 1812.

36. *The War,* 26 Sept. 1812; *Columbian Centinel,* 9 Sept. 1812.

37. An account of the Chicago massacre and the sufferings of the survivors, is contained in Mrs. John Kinzie, *Wau Bun, the Early Days in the Northwest,* 159-226. Mrs. Kinzie had been married to Capt. Daniel McKillip, a Loyalist officer of the New Settlement who was killed at the battle of Fallen Timbers. She remarried to fur trader John Kinzie. Boucherville, *Journal,* 121n. Capt. Heald's report of the Fort Dearborn action is found in John Russell, Jr., (Comp.) *The History of the War,* 174-76.

38. Memorial of Niagara residents to Prevost, 16 Dec. 1812, cited in Tupper, *Brock,* 298; [Procter and Procter], "Campaigns," 410.

39. Militia General Order, 18 Aug. 1812, *DHCNF* 1812, Vol. 3: 188. This court of inquiry found that several officers had wantonly deserted their posts. Eight officers of the 1st and 2nd regiments of Essex Militia were superseded with three subordinate officers broken into the ranks. Militia General Order, 23 Jan. 1813, *DHCNF* 1813, Vol. 1: 46.

40. Brock's Proclamation, 16 Aug. 1812, *The War,* 12 Sept. 1812; Warren to Lord Viscount Melville, 18 Nov. 1812, cited in John K. Mahon, "British Command Decisions of the War of 1812," 222.

41. Brock to Prevost, 2 Dec. 1811, Tupper, *Brock,* 125; Brock to Liverpool, 29 Aug. 1812, *DICSD,* 192-93.

42. *NOW* 1, 53; Madison's address to Congress, 4 Nov. 1812, *The Annual Register or A View of the History, Politics and Litertature for the Year, 1812,* 444-45.

43. G. Glenn Clift, *Remember the Raisin!,* 20.

6

STALEMATE

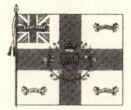

"I feel it an object to know, at least to see, a country that may be the scene of action."[1]

Procter to Brock, 29 August 1812

"The Indians ... have their fears that this territory may again be ceded to the Americans."[2]

Procter to Brock, 30 September 1812

WITH BROCK'S DEPARTURE on 19 August, Procter resumed command on the Detroit frontier. There was much to be done. He prepared to send an expedition against Fort Wayne, Indiana, but on receiving Brock's express of 24 August to suspend offensive action, he postponed that operation. In the meantime, he had to organize Michigan Territory, deal with the prisoners, and secure the surrendered posts and inventory.[3]

Subsequent to accepting the surrender of McArthur and Cass, Capt. William Elliott proceeded down Hull's Road with two militiamen and a warrior to take charge of the remaining American posts. In complying with the terms of Hull's capitulation, McArthur endorsed the authenticity of Elliott's mission on the back of Hull's letter, instructing Brush to surrender his command. On 17 August, as Elliott approached Frenchtown, he was apprehended by a detached picket and taken blindfolded into the Wayne Stockade, where "the gate [was] shut and nailed up." On learning of Elliott's business, Brush summarily pronounced Hull's documents forgeries, and Elliott a spy who was to be hanged. In the ensuing row, Brush's men threatened to shoot their commander rather than allow Elliott's execution. The British emissaries were confined in a blockhouse for the night. The following morning, fugitive renegades from Detroit, Simon Zealotus Watson, and Andrew Westbrook, confirmed the validity of Elliott's mission. Brush and his colleagues packed up, stole some horses from the villagers, and with the utmost expedition headed for Ohio. Within 12 hours, they reached the Maumee Rapids blockhouse. The next day, Lt. Col. Anderson released Elliott and surrendered the Wayne Stockade, and the 2nd Michigan Regiment, to him. Lt. Benoit Bender arrived with boats to ferry the public property, a small howitzer, over a hundred stand of arms, 46 barrels of flour, and miscellaneous stores and equipment to Amherstburg.[4]

On 19 August, Capt. Peter Chambers and a party of warriors under Matthew Elliott and Tecumseh joined Capt. Elliott at Frenchtown. Chambers had served the 41st since the age of 15. At 24, he was energetic, forceful, and ambitious. He had barely assured the Raisin River inhabitants of British protection when Col. Anderson's distraught wife went to him, begging that he halt the warriors from ransacking her house. The unruly Natives ignored his directions and he could only watch helplessly as the Wyandot despoiled the village in what he described as "one universal scene of destruction." Chambers urged Matthew Elliott and the other officers of the Indian Department to interfere, "but when they did, it was so little as to be of no avail." He was direct in laying blame for the Natives' misconduct, writing, "The disgraceful scenes could have been in a great measure prevented had the proper officers exerted the necessary controul [sic]." Although Matthew Elliott was the senior member of the Indian Department present, he was unwell, and it was Capt. Thomas McKee and Tecumseh who made attempts "to put a stop to scenes so shocking and disgusting." Even they could not totally contain the disorder as the warriors pillaged homes and absconded with "a great number of horses." Before leaving, Chambers ordered the destruction of the Wayne Stockade and the two detached blockhouses.[5]

On 21 August, Chambers proceeded to the Maumee Rapids and destroyed the blockhouse recently evacuated by Capt. David Hull (nephew of the late American commander). Given the warriors' misconduct at the Raisin, the British officer intended to send them back, but "a scoundrel by the name of Amable Bellair" told him that there were 180 Americans at the rapids so he took the allies along. On arrival, he found that Brush's party had passed through the day before, leaving behind a few convalescents, 77 barrels of pork, 18 of flour, seven of whiskey, and two of salt. As he loaded these goods onto the waiting boats, the braves despoiled private property, destroying all but one home in this predominantly American community of 30 families. One unfortunate settler complained to Procter that the warriors defaced his wife's tombstone and tore down the picketing around her grave, adding, "It is not for me to implicate the gentlemen who commanded the expedition, yet I am of the opinion that they might have prevented it." These stories filtered back to the republic and were embellished in newspapers: "Even the tomb was not held sacred; dead bodies were unearthed and stripped of their scalps by the Indians, who after robbing the dead, cheated their employers by selling these trophies at the same as if torn from the living!"[6]

This time, it was Tecumseh and Roundhead who restrained the tribesmen. Nonetheless, as the captured stores were loaded on three of Lt. Bender's boats and some canoes, the warriors plundered them. Worse yet, they murdered and scalped one of Bender's *Canadien* boatmen and shot at another. Chambers returned to Amherstburg with the loot on 23 August only to learn that the warriors had stolen his horse during his absence. He stormed off for what one observer termed, "a very serious quarrel" with Matthew Elliott. A few days later, Procter wrote Brock, not coincidentally, "I take it upon myself to permit [brevet] Maj. Chambers to return to Niagara, recollecting that active officers of his rank may be wanted there." Procter, chronically undermanned, sent Chambers away for the sake of maintaining harmony within the alliance.[7]

The Natives' conduct had indeed been disorderly since the fall of Detroit. They helped themselves to more than three hundred horses in Michigan within two days, contrary to the guarantees of private property specified in the terms of the capitulation. Robert Nichol remonstrated that within 10 days of the surrender, "There was scarcely a house on either side of the river that has not been robbed by them. They have already taken the greater part of the captured horses and cattle, and without our being able to prevent it." Lt. Edward Dewar complained that "their conduct becomes outrageous in proportion to the impunity with which they offend." After warriors purloined eight of his army boats, Dewar sent some dockyard men to recover one that was abandoned in the river, but the braves forcibly seized it, too. When a resident on the Canadian side demanded the return of his stolen horse, the warriors complied, after running swords through the unfortunate animal. Dewar lamented that the government would have to reimburse the inhabitants on the Canadian side for about 50 stolen horses, observing that the soldiers' selling liquor to the Natives did not help to curb their misconduct.[8]

Despite their proven performance as instruments of terror during the Detroit campaign, the warriors proved difficult to control. Their societies did not possess the organizational control the British officers expected. At Michilimackinac, Capt. Roberts also reported difficulties in mobilizing the braves. After recovering from their victory drinking binge, most of them went home to their starving families with their presents and booty. Roberts wrote, "The spark which gave life to everything at the commencement of operations seems to have nearly expired.... Private views and individual jealousies have overcome every other sentiment."[9]

The weak military presence on the Detroit River produced the double effect of continued British reliance on the tribesmen as auxiliary fighters while limiting the means by which to control their excesses. Brock could only suggest discreet circumvention of Elliott as a means to contain the disorder, "Col. Elliott is a respectable gentlemanly man, but he by no means possesses the influence over the Indians that Capt. McKee does. I recommend to you to promote a good understanding with and between them and to observe a conciliatory deportment towards the latter." Procter confirmed Brock's opinion, crediting McKee and Tecumseh for exerting what little control was possible at Frenchtown and on the Maumee. He deplored the inefficiency that resulted from Elliott's jealousy of McKee's influence as producing "imbecility" in the Indian Department. Unfortunately, the frequently intoxicated McKee was seldom available for service. Procter recognized his influence among the tribes and and expressed the hope that his personal influence "may restrain him in his greatest failing." A Detroit resident witnessed McKee's performance:

The Indians were commanded by a half-breed named McKee. Once in a while ... Indians would venture into town ... at the sight of which ... timid citizens would be alarmed.... McKee would go in the street and give a few tremendous yells at the sound of which the Indians would gather around him and he would order them back into camp and they would instantly obey him. At times when the Indians would come to town, McKee would be so drunk, he would have to be assisted into the street and held upright by some citizens, but notwithstanding, his earthly yells (he had a voice like a lion) would bring all the Indians around him, and he would order them back to camp.[10]

In short, with Elliott ineffective and McKee uncertain, there was no one in the Indian Department to adequately control and direct the Natives. Even Tecumseh and Roundhead possessed limited powers in this regard. Procter had high regard for one other other chief, John Norton, of the Grand River Mohawk. He was remarkably intelligent, speaking no fewer than 12 Native languages in addition to English, French, Spanish, and German. Although adept in the use of the scalping knife, Norton exerted a restraining influence over the warriors, and Procter repeatedly sought his aid.[11]

Maj. Gen. Roger Sheaffe, Brock's deputy, compounded Procter's dilemma concerning Native misconduct by writing, "The General [Brock] expects that all prudent and proper measures are adopted for the protection of the inhabitants on both sides of the streight [sic] from the depredations and lawless violence of the Indians which he trusts will be in a great measure checked by employing the influence of the officers of the Indian Department and the authority of the chiefs." Given the limited effectiveness of the Indian Department, Procter proposed to use "the rigour of the law against Indians detected in committing depredations," but Brock, through Sheaffe, discouraged the measure "in the most forceful manner," as "it would only produce the effect of increasing a hundredfold the evil, instead of remedying it and might eventually bring the most calamitous consequences on ourselves and give a mortal blow to our intentions with the Indian Nations in that quarter." As a result of these succinct but somewhat contradictory directions, the tribesmen continued in their misbehaviour for the duration of the British occupation. Procter and the military presence would become unpopular on both sides of the river for their failure to deal with this lawlessness. Given his few regulars, Procter would repeatedly attempt to mobilize the tribesmen, as much to rid the settled areas of disorder as to disrupt American preparations. Almost immediately after the capitulation, the power of the Natives held sway.[12]

Nor was misconduct the worst that Procter could expect from his allies. The militiamen of the Raisin River had been released on parole; however, Procter confined Capt. Hubert Lacroix, an active officer of Frenchtown on charges of treason, since he was born in Montreal. The

difficulty arose when Tecumseh, a personal friend of Lacroix, intervened and demanded the release of the *Canadien*, threatening to abandon the alliance if his demand was not met. Procter complied for the
sake of harmony, this being the first (but not last) time that the war
chief got his way with the weak British presence.[13]

Although Procter was unable to protect the inhabitants' property,
he managed to protect the inhabitants themselves. The *Buffalo Gazette*
carried the following report from Detroit fugitives on 22 September:

Yesterday a flag arrived from Fort Erie, bringing over Aaron Greely Esq., late
Surveyor General of the Michigan Territory.... They arrived on board the
Adams ... after the remarkably short passage of 33 hours. We are authorized
by Mr. Greely to state the British officers and Indian agents do everything
in their power to prevent the Indians from committing acts of cruelty. Mr.
Greely also contradicts in express terms the report that the British either gave
or offered six dollars or any other sum for SCALPS, but on the contrary,
discountenanced the Indians by all possible means from acts of cruelty.[14]

Given his shortage of troops to maintain order, the British commander was anxious to establish working relations with the inhabitants
of the conquered territory. Aside from his short proclamation, Brock
had provided little guidance with regard to the civil administration of
Michigan, leaving Lt. Col. Robert Nichol to assist in its organization.
Nichol reported to Brock:

It has been found absolutely necessary to organise the civil government.
Under existing circumstances, I have advised Col. Procter to assume the
administration until your pleasure is known, to which he has agreed and the
necessary arrangements thereto have been adopted and promulgated. In
Judge Woodward, who has been appointed secretary *pro tem* he will find an
able coadjutator.... I do not think a more judicious choice could have been
made. In all the discussions which took place on this subject, Col. Procter
did me the honour of consulting me.[15]

As Chief Justice Augustus Woodward was the single American official to remain in Michigan, Procter had few contenders from whom to
pick. The magistrate approached Procter to seek "clarification" on the
legal status of the ceded territory. Procter wrote Brock, "Immediately
after your departure hence, a difficulty was encountered regarding the
administration of the laws of this territory as announced in your

proclamation of the 16th instant." The British commander was respectful of Woodward, soliciting his advice in drafting a guideline for the civil administration of Michigan. Specifically, he asked for the geographical limits of the territory, its settled parts, and the composition of its administration and government. Woodward replied "with great pleasure" that same day, providing a detailed brief, noting that office holders could continue in their duties but not those federally employed. With the input of Woodward and Nichol, Procter issued his "Regulation for the Civil Government of the Territory of Michigan." This document affirmed the "ceded" status of the territory and outlined its executive, legislative and judicial framework with Procter as governor and Woodward as secretary.[16]

For his part, Woodward did not take kindly to military dictatorship, be it American or British. Despite his conciliatory intentions, Procter could not realistically expect full co-operation from the calculating judge, an outspoken advocate of democratic rights who disdained anything that smacked of arbitrary authority. Thus began Procter's entanglements with Woodward's formidable arsenal of legalistic bombast that invoked authorities ranging from the Book of Leviticus to the edicts of Charlemagne. Nonetheless, by late August, Nichol reported that public confidence had been "partially restored" with "business again going on."[17]

Woodward was well known to the British officers, especially to Capt. Muir of the 41st, who spent some years at Amherstburg before the war. In 1806, Muir created a minor international incident when, in co-operation with the American garrison, he and Ensign John Lundie crossed to Fort Detroit in order to arrest a British deserter (an illegal act but one sanctioned by local custom between the two garrisons). After refreshing themselves in the fort, the two officers, accompanied by several American colleagues, entered a private home and laid hands upon the culprit. As they dragged him off by the shoulders, the local baker came upon the scene and grabbed the victim by the limbs, upon which the assailants threatened to "run him through" and "blow out his brains." The heroic baker retorted with, "Fire and be damned, you ruffians!" Meanwhile, other residents were attracted by the commotion. The alarmed folk quickly spread the story that seven hundred warriors were lurking in the neighbouring woods, ready to massacre the peaceable townspeople. The cry "Murder! Fire! Indians!" was instantly taken up as the citizens rushed upon the intruders, armed with firearms, farm implements, and buckets of water. Despite attempts by the American officers to protect their British counterparts, the throng set upon the aliens. In the ensuing scuffle, Ensign Lundie tried to shoot one of them, while Muir took aim at the deserter but shot himself in the leg instead. The uproar intensified as Lt. Porter Hanks, subsequently commander at Fort Michilimackinac, ordered the citizens to disperse to their homes or he would drive them there with a detachment from Fort Detroit. Abraham Hull, the governor's son, chastized the citizens as "a parcel of rascals" who "ought all to be put in jail." The younger Hull further asserted that if they did not retire, he would level the fort guns on the town and "blow them all to hell!" As a result of this singular transaction, the town marshall arrested Muir, Lundie, Hull, Hanks and Lt. Henry Brevoort (master of *Adams* in 1812), charging the lot with assault and battery, and disturbing the peace.[18]

Muir and his companion appeared before Judge Woodward who found them guilty. The chief justice used the occasion to assert legal muscle against two of his favourite enemies, an undemocratic British institution, and military establishments in general. He awarded Muir a stiff fine of $44.60, and 17 days imprisonment to boot. Woodward sentenced the unfortunate ensign a staggering fine of $8888 plus a hefty six months in jail (meaning perpetual imprisonment). The ridiculous sentences were contested by the territorial council which pointed out that by statute, Woodward could neither imprison the men nor fine them more than $100. Governor Hull also intervened, unsuccessfully. He became so flabbergasted with Woodward's heavy-handed dealings that for a long time he would not speak to his chief justice. In the end, an embarrassed Woodward accepted the dictates of law and fined both men a few cents each, commuting the jail terms. Muir, now commandant of Fort Detroit, undoubtedly remembered the affair.[19]

Despite Woodward's past reputation, Governor Procter's relations with this champion of Jeffersonian democracy started off well, Procter "and the gentlemen of his family" politely inviting the judge to social gatherings and lending him scarce American newspapers. However, the eccentric Woodward developed second thoughts about his interaction with the occupying army. To ease his conscience (and any legal unpleasantness that may result), Woodward declared the delicacy of his situation to Secretary of the Treasury Albert Gallatin, stressing that his actions in co-operating with the enemy were "commanded by philanthropy." He concluded his letter by writing, "I flatter myself that the course which I have adopted will be approved; or, if not, that I shall be early apprized [*sic*] of it."[20]

As Michigan was British territory, Procter administered oaths of allegiance to the residents. Most of the *Canadiens* of the Raisin River were agreeable to this measure, and Procter observed that they would "cheerfully take up arms" for the Crown, if ordered. However, others resisted his efforts, and he intended to deport some "dangerous characters" who corresponded with the American army. But as the only available vessel, *Ellenor*, was not seaworthy, he hesitated, stating, "I do not choose to take responsibility of drowning them tho' they may deserve to be hanged."[21]

Procter then turned his attention to the practical concerns of the oncoming winter. In response to his request for a brief on foodstuffs, Lt. Dewar reported that despite a bumper crop of wheat in 1812, the actual harvest would be half that of other years, while Indian corn and potatoes would be a mere quarter of normal yields. The militiamen's absence from their farms had impaired the harvest, a situation aggravated by abnormal rains that either rotted crops in the fields or made harvest difficult. Many of the cattle and hogs were consumed during the Detroit campaign or wantonly butchered by the tribesmen. As the Detroit region had never been self-sufficient in foodstuffs Procter had to consider outide sources since the concentration of combatants would create serious food shortages during the winter for civil, military, and Native communities alike. In addition, Procter also had to resupply the distant outpost of Michilimackinac before the close of the navigational season.[22]

The Provincial Marine ferried the Ohio militiamen to their home state across Lake Erie to ensure their safety from molestation by the warriors. Brush and his companions had already spread the alarming news of Detroit's capture, causing the hasty abandonment of small lakeshore settlements. The distressed refugees congregated at Cleveland, a hamlet of 10 rude log dwellings. The subsequent arrival of the paroled militiamen in the sparsely populated areas further heightened the sense of panic. Such were the apprehensions at Cleveland that the disembarking militiamen were initially reported as "300 British soldiers and 600 Indians." Desperate military preparations were undertaken as women and children fled for safety. Pennsylvanians also sprang to action, and gathered at Erie for the relief of Cleveland. Two thousand additional militiamen assembled at Dayton, Ohio, while Brig. Gen. James Winchester placed on alert his fifteen hundred Kentucky volunteers at Cincinnati. Procter actively contributed to this turmoil, sending *Queen Charlotte* (known to Americans as "the terror of the lake") to cruise between Cleveland and Sandusky for the sole purpose of creating "alarm."[23]

One Ohio resident related the following anecdote to describe the anxiety on the American lakeshore during the fall of 1812:

On the night of the 11th of August, 1812, the people of Conneaut were alarmed by a false report that the British were landing from some of their vessels. A sentinel, placed on the shore, descrying boats approaching, mistook them for the enemy. In his panic, he threw away his musket, mounted his horse, and dashing through the settlement cried out with a stentorian voice, "Turn out! Turn out! Save your lives! The British and Indians are coming and will be on you in fifteen minutes!"

The people aroused from their beds, fled in the utmost terror to various places of covert in the forest. By that soothing attention mothers know how to bestow, the cries of the children were measurably stilled; but one little dog, apart from his companions kept up a continual and unmitigated yelping. Various means having in vain been employed to still him, until the patience of the ladies was exhausted, it was unanimously resolved that that particular dog should die, and he was therefore sentenced to be hanged without benefit of clergy. With the elastics supplied by the ladies, for a halter, and a young sapling, for a gallows, the young dog passed from the shores of time to yelp no more.[24]

While Procter braced himself for the next American advance, Brock faced a more immediate threat on the Niagara frontier. Prevost had foiled his intention of sweeping the American facilities on the lakes on the one hand, and refused to send him troops, on the other. Thus Brock had little choice but to juggle his weak detachments throughout the colony, concentrating them in threatened areas. As a consequence, he could not send Procter the entire 41st as planned. Having already withdrawn from Amherstburg those elements that accompanied him on the Detroit expedition, he asked Procter for additional troops. These included the detachments under Chambers, Bullock, and the artillerymen of the fort with all the spare ordnance. Furthermore, he suggested that Procter himself might return to Fort George. Although Brock asked that the news of Prevost's armistice be concealed from the Native chiefs, they learned of it through their networks. Eight hundred of the assembled braves returned immediately to their villages. Disgusted, Tecumseh and the Prophet resumed their work on the Wabash, suspicious of the British commitment.[25]

Unable to dissuade the warriors from leaving, Procter received reports of American preparations and was convinced that hostilities would be renewed. He chose to remain at Amherstburg. He used the interlude of the armistice in late August to personally examine northern Ohio, accompanied by Matthew Elliott and Robert Nichol, "to know, at least to see a country that may be the scene of action." By meeting the advancing enemy in Ohio, he would adhere to Brock's strategy of pre-emptive strikes, while simultaneously demonstrating British intentions of securing the Ohio country as a Native preserve. The British commander ascended the Maumee as far as the rapids and explored the Sandusky River, finding both areas deserted. At the latter place, he received the first news of the fall of Fort Dearborn.[26]

On returning to Detroit, Procter was approached by Judge Woodward to rescue the survivors of Fort Dearborn, reportedly 23 soldiers and 11 civilian captives. Procter replied that he would "with the most effectual means in my power ... release from slavery the unfortunate individuals." He directed Elliott and McKee to secure the co-operation of the chiefs in recovering any prisoners in Native hands. Although the tribesmen immediately ransomed some, they had taken most of their captives deep into the interior. These were not located until March 1813, when Robert Dickson liberated 17 soldiers, four women, and a few children in camps west of Lake Michigan. One soldier, James Van Horne, was still a prisoner in Illinois Territory the following spring when a *Canadien* brought word that Procter had "sent a proclamation to the Indians to send all the prisoners to Detroit." Only in late June of 1813 was he ransomed at Michilimackinac. An orphaned boy, 6 years of age, was not recovered until September 1813.[27]

During his reconnaissance of Ohio, Procter also learned that Native warriors were besieging Fort Wayne, Indiana. Subsequent to the capture of Detroit, the Native confederacy under Tenskwatawa's influence had unilaterally undertaken co-ordinated assaults against the remaining American posts in the Northwest. As the Fort Wayne garrison held out against repeated attacks, the Native insurgents realized that they could not succeed against fortified posts without British artillery support. In desperation, they improvised with "quaker guns," bored out logs reinforced with iron hoops. They approached Procter for assistance, but the British commander was constrained by Prevost's directions. He proposed to send Matthew Elliott to restrain Native excesses, but as the old frontiersman was sick with lumbago (rheumatism in the loins), Procter sent interpreters instead.[28]

Despite the allied pre-eminence in Michigan, Prevost was not enthusiastic about the newly acquired territory. Far from supporting offensive movements aimed at securing a Native homeland, he urged the abandonment of that which had been gained, writing to Brock, "You will therefore be pleased, subject to the discretion I have given you ... to take immediate steps for the evacuation of that post [Detroit], together with the territory of Michigan. By this measure you will be enabled to withdraw a greater number of troops from Amherstburg." Clearly Prevost was not interested in further conquests or even consolidating existing ones. He placed Brock in the difficult position of either abandoning Michigan or committing scarce troops in its occupation. Having sent Brock a single regiment, the 49th, the governor adamantly refused to send any more troops, writing, "I have already afforded you reinforcements to the full extent of my ability; you must not, therefore, expect a further supply of men from hence until I shall receive from England a considerable increase." [29]

To further discourage adventures in the west, Prevost asked Brock to conduct a diversion on the Niagara frontier in case Lower Canada were attacked. Brock's own force was so inadequate and scattered that he replied, "I am at a loss to know in what manner I can possibly act so as to produce the effect expected." Although Prevost's passive strategy was diametrically opposed to that of Brock, his actions were driven by the British government's inability to send immediate aid. Moreover, the British cabinet was convinced that the repeal of the British Orders in Council would soon end the war. Even Prevost observed on London's pacific "infatuation." [30]

Although Prevost complained about home government policy, his overall strategy remained unmistakably defensive. He concentrated most of the British forces in Lower Canada, which was barely threatened. Indirectly chastising Brock, the commander-in-chief even hinted that if Hull had not invaded British soil, he would have considered the capture of Michilimackinac "in violation" of orders. Procter, who had the opportunity to join his family at Fort George and abandon Michigan, chose to stay at his post, backing Brock's intention to stand by the Native cause. He warned that the evacuation of Michigan would leave the inhabitants totally at the mercy of the tribesmen and would probably bring about their defection, writing to Brock that the Natives "have their fears that this Territory may again be ceded to the Americans; and in the event of which they will, I am confident, look upon us as their betrayers, and worst enemies. Our retention of this

Territory is I believe, as much as they would require." Brock agreed. On hearing of renewed American concentrations in the west, he directed Procter to remain at Detroit and forwarded his family and baggage there to join him.[31]

The decision by Brock and Procter to maintain Michigan against the wishes of the governor prepared the ground for subsequent events. Despite the shortage of soldiers, Brock believed that the wilderness, the Native alliance, the British command of Lake Erie, and an aggressive defence by Procter would combine for a desperate but effective stand in the Detroit country. In exchange for the regulars Procter had sent to him, Brock forwarded two half-manned flank companies of the Royal Newfoundland Regiment to double as marines and infantrymen. Although Procter did not receive the regiment he had been led to expect, he was satisfied that Brock had done all he could to support him. Procter had no choice but to make up for his shortage of regulars with militiamen and Native warriors as auxiliary fighters.[32]

Brock's purpose in ceding Michigan Territory to the Crown became clear as he argued for its incorporation as a Native homeland. Having already primed the British government, he now sought Prevost's support:

I shall suspend under the latitude left by your Excellency to my direction, the evacuation of Fort Detroit. Such a measure would most probably be followed by the total extinction of the population on that side of the river, or the Indians, aware of our weakness and inability to carry on active warfare would only think of entering into terms with the enemy. The Indians, since the Miami affair of 1793 [i.e., the battle of Fallen Timbers, 1794] have been extremely suspicious of our conduct, but the violent wrongs committed by the Americans on their territory have rendered it an act of policy with them to disguise their sentiments. Could they be persuaded that a peace between the belligerents could take place without admitting their claim to an extensive tract of country, fraudulently usurped from them, and opposing a frontier to the present unbounded views of the Americans, I am satisfied in my own mind that they would immediately compromise with the enemy. I cannot conceive a connexion so likely to lead to more awful consequences....

Should negociations for peace be opened I cannot be too earnest with your Excellency to represent to the King's ministers, the expediency of including the Indians as Allies, and not leave them exposed to the unrelenting fury of their enemies.[33]

With Brock holding firm in Michigan, it was up to Tecumseh to assert Native influence in the remainder of the Northwest. Although the Native insurgency caused widespread alarm, Tecumseh's confederacy made virtually no military progress against the Americans. The warriors managed to burn one of the corner blockhouses of Fort Harrison, but its commander, Capt. Zachary Taylor (a future U.S. president) succeeded in holding the fort until relieved by a force of six hundred mounted rangers. Two days later, Fort Wayne was likewise relieved, although the tribesmen destroyed the outlying homes and buildings, killing three soldiers outside the fort. Through these desperate efforts, the Americans managed to maintain their toehold in the Northwest.[34]

Recognizing the difficulties in reducing fortified posts, even small stockades, the chiefs appealed to Procter for help. He was willing to oblige, but Prevost's restrictive orders still precluded his co-operation. Although the armistice had specifically excluded the Detroit frontier, the governor insisted on a strictly defensive posture on all fronts. Directed to suspend offensive operations on the one hand but ordered to contain atrocities on the other, Procter acted on his own initiative. When the armistice expired on 10 September, he sent off a force against Fort Wayne, asserting that he wished to avert a recurrence of the Fort Dearborn massacre. Brock supported the venture as "strengthening a defensive position" but was unequivocal in reaffirming Prevost's injunctions. "Your operations are to be confined to measures of defence and security ... not ... conquest." He endorsed Procter's, humanitarian motives to Prevost, arguing once more for support of the Natives: "The Indians were likewise looking to us for assistance. They heard of the armistice with every mark of jealousy, and had we refused to joining them in the expedition it is impossible to calculate the consequences. I have already been asked to pledge my word that England would enter no negotiations in which their interests were not consulted, and could they be brought to imagine that we should desert them, the consequences must be fatal."[35]

On 14 September, the Fort Wayne expedition set off under Muir's command in *Salina* and Bender's boats. It included 150 men of the 41st with two officers, a small artillery detachment under Lt. Felix Troughton, engineer officer Capt. Matthew Dixon, and a hundred militiamen with 12 officers under William Caldwell. Matthew Elliott, Thomas McKee, Roundhead, and Splitlog led some eight hundred

Richardson's *War of 1812*

Brig. Gen. James Winchester led the second American attempt against British positions in the Detroit country. His disastrous defeat at Frenchtown convinced the American government to adopt a systematic approach to the conduct of the war.

warriors, mainly Wyandot augmented by two hundred recently arrived Ottawa and Ojibwa from Michilimackinac. This force was joined by 47 *Canadien* drivers of the Raisin River, with cattle and pack horses.[36]

Muir's expedition ascended the Maumee in boats as far as the rapids, where it conducted a 10-mile portage. Although the low water levels greatly impeded progress, the tiny army advanced to within 40 miles of Fort Wayne. Suddenly it blundered into the reconstituted Northwest Army, which had already relieved Fort Wayne and was advancing down the Maumee. Splitlog reported the American force as 2500 men, located only two miles away. On 25 September, Native scouting parties from the opposing sides collided, producing a handful of casualties in either group. Muir, whose expedition might be cut off and overwhelmed, was in a potentially embarrassing situation. It had taken him three days to haul his cumbersome guns eight miles. He alerted Procter to take precautions, as the large American force was undoubtedly aimed at Detroit or Amherstburg.[37]

Muir then engaged in inconclusive consultations with his allies to determine the best course of action as Elliott, Roundhead, and the shaman conjurers proposed alternate plans. Hampered in his movements by the guns, Muir loaded them into the boats and sent them down river. Perceiving this action as indicative of his desire to retreat, the Lake Indians abandoned the expedition *en masse*. At this point, scouts captured an American soldier who described the American force under Brig. Gen. James Winchester as three thousand strong with cavalry and artillery. With only half the Native force remaining, Muir considered it "madness" to engage the enemy, but the medicine men, who had been conjuring all night, dreamed that the allies would be successful in battle and now insisted on fighting. Muir had had enough. He ordered a retreat to the decrepit Fort Miamis, arriving there in good order on 30 September. He blamed the expedition's failure on the armistice, which had delayed the operation until it was too late. Procter agreed, calling Prevost's effort "short-sightedness." In later years, he assessed the effect of the actions of the commander-in-chief: "This want of co-operation had a most unfavourable effect upon the minds of the Indians and was an impolitic and unmanly desertion of them." Forced to explain British intentions to the chiefs, Procter called a grand council in October 1812 and managed to retain the support of the assembled leaders, although Tecumseh remained aloof.[38]

As Procter had sent the better part of his disposable force on the expedition, Muir's news of the American advance caused him "no little anxiety" for its safe return. He asked for any of the 41st who might be spared, and sent *Queen Charlotte* to northern Ohio, once more to "cause an alarm" between Cleveland and Sandusky. On 3 October, much to Procter's relief, Muir's force returned to Amherstburg with negligible losses. Procter praised the "brave little band"; however, the mediocre performance of the warriors prompted him to write: "If I had not already been convinced of the necessity of an independent regular force to ensure the effectual assistance of the Indians, the history of this expedition would have confirmed me in this opinion." Convinced that British retention of Michigan Territory was essential to retain Native support he added, "The Indians hesitated some time whether they should again confide in us [after Prevost's Armistice]. They have their fears that this territory may be again ceded to the Americans."[39]

With the navigation season rapidly drawing to a close and the stock of foodstuffs running low, Procter focussed on the pressing matter of provisioning for the winter. In order to secure the produce of the Raisin River settlement, he directed the commissariat to establish a station in the village, protected by a party of warriors. Even this was not an easy task, as the Wyandot at Brownstown refused Elliott's directions to go there. Lt. Dewar ended up circumventing the Indian Department and crossing to Brownstown, where he convinced Roundhead to provide 14 warriors. Once established at Frenchtown, the commissariat, assisted by 20 militiamen, purchased 86 head of cattle and about three thousand bushels of wheat. Meanwhile, Capt. Roberts reported that the supply vessel destined for Michilimackinac with two hundred barrels of pork and three hundred barrels of flour was believed lost on Lake Huron and that he was desperately short of provisions. As the commissariat stocks were almost depleted, Procter released what provisions he could before the ice set in.[40]

British control of the Upper Lakes had paid immense dividends thus far, facilitating troop movements, tactical operations, arms shipments, and resupply activities. Hull's surrender prompted the American government to challenge this mastery. One of the paroled prisoners from Detroit, Daniel Dobbins, late master of the captured *Salina*, first took news of Hull's disaster to Washington. The government responded to his report (and unemployed state) by commissioning him to construct vessels of war at the lakeside village of Erie, Pennsylvania, a task he undertook immediately. In addition, the commander on the Great Lakes, Commodore Isaac Chauncy (USN) dispatched a naval presence to Black Rock, New York on 7 September. He directed Lt. Jesse Elliott (USN) to assess the situation on Lake Erie, select a site for a naval facility, purchase and convert any locally available merchant vessels into gunboats, lay down the keels for two vessels of three hundred tons, and build six gunboats of 40 feet. Elliott, heading a work gang of 320 men including 30 carpenters and a master builder, was to build accommodations, harbour defences, and a powder magazine at his preferred location. President Madison announced to Congress in September that he had undertaken steps to seize command of the lakes to secure "peace with and control over the savages."[41]

The American naval presence on Lake Erie produced immediate and dramatic results. The British brigs, *Detroit I* (formerly *Adams*) and *Caledonia* had been busily ferrying captured ordnance from Detroit to Fort Erie. *Detroit I* of six guns (pierced for 16) was commanded by Lt. Rolette, while *Caledonia*, mounting a pair of 4-pdr. guns on pivots, was captained by Sailing Master Robert Irvine. These vessels were at Fort Erie on 7 October, waiting to off-load their cargoes. From the opposite side of the Niagara River, Lt. Elliott observed the British activity and prepared to capture these cartel vessels. Before dawn on 9 October, he led boarding parties that surprised the brigs while they lay at anchor. *Caledonia* was taken intact to the U.S. side loaded with furs belonging to the Northwest Company and 30 American prisoners in the hold. The Americans were less successful with *Detroit I*, encountering difficulties negotiating the vessel against the current of the Niagara River. They abandoned her off Squaw Island where she was subsequently destroyed by artillery fire from both sides of the river. Her cargo lost to the British included four or five 12-pdr. guns, a large quantity of shot, and two hundred muskets, all captured at Detroit and destined for Fort George and Kingston. Elliott managed to save all pieces of ordnance from the vessels and mounted them at Black Rock to protect his germinating naval facilities.[42]

In predicting that Elliott's exploit would create "incalculable distress," Brock appreciated the drastic change that occurred on Lake Erie. The British marine establishment had lost two brigs, while the Americans gained one for their embryonic navy. Displeased with the security afforded the vessels, Brock relieved Maj. Armaud of the 41st of his command of the fort. Armaud's name subsequently disappeared from army records.[43]

Brock could no longer contain his dissatisfaction with Prevost's passive strategy: "I shall refrain as long as possible, under your excellency's positive injunctions, from every hostile act, although sensible that each day's delay gives him [the enemy] an advantage." Procter was also alarmed by the loss of the two vessels, and at the insistence of Lt. Rolette (who had been exchanged after his capture), he undertook the construction of two shallow draft gunboats to guard against future cutting-out operations. Prevost's passivity proved to be a critical miscalculation that allowed the Americans to establish offensive springboards on the waterways.[44]

It is uncertain whether Procter received his chief's final letter, a draft of which was found among his effects. It defined Procter's strategic doctrine for the following year. Strangely, it contained the unmistakable tone of parting:

The unfortunate disaster which has befallen the Detroit and Caledonia will reduce us to great distress.

An active, interesting scene is going to commence with you. I am perfectly at ease with the result, provided we can manage the Indians and keep them attached to our cause, which in fact is theirs.

The fate of the province is in your hands. Were it not for the positive injunctions of the commander of the forces, I should have acted with greater decision. You of course will adopt a very different line of conduct. The enemy must be kept in a state of constant ferment. If the Indians act as they did under Tecumseh, who probably might be induced to return to Amherstburg, that army [the Northwest Army] will very soon dwindle to nothing ... harass him continually. May every possible success attend you.[45]

At this point, Procter suffered an extended news blackout. Brock was killed on 13 October at Queenston, at the forefront of a failed charge to recapture the heights occupied by the invading Americans. The commander of Upper Canada was posthumously knighted for his vital contributions, aptly remembered as "the Saviour of Upper Canada." Procter would not learn of Brock's death or of the subsequent British victory for three full weeks. John Askin of Sandwich found it odd that the British commander had to beg for news of a public nature from the residents' private mail. This method of gathering information proved to be less than reliable, as Procter received an alarming report through Mr. McKenzie (the same gentleman whose magnified report of warrior numbers had so unnerved Hull) of the uncertain outcome to the American invasion at Queenston. Apprehensive that Fort Erie may have fallen, Procter directed *Lady Prevost* to approach port cautiously. He also sent Lt. Thomas Barnard of the 41st with a militia officer and some Wyandot to gather news on the Niagara frontier. Finally, Procter learned of events to the east from an official letter dated 30 October from his new superior, Maj. Gen. Roger Sheaffe. With the onset of winter, Procter would get minimal information or reinforcements. Brock's death was a particularly distressing event for Procter. All his plans were governed by the assumption that Brock would do whatever possible to support his efforts in the west. Procter was left to carry out an ambitious strategy based on the promise of a dead man.[46]

After Brock was killed, Sheaffe repelled the American invasion at Queenston and arranged an armistice on the Niagara frontier. This latest truce worked to the Americans' advantage as they used it to safely transport by water naval stores from Black Rock to Erie, a task that would have been difficult to accomplish by land. Thus the advantage of British naval superiority on Lake Erie was effectively nullified for a few days, facilitating the establishment of a second American naval facility on Lake Erie.[47]

In the meantime, Edward Couche, deputy commissary general, noted that it was too late in the year to transport to Amherstburg the eight hundred barrels of badly needed flour accumulated at Fort Erie. As a substitute, he sent £2000 in hard coin and £1500 in army bills, writing Robert Gilmor, his representative at Amherstburg, that "every means in your power may continue to be used to procure supplies of provisions from all quarters within your reach." Procter's allied force would have to survive winter on local produce.[48]

The British commander faced a provisioning crisis as displaced warriors from Indiana converged on Amherstburg with their families. Their homes burned by American raiders, their third consecutive harvest lost, and their way of life uprooted, some eight hundred refugees descended on the British camp. Although the local Wyandot could sustain themselves, the refugee families were entirely dependent on the commissariat for provisions. On 10 October, Procter sent Lt. Dewar and Roundhead on a reconnaissance of the Maumee area to investigate what abandoned crops might be available in that area. They reported no Americans near the rapids and estimated eight thousand bushels of corn and two hundred cattle in the immediate vicinity. Having already prohibited the distillation of grain whiskey, Procter resolved to send the tribesmen to feed on the Maumee corn. By so doing, he would relieve the pressure on the hard-pressed commissariat while denying those foodstuffs to the advancing Americans. Matthew Elliott was reluctant to comply, delaying his departure ten days until 29 October, when he finally set off "in agitation." By this time, the commissariat store was reduced to two days' stocks of food.[49]

While Procter contended with mounting logistical headaches, the second American Northwest Army edged forward. Brig. Gen. James Winchester commanded two thousand hastily recruited Kentucky volunteers at Fort Wayne and called on Governor Meigs to provide two additional Ohio regiments for an advance on the Maumee Rapids. A veteran of the Revolutionary war, Winchester had gained some reputation as an Indian fighter before retiring on his Tennessee plantation. Commissioned in the U.S. Army in 1812, he commanded little respect from the undisciplined volunteers that he led. The free-minded frontiersmen were contemptuous of his attempts to instill discipline. One common soldier recorded his impressions:

All despised him [Winchester] and were continually playing some of their tricks off on him. At one encampment they killed a porcupine and skinned it and stretched the skin over a pole that he used for a particular purpose in the night, and he went and sat down on it, and it likely to have ruined him. At another encampment they sawed his pole that he had for the same purpose nearly in two, so that when he went to use it in the night, it broke in two and let his Generalship, uniform and all fall backwards in no very decent place, for I have seen his Regimentals hanging high upon a pole the next day taking the fresh air.[50]

The matter of Winchester's leadership was resolved when Secretary of War Eustis revoked his appointment as commander of the Northwest Army in favour of Indiana Governor William H. Harrison. The "hero of Tippecanoe" was immensely popular with trans-Appalachian settlers. In order to assure his selection as commander, the government of Kentucky made him a major general in the militia to outrank Winchester and lobbied Washington. Confirmed in his new capacity, Harrison's mission was to secure the frontier from Native inroads, recapture Detroit, and then advance into Upper Canada as far as his "judgment would justify." His budget for provisions and materiel was virtually unlimited. The American general was eager to comply with his orders, writing to Governor Isaac Shelby of Kentucky, "We are amply supplied by bayonets and our spirits are roused to the highest pitch. Indignation and resentment fires in every breast." Commanding some eight thousand men (mainly volunteers and militiamen from Kentucky, Ohio, Pennsylvania and Virginia), Harrison had reasons for optimism as Americans looked to him to reverse Hull's disgrace.[51]

Thirty-nine years of age, Harrison came from a wealthy Virginia family. He had studied to be a doctor but joined the army in 1791 as an ensign and served as an aide-de-camp to Brig. Gen. Anthony Wayne on the Fallen Timbers campaign. Resigning his commission in 1798, he became governor of Indiana from 1800 till 1812. During this time, he expropriated massive tracts of land from the Natives by treaty, earning Tecumseh's undying enmity. Riding high in the public estimation after the battle of Tippecanoe, the ambitious Harrison was eager to win national fame.[52]

After relieving Fort Wayne on 12 September, Harrison launched numerous search and destroy missions against the Native villages of the region. Finding these communities deserted, his raiders torched homes and destroyed the crops of corn, wheat, barley, buckwheat, oats, pumpkins, melons, and potatoes, leaving Native families to face a winter of starvation. Like the warriors, they showed little respect for sex, age or even the dead. Although Harrison tried to identify the peaceful tribes, directing their removal to secure camps, the frontiersmen generally viewed the Natives as "bloodthirsty savages" who deserved no mercy. One of them described the treatment of a Native couple found in the open prairie:

The next morning, in a fog, our company of spies met two Indians, as we supposed and our captain fired upon them. Many of us, before he shot, begged for mercy for the Indians, as they wanted to surrender. But Judy, one of the spies, said anyone will surrender when they cannot help it, and that he did not leave home to take prisoners. I saw the dust rise off the Indian's leather shirt when Judy's bullet entered his body. The wounded Indian commenced singing his death song, the blood streaming out of his mouth and nose.... The Indian shot Wright and expired. The other Indian, supposed to be a warrior, proved to be a squaw; but before this fact was known, many guns were fired at her. It is singular that so many guns fired at the squaw missed her, but when the whites surrounded her and knew her sex, all was over. She cried terribly, and was taken prisoner and at last delivered over to her nation.[53]

With the "back Indians" neutralized, Harrison hoped to conduct a lightning attack on Detroit with a corps of mounted men; however, natural obstacles impeded his progress greatly. The difficulties of transporting men and equipment through the wilderness placed an immense strain on a logistics system that was noteworthy for its lack of organization. Nonetheless, his army plodded forward in three divisions. Under Harrison's personal direction, the right wing consisted of three militia brigades from Pennsylvania, Ohio, and Virginia. Before the artillery from Pittsburgh could be moved forward, this wing had to build roads and causeways over great distances through the Black Swamp, tormented all the while by swarms of voracious mosquitoes. The centre wing consisted of twelve hundred Ohio militiamen and eight hundred mounted infantrymen from Kentucky under Brig. Gen. Edward Tupper. It was to advance from southern Ohio, building depots and moving forward the voluminous contracted foodstuffs. The third wing under Brig. Gen. Winchester consisted of the 17th U.S. Infantry and twelve hundred Kentuckians. It was to proceed down the Maumee. The overall aim was to move the base line forward so that all columns would converge on the rendezvous point of the Maumee Rapids. Once there, Harrison intended to amass troops, forage, ordnance, and a million rations (to sustain ten thousand men for one hundred days) for a massive "*coup de main*" against Procter's positions.[54]

The American advance was pitifully slow, hampered by physical conditions and incompetence. Private Elias Darnell recorded, "The water in the wagon ruts was the only drink we could get to cool our scorching thirst and but very little of that." The men, dressed in their light homespun clothing, were wholly unprepared for the cold winter. Harrison appealed to the citizens of Kentucky for help: "Can any patriot sleep easy in his bed of down, when he reflects upon the situation of a centinel [sic] to the cold of a winter's night in Canada, in a linen hunting shirt?.... Will the amiable fairer sex suffer their brave defenders to be mutilated by the want of mittens and socks, which they can with so little exertion, procure them.... Blankets, overalls, roundabout jackets, shoes, socks, and mittens are the articles wanted."[55]

Winchester's wing was the fighting corps within the Northwest Army. After colliding with Muir's expedition, the American general became as alarmed as his adversary. Exaggerated reports of the allied strength caused him to fortify a temporary position. On learning of Muir's withdrawal, Winchester resumed his march, averaging a miserable five miles per day. His column halted to build a secure post at the confluence of the Maumee and the Auglaise rivers (the site of Fort Defiance, constructed in 1794 as a counterpoint to the British Fort Miamis). Then, on the 28th of October, an almost incessant downpour began that continued for a month, virtually halting American movements. The region turned into an enormous morass, horses sinking into the marshy ground to their knees, wagons to their hubs. The malnourished troops suffered terribly from disease, especially pneumonia, measles, typhus, intermittent fever, and dysentery. These ailments abated only to be replaced by the effects of cold, rheumatism and frostbite. Discipline among the volunteers (such as it was) lapsed and sometimes collapsed entirely. At one point, Winchester's troops mutinied for lack of provisions, and Harrison had to personally quell the disorder. He did so by appealing to the personal pride of the tough frontiersmen: "If you fellow soldiers from Kentucky, so famed for patriotism, refuse to bear the hardships incident to war and to defend the rights of your insulted country, where shall I look for men who will go with me." Although the insubordination subsided, discipline in Winchester's column remained tenuous, at best. False alarms in the camps were frequent, and several men were accidentally shot by their jittery (and often drunken) companions.[56]

Tupper's wing also experienced serious internal problems. Discontent with his leadership caused three hundred mounted men to desert; the remainder refused to march. Harrison ordered Tupper's arrest pending an investigation of his conduct, but the exigencies of the moment precluded immediate action. Tupper's column sufficiently pulled itself together to reach McArthur's Blockhouse by early November, from which a company of spies dashed forward to reconnoitre the Maumee Rapids.[57]

Meanwhile, Matthew Elliott arrived at the Maumee Rapids on 7 November with 250 Potawatomi and Delaware "after a most unpleasant voyage." Additional Natives arrived there by land. Elliott's arrival coincided with that of Tupper's spies, who captured interpreter Andrew Clark while he was hunting wild turkey. Alarmed at Clark's abduction, Elliott reported the enemy marching on the rapids in number, requesting the support of regulars with artillery while he collected the braves. The Americans spirited Clark off to Tupper's headquarters where they made him to understand that his continued well-being was dependent on his willingness to be talkative. From Clark's statements, Tupper reported to Harrison that the British foraging party consisted of five hundred Ojibwa, Ottawa, Potawatomi, and Wyandot warriors, 50 militiamen, and members of the Indian Department. Their shipping consisted of two gunboats, six bateaux, and a schooner. Fort Detroit, stripped of its guns, was garrisoned by a mere 50 regulars. Fort Amherstburg was said to be manned by five hundred regulars and two hundred militiamen. Few warriors remained in the Amherstburg area, having received their annual presents and gone home.[58]

Armed with Clark's vital intelligence, Tupper advanced his main body of six hundred mounted men, intent on surprising Elliott's foraging party. On 14 November, he came upon the Natives dancing and drinking. Tupper hoped to encircle them and capture the British shipping but his scouts could not find a suitable ford across the river. Meanwhile, the braves under Elliott and Splitlog managed to cross over and skirmished with the American rear, both sides sustaining a handful of casualties. Although Tupper reported, "Nothing but the situation of the river prevented our making a complete slaughter of their whole force, and securing their gunboats and bateaux loaded with corn," it was his force that retreated in a half-starved, exhausted, and disheartened state.[59]

While Tupper's action failed to achieve its defined purpose, his sudden advance convinced Elliott that the American main force was not far behind, causing him to abandon the rapids. The Natives were also shaken by the American presence. In the encounter with Tupper's men, eight of their number had been killed. Retreating through Frenchtown, the Wyandot chiefs presented François Navarre, a principal resident, with a letter:

FRIENDS! LISTEN!
You have always told us you would give us any assistance in your power.
We therefore, as the enemy is approaching us, within twenty-five miles, call upon you all to rise up and come here immediately, bringing your arms along with you.
Should you fail at this time, we will not consider you in the future as friends, and the consequences may be very unpleasant.
We are well convinced you have no writings forbidding you to assist us.
We are your friends at present.

ROUNDHEAD
[an emblem resembling a horse]

WALK IN THE WATER
[an emblem resembling a turtle][60]

The *Canadiens* of Frenchtown had enjoyed close relations with the neighbouring tribesmen in the past. Alarmed by the threat, the settlers sought assistance from Judge Woodward on their "delicate matter." While there was no immediate consequence to the threat, the incident marked the beginning of unfriendly relations between the Frenchtown residents and the Natives.[61]

Elliott left the rapids on 8 December by boat. His expedition was marred by personal tragedy and mishap. On 22 November, his son, Alexander, had been killed by hostile tribesmen. Furthermore, Elliott's schooner, *Salina*, became entrapped in the ice pack during the return voyage. He continued the journey over the ice on foot, arriving at Amherstburg nine days later, dutifully bearing his son's frozen body.[62]

Procter's intention of stripping the rapids area of its produce was only partially realized, as American scouts reported six to ten thousand bushels of corn still unharvested later that month. Hard-pressed for food, Procter sent off sleigh parties to recover the cargo of *Salina*, and to collect all the cattle, hogs, and corn on the deserted islands in Lake Erie.[63]

The Americans were also encountering difficulties. By late November, the advance through the Black Swamp had badly floundered. Harrison had hoped to arrive at the rapids by early October and overrun the British positions before winter. However, his troops were still struggling toward their destination over the snow-covered ground, lacking shelter, food, clothing, blankets, and shoes. Winchester's column built 60 pirogues (a kind of dugout canoe) with which to descend the river which was now frozen. Undaunted, the soldiers constructed sleighs, but the beasts of burden died from lack of forage. The men then fabricated harnesses with which they hauled the sleds themselves. On Christmas Eve, a timely supply of flour arrived to alleviate the starvation conditions; however, the volunteers were gloomy. "It seemed the very elements fought against us," wrote volunteer Elias Darnell. "This division had lost over 100 lives without yet seeing the enemy with over 300 more sick from cold and malnourishment.... The distance to Canada, the unpreparedness of the army, the scarcity of provisions and the badness of the weather, show that Malden cannot be taken in the remaining part of our time." The impending expiration of the six-month term of enlistment for the volunteers was a serious concern as Harrison's autumn campaign became a winter one.[64]

At this time, *The War* reported the British occupation of Michigan in a remarkably candid and factual manner. American passengers in the schooner, *Ellen*, arrived at Black Rock from Detroit and described the Natives as "troublesome" — they had "plundered many houses and taken every horse they could find in the neighbourhood of Detroit." They added, "No Indian murders have been heard of at or near Detroit. The British officers had in every instance treated American prisoners and other Americans well." The prisoners who were recaptured on *Detroit I* also acknowledged Procter's humane treatment: "It is much feared that the savages will massacre all the Americans at Detroit. The above gentlemen did not understand that any scalps were paid for by the British. The British commanders had in several instances ransomed American prisoners taken by the Indians."[65]

The decade that Brock and Procter spent in the Canadas had brought them into close contact with the commercial interests of the fur trading magnates of Montreal. The British officers came to understand the interdependencies among the fur trade, the Natives, and the waterways, recognizing the economic unity of the Great Lakes as the basis for a lasting partnership in a commercial empire. This common interest produced a natural alliance of the two military officers, the merchants, and the Indian Department officials. Their combined aim was to regain the area north of the Ohio River, restore that land to the Natives, and maintain the entire Great Lakes region as a British sphere of influence. By ceding Michigan to Britain and arguing for recognition of a Native homeland, Brock had already taken significant steps towards the realization of this vision. With Brock gone, the torch fell to Procter, who in the early winter of 1812-13 prepared a draft document in which he declared the expansionist objective. His lengthy report demonstrates an astute understanding of the strategic issues relative to the Great Lakes basin. His analysis is noteworthy for its insight that went well beyond the scope of a military commander. It was, in fact, the blueprint for a commercial empire and a Native state within the British mercantile system.

Procter's argument began with the premise that the Western District was virtually surrounded by American territory. By itself, this area was not only militarily vulnerable but of "little value to Britain unless accompanied by the lands of the northwest." Furthermore, he predicted that American settlement of the Northwest region would most certainly rupture relations between Britain and "the western nations, the most powerful and the most warlike of the Indians," in which case, the fur trading commercial empire would disintegrate.

To avert these calamities, Procter proposed the retention of the British territories actually occupied at the time, with a "boundary line drawn from the bottom of Lake Erie westward to the Mississippi." By retaining "the most beautiful and most valuable part of North America, an extensive tract of the most temperate and healthy climate, of soil and picturesque surface," he argued that Britain would have access to boundless quantities of strategic resources denied by the closed European and American markets, specifically, "timber, tar, wheat, copper, lead, hemp, hides, [and] furs." The resulting stimulation to British trade would create a "nursery of seamen and ships and the surest way of perpetuating the naval power of Britain."

On the subject of the fur trade, Procter viewed a restoration of the economic unity of the Great Lakes basin as providing a secure and convenient water connection between the Canadas, Hudson's Bay, the Mississippi, and the territories beyond. He stressed that failure to occupy the Northwest would result in the permanent loss of Native loyalty, as the tribesmen would be left to "the vengeance ... of an unwieldy and discordant Republic, subject to all the troubles and vicissitudes that may take place." The net consequence, according to

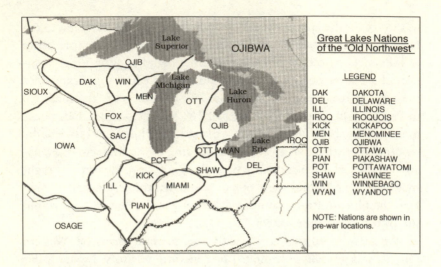

Procter, would be a virtually defenceless British North America. Furthermore, the Natives would be left with a legacy of betrayal and abandonment. They would forever regard Britain as "a deceitful ally whose friendship is harmful and whose alliance is destruction."[66]

It is worth observing that by confining the boundary line from the bottom of Lake Erie to the Mississippi, Procter's conception of a Native state embraced only the Michigan and Illinois Territories. Native expansionists, on the other hand, were determined to recover all lands north of the Ohio River, or at least those beyond the boundary line established by the Treaty of Greenville (roughly mid-way between the Ohio River and Lake Erie). By adopting the most modest of three possibilities, Procter excluded Ohio and Indiana, areas of dense tribal population. Allied Native leaders would certainly insist on a more aggressive line. Yet Procter had to balance their expectations against Prevost's disinterest in all three options. Far from embracing offensive plans, the governor was prepared to abandon Michigan and the Western District in favour of a concentrated defense. Although the American offensives of 1812 were aimed exclusively at the upper province, Prevost retained most of the British troops in the lower one. Bound by Brock's commitment to the Natives, Procter was left to counter Harrison's army of seven thousand men with fewer than four hundred troops.

Procter moved his treatise on the Northwest beyond the bounds of a theoretic vision. As early as 26 November, he wrote Sheaffe that by

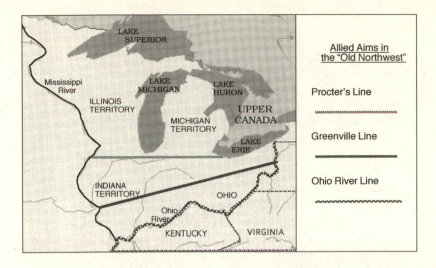

converting Michigan into "the resort of the Indians," he would leave "no inducement" for the Americans to advance. With a British administration installed in the ceded territory, he demanded oaths of allegiance from the residents. The British commander urged the isolated settlers of Michigan, especially "the unfortunate [French-]Canadians," to move, predicting with tragic clarity that "the advance of the enemy can cause only misfortune and distress."[67]

Still locked in its struggle with Napoleonic France, the British government nonetheless gave Brock's argument a favourable hearing, and adopted the notion of a Native state. However, with critical battles still to be fought in Europe, Britain was hard pressed to back the commitment in material terms. In November 1812, Napoleon fled Russia, his *grande armée* demolished. Although this disaster opened prospects for his overthrow, his military capability remained formidable.

American observers expressed reservations about their own winter conflict. *The War* openly declared American reverses as symptomatic of mismanagement, adding, "If it is the determination of the Government to attempt the reduction of Canada, something like a system should be pursued in the operations of the army." Despite its snail-like pace, the progress of the reconstituted Northwest Army was certain. Harrison savoured the opportunity to sweep away the small, mixed, allied force in his path. If he could effect a winter concentration at the Maumee Rapids, British naval superiority would be neutralized. Procter's command was to be severely tested.[68]

NOTES

1. Procter to Brock, 29 Aug. 1812, *SBD* 1: 510.
2. Procter to Brock, 30 Sept.1812, *SBD* 1: 524.
3. Procter to Brock, 24 Aug. 1812, NAUS, *MIC*, 104-05; Brock to Procter, 25 Aug. 1813, Tupper, *Brock*, 300.
4. Capt. William Elliott to Procter, 22 Aug. 1812, NAC, RG 8, C 688A: 211; Walker, *Journal*, 35; Cruikshank, "General Hull's Invasion of Canada in 1812," 287; Charles Askin, "Charles Askin Journal," *JAP* 2: 724.
5. Chambers to Procter, 24 Aug. 1812, NAC, RG 8, C 688A: 129; Charles Askin, "Charles Askin Journal," *JAP* 2: 723-24.
6. Louis Bond to Procter, 27 Dec. 1812, *MPHC* 8: 638; *The War*, 17 Oct. 1812.
7. Chambers to Procter, 24 Aug. 1812, NAC, RG 8: C 688A: 129; Charles Askin, "Charles Askin Journal," *JAP* 2: 724-27; Procter to Brock, 26 Aug. 1812, *SBD* 1: 495.
8. Charles Askin, "Charles Askin Journal," *JAP* 2: 724; Nichol to Brock, 25 Aug. 1812, Tupper, *Brock*, 290; Dewar to Procter, 28 Aug. 1812, *SBD* 2: 512-13.
9. Roberts unaddressed, 16 Aug. 1812, *DICSD*, 152.
10. Brock to Procter, 17 Sept. 1812, Tupper, *Brock*, 311; Procter to Sheaffe, 20 Nov. 1812, NAUS, *MIC*, 19-21; Recollections of Aura P. Stewart, *MPHC* 4: 327.
11. John Norton (Teyoninhokarawen or Snipe) (c.1784-c.1825) was born of a Scottish mother and Cherokee father. He received a classical education in England before returning to the Canadas as a private soldier. After 1791, he became a fur trader and interpreter with the Grand River Mohawk. Appointed "Captain of the confederate Indians" by Sheaffe after his part in the battle of Queenston Heights, he also led the Mohawk at the battles of Beaver Dams and Chippawa. He repeatedly rushed to the west but did not participate in any of Procter's engagements. After the war, he went to England and wrote a very complete account of the war. This manuscript remained unpublished until 1960. Norton settled on the Grand River and is believed to have died among the Cherokee or in Mexico. *DCB* 6: 550-53.
12. Sheaffe to Procter, 1 Sept. 1812, *SBD* 1: 516; Sheaffe to Procter, 24 Sept. 1812, NAUS, *MIC*, 110-13. Roger Hale Sheaffe (1763-1851), was born in Boston and was a classmate of Prevost at the military academy of Chelsea, England. He entered the army in 1778 as an ensign in the 5th Foot. After serving in Ireland, he accompanied that regiment to Quebec in 1787. Ten years later he transferred to the 49th, serving with

that corps in Holland. Sheaffe succeeded Brock as lieutenant colonel of the 49th, accompanying that regiment to the Canadas in 1802. His harsh dealings with the men prompted a near mutiny at Fort George the next year, for which Brock criticized his "little knowledge of mankind" and his "indiscreet and injudicious" dealings with the lower ranks. Nonetheless, on 4 June 1811, Sheaffe was promoted to major general. Sheaffe was made a baronet for his successful counter-attack at Queenston Heights and succeeded Brock as administrator and military commander of Upper Canada. Although Sheaffe pressed forward with the construction of new vessels on the lakes, his illness during the first two months of 1813 probably hindered progress in this regard. Sheaffe's role in the defence of York in April 1813 generated much criticism, leading to his removal in June and his subsequent recall to England. According to Prevost, he "lost the confidence of the province by the measures he had pursued for its defense." Sheaffe rose to full general in 1838 and died in Edinburgh. *DCB* 8: 793-96.

13. Au, *War on the Raisin,*17.
14. *DHCNF* 1812, Vol. 1: 287.
15. Nichol to Brock, 25 Aug. 1812, Tupper, *Brock,* 290.
16. Procter to Brock, 24 Aug. 1812, *SBD* 1: 479; Procter to Woodward, 20 Aug. 1812, Woodward to Procter, 20 Aug. 1812, Procter's Proclamation, 21 Aug. 1812, *MPHC* 36: 258-67.
17. Nichol to Brock, 25 Aug. 1812, Tupper, *Brock,* 290-91.
18. Maj. Alex Campbell's Report, 5 Jan. 1806, *MPHC* 15: 30-32; Lt. Col. James Grant to Military Secretary James Green, 19 Oct. 1806, James Abott and William M'Scote to Acting Governor Stanley Griswold, 14 Dec. 1805, William Wirt Blume, *Transactions ot the Supreme Court of the Territory of Michigan,* 1805-1814 2: 87-90; Silas Farmer, *History of Michigan,* 183-84.
19. Woodford, *Woodward,* 84-86; Lt. Col. Grant to Green, 26 July 1806, *MPHC* 15: 37-38.
20. Procter to Woodward, nd., and Miscellaneous Papers, *MPHC* 8: 636-37; Woodward/Procter correspondence, *TPUS* 10, 399-411; Woodford, *Woodward,* 114.
21. Procter to Sheaffe, 28 Nov. 1812, NAUS, *MIC,* 22-26.
22. Dewar to Procter, 28 Aug. 1812, *SBD* 1: 511-12.
23. Cleveland citizens to Brig Gen. Perkins, 22 Aug. 1812, cited in *Trump of Fame,* 2 Sept. 1812, WRHS, Tract No. 92: 46-47, 52; Winchester to Meigs, 22 Sept. 1812, Knapp, *Maumee,* 137; Procter to Brock, 30 Sept. 1812, NAC, C 677: 100. James Winchester (1752-1865) was native to Maryland. He was an active junior officer during the Revolutionary War. In 1785, as an influential landowner in Tennessee, he earned a

reputation as an Indian fighter in North Carolina. Made a brigadier general in the U.S. Army on 27 Mar. 1812, he briefly commanded the Northwest Army. *WAMB*, 484-85; *DAB* 10: 378.

24. Cited in *Saga of the Great Lakes*, 133-34.

25. Brock to Procter, 25. Aug. 1812, Tupper, *Brock*, 300-01; Niagara residents' memorial to Prevost, 16 Dec. 1812, cited in Tupper, *Brock*, 297-98.

26. Brock to Procter, 25 Aug. 1812, NAUS, *MIC*, 108; McAfee, *Late War*, 126; Procter to Brock, 29 Aug. 1812, 9 Sept. 1812, *SBD* 1: 510, 520.

27. Woodward to Procter, 8 Oct. 1812, Procter to Woodward, 10 Oct. 1812, Procter to Evans, 28 Oct. 1812, *MPHC* 15: 160-61, 163, 172; James van Horne, *A Narrative of the Captivity and Sufferings of James Van Horne*, 14-16; Dickson to Freer, 16 Mar. 1813, Capt. Bullock to Freer, 28 Sept. 1813, *MPHC* 15: 259, 393. The massacre at Fort Dearborn was the first instance in the war that the American government ascribed Native barbarity to British direction. The *Niles Weekly Register* deliberately distorted the narrative of one survivor, Mrs. Helm, to include fictitious details, "Col. Procter, the British commmander at Malden, bought the scalps of the murdered garrison of Chicauga [*sic*] ... she boldly charged him with his infamy in his own house." Blanchard, *Northwest*, 288.

28. Procter to Brock, 9 Sept. 1812, *SBD* 1: 520.

29. Prevost to Brock, 14 Sept. 1812, Tupper, *Brock*, 308-09.

30. Prevost to Brock, 14 Sept. 1812, Tupper, *Brock*, 308-09; Brock to Prevost, 18 Sept. 1812, *SBD* 1: 594.

31. Procter to Brock, 30 Sept. 1812, *SBD* 1: 524; Sheaffe to Procter, 1 Sept. 1812, *SBD* 1: 516. Procter's wife and most, if not all, the offspring arrived at Amherstburg and stayed there for the duration of the British occupation.

32. Brock to Prevost, 28 Sept. 1812, 9 Oct. 1812, *SBD* 1: 596-98, 599-601.

33. Brock to Prevost, 28 Sept. 1812, *SBD* 1: 596-97.

34. Capt. Taylor to Harrison, 10 Sept. 1812, *The War*, 10 Oct. 1812; Elias Darnell, *A Journal Containing an Accurate and Interesting Account of the Hardships, Sufferings Battles, Defeat and Captivity of those Heroic Kentucky Volunteers and Regulars*, 16.

35. Procter to Brock, 10 Sept. 1812, Brock to Procter, 17 Sept. 1812, Tupper, *Brock*, 307, 310; Brock to Prevost, 18 Sept. 1812, *SBD* 1: 592-94.

36. Charles Askin, "Charles Askin Journal," *JAP* 2: 728-29; Procter to Brock, 10 Sept. 1812, Tupper, *Brock*, 307-08.

37. Muir to Procter, 26, 30 Sept. 1812, *MPHC* 15: 148-49, 151-54.

38. *Ibid.* 151-54; [Procter and Procter], "Campaigns," 414; Lt. J. Barnard to Sheaffe, 31 Oct. 1812, *SLB*, 297.

39. Procter to Brock, 30 Sept. 1812, *MPHC* 15: 150; Procter to Sheaffe, 1 Oct. 1812, *SBD* 1: 524-25; Procter to Brock, 3 Oct. 1812, *SBD* 1: 527.

40. Dewar to McDonnell, 19 Oct. 1812, *MPHC* 15: 169-72; Roberts to Procter, 28 Oct. 1812, NAUS, *MIC,* 114; Procter to Sheaffe, 30 Oct. 1812, *MPHC* 15: 175.

41. W.W. Dobbins, *The Battle of Lake Erie,* 9; Chauncy to Elliott, 7, 24 Sept. 1812, cited in R. Jarvis, *A Biographical Notice of Commodore Jesse D. Elliott,* 16-17; Madison's address to Congress, *The War,* 31 Oct. 1812.

42. Elliott to Secretary of the Navy, 9, 10 Oct. 1812, *DHCNF* 1812, Vol. 2: 45-47; *Quebec Mercury,* 27 Oct. 1812; Report of a Court of Inquiry, Maj. Ormsby, President, 27 Oct. 1812, NAC, C 728: 151-58. A subsequent American account diminished the value of the cargoes to $8-10,000 in deer, bear, and buffalo skins. *The War,* 31 Oct. 1812. Robert Irvine, of the Provincial Marine, was promoted to lieutenant after his spirited defence of the *Caledonia* against Elliott's boarding party.

43. Brock to Prevost, 11 Oct. 1812, Tupper, *Brock,* 324-26; Merritt, *Journal, SBD* 3: 557.

44. Brock to Prevost, 11 Oct. 1812, Tupper, *Brock,* 326; [Procter and Procter], "Campaigns," 410; Procter to Sheaffe, 28 Nov. 1812, NAUS, *MIC,* 22-26.

45. Brock to Procter, nd., Tupper, *Brock,* 326-27.

46. Procter to Sheaffe, 30 Oct. 1812, *MPHC* 15: 174; Sheaffe to Prevost, 3 Nov. 1812, *SLB,* 299; John Askin, Sr., to Charles Askin, 28 Dec. 1812, cited in Richardson, *The War of 1812,* 300.

47. Tupper, *Brock,* 358.

48. Edward Couche to Robert Gilmor, 18 Nov. 1812, *MPHC* 32: 555.

49. Dewar to McDonnell, 19 Oct. 1812, Elliott to Claus, 28 Oct. 1812, Procter to Sheaffe, 30 Oct. 1812, 9 Nov. 1812, *MPHC* 15: 169-70, 173-75, 178-79.

50. Winchester to Meigs, 22 Sept. 1812, Knapp, *Maumee,* 137-38; War of 1812 Diary of William B. Northcutt, cited in Glenn Clift, *Remember the Raisin!,* 176.

51. Eustis to Harrison, 17 Sept. 1812, *MLWHH* 2: 136-37, *NOW* 1: 53; *The War,* 3 Oct. 1812.

52. *WAMB,* 166-67.

53. Harrison to Campbell, 25 Nov. 1812, *MLWHH* 2: 229; Darnell, *Journal,* 18-19; Memoir of Governor Reynolds, cited in Blanchard, *Northwest,* 295. The American raids were aimed at the Potawatomi villages on the Elkhart and St Joseph's Rivers; the Miami settlements at the forks of the Wabash; the Ottawa towns on the Blanchard River, Ohio; several Potawatomi, Kickapoo, and Piankashaw towns near Peoria, Illinois; two Kickapoo villages near Salt River, Illinois;

Prophetstown; the Winnebego/Kickapoo villages at Wild Cat Creek, Indiana; and the Miami/Delaware towns on the Missenewa River. Various correpondence *MLWHH* 2: 143-249; Tanner, *Atlas of Great Lakes Indian History*, 108-10; McAfee, *Late War*, 125-30.

54. Harrison to Eustis, 21 Sept. 1812, 12 Dec. 1812, *MLWHH* 2: 146, 242; *NOW* 1: 60.

55. Darnell, *Journal*, 12; Harrison to the people of Kentucky, 25 Sept. 1812, cited in *The War*, 17 Oct. 1812.

56. Darnell, *Journal*, 26; McAfee, *Late War*, 146.

57. McAfee, *Late War*, 149-50; *NOW* 1: 61.

58. Elliott to Ironside, 10 Nov. 1812, Elliott to St. George, 11 Nov. 1812, *MPHC* 15: 179, 182; Perkins to Harrison, 22 Dec. 1812, WRHS, Tract No. 92: 92-93; Reginald Horsman, *Matthew Elliott, British Indian Agent*, 203; Tupper to Meigs, 9 Nov. 1812, Knapp, *Maumee*, 146-47; Tupper to Harrison, 10 Nov. 1812, *MLWHH* 2: 205.

59. Tupper to Harrison, 16 Nov. 1812, *MLWHH* 2: 216-21; Elliott to St. George, 11 Nov. 1812, *MPHC* 15: 182. This skirmish was grossly misrepresented in the American press. One account pegged the enemy at 1500 to two thousand strong, including three hundred British regulars with 14 redcoats and 70 warriors killed. This allied force was to have escaped by plunging into the river with Tecumseh taken captive. *The War*, 26 Jan. 1812.

60. Procter to Sheaffe, 26 Nov. 1812, NAUS, *MIC*, 17-29; U.S. Congress, *Barbarities of the Enemy*, 132.

61. Raisin River residents to Woodward, 23 Nov. 1812, U.S. Congress, *Barbarities*, 133; Dewar to McDonnell, 19 Oct. 1812, *MPHC* 15: 171.

62. Horsman, *Matthew Elliott*, 203.

63. Procter to Sheaffe, 28 Dec. 1812, NAUS, *MIC*, 131.

64. *NOW* 1: 60; Darnell, *Journal*, 40; Procter to Sheaffe, 26 Nov. 1812, 28 Dec. 1812, NAUS, *MIC*, 27, 131.

65. *The War*, 31 Oct. 1812.

66. Procter Papers, NAUS, *MIC*, 272-76. The historical context to a British commercial empire in the Northwest Territory is explored by Donald Creighton in *Empire of the St. Lawrence*. Lord Simcoe's earlier designs on the Northwest are concisely discussed in Malcolm MacLeod's "Fortress Ontario or Forlorn Hope? Simcoe and the Defence of Upper Canada," 149-78. The evolution of the Native connection (with reference to Procter's vision) is examined in Robert Allen's *His Majesty's Indian Allies*. The diplomatic history of the conflict over the Northwest is explored in A.L. Burt's *The United States, Great Britain and British North America: From the Revolution to the Establishment of Peace after the War of 1812*. Procter's thesis is also found in in OA MS-109,

Microcopy No. T-836. After the war, Procter publicly affirmed his intention to make the uncultivated parts of Michigan "completely an Indian country ... a permanent bulwark for the upper province." [Procter and Procter], "Campaigns," 424.

67. Procter to Sheaffe, 26 Nov. 1812, NAUS, *MIC*, 27-29.
68. *The War*, 24 Oct. 1812.

7

CALM BEFORE THE STORM

"Permit me to express a hope that before the season closes, there may be a considerable increase to my force here." [1]

Procter to Brock, 16 September 1812

ALTHOUGH PROCTER'S SITUATION was potentially precarious, it was not unduly threatening in the fall of 1812. His most immediate concern related to logistics. Situated at the end of a long and uncertain supply line that was closed for the winter, his command was beginning to feel the effects of wartime shortages. British deserters on the Niagara frontier reported conditions in Upper Canada as "deplorable": flour and salt were simply unavailable, and mortality rates were rising from the combined effects of malnutrition and disease. Procter had previously been mildly concerned by his shortfall of regular soldiers, but the limitations of his auxiliaries and the renewed American advance now caused him to demand fulfillment of Brock's original promise to send the entire 41st, the regiment he had nurtured into an efficient corps over a decade as its commander. [2]

Most members of the 41st had been in Canada since 7 November 1799, longer than any other British regiment. The soldiers were slated to return to England in May 1812, but as the threat of war loomed, Prevost cancelled their departure. The troops, scattered across posts at Chippewa and forts Amherstburg, Erie, George, and York, had suffered considerable hardship in the backward colony of Upper Canada. Even before the war, Procter had complained that the men were not paid their meager wages. With the outbreak of hostilities, Brock had planned to concentrate the entire 41st at Amherstburg, "as we cannot be too strong in that quarter," but Prevost's strategy frustrated that plan. Procter bemoaned the fact that his unit was "pulled to pieces," misemployed, and consequently in a "fallen state." The British commander experienced the double frustration of the continued dispersion of his regiment while his own command, the Right Division, remained seriously undermanned.[3]

At this time, 970 soldiers of the 2,320 regular troops in Upper Canada were men of the 41st. Only 270 of these were with Procter. In December, his division counted 367 men and 12 officers (including surgeons). In addition to the soldiers of the 41st, he had 70 of the Royal Newfoundland Regiment under Capt. Robert Mockler, 25 artillery-men under Lt. Felix Troughton, and a handful of support staff. Fort Detroit was garrisoned by 114 men under Muir. Aside from a detachment of 17 soldiers with Procter at Sandwich, the remaining troops garrisoned Fort Amherstburg under Lt. Col. St. George. Although Procter appreciated the American threat on the Niagara frontier, his letters began to reflect a chronic shortage of regulars.[4]

The British commander needed more than troops of the line. He lacked the regimental staff (that of the 41st remained at Fort George) as well as a district command staff to co-ordinate the diverse activities within an enormous region. He lacked a brigade-major, staff adjutant, clerks, provost marshal, aide-de-camp (Lt. MacLean was acting), and after the death of Lt. Dewar, a deputy assistant quartermaster. He asked Sheaffe for the regimental headquarters of the 41st so that he could "be of some service to the corps" he had served so long. Worse yet, of his six line officers, the two senior captains were sick. Muir was so ill that Procter feared he would never be fit for duty, while he termed Tallon's health, "precarious." This weak command structure threatened regimental housekeeping functions, an ominous circumstance.[5]

There was a limit to the amount of inattention the men of Procter's command could endure. Although the men readily accepted discipline and hardship, their needs could not be ignored indefinitely without adverse effects. The Right Division was short of food and money, as well as items ranging from general orders to barrack furniture, bedding, cooking utensils, writing paper, and winter clothing. Even heating fuel was scarce, the Amherstburg garrison travelling as far as Detroit to obtain seasoned firewood. Overloaded with administrative headaches and lacking a proper headquarters staff, Procter was forced to make arbitrary decisions, alienating some of the local residents. Magistrate and doctor Robert Richardson (father of John Richardson) complained in a private letter that "commanding officers expect everything to be done as they wish, sometimes without law or reason."[6]

Given his shortage of steady regulars, Procter continued to improvise with militiamen who proved useful on short periods of duty so long as their families and crops were not threatened. The British commander called out three hundred of them during the Fort Wayne expedition. They also assisted the commissariat in foraging activities on the Raisin and Maumee rivers. A company of Essex militiamen had also served on the undermanned Provincial Marine vessels. During the winter, Procter retained only 30 militiamen as dispatch riders to keep up communications between the far-flung posts at Raisin River, Amherstburg, Detroit, Sandwich, and Fort George.[7]

One area in which Procter had no deficiency was artillery. The guns of the Right Division were decidedly superior to those of Harrison. In addition to the 30-odd guns mounted on the ramparts of Fort Amherstburg, Procter also had a field train of some 10 pieces of various calibers. Eight additional 24-pdr. guns remained on the Amherstburg dock, waiting to be shipped down the lake, Fort Detroit having been stripped of all but four 6-pdr. guns.[8]

Relations between the Natives and the military establishment remained tenuous, at best. The individualistic impulses of the warriors hindered their inclination to act in concert, even among themselves. "Decency is preserved between the chiefs but I can never produce cordiality," wrote Procter. The warriors had proven their utility as a vehicle of terror, particularly in ambuscade, as the Detroit campaign had demonstrated. Yet they were difficult to command, as Muir and Chambers discovered. They came and went as they pleased, fickle and easily influenced by example, rumour, and omen. Procter could never be sure how many warriors would accompany his soldiers on a mission or when they would desert. Those Natives who remained about Amherstburg during the winter expected to be well fed with provisions that were as scarce as they were expensive to transport. Harrison's successful fall campaign against the villages in Indiana made clear the tribesmen's limitations in independent operations. Yet despite these disadvantages, the warriors were certainly preferable as allies than as enemies. In fact, given the shortage of regulars on the Detroit frontier, their military services were invaluable.[9]

Although Tecumseh was a brave and capable leader, his confederacy lacked the political organization and collective will to establish and maintain a Native state. The Shawnee war chief had remained on the Wabash since Prevost's armistice, suspicious of the British commitment. During the winter, Procter reported him still aloof, disgusted at the failure of the Fort Wayne expedition, and incapacitated by sickness. Procter wrote in mid-January that the Native leader had "scarcely recovered his health." He had no idea when or if Tecumseh would return. Although most of the "Lake Indians" dispersed to their villages for the winter, the refugee tribesmen from Indiana joined the local Wyandot along the Detroit River. In fact, Procter was so weak in regulars that Native warriors were numerically his strongest arm. Despite their potential value, Procter was apprehensive of this imbalance, writing to Sheaffe, "The aid we may expect from the Indians will always be in proportion to their confidence in our strength and which they are too sensible is but small." 10

The tribesmen who sought refuge from the American inroads became increasingly dependent on their allies. Having lost their livelihood, they went to Amherstburg with their families for both provisioning and the prospects of revenge. Procter was painfully aware of Brock's commitment, writing to Sheaffe, "The Indians conceive our government pledged to their interest. Indeed, General Brock made the chiefs every assurance of it.... Should this not be the case, the greatest of evils must result." At Montreal, fur baron James McGill also emphasized the necessity of properly sustaining the alliance, writing to Prevost, "The Indians are the only Allies who can aught avail us in the defence of the Canadas. They have the same interest as us, and alike are objects of American subjugation, if not extermination." 11

At this time, British commanders learned of American naval preparations on Lake Erie. In late October, Procter received a disconcerting letter from Maj. Thomas Evans of Sheaffe's staff, who reported five vessels under construction at Erie. Evans added that Lt. Jesse Elliott employed two hundred carpenters in cutting down several merchant schooners into gunboats at Black Rock to join *Caledonia*. For years, the Upper Canada Provincial Marine vessels were under the command of the venerable Commodore Alexander Grant, one-time president of the Executive Council of Upper Canada. Shortly before the war, Brock replaced the 80-year-old mariner with Commodore George Benson Hall, who now managed the affairs of the Lake Erie squadron.12

In the fall, Prevost, aware of the need to retain command of the lakes, had directed the construction of one large naval vessel at Amherstburg and two more at York and Kingston. His acting deputy quartermaster general, Capt. Andrew Gray, visited Amherstburg and ordered materials for a ship of 18 guns, larger than any existing vessel on the Upper Lakes. Sheaffe promptly identified to Prevost those resources the Provincial Marine could not furnish. The commander-in-chief transmitted requisitions to London for armaments, seamen, and hardware during the winter and urged speedy attention to their supply in the new year. It was early January before carpenters, boat-builders, joiners, and blacksmiths were sought out for Amherstburg in the Long Point settlements. These backwoods builders were hardly skilled craftsmen. Procter chafed to Sheaffe over the delays in con-struction arising from the absence of competent artificers, stressing, "Nothing can be more gratifying to me than to find effectual measures taken to ensure superiority on the lakes, so requisite to the security of the country. Every exertion is making and shall be preserved in as far as depends on me to attain that object."[13]

Although the British squadron on Lake Erie was a sad apology for a fighting force, it had maintained control thus far by virtue of its very existence. Since the loss of the brigs *Caledonia* and *Detroit I* and the schooner *Salina*, it consisted of three war vessels and three commercial craft armed as gunboats:

- *Queen Charlotte*: Ship-rigged, launched 1809, eighteen 24-pdr. carronades,
- *Lady Prevost*: Schooner-rigged, launched 1812, ten 12-pdr. carronades and two long 6-pdr. guns,
- *General Hunter*: Brig-rigged, launched 1806, four long 6-pdr. guns and two 18-pdr. carronades,
- *Chippawa*: Converted schooner, launched 1810, (probably ex-*Cuyahoga Packet*), two 8 in. howitzers,
- *Little Belt*: Converted sloop, launched 1810, ex-*Friend's Goodwill*, one long 12-pdr. gun and one 24-pdr. carronade,
- *Erie*: Converted sloop, captured at Michilimaclinac, one long 12-pdr. gun and one 12-pdr. carronade.

In addition, several privately owned vessels, *Mary*, *Ellen* (*Helen* or *Ellenor*), *Miamis*, and *Nancy*, could be impressed as transports plus the smaller *Ottawa*, *Thames*, and *Dover*.[14]

Serious as the loss of the brigs at Fort Erie had been, Procter considered it "not an entirely unfortunate circumstance" as it drew attention to the "imbecility" of the of the Upper Lakes marine management before it was too late. As early as November 1812, he emphasized the need for a proper naval presence on Lake Erie in response to American preparations. Yet, progress toward converting the Provincial Marine into a fighting force remained slow. Procter had mixed views of Commodore Hall's recruiting journey to Quebec City in January 1813, "least it be a product of a half measure." [15]

Despite Procter's warning, Prevost's office took no steps to allocate naval officers, sailors, gunners, and marines for the Amherstburg station. Commodore Hall's return of 2 October showed his establishment as four officers, 44 crewmen, 25 landsmen and boys, and 74 amphibious soldiers of the Royal Newfoundland Regiment acting as marines. His proposed manning establishment for the spring was a modest four officers, 87 crewmen, and 21 landsmen and boys, minus 28 marines he declared redundant. As none of these were navy men, Hall wrote, "The want of seamen for His Majesty's Vessels is already severely felt, none of them have more than a sufficient number to navigate them in peaceable times." Yet, he showed little interest in converting his motley force into a fighting squadron by pressing his case for professional seamen. Fully aware that the very existence of the Right Division depended on mastery of Lake Erie, Procter urged a proper naval presence to meet the growing American threat. "I have taken it for granted that we are to receive officers and seamen from the only adequate source, the Royal Navy," he wrote to Sheaffe. [16]

Others echoed Procter's concerns. "By land our success has exceeded our hopes," observed Chaiman Thomas Scott in his provincial legislative council address: "Not so is our warfare on the lakes. Whether this is to be attributed to inferiority of strength on our part, to accident, which the wisest and bravest can neither foresee nor prevent, or to the experienced naval commanders, we presume not, even to hint an opinion." Sensing the lack of vigour in naval preparations, Robert Nichol, lamented, "Alas, we are no longer commanded by Brock.... Confidence seems to have vanished from our land and gloomy despondency has taken its place.... Efforts will be unavailing against bad management and despondency in those who ought to be better qualified to fill the high and important situations they hold." Rector Strachan was more direct in laying blame at Prevost's doorstep. "The people of Upper Canada have wept at the infatuation of the

Commander-in-Chief," he wrote, "to find that he who was sent to protect them has proved their greatest foe.... England expects every man to do his duty but what will she say when she discovers that our Commander-in-chief has ordered us not to do our duty and censured us when we have done it."[17]

During the winter, Maj. Gen. Sheaffe was seriously ill for two months, a circumstance that probably contributed to the lethargy in naval preparations. Sheaffe faced other serious problems. In inheriting Brock's responsibilities, he realized the gaping chasm between Brock's strategy and that of Prevost. With his small force thinly spread across Upper Canada, Sheaffe could do little for Procter. His aide, Maj. Glegg, wrote, "Our friend, Major General Sheaffe is much changed of late. There appears at times an irresistible melancholy on his mind, which is very distressing. I have reason for knowing that his expectations from below are by no means flattering." As the war moved into 1813, Sheaffe would have to align an ambitious defence plan with the slim resources dedicated to its attainment.[18]

Compounding the ever-mounting problems at Amherstburg, Procter learned of subversive goings-on in the territory, namely that "the worthies of Detroit communicate with the enemy." Furthermore, Roundhead reported treacherous activity of two Raisin River residents and demanded their removal to Amherstburg. Procter feared that they would leak intelligence of his weakness to the enemy. His concerns were well founded as Michigan residents had been passing information to their countrymen for months. During the Fort Wayne expedition, informers correctly described British dispositions. "Malden is almost destitute of troops," an American artillery officer at Pittsburgh reported to Maj. Gen. Elijah Wadsworth of the Ohio militia, "If this story be correct, you have a fine opportunity of falling in behind the enemy and perhaps of taking Detroit or Malden."[19]

During the winter of 1812, Harrison's ponderous columns continued to trudge toward the rapids. His numbers were suddenly augmented by those militiamen captured and paroled at Detroit and exchanged for the prisoners taken on a captured British vessel. After the American commander amassed a million rations, he hoped to conduct a winter assault on Amherstburg by February or March of 1813. As an alternative, he offered Acting Secretary of War James Monroe (Eustis having resigned on 3 December 1812), the option of concentrating his army in northern Ohio to await successful naval operations on Lake Erie. Monroe left it to Harrison to either capture Fort

Amherstburg or destroy the Provincial Marine vessels while they were ice-bound.[20]

Upon being given the option (and responsibility) of deciding the concept of operations, Harrison's confidence suddenly wavered. Like Hull, he complained about the tardy American activity on the Niagara frontier, writing, "I have indeed no doubt that we shall encounter at Malden the very troops which contended with General Van Rensselaer at the heights of Queenston." Furthermore, he pointed out, "My reaching Malden during the winter depends upon a circumstance which I cannot control, viz: the freezing of the straight [the Detroit River] in such a manner as to enable me to pass over the troops and artillery." Learning from Hull's experience, he was convinced that the retention of Detroit was dependent on the reduction of Fort Amherstburg.[21]

Despite his reservations, Harrison still hoped for a successful winter campaign. He expected that the Northwest Army would be ready to advance from the rapids by 20 January 1813. With the advantage of virtually unlimited spending power, plus complete freedom to determine the timing and objective of the campaign, he adopted a cautious strategy: "My plan of operations has been, and now is, to occupy the Miami [the Maumee] Rapids and to deposit there as much provisions as possible; and to move from thence with a choice detachment of the army and with as much provision, artillery and ammunition as the means of transportation will allow, make a demonstration towards Detroit and by a sudden passage of the strait upon the ice, an actual investiture of Ft. Malden." Upon securing the Detroit frontier, Harrison planned to join the American force on the Niagara frontier and overrun that region as well. With 6300 effectives against Procter's small mixed force, his plan showed promise.[22]

Fortunately for Procter, Harrison was not in a position to capitalize on the weak British position. The American columns continued to be constrained by physical difficulties, corruption, and chaotic organization. Harrison blamed his slow but costly advance on "the imbecility of the public agents and the villainy of the contractors." Although he expressed confidence in a successful winter campaign, his army was abysmally equipped. The men of Winchester's wing were still in their summer clothes, linsey hunting shirts, Kentucky jeans, and moccasins. It was not until well into December that the ill-clad men received winter clothing. Even these were not army issue but blankets, knit socks, and hunting shirts forwarded by the women of Kentucky in response to Harrison's appeals and the despairing letters of their men. A volunteer, Pte. Nathan Newsom, recorded his impressions of the campaign:

The army at this time far more presents an object of charity ... rather than the grandeur, dread, and reverence which must necessarily mark an invading army which can reasonable expect to meet with success and honor. Nearly one half sick, nearly the other half ... almost naked.... It is ardently wished by every naked man in camp that something would arrive where with he might cover his nakedness, keep his body warm and his feet dry so that he would be able to do his duty as a soldier.[23]

Despite immense difficulties, Harrison continued to make steady progress. He had neutralized the "back Indians" of Indiana Territory, while Wadsworth consolidated areas east of the Maumee. On 29 November, a party of Americans engaged in a minor skirmish with a Wyandot war party on Bull Island in Sandusky Bay. With these braves driven off, the Lower Sandusky area was secured, and the Americans planned to build a small fort there. The buffer zone between the belligerents was gradually shrinking. By 13 January 1813, Procter received word of Winchester's occupation of the Maumee Rapids three days previously; several false alarms of his further advance followed. Bracing for the inevitable conflict, Procter wrote "We have no choice but to employ every description of force within our reach."[24]

Unknown to Procter, the American organization for war was undergoing significant changes. Congress convened on 2 November and immediately turned its attention to repairing the damage of Hull's surrender. Eustis resigned and James Monroe was designated his temporary replacement. In addition to the naval preparations already undertaken, the American government authorized an increase of twenty thousand men to the U.S. Army. The War Hawks held sway in Congress, and Prevost's worst nightmare, of united American opinion, was realized. Henry Clay could now press his designs with a moral justification by citing British-Indian victories in the Northwest:

Canada innocent? Canada unoffending? Is it not in Canada that the tomahawk of the savage has been moulded into its death-like form? Has it not been from Canadian magazines, Malden and others, that those supplies have been issued? Supplies which have enabled the savage hordes to butcher the garrison of Chicago and to commit other horrid murders? Was it not by the joint co-operation of Canadians and Indians that a remote American fort, Michilimackinac, was assailed and reduced while in ignorance of war? What does war represent? The united energies of one people arrayed against the combined energies of another.[25]

Ignorant of the new U.S. determination, allied expansionists pressed their vision. "What the Indians dread is the restitution of this territory to the states," argued Procter to Sheaffe. "If it should be ceded, we sacrifice their interest and nothing will satisfy them." Others echoed his position. Fur trader John Askin of Sandwich asserted, "However we might wish for peace, it should not be on the conditions of giving back the posts we took, a war should be much preferable, for should it take place we will lose the Indians and the trade and in a very few years Canada with it; but that a peace can be made without the concurrence of the Indians I can't think possible. Surely England will not abandon a people to whom we are not only indebted for the preservation of our posts but also for the taking of those we got." [26]

At this time, Prevost found a mechanism to justify withholding regulars in Lower Canada. The influential fur trading magnates of Montreal had been agitating for a stronger British presence in the west, and given Prevost's refusal to provide regulars, they approached him with an alternate proposal, arguing that the American "gigantic assemblage" could only be resisted through the generous and competent organization of the Native tribes to the west of the Great Lakes. To head the endeavour, they recommended Robert Dickson, an "indefatigable ... enthusiast in the British and Indian cause." Prevost readily seized on this relatively cheap method of demonstrating his support for the Right Division while keeping his regulars in the lower province. He commissioned Dickson to hire five officers and 15 interpreters to mobilize a thousand warriors for war. Armed with silk standards, medallions, and funds, Dickson set off on his mission. Prevost could thus report to London that Detroit was securely protected by hordes of western warriors. [27]

By this time, the British government expected more than a token effort in the west. Lord Bathurst, the new minister for war and colonies, had studied Brock's arguments for a Native homeland and officially committed the British government to the cause, writing to Prevost, "I so entirely concur in the expediency contained in the suggestions ... as to the necessity of securing the territories of the Indians from encroachment that I have submitted it to His Majesty's secretary for foreign affairs, in order that whenever negotiations for peace may be entered into, the security of their possessions may not be either compromised or forgotten." The expansionist vision had become endorsed as a matter of official British policy! [28]

By acceding to Brock's diplomatic objectives, London not only affirmed the British commitment to a Native state but implicitly approved of the military initiatives undertaken thus far in the west. Furthermore, the British government knowingly committed itself to the responsibility of sustaining the Native alliance in material and diplomatic terms.

NOTES

1. Procter to Brock, 16 Sept. 1812, *SBD* 1: 523.
2. *The War*, 2 Feb. 1813; Lomax, *The 41st*, 365. Procter remained senior lieutenant colonel of the 41st during the war. When the second battalion of the 41st was raised, William Evans became lieutenant colonel of the regiment, in Aug. 1812. Lomax, *The 41st*, 365.
3. Baynes to Brock, 21 May 1812; Brock to Military Secretary Freer, 9 Mar. 1812, Brock to Baynes, 12 Feb. 1812, Tupper, *Brock*, 176, 158, 150; Procter to Lt. Col. Cecil Bishopp, 8 March 1813, NAUS, *MIC*, 64.
4. Prevost to Bathurst, 24 Aug. 1812, *SBD* 1: 491; Adjutant General's Return, 21 Dec. 1812, *MPHC* 15: 208; Strength Return of Fort Detroit, *MPHC* 32: 551.
5. Procter to Sheaffe, 30 Oct. 1812, *MPHC* 15: 175; Procter to Sheaffe, 23 Dec. 1812, NAUS, *MIC*, 135.
6. Procter to Sheaffe, 26 Nov. and 31 Dec. 1812, NAUS, *MIC*, 27-29, 35-36; Byfield, *Account*, 24; Robert Richardson to John Askin, 7 Feb. 1813, *JAP* 2: 13. The proximity of the American border remained a constant temptation for the soldiers to desert the harsh conditions of army life. They enlisted for five-year terms, privates being paid $5 a month plus rations, quarters, and necessities. Discipline in the British Army could be severe. Floggings with the whip steeped in brine were common. One soldier was awarded 1500 lashes for some offence. During the punishment, he seized a sword. After he was overpowered and disarmed, the sentence was completed and the man was tried for mutiny, found guilty, and shot! Brock personally apprehended 20 would-be mutineers of the 49th in 1803, ordering the execution of seven of them. Tupper, *Brock*, 26-35.
7. Procter to Brock, 9 Sept. 1812, *SBD* 1: 520-21.
8. Upper Canada Ordnance Return, 31 Mar. 1813, *MPHC* 15: 265; Interpreter Clark's interrogation, Tupper to Meigs, 9 Nov. 1812, Knopf, *Document Transcripts* 2: 102. The ordnance of Fort Amherstburg consisted of twelve 18-pdrs., three 12-pdrs., five 9-pdrs., four 6-pdrs., and two 3-pdrs. (not counting the field train). Upper Canada Ordnance Return, 15 Dec. 1812, *MPHC* 15: 200.

9. Procter to Sheaffe, 13 Jan. 1813, NAUS, *MIC*, 39-43. A thorough analysis of British-Native military relations (and the inherent problems) is found in Colin Calloway, *Crown and Calumet.*

10. Procter to Sheaffe, 13 Jan. 1813, 20 Nov. 1812, NAUS, *MIC*, 39-43, 19-21. Tecumseh's movements during the winter of 1812-13 are unclear. One of his biographers has him at Amherstburg in mid-December, recovering from a leg wound sustained at the battle of Maguaga five months previously. Yet he has Tecumseh accompanying Muir's Fort Wayne expedition. Both assertions are unlikely. Tecumseh was well enough to accompany Brock's Detroit campaign and the mopping-up detail at Frenchtown and the Maumee Rapids. His wound in August was a minor one that would have healed well before December. Brock wrote in his final letter that Tecumseh "probably might be induced to return to Amherstburg," and Procter barely mentioned his name during the winter. The evidence strongly points to Tecumseh's having left the alliance in late August 1812, not to return to Amherstburg until mid-April 1813, after learning of the allied victory at Frenchtown, Harrison reporting him on the Wabash in late December. Edmunds, *Tecumseh and the Quest for Indian Leadership*, 187; Brock to Procter, nd., Tupper, *Brock*, 326-27; Harrison to secretary of war, 24 Dec. 1812, *MLWHH* 2: 252.

11. R. David Edmunds, *The Potawatomis, Keepers of the Fire*, 192; Procter to Sheaffe, 28 Nov. 1812, NAUS, *MIC*, 22-26; McGill to Prevost, 19 Dec. 1812, NAC, C 257: 31.

12. Evans to Procter, 21 Oct. 1812, NAUS, *MIC*, 122. George Benson Hall (1780-1821) was born in Ireland. He was a subordinate officer in the Royal Navy for four years before arriving in Canada in 1802 to serve on a government vessel on Lake Ontario. Two years later, he was given command of *General Hunter*, and in 1811, *Queen Charlotte*. The next year, he succeeded Alexander Grant as commodore of the Lake Erie Squadron. Hall commanded the Sandwich batteries during the Detroit campaign and proceeded to Quebec City during the winter of 1812 in an unsuccessful effort to recruit seamen and artificers. His vessels supported Procter's first Maumee expedition but Hall refused to serve under Barclay in the battle of Lake Erie. Accompanying Procter's retreat up the Thames, he became naval storekeeper at Montreal. After the war, Hall assumed civic duties at Amherstburg but died leaving his family financially distressed. *DCB* 6: 308-09.

13. Gray's requisition of materials, 24 Nov. 1812, *MPHC* 15: 189; Sheaffe to Prevost, 16 Dec. 1812, *SBD* 1: 661; Myers to Talbot, 2 Jan. 1813, *DHCNF* 1812, Vol. 3: 26-27; Procter to Sheaffe, 13 Jan. 1813, *SBD* 2: 3.

14. Prisoner Embarkation Return, 26 Aug. 1812, *SBD* 1: 497; K.R. Macpherson, "Naval Service Vessels on the Great Lakes, 1775-1875," 175-76; K.J. Bauer, "U.S. Warships on the Great Lakes," 60.

15. Procter to Sheaffe, 28 Nov. 1812, Procter to Sheaffe, 13 Jan. 1813, Procter to Evans, 13 Jan. 1813, NAUS, *MIC*, 26, 38, 39.

16. Hall's Establishment Return, 2 Oct. 1812, *SBD* 1: 557; Hall to Myers, 27 Oct. 1812, NAC, C 728: 110; Procter to Sheaffe, 13 Jan. 1813, *SBD* 2: 3.

17. Address by Thomas Scott, 17 Nov. 1812, *SBD* 2: 57; Nichol to Talbot, 18 Dec. 1812, *TP*, 170; Strachan to James McGill, nd. Nov. 1812, Spragge, *Strachan Letter Book*, 27.

18. Glegg to William Powell, 10 Jan. 1813, *DHCNF* 1813, Vol. 1: 34.

19. Procter to Reynolds, 23 Dec. 1812, 11 Jan. 1813, NAUS, *MIC*, 30-31, 37; Maj. Amos Stoddard to Wadsworth, 28 Sept. 1812, WRHS Tract No. 92: 71.

20. Patricia Fife Medert, *Raw Recruits and Bullish Prisoners*, 77; Harrison to Monroe, 12 Dec. 1812, *MLWHH* 2: 240-41; Monroe to Harrison, 26 Dec. 1812, *MLWHH* 2: 265.

21. Harrison to Monroe, 4 Jan. 1813, *MLWHH* 2: 293-99.

22. *Ibid.*, 293-99.

23. *Ibid.*, 297; Nathan Newson Journal, cited in R.E. Banta, *The Ohio*, 222; Clift, *Remember the Raisin!*, 39.

24. Wadsworth to Stoddard, 4 Oct. 1812, WRHS Tract No. 92: 75; Procter to Sheaffe, 13 Jan. 1813, *SBD* 2: 3.

25. George D. Prentice, *Henry Clay*, 98-99.

26. Procter to Sheaffe, 28 Nov. 1812, NAUS, *MIC*, 26; John Askin to Charles Askin, 28 Dec. 1812, cited in Richardson, *War of 1812*, 301.

27. McGill and McGuillivray to Prevost, 19 Dec. 1812, *MPHC* 15: 203. Robert Dickson (c.1765-1823) was born in Scotland. Engaging in the fur trade, he married a Sioux woman and became the best-known trader on the Upper Mississippi. He led a band of western warriors against Fort Michilimackinac and sent a contingent of Menominee to Amherstburg in time to engage in the fighting on the Canards River. In 1813, Prevost placed him in charge of the western nations and he led 1400 of them to co-operate with Procter against Fort Meigs. He remained active in operations on the Upper Mississippi until war's end, dying on Drummond Island. *DCB* 6: 209-11.

28. Bathurst to Prevost, 9 Dec. 1812, cited in Alfred T. Mahan, *Sea Power in Relation to the War of 1812*, 2: 100n.

8

BLOOD AND ICE: FRENCHTOWN

"With my inadequate means, the game will be a difficult one however I will do my best."[1]

Procter to Sheaffe, 13 January 1813

DESPITE DEEP SNOW, cold, malnutrition, disease, and insubordination, Winchester's wing stumbled forward to arrive at the Maumee Rapids on 10 January 1813. Once there, he directed the building of huts and a large storehouse (Fort Deposit) on an eminence known as Presque Isle Hill. The soldiers found much of the corn still unharvested in the abandoned Native fields, a cheering sight for men who had lived for weeks on a meager diet augmented with hickory roots and wild fruit. The Americans immediately gorged themselves on homony (corn pounded, sifted and boiled into a meal). In keeping with Harrison's directions, Winchester remained at the rapids to await the other wings.[2]

Then a minor incident put into motion a series of dire events. Upon arriving at the rapids, Winchester's men had driven off the Native scouts from the adjoining woods. The fleeing warriors promptly reported the American presence to Procter, who directed that the Raisin River settlement and its produce be secured from American inroads. On the evening of 13 January, two Frenchtown residents appeared at Winchester's headquarters with a letter from Isaac Day, an American settler of their village who had been secretly selling flour to one of Harrison's contractors. Day reported that the British were aware of the reoccupation of the rapids and were removing suspected collaborators from Frenchtown. He proposed that a small party of horsemen with arms and ammunition for thirty men would be adequate to secure the three thousand barrels of wheat and flour in the community. Day estimated the combined allied strength in the Amherstburg area as less than a thousand British, "French," and Native warriors. Frenchtown was said to contain only fifty militiamen and less than a hundred braves. In Day's opinion, five hundred Americans could permanently garrison Frenchtown and protect its residents and foodstuffs. The next day, another messenger arrived at the rapids, followed by two more on the 16th. The last courier reported the allied strength at two companies of militiamen and two hundred warriors. The British were said to be preparing to burn down the settlement.[3]

Another clandestine informer reported that the British intended to rendezvous at Frenchtown to drive the Americans from the rapids. In response, Winchester called a council of officers which overwhelmingly decided to conduct a pre-emptive strike on Frenchtown. Lt. Col. John Allen, foremost lawyer of Kentucky, delivered a passionate address indicative of the sentiments guiding the meeting: "Can we turn a deaf ear to the cries of men, women and children, about to perish under the scalping knife and tomahawk of the savage?.... Will it be said that a thousand freemen are unequal to a contest with three hundred savages and slaves?.... The Lion ... will either send a second detachment, in which case both may be separately beaten, or he will put his whole force in motion, and thus furnish us with a sufficient excuse for falling back upon on our own army which cannot be far in our rear."[4]

Lt. Col. Samuel Wells, commanding the regulars of the 17th U.S. Infantry, seems to have objected to the venture as hazardous but his opinion was overruled. Emotional appeal stifled rational military judgment as the Americans looked forward to an easy victory. Yet the undertaking was potentially hazardous as Frenchtown was 35 miles from the rapids but only 18 from Fort Amherstburg. With the other American columns lagging, it was doubtful that the left wing could hold its ground in an exposed forward position. Nonetheless, the men were rested and fed. With more winter clothing arriving on 15 January, the hardy Kentucky men were eager to fight. Convinced that Harrison would soon reinforce his advance, Winchester immediately sent 550 men to Frenchtown under Lt. Col. William Lewis. He explained to Harrison: "Nothing will reconcile an extension to the period of service of the volunteers but progressive operations." Having endured severe hardships and boredom since August 1812, the men were anxious to return home but also eager to strike a blow at the enemy before doing so. On learning of these unexpected developments, Harrison was not unduly alarmed but promptly rushed troops from Upper Sandusky to Winchester's support.[5]

On 17 January, two battalions of Kentucky volunteers (those of majors George Madison and Benjamin Graves) under the command of Lt. Col. Lewis, advanced 18 miles and spent the night in the small *Canadien* settlement of Presque Isle (modern-day Toledo). They were joined by a reinforcement of 110 men from the rapids under Lt. Col. Allen, bringing the total number of the strike force to about seven hundred men. As one participant put it, the sight of this hamlet on the south bank of the Maumee "filled each heart with emotion, cheerfulness and joy as we had been nearly five months in the wilderness." Winchester's command of thirteen hundred men was now evenly split at two locations. That night, yet another messenger arrived from the Raisin River settlement to say that four hundred warriors and two companies of "British" occupied Frenchtown. Matthew Elliott was understood to be bringing additional reinforcements to that place the following morning, preparatory to attacking the American encampment at the rapids. As Frenchtown was equidistant from Amherstburg and Presque Isle, Lewis hoped to pre-empt the British junction by striking at Frenchtown first, "to conquer or die." Advancing rapidly over the lake ice on the 18th, the Americans arrived at their destination in the mid-afternoon, joined by a company of Raisin River militiamen, an act the Natives observed and would remember.[6]

Alerted to the American advance by Native scouts, the allied force was in position to receive the attack. Maj. Ebenezer Reynolds of the 2nd Essex Regiment formed his two companies of militiamen (a hundred men) under captains William Elliott and Alexis Maisonville in the village facing the river. Supporting him were four hundred warriors (mainly Potawatomi and Wyandot) plus a 3-pdr. howitzer under the direction of one bombardier Kitson. The action began at 3 PM at a distance of one-quarter mile with the howitzer firing upon the Americans. Defying the "mouse cannon," the Kentuckians jeered back with crowing and barking noises. Lewis ordered the long drum roll, signifying the order to charge. Although the 80-yard river was extremely slippery, the Kentucky men maintained their charge in good order, dislodging the defenders from the village and loping off after the warriors in the adjoining woods to the northeast. Reynolds's party retreated slowly, the warriors covering the withdrawal of the 3-pdr. howitzer that kept up a continuous fire over a two-mile stretch. Lewis reported one Potawatomi and two militiamen captured in the village plus at least 15 braves killed. The allies drew off and regrouped at the house of a *Canadien* at Sandy Creek, a few miles to the north. Reynolds hastened on to Sandwich to notify Procter of the action.[7]

The Native warriors showed more respect for the tough Kentucky frontiersmen than for the Ohio settlers. A *Canadien* of the Raisin River recalled that when the Kentuckians came into view, an old Indian sat by a fire smoking his pipe, calmly observing "Ho, de Mericans [*sic*] come; I suppose Ohio men come, we give them another chase." On seeing the enemy up close, he suddenly exclaimed, "Kentuck, by God!" seized his gun, and ran off into the woods.[8]

The American pursuit continued until nightfall. In his detailed return, Lewis reported 12 Americans killed (found scalped next day) and 55 wounded (two fatally). Most of these casualties were sustained in the woods during the pursuit of the elusive warriors. Despite their losses, the Kentuckians were elated. On learning of the American victory, Winchester hastened to Frenchtown with 250 regulars under Lt. Col. Samuel Wells. He also sent forward drivers with a drove of two hundred hogs and some cattle. These beasts would become unwitting players in the tragic events that followed.[9]

While forced to yield the village, the allied defenders gave a good account of themselves, having received the attack and withdrawn in good order, making their enemy pay dearly for their victory. The American casualties served to detain the entire force at Frenchtown. As Winchester subsequently observed, he would have withdrawn the troops but lacked conveyance for the wounded. The battle of the 18th was one of the few cases during the war in which Canadian militiamen engaged the enemy without the assistance of a force of regulars, the single professional soldier present being Bombardier Kitson. Likewise, the Potawatomi braves fought stubbornly, inflicting dozens of casualties on the enemy once they were drawn into the woods. Procter later praised their diligence in covering the withdrawal of the gun.[10]

The Americans settled in at Frenchtown, burying the dead in a common grave. With the recently arrived regulars, Winchester commanded a force of almost a thousand men, mainly Kentuckians. These consisted of nine companies of the 1st, 2nd, and 5th Kentucky Regiments; six companies of the 1st Kentucky Rifles; three companies of the 17th U.S. Infantry (raised mainly in Kentucky), and a handful from the 19th. Several dozen local residents who participated in the earlier battle might also be counted upon to fight again, if the need arose. Winchester was disappointed at the extent of booty captured in the commissariat store, 30 barrels of flour, a ton of beef, and twelve blankets. He estimated a further four hundred barrels of flour and some beef as available for purchase in the settlement. Considering the ground unfavourable for defence, he sought axes, artillery, and fixed ammunition from Harrison, adding, "No pains or reasonable expense shall be spared to acquire the necessary information concerning the enemy." [11]

Winchester did not take measures to ensure that the men were properly bivouacked. The seven hundred Kentucky volunteers occupied the homes and gardens enclosed by the village picketing while the regulars pitched their tents well outside the enclosure. After their long ordeal in the wilderness, the soldiers enjoyed the peaceful comfort of this backwoods village. "We almost seemed to forget that we had a care in the world," recalled volunteer Elias Darnell. A contemporary observer wrote: "There were all the conveniences and luxuries of an old settlement, [boiled] cider and apples in abundance and to a soldier ... the sight of a woman is not the most uncomely sight to be conceived of. They rested in a state of too great security." [12]

After being lionized by the grateful villagers, feasting on sugar loaf and whiskey, the officers and men bunked down for the night. Winchester took up quarters in the home of François Navarre on the south side of the river, almost a mile from the troops. In his words, "Not to discommode the wounded men, who, with Colonel Lewis's corps, occupied the houses on the north side of the river, I, at some personal risk, took quarters for myself and suite, in a house on the southern bank, directly fronting the troops." Wells's four companies of regulars encamped in an open field outside the enclosure, downstream from the village. These men were both totally exposed and physically separated from the main body by over four hundred yards. There was some talk among the officers of preparing breastworks and moving to better ground, but nothing was done. Having sent patrols as far as Brownstown on the 21st without seeing any sign of the enemy, Winchester did not perceive any immediate danger. [13]

On the evening of the 21st, the Americans sent out no spies or patrols as "it was too cold." For his part, Winchester viewed security arrangements as matters "of routine and constant use," seemingly assuming that they would happen on their own. The fixed ammunition that arrived that day was not distributed but stored in

Winchester's quarters. Alarmed by the lack of precautions, Wells directed his officers to remain alert, as they would probably be attacked. He then returned to the rapids "on some business." That evening, members of the Navarre family repeatedly warned the American officers that a large enemy force had crossed the Detroit River below Grosse Isle and was marching on Frenchtown. Winchester and his officers dismissed these reports as "conjecture," refusing to believe that Procter could mount an attack so quickly. Several additional *Canadiens* and friendly Natives also cautioned the Americans of an impending British strike, but all warnings were discredited as "impossible rumour." [14]

On learning of the American victory of the 18th, Harrison wrote Acting Secretary of War Monroe that he was sending a battalion of Ohio militiamen and one field piece to reinforce Winchester. "It is absolutely necessary to maintain the position at the Raisin River and I am assembling troops as fast as possible for the purpose," he wrote. "Our affairs in every respect wear a flourishing aspect. I fear nothing but that the enemy may overpower Genl. Winchester before I can send him a sufficient reinforcement." Although surprised at Winchester's move, Harrison arrived at the Maumee Rapids on the 19th, and gathering men and materiel, directed Winchester "to maintain the position on the Raisin River at any rate." At this time, Monroe wrote Harrison, urging the reduction of Amherstburg and recapture of Detroit but warning against "any rash enterprize." To be clear on the division of responsibilities for the consequences, he added, "He [the president] reposes entire confidence in your judgment." [15]

At 2:00 AM on the 19th, Maj. Reynolds arrived at Procter's Sandwich headquarters to alert him of the recent action. Having already received several false alarms of the American advance, the British commander was ready and acted decisively. His circumstances were potentially dangerous, as Winchester would doubtlessly be reinforced for a further advance. His regulars were few and time did not allow for the mustering of the more distant militiamen. Most of the Native warriors had left for their winter camps. The warriors, militiamen, and even the regulars were unproven in a general engagement. In tactical terms, attacks on villages were inadvisable unless the assailants possessed superior numbers. Nonetheless, Procter's only chance lay in eliminating Winchester's force before it could unite with the other wings. The British commander wrote, "I deemed it requisite that he should be attacked without delay and with all and every description of force within my reach." [16]

The soldiers of the Fort Amherstburg garrison were celebrating Queen Charlotte's birthday with "*les jeunes gens de la côte* [the young people of the coast]" in Mrs. Draper's Tavern when Lt. Col. St. George appeared in combat attire and announced, "My boys, you must prepare to dance to a different tune; the enemy is on us and we are going to surprise them." Rapidly collecting his force, Procter left only a militia company of the 2nd Essex Regiment under the command of the bedridden Muir at Fort Detroit and a corporal's guard of artillerymen and invalids as a skeleton garrison under Col. James Baby at Fort Amherstburg. The British commander moved so quickly that the Kent militiamen could not participate, his call-out notice only arriving at Raleigh on the Thames at 11:00 that morning.[17]

The same day, leading elements of the British force advanced to Brownstown. This body consisted of a company of the 41st under Capt. Joseph Tallon, a detachment of artillerymen, and the crewmen of the idle provincial marine vessels. The men hauled three 3-pdr. guns and three small howitzers through the deep snow on sleds. At Brownstown, they met the retreating warriors from Frenchtown and the remaining regulars from Detroit and Amherstburg, plus additional militiamen, provincial mariners, and Natives. Procter's combined force counted 336 regulars of all ranks; 212 militiamen of the 1st and 2nd Essex regiments; 19 men of the Indian Department; 28 Provincial Mariners (595 men from ten different corps) and about six hundred braves under Roundhead, Splitlog, and Walk-in-the-Water, making a total of almost twelve hundred combatants. On the 21st, the allies advanced to Swan Creek, six miles from Frenchtown. Bivouacking there for the night, the men kindled fires and slept with their numbed feet near the flames to keep from freezing in the blistering cold. Procter broke camp in the morning darkness of the 22nd, and resuming the march, arrived before Frenchtown by dawn, to see puffs of smoke curling lazily from the fires of the unsuspecting village.[18]

In profound silence, Procter deployed his undetected force into battle order, a line of a half-mile arc, some 250 yards north of the American camp. Drawn up along a ravine, the regulars held the centre position, flanked by Natives on the right and the militiamen and more braves on the left. With muskets freshly primed, the allied force was preparing to charge the sleeping camp just as the drummers beat the reveille. Suddenly, an American sentry discharged his musket and felled a British grenadier named Gates, killing him instantly (the musket ball literally entered one ear and emerged from the other). In the

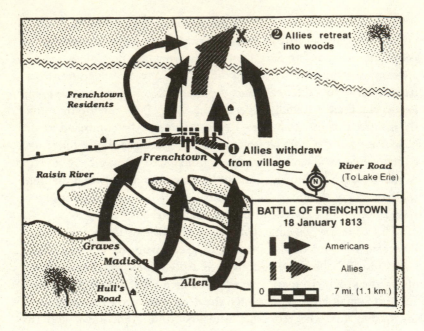

Frenchtown Residents

② Allies retreat into woods

Frenchtown

① Allies withdraw from village

Raisin River

River Road (To Lake Erie)

N

Graves
Madison

Allen

Hull's Road

BATTLE OF FRENCHTOWN
18 January 1813

Americans

Allies

0   .7 mi. (1.1 km.)

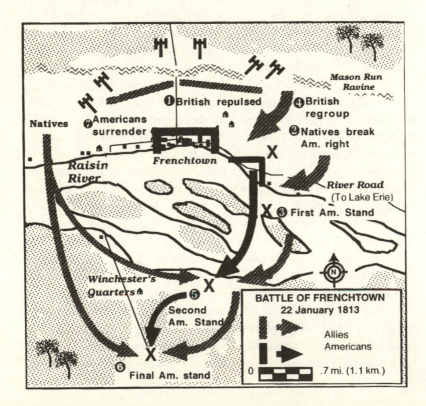

Natives

① British repulsed

④ British regroup

⑦ Americans surrender

② Natives break Am. right

Mason Run Ravine

Raisin River

Frenchtown

③ First Am. Stand

River Road (To Lake Erie)

N

Winchester's Quarters

⑤ Second Am. Stand

⑥ Final Am. stand

BATTLE OF FRENCHTOWN
22 January 1813

Allies
Americans

0   .7 mi. (1.1 km.)

words of young John Richardson, "The army drew up and formed the line of battle in two adjoining fields and moved down towards the enemy 20 or 30 paces in front and the Indians on our flanks. We had got tolerably near their camp when we heard their reveille drum beat (so completely lulled into security were they that they had not the most distant idea of an enemy being near) and soon after we heard a shot or two from the centinels [sic] who had by this time discovered us. Their camp was immediately in motion." [19]

American participants confirmed that two minutes into the beating of reveille, their sentinels fired off three guns in quick succession. Then, according to Elias Darnell, "The British immediately discharged their artillery loaded with balls, bombs and grapeshot, which did little injury. Then they attempted to make a charge on those within the pickets but were repulsed with great loss." Although terrifying, most of the artillery rounds passed overhead, the gunners' aim being based on guesswork in the semi-darkness. The early morning light also caused the British officers to mistake the five-foot puncheon fences of split oak rails for formed lines of infantry. Three sides of the village were encompassed by this picketing, which provided excellent cover for the defenders against an attack from the north, east, or west. The action became general and was warmly contested for half an hour, during which the exposed British centre suffered heavy casualties, especially near the guns. [20]

The artillery and musket fire generated a continuous roar that was complemented by the warriors' frightful war shrieks. As the din and smoke of battle enveloped the scene, participants witnessed instances of courage, accident, and even humour. Provincial Mariner Robert Irvine single-handedly recovered one of the guns that had been advanced too close to the picketing. Just as he returned to the safety of the British lines, a painful musket ball penetrated his heel. Amid the confused fighting, John Richardson found that someone had stolen his flintlock, and he struggled frantically to repair a defective one as the battle raged around him. His younger brother, Robert, aged 14, screamed from the excruciating pain of a severe wound to the knee. Yet, his great concern was that his father, a hospital assistant attached to the division, not learn of his injury, having forbidden Robert to join the expedition. Private Shadrach Byfield was felled by a sharpshooter's ball in the neck and someone yelled, "Byfield is dead!" Dazed, the British soldier, replied, "I believe I be." Drifting off, he asked himself, "Is this death or how men die?" The wound, however, was not fatal.

He crawled to the rear. A companion offered him a shirt tail as a bandage, and he survived to fight again. Charles Frederick Rolette of the Provincial Marine received a musket ball in the forehead but a bandanna he wore for a splitting headache absorbed the impact of the round. He, too, survived with a nasty swelling (and no doubt, a headache of superlative proportions).[21]

On the American right, the warriors managed to gain the cover of a barn and some fencing, from which they and the British centre maintained an effective crossfire on the exposed American regulars who, after 25 minutes, gave way. Winchester joined the troops and tried vainly to form them under the riverbank, while colonels Lewis and Allen led two companies from the pickets to assist the regulars in inclining toward the centre. As the Kentuckians fell back, the fleet-footed braves surged forward. The Natives continued to gain the Americans' rear, turning the withdrawal into a rout as the mass of panic-stricken troops rushed wildly across the river. In this *mêlée*, the officers made a second attempt to form the ranks along some fences 60 yards south of the river, but most of the men continued their headlong dash down a narrow lane. It was here that Lt. Col. Allen, wounded in the thigh, stopped to rest on a log. A Wyandot chief approached with a view to capturing him but another warrior advanced menacingly towards Allen, who cut down the assailant with his sword. The surrounding Natives immediately killed the American.[22]

Taking few prisoners, the mounted Wyandot hunted down the exhausted Kentuckians as they struggled in two feet of crusted snow. A third attempt by the officers to rally the men a mile and a half from the action also failed, many of the frantic soldiers having discarded their arms in utter disarray. Few survived. Yelling their bloodcurdling scalp halloo, the warriors slaughtered them wholesale. Even some of the Americans who laid down their arms were systematically tomahawked and scalped. The Kentuckians offered horses, valuables, and huge sums of money to be turned over to the British. One hysterical prisoner offered to show his captors "a great many white men" if they let him live, but the warriors killed him. According to volunteer Willam Atherton, the Americans who showed courage were spared, but those who demonstrated unmanly fear were summarily slain. About two miles south of the river, the road came upon an open field where most of the remaining fugitives were captured or killed. At this point, the surviving senior officer, Maj. Elijah McClenahan, took his son by the hand, and with Capt. Michael Glaves, made good their escape along the lakeshore.[23]

Meanwhile, the Kentucky militiamen, sheltered behind the pickets, held their own. Although American participants generally described the artillery fire as passing overhead, some parts of the pickets were "completely shattered by the enemy's shot." After two and a half hours, the Americans had withstood and repulsed three frontal assaults, inflicting heavy casualties on the unsheltered line of red coats. The British guns in the centre were within 50 yards of the oak palisades, silenced as the frontier sharpshooters picked off the gunners. Capt. Joseph Tallon of the 41st led the third charge against a picketing that bristled with the muzzles of Kentucky firelocks. No fewer than 111 British soldiers were cut down by the concentrated musketry, including Tallon himself. The Kentucky volunteers, sheltered by the palings, could take "cool and deliberate aim" at the enemy through loopholes in the fencing.[24]

Observing his faltering lines, Procter ordered the frontal assaults to cease and withdrew the assailants to regroup on the far left, behind the shelter of a group of farm buildings. An intense struggle developed over possession of these structures. St. George was wounded four times while attempting to occupy one of the barns. A young American ensign, William Butler, performed an act of individual heroism, twice running to the barn to set it on fire. Although his clothes were riddled with shot he returned unharmed to his lines. Eventually, the British soldiers gained the cover of several of these outbuildings. From this new position, one or two British 3-pdr. guns fired at the American right. Two other pieces remained on the British right to annoy the men behind the picketing, but American marksmen picked off the horse and driver of the ammunition sleigh, silencing those guns. With the battle stalemated, Procter awaited the return of the warriors from their pursuit and pondered his next move while the Americans breakfasted on milk and fresh crusty bread.[25]

Among the returning Wyandot (some of whom bore up to nine scalps each) was Winchester, captured by a warrior known as Brandy Jack. When a group of Potawatomi threatened to murder his captive, Brandy Jack seized his war club, declaring that they would have to kill him first. Roundhead took charge of the American general, and took him, along with his 16-year-old son and Lt. Col. Lewis, to Procter. Some weeks later, the *Morning Chronicle* of London reported the event: "The Indian according to the laws of nations and courtesy due to the prisoners of war, stripped the Americans commander of his fine waistcoat and shirt and then daubed his skin with paint. In this ludicrous state, having dressed himself in his regimentals, he [Roundhead] presented him to Colonel Procter who with difficulty succeeded in getting the discomfited general his coat, sword and hat." [26]

Aware of the potent fear of Native savagery, Procter demanded that Winchester give up his remaining men, "that unless done quickly, the buildings adjacent would be immediately set on fire and no responsibility would be taken for the conduct of the savages, who were then assembled in great numbers." As the warriors had already partially penetrated the south side of the village and made several attempts to burn out the Americans, Winchester wrote a note to the defenders, telling them of his capture and directing them to surrender. He later maintained that although he "intended" conditions, he could not recollect having made any. [27]

The command of the Americans within the picketing had devolved on Maj. George Madison. A future governor of Kentucky, the 49-year-old Madison was a veteran frontier fighter who left his duties as state auditor to join in the war effort. He considered the order to surrender nonbinding as Winchester was a prisoner. Nonetheless, he agreed to a ceasefire and opened discussions with the British. Three separate parleys under flags of truce occurred between the two sides as Madison insisted upon conditions to accompany the surrender, including that the wounded be cared for, that the troops be protected from the warriors, and that the officers have their sidearms restored as private property. Annoyed by the delays, Procter snapped, "Do you mean to dictate to me?" to which Madison retorted, "I mean to dictate for myself and we prefer selling our lives as dearly as possible, rather than be massacred in cold blood." American accounts assert that verbal agreement regarding the safety of all prisoners was achieved, while Procter maintained that Winchester surrendered his force at discretion. In either case, the action terminated by 11 AM with an agreed surrender. [28]

Both Madison and Procter had been bluffing. With his regulars badly cut up, and having received a report that Harrison's troops were marching on Frenchtown, Procter had no time to waste. On the other hand, Madison could not hold out much longer. With the main supply of ammunition captured at the Navarre house, the Americans were reduced to a mere two or three cartridges apiece. Madison marched out his men and ordered them to ground their arms while the warriors moved in and helped themselves to the booty of small arms, tents, and cooking utensils. [29]

Despite his victory, Procter's situation was, as he put it, "embarrassing." He had five hundred able-bodied prisoners to guard, more than his disposable non-Native force, at a time when Harrison's reinforcements were reported close at hand. In the British commander's view, these prisoners "could not have been expected to stay idle." Encumbered with them, plus the numerous wounded of both armies, his force was in no condition to conduct another engagement or even a fighting retreat. The expectation of Harrison's advance seemed general; Private Shadrach Byfield recalled a British surgeon urging the wounded men to flee as "We shall be all taken!" Procter's means for meeting a fresh enemy were as limited as the perceived situation was pressing.[30]

John Norton was on the Thames River at Delaware when he encountered an express announcing Harrison's advance. Joining Procter some days later, he learned of the circumstance that prompted the sudden British retreat:

An inconsiderable party of Wyandot having collected together a drove of
cattle and hogs belonging to the army under General Winchester ... were
discovered approaching the River Raisin on the ice by the militia on the
lookout. Apprehension, or the reflection of the sun changing the appearance
of the objects, the hogs were mistaken for infantry, the horned cattle for
cavalry, and the Wyandot, who were mounted and were observed to be
riding from one extremity of the line to the other were allowed to be
General Harrison and his staff as they appeared to be occupied in preserving
regularity in the line of march. On arriving at Frenchtown, all appeared in
their proper characters but the express had been dispatched by the zealous
and vigilant observer and he to whom it was entrusted travelled with such
diligence that the *éclaircissement* never overtook him.[31]

The following day, Winchester prepared a remarkably detached account of the battle. He was, he said, suddenly attacked by a superior force in an "unequal contest." Incredibly, he declared, "However unfortunate may seem the affair of yesterday, I am flattered by a belief that no material error is chargeable upon myself." He blamed the defeat on Harrison's failure to provide timely reinforcements from the Maumee Rapids, where he had arrived two days before the engagement. Indeed, the surviving officers held the opinion that they were expecting Harrison's advance and that a single battalion would have meant an American victory. Winchester reported 487 men and 35 officers captured, for a total of 522 prisoners, plus more in Native hands.

Two weeks later, in a more detailed return, he reported 397 men killed and missing and 547 prisoners for a total of 911 casualties (not counting 33 who escaped), approximating Harrison's estimate of a thousand Americans engaged.[32]

Allied casualties were considerably fewer. Nonetheless Procter's army sustained heavy losses with a total of 185 men or two-fifths of the entire White force being wounded. Most of these were regulars of the 41st, with 18 killed and 127 wounded (49 percent casualties among the rank and file, the highest proportion ever sustained by the 41st in an engagement). Among the Indian Department, militia, and Provincial Marine, five were killed and 34 wounded. St. George's wounds precluded his further service on the frontier. The 11 other wounded officers included Lt. Troughton of the artillery, Capt. Tallon and Lt. Clemow of the 41st, and lieutenants Rolette and Irvine of the Provincial Marine. In a letter to the secretary of war, Winchester reported that Procter was also wounded, though the British commander made no mention of injury.[33]

Only rudimentary medical attention could be provided on the field, wounds being simply plugged with lint and tightly wrapped with linen bandages to halt the bleeding. Like Lewis on the 18th, Procter lacked adequate transport with which to remove the wounded. While the British commander had little time to lose, he arrested five residents who were identified as having taken up arms against his army.[34]

Then, acting on the false report that Harrison was only eight miles away, Procter ordered a retreat. "It was consistent with prudence and humanity to march off with the prisoners without delay," he wrote. "It was necessary to leave the [American] wounded behind because every sleigh was at Brownstown bringing over our own wounded." Procter was certainly aware of the dangerous state of the Natives, having written some months before: "It is impossible to save any prisoner and the attempt has endangered the lives of several of our people where the Indians have lost their lives."[35]

Shortly after noon on the 22nd, Procter broke camp and marched to Amherstburg. Sleigh parties followed with the wounded. Approximately 64 severely injured Americans remained in the village under the care of their surgeons, doctors John Todd and Gustavus M. Bower, assisted by a few attendants and three interpreters under Maj. Reynolds and Capt. Elliott. As was their custom after a battle, the tribesmen prepared for a "frolick," for which the Indian Department drew them off to Stoney Creek, six miles away.[36]

The British main body arrived at Amherstburg with the prisoners at midnight that same day. "When we got to Malden, the firing was almost incessant," one participant observed. "It seemed that the whole face of the country was covered with Indians, rejoicing over a vanquished enemy." It was not just the Natives that were emotionally charged. "The people of Canada could only regard them [the prisoners] as a band of banditti who, without cause or provocation, had invaded their territory, murdered their husbands and children, and when they had it in their power, plundered their property," wrote Procter. "The women of Amherstburg were only restrained by the magistrates and officers from assaulting the prisoners when they came in."[37]

Accommodation for this huge influx of men was limited, and the unwounded prisoners were corralled into a wood yard. The next day, their guards gave them shelter from a freezing rain in a warehouse, and on the 25th further removed them to the Sandwich jail. The small hospital at Fort Amherstburg was so crowded with injured British soldiers that some of the patients had to be quartered in the barracks. Unable to accommodate and feed the large numbers, Procter was anxious to send the Kentucky militiamen home on parole, but his fears of Native atrocities precluded their release in Michigan. He sent them to Fort George by way of the Thames.[38]

The Americans marched off under guard on 26 and 27 January. In the course of their journey, they encountered the light company of the 41st, bound for Amherstburg. The nature of the banter between the two parties as related by Elias Darnell of Kentucky demonstrated the universal camaraderie of common soldiers, "They [the British soldiers] appeared to be very sociable, generally of Irish descent. One of their officers said, 'In a few weeks, they would drive General Harrison and all his army along there.' 'Yes,' replied James Allen, 'before that time your Irish hides will be riddled so that they would not hold hickory nuts'." A total of 512 American prisoners arrived at Fort George on 10 and 11 February to be paroled and released across the Niagara River. Winchester and the regulars were sent on to Quebec.[39]

By all accounts, the battle of Frenchtown was a bitterly contested and bloody struggle. Cruelties were not confined to the warriors as Richardson noted foul fighting on the part of the Americans, as well. "I was a witness of a most barbarous act of inhumanity on the part of the Americans who fired upon our poor, wounded, helpless soldiers who were endeavouring to crawl away on their hands and feet from the scene of the action and were thus tumbled over like so many hogs," he wrote to his uncle. Capt. Billy Caldwell of the Indian Department saved an American officer from being tomahawked but while conducting his prisoner to safety, the latter sprang upon his benefactor and slit his throat ear to ear. Since the cut was shallow, Caldwell was able to overpower and kill his assailant.[40]

Procter also disapproved of the Kentuckians' methods. His regulars were so disdainful of their practice of mixing buckshot with musket rounds in their cartridges that they refused to use captured ammunition in the heat of battle. Shadrach Byfield confirmed that some of the Americans loaded their pieces with cartridges that contained nine buckshot, in addition to a musket ball. While expressing contempt for the frontiersmen, Procter observed, "My opinion of the enemy is not any more favourable than it was.... They were armed with knives and tomahawks, and some of them used them. They fired on the wounded as they lay on the ground. Every art, every means has been employed to prejudice and influence these misguided people against us."[41]

The Kentuckians' rugged reputation was enhanced by their unkempt appearance. "They had the air of men to whom cleanliness is unknown," wrote John Richardson, "and their squalid bodies were covered by habiliments that had evidently undergone every change of season and were arrived at the last stage of disrepair ... their long hair fell matted and uncombed over their cheeks; and these together with the dirty blankets wrapped around their loins to protect them against the inclemency of the season and fastened by the broad belts, into which were thrust axes and knives of an enormous length gave them an air of savageness which in Italy would have caused them to pass for brigands of the Apennines." The Kentucky backwoodsmen prided themselves on being "half horse and half alligator, tipped with snapping turtle." A New Englander considered them "decent fellows, yet the large knife and hatchet ... with their dress gave them a rather savage appearance." Their wild looks and backwoods habits (including scalping) spawned exaggerated stories. Volunteer William Atherton learned the extent to which rumour had preceded them. As a prisoner in Quebec City, he and his companions were put on public display. Among the curious spectators, one gentleman examined them closely and suddenly exclaimed, "Why, they look just like other people!"[42]

On the morning of the battle, Harrison was on Hull's Road, between the rapids and Frenchtown, hastening toward the action with nine hundred men. At noon, he received word from fugitives that Winchester's wing was totally defeated, and he halted the advance, sending 170 men to within 12 miles of Frenchtown to assist other survivors. Although embarrassed by the disaster, Harrison distanced himself from the outcome, maintaining that Winchester's movement "was made not only without any authority from me but in opposition to my views." Based on initial reports from Maj. McClanahan and fleeing Frenchtown residents, Harrison estimated the dead in the battle as up to eight hundred. He reported Winchester cruelly butchered, "killed, scalped and his bowels taken out." Fearful of a further British advance, Harrison fell back on the rapids. Once there, he destroyed Winchester's accumulated stores, baggage, and facilities and continued his retreat to the Sandusky River. Thus, because of faulty intelligence, Procter and Harrison simultaneously fled in opposite directions, prompting the new secretary of war, John Armstrong, to call them "the terror of each other."[43]

Back at Frenchtown, the wounded Americans (variously estimated between 48 and 80 men), were quartered in two houses. One of the attendants, Elias Darnell, wrote, "The British said, as they had a great many of their wounded to take to Malden that evening, it would be out of their power to take ours before morning, but they would leave a sufficient guard, so that they should not be interrupted by the Indians." That evening, some prowling warriors tried to burn the commissariat building and Darnell helped "two British officers" to extinguish the flames. Although Procter may have intended to remove all the prisoners once sleighs became available, it is more likely that he expected these prisoners to fall into Harrison's hands, anticipating the latter's advance. Indeed this was the general expectation. Darnell observed Maj. Reynolds walking about the village, looking apprehensively up the road, and concluded that he was awaiting Harrison's men. Surviving American officers also stated that they expected Harrison's arrival on the day of the battle.[44]

With nightfall, a desolate gloom settled over the largely deserted village. Anticipating further conflict, Procter had ordered the area residents to remove to Detroit for safety. Some were only too happy to oblige; others fled to Ohio. Only a few *Canadiens* remained in the village. By next morning, Reynolds and the interpreters had disappeared, as well. According to Darnell, Elliott had called them away. One of the attendants, an orderly sergeant named John Dawson, observed that two of the three interpreters had been called away and the remaining one asserted "he could not talk Indian!"[45]

Between daylight and sunrise of the 23rd, some two hundred warriors entered Frenchtown. They robbed the wounded of their clothing,

tomahawked those who were unable to move, ordered the remainder
outside, and set fire to the two homes that had served as hospitals. All
who could walk were marched down the road. Those who failed to keep
up were murdered, leaving the road "strewn with mangled bodies."
According to Alexis Labadie, a local *Canadien*, the mutilated, truncated
corpses were devoured by hogs that appeared "to be rendered mad by
so profuse a diet of Christian flesh." Capt. Nathaniel Hart (brother-in-
law to Henry Clay) offered one warrior $100 to be taken to Amherst-
burg. The warrior placed him on a horse but another murdered him en
route. Several captives met a similar fate, including William Butler,
who had distinguished himeslf the previous day.[46]

Surgeon's mate Gustavus M. Bower was protected by an Ottawa
chief named M'Carty, who mounted him on a horse. Bower noticed a
group of four prisoners, of whom one, Jason Blythe, bargained with a
warrior to be taken to Amherstburg, only to be tomahawked, stripped,
and scalped. When another private, Charles Searls, engaged in a political argument with his captors, he too was tomahawked. Bower saw
three additional captives murdered in a like manner before the survivors reached Brownstown at midnight to be lodged in the Wyandot
council house.[47]

Doctor John Todd, an American surgeon and witness to the atrocities, stated that Capt. William Elliott assured Capt Hart (his long-
time personal friend) that he would send his personal sleigh next
morning and accommodate Hart in his own home. Elliott left
Frenchtown the evening of the battle. At Stoney Creek, Todd encountered Elliott and told him of the murders at Frenchtown, insisting that
the survivors might yet be saved. Elliott replied that as the sleighs were
already in use, none were available. Todd reported that on hearing of
the brutal killings, Elliott and a British surgeon became "much exasperated, asserting that it was impossible to restrain the savages."[48]

Upon arriving at Amherstburg, Todd was given free access to the
hospital, dispensary, and "as comfortable rooms as could be procured."
He estimated that ten Americans had escaped Native captivity to
Amherstburg, including "one poor fellow brought in scalped alive."
Todd urged the release of the remaining wounded men, but Capt.
Elliott is said to have replied, "The Indians are excellent surgeons,"
attributing the murders to the Native custom of seeking revenge for
losses. Todd rejected suggestions that the warriors had been drunk,
since the "massacre" was deliberate and methodical. He added, "With
few exceptions, I was treated respectfully by the British officers, save

the abuse which was lavished on my government and that was not sparingly bestowed."[49]

Several explanations emerged to account for the atrocities of the 23rd. The Potawatomi chief, Blackbird, attributed the act of refusing burial to the dead Kentuckians as revenge for similar American acts. "The way they treat our killed and the remains of those that are in their graves to the west make our people mad when they meet the Big Knives," he declared. "Whenever they get any of our people into their hands, they cut them into small pieces." Rector Strachan explained the indignities to the dead as brought on by the butchering of a warrior's body by the Kentuckians in the action on the 18th: "The American troops ... literally tore him to pieces which so exasperated the Indians that they refused burial to the Americans killed on the 22nd." Procter confirmed this incident, describing the body of the warrior as "pierced with wounds without number ... apparently every American that had passed the corpse had thrust his bayonet into it." Furthermore, on examining the bodies of dead American officers, the British commander asserted, "Their commission was found bound up with a bloody scalp ... tied about their neck."[50]

Judge Woodward hinted in his letter to Procter that American barbarities were indeed a principal cause of the defilements: "When an engagement has taken place, the fury of the savage mind at the sight of blood, and in reflecting on the dead they lose, and perhaps on the retaliatory treatment of prisoners or of the dead, which their cruel mode of warfare produces, is always likely to drive them to an ignoble revenge on their prisoners." The events at Frenchtown marked a shift in the conduct of the war in the west as the struggle adopted a brutal dimension. Given the desperate condition of many Natives, they could hardly be expected to observe the European conventions in a veritable war of survival.[51]

The Frenchtown collaborators also contributed to the Native backlash. Not only had the *Canadiens* failed to respond to the Wyandot request for assistance after their retreat from the Maumee Rapids but some of them fought on the American side in the action of the 18th. Harrison acknowledged, "Many of them had sallied out of their houses upon the arrival of Col. Lewis with their arms in their hands and even in the opinion of some of our officers won the palm of valor from our troops. They attacked and killed the struggling Indians wherever they met them." Furthermore, Procter gained definitive proof of their collaboration with the Americans through captured correspondence. In the words of Judge Woodward, these "were calculated to draw down the vengeance of the enemy."[52]

The events of the 22nd and 23rd became melded, distorted, and enormously magnified. A later American secretary of war, Alexander J. Dallas, would publicly declare, "While the British officers and soldiers silently and exultantly contemplated the scene, some of the American prisoners of war were tomahawked, some were shot and some were burnt." Timothy Mallary, a survivor of the massacre, managed to escape Native captivity to Amherstburg where he allegedly witnessed British officials paying James Girty (son of the notorious frontiersman, Simon Girty), $3 a week to receive scalps from the warriors. He added, "I saw here about a half a bushel of scalps in a kettle!" For his part, Procter expressed regret at "instances of Indian barbarity, but the example was set by the enemy and they came to seek them. I know we shall be vilified for the truth is not in them."[53]

War propaganda aside, this was the worst example of Native misconduct while acting in concert with a British force during the war. According to John Norton, the warriors were extremely slow in delivering up prisoners and did so "only after repeated intercession in their behalf by the British officers." Procter personally intervened to secure the release of a young officer from a reluctant Potawatomi warrior, writing, "I had much difficulty in bringing the Indians to consent to the sparing of their lives."[54]

Officially, Procter acknowledged the contribution of the warriors: "The zeal and courage of the Indian Department were never more conspicuous than on this occasion." With Robert Dickson, Tecumseh, and John Norton absent and McKee rendered *hors de combat* from his intemperate and debilitating habits, Procter declared Matthew Elliott's role as "very much improved" and urged his retention with an increased salary. Nonetheless, allied relations continued to fester. Norton noticed the growing rift, commenting, "I was much troubled at perceiving in the Indian Department of this neighbourhood a strong dislike to the General ... apprehending that by the insinuation which their ill-nature might urge them to throw out, they might seriously injure the service."[55]

By any standard, Winchester's advance was an unmitigated disaster in which he blundered badly and repeatedly. Capt. Eleazar Wood, a promising West Point graduate, described Winchester's enterprise as "rash in conception and hazardous in execution.... Winchester was destitute of every means of supporting his corps long at the Raisin River, was in the very jaws of the enemy and beyond the reach of succor. He who fights with such flimsy pretensions to victory, will always be beaten and eternally ought to be." Although Armstrong itemized eight tactical blunders committed by Winchester, he considered Harrison responsible as commander-in-chief. Only Harrison's immense popularity saved him from dismissal.[56]

For his part, Harrison maintained, "Never were the affairs of an army in a more prosperous situation than ours before ... the Raisin River." He speculated that if Winchester had remained at the rapids for another week, he could have concentrated five thousand men for an overwhelming advance. He attempted to minimize the effect of the disaster by writing to Governor Meigs, "Unless the weather is unfavourable, I shall certainly give the enemy an opportunity of measuring their strength with us in another contest." In fact, he was in no condition to resume offensive action. The remaining Kentucky and Ohio volunteers were preparing to return home, their six-month terms of enlistment almost expired. In order to prevent the complete disintegration of the Northwest Army, their state legislatures offered sizable bounties for those volunteers who chose to remain.[57]

The annihilation of Winchester's army was a particularly heavy blow to Kentucky, severely dampening war fever in that state. Governor Isaac Shelby described the impact of this disaster:

Col. Wells arrived at this place on the evening of the 2d inst. with the distressing intelligence of the defeat of Gen. Winchester's detachment. This melancholy event has filled the state with mourning and every feeling heart bleeds with anguish. The Legislature in this state was on the point of rising at the moment when Col. Wells arrived but continued their session during the whole of the third. [In] Consequence of the intelligence contained in your despatches ... [the legislature] passed an act, authorizing the Organization of three thousand Militia for any term not exceeding Six Mos. for any service of the United States.[58]

The political leaders of Kentucky had been instrumental in securing the war vote. They insisted on the employment of their volunteers with Harrison as commander and urged wide latitude from Washington in the prosecution of the campaign. Fearful of being left out of the glory, they had rushed in huge contingents, only to see them decimated, captured, and killed. Henceforth, the number of Kentucky volunteers dropped off sharply, and Shelby resorted to the unpopular draft to complete state quotas. Anticipating a quick and easy victory, Kentuckians were psychologically unprepared for such a complete reversal of expectations. Their leaders, now resigned to a prolonged, difficult, and bloody conflict, adopted the emotional war cry, "Remember the Raisin!" to raise new levies. That vehement War Hawk, Henry Clay, now called for an "efficient war" to be pursued with "utmost vigor until a peace is negotiated from Quebec or Halifax," but even he added, "If we fail, let us fail like men." [59]

Procter's victory was one of the most complete of any in the war. Having wiped out the fighting core of the Northwest Army, he had effectively foiled Harrison's winter offensive. The British success was largely attributable to the Natives' successful onslaught on the American right and their very presence as an instrument of terror. The British commander would remember their critical contributions, particularly that of the loyal Wyandot:

These people form a singular exception to the degeneracy which usually attends the intercourse of the Indian with the white. The Wyandots have all the energy of the savage warrior, with the intelligence of and docility of white troops. They are Christians and remarkable for their orderly and inoffensive conduct; but as enemies, they were among the most dreadful of their race. They were all mounted; fearless, active, and enterprising; to contend with them in the forest was hopeless, and to avoid their pursuit, impossible. They were led by Roundhead, who, next to the celebrated Tecumthe [sic], was the most distinguished and useful of all the chiefs. [60]

The American war effort as a whole had floundered badly. Nothing was gained, and even the attempt to recover Michigan resulted in another disaster. Two decisive defeats in the west plus the one at Queenston Heights had made glaringly apparent the incompetence of the war office. President Madison found a new secretary of war in Maj. Gen. John Armstrong, who assumed office on 5 February 1813. A respected professional soldier, Armstrong had advocated a concentrated thrust against Montreal versus the dispersed operations along the frontier. He concluded that a rupture of British communications on the upper St. Lawrence would starve Upper Canada into surrender. Once in office, though, Armstrong changed his mind, preparing strong assaults, facilitated by naval superiority on the lakes, against Kingston and forts York, George and Amherstburg. Success in any of these actions would be detrimental to Procter's command, which now suffered an acute shortage of regulars.

In far-off London, strategic planners continued to be preoccupied with the final stages of the Napoleonic struggle. Although the British government had embraced the political goal of a Native state, military leaders, notably the Marquis (soon to be Duke) of Wellington, advised the minister for war and colonies that Prevost ought to confine his activities to defensive measures as he had insufficient forces to take and hold new territory.[61]

NOTES

1. Procter to Sheaffe, 13 Jan. 1813, NAC, C 678: 25; Atherton, *Narrative of the Suffering and Defeat of the Northwest Army Under General Winchester*, 31.
2. Winchester to President Madison, nd., *NOW* 1: 197-98.
3. Isaac Day to Harrison, 12 Jan. 1813, *MLWHH* 2: 307-08; William Atherton, *Narrative*, 32.
4. Winchester to Harrison, 17 Jan. 1813, *MLWHH* 2: 314; Darnell, *Journal*, 46; *NOW* 1: 67-69.
5. Darnell, *Journal*, 45; Samuel Wells to Thomas Cushing, 9 Feb. 1813, *MPHC* 40: 504; Winchester to Harrison, 17 Jan. 1813, *MLWHH* 2: 314; Atherton, *Narrative*, 32; Harrison to Meigs, 19 Jan. 1813, *MLWHH* 2: 315.
6. Darnell, *Journal*, 46-47.
7. Brown, *Campaigns*, 148; Darnell, *Journal*, 48-49; Lewis to Harrison, 20 Jan. 1813, *MLWHH* 2: 321.
8. Darnell, *Journal*, 47.
9. Lewis to Winchester, 20 Jan. 1813, *MLWHH* 2: 319-24; Richardson to Charles Askin, 4 Feb. 1813, cited in Richardson, *War of 1812*, 302; Atherton, *Narrative*, 33-40; Winchester's General Order, 19 Jan. 1813, cited in Au, *War on the Raisin*, 30.
10. Winchester to Seretary of War, nd., *NOW* 1: 199; Procter to Sheaffe, 25 Jan. 1813, NAC, C 678: 46.
11. Winchester to Harrison, 21 Jan. 1813, *MLWHH* 2: 325.
12. Darnell, *Journal*, 48-50; Elijah Whittlesey to his wife, 25 Jan. 1813, WRHS, Tract No. 92: 102.
13. Winchester and Maj. Madison to Armstrong, nd., 1813, *NOW* 1: 199-200; Darnell, *Journal*, 50. Although Wells subsequently went to great lengths to distance himself from the command blunders, his sense of elitism may have contributed to the subsequent diasaster. He insisted that his regulars remain outside the enclosure, "military etiquette, calling for his regulars to assume the place of honour, to the right of the militiamen." Au, *War on the Raisin*, 31.

14. Winchester and Maj. Madison to Armstrong, nd., *NOW* 1: 200; Darnell, *Journal*, 50-52; McClenahan to Harrison, 26 Jan. 1813, *MLWHH* 2: 338-41; Atherton, *Narrative*, 40-42.

15. Harrison to Monroe, 20 Jan. 1813, *MLWHH* 2: 317; Harrison to Winchester, 20 Jan. 1813, Charles S. Todd and Benjamin Drake, *Sketches of the Civil and Military Services of William Henry Harrison*, 56; Monroe to Harrison, 21 Jan. 1813, *MLWHH* 2: 326.

16. Procter to Evans, 24 Jan. 1813, NAUS, *MIC*, 226; Procter to Sheaffe, 25 Jan. 1813, NAC, C 678: 46.

17. Reynolds narrative, cited in Coffin, *The War and its Moral*, 203; James Baby to Capt. Jacob, 19 Jan. 1813, *SBD* 2: 5; John Askin to William Powell, 25 Jan. 1813, *DHCNF* 1813, Vol. 1: 50.

18. Governor Edwards to Meigs, 2 Feb. 1813, Knopff, *Document Transcripts* 2: 102; Right Division Return, 22 Jan. 1813, *SBD* 2: 10.

19. Byfield, *Account*, 16; John Richardson to Charles Askin, 4 Feb. 1813, cited in Richardson, *War of 1812*, 302. Decades later, Richardson criticized Procter for "firing his three pounders in answer to the alarms of the sentinels" rather than charging the enemy at the point of the bayonet. This view emanated from the opinion of his father, Robert Richardson, a hospital assistant attending the wounded in the rear of the field. While this unqualified opinion has been freely repeated in subsequent works, eyewitness accounts agree that the British officers, believing the Americans to be bivoucked outside the fence, mistook the pickets for their formed lines. Robert Richardson, Sr., to John Askin, 7 Feb. 1813, *JAP* 2: 749; Byfield, *Account*, 16; Darnell, *Journal*, 43.

20. Byfield, *Account*, 16; Darnell, *Journal*, 52; Hunt, *Memoirs*, 43; Atherton *Narrative*, 43; Procter's Report to Sheaffe, 25 Jan. 1813, NAC, C 678: 46; Au, *War on the Raisin*, 30.

21. Richardson, *War of 1812*, 137; John Richardson to Charles Askin, 4 Feb. 1813, cited in Richardson, *War of 1812*, 304; Byfield, *Account*, 17-18; Reynolds narrative, cited in Coffin, *The War and Its Moral*, 204.

22. Atherton, *Narrative*, 44-45; McClenahan to Harrison, 26 Jan. 1813, *MLWHH* 2: 338-41.

23. *Niles Register*, 5 June 1813; McClenahan to Harrison, 26 Jan. 1813, *MLWHH* Vol. 2: 338-41; Atherton, *Narrative*, 46-50.

24. Brown, *Campaigns*, 149; John Richardson to Charles Askin, 4 Feb. 1813, cited in Richardson, *War of 1812*, 302; Darnell, *Journal*, 52-53.

25. Mockler, Bender, *Bender CM*, 22, 40; Atherton, *Narrative*, 48-49.

26. Byfield, *Account*, 18; Reynolds narrative, cited in Coffin, *The War and its Moral*, 204; *Morning Chronicle*, 23 Apr. 1813.

27. Winchester to Monroe, 23 Jan. 1813, *MLWHH* 2: 327-28; Winchester to Armstrong, nd., 1813, *NOW* 1: 201.

28. McAfee, *Late War*, 215-16; Hunt, *Memoirs*, 42; Labbadi to Harrison, 11 Feb. 1813, *MLWHH* 2: 360-62; Atherton, *Narrative*, 50-53.

29. Darnell, *Journal*, 54-56. The warriors appropriated most of the captured inventory, Procter's Field Train Department managing to secure only 397 muskets and some lesser stores. Return of Captured Stores, 25 Jan. 1813, NAC, C 678: 46.

30. Byfield, *Account*, 18. One account mentions a Native scout reporting Harrison 10 miles from Frenchtown. Ernest Cruikshank, "Harrison and Procter," 162.

31. Norton, *Journal*, 317.

32. Winchester to Monroe, 23 Jan. 1813, *MLWHH* 2: 328; Winchester to Armstrong, nd., 1813, *NOW* 1: 197-200; Statements of majors Madison, Eve, and Garrard, and Lt. Col. Lewis, nd., 1813, *NOW* 1: 201-05; Winchester to Monroe, 11 Feb. 1813, cited in Cruikshank, "Harrison and Procter," 163; Harrison to Meigs, 24 Jan. 1813, *MLWHH* 2: 331.

33. Right Division Return, 22 Jan. 1813, *SBD* 2: 10-12; Lomax, *The 41st*, 68; Winchester to Monroe, 11 Feb. 1813, Russell, *The History of the War*, 229.

34. Au, *War on the Raisin*, 45. Of the the five Americans arrested, Procter dealt rigorously with two, Whitmore Knaggs and Capt. Hubert Lacroix, the latter having eluded his grasp the previous fall. Both men were imprisoned in Quebec City and eventually released. Procter to Brenton, 13 July 1813, *MPHC* 15: 338.

35. Procter to Sheaffe, 28 Nov. 1812, NAUS, *MIC*, 22-26. Procter subsequently considered himself "misled" by the scout's report. Norton, *Journal*, 314. Some early American histories have judged Procter's actions with balance: "There is no doubt that General Procter intended to keep his promises but the wounded men were left on the ground without sufficient guard.... Procter did protect those who could walk." N.S. Shaler, *Kentucky*, 162-63.

36. Coffin, *The War and Its Moral*, 206; Medard Labadie to Harrison, Feb. 26, *MLWHH* 2: 360-62.

37. Atherton, *Narrative*, 75; Byfield, *Account*, 18; Procter Papers, Note to file, nd., NAUS, *MIC*, 143.

38. Atherton, *Narrative*, 57; Byfield, *Account*, 18.

39. Atherton, *Narrative*, 113; Darnell, *Journal*, 67-76; Clift, *Remember the Raisin!*, 94-95; Procter to Sheaffe, 25 Jan. 1813, NAC, C 678: 46. The prisoners marched off on the 284-mile march, running to keep from freezing. Irregularly fed, they foraged for apple peels and frozen potatoes. Darnell, *Journal*, 71-76.

40. John Richardson to John Askin, 4 Feb. 1813, cited in Richardson, *War of 1812*, 303.

41. Henry Procter, Sr., *Bender CM*, 130; Byfield, *Account*, 13; Procter to Sheaffe, 1 Feb. 1813, *MPHC* 15: 235-36.

42. Richardson, *War of 1812*, 140; Walker, *Journal*, 6; Atherton, *Narrative*, 125.

43. Harrison to Meigs, 24 Jan. 1813 and Harrison to Monroe, 24 Jan. 1813, *MLWHH* 2: 329-35; *NOW* 1: 166n. John Armstrong (1758-1843) was born in Pennsylvania. He served in the Revolutionary War as a staff office and became a U.S. Senator (1800-1804) before becoming Minister to France (1804-11). Appointed brigadier general in 1812, he commanded the defences of New York City, before being selected as secretary. Although his direct manner made him unpopular with the politicos of the Madison administration, he was competent in military science. After an assessment of Harrison's ponderous operations, he directed the latter to remain on the defensive until naval control of Lake Erie was assured. Armstrong had to resign in September 1814 after the capture of Washington. His two-volume work, *Notices of the War*, while self-serving, provides a good overview of American strategy and operations. *WAMB*, 12.

44. Darnell, *Journal*, 57-60; Statements of Maj. Madison, Lt. Col. Lewis and Capt. Garrard, nd., cited in *NOW* 1: 204-05.

45. James Knaggs, Memoir, *MPHC* 17: 222; Affidavit of John Dawson, 13 Apr. 1813, U.S. Congress, *Barbarities*, 146-47. The account of Robert Reynolds of the Fort Amherstburg commissariat is very confused. Reynolds maintained that as he was hauling off the wounded, Harrison (who was then on his return to the Maumee Rapids) pursued them to Brownstown. Reynolds offers no explanation of his hauling away 23 British corpses on the 22nd, while leaving the dozens of American wounded soldiers at Frenchtown. As brother to Maj. Ebenezer Reynolds, he undoubtedly knew why British officials abandoned the village by the morning of the 23rd, but his account is silent on that point. Being 83 years of age when he narrated his reminiscences, Reynolds may be excused for his fuzzy memory. Byfield, *Account*, 16; Reynolds narrative in Coffin, *The War and Its Moral*, 206.

46. Darnell, *Journal*, 59-63; Alexis Labadie deposition, 6 Feb. 1813, *Barabarities*, 131; Atherton, *Narrative*, 58-74. Months later the number of destroyed Frenchtown homes grew from two to four. Petition of John Anderson, George McDougall, and G. Godfroy to Governor Cass, 19 Oct. 1813, *MLWHH* 2: 587.

47. Bower to Jesse Bledsoe, 24 Apr. 1813, Knapp, *Maumee*, 150-51.

48. Todd to Jesse Bledsoe, 2 May 1813, U.S. Congress, *Barbarities*, 141-43.

49. U.S. Congress, *Barbarities*, 142-45.

50. Speech of Blackbird to Claus, 15 July, 1813, cited in Cruikshank, "Harrison and Procter: the River Raisin," 141; Strachan to Thomas Jefferson, 30 Jan. 1815, cited in Coffin, *The War and Its Moral*, 283; Procter Papers, Note to file, nd., NAUS, *MIC*, 143-44.

51. Woodward to Procter, 2 Feb. 1813, *MPHC* 36: 291; *The War*, 6 Apr. 1813. While deplorable, the murder of prisoners was not a uniquely Native custom and certainly not confined to this period. Post-combat stress disorder has been documented since ancient Greek times.

52. Harrison to Monroe, 26 Jan. 1813, *MLWHH* 2: 337; Woodward to Monroe, 22 Mar. 1813, *TPUS* 10: 435.

53. Acting Secretary of War Alexander J. Dallas, *An Exposition of the Causes and Character of the War* (pamphlet), 59; Mallory, *Narrative*, 89; Procter to Sheaffe, 1 Feb. 1813, NAC, C 678: 61. The *Chillicothe Journal* of the day stated, "Those who surrendered on the field were taken prisoner, those who attempted escape were tomahawked." Modern American works are circumspect in their assessment of the episode. One states: "They murdered a few of the prisoners and on the morning of 23 January 1813, a few others were killed. Some of those who were not murdered were taken to Fort Malden, but most were forced to travel to distant Indian villages." *Chilicothe Journal*, 25 Feb. 1813, cited in Edgar, *Ten Years*, 173; Gilpin, *The War of 1812 in the Northwest*, 170.

54. Norton, *Journal*, 315; Procter to Sheaffe, 25 Jan. 1812, NAC, C 678: 46.

55. Procter's to Sheaffe, 25 Jan. 1812, NAC, C 678: 46; John Askin to William Powell, 25 Jan. 1813, *DHCNF* 1813, Vol. 1: 49; Procter to Sheaffe, 8 Apr. 1813, NAUS, *MIC*, 73-74; Norton, *Journal*, 315.

56. *NOW* 1: 85-95; Eleazar Wood diary, cited in McAfee, *Late War*, 234.

57. Harrison to Monroe, 26 Jan. 1813, 338; Harrison to Armstrong, 11 Feb. 1813, 357; Harrison to Meigs, 24 Jan. 1813, *MLWHH* 2: 338, 357, 329-30; Acts of Ohio and Kentucky Legislatures, *The War*, 16, 23 Feb. 1813.

58. Shelby to Harrison, nd., cited in Au, *War on the Raisin*, 58.

59. Hammack, *Kentucky*, 38, 54, 59, 111. *The War*, 16 Feb. 1813, declared Winchester's defeat a "great national disaster." Indeed, it ranks with St. Clair's defeat and the battle of the Little Big Horn as the worst calamity to befall an American army. By ironic coincidence, George Custer was a native of Monroe, Michigan, previously known as Frenchtown.

60. [Procter and Procter], *Lucubrations*, 335.

61. Wellington to Bathurst, 10 Feb. 1813, cited in John K. Mahon, "British Command Decisions," 224.

III

THE TIDE TURNS

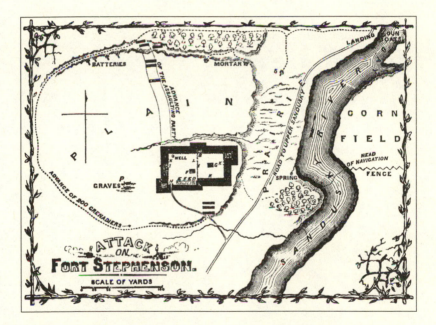

ATTACK ON FORT STEPHENSON.

SCALE OF YARDS

9

AFTER FRENCHTOWN

"The operations of the British commander are marked with the same minute correctness of judgment in this instance and the same boldness of conception and execution which distinguished, in the former instance, his illustrious predecessor, General Brock. It is a military movement of equal, and in fact greater splendor. His allies, however, will plant a thorn in his heart."[1]

Woodward to the secretary of war, 31 January 1813

TO FULLY UNDERSTAND the series of events that followed the battle of Frenchtown, one must go back some weeks before the engagement. Territorial Secretary Woodward had received no response from Washington regarding his concerns about working with the British occupiers. As a result, in early January, he resolved to go to Washington to discuss the matter with federal officials. The Detroit residents, however, urged him stay on to protect their interests. Thus, Woodward remained at Detroit during the actions on the Raisin River.[2]

Returning to Detroit after the battle of Frenchtown, Procter learned from Muir of a new threat, this one to his rear. "The advance of Winchester's army gave opportunity to a part of the inhabitants of the Michigan Territory to display their hostile intentions toward our government," he wrote. "A number of them were prepared, I have reason to believe, in the event of my having failed in my attack on the enemy to rise and possess themselves of Ft. Detroit, in which, at the time, I could afford a garrison of militia only." Apprehensive of

Harrison's advance against his weakened command, the British commander became greatly alarmed of this reported subversive activity.[3]

Procter was further upset with the lack of co-operation he received in identifying the culprits. Some residents produced at least two affidavits concerning an alleged plot; however, these were so vague in substantive specifics as to be virtually useless. The most meaningful statement concerned a man named Sopher, who was said to have declared, "We can scare the Devil out of them [Muir's weak garrison at Fort Detroit]!" Woodward conceded, "The absence of nearly the whole garrison from the fortress of Detroit would naturally lead to expressions from incautious men, which, however innocent in themselves, when borne by the officious tale bearer, and magnified by the malignant heart, might involve the community in destruction." He acknowledged that events suddenly soured relations with the occupiers as they "served to shake the confidence of the British officers in our inhabitants."[4]

An angry Procter threatened to deport some 29 of the "conspirators," along with those residents born under the American flag who refused to take the oath of allegiance. While he stewed, Woodward wrote an account of Winchester's defeat to the secretary of state, knowing Procter would censor it. He itemized Winchester's errors and concluded, "The superiority of generalship beyond all doubt belongs to the British commanders."[5]

Then on 1 February 1813, some residents of Detroit, under the aegis of Woodward, presented Governor Procter with a set of resolutions relating to the contemplated deportation. They termed his intention a "flagrant and gross violation" of the capitulation which guaranteed protection to persons and private property. Their resolutions urged that any guilty parties should be dealt with individually without a mass expulsion. Although the legalistic and demanding tone pointed to Woodward's collusion, if not authorship, his name did not appear among the signatures. The demands from the Detroit citizens delivered by the territorial secretary came at a most inopportune time.[6]

Nonetheless, Woodward approached Procter with the complicated mess, armed with his vast array of jurisprudential precedents relating to the administration of conquered territories, posing as a passive moderator in the proceedings. Furthermore, Woodward raised the subject of recent events at Frenchtown to press his claims. He certainly overstepped the bounds of discretion by accusing Procter of personal responsibility for the atrocities of the 23rd. His allegations included the tomahawking, shooting, scalping, and burning of wounded prisoners at Frenchtown, as well as the destruction of private homes. Woodward concluded by proposing conditions to ensure the future protection of citizens. His terms included a sizable increase to the Detroit garrison, the arming of Michigan citizens, the provision of 18 American hostages, the designation of six American commissioners to investigate treacherous activity, and exclusion of the Natives from Detroit.[7]

On hearing Woodward's accusations and demands, Procter's patience broke. Indignant that a conquered people were dictating terms to him, he became further incensed at their boldness in accusing him of personal responsibility for atrocities. In his mind, the judge had compromised his position as territorial secretary. Relations between the two men deteriorated rapidly. Procter singled out Woodward's role as "artful, designing and ambitious. Of the impropriety of this man's conduct, I certainly cannot entertain a doubt. In such a man, I could not place confidence." As word of Woodward's actions spread, relations with the British military establishment further cooled. Woodward wrote, "From the period of the Raisin River a reciprocal distrust and aversion was growing between the British officers and our inhabitants." Any pretense at a benevolent occupation was ended.[8]

As a frontier society, the Detroit region had its share of indiscreet braggarts and would-be heroes. While the hostile intentions and actions of the Frenchtown residents were clearly established through captured letters, it is probable that the alleged plot at Detroit was confined to a few men and constituted little more than jug-passing, tavern bravado. Nonetheless, given his precarious hold on the frontier, Procter could not afford to dismiss the reported conspiracy. His exasperation was complete on concluding that his territorial secretary could no longer be trusted in his public duties. Although Procter documented the episode, Sheaffe misplaced the package and the legal process ended there.[9]

It was during this awkward time that an emissary from Harrison was brought before an extremely ill-tempered Procter. A week after the battle of the 22nd, Harrison sent Dr. Samuel McKeehan, a surgeon of the 2nd Ohio Regiment, to Amherstburg with two *Canadien* guides, furnished with a letter for Procter and $100 in gold. His mission was to determine the fate of Winchester's army, assist the wounded, return with Winchester's dispatches, and report on his "proceedings" in the British camp.

McKeehan set off on in a carriole sleigh under a flag of truce and spent the first night in a deserted cabin near the Maumee Rapids. About midnight, hostile warriors killed one guide, wounded McKeehan in the foot, and relieved the doctor of his valuables. His captors marched the would-be emissary to Capt. William Elliott at Frenchtown, who conveyed him to Fort Amherstburg. The unfortunate McKeehan then found himself before a less than jovial Procter, who summarily accused the good doctor of being a spy. Procter "swore, by God, that the flag and papers were only a pretext to cover some dishonourable service." Being short of medical staff, Procter directed McKeehan to tend the American wounded. Then on 2 March, he arrested the American for carrying on some "private correspondence." Procter sent him to Montreal, to be chucked unceremoniously into a damp dungeon, ten feet underground, for more than a month. Finally, in early May, McKeehan was released and told to get about his business. Thus Procter concealed his weakness from his enemy until he was reinforced. For the sake of form, he eventually sent Dr. Bower to Harrison in place of McKeehan, writing to Sheaffe, "I shall keep the gentleman and send some person to him." [10]

Returning to the Woodward saga, Procter concluded that the petition by the residents was an attempt to divert attention from the matter of their fifth column conspiracy. On 4 February, fearing a general insurrection, he suspended civil liberties, placing Michigan Territory under martial law. After more stormy, deadlocked discussions, Woodward retaliated by asking for his passport. By this time, Procter had learned that Harrison could not follow up Winchester's vanguard movement, and the colonel's rage seems to have abated. Through his aide, Lt. MacLean of the 41st, he asked Woodward for evidence to substantiate the allegations of a massacre on the 23rd. This development put Woodward back on the attack. He produced a number of sworn statements from the Frenchtown residents and again requested his passport. [11]

On seeing the affidavits, Procter, mistrustful as ever, conducted his own investigation. His findings, detailed in an undated draft document in his handwriting that was captured among his effects on 5 October 1813, constitute the only detailed British account of the murders of 23 January. Procter noted that the Frenchtown residents gave the warriors rum to make them "drunk ... an easy slaughter on the arrival of Harrison." The interpreters said they left the village "either from fear of the Natives, as they say, or perhaps they had got more or less drunk likewise" and feared capture. As sleighs were unavailable, the warriors undertook to move the injured Americans themselves. Two mortally wounded prisoners who could not be moved were killed, as were two more who could not keep up with the march. One American engaged in an argument with a warrior who killed him. Another warrior killed a *Canadien* resident during a dispute over a pig. No prisoners were burned in the houses on the 23rd although the Americans burned some structures in the action of the previous day. A wounded *Canadien*, Pascal Rheume, had crept into one home and died of his injuries. His remains were identified there after that house was set on fire. Procter acknowledged that homes were torched on the 23rd "lest they should become a covert for the enemy," but only after the Natives had removed the prisoners. He attributed the exaggerated versions of a massacre to "two exhausted, panic-stricken, female fugitives" who fled to Detroit, whose "imagination was more vivid than their judgment was correct." [12]

In his draft report, Procter admitted five prisoners were murdered, insisting that even these had not been dispatched from motives of "cruelty or revenge," as there were "very few [warriors] slain." He noted, "The Indians when any of their chiefs or principal men are killed, from some religious or superstitious observance, deliver a prisoner to the family of the deceased, who, if they choose to put him to death as a gratification to the shade of him that fell." Allowing "no ground or foundation" to the story of a general massacre, Procter concluded with, "But what a strange tale!" Although he downplayed the extent of the atrocities, he acknowledged, "Both our civil and military officers ... were much shocked that such an event should have happened." [13]

By 15 February, Woodward and Procter were no longer on speaking terms, their pride having been injured in the mutual recriminations. The next day, Lt. MacLean called Woodward to Sandwich to discuss the Frenchtown affair, noting that Matthew Elliott had summoned several other witnesses to be present. Woodward did not attend, and in further defiance of Procter's authority wrote to James Baby that he received MacLean's invitation too late to be able to comply. He added that at the last meeting, Procter had demonstrated "an intemperance of demeanor unbecoming an officer of rank as it is indecorous in the character of a gentleman." He announced that he would not wait on Procter until the latter refrained from such offensive conduct. [14]

That same day, MacLean sent Woodward another letter, politely requesting his attendance at Procter's office at 10 AM on the 19th.

This etching depicts the popularized American view of the massacre at Frenchtown, 23 January 1813. Drunken Natives are shown murdering, scalping indiscriminately and setting fire to Frenchtown homes. Procter's army is incorrectly shown encamped in the background, looking on.

Although Woodward complied, this meeting achieved nothing beyond more "animated discussions." Procter issued Woodward his passport, glad to be rid of the troublesome and eccentric judge who had shifted the order of business from treachery to massacre to indecorous behaviour. On 24 February, Woodward presented his "best compliments and sincere wishes for the personal happiness of General Procter and family," and departed for Fort George. The episode ended with Procter suspending his threatened mass deportation, although he sent off the worst offenders from Detroit, "that depot of treachery." [15]

But tales of a horrific massacre did not subside. Survivors spread the story of a slaughter consequent to Procter's failure to send the promised sleighs for the wounded on the 23rd. "The most horrid scenes of cruelty imaginable" were said to have occurred, and Procter's "sacred promise was sacrificed on the altar of savage barbarity to the god of murder and cruelty." Since some of the Americans remained in Indian hands, the extent of the massacre became difficult to establish. The very fact that at least a dozen Kentuckians survived to provide first-hand descriptions of the atrocities indicates that the massacre was not general. Nonetheless, a wide discrepancy separated the five admitted as murdered in Procter's report and the dozens estimated in American accounts.[16]

In order to determine the exact number of murdered prisoners, Procter directed Ensign Isaac Baker, an American surgeon, to prepare a detailed return. Baker's report, while imprecise, was the most detailed of any. He listed 22 men murdered, only seven of whose names were known. He later identified four additional officers and "a number of privates." Baker's numbers grew with the telling. Once he was safely on American soil, he doubled the number of massacred soldiers to 60, adding that "massacres were not only committed on the 22nd and 23rd, but also on the 24th, 25th and 26th, and even three weeks afterwards." He acknowledged the kindness of a dozen Detroit residents, particularly Judge Woodward, in purchasing captives from the Natives and providing the destitute men with clothing. Procter ordered that the practice of buying captives for upwards of $80 dollars be stopped, as it had the effect of inflating prices, making it more difficult for the cash-strapped officials to recover prisoners. Isaac Baker acknowledged British efforts in rescuing Americans from Native captivity, naming James Baby, Matthew Elliott, and Adam Muir as the agents, adding that some three dozen Americans remained in Native hands. Although Winchester was undoubtedly aware of the massacre allegations, he made no mention of it. On the contrary, he expressed to Procter "a high sense of gratitude for the polite attention shown to myself, as well as for the humanity and kindness, with which you [Procter] have caused the prisoners to be treated."[17]

Independent British observers viewed the sordid massacre stories as magnified. Capt. William Merritt, an Upper Canadian dragoon officer, arrived at Amherstburg with dispatches some days after the events. He acknowledged the incidence of "deliberate murder" at Frenchtown but declared, "The circumstance has been much exaggerated." John Norton considered the stories manufactured for diversionary purposes: "Some of the Americans accused of having been concerned in the conspiracy fabricated many stories of cruelties exercised by the Indians on the prisoners taken at Frenchtown." Wartime propaganda was common, and the massacre story served not only to distract attention from yet another defeat for the War Hawks but to animate those who were becoming war weary. One monstrous fabrication had warriors hurling five hundred Americans to their deaths over Niagara Falls after the battle of Queenston Heights. The magnified stories had their effect.

According to Governor Isaac Shelby of Kentucky, "Our enemy can never be taught the rules of civilized warfare but by retaliation."[18]

Although the entire Raisin River affair is best remembered for its horrors, many of the Americans received humane treatment from their Native captors. Isaac Baker had been protected on the 23rd by an Ottawa chief named Watusson, a descendent of the famous war chief, Pontiac. Watusson treated Baker kindly, delivering him safely to Detroit where he sold his captive to a resident for $200. After the American reoccupation of Detroit, Baker again encountered Watusson and the two met "like brothers." Another rarely mentioned episode concerned Brandy Jack, the Wyandot captor of Winchester on the 22nd, who was also present at the events at Frenchtown the following day. On perceiving that houses containing wounded men were engulfed in flames, "Brandy Jack forced in the doors and caught hold of John Green [an American prisoner] and draged [*sic*] him from the house, took him to a Frenchman's house and the next day, hired a horse and train, as sleighs were called by the French, and took Green to Detroit."[19]

Although Tecumseh deplored maltreatment of captives, many tribesmen clung to ancient traditions that condoned cruelty to prisoners, fully prepared to endure such treatment themselves:

The prisoner has victuals ... and while he is at his repast, a consultation is held and if it be resolved to save his life, two young men untie him and taking him by the hands, lead him to the person into whose family he is to be adopted and there he is received with all imaginable marks of kindness. He is treated as a friend, as a brother, as a husband.... But if his sentence is death, how different their conduct! The dreadful sentence is no sooner passed than the whole village set [*sic*] up the death cry ... while they make the necessary preparations for rioting in the most diabolical cruelty. They first strip him and fixing two posts in the ground [they tie him to the stakes by the limbs]. In this posture, they burn him all over the body, sometimes first daubing him with pitch. The whole village, men women and children assemble round him, every one torturing him in what manner they please, each trying to outdo the other in cruelty as long as he has life.... The remainder of the day and the night following is spent in rejoicing.... Sometimes they fasten them to a single stake and build a fire around them. At other times, they cruelly mangle their limbs, cut off their fingers and toes, joint by joint and ... scald him to death.[20]

American first-hand accounts reflect the mixed treatment prisoners received. William Atherton described his Native captors as "brave, generous, hospitable, kind and honest," but he did not think much of their harsh lifestyle. Another captive, Joseph Fandrée, was taken north to a village near Lake Huron. A prisoner there for four years, he told of four or five others still in captivity. Elias Darnell was adopted into the family of a dead warrior. Although offered a choice of wives, Darnell declined the prospect and escaped to join his captive comrades at Amherstburg.[21]

Another prisoner, Timothy Mallary, attested to the good treatment he received. He was adopted into a Potawatomi family at River Rouge as a replacement for a warrior who had been killed in the action of the 22nd. In the course of his adoption, he was dressed, shaved, and otherwise prepared as a warrior. The squaws took special care to conceal him during drunken orgies as the warriors, in their excited state, would have killed him and his companions, Maj. Graves and two other men. John Davenport who was likewise converted in physical appearance to resemble his "copper-colored brethren," reported favourably on his treatment. Like Darnell, he was presented with several squaws as candidates for "conjugal felicity" before he escaped to Amherstburg. Younger captives, such as 21-year-old Atherton, generally fared well, some opting to remain with their new families as a matter of choice. Older prisoners showed a persistent desire to return to their accustomed lifestyles, and some were killed during senseless political arguments.[22]

Procter's recent experiences with legal matters in both civil and military capacities prompted him to renew his demands for an officer of the Adjutant General's Department. "I am often oppressed with [legal] business, and at times rather embarrassed," he wrote. Frustrated in his dealings with Woodward, he complained, "I have been and still am with a numerous force to oppose in my front, avowed disaffection in my rear, and with a very inadequate force, in a ceded country, invaded. I am to be straitened and shackled in my efforts to rid the country entrusted to my care of treacherous and dangerous characters by the forms of civil courts which [I] conceive to be suitable only to countries in safety and where loyalty predominates." In desperation, he considered arming the *Canadiens* of the Michigan Territory. Procter abandoned the idea of expelling those Americans who refused to take the oath of allegiance, proposing to administer oaths of neutrality instead. He pressed his demand for the 41st to assure the security of the district, writing, "We shall do our duty, but that will not save the country."

Replacements for his recent casualties consisted only of the light company of the 41st and a few artillerymen. At their departure from Fort
George on 2 February, Capt. Chambers observed, "There was not an
individual of it, but was in a state of perfect sobriety," apparently a
compliment.[23]

Meanwhile, Woodward trekked to New York to undertake his campaign of revenge against the British military dictatorship of Michigan.
From the safety of American soil, he wrote to Acting Secretary of State
James Monroe, reviewing his role in the administration of Michigan
Territory under British rule. Free to write without the fear of British
censorship, Woodward repeated his previous assessment that Winchester's advance had been as "erroneous and indiscreet in substance as
it was weak and defective in its execution," while "the operations of
General Procter were distinguished by the same boldness of conception, the same nicety of judgment, the same vigour of execution which
characterized his immediate and far-famed predecessor, General Brock."
Anxious to divert attention from his dealings with the occupiers,
Woodward denounced the British occupation. His principal complaints
related to the attrocities of the 23rd of January and Procter's threatened
expulsion of the Detroit residents.[24]

The U.S. press welcomed Woodward's arrival with firsthand news
from the conquered territory. The documents he gathered for the
Frenchtown massacre investigation appeared on the front pages of
major newspapers. This publicity prompted the American government
to examine the allegations as a matter of national and political interest.
Consequently, in May 1813, the first order of business of the Thirteenth United States Congress was a resolution calling for a committee
to investigate British barbarities. Of the nine categories of alleged outrages, the Detroit frontier qualified for three: violations of flags of truce
(McKeehan), ransom of American prisoners, and massacre and burning
of American prisoners.[25]

Although the report included alleged atrocities on the Atlantic
seaboard, the most shocking findings related to the "massacre at
Frenchtown." These events were graphically described in dozens of
affidavits by eyewitnesses and secondhand reports, occupying no less
than 30 pages or one sixth of the document. It was published in serial
form by leading newspapers and also in book form, receiving wide circulation. The Madison administration used it to stifle partisan strife,
distract attention from incompetent management, and gain emotional
support for a war that was hardly popular. Some American newspapers

acknowledged the accusations as "vaguely proved," and the *Federal Republican* noted that the atrocities were the same as those observed towards the Natives "by the Christian soldiers of Mr. Madison." Nonetheless, the War Hawks turned the slogan, "Remember the Raisin!" into a war cry.[26]

Native atrocities, a sensitive point with both Prevost and London, also made for great political hay in embarrassing the British alliance. American political leaders used this issue to depict British leadership as barbaric and unprincipled in allying with "savagery." The preamble in "Barbarities of the Enemy" argued this point as follows: "The massacre of the 23rd January, after the capitulation, was perpetrated without any exertion on their part to prevent it; indeed, it is apparent from all the circumstances, that if the British officers did not connive at their destruction, they were criminally indifferent about the fate of the wounded prisoners. But what marks more strongly the degradation of the British soldiers, is the refusal of the last offices of humanity to the bodies of the dead." Capitalizing on the propaganda value of the matter, President Madison declared to his countrymen:

They [the British] have not, it is true, taken into their own hands the hatchet and the knife, devoted to indiscriminate massacre; but they have let loose the savages armed with these cruel instruments; have allured them into their service and carried them into battle by their sides, eager to glut their savage thirst with the blood of the vanquished, and to finish the work of torture and death on maimed and defenceless captives and what had never been seen before, British commanders have exorted victory over the unconquerable valour of our troops by presenting to the sympathy of their chief awaiting massacre from their savage allies.[27]

Thus began the demonizing of Procter as the bloodthirsty agent of "fiend-like depravity," even though his personal involvement or approval remained totally unsubstantiated. An American officer who met Procter briefly after the capture of Detroit would describe him several decades later as "the meanest looking man I ever saw. He had the counteneance in which that of the murderer and cowardly assassin predominated; nor did he belie his appearance."[28]

John Strachan, that fierce loyalist Rector of York, examined "Barbarities of the Enemy" and responded with a spirited denunciation to Thomas Jefferson, rejecting all nine points of accusation as transparent hypocrisy. On the subject of Native cruelties, he pointed out that the tribesmen had been defending their lands, the first scalp of the war was taken by the Americans on the Canards River, the overwhelming number of prisoners returned home safely, some British soldiers at Frenchtown had been killed by the warriors while protecting prisoners, and that Kentuckians also used tomahawks and scalping knives, "burning warriors alive as a pastime."[29]

While this war of words escalated, Procter received some good news. In March, Brevet Lt. Col. Augustus Warburton arrived to replace the incapacitated St. George (who convalesced at Amherstburg till July when he was sent to England for medical attention). Although unfamiliar with Upper Canada and not of the 41st, Warburton relieved Procter of some of his staff duties. Sheaffe pronounced Procter's victory "brilliant," while Prevost issued a general order highly complimentary to the Right Division. Furthermore, Capt. McDouall of Prevost's staff informed Procter that the remainder of the 41st would be sent to him as soon as Lake Erie became navigable. These would enable Procter to adopt a "formidable attitude" by which to give "a good accounting of the bragadoccio Harrison." In addition, Dickson would have chief command of all the Indians, "subject only to your [Procter's] orders."[30]

Moreover, Prevost appointed Procter and John Vincent (commander of the Centre Division) brigadier generals, an administrative rank subject to formal promotion to major general by the Prince Regent. On 9 February, Prevost wrote Procter, complimenting his adroit leadership and promising to present his "singular judgment and decisive conduct" before the British monarch. Other accolades followed. Procter and his command received the unanimous vote of thanks of the Upper Canada House of Assembly as well as that of Lower Canada. The guns of Quebec boomed out salutes in honour of his victory. Procter's name appeared in English newspapers, while private interests prepared a caricature of Winchester's capture, dedicating it to President Madison. Procter was a hero.[31]

The battle of Frenchtown also had a tremendous uplifting impact on the Native allies. Robert Dickson, the most influential non-Native among the western nations, passed through Detroit and commented, "I have to observe that since the battle of the 22nd ultimato that the Indians are flocking in and they all entertain the highest confidence in Colonel Procter and His Majesty's troops." Although Procter recognized that his victory was largely attributable to the warriors, his confidence in their support remained qualified, "The Indian force is a strong aid when there is a probability of success but any reverse would

General Winchester at Frenchtown. This caricature from the *Morning Chronicle* of London shows Roundhead, attired in Winchester's regimentals, presenting a painted Brig. Gen. Winchester to an embarrassed Procter. It was "dedicated to Mr. President MAD I SON."

quickly disperse it. Our militia force depends also on success, in a great measure. I have had some little experience of both."[32]

At Quebec City, Prevost issued a general order that could only serve to undermine Procter's efforts at bolstering Native confidence: "His Excellency disapproves of any co-operation with the Indians not connected with the system of defence of the province." With scant regard for Procter's circumstance and the official commitment to a Native homeland, Prevost allowed this directive to be published in the *Quebec Gazette.* The tribesmen would certainly have learned of his pronouncement through American subversives or from sympathetic officials like Elliott. Thus, while Procter was struggling to demonstrate British fidelity in the Native interest, Prevost virtually disavowed the objective of a Native homeland as a matter of public record.[33]

In Ohio, Winchester's defeat revived widespread alarm among residents who had returned to their settlements. Hysterical fugitives from the Raisin River arrived at the hamlet of Lower Sandusky. These refugees generated such panic among the local settlers that they hastily gathered their valuables and set off in a convoy of sleighs and carts for Cleveland and Upper Sandusky, arriving there "half-naked and destitute."[34]

Anxious to neutralize the moral effects of his late reverse, Harrison still hoped to deliver a blow against the enemy before the ice melted. When he received word on 8 February that two hundred braves were rounding up cattle at the mouth of the Maumee River, he almost repeated Winchester's blunder. With 1100 men and a 6-pdr. gun, he marched towards Presque Isle in two detachments, arriving there before dark. At the deserted settlement, Harrison learned that the Natives had fled to British territory. With his force united, the American commander resolved to advance to the Raisin River. Warm temperatures hampered this movement as horses and cannon broke through the lake ice. Halting, Harrison sent spies to Frenchtown to gather intelligence; they returned next day with a *Canadien*, who reported that the warriors had withdrawn from the village.[35]

Frustrated in his design, Harrison fell back on the Maumee Rapids, postponing offensive plans since the terms of service for many of the Ohio and Kentucky volunteers expired on 23 February, as did the enlistments from Virginia and Pennsylvania. By 30 March, the Northwest Army had dwindled to fewer than two thousand soldiers. While Harrison prepared to embark on a fresh recruiting drive, one of his subordinates, Col. Duncan McArthur (not notable for his loyalty to Hull), complained to the secretary of war about the lack of progress in prosecuting the war in the Northwest.[36]

Before leaving to visit his family and recruit his army, Harrison made one final attempt to strike at his enemy. His plan, a bold one, was to send an élite strike force of hand-picked men to blow up the ice-bound *Queen Charlotte* at Amherstburg. To command this secret mission, he selected Capt. Angus Langham of the 19th U.S. Infantry. With the incendiary materials prepared, Harrison paraded and addressed the detachment of 68 regulars, 120 Pennsylvania and Virginia militiamen, and 24 friendly tribesmen. They were to travel across Lake Erie in 30 sleds, accompanied by some local guides. The expedition set off for the lake by way of Lower Sandusky but encountered discipline problems almost immediately when the Natives consumed more than their normal allowance of rum ration. Drunk and ill tempered, they struck a Black servant in the head with their tomahawks, severely wounding him.[37]

On the morning of 2 March, Langham disclosed the secret details of his mission to the men. Upon learning the objective, 20 soldiers fell out, along with half a dozen warriors. Undeterred, Langham resumed the unlucky march. Near Sandusky Bay, one of the sleds broke through the ice. His men also captured a prowling Native, who was nearly executed before being identified as a member of the expedition. Then, the general alarm was sounded in response to the report of a column bearing down from the north. The men flew to arms, only to learn that the sighting was merely a mirage created by the sun's reflection on the ice. That evening, they bivouacked on a small island. Shortly after they turned in, one of the guards accidentally discharged his musket, creating renewed alarm. Having fully briefed his command on the need for absolute security, Langham threatened to execute the guard but relented. Next day, the detachment advanced to South Bass Island but beyond there the ice was melted. Langham consulted his officers, guides, and men, the majority of whom favoured abandonment of the mission. Accordingly, they made for Presque Isle on 5 March where they met Harrison. Satisfied that the broken ice would prevent a British advance until the opening of the navigation season, the American commander left the construction of a fortification at the Maumee Rapids to Brig. Gen. Joel Leftwich, and departed southward on 7 March.[38]

On the Detroit River, Procter continued to struggle with his manpower shortages. In an effort to maximize the potential of the warriors, "a powerful but uncertain aid," he proposed to employ them as a mounted harassing and foraging corps that would act in concert with a fencible battalion of rangers raised from militiamen of the colony. He had first raised this issue with Sheaffe in November and documented his proposal in early January, writing, "The Indians in Council have formally requested the aid of such a Corps as were attached to and acted with them, during (as it was called) the Revolutionary War and that Capt. Caldwell whom they well know and think highly of, may be, I am convinced, of the highest utility both in restraining and directing the hostility of the Indians to the proper objects."[39]

William Caldwell, a veteran of Butler's Rangers, went to Montreal to argue for the formation of the unit, but Prevost squelched the plans as "more extensive than were ever contemplated." He discouraged Procter from pursuing the project by authorizing only one or two companies as an "experiment." Instead of the five hundred members that Procter anticipated, Sheaffe was limited to authorizing the embodiment of only 60 men, and even that company "to be reported upon." By extensive, Prevost meant that the plan was too expensive. Sixty rangers could not effectively control hundreds of warriors; therefore, the experiment could never prove itself. Procter's plan to raise members from all areas of Upper Canada was also undermined as the recruitment zone was limited to the Western District.[40]

Procter had hoped to solve a number of problems with a ranger battalion. As a mobile corps, the rangers could have acted in close concert with the tractable and mounted Wyandot who initially proposed the project. With a mobile force, Procter could have relieved pressure on the commissariat by having the braves feed off enemy territory. Since the rangers would have been paid as regulars, full-time volunteers would have manned its ranks and Procter could have avoided calling away the militiamen from their farms. Furthermore, with an allied mounted corps, Procter could circumvent his reliance on Elliott. Despite its merits, the imaginative scheme was aborted, and Procter remained stuck with too few regulars, an aged and ailing Elliott, a short-service militia, a makeshift marine establishment, and warriors of intermittent reliability.

Prevost's role at this time with regard to defence in the west was curious. He seems to have adopted part of Brock's strategy for the defence of the Canadas, writing to the minister of war, "My opinion of the propriety of defending with all the means at my disposal the frontiers of the Canadas led me to an opposite line of conduct to that pursued by my predecessor [Sir James Craig], whose sole object appears to have been directed to the concentration of his force at Quebec." He stated his intention "to preserve the superiority of the British naval force upon the lakes, so essential to the defence of Upper Canada." Furthermore, he accepted the official position that "whenever negotiations for peace may be entered into, the security of the Indian possessions may not be compromised or forgotten." Yet Prevost confided to Sheaffe the "offensive demonstrations for the recovery of their [the Natives'] territory" as nothing more than "a powerful diversion" to keep the Americans from attacking critical areas to the east.[41]

The land war remained centred in the west. Since the outbreak of hostilities, there had been two American armies in existence. The Northern Army had made a poor showing on the Niagara frontier. The second one, the Northwest Army (under Hull, Winchester, and Harrison) actually lost immense reaches of territory. With the continued American emphasis on the frontiers of Upper Canada and official endorsement of the Native homeland, Procter rightly expected a due share of resources.

In fact, reinforcements from England were en route. In March, Bathurst notified Prevost that nine full regiments were bound for the Canadas from Ireland, the West Indies, Malta, and Halifax. Sir James Yeo of the Royal Navy was also en route with 450 seamen to take charge of the Provincial Marine. Given this heartening news, Prevost released some of the troops for Upper Canada: half a company of artillerymen, the 8th Foot, six companies of the 104th Foot, and four companies of Canadian Voltigeurs. Prevost even directed Sheaffe (in a postscript) to "push on to Detroit the companies of the 41st Regt. [almost five hundred effectives] that you have detained on the Niagara Frontier." Oddly, Adjutant-General Baynes's directions for the redistribution of troops in Upper Canada of the same date related only to movements of the 1st, 8th, and 104th regiments, with no mention of the 41st transferring to Amherstburg. Although Sheaffe promised Procter "all of the 41st" would be forwarded "with all possible expedition," they stayed on the Niagara frontier.[42]

Despite his directions, the commander-in-chief was specific in his instructions to Sheaffe on the matter of troop deployments:

The fatal effects of dividing and dissipating a force have been so frequently illustrated of late that I am under little apprehension of your not feeling that it is by concentrated means alone adequate efforts can be produced. I am satisfied that the application of this principle may be safely left to your prudence and judgment aided by the perfect knowledge of the country which you possess. Convinced that it is impossible I can free you from any embarrassments which will inevitably arise from circumstances inseparable from the war we are carrying on, as they can neither be foreseen nor provided for, it only remains for me to assure you that I have every disposition for putting the most liberal construction on your measures for the promotion of the public service, in every difficulty that may occur, and for making on all occasions the most favourable report of them, founded on those principles to His Majesty's Government.[43]

The policy of the commander-in-chief was clear. Sheaffe was to hold the troops in the Niagara region and the governor would protect him from political embarrassments that might arise from reverses in the west. In place of Brock's flexible defence that called for elastic concentrations to strike at critical objectives, Prevost advocated static concentration to protect vital avenues from invasion. Thus, Procter would get the benefit neither of an entire regiment nor of temporary concentrated support. Prevost was certainly aware of Procter's desire to honour the official commitment of a Native state; however, he showed a marked reluctance to back up that commitment in material terms. In his customary evasive, obtuse vernacular, he wrote Procter, "I am extremely concerned to inform you that it is not possible for me to comply with your request at this moment to the extent you require, consistent with the system of defensive warfare which circumstances have compelled me to pursue and which I must persevere."[44]

Prevost's strategy for a "diversion" was limited to rousing the western warriors through Robert Dickson. In a clear attempt to circumvent Elliott's influence, he appointed Dickson deputy superintendent of Indian affairs "in the Michigan and conquered territory," without retiring Elliott, "entrusting the management of those distant tribes of Indians [west of Lake Michigan] to other hands than those that are presently employed in the Indian Department at Amherstburg." He also urged Sheaffe to vest sufficient authority in Procter regarding Indian goods that "His Majesty's bounty may flow through the channel in which it was intended." Contrary to Procter's assessments, Prevost reported to London that the movement of the "confederate nations from the Wabash to the River Raisin under Tecumseh" and "several warlike tribes with Mr. Dickson" would alone be formidable enough to deal with the Northwest Army. Having issued these pronouncements, the commander-in-chief once more exhorted Procter to "soften the ferocity" of the warriors.[45]

Prevost's role is even more difficult to fathom in his creative portrayal of events to the minister for war and colonies. "I have desired that Tecumseh ... should be employed in interrupting the communication with Major General Harrison's army," he wrote Lord Bathurst. "The Indian Chiefs Roundhead and Norton with about 800 warriors supported by a chosen band from the 41st Regiment co-operate with Tecumseh ... to render it [the American army] an easy prey for the Indian force coming from the southward under Mr. Dickson." In reality, Roundhead could not move the Natives forward without a sizable force of British regulars; Tecumseh was absent and uncertain; Norton spent only brief periods with the Right Division, being needed on the Niagara frontier; and Dickson would not appear at Amherstburg till the late summer. Prevost's credible-sounding assessment of the upcoming campaign was fanciful, to say the least.[46]

Procter's experiences prompted a less promising assessment. Fully aware of the dangers of excessive reliance on the tribesmen, he continued to press for regulars. The British commander received unexpected support in this regard from the principal inhabitants of the Western District, who presented Prevost with a comprehensive petition aimed at enlarging the size of local garrisons. The memorial reviewed the strategic value the straits of Detroit, warning of the growing enemy threat at the Maumee Rapids. It also noted that because of the militiamen's absence from their farms, very little wheat been sown, creating "great scarcity" in the ensuing season, and consequently, the men had to be left on their farms to grow spring crops of Indian corn and oats. Reminding Prevost of Brock's intention to station no less than 1600 British troops at Amherstburg, the residents argued that only a strong British garrison could rectify the problems enumerated. The signatories included the militia leaders, civic and religious heads, and principals of the Indian Department, along with the merchants of Sandwich, Amherstburg, New Settlement, and the Thames country. In short, it was a unanimous statement of concern from the residents on the glaring deficiencies in the defence of the Western District, one that fully supported Procter's views. Prevost responded with assurances.[47]

During this time, Procter restructured his division. After the battle of Frenchtown, he received both flank companies of the 41st (the Grenadiers and the Light Company) and a few artillerymen. The Grenadiers arrived through the intervention of Prevost's aide, Capt. Robert McDouall, who in March observed first hand the situation at Amherstburg and urged Brig. Gen. Vincent to alleviate Procter's shortages. Thus in April, Procter commanded 520 regulars (all ranks) and had recourse to about 450 militiamen who could be employed for brief periods. The braves numbered about 800.[48]

Inadequate as this force was, Procter had difficulty sustaining even that. The empty war chest meant that his concerns were the last to be considered. As a result of the general shortage of cash, his troops went unpaid. To compound matters, the shortage of merchandise and provisions at Amherstburg inflated prices to exorbitant levels. Procter grimly observed, "Circumstances have unfortunately placed the soldiers in the power of the shop or storekeepers here." The British commander also drew attention to the dissatisfaction of Indian Department officers with irregular payment of their wages. On their behalf, he sought permission for the local commissariat to approve payment, thereby avoiding the lengthy process of seeking authorizing signatures at York.[49]

Despite shortages, Procter had thus far managed to survive not only the enemy threat but the deprivations of a harsh winter, as well. The alliance remained intact. With the ice breaking up, he could look forward to being resupplied from the newly established depot at Long Point where quantities of flour and Irish pork awaited the opening of the navigation season. In addition, about half the Raisin River residents had returned to their farms, and the commissariat was again making purchases there.[50]

Although Procter was disappointed at the meager support apportioned his command, he had little choice but to continue to use his small mixed force to defeat his enemy piecemeal. He would have to strike aggressively before Harrison could bring overwhelming forces to bear on the Right Division. His task would be particularly difficult if someone did not soon take an active interest in naval affairs on Lake Erie. By 3 April 1813, Secretary of War Armstrong laid out the blueprint for American success in the Northwest, directing Harrison to suspend offensive operations because "our first object is to get command of the Lakes."[51]

On the British side of Lake Erie, naval affairs took a turn for the worse in March, when Capt. Andrew Gray, tabulating manning requirements for the Provincial Marine, identified the need for nine officers on Lake Ontario but none for Lake Erie. Ignoring Procter's insistence that naval men and officers were needed, he based his estimate on nothing more than "the favourable opinion I entertain of Capt. Hall [commander of the Lake Erie Squadron] as an officer." In a detailed breakdown of crews by vessel, Gray went on to state that only 170 men were needed for the four vessels on Lake Erie (including the new ship under construction, *Detroit*), while the Lake Ontario squadron of seven vessels would require 445 seamen. Then, by counting the existing crews of both squadrons, he identified the net additional requirement for seamen on both lakes as 465, leaving only 20 sailors for the Amherstburg station. In assessing the enemy threat on Lake Erie, Gray seemed to be ignorant of American preparations, asserting, "It is therefore uncertain what their means may be at the opening of navigation. There is no reason to suppose that they will be enabled to meet us on the lake, as from all information we have been able to procure, their efforts have been confined to small craft and gunboats."[52]

If British strategists were unaware of American naval developments on Lake Erie, the *Buffalo Gazette* of 30 March enlightened them with the following news: "Last week, Capt. Perry of the U. S. Navy arrived ... on his way to Erie, Pa. to superintend the completing and fitting out a naval force at that place. The Captain, we understand, will command the American force on Lake Erie the ensuing summer." If that wasn't enough for astute British spies, the 13 April issue provided further details: "A number of ship carpenters passed thro' this place for the navy yard at Erie. Last week several sailors also passed this village for the same place. Ship carpenters and sailors recently passed Pittsburgh destined for Erie."[53]

At this time, Erie (formerly known as Presque Isle) was a village of 47 houses, some 300 residents, and a tavern known as Duncan's Erie Hotel. Daniel Dobbins, joined by experienced shipwrights, undertook the construction of gunboats there during the winter. On 27 March, Master Commandant Oliver Hazard Perry (USN) arrived to take command, finding three gunboats on the stocks, and the keels of two 20-gun brigs laid down. Surprisingly, the high command in the Canadas expressed no concern over these developments. While Procter prepared to break up Harrison's preparations in Ohio, the menacing naval presence to his rear steadily grew.[54]

Procter went ahead with those marine preparations within his control. The keel of the new ship at Amherstburg was laid down in January 1813, while two decked gunboats took form at the Forks of the Thames. Capt. Peter Chambers, Procter's new quartermaster, inspected the work on the Thames and complained that the artificers sent by Col. Talbot, while well paid, proved to be a worthless lot, being "mere hewers of wood" who refused to work, preferring to create trouble among the other workmen. In his usual direct manner, Chambers threatened to use the "full force of the law" against them, and Procter had to divert labourers from work on *Detroit* to hasten the completion of the gunboats.[55]

Although the Frenchtown disaster greatly embarrassed Harrison, his frontier volunteers still held him in high regard. On behalf of the discharged Kentucky enlistments, the officers presented their commander with a statement of confidence: "We shall carry back to our friends and our country, a confirmation of their high opinions of your military worth, which were formed at first acquaintance. And should the circumstances again call us to the field, we should be highly gratified at being placed under your command." For his part, Harrison seemed to have second thoughts about relying on irregular troops, writing to Armstrong, "If I had 2,000 regular troops, after the defeat of General Winchester, instead of 4,000 militia, we should have been in possession of Malden and the fleet of the enemy. I greatly fear that the naval superiority on the Upper Lakes will not be obtained."[56]

In Ohio, McArthur and Cass (who were free to take up arms once more) responded to the dampened enthusiasm for the war with a renewed recruiting drive. Their rhetoric was quite different from that which had drawn the previous contingents as appeals for conquest and glory were displaced by those of survival and dignity: "Our government is engaged in no schemes of aggrandizement, no plans of ambition.... Are you prepared to have your midnight slumbers awakened by the Indian yell, and the conflagration of your own dwellings gleam upon the last act of savage barbarity? These evils can only be averted by a vigorous prosecution of the war."[57]

NOTES

1. Woodward to Acting Secretary of War Monroe, 31 Jan. 1813, *MPHC* 15: 234.
2. Detroit citizens to Woodward, 6 Jan. 1813, *MPHC* 8: 639.
3. Procter to Sheaffe, 4 Feb. 1813, NAC, C 678: 70; Procter to Maj. Ebenezer Reynolds, 11 Jan. 1813, NAUS, *MIC,* 37.
4. Statements of John Whipple and Nathaniel Goldwaite, 1 Feb. 1813; Woodward to Monroe, 22 Mar. 1813, *TPUS* 10: 435, 438-40.
5. Lt. William Jones to Henry Brevoort and William McComb, 1 Feb. 1813, George McDougall to Woodward, 2 Feb. 1813, *MPHC* 8: 639-40; Woodward to Monroe, 31 Jan. 1813, *MPHC* 15: 234.
6. Petition of Detroit residents to Procter, 1 Feb. 1813, *MPHC* 15: 241-43.
7. Woodward to Procter, 2 Feb. 1813, *MPHC* 36: 290-94.
8. Procter to Sheaffe, 4 Feb. 1813, NAC, C 678: 70; Woodward to Monroe, 22 Mar. 1813, *TPUS* 10: 436.
9. Sheaffe to Freer, 20 Mar. 1813, *MPHC* 15: 261.
10. Harrison to McKeehan, 31 Jan. 1813, *MLWHH* 2: 346; McKeehan narrative, 24 May 1813, *MLWHH* 2: 461-63; McKeehan to Dearborn, 4 June 1813, U.S. Congress, *Barbarities*, 68-71; McKeehan correspondence, *DPCUS* 1813-14, Vol. 2: 2202-04; Procter to Sheaffe, 2 Feb. 1813, NAC, C 678: 61.
11. Procter's Proclamation, 4 Feb. 1813, *TPUS* 10, 428; Woodward to Procter, 6 Feb. 1813, *MPHC* 36: 294; McLean to Woodward, 9 Feb. *MPHC* 36, 294; various documents on "Frenchtown Massacre," U.S. Congress, *Barbarities*, 123-32.
12. Procter Papers, Note to file, nd., NAUS, *MIC,* 141-48.
13. *Ibid.* 146-148; Darnell, *Journal,* 55. Although the truth relating to the "massacre" is frustratingly elusive, Peter Clarke's history of the Wyandot independently supports some of Procter's assertions. It affirms four American efforts at setting a barn on fire on the 22nd; the final one succeeded. It also confirms Procter's findings relating to Pascal Rheume's body. Clarke, *Wyandots,* 109-10.
14. Woodward to James Baby, 15 Feb. 1813, McLean to Woodward, 16 Feb. 1813, Woodward to Procter, 18 Feb. 1813, *MPHC* 36: 99, 297-98, 299.
15. Woodward to Monroe, 22 Mar. 1813, *TPUS* 10, 436; McLean to Woodward, 18 Feb. 1813, Woodward to McLean, 19 Feb. 1813, Procter to Woodward, 19 Feb. 1813, Woodward to Procter,

24 Feb. 1813, *MPHC* 36: 299-300; Procter to Sheaffe, 1 Feb. 1813, *MPHC* 15: 235.

16. Mallary, "Narrative," 81; Davenport, "Narrative," 91. Both these accounts are appended to Darnell's *Journal.*

17. Isaac Baker to Harrison, nd., and 25 Feb. *MLWHH* 2: 327, 371-75; Isaac Baker Narrative, John Russell, *History of the War*, 229-331; Procter to Sheaffe, 25 Jan. 1813, *SBD* 2: 8; Procter Papers, Note to file, nd., NAUS, *MIC,* 143; Baker to Winchester, 26 Feb. 1813, U.S. Congress, *Barbarities*, 133-36; Winchester to Procter, 29 Jan. 1813, *MPHC* 15: 230.

18. Merritt, *Journal, SBD* 3, Pt. 2: 567; Norton *Journal*, 314-15; Procter to Sheaffe, 1 Feb. 1813, NAC, C 678, 61; White, *American Troops*, 87; Shelby to Harrison, *MLWHH* 2: 399.

19. Hunt, *Memoirs*, 23, 28.

20. Henry Trumbull, *Indian Wars*, 109-10.

21. Darnell, *Journal*, 64; Monroe to Charles Bagot, 28 Jan. 1817, *MPHC* 16: 563.

22. Mallary, "Narrative," 87-88; Davenport, "Narrative," 96-99; Atherton, *Narrative*, 104. Some Native captives became surprisingly acclimatized to their new lifestyle. John Hunter, an American captive of the Osage nation, after hearing Tecumseh's oration on the need for concerted Native resistence to American encroachment, wrote, "There was nothing I then desired as that of being a warrior, and I even envied those who were to achieve those important objects, the fame and glory that would rebound as a necessary result." "Hunter's Memoirs," cited in Ferdinand Brock Tupper, *Family Records*, 195-99.

23. Procter to Baynes, 31 Jan. 1813 and Procter to Sheaffe, 1 Feb. 1813, *MPHC* 15: 232-33, 235-36; Procter to Sheaffe, 21 Feb. 1813, NAUS, *MIC,* 62; Ensign Smith to Robert Hillhouse, Feb. 2, 1813, *MPHC* 32: 547.

24. Woodward to Monroe, 22 Mar. 1813, *MPHC* 36: 303-09.

25. The introduction to *Barbarities* was presented to Congress on 13 July 1813 as "The Spirit And Manner In Which The War Is Waged By the Enemy," found in *DPCUS* 1813-14, Vol. 2: 2239-347. It was published in book form under the same title on 31 July 1813. For more potent effect, it was republished in 1814 as *Barbarities of the Enemy.*

26. Various letters regarding Woodward, Mar.-Apr. 1813, *MPHC* 36: 309-14; *Federal Republican*, nd., cited in Irving Brant, *James Madison*, 151-52.

27. U.S. Congress, *Barbarities*, 8-9; President Madison's address, 4 Mar. 1813, *Annual Register* or *A View of the History, Politics and Literature for the Year 1813*, 395.

28. Henry B. Brackenbridge, *History of the Late War*, 91; Hatch, *Chapter*, 116-17.

29. John Strachan to Thomas Jefferson, 30 Jan. 1813, Coffin, *The War and Its Moral*, 273-85.

30. General Orders, 8 Feb. 1813, 1 Mar. 1813, *DHCNF* 1813, Vol. 1: 60, 84; McDouall to Procter, 29 Mar. 1813, NAUS, *MIC*, 65.

31. Prevost to Procter, 9 Feb. 1813, *DHCNF* 1813, Vol. 1: 62; Sheaffe to Procter, 30 Jan. 1813, *SLB*, 335; Resolutions of the Upper and Lower Canada Houses of Assembly, 8 Feb. 1813, *MPHC* 32: 549; Procter to speakers of the Houses of Assembly, 17 Mar. 1813, 5 Apr. 1813, NAUS, *MIC*, 61, 64; caricature print by S. Knight, Sweetings Alley and Cornhill, London, 3 May 1813, NAC, C 123432. Augustus Warburton (1781-1837) was born in Ireland and commissioned in the 4th Foot. He gained a captaincy in the 60th Foot before being appointed brevet lieutenant-colonel and inspecting field officer of the Lower Canada militia in 1811. Arriving in Upper Canada the following year, he replaced the incapacitated St. George, but his primary function was to serve as Procter's second in command. Lomax, *The 41st*, 86.

32. Dickson to Prevost, 15 Feb. 1813, NAC, C 257: 52; Procter to Sheaffe, 2 Feb. 1813, NAC, C 678: 61. John Vincent (1764-1848) was born in Ireland and commissioned in the army in 1781. He joined the 49th Foot two years later, accompanying that corps in the West Indies, Holland, and Copenhagen before coming to the Canadas in 1802. Shortly after war broke out, he was transferred to Fort George. He commanded at the actions of Fort George and Stoney Creek in 1813. With Procter, he was largely responsible for holding Upper Canada in the fall of 1813, contrary to the directions of Prevost and de Rottenberg. Relieved of his duties as commander of the Centre Division in fall of 1813, Vincent commanded briefly at Montreal before returning to England for health reasons next year. He rose to lieutenant general in 1825 and full general in 1841. Vincent died in England at the ripe age of 83. *DCB* 7: 888-89; Henry J. Morgan, *Sketches of Celebrated Canadians*, 196.

33. [Stephen Sewell], *Letters of Veritas*, 61.

34. Harrison to Armstrong, 12 Mar. 1813, *MLWHH* 2: 383.

35. Harrison to Armstrong, 11 Feb. 1813, *MLWHH* 2: 356-57; Larry Nelson, *Men of Partiotism Courage & Enterprise! Fort Meigs in the War of 1812*, 43.

36. Harrison to Armstrong, 11 Feb. 1813, *MLWHH* 2: 356-58; McArthur to Armstrong, 30 Mar. 1813, *MPHC* 40: 510-11; Nelson, *Fort Meigs*, 43.

37. Nelson, *Fort Meigs*, 46.

38. Harrison to Armstrong, 12 Mar. 1813, *MLWHH* 2: 383; Nelson, *Fort Meigs*, 46-48.

39. Procter to Sheaffe, 28 Nov. 1812, NAUS, *MIC,* 22-26; Procter to
    Sheaffe, 13 Jan. 1813, *SBD* 2: 4; Mounted Corps Instruction,
    5 Mar. 1813, *SBD* 2: 28-30.
40. Prevost to Sheaffe, 27 Mar. 1813, *MPHC* 15: 264.
41. Prevost to Bathurst, 19 Mar. 1813, *DHCNF* 1813, Vol. 1: 125; Prevost
    to Sheaffe, 27 Mar. 1813, *MPHC* 15: 264.
42. Bathurst to Prevost, 12 Mar. 1813, *MPHC* 15: 255-57; Prevost to
    Sheaffe, 27 Mar. 1813, *MPHC* 15: 264-65; General Order, 27 Mar.
    1813, *DHCNF* 1813, Vol. 1: 136-37; Sheaffe to Procter, 6 Apr. 1813,
    SLB, 365.
43. Prevost to Sheaffe, 27 Mar. 1813, *MPHC* 15: 263.
44. *Ibid.,* 263-65; Prevost to Procter, 25 Feb. 1813, NAUS, *MIC,* 63.
45. Prevost to Sheaffe, 27 Mar. 1813, *MPHC* 15: 264.
46. Prevost to Bathurst, 27 Feb. 1813, *MPHC* 25: 431.
47. Western District Memorial to Prevost, 26 Feb. 1813, *MPHC* 15:
    250-52; Sheaffe to Freer, 8 Apr. 1813, *MPHC* 15: 271.
48. Myers to Baynes, 10 Mar. 1813, *DHCNF* 1813, Vol. 1: 103. Robert
    McDouall (1774-1848) was born in Scotland. He purchased an
    ensigncy in the 49th Foot in 1791, serving in Egypt and Coppenhagen
    before coming to Canada in 1810 as a captain. Prevost selected him as
    aide-de-camp in 1812, and he was promoted to major in the Glengarry
    Light Infantry Regiment on 24 June 1813. It is clear from his letters to
    Procter that the two were close friends, McDouall's special references to
    one of Procter's daughters suggesting a personal interest. He seemed to
    be Procter's sole ally at Prevost's headquarters, inspecting matters at
    Amherstburg in early 1813 and repeatedly urging that reinforcements
    be sent to that quarter. *DCB* 7: 556-58.
49. Procter to Sheaffe, 13 Apr. 1813, NAC, C 678: 228; Procter to Sheaffe,
    5 Apr. 1813, NAC, C 257: 75.
50. Robert Gilmor to McLean, 27 Mar. 1813, *MPHC* 32: 557.
51. Armstrong to Harrison, 3 Apr. 1813, *MLWHH* 2: 412.
52. Gray to Prevost, 12 Mar. 1813, *DHCNF* 1813, Vol. 1: 107-11.
53. *Buffalo Gazette,* 30 Mar., 13 Apr. 1813, cited in *DHCNF* 1813, Vol. 1:
    141, 153. Oliver Hazard Perry (1785-1819) was born in Rhode Island
    and became a midshipman in the U.S. Navy at the age of 15. He
    served in the West Indies and the Mediterranean, being commissioned
    lieutenant in 1810. With the outbreak of war, he volunteered for fresh-
    water service under Commodore Isaac Chauncey, who assigned him
    command on Lake Erie. *WAMB,* 318.
54. Charles J. Dutton, *Oliver Hazard Perry,* 61, 76-77.
55. Procter to Sheaffe, 28 Nov. 1812, NAUS, *MIC,* 22-26; Chambers to
    Procter, 25 Mar. 1813, *MPHC* 32: 552.

56. The Kentucky Volunteers to Harrison, *The War*, 16 Mar. 1813;
Harrison to Armstrong, 28 Mar. 1813, *MLWHH* 2: 404.

57. McArthur and Cass to the Young Men of Ohio, 2 Apr. 1813, *The War*,
27 Apr. 1813.

10

BUNGLE IN THE MUD: FORT MEIGS

"This is the most extraordinary wet season; the like has not been seen for many years." [1]

Diary of Thomas McCrae, 4 May 1813

ALTHOUGH PROCTER monitored Harrison's movements after the battle of Frenchtown, he, like his adversary, was unable to act offensively. Yet, even without a visible threat, an alarmed Harrison retreated. Considering the Maumee Rapids position untenable, he destroyed Fort Deposit, along with 12 tons of flour and 15 tons of salt pork that had been labouriously accumulated there. The American commander then fell back on the Portage River, 18 miles to the east. [2]

In March 1813, Roundhead reported Harrison's reoccupation of the Maumee Rapids and urged Native leaders to conduct an immediate attack on the American encampment. Procter could not comply, constrained as he was by Prevost, who in turn reported to Lord Bathurst: "I did not think it prudent to allow Col. Procter to move forward ... to dislodge the American army because I considered the movement hazardous." John Norton tried to convince the chiefs to attack on their own, but they haggled in council until the spring thaw made movement difficult. With Tecumseh still in Indiana (since August), Walk-in-the-Water was able to convince the other chiefs not to advance without British support. In Norton's words, "We had too many ceremonies to go through." [3]

Immensely popular with his followers, Maj. Gen. William Henry Harrison, the "hero of Tippecanoe" made little progress toward recapturing Michigan until Perry's decisive victory allowed his occupation of the Detroit country.

The indecision among the allies allowed Harrison to initiate construction of a massive fortification atop an elevated bluff on the east bank of the Maumee Rapids. Named Fort Meigs after the Ohio governor, it was designed by two West Point graduates, Capt. Charles Gratiot and Capt. Eleazar Wood (U.S. Army Engineers). Of imposing proportions, its roughly octagonal form eventually covered nine acres. Stout 15-foot pickets were embedded three feet, punctuated by seven large blockhouses and four large batteries to enfilade the approaches. The walls were further strengthened by clay breastworks thrown up against both sides of the palisade base, and the surrounding area cleared of timber and bushes, which were collected as a perimeter abatis.[4]

Harrison was intent on building an impregnable base as a springboard for subsequent operations. With unlimited spending power still at his disposal, he planned to overwhelm Fort Amherstburg through sheer force. As he wrote to the secretary of war, "We have no alternative but to make up by numbers the deficiency in discipline." Through a determined effort, he planned to conclude the campaign within two months. In outlining his latest plans, he contested Armstrong's directions, preferring a land campaign from Fort Meigs rather an amphibious one from Cleveland. Instead of professional soldiers, he planned to use mounted Kentucky volunteers, whom he considered "superior to any militia that took the field in modern times."[5]

The secretary of war disagreed with Harrison. (Given two disasters in the west, Congress recognized the limitations of volunteers and was adverse to further experimentation with undisciplined troops.) He "clearly and distinctly" made Harrison to understand that the government decision to form 52 regular regiments was "expressly in the view of superseding hereafter, the necessity of employing militia except in moments of actual invasion." No less than seven regiments of regulars (some seven thousand troops) were earmarked on paper for Harrison. Furthermore, Armstrong was adamant about an amphibious crossing, calling it "easy, safe and economical," declaring Harrison's land campaign "difficult, dangerous, and enormously expensive." In no uncertain terms, Armstrong demanded weekly and monthly reports on equipment, supplies, provisions, ammunition, strength, discipline, and health as well as returns for horses and oxen, noting that "no return of any description" had ever been received from Harrison's headquarters.[6]

Armstrong's intent was unmistakable. Despite vast expenditures, the trans-Appalachian levies of the Northwest Army had achieved nothing toward conquering Canada or even recovering Michigan Territory. Its failures became a political millstone at Washington, and future operations were to be conducted in a professional manner with a view to producing definitive results. As the first step, the secretary of war put Harrison in his place by teaching him the first duty of a soldier. The exchange between the frontier leader and the professional soldier marked the beginning of an animosity between the two men.

Harrison represented the democratic ideal of the American citizen soldier, "the first qualification being valour; the second, ambition; and the third health," while Armstrong demanded obedience, regularity, and discipline.[7]

Armstrong had good reasons for taking control, sensing the political storm that was brewing in Washington. Indeed, in April, congressmen demanded an inquiry "into the causes of the failure of our arms on the Northern and Northwest frontiers." Although the motion was not carried, the secretary of war could ill afford further disasters. In contrast to the freedom of action to which Harrison had become accustomed, Washington now took control of the composition and strategy of the Northwest Army.[8]

Fort Meigs was garrisoned by 1200 men, mainly volunteers, with an equal number expected from Kentucky. As the men laboured at building defences for this isolated post, boredom set in and discipline lapsed. One garrison order directed: "Fighting is ... forbidden ... unless authorized." With Harrison absent and Capt. Wood detached to build Fort Stephenson on the Lower Sandusky, command devolved upon Brig. Gen. Joel Leftwich, a militia officer from Virginia. Under his command, discipline collapsed entirely. Leftwich allowed the troops to remain in their quarters all day. His rationale was that if he "couldn't make the militia do anything, they might as well be in their tents as to be kept out of the mud and water." Work not only halted but regressed: timber for pickets was consumed as firewood, and once this source became depleted, the men tore down sections of the picketing for fuel! Returning from Fort Stephenson, Capt. Wood was horrified at the state of affairs allowed by the "phlegmatic, stupid old granny" of a general. He assumed command and progress resumed. Even then, the men had to be watched closely. One private threatened to blow up the magazine and desert to the enemy. A court martial ordered him "confined, tied to a post or log in a tent by himself one month ... have a handcuff on his right hand ... ride a wooden horse 30 minutes once a week for one month with a 6-pdr. round shot fastened to each foot ... wear a ball and chain the whole time ... have one eye brow and one side of his head shaved and ... be fed on bread and water only."[9]

As Fort Meigs took form, the Americans perceived signs of an impending assault on their stronghold. Warriors reappeared to snipe at work parties that ventured into the woods. On 3 April, four men arrived from Detroit to report vigorous preparations at Fort Amherstburg, that six hundred British regulars, seven hundred militiamen, and five hundred warriors were indeed preparing for an invasion of Ohio. Five days later, a war party of 15 braves ambushed a timber-cutting detail, killing one member and capturing two more. A dozen *Canadien* exiles from the Raisin River pursued the fleeing Native canoes, overtaking them five miles down the Maumee. In the obstinate struggle that ensued, most of both parties became casualties before the survivors broke off the engagement to return home. On 18 April, an American mounted party dashed to the Raisin River and returned with three *Canadiens*, who notified the Americans that Tecumseh had passed through the village on his way to Amherstburg. The informers also reported that Procter promised the Natives possession of Michigan Territory as their homeland, having learned of his government's decision to support Native wishes at peace talks.[10]

For his part, Procter knew that each day he delayed the expedition, his task of dislodging the defenders of Fort Meigs would become more difficult. Aside from the purely military threat posed by this post, its very presence in the heart of Native territory served to demoralize the tribesmen. Procter hoped to reduce the American fort before the fresh levies expected from Kentucky arrived. "If I tamely permit the enemy to wait his reinforcements and mature his plans, he will become too formidable," he wrote, "I have therefore resolved to cripple him without further delay than is requisite to have the cooperation of Tecumseh four or five days. I most heartily wish Mr. Dickson was here." Although he called on Tecumseh to join in the attack, the war chief was not quick to comply. On 3 April, Procter sent some provisions to induce his return but six days later he wrote, "Of Tecumseh, I have not heard lately."[11]

With the ice broken up by mid-April and his wounded soldiers largely recovered, Procter continued to be delayed by excessive rains. He also awaited two promised companies of the 41st. Sheaffe released these, and they actually advanced as far as Ancaster before being recalled. As York had been captured by the Americans, Lt. Col. Myers wrote Procter that the troops were "extremely wanted" at Fort George. Myers added that if Procter could part with five hundred warriors, they could be useful on the Niagara frontier. Further, Myers asked that no more prisoners be sent, as the Centre Division had no means by which to deal with them. Procter was to dispose of them locally.[12]

On 16 April, Tecumseh and the Prophet arrived with a dozen braves. The war chief asked Procter to wait five additional days for the arrival of four hundred Shawnee, Potawatomi, Kickapoo, and Sac warriors, bringing the combined Native strength to a respectable 1200. On 23 April, Procter embarked his regulars aboard *Lady Prevost, General Hunter, Chippawa, Mary, Nancy, Miamis,* and his new gunboats, *Eliza* and *Myers.* The regulars counted 423 men of the 41st, 63 of the Royal Newfoundland Regiment; 31 artillerymen and 16 of other corps for a total of 533 officers and men. The militiamen, 462 all ranks, crossed Lake Erie in bateaux while Tecumseh led the Native contingent over-land to the Maumee River. The invasion of Ohio had begun.[13]

The British force arrived at Maumee Bay that same day. Next morning, the expedition was joined by the warrior contingent at Swan Creek some miles upriver. While a detachment went forward to select battery sites, Procter established the main camp among the ruins of old Fort Miamis as the Winnebago and Kickapoo rounded up stray cattle, pigs, and horses. On the 27th, Procter and his staff conferred with the Native chiefs and developed a plan of operations for the siege, while Harrison directed the advancing brigade of Kentucky militiamen under Brig. Gen. Green Clay to hasten to Fort Meigs.[14]

By 29 April, the British 24-pdr. guns, each weighing almost two tons, had been hauled laboriously into position over mud-soaked ground by two hundred men apiece. While the soldiers toiled through an incessant rain from nightfall to 3 AM, the engineer officer directed the completion of four protective emplacements for the guns, desig-nated the King's, Queen's, Sailors', and Mortar batteries. Procter also ordered up *Eliza* and *Myers*, mounting 9-pdr. guns, to further augment the artillery. The following day, four Ottawa boys captured the mail from Sandusky, driving off the terrified attendants.[15]

In the early morning of 1 May, on a signal shot from *Myers,* the British guns laid down a heavy bombardment on Fort Meigs. Two 24-pdr. guns (the ones Hull had painstakingly fitted onto carriages), an 8-inch howitzer, a 5 1/2-in. mortar and three 12-pdr. guns rained metal on the American fort. Observing the British preparations, Harrison, on the advice of his engineers, had directed a continuous relay of a third of the garrison to throw up a 12-foot high traverse or mound of earth to protect the men, horses, and vital supplies. Thus protected, the Americans burrowed into the ground on the sheltered side. The British guns produced no breach in the walls, and by 3 May, the warriors became impatient. Tecumseh issued Harrison a written challenge: "I have with me eight hundred braves. You have an equal number in your hiding place. Come out with them and give me battle; you talked like a brave when we met at Vincennes [in 1811], and I respected you; but now you hide behind logs and in the earth like a ground hog. Give me your answer." Through Chambers of the 41st, Procter also demanded the surrender of Fort Meigs, to spare the "effusion of blood"; the American commander responded with a refusal.[16]

Perceiving Harrison's traverse, Procter enfiladed the fort. He ordered the construction of two additional batteries for a 6-pdr. gun, a 5 1/2-in. howitzer and a 5 1/2-in. mortar in the shelter of a ravine on the fort side of the river, within three hundred yards of the American defences. To protect these works, he detailed two militia companies, a contingent of braves, and both flank companies of the 41st under Capt. Richard Bullock and lieutenants Harris Hailes and Angus McIntyre. Harrison countered with lateral traverses. The British gunners concentrated their crossfire of hotshot against two blockhouses known to contain ammunition. Nonetheless, heavy rains saturated the green timbers to frustrate incendiary efforts. The soil turned into a slimy paste that reached to the ankle, extinguishing the sizzling fuses of the bombs to render them harmless. Although the roofs of all the blockhouses were destroyed, exposing the salted beef and pork of the garrison to rain spoilage, the pickets remained intact. Frustrated, Procter observed, "If we knew how to burn them, Mr. Harrison's army would have been destroyed long since."[17]

According to Capt. Daniel Cushing, who was commanding the American artillery, the British batteries lobbed over 1100 rounds of hotshot, coldshot, bombs, and shells during the first five days of May. Short of ammunition, the fort gunners responded sparingly. To supplement this shortage, Harrison was said to have offered his soldiers a gill (four ounces) of whiskey for each British round shot or bomb delivered to an artillery officer. Most of the British ballista in the fort were recovered in this manner. Meanwhile, the warriors climbed into the trees and sniped at anything that moved, particularly as the defenders tried to fetch water from the river, since there were no wells in the fort. Although the cannonading produced limited structural damage, several dozen defenders were killed or wounded during the siege. The heavy 24-pdr. shot passed through the pickets, but the gaps were quickly patched, and the walls held firm.[18]

On 4 May, at 11 PM, Harrison received word that Brig. Gen. Green Clay's brigade of 1200 Kentucky volunteers was located just two hours upriver. The American commander decided to employ the fresh contingent to silence the troublesome British batteries. The next morning, his messenger arrived at Clay's headquarters in a breathless state with

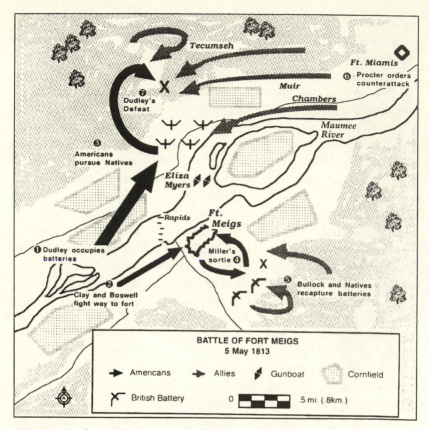

BATTLE OF FORT MEIGS
5 May 1813

Harrison's plan. Clay was to land eight hundred men under Lt. Col. William Dudley on the west bank of the river, spike the cannon, destroy the gun carriages, and cross the river to Fort Meigs, while Clay and his remaining four hundred men were to land on the opposite bank and fight their way into the fort. Concurrent with these movements, Harrison would co-ordinate a garrison sortie against the British batteries adjacent to Fort Meigs. The instructions appeared simple enough; everything depended on their execution.[19]

In preparing his men for the impending battle, Clay was aware of past American disasters arising from the militimen's lack of discipline. He addressed his brigade, exhorting the men on the importance of obedience: "Discipline and subordination mark the real soldier and are indeed the soul of an army.... It is upon you, your subordination and discipline I rely for a successful issue of the present campaign. Without this confidence and support, we shall achieve nothing honourable or useful. The same destiny awaits us both.... Should we encounter the enemy, remember the dreadful fate of our butchered brothers at the River Raisin, that British treachery produced their slaughter." The Kentucky men boarded their boats and set off on their mission.[20]

On the morning of 5 May, Dudley successfully executed the first part of the plan. Gliding down the Maumee, he landed the men of the 12 lead boats, and by 8 AM, had driven off the British artillerymen, carrying the batteries and spiking the cannon as planned. As the Kentuckians lingered, sniping warriors drew the column of Maj. James Shelby (son of Governor Shelby) into the woods. Eager to avenge their fallen comrades at Frenchtown, the Kentuckians charged madly after the Natives, bellowing their battle cry, "Remember the Raisin!" The braves lured them some two miles into the bush. Perceiving this movement, Dudley reluctantly brought up the balance of his command.[21]

From the opposite bank, Harrison monitored events through a spyglass. Almost beside himself, he yelled to the detachment to return, but they could not hear him across the river. The American commander offered an immense reward of $1000 for any man who could cross the river and bring Dudley's men back. One officer made the attempt but failed to negotiate his craft through the current. Then it happened; the ambushers became the ambushed. On learning of Dudley's movements, Procter mobilized his entire force to retake the batteries. Three companies of the 41st, commanded by Capt. Muir and supported by the militiamen, advanced on the Kentuckians along the river, while the warriors under Tecumseh encircled them in the woods. Simultaneously, Chambers led a wing that not only retook the batteries at the point of bayonet but completed the envelopment by cutting off the Americans' retreat to the boats. The Kentuckians in the bush suffered heavy casualties at the hands of the warriors. Dudley was among those killed and scalped. His remaining men were exhausted from their manoeuvres in the deep mud. Dazed at the sudden turn of events, they laid down their weapons, three hours after landing. "Damn your eyes, ground your arms or you will be slain' brought me hastily to my senses," recalled one participant, "Down went gun, off went knapsack, to hastily disappear beneath the mud and water, then ankle-deep where I stood, and with my full weight I aided their exit from further service, pressing them as deeply into the mud as possible." The allied counterattack annihilated Dudley's force; only 150 Kentuckians escaped to the shelter of the fort.[22]

While Dudley's detachment struggled, the remainder of Clay's force, under Lt. Col. William Boswell, fought its way to Fort Meigs, assisted by a garrison sally which conducted most of the men to safety. In the meantime, Capt. Bullock observed Dudley's occupation of the British fieldworks on the opposite bank and prepared to move his men to Procter's support. While he was drawing off from his batteries, Lt. Col. John Miller (not to be confused with Lt. Col. James Miller of Maguaga fame) led 350 regulars in a sortie against Bullock's artillery. Miller managed to occupy the batteries and spike the guns, capturing Bullock's two lieutenants and 42 privates of the light company before the surprised allies could rally.[23]

Chambers of the 41st described "a dreadful slaughter" which occurred when the prisoners were herded into the British encampment at the dilapidated Fort Miamis. "The Indians could not be repressed," he wrote. "One of our men was shot in the act of saving the prisoners. By great exertions, we succeeded in sending four or five hundred prisoners on board the vessels [at Swan Creek]." Pte. Shadrach Byfield bore witness to the disorder. He saw one American scalped alive and confirmed that the warriors fired on the British guard, killing one redcoat, identified by John Richardson as Pte. Russel, "an old and excellent soldier." Some two dozen Americans were killed before the combined efforts of Tecumseh, Elliott, McKee, and the guard halted the bloodletting.[24]

Once again, Procter's weakness in regulars emboldened the vengeful impulses of the braves. A surviving prisoner described the scene:

On our approach to the old garrison.... I perceived that the prisoners were running the gauntlet and that the Indians were whipping, shooting and tomahawking the men as they ran by their line.... As I entered the ditch around the garrison, the man before me was shot and fell, and I fell over him.... How many lives were lost in this place I cannot tell, probably between twenty and forty.... When we got within the walls, we were ordered to sit down.... A new scene commenced.... An Indian painted black, mounted on the dilapidated wall shot one of the prisoners ... and drew his tomahawk, with which he killed two others.... The men ... trampled upon me so that I could not see what was going on.... The confusion and uproar at this moment cannot be adequately described.... The British officers and soldiers seemed to interpose to prevent the further effusion of blood.... Their expression was "Oh, nichee, wah!" meaning "Oh, brother, quit!".... Comparative calm ensued.... About this time, but whether it was before or after, I do not distinctly recollect Colonel Elliott and Tecumseh rode into the garrison. When Elliott came to where Thos. Moore of Clark county stood, the latter inquired "if it was compatible with the honor of a civilized nation ... to suffer defenceless prisoners to be murdered by savages."... Elliott was an old man; his hair might have been termed, with more propriety, white than gray, and to my view he had more savage in his countenance than Tecumseh. This celebrated chief was a noble, dignified personage.... We were taken in open boats about nine miles down the river to the British shipping.[25]

Another survivor of Clay's force provided a corroborative account of the disorder amid the rubble of Fort Miamis: The "prisoners ... were conducted to ... Fort Miami, to which they give the appellation of 'slaughter pen' and there ordered to sit down. The Indians now commenced their barbarities in presence of British officers. Several of the officers and men were shot by the Indians who surrounded them, while others were selected and dragged out with tomahawks buried in their skulls. About forty persons were butchered in this way when an end was put to the savage cruelty by the interference of Col. Elliott, who, it appears, had complete control over Procter's allies."[26]

John Norton's description of the *mêlée* was based on the observations of witnesses. "An act of cruelty was here perpetrated so suddenly as to prevent the interference of the humane," he wrote, "A worthless Chippewa [Ojibwa] of Detroit, having with him a number of wretches like himself, who had not the courage to kill their enemies while in arms, but yet desirous of obtaining the repute of having killed them, they assailed the unfortunate prisoners and killed a sentry of the 41st that stood forth in their defence. They had created great havoc before their ungenerous fury could be restrained." Ensign James Cochran, who would join the Right Division shortly, identified the instigator of these murders as "a villain called Split Nose, a petty chief of the Chippewas ... a sneaking ruffian whom I met with a few months after." Even after the bloodletting was halted, neither Tecumseh nor Elliott could prevent the abduction of the younger men for adoption purposes.[27]

The Americans' efforts to spike the cannon met with marginal success as they had nothing but ramrods to force into the touch holes. The obstructions were easily bored out and the guns prepared for action, but the continuing heavy rains over the next four days greatly limited the effectiveness of the renewed bombardment.[28]

On the afternoon of the battle, the besiegers, observing a white flag over the fort, supposed that Harrison wished to capitulate. Harrison's

Tecumseh's features in this portrait are unsupported by documented description. Appearing in a 1902 reprint of John Richardson's *War of 1812*, it is one of several largely mythical depictions.

purpose was not to discuss surrender, though. It was to negotiate a prisoner exchange. The next day, the two commanders met for the first time in a parley on the beach in front of the fort and eventually concluded a written agreement to exchange 21 American prisoners for the two British officers (Hailes and McIntyre) and 39 British privates held by Harrison. None of the exchanged men was to engage in military service other than garrison duties for a month. In addition, since Procter was instructed to dispose of prisoners locally, he agreed to release the Kentucky militiamen on parole on the north shore of Lake Erie. Once again, the British commander went to the trouble of transporting his captives to safety, promising to keep the tribesmen away. Although Procter proposed a further prisoner exchange of Wyandot, Seneca, and Delaware braves for an equal number of Kentucky men, Harrison referred that offer to his government. Harrison took advantage of this interlude in the fighting to secure Clay's ammunition boats.[29]

Two days after the battle, Richardson described the "ludicrous and revolting" scenes in the warriors' encampment as they examined the immense quantities of captured loot:

In varying directions were lying the trunks and boxes taken in the boats of General Clay's division and the plunderers were busily occupied in displaying their riches, carefully examining each article and attempting to divine its use. Several were decked out in the uniforms of the officers.... Some were habited in plain clothes; others had their bodies clad in clean white shirts.... Their tents were ornamented with saddles, bridles, rifles, daggers, swords and pistols.... Such were the ridiculous parts of the picture; but mingled with these, and in various directions, were to be seen the scalps of the slain drying in the sun, stained on the fleshy side with vermilion dyes and dangling in the air, as they hung suspended from their poles to which they were attached; together with hoops of various sizes, on which were stretched portions of human skin taken from various parts of the body, principally the hand and foot, and yet covered with the nails of those parts; while scattered ... were visible the members from which they had been separated, and serving as nutriment to the wolf-dogs by which the Indians were accompanied.[30]

The restless tribesmen drifted off with their booty, as was their custom after an engagement. According to Chambers, all that remained were "ten Indians including Tecumseh and very few of the militia." The British commander acknowledged, "Before the ordnance could be withdrawn from the batteries, I was left with Tecumseh and less than twenty chiefs and warriors," adding, "Under present circumstances at least, our Indian force is not a disposable one, or permanent, tho' occasionally, a most powerful aid." On the 9th, two American-born crewmen from the British gunboats defected (at least five switched sides during the siege), reporting that between 1600 and two thousand braves had deserted. They attributed the reason for the Natives' departure to their belief that Harrison's flag of truce signified a surrender and that Procter was denying them their share of the spoils of Fort Meigs.[31]

It was not just the warriors who abandoned the expedition. Half the militiamen left for home after six of their officers presented Lt. Col. Warburton with a petition on 6 May. The document presented their situation:

From the situation of our district last fall, but very short crops of grain were put in the ground, and these, small as they were, will be rendered still less by the unfavourableness of the last winter. Under these ... appearances, the farmer had only the resource left of putting in crops of spring wheat and should they be kept here any longer, that of corn will also be out of their power and the consequence must be a famine next winter. Indeed the men are now detained with the greatest reluctance, some have already gone and we are apprehensive that it will not be in our power to detain them much longer.[32]

The militiamen's position was neither surprising nor unique. They had warned Prevost of the implications for the harvest some months earlier. They knew that without spring planting, their families would simply starve in the ensuing winter. The issue was not one of loyalty but of raw survival. Their circumstances seemed to be general in the Canadas. Lt. Col. Mahlon Burwell described a similar problem among the Long Point militiamen that spring: "The inhabitants are in the midst of their planting and it will be like drawing their teeth to call them out until they are done." Prevost himself acknowledged the widespread nature of the problem. "The militia have been considerably weakened by the frequent desertions of even the well disposed part of them to their farms, for the purpose of getting seed into the ground before the short summer of this country has too far advanced."[33]

Abandoned by three-fourths of his force, Procter found himself in the embarrassing circumstance of surrounding an enemy whose numbers exceeded his own. Even his regulars were suffering from ague, dysentery, and exposure. He had to raise the siege before Harrison took advantage of his weakness. On the morning of 9 May, the British com-

mander ordered a parting bombardment before dismantling his batteries at 10 AM. By noon the 13-day siege was ended, as the allied force
sailed downriver.[34]

Harrison put the best slant on his miscarried scheme of the 5th.
"The General has ascertained that the number of regular troops with
the enemy are really contemptible," read his general order. "Nine-
tenths of his force are Indians and Canadian militia who are the worst
in the world." Some days later, though, he could not contain his disappointment with the insubordination of the frontiersmen. In an
address to the troops, he blamed their impulsiveness for the disaster
that befell Dudley's corps, pointing to the mistaken notion that "valor
can alone accomplish anything."[35]

In his official report, Procter praised his force: "The courage and
activity displayed throughout the whole scene of action by the Indian
chiefs and warriors contributed largely to our success." Procter had given
the brevet rank of major to his six line captains since militia officers
of equal rank were present. Obviously pressing for their promotions
(particularly for Muir and Chambers), he warmly commended their performance to Prevost: "Some of them are old officers, all of them deserv-
ing. Any mark of Your Excellency's approbation would be extremely
grateful to me." Procter also credited the efforts of lieutenants Richard
Bullock (41st) and John LeBreton (RNR). It was on this occasion that he
recommended young John Richardson for promotion along with his
own son, Henry Procter, Jr., and the two other gentleman volunteers
with the 41st, all of whom had joined the regiment the preceding summer. Subsequently, Richardson expressed his displeasure at the fact that
all four were recognized equally and without distinction, maintaining
that he had been in the thick of the action with Chambers on the 5th,
while Henry Procter, Jr., remained in camp, unexposed to danger.[36]

The two sides sustained widely disproportionate casualties.
Procter's regulars suffered only 13 dead and 36 wounded. Militia losses
amounted to four wounded and only one, Lt. Laurent Bondy, killed.
The captured 39 British privates and two lieutenants were exchanged.
Native losses were unrecorded but considered light. In contrast, the
Americans counted 81 killed, 270 wounded, and 547 prisoners in
British custody, with more in Native hands.[37]

Harrison sent three reports to Armstrong. In the first hasty dispatch, he declared "another disaster to the Kentucky troops, not indeed
bearing any comparison to that of the Raisin River in point of killed
and wounded but exceeding it in the number of prisoners." In his sec-

ond, he focussed on the bravery of the men on the east side of the river, reporting the captured Americans as an administrative matter for Washington to sort out. In his third report to Armstrong, Harrison identified only 50 of Dudley's men killed and fancifully suggested that "a considerable number" of Dudley's troops had "retreated up the river to Ft. Winchester" when in fact, they were taken prisoners of war as stated in his initial report. He further misrepresented the facts by suggesting "great loss" on the part of the besiegers. Clay also avoided mention of Dudley's disaster in his report.[38]

News of this latest catastrophe produced a further dampening effect on American recruiting efforts. The casualties of the 5th again occurred largely among the Kentucky draftees and at the start of their six month term. Harrison's fighting men were becoming disenchanted with military service. They continued to go without blankets, clothing, cooking utensils, and other essentials. As the discharged and paroled men plodded home to Kentucky to tell their sad and horrific stories, it became increasingly difficult to rouse men for the war effort. Even that veteran warrior, Governor Isaac Shelby, conceded to Henry Clay, "I am free to declare to you that as an individual, my confidence in the administration has greatly abated. And I shall feel but little inclination in future to see a greater proportion of the best blood of Kentucky than is required by law put to hazard in the general cause of war." [39]

Thus far, Procter's strategy of beating his enemy piecemeal had held the Americans in Ohio. Nonetheless, while his latest tactical victory shattered the third consecutive Northwest Army, he had failed to dislodge his enemy, and Fort Meigs remained as a secure base for offensive operations. Harrison and his engineers had done an admirable job on its defences. The American presence in Ohio was tested and held firm, producing a visible effect on the tribesmen of the area. Local chiefs of the Delaware, Seneca, and Shawnee nations came forward, offering their services to the Americans. Furthermore, Procter's failure to destroy the fort became a new source of friction among the allies, as the Natives insisted on fulfilment of Brock's promise that their lands would be recovered. Meanwhile Harrison's overall position was clearly gaining strength as he prepared for his final drive into Upper Canada.

On returning to Amherstburg, Procter received uplifting correspondence directly from Prevost. The latter announced the impending arrival of Sir James Yeo and 450 seamen and officers for lake service. Furthermore, Prevost wrote, "And I shall not fail to supply you with whatever you may stand in need of as soon as your wants are made known to me." This encouraging letter gave Procter good reason to believe that the worst was over. With soldiers, seamen, and supplies, he could maintain the struggle.[40]

Once again, Procter outlined his pressing needs. Conspicuous in the prewar years for his attention to the men's comfort and discipline, he identified "a deficiency or want even of necessaries for the men," itemizing pork, money, uniforms, barrack furniture, bedding, and cooking utensils. He stressed the need for two more commissariat clerks as the two existing ones were literally sick from anxiety and fatigue. The British commander complained that both regulars and Indian Department officers were paid irregularly, warning that the lack of necessities was "injurious to the service." Reduced to expediting detailed requisitions himself, Procter had serious shortages indeed.[41]

Brutal as life was for the common soldier, Procter understood that if his basic needs went unsatisfied, he would cease to be effective, and regimental efficiency would suffer and eventually fail. Events had repeatedly proved to him that only his regulars were absolutely reliable. Without their disciplined core, the efforts of militiamen and warriors would be neutralized. He reported that his Native allies were "not half fed" and would have deserted, had they not been "warm in the cause." With still only half the 41st at Fort Amherstburg, Procter's letters were becoming blunt: "Your excellency will perceive that the reinforcement you intended has not been sent; nor do I expect to receive any whilst any circumstance may seem to justify their detention." In addition to his shortages of gun powder, Indian goods, artificers, dockyard work-men, and sailors, Procter lacked Irish pork, sending only flour, corn, and tallow to Michilimackinac in *General Hunter*. Nonetheless, he remained optimistic, writing, "There cannot be a doubt of our future success."[42]

Brig. Gen. John Vincent, of the Centre Division, acknowledged Procter's extreme circumstance and forwarded a company and the headquarters of the 41st to Fort Erie for embarkation to Amherstburg "under a confident persuasion that reinforcements are near at hand to replace them." Learning of this augmentation to his command, Procter, hoped to be free of relying on the militia organization "or any portion of it." With the certain news that reinforcements were actually on the way, he paraded the Essex and Kent militiamen on 4 June, the King's birthday, disarmed them and dismissed them to their homes, leaving some feeling of resentment among the members. The demands of military expediency had come into conflict with their pressing need to support their distressed families. These divergent interests became an unfortunate feature of the war on a front where professional soldiers continued to form a minority of the combatants.[43]

Misfortune intervened once more. As *Queen Charlotte* approached Fort Erie to pick up the soldiers and provisions, the countryside was found to be in American hands; Fort George and Fort Erie had been captured on 27 May. The pork at Point Abino near Fort Erie had been destroyed and the British troops were nowhere to be seen. Vincent could only send a drove of cattle with six militiamen down the Thames to alleviate the pressing shortage of meat at Amherstburg. The long-awaited reinforcement destined for Procter had included not only the elements of the 41st but two additional companies of the Royal Newfoundland Regiment plus three part-companies of the Glengarry Fencible Regiment. These units, already weakened during the engagements of the 27th, were ordered to join the retreat to Burlington.[44]

To compound these adverse developments, the earlier capture of York produced other headaches for Procter. During the attack there, the ship stores and hardware at the naval storehouse, most of it destined for the new ship at Amherstburg, had been destroyed or captured. As British North America possessed virtually no manufacturing capability for such items, they were difficult to replace. Contemporary participant William Dunlop described their movement once they arrived from England: "Every kind of Military and Naval stores, every bolt of canvas, every "rope yarn," as well as the heavier articles of guns, shot, cables, anchors, and all the numerous etceteras for furnishing a large squadron ... had to be brought from Montreal ... and in summer by flat-bottomed boats which had to tow up the rapids ... exposed to the shot of the enemy without any protection." Furthermore, as the British soldiers retreated from York, they burned the new frigate, *Isaac Brock*, on the stocks. Since this vessel would have given decided superiority to the British side on Lake Ontario, its destruction meant that minimal naval resources could be spared for Lake Erie. Worse yet, Vincent reported that the Americans were expected to complete "two brigs and six large gun boats" at Erie in three weeks. Indeed, two 20-gun brigs had been launched on 24 May. These combined developments suddenly placed the Right Division into a potentially perilous strategic situation as the results of the British failure to sweep the American positions on the lakes in the fall became painfully apparent.[45]

At Amherstburg, marine preparations continued to move forward slowly. Although *Eliza* and *Myers* were launched, the new ship, *Detroit*, was far from finished. Without this vessel, the British squadron would have no chance against the enemy brigs known to be nearing completion. Master Builder William Bell was short of artificers, hardware, and money. Still worse, *Detroit* lacked sails, cables, hardware, cordage, and cannon. These would never arrive, having been destroyed or captured at York. Procter repeated his need for sailors as he could not even man the gunboats to cruise the Ohio coastline. The threat of the American preparation at Erie was certainly known to the British side as Lt. Col. Myers reported to Prevost's office the certainty of two vessels of 20-guns each and five gunboats there, along with others at Black Rock.[46]

If Myers's letter did not signify a clear need for decisive action, Procter took steps to ensure that Prevost understoood the seriousness of his situation. In May, Prevost's provincial aide-de-camp for Lower Canada, Col. Pierre de Boucherville (brother of entrepreneur Thomas Verchères de Boucherville), conducted an information gathering visit to Amherstburg. Preferring not to communicate sensitive details in writing (given the American occupation of the Niagara Peninsula), Procter briefed him so that "The Colonel can speak fully.... Presque Isle [Erie] and Cleveland will naturally become the subject of much attention."[47]

Strangely, after acknowledging the tours and conferences that Procter arranged for him, Boucherville lamely reported to Prevost that since he was merely a "bearer of dispatches," Procter's letters "must be more correct than the communications that I can give." In his useless report, Prevost's aide "found the troops in high spirits ... but the disaffections of the settlers is shocking and deserves an exemplary chastisement." As a finishing touch to his farcical brief, Boucherville closed with some appropriate political fawning: "I ... assure Your Excellency that my attachment to your person will be as lasting as my existence and beg of Your Excellency a continuation of favour in employing me, where and when ever honour or renown can be obtained." If indeed he was no more than a highly paid bearer of letters, one wonders why he wasted Procter's time in "several conferences" or, for that matter, why Prevost sent him in the first place. This sort of help was not what Procter required.[48]

At this point, much depended on Prevost's decision. The substantial resources (including nine regiments) promised by Bathurst had largely arrived, and more were en route. Significantly, even Bathurst observed on Prevost's policy that left such scant resources for the defence of Upper Canada: "I cannot but express a hope that you may have been enabled to make such detachments to the Upper Province as to meet the corresponding efforts of the enemy." In response to American naval activity on the lakes, he designated Sir James Yeo, with 450 seamen, for freshwater service. Bathurst even offered to place the crews of the empty transports at Prevost's disposal if they could be of "material service." His intention was clear. Upper Canada was to be reinforced and "the necessity of maintaining naval superiority on the lakes" was paramount.[49]

Not much of the King's bounty came Procter's way, but he still anticipated a successful outcome, concentrating the displaced tribesmen along the Detroit River. Since Tecumseh chose to remain with his allies, the British commander settled his band at the mouth of the Huron River near Frenchtown, while Main Pock and the Potawatomi occupied a site 20-miles upstream. Although the Ojibwa returned to their scattered camps, the Ottawa located on the Rouge River near Detroit. The Wyandot maintained their lands in the vicinity of Amherstburg and Brownstown, joined by the Miami. Tecumseh alternated his headquarters among Bois Blanc Island, the Huron River, and Matthew Elliott's estate. Disgusted by meagre provisioning and ignored by the warriors, Tenskwatawa withdrew to a well-hidden location on Cedar Creek, near the New Settlement.[50]

Procter ordered the Indian Department to Detroit, "making the territory completely an Indian country," even contemplating a British marine presence on Lake Michigan to contain American influence in that quarter. Despite his few regulars and the growing naval threat on Lake Erie, Procter adhered to the promise of a Native homeland.[51]

NOTES

1. Thomas McCrae Diary, 4 May 1813, *DHCNF* 1813, Vol. 1: 220.
2. Elijah Whitlesley to his wife, 25 Jan. 1813, WRHS, Tract No. 92: 103.
3. Prevost to Bathurst, 27 Feb. 1813, *MPHC* 25: 431; Norton, *Journal*, 314.
4. Nelson, *Fort Meigs*, 40-41; William M'Carty, *History of the American War of 1812*, 76.
5. Harrison to Armstrong, 17 Mar. 1813, *DPCUS* 1813-14, Vol. 2: 2390.
6. Armstrong to Harrison, 4 Apr. 1813, *DPCUS* 1813-14, Vol. 2: 2391.
7. *The War*, 9 Jan. 1813.
8. Motion by Congressman Miller, 18 Apr. 1813, *DPCUS* 1813-14, Vol. 2: 2030.
9. Nelson, *Ft. Meigs*, 55-56; Daniel Cushing Diary, *Fort Meigs and the War of 1812*, 109.

10. Cushing, *Diary*, 103-14; Harrison to Armstrong, 21 Apr. 1813,
    MLWHH 2: 422; Report from the Miami Rapids, 9 Apr. 1813, *The
    War*, 27 Apr. 1813. Accounts contain a report of "doubtful authority"
    that as an inducement for Native participation against Fort Meigs,
    Procter promised the Prophet control of Michigan territory and
    Harrison would be delivered to Tecumseh as a prisoner in petticoats. As
    Procter never mentioned the Prophet as a key personality in any of his
    letters, this story probably originated as an extension of his promise to
    give the tribesmen control of the Northwest. McAfee, *Late War*, 273;
    Blanchard, *Northwest*, 309.

11. Procter to Sheaffe, 3 Apr. 1813, NAC, C 678: 167; Procter to Sheaffe,
    17 April 1813, NAC, C 678: 230; Norton *Journal*, 315.

12. Procter to Sheaffe, 3, 17 Apr. 1813, NAC, C 678: 167, 230; Myers to
    Procter, 29 Apr. 1813, *DHCNF* 1813, Vol. 1: 184.

13. Procter to McDouall, 16 Apr. 1813, NAUS, *MIC*, 85-87; British
    Embarkation Return, 23 Apr. 1813, NAC, C 678: 253; Edmunds, *The
    Shawnee Prophet*, 133.

14. Chambers Diary, 24-27 Apr. 1813, *MPHC* 15: 289-90. Fort Miamis was
    built by Lieutenant Governor Simcoe on American Territory in 1794.
    The British abandoned it two years later, and by 1813 it was in ruins.
      Green Clay (1757-1826) was a Virginian by birth who engaged in
    extensive land speculations in Kentucky before the war. In 1812, he
    was appointed major general in the state militia. He resumed his
    commercial and farming enterprises the next year. *DAB* 4: 628.

15. John Richardson, *Eight Years in Canada*, 135; Knapp, *Maumee*, 164;
    Todd and Drake, *Harrison*, 75; Chambers Diary, 30 Apr. 1813, *MPHC*
    15: 290; Richardson, *War of 1812*, 148.

16. Todd and Drake, *Harrison*, 75; Knapp, *Maumee*, 164; Hatch, *Chapter*,
    115; Thomson, *Sketches of the Late War*, 110.

17. James B. Finley, *Life Among the Indians*, 213; Procter to Prevost,
    9 Aug. 1813, *MPHC* 15: 349. Richard Bullock was a lieutenant of the
    41st in 1796 and captain in 1809. He was present at the battle
    of Queenston Heights and joined the Right Division in mid-1813.
    Shortly before the Thames retreat, Procter sent him to take command
    at Michilimackinac, where John Askin, Jr., described him as imperious,
    a "d—d scoundrel ... tormenting all about him ... fit only to drive
    miscreants and [he] knows very little or pretends to, the difference
    between gentlemen and blackguards." Bullock retired from the army
    in 1826. His son and namesake, Lt. Richard Bullock, also of the 41st,
    was one of the few line officers to avoid capture after the battle of
    Moraviantown. Lomax, *The 41st*, 65; John Askin, Jr., to John Askin,
    26 Oct. 1813, *JAP* 2: 771.

18. Brown, *Campaigns*, 45; Cushing, *Diary*, 116-17.

19. Clay's Report to Harrison, 9 May 1813, *MLWHH* 2: 440-42; Slocum, *The Ohio Country, 1783-1815*, 237.

20. Clay's General Order, 5 May 1813, Gilbert Auchinleck, *A History of the War Between Great Britain and the United States*, 183-84.

21. Clay to Harrison, 9 May 1813, *MLWHH* 2: 440; Nelson, *Ft. Meigs*, 76; Joseph R. Underwood Narrative, cited in Knapp, *Maumee*, 168.

22. Harrison to Armstrong, 5 May, 1812, *MLWHH* 2: 432; Richardson, *War of 1812*, 150-51; Thomas Christian account, cited in Nelson, *Fort Meigs*, 77.

23. Richardson, *War of 1812*, 152; Harrison to Armstrong, 5, 9, 13 May 1813, Clay to Harrison, 9 May 1813, *MLWHH* 2: 431, 432, 443, 439; Byfield, *Account*, 12. John Miller (1781-1846) was born in Virginia. A major general of the Ohio militia, he became colonel of the 19th U.S. infantry during the war and commanded the troops occupying the Western District in 1814. In 1825, he became governor of Missouri. *DAB* 6: 628.

24. Chambers Diary, 5 May, 1813, *MPHC* 15: 291; Byfield, *Account*, 13; Richardson, *War of 1812*, 154; McAfee, *Late War*, 174.

25. Joseph R. Underwood Narrative, cited in Knapp, *Maumee*, 170-71.

26. Anonymous correspondent, 20 May 1813, cited in *The War*, 8 June 1813.

27. McAfee, *Late War*, 272; Norton, *Journal*, 321; Cochran, *Narrative*, NAC, MG 40, G4, File 2, 35; Cochran, *Notes*, NAC, MG 40, G-4, File 1, 88.

28. Richardson, *War of 1812*, 152; Cushing, *Diary*, 118-19.

29. Harrison to Armstrong, 13 May 1813, *MLWHH* 2: 443; Richardson, *Eight Years*, 138; Harrison-Procter Agreement, 7 May 1813, NAC, C 678: 250-52.

30. Richardson, *War of 1812*, 159.

31. Chambers Diary, 5 May 1813, *MPHC* 15: 291; Procter to Prevost, 14 May 1813, NAC, C 678: 261; Harrison to Armstrong, 13 May 1813, *MLWHH* 2: 443; Cushing, *Diary*, 119.

32. Militia captains to Procter, 6 May 1813, NAC, C 678: 259.

33. Burwell to Talbot, 21 May 1813, *TP*, 191; Prevost to Bathurst, 26 May 1813, NAC, CO 42: 150.

34. Cushing, *Diary*, 119; Brackenbridge, *Late War*, 100.

35. Harrison's General Order, 6 May 1813, Cushing, *Diary*, 21; Harrison's General Order, 9 May 1813, *MLWHH* 2: 437.

36. Procter to Prevost, 14 May 1813, NAC, C 678: 261; Richardson, *War of 1812*, 167. Henry Procter, Jr., (1795-?), was the son of Maj. Gen. Procter. He and John Richardson were among the four gentleman volunteers accepted into the 41st shortly after the outbreak of war, accompanying the Right Division on its major engagements. The elder

Procter recommended all four for advancement, but John Richardson was the first to be promoted. Procter was displeased with his singular elevation, one contrary to his judgment: "Mr. Richardson whom I find promoted over the faculty here who have invariably shown zeal and ability which he has not." Some three decades later, in the course of his research for *The War of 1812*, Richardson learned of Procter's comments and criticized his former commander without reserve. Procter to Myers, 23 May 1813, NAC, C 678: 307; Richardson, *War of 1812*, 167-68.

37. British Casualty Return, 5 May 1813, *MPHC* 32: 559; British Return of American Prisoners, 5 May 1813, *MPHC* 15: 278.

38. Harrison to Armstrong, 5, 9, 13 May 1813; Clay to Harrison, 9 May 1813, *MLWHH* 2: 431-32, 439, 442, 443.

39. Cass to Armstrong, 24 May 1813, *MPHC* 40: 526; Shelby to Clay, 16 May 1813, cited in Hammack, *Kentucky*, 68.

40. Prevost to Procter, 7 May 1813, *SBD* 2: 32-33.

41. Procter to Sheaffe, 5 Apr. 1813, NAC, C 257: 75; Procter to Sheaffe, 13 Apr. 1813, NAC, C 678: 228; Procter to Lt. Gen. J.C. Sherbrooke (Colonel of the 41st), 15 June 1813, NAC, C 679: 104.

42. Procter to Baynes, 14 May 1813, NAC, C 678: 257-61; Procter to Baynes, 23 May 1813, *MPHC* 15: 302.

43. Vincent to Prevost, 19 May 1813, *MPHC* 15: 299; Procter to Myers, 23 May 1813, NAC, C 678: 307; Clay to Harrison, 20 June 1813, cited in Knapp, *Maumee*, 207; Robert Reynolds narrative, Coffin, *The War and Its Moral*, 211.

44. Vincent to Prevost, 2 June 1813, NAC, C 679: 2; Capt. McDouall to Procter, 4 June 1813, *DHCNF* 1813, Vol. 2: 300.

45. William Dunlop, *Recollections of the American War*, 35-36; Vincent to Baynes, 14 June 1813, *SBD* 2: 156.

46. Myers to Baynes, 20 May 1813, *MPHC* 15: 300.

47. Procter to Prevost, 4 June 1813, NAC, C 679: 14.

48. Boucherville to Prevost, 4 June 1813, NAC, C 679: 88.

49. Bathurst to Prevost, 12 Mar. 1813, *MPHC* 15: 255-56. The first significant reinforcements to arrive since the start of war included the 19th Regiment of Light Dragoons plus large detachments of artillerymen and marines. The nine infantry units were the 1st, 13th, 70th, 89th, 103rd, 104th, De Meuron's (Swiss), De Wattville's (Swiss), and the Second Battalion of the 41st,

50. McAfee, *Late War*, 281; Tanner, *Atlas of Great Lakes Indian History*, 116.

51. Procter to McDouall, 14 May 1813, NAC, C 678: 240.

II

FRONTAL WARFARE

"I have only to say that I have manned the fleet and armed the Detroit, and that I look hourly for the enemy in two points, in considerable numbers and must therefore meet him with a divided, with a reduced force. I begin to think I shall never have an opportunity of meeting the enemy on terms of equality. He will have more thousands than I can produce hundreds of regulars, my only real reliance. A supply of seamen ... would give us a fair prospect. Our only consolation must be in doing our duty." [1]

Procter to Baynes, 19 August 1813

WHILE THE ALLIED VICTORY on the Maumee derailed Harrison's preparations, Fort Meigs remained a strategic threat to the allies. As a launching pad for offensive operations, it was within striking range of Procter's positions. Furthermore, its very presence constituted a threat to the Natives' cherished dream of a homeland in Ohio. While Procter appreciated the danger posed by the American fort, he had to devote increased attention to the even more ominous developments at the other end of Lake Erie. Through the new depot at Long Point the Right Division maintained a tenuous provisioning artery, but Procter worried that the American navy would sever this communications lifeline. Although the Provincial Marine establishment on the Great Lakes reported to the governor-general through the quartermaster-general department, responsibility for the operation and very survival of the Lake Erie Squadron had essentially fallen to Procter by default.

Supply considerations forced Capt. Robert Heriot Barclay to engage his adversary on Lake Erie. He was painfully aware that the outcome would determine the future of the land campaign in the Detroit country.

It was with no small sense of relief to Procter that the Royal Navy hove into Amherstburg harbour on 6 June 1813. Capt. Robert Heriot Barclay (RN) had been a naval lieutenant at Bermuda in February 1813, when Admiral Warren sent him to Lake Ontario in response to Prevost's urgent request for a naval presence on the Great Lakes. Although 28 years of age, the Scottish-born Barclay was a seasoned veteran who had been at sea since the age of 12. He lost an arm in action against the French at Moir Montier Roads and served under Nelson at the battle of Trafalgar. Arriving at Kingston in early May, he took command of the vessels on Lake Ontario but was superseded within days by 31-year-old Commodore Sir James Yeo (RN), the newly arrived commander on the lakes. Yeo first offered the Lake Erie squadron to Capt. William Mulcaster (RN), who declined because of the poor condition of that flotilla, and then ordered Barclay to take command.[2]

Accompanying Barclay were three naval lieutenants, a surgeon, a purser, a master's mate, and only 19 seamen. Twelve of them were colonial mariners discharged by Yeo from the Lake Ontario Squadron.

Commanding the inland navy, Sir James Lucas Yeo carefully avoided decisive actions on Lake Ontario. Considering Lake Erie of secondary importance, he gave Barclay scant resources and blamed Procter for the defeat at Put-in-Bay.

Barclay described the remainder as "the most worthless characters that came with him [Yeo]." The party arrived on the Niagara frontier in time to join Vincent's retreat from Fort George and marched on to Long Point. Arriving there on 1 June, they found the armed schooners, *Lady Prevost* and *Chippawa*, plus the transport, *Mary*, at anchor. Taking command of these vessels, Barclay examined the crews, mainly *Canadien* mariners, and immediately wrote Yeo seeking a reinforcement of "good seamen." Then Barclay weighed anchor for Amherstburg where Procter welcomed him and briefed him on marine matters.[3]

From Amherstburg, Barclay wrote a second letter within a week to Yeo requesting seamen before setting sail for a firsthand look at the enemy. With *Queen Charlotte*, *Lady Prevost*, and *Chippawa*, he conducted a reconnaissance of Erie, assessing that situation as "gloomy." He reported two "corvettes" launched and "in a very forward state, indeed," their lower masts in place. He concluded that these, with the four gunboats and two smaller schooners in the harbour, were greatly superior to his own flotilla. Barclay wrote yet another letter to Yeo, emphasizing his urgent need for seamen. In place of sailors, Barclay received a haughty reprimand from Yeo for poor form that called Barclay's language "too peremptory from a junior to someone so much higher in rank." By addressing the matter of protocol, Yeo conveniently diverted attention from the long-standing issue of manning the Lake Erie Squadron, though it clearly fell under his responsibility as commander on the lakes. Alarmed by the advanced American preparations, Barclay also wrote Vincent for an immediate reinforcement of troops "to enable General Procter to join with me in an attack on Presque Isle [Erie] and destroy the enemy vessels before they can get ready." Then he fixed a course for the east end of the lake to investigate the reported presence of the Black Rock vessels.[4]

Meanwhile, Barclay's antagonist, Master Commandant Oliver Hazard Perry (USN) had been at work since March. Twenty-seven years of age, this Rhode Islander was "a man of lofty stature, strongly built, with dark eyes, an irrististable smile and an air of freshness, health and contentment." In early June, with the Niagara frontier in American hands, Perry undertook to unite Elliott's vessels at Black Rock with those at Erie. In addition to the captured brig, *Caledonia,* Elliott's flotilla included four cut-down commercial schooners converted into gunboats: *Ohio, Amelia* (formerly *General Wilkinson*), and *Somers* (formerly *Catherine*), plus the sloop *Trippe* (formerly *Contractor*). After arming these with guns from the shore batteries on the Niagara River, Perry warped them against the river current into Lake Erie. In the open water, he hugged the shoreline to elude Barclay's vessels. On at least two occasions, the American vessels almost blundered into Barclay's stronger squadron but a heavy fog obscured visibility for both sides. On 18 June, Perry's vessels scurried into Erie harbour just as the British squadron appeared. His united fleet boasted the Black Rock vessels plus the sister brigs, *Niagara* and *Lawrence,* and the schooners, *Ariel, Scorpion, Tigress,* and *Porcupine.*[5]

The United States Navy had acted decisively on Lake Erie. With the keels for three gunboats laid down by Daniel Dobbins at Erie before the winter, shipwright Henry Eckford arrived in January 1813 to expedite construction. On 3 March 1813, Congress approved additional construction of whatever vessels were necessary to secure command of Lake Erie, and ship designer Noah Brown arrived to cut timber for two brigs. The energetic Perry also arrived that month to take command some two months before his British counterpart. Construction proceeded so rapidly that green timbers were used for the vessels. Brown's design for the brigs was totally functional, as the vessels were required for only one battle. With political decision, energetic leadership, competent builders, and ample finances, the Americans at Erie also enjoyed a tremendous logistical advantage. Naval stores were forthcoming through secure lanes from the New York and Philadelphia navy yards, while miscellaneous iron hardware was readily available from Pittsburgh.[6]

While Perry pressed forward his preparations, the secretary of war initiated co-operative efforts at Cleveland for the construction of troop-carrying boats for the Northwest Army. "These boats will be of the kind known as Schenectady boats, narrow and sharp ahead, and flat-bottomed," Armstrong wrote to Capt. Thomas Jessup, the project officer. "They will carry from forty to fifty men each, with their baggage, arms and accouterments and provision for the voyage.... If workmen cannot be found in Cleveland and other places on the Lake, you will take them from Pittsburgh." By May 1813, Jessup reported 15 boats ready with materials prepared for an additional 30.[7]

Barclay reported his findings at Erie to Procter and the two agreed that the vital objective was the enemy naval facility. Consistent with his strategy of pre-emptive strikes, Procter planned an allied assault in co-operation with his naval colleague. He needed one element to successfully execute the scheme: regulars. With the latest detention of the promised troops in May, Procter would have left his forts virtually defenceless to conduct an operation at the east end of the lake. Vincent of the Centre Division wrote that with Fort Erie in American hands, there was little point in sending troops to Amherstburg, as they would only magnify Procter's "distress" (meaning his shortage of foodstuffs). Nonetheless Barclay convinced him of the urgency, and Vincent wrote, "I think it so necessary that the remainder of the 41st Regiment should be forwarded immediately for the purpose of destroying this fleet at Presque Isle that I shall not hesitate in giving every assistance to Captain Barclay." Procter increased the pressure, noting that he had announced the impending arrival of the regulars to the Native chiefs in council, adding, "It might have the worst effect, were they to conceive I was deceiving or amusing them."[8]

Procter also seconded Barclay's arguments to Prevost's office on 10 June, seeking the 41st "without delay to ensure the safety of the district." He received (Brevet) Lt. Col. C. William Shortt of the 41st, but men only trickled in. "I stand very little chance here at the end of the line, if I am to receive only reinforcements that can be spared," he complained. "The cry has always been against sending men here." Procter retaliated by expressing a reluctance to forward requested warriors to the Centre Division: "I should run some risk in parting with any more. You have some very fine fellows among them, whom perhaps I may miss."[9]

Once more, Capt. Robert McDouall intervened on Procter's behalf, placing the situation on Lake Erie clearly and convincingly before Prevost. The commander-in-chief informed Procter that he had directed the newly appointed commander in Upper Canada, Maj. Gen. Baron Francis de Rottenberg, to "push on the remainder of the 41st." He also promised Procter £1000 in hard currency, £2000 in army bills, salt pork, shoes, clothing, entrenching tools, and naval stores. He concluded his letter with the rousing exhortation, "Bring forward the united power of both services to crush the enemy's endeavours to obtain an ascendancy on Lake Erie." Meanwhile, he presented a glowing image of developments to London, describing the "judicious arrangements" of that "distinguished leader [Procter]" as preparatory to a successful advance on Fort Meigs. On 24 June, Prevost sent another request to Admiral Warren at Halifax for sailors, specifically for Barclay's vessels.[10]

Procter summarized the increasingly complex vortex of problems that swirled around him:

We are well aware of the necessity of giving the first blow, indeed we owe everything to our having done so. Captain Barclay has, I believe, written urgently to Sir James Yeo on the necessity of our having seamen without delay. If I had a regular force, on which alone I could place any reliance, I could give impulse to my Indian force that would enable them to feed at the enemy's expense. At present, they are not half fed and would leave us if they were not warm in our cause. The want of meat does operate much against us, as does the want of Indian arms and goods. In short, our wants are so serious that the enemy must derive great advantage from them alone. Surely, Mr. Couche need not have kept us so entirely without money as well as meat. I am however full of hope that we will stand our ground.[11]

Procter and Barclay held out hope that with Vincent's co-operation, McDouall's representations, and Prevost's directions, the situation might yet be salvaged. They moved ahead with preparations against Erie, loading the field train on the heavy vessels. At this point, Yeo transmitted a verbal answer to Barclay's requests for seamen to the effect that he would send none. Undeterred, Procter and Barclay pushed forward with the Erie expedition, as the destruction of the American navy in port would obviate the glaring need for seamen. Everything depended on the timely arrival of the regulars.[12]

The frequent appeals for aid from Amherstburg were having one effect: the horses of Procter's dispatch riders were "completely done up." The naval situation became so serious that by early June, small American supply vessels could coast along the Ohio shoreline in relative safety. The gunboats could have had ample employment in intercepting these but the inadequate crews had their hands full in manning the vessels for transport service after being released from the Maumee expedition.[13]

The continued American occupation of the Niagara peninsula was producing visible effects at Amherstburg. The commissariat had to convey uphill all goods and provisions to Long Point by land, a formidable task for its overworked establishment. The warriors on the Detroit frontier, having lived for weeks on short rations of bread and smoked whitefish, would not move for want of provisions. Disappointed at the inconsiderable British presence and the paltry provisioning, they became bolder. "The Indians were constantly endeavoring to come on board the prison ship to massacre us," wrote James Van Horne, a prisoner confined on a hulk at Amherstburg. "The British had to bring their armed vessels alongside to protect us." The departments, like the troops, went unpaid. In frustration, Procter wrote, "I do not like writing where I must dwell so much on wants. We are looking anxiously in every direction."[14]

At this critical juncture, Maj. Gen. Rottenberg arrived on the scene from Montreal to replace Sheaffe. If Procter and Barclay had any hopes that his presence would improve their prospects, they were abruptly disappointed. Rottenberg's first decision was to override Vincent's recommendation and countermand Prevost's direction by once again detaining the balance of the 41st on the Niagara frontier. His justification was to conduct a raid on Black Rock, a place no longer of any strategic value since Perry had removed the vessels to Erie. Not only did this attack of 11 July tie up the troops needed for the Erie expedition but it cost 39 British casualties including Lt. Col. Cecil Bisshopp, an active officer on the Niagara frontier. The negligible gains from this operation amounted to the destruction of a commercial schooner and the capture of four cannon, along with miscellaneous stores. Vital resources were squandered for an objective of questionable value while the strategic threat on Lake Erie mounted.[15]

Procter had to start all over in educating a new superior about his increasingly dangerous situation. In his first letter to Procter, Rottenberg established his views on defence in the west, declaring that if a British retreat from the Niagara region became necessary, the Right Division was to fall back on Lake Huron and proceed to Lake Superior. From there, it was to paddle via Lake Nipissing and the Ottawa River to Montreal using the traditional *voyageur* route. In place of the long-promised regulars, Rottenberg designated a reinforcement of a solitary company for Procter and even that, only when he was reinforced. By his letter, the military commander of Upper Canada identified his responsibilities as confined to the Niagara frontier and below while Procter was essentially on his own. Rottenberg did not mention the consequences of a retreat for the Native alliance, or for the inhabitants of the Detroit country.[16]

Angered by Rottenberg's letter, Procter penned his response immediately. Although he maintained his professional decorum and sense of nominal loyalty, he complained directly to Prevost. He expressed disappointment that the continued detention of troops exacerbated the already serious mismanagement on Lake Erie. He wrote, "If I had received from the Niagara Line the reinforcements which you had directed be sent, I should by this time have had it in my power, by the destruction of the enemy's vessels in the harbour of Presque Isle to have placed the Dock Yard and Post of Amherst in a state of security, that under existing circumstances, it cannot be said they are in at present." Still hopeful, he added, "Tho' certainly more difficult to be effected, it may not be too late, if agreeable to requisition, the remainder of the 41st be immediately sent to Long Point."[17]

As each critical day blurred into the next, Procter concluded that the lost opportunity for reducing Erie might prove fatal and pointedly declared the cause in a private letter to his friend, McDouall. "I have only to say the detention of the force ordered here by the Commander of the Forces has prevented this district being in a state of security," he lamented. Procter added that he would make no "attempt on Presque Isle except I have the whole of the first battalion [of the 41st] which I have reason to believe there is not any real intention of sending me, notwithstanding his Excellency's orders." Procter's confidence in his superiors was clearly shaken.[18]

The commander of the Right Division peered anxiously at enemies in two quarters. Although an American naval victory would automatically serve to isolate and starve his division, he could not ignore the growing military threat in Ohio. By this time, Harrison felt bold enough to send 150 Kentucky horsemen under Col. Richard Johnson to the defenceless Raisin River settlement for intelligence. Guided by a local resident, the party arrived at midnight on 29 June. The Kentuckians interrogated residents about enemy movements and spirited away five suspected British sympathizers. Johnson reported that Procter was incapable of undertaking offensive operations against either Fort Meigs or Erie. The settlers also provided information on a war party of 20 braves passing down toward Ohio to steal horses. The Americans gave chase but were unable to overtake the marauders. Learning of Johnson's mission and the near interception of the war party, Procter wrote to Prevost, "I am sorry to say that from the repeated and recent treacheries of the inhabitants of the Raisin River Settlement, it will not be in my power to preserve it." He declared, once again, that the reinforcements, money, and supplies had not arrived. To underscore his demand for sailors, Procter reported with certainty that the Americans were concentrating 11 vessels at Erie.[19]

Barclay echoed Procter's concerns to Prevost. In comparing the strengths of the rival flotillas, he acknowledged Perry's as superior. The British naval commander reported 268 crewmen on his vessels. Of these, 160 were soldiers loaned by Procter, the remainder, members of the Provincial Marine, augmented by his handful of sailors. With *Detroit* almost ready to launch, Barclay itemized his glaring deficiencies in seamen, ordnance, ammunition, and naval stores. "The exigencies of the service on Lake Ontario will not admit of ... sending many seamen," he wrote to Prevost, "It will require 250-300 seamen to render His Majesty's squadron perfectly effective." Like Procter, Barclay became direct in his writing, pointing out that his means had been "entirely misrepresented." He also revealed Rottenberg's interference in its proper light, noting that Procter "perfectly coincided in the propriety" of descending on Erie but that Rottenberg "had given him to understand that no assistance could be given from that quarter." Thus, went on Barclay, Procter "was obliged to desist from an enterprise for which he had not sufficient numbers to make success even probable." Barclay concluded by stating the obvious: "If the enemy do gain an ascendancy on this lake, all supplies must necessarily be cut off."[20]

In early July, Procter lost his solitary sympathetic ally at headquarters when Prevost sent Capt. McDouall to London. In his absence, the governor intercepted one of Procter's letters to McDouall. The commander-in-chief responded, writing Procter with some impatience that he had done everything possible to support the Right Division. Further, he directed his subordinate to rectify his deficiencies in naval stores and ordnance at the expense of the enemy, adding the taunt, "I am much mistaken if you do not find Capt. Barclay disposed to play that game." With further presumptuousness, he "concluded" the whole of the 41st was under Procter's command but that the British commander would communicate to him "with the characteristic frankness that distinguishes a zealous and good soldier."[21]

Even before Procter received this letter, he wrote Prevost with the unsolicited "frankness" of urgency. He declared flatly that Prevost's efforts for the Right Division were "of no avail" and revealed Rottenberg's role in the Erie fiasco without mincing his words: "By my Brigade Major, I also was informed that the Major General [Rottenberg] could not act in conjunction with me and Captain Barclay." Procter pointed out that had the commander-in-chief's instructions been obeyed, he could have not only destroyed the Erie vessels but supported the Centre Division with a powerful diversion. Baring all, he also disclosed Rottenberg's wild retreat proposal. "Retreat has never once occurred to me," Procter wrote. "The very attempt would make the Indians our enemies." Procter clung to the alliance as much out of necessity as fidelity.[22]

Prevost rebuked Rottenberg for his retreat proposal, but the latter was either ignorant or feigned ignorance of the priorities of naval superiority and the Native alliance. Like Yeo, he avoided the critical issue by leaning on protocol, replying to Prevost, "I join with Your Excellency in admiring the spirit of General Procter in rejecting the idea of a retreat but I cannot help observing that it would have been fair in that officer ... to state his objection to me circumstanced as he is in regard to his Indian forces." As the Centre Division had been reinforced by two more regiments (the 8th and 104th), his prompt action in forwarding the remaining companies of the 41st could have still been useful against Erie, but this was not to be.[23]

Prevost was certainly aware of the need for seamen and naval materiel on Lake Erie, having specifically represented Barclay's needs to Admiral Warren. As well, although he was conversant with the adverse effects of the American spring offensives, he trivialized Barclay's warning of the naval threat:

The ordnance, ammunition and other stores for the service on Lake Erie had been deposited at York for the purpose of being transported to

Amherstburg but unfortunately were either destroyed or fell into the Enemy's hands when York was taken by them and the subsequent interruption of the communication by their occupation of Ft. George has rendered it extremely difficult to afford the supplies that Captain Barclay requires which are however in readiness to forward to him whenever circumstances will admit of its being done with safety.

I have reason to think that the report Captain Barclay has received of the American force is an exaggerated one as I do not find even from their own papers that they have any other description of vessels on Lake Erie besides the two corvettes and the schooners.[24]

Barclay realized that his squadron might have to engage a superior enemy. On 29 July, he officially declared his inadequacies to Procter — *Detroit* lacked sails, hardware, guns, and stores. Most important, Barclay stressed his need for seamen, "The ships are manned with a crew, part of whom cannot even speak English, none of them seamen and very few in number." He also identified a need for good shipwrights to finish *Detroit*, as the builder, William Bell, declared his gang of workmen "ignorant of their profession." Despite this unpromising assessment, Barclay estimated that his unmanned, unarmed, and unprovisioned flagship would be ready to launch in 10 days.[25]

After the collapse of the plan against Erie, Procter and Barclay discussed their remaining options. They agreed that Barclay would sail to Long Point to take on any reinforcements and then blockade the enemy vessels in Erie harbour. Any seamen who arrived at Amherstburg would be placed aboard *Detroit*, which would be armed with what guns were available locally. The flagship would then join Barclay at Long Point. In the meantime, Procter would strike at northern Ohio to retard Harrison's buildup and capture supplies, as directed by Prevost.[26]

Procter suddenly found himself contending with a massive new dimension as Prevost's scheme of mobilizing the western nations came to fruition. Detroit resident John Hunt witnessed the imposing scene:

It was in June that I saw one of the wildest and most grand and beautifull [*sic*] Indian sights that I ever beheld. Col. Dickson of the British Indian Department had been on the Upper Mississippi and Green Bay Country collecting Indians to fight for them. About twelve or fifteen hundred warriors came down the river one very beautiful morning, all in birch canoes with the British flag flying, singing their war songs and as they approached

the head quarters of Genl Proctor at Sandwich, at a signal given, they commenced fiering [*sic*] their guns and turned the bows of their canoes towards
Sandwich or Canada shore, landing in beautiful order one after the other....
They were met upon landing by a part of the 41st ... with their bands and
colors flying, the Indians forming in squads of fifty, each squad painted
differently all over their bodies as they were nearly in the nude state. They
thus advanced escorted by the troops, dancing and singing their war dance
until they reached the house of General Proctor where a speech was made
to the Genl. in which they said all they asked was to get a chance to fight
the Long Knives at Fort Meigs that fort not being very strong.... All they
wanted to show their British Father the bravery of the Indian Warrier [*sic*].[27]

Robert Dickson's arrival with a horde of Menominee, Winnebago,
Ojibwa, Sioux, Ottawa, Sac, and Fox tribesmen introduced a drastic
change to affairs at Amherstburg. The combined Native coalition now
consisted of more than three thousand warriors, outnumbering the
regulars by six to one. Hopelessly ill-equipped to feed this immense
concentration, Procter was obliged to employ the new arrivals immediately or risk losing them. Given the pressing food shortage, his preferred objective was Harrison's supply depot on the Upper Sandusky
River, but the Native leadership disagreed. Through Tecumseh, they
insisted on another attempt against Fort Meigs. Procter wrote, "I had
... the mortification to find instead of the Indian force being a disposable one, or under my direction, our movements should be subject to
the caprices and prejudices of the Indian body, to the degree in which
my regular force was disproportionate to their numbers." Although
Procter avoided pointing fingers, he did suggest the source of this particular problem. He observed that Dickson's contingent was "restrain-
able and tractable to a degree I could not have believed possible" but
that they became "contaminated by the other Indians," meaning
Tecumseh's followers.[28]

Thus far, the western nations had not been threatened directly by
American encroachment. Many of these newly arrived warriors had
scarcely seen a White man. Their reasons for following Dickson to
Detroit had more to do with economics. An extended drought destroyed
the tribesmen's crops and forced the migration of large game north-
ward. As Dickson had already afforded them some relief, they now
accompanied him to Detroit ready to fight but expecting further provisioning for their starving families. According to Richardson, these
warriors were "of the fiercest character." He described one particular

Sac chief who had been invited to breakfast with the officers. "In the course of the meal, to impress upon the minds of his hosts the particular virtues of his tribe; and in order to demonstrate more fully the extent to which they carried their disregard of pain and death, [he] drew forth a sharp knife from its sheath, and having cut a piece of flesh out of one of his thighs, threw it contemptuously away, exclaiming that he gave it to the dogs."[29]

On 12 July, Prevost droned on with another batch of promises for Procter, including money and arms for the Natives. Significantly and for the first time, his list included "some petty officers and seamen." Procter, tired of unfulfilled promises, complained to him that the 41st were being forwarded so slowly and sparingly as to actually defeat their purpose in being sent. He closed his letter on a bitter note: "I have no hope of any aid from the Centre Division, where our situation has been little understood, or has ever been a secondary consideration."[30]

It was not until 18 July that Rottenberg suddenly awoke to the danger on Lake Erie. He wrote Barclay, "A force of nearly four hundred men are directed to march in successive divisions upon Long Point, as detailed in my letter to General Procter of this day's date. I am fully impressed with the indispensable necessity of an attack upon Presque Isle [Erie] and should have co-operated long ago, had I possessed the means of so doing. I trust it will not yet be too late, and that you will lose no time in making your arrangements for taking up the troops from Long Point." Even if four hundred men arrived promptly in a body, it was already too late. The field train had been removed from Barclay's vessels, which were now being readied for blockading operations. Furthermore, spies alerted Perry to British intentions and he hastily reinforced and fortified Erie. With the Right Division preparing to invade northern Ohio, the time for the reduction of the American naval base had passed.[31]

The combination of delays, empty promises, and missed opportunities seriously threatened the British positions in the Detroit country. Too late to be useful for pre-emptive strikes, the long-promised reinforcements arrived piecemeal over three weeks, mostly after Procter had already concluded his second Ohio expedition: 10 men on 24 July; 52 on 27 July; 115 on 2 August; 128 on 5 August; and 93 on 10 August.[32]

Another attempt against Fort Meigs made little sense to Procter. In May, his 24-pdr. guns had failed to breach the fort walls. As Barclay's principal vessels were at Erie, unavailable to transport the heavy guns, a renewed assault on the strengthened fort with light pieces bore little promise. These misgivings did not deter Tecumseh, who insisted that the American fort could be carried by stratagem. Since his braves had the overwhelming advantage in the bush, he proposed a *ruse de guerre* to decoy the garrison into the woods while their allies stormed the open fort gate. As the warriors would accompany him on to no objective other than Fort Meigs, Procter had little choice but to comply. His weakness in regulars allowed Tecumseh to determine the strategic objectives of the Right Division.[33]

Procter embarked about five hundred regulars in small craft, while the Native coalition of three thousand warriors took the land route to the rendezvous on the Maumee. Dickson led the western tribes; Tecumseh led the Wabash warriors while Roundhead led the Lake Indians. Procter reflected on the colourful gathering:

The encampment of this large body of warriors with their women and children presented a singularly wild and imposing spectacle. They were perhaps a more numerous assemblage of the Indian nations than had ever united in arms in a common cause; and the peculiar customs and appearance of the various tribes ... added not a little to the interest of the scene. By night the effect was almost indescribable. The blazing fire, throwing its red glare upon its swarthy figures which danced or regrouped in indolence around it, the sound of the war-song, the shout, the yell, strangely varied at intervals by the plaintive cadence of the Indian flute, or the hollow tone of the Indian drum, the dark foliage of the forest, slumbering in the Canadian night and half-hidden, half-revealed, as the light of fires shot up to heaven, or sunk into gloomy embers.[34]

On 20 July, American scouts from Fort Meigs reported the first British vessels arriving in the Maumee. The next day, the allied host surrounded Fort Meigs. The commander of the post, Brig. Gen. Green Clay sent a messenger through the encircling lines to Harrison on the Sandusky River, alerting him of the enemy venue. Clay had previously received word of the British approach through two refugees from Detroit. One of them, a former member of Dudley's command, had effected his escape from Native captivity in northern Michigan. The informers reported that Procter's militiamen were disarmed but that a thousand regulars were expected from the Niagara frontier.[35]

During the second siege of Fort Meigs, only isolated small-arms skirmishing occurred between the allies and the two thousand defenders.

On the late afternoon of Monday, 26 July, the American garrison heard extremely heavy firing on the Sandusky Road a half mile east of the camp. The tumult was a deception in which a thousand warriors, Capt. William Derenzy's Light Company, and a few militiamen conducted a mock battle. The aim was to deceive Clay into believing that American reinforcements had arrived, inducing a sally from the fort that would then be annihilated. According to John Richardson, lurking in the woods with the ambush contingent, the firing became "so animated that we were half in doubt ourselves whether the battle was a sham one or a real." Clay, however, was not deceived, as Harrison had sent him recent updates. "The supposed object was to draw out our troops from the garrison, thinking we had a reinforcement coming in," wrote one of the defenders, "but we were too well aware of their intention to be taken in by their British and savage intrigue." The exercise in subterfuge arrived at a dampened conclusion with the onset of a tremendous downpour, described by one American as "the heaviest thunder shower that I ever experienced," Fort Meigs being "completely inundated." On 30 July, the allies descended the Maumee River, their destination a mystery to the garrison. This second attempt against Fort Meigs netted scant trophies, some unwary stragglers, and a few head of cattle.[36]

Tecumseh's failed scheme did little to cement relations between the allies. Procter could not afford to linger in Ohio much longer with the uncertain naval situation; however, Amherstburg's failing supply system would offer little inducement for the newly arrived warriors to remain on the frontier. The Indian Department leaders openly declared that without some kind of victory, the Natives would desert the expedition. Facing abandonment once more, Procter acquiesced and decided to sail up the Sandusky River to attack Fort Stephenson.[37]

Although not a significant post, the newly constructed Fort Stephenson (modern-day Fremont), guarded the supply depot of Upper Sandusky, Procter's probable objective. Located 40 miles from Lake Erie, it stood on rising ground within sight of the Sandusky River. The fort was surrounded by a stockade of 16-foot posts with bayonets embedded in their tops. A seven-foot ditch and 19-foot high glacis earthworks encompassed the fort. It was garrisoned by 160 men and seven officers, regulars of the 17th U.S. Infantry. Upriver, from his headquarters at Seneca, Harrison declared that post "untenable ... with nothing of value but 200 barrels of flour." When he ordered its commander, Maj. George Croghan, to evacuate his garrison, Croghan replied, "We are determined to defend this place and by Heaven we will." The 21-year-old Croghan had been a volunteer aide to Harrison on the Tippecanoe campaign. Commissioned at the outset of the war, he served under Winchester before earning a promotion to major for his distinguished services at the first siege of Fort Meigs. Croghan was determined to earn further laurels.[38]

On 31 July, Procter's force gathered in Sandusky Bay in *Eliza*, *Myers*, *Nancy*, *Ellen*, and a number of bateaux to await the warriors approaching overland. The tribesmen arrived but in disappointing numbers, prompting him to lament, "We could not muster hundreds of Indians than I might reasonable have expected thousands." Although some war parties scoured northern Ohio, hoping to ambush any American movements, most of the warriors had deserted. "The greater part of the Indian warriors objected to having an American army at the Miami between them and their families which remained in the neighbourhood of Amherstburg, defenceless and unprotected by the warriors," wrote John Norton. "Among these, the celebrated Tecumseh took the lead. The main body therefore returned to Amherstburg. A few hundred warriors ... proceeded with the troops which followed General Procter." By Procter's assessment, "The Indian force is seldom a disposable one and only found useful in proportion as we are independent of it." He led his diminished numbers upriver and appeared before Fort Stephenson on 1 August.[39]

After an exchange of salutes between Croghan's solitary 6-pdr. gun, "Old Betsey," and those of *Eliza* and *Myers*, Procter disembarked his troops. He sent Capt. Chambers, Matthew Elliott, and Robert Dickson to deliver the customary demand for surrender in order to "spare the effusion of blood." Croghan's emissary, Ensign Edmund Shipp, responded with the customary refusal, asserting that the fort would be defended to the "last extremity." To dramatize the British ultimatum, Elliott said to Shipp, "You are a fine young man. I pity your situation. For God's sake, surrender and prevent the dreadful slaughter that must follow resistance." As Shipp turned aside, a warrior sprang forward and tried to wrest his sword while Elliott completed the charade by pretending to release the young officer, expressing great anxiety for his safe return to the fort.[40]

With the parley concluded, the gunboats bombarded the fort, joined by a 6 1/2-in. howitzer from the shore. Early on the morning of August 2, Procter ordered three more 6-pdr. guns ashore. These opened fire within 250 yards of the fort. That same morning, Matthew Elliott approached Procter and told him, "Unless the fort was stormed,

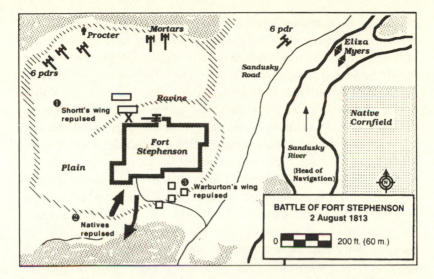

we should never be able to bring an Indian warrior into the field with us and that they proposed and were ready to storm one face of the fort if we attempted another." As Procter was reinforced that day by Lt. Col. William Evans of the 41st and 115 soldiers from Long Point via *Chippawa*, he considered an assault.[41]

In assessing the strength of the fort, the British officers underestimated the garrison as consisting of 50 men who could be overwhelmed by a frontal attack. Given the insistence of the warriors and the willingness of his officers, Procter decided to try. The plan called for a two-hour bombardment followed by a diversionary attack by soldiers and warriors on the south side, while the main assault would be directed against the north-west angle. Croghan observed that the British guns concentrated their aim on that corner of the fort and ordered his men to reinforce it with bags of flour and sand to prevent any breach in the walls.[42]

The main attack was to be led by Brevet Lt. Col. William Shortt, related to Procter through marriage. At 4 PM, he led 350 men (mainly of the light and battalion companies of the 41st) in three equal divisions in echelon against the fort. The first division under Lt. John Gordon approached the walls with Shortt in the lead. This body was so enveloped in the thick artillery smoke that it advanced within 20 paces of the walls before the defenders detected its presence.[43]

Ignoring the brisk small arms fire of the garrison, Shortt's column pressed forward into the ditch. Once there, Shortt found no breach in the palings. He pressed the attack against the 16-foot pickets, though his men lacked scaling ladders. American participants have Shortt exhorting his men with "Give those damned Yankee rascals no quarter." At that moment, a masked port in the corner blockhouse was opened and the 6-pdr. gun, previously arranged in a raking position on the ditch, belched forth its contents: a half charge of powder with a double charge of leaden slugs, nails, and jagged pottery. The effect of the shot upon the dense mass of assailants at the range of 30 feet was devastating. Dozens of soldiers were killed or wounded by the single discharge and the accompanying musketry. Shortt was felled in the act of preparing a white handkerchief for a ceasefire. The "good old soldier," Muir, was knocked down by a musket ball that grazed the top of his head. As the redcoats recoiled, Lt. John Gordon took command, rallied the survivors, and impetuously renewed the attack. Wounded in the chest while hacking at the pickets with his sabre, the young officer continued to "animate his men with his example" until he was cut down by a wound to the head. A second artillery discharge accompanied by a volley of small arms fire produced similar results, leaving nearly all the men who entered the ditch dead or wounded.[44]

Meanwhile, the 160-man column under Warburton (mainly grenadiers of the 41st and some battalion men) arrived in position late, after Shortt's column had already been repulsed. Nonetheless, this body proceeded to the designated point of attack by way of a sheltering ravine that ran parallel to the south wall of the fort. Warburton's four divisions were commanded by lieutenants William Gardiner, Richard Bullock and Benoit Bender and Ensign Procter, all of the 41st. After advancing about a hundred paces along the ravine, this column encountered heavy musket fire, upon which the men of all four divisions broke for the cover of the woods some three hundred yards to the rear. Warburton, some dozen grenadiers, and three officers (Chambers, Bender, and Ensign Procter) found themselves pinned down by musketry behind a slight rise 20 paces from the fort. The balance of the troops remained out of range, oblivious to the commands of their officers. The warriors ran off into the woods at the first fire, unaccustomed to direct assaults on forts.[45]

Procter ordered Warburton to retire, but the latter expressed a reluctance to do so till nightfall. Chambers' response was more colourful. Within the hearing of the men, he yelled out that if Procter wanted them, "he might come and get them himself," as they would not expose themselves. Although the entire column sought cover, Chambers, wounded in one leg and with an annoying thorn in the boot of the other, took time to inspire Lt. Bender, who was sheltering himself. "If I had a leg to kick him, I would do it," he later recounted. Despite such talk, the assailants were in a precarious fix, Warburton noting that should the enemy conduct a sally, they would "cut but a poor figure."[46]

Private Shadrach Byfield managed to outrun the enemy fire. Jumping into a battery, he found Procter there, weeping and exclaiming, "Good God! What shall I do about the men!" The British commander came to the rear of Shortt's position to help with the wounded, but the forward elements of the two columns could do little more than remain under cover. As the stand-off continued in the hot sun, the garrison lowered water to the outside in response to the agonized calls of the wounded British soldiers. The assailants remained pinned down till 8 PM. Then, with the moonlight obscured by cloud cover, they withdrew under light musket fire, the warriors helping to bear off the wounded. The allies, particularly the 41st, sustained heavy casualties during the half-hour encounter. Procter recorded 26 men confirmed killed, 29 missing (most of whom were also killed), and 41 wounded. The fatalities included Shortt and Gordon and an interpreter of the Indian Department. Three other line officers were slightly wounded.[47]

Procter reported that the "brave assailants ... had been carried away by a high sense of honour to urge too strongly, the attack." His disappointment in the heavy losses was great, and he later admitted that "The business had entirely failed." The unexpected fire from the masked 6-pdr gun at point-blank range only partly explains the heavy casualties. The stubborn persistence of Shortt's column in storming unbreached walls was unusual. Richardson later blamed Procter for furnishing the men with axes that were dull from use. Aside from the questionable premise that the responsibility for sharpening axes falls to a general officer, his explanation ignored the intense fire that would have swept men away had they brandished sharpened axes or dull ones.[48]

A more plausible explanation for the suicidal assault lies in the internal politics of the officers. That the previous smart actions of the Right Division had gone unrecognized in the form of officer promotions served to magnify the rivalry between captains Muir and Chambers. The first personal slurs began after the battle of Frenchtown when Chambers spread stories about Lt. Bender (Muir's brother-in-law) hiding from the American fire. Chambers' insinuations continued for months until finally Bender was forbidden to dine in the mess with his brother officers, and he demanded a court martial. The full extent of this rift is not known, but the lines were clearly drawn between Muir,

Bender, MacLean, and Ensign Procter on the one hand and Chambers, Tallon, Mockler, and Ensign Richardson on the other. Chambers' role was particularly noteworthy. When he harshly criticized Procter's aide, Lt. McLean, the general counselled him in writing that "reproof" is a more effective technique of leadership than "resentment" and "more in the true spirit of the service." Prior to the assault on Fort Stephenson, Chambers was a prominent player in the bravado concerning the "warm work" to follow, predicting that "many of the officers would shake in their shoes."[49]

Fearful that his weakened force would be cut off by Perry or Harrison, Procter conducted a hasty departure at 3 AM on 3 August, leaving behind a bateau loaded with miscellaneous stores. He also left his dead and some of the wounded who could not be recovered. The American defenders had only one man significantly wounded during the assault. Detroit resident John Hunt recalled the British "came home cursing Major Croghan and saying he loaded his guns with nails, slugs and everything and anything that came to hand." Muir, the top of his head disfigured by a musket ball that riddled his cap, asserted, "Look here boy, what the Yankees done at Fort Stephenson. They came near scalping me!" The second Ohio expedition was a miserable affair, producing an adverse effect on the *esprit de corps* of the Right Division while widening the rift between the allies.[50]

From Amherstburg, Procter sent Lt. John Le Breton (Royal Newfoundland Regiment) to Fort Stephenson to inquire about the missing and to seek the return of the wounded soldiers on parole. Harrison replied that he referred the prisoner issue to his government and that the wounded received "every aid that surgical skill could give." When the American commander heard the cannonading of 2 August, he realized that Procter had only light artillery and resolved to raise the siege with about a thousand men. Procter subsequently learned from Lt. Le Breton that his adversary was only three miles distant on the night of the attack and could have cut off Procter's retreat had he advanced. Two thousand Ohio volunteers also converged on Fort Stephenson within days. On the very day of the battle, Perry was bringing his vessels into Lake Erie. Procter's retreat had been a timely one.[51]

In his report, Procter attributed the fruitless results of his expedition to his fickle allies:

The troops, after the artillery had been used for some hours, attacked two faces, and impossibilities being attempted, failed. The troops maintained the greatest bravery ... but the Indians who had proposed the assault, and had it not been assented to, would have ever stigmatized the British character, scarcely came under fire, before they ran off out of reach. A more than adequate sacrifice having been made to Indian opinion, I drew off the brave assailants who had been carried away by a high sense of honour to urge too strongly the attack.... You will perceive that my Indian force is seldom disposable, never to be relied on in the hour of need, and is only found to be useful in proportion as we are independent of it.[52]

Richardson confirmed Procter's assertion that the attack was made at Native insistence: "Annoyed by the failure of his cherished scheme [the ruse at Fort Meigs], Tecumseh urged upon General Procter the necessity of doing something before our return, and ... it was determined to change the theatre of operations to Sandusky." The single consequence of Tecumseh's ambush schemes occurred when a war party attacked a troop of American dragoons near Lower Sandusky. The horsemen flushed the braves from their concealment and killed all but one of the 12. The survivor, an Ojibwa named Ocamau, was "literally cut to pieces ... receiving wounds in the face, head, breast and back"; he died from his injuries a few years later. This strategically insignificant incident had a depressing effect on the already sagging Native morale, prompting Procter to seek a troop of the 19th Dragoons to counteract the warriors' "dread of cavalry."[53]

The steady American advance in northern Ohio also dismayed the neutral Natives of the locality as some four hundred Delaware, Shawnee, Mingo and Seneca warriors offered their services to Harrison. Several previously neutral chiefs (Crane, Big Snake, Black Hoof, and Anderson), openly declared for the Americans while even pro-British chiefs such as Walk-in-the-Water waited for the chance to switch sides. So great was the despondency among the warriors that even Tecumseh proposed to abandon the alliance, complaining that the promised British reinforcements had not arrived and that the braves were merely used to "start the game." Frustrated at the poor provisioning of his warriors and the lack of success, he gathered the Wyandot, Shawnee, and Ottawa leaders and proposed to leave the British. Representatives of the other tribes, notably the Sioux and Ojibwa, reminded Tecumseh of his leading role in the alliance and dissuaded him from deserting. Nonetheless, many of Dickson's western warriors returned to their homes. The Sac chief, Black Hawk, departed, stating, "I was now tired of being with them, our success being bad, and having got no plunder." The majority of the Sioux and Menominee under chief Weenusate (or Tomah) also departed on 18 August, paddling their canoes to Michilimackinac where Capt. Roberts complained they remained till late September, awaiting presents.[54]

The consequences of an inadequately supported Native alliance became glaringly apparent. The confederacy had contributed substantially to past British successes. Ironically though, as the number of braves increased, their military effectiveness diminished. Harrison's cautious advance had effectively neutralized the benefits of ambuscade and guerrilla warfare. His strategy of "seize and hold" forced concentrated engagements against fortifications in which the warriors' individual form of fighting was disadvantaged. The lack of tactical success in turn deprived the braves of their motivating influences — plunder, scalps, revenge, and personal glory. The warriors viewed success in terms of victory on the battlefield, lacking the stamina necessary for sieges and sustained operations. Moreover, Native confidence in their allies was shaken by their failure to reduce fortifications. Harrison's steady advance had done much to negate the impact of Native terror.

Although Tecumseh remained with the British camp out of necessity, he typified Native attitudes in measuring the depth of British commitment in direct proportion to the visible British presence at Amherstburg. The war chief considered the ongoing shortages as proof of British duplicity. Driven from their villages and hunting grounds, the braves and their families were entirely dependent upon the commissariat for vast amounts of food that were not forthcoming. Under these unhappy circumstances, the influence of septuagenarian Matthew Elliott and the other Native leaders diminished progressively.

To the British officers, the Native allies (who, with their families numbered in excess of ten thousand) had become a tremendous burden. The demands for feeding this multitude fell to a commissariat that was already in critical straits. Upper Canada was seriously short of food, much of it smuggled in from the eastern American states. The sheer logistics of transporting these voluminous provisions overland and uphill to Long Point was tremendous. Also, the braves were angered to learn that paroled American prisoners reappeared in arms against them, creating another source of friction. The Native custom of selling American prisoners created embarrassing difficulties for the cash-strapped officials. It was only in the summer of 1813 that Procter was authorized to pay the paltry sum of $5 per captive. Prior to that time, British officials purchased Americans prisoners largely through private funds. The officers viewed Native atrocities as barbaric and cowardly acts, further straining relations between the allies. In military terms, they considered the braves undisciplined, insubordinate, unreliable, and useless in storming fortifications. Prevost's scheme of converting the western nations into "an impenetrable barrier" merely brought them to Procter's doorstep where the allied dissensions were magnified by inadequate provisioning.[55]

Events of the summer placed the allied expansionist objective and the alliance itself into jeopardy. The assembled warriors at Amherstburg sensed that Procter had lost the initiative but still looked to the British commander for provisioning, material support, and overall leadership. Past victories had provided Tecumseh with an opportunity to transform the confederacy from a military coalition into a rudimentary political entity aimed at asserting ownership of the Northwest. Despite his best efforts, he had failed. As the balance tipped against the allies, the notion of a Native state became endangered. Yet, more than ever, the two camps remained mutually reliant.

Procter still hoped to salvage the situation, begging for regular troops, his ultimate reliance. "Even the Second Battalion of the 41st tho' weak would be extremely acceptable," he wrote dogmatically to Prevost. Lacking three hundred men with whom to garrison Frenchtown, he abandoned that post. The British commander's letters began to betray doubts, as he wrote, "I have never desponded, nor do I now, but I conceive it my duty to state to your excellency the inadequateness of my force." Having lost the initiative on land, Procter had to devote his attention completely to pressing naval matters.[56]

During the Sandusky expedition, Barclay made a simultaneous attempt to contain Perry's fleet at Erie. The sandbar at the mouth of the harbour limited passage to vessels of a seven-foot draught, so Perry's brigs could not cross over with guns in place. Perceiving this circumstance, Barclay planned to blockade his adversary in port. He relaxed his watch on 19 and 20 July to pick up any soldiers or sailors who might have been forwarded to Long Point and resumed his blockade the following day. From Long Point, he wrote Yeo, "Captain Finnis [second in command] agrees with me that to risk an action with a very inferior a force would be imprudent and impolitic in the highest degree as in the event of any of HM vessels falling into enemy hands, *Detroit* would be of less use and their squadron would remain decidedly superior." Then, on 29 July, Barclay again weighed anchor for Long Point, remaining absent for almost a week, apparently because of bad weather. Resupply and repair considerations may also have accounted for his departure. Local traditions even attribute a romantic liaison on Barclay's part to explain his extended absence. In any event, Barclay resumed his blockade on 4 August to find that his adversary had emerged onto Lake Erie. If Barclay relaxed his blockade as a matter of choice, he committed a severe error in judgment.[57]

Perry had taken full advantage of Barclay's departure. Receiving seamen from the idle ships of the Atlantic seaboard, he acted vigorously to bring his vessels onto the lake. His enterprising engineers devised cumbersome but effective contraptions called camels (submerged pontoons) to float the brigs into deep water. Unshipping the guns to lighten the vessels, they pumped out the water from the camels, which raised their charges sufficiently to float them over the bar. By 4 August, *Lawrence* was on the lake, protected by the gunboats. Although Barclay reported his enemy "in a formidable state of preparation," he was unaware that *Lawrence* was unarmed, while her consort, *Niagara*, was in the undignified position of being stranded on the bar, also without guns. Barclay judged it best to withdraw to Amherstburg and await the completion of his flagship. As he sailed into the sunset, the American Navy roamed Lake Erie at will. Perry's heavily gunned brigs were the largest vessels to appear on the Upper Lakes to that time.[58]

Perry received accurate information on Barclay's squadron from nine deserters from *Queen Charlotte* who jumped ship during the blockade of Erie. Furthermore, the Raisin River residents continued to correspond with American officials. In Procter's words, "The effrontery of these people equals their want of principles." He arrested and deported at least one informant, John Kinzie, for "treasonable correspondence with the enemy." For his part, Perry guarded against British spies by directing the keepers of the Erie public houses to report any strangers in the lakeshore village.[59]

By Barclay's report of 24 July, the Lake Erie squadron contained 42 guns and only 267 crewmen. His squadron was deficient two hundred men and his flagship was unmanned and unarmed. While Barclay awaited additional seamen, he trained his crews at the ropes and guns, hoping that someone would respond to his needs. He had appointed naval officers to command the principal vessels, relegating their colonial counterparts to secondary posts, to which George Benson Hall, the former commodore, took offense. Desperate for experienced offi-

This is a postwar painting of Commodore Oliver Hazard Perry, whose decisive victory on Lake Erie left Procter no option but to retreat. It jeopardized Native aspirations for a sovereign state, and plunged British-Native relations into crisis.

cers, Barclay approached the slighted Hall for a "decided answer" as to whether he would serve on board the vessels or not. Hall, nurturing his grudge, smugly replied that he was always ready to serve in the station to which he was appointed by Prevost and confirmed by Yeo, meaning the dockyard. Barclay immediately suspended Hall without pay, prompting the latter to register his grievance with Prevost's office. The governor not only confirmed Hall's appointment as superintendent of the Amherstburg Dockyard, but chastised Procter for allowing Barclay to suspend him. Furthermore, in a clever exercise of deceit, Prevost directed that "no disposition of the naval force made by the senior officer commanding HM vessels on Lake Erie" was to be made without the "concurrence and approbation of the general officer commanding the Right Division." Procter again found himself saddled with the responsibility for the wretched marine establishment on Lake Erie.[60]

Meanwhile, Amherstburg was rapidly running out of food. Perry's warships had ruptured the supply line to Long Point while the bad state of the King's Road precluded land conveyance. Although promised "beef on the hoof" from Long Point, Robert Gilmor, deputy assistant commissary-general at Amherstburg, feared that supply would not keep up with demand and reported the alarming prospects to his superior, Edward Couche. Gilmor described a countryside bereft of cattle, adding, "I am really out, I have sent Mr. Reynolds to purchase the whole of the flour and corn ... in Michigan Territory ... and Sandwich." The logistical problems of feeding no fewer than fourteen thousand mouths per day were further exacerbated by shortages of staff and money.[61]

In far-off London, the future George IV (Prince Regent in place of his unstable father), directed the recall of Sheaffe and Rottenberg "with a view to other employment." The designated commander of Upper Canada, Lt. Gen. Gordon Drummond, while capable, energetic, and familiar with Canada, would not arrive for another six months. Procter gained little solace in his difficulties to know that the Prince Regent was "fully sensible to the judgment, spirit, and perseverance manifested by Major General Procter in the course of his arduous exertions to keep in check Major General Harrison's army."[62]

The army senior officer promotion list of 13 August did not contain any of Procter's officers. Procter himself was made major general retroactive to 4 June, but the 27 promotions within British North America reflected only one former member of his command, Col. St. George, who had returned to England for medical attention. Given their spirited actions on the frontier, the officers of the Right Division were disappointed. Furthermore, the elevation of their commander probably raised unpleasant suspicions in their minds.[63]

Just as the *esprit de corps* of the Right Division was ebbing, Americans rejoiced at news of the battle of Fort Stephenson. Insignificant as the strategic results of this engagement may have been, Croghan was promoted and raised to hero status. Perry's entry onto Lake Erie attracted far less attention but produced infinitely more dramatic results. There would be no more British incursions into Ohio. Even if the Americans did nothing, the Right Division would either starve or retreat. Once again, Procter itemized the neglects of his command but seamen increasingly headed his list. He acknowledged that he was on the strategic defensive on both land and sea as the Americans could engage him on their terms. Meanwhile, Harrison sent invitations to governors Shelby and Meigs to personally lead their militiamen in the final drive on Fort Amherstburg.[64]

NOTES

1. Procter to Baynes, 19 Aug. 1813, NAC, C 679: 456.
2. Barclay, *BCM*, 298. Robert Heriot Barclay (1785-1837) was born at King's Nettle, Fife, Scotland, the son of a clergyman. He joined the Royal Navy at the age of 12 as a midshipman and in 1805, he was commissioned lieutenant. In the 1808 action at Moir Montier Roads, while serving aboard the 38-gun frigate *Diana*, Barclay's left arm was shattered by a swivel shot and had to be amputed. On Lake Erie his rank was commander, but as the commander of a squadron, he is generally called captain. American newspapers erroneously identified him as the son of Thomas Barclay, commissioner-general for British prisoners at New York. *The War*, 5 Oct. 1813; *DCB* 7: 45-46.

   Commodore Sir James Lucas Yeo (1782-1818) went to sea at the age of 10. Within five years, he became lieutenant and seven years later, commander. At the age of 25, Yeo was post captain and was knighted three years later for his actions in South America against the French. In 1812, Yeo was acquitted of charges arising from his running a vessel aground in the Bahamas the previous year, and he was appointed to command on the Great Lakes. Arriving in Canada in May 1813, he immediately joined Prevost in a failed amphibious operation against Sacket's Harbour. Yeo maintained a tenuous British presence on Lake Ontario for the duration of the war but died of fever and "general debility" in 1818 off the African coast, at the age of age 35. *DCB* 5: 874-77.
3. Barclay, *BCM*, 299; Barclay to Yeo, 1 June 1813, NAC, C 679: 20.
4. Barclay to Yeo, 7 June 1813, cited in Malcomson and Malcomson, *HMS Detroit, The Battle For Lake Erie*, 39; Barclay to Yeo, 17 June 1813, NAC, C 730: 10; Barclay, *BCM*, 300; Barclay to Vincent, 17 June 1813, NAC, C 730: 10.
5. Barclay, *BCM*, 300; Dutton, *Oliver Hazard Perry*, 85. 223.
6. Brown, *Campaigns*, 41-42; Frederick C. Drake, "A Loss of Mastery: The British Squadron on Lake Erie, May-September, 1813," 55-56; Alfred Mahan, *Sea Power* 2: 68.

7. Armstrong to Jessup, 9 Mar. 1813, *DPCUS* 1813-14, Vol. 2: 2388; Jessup to Dr. Goodlet, 30 Apr. 1813, cited in Drake, "A Loss of Mastery," 55.

8. Vincent to Prevost, 4 June 1813, NAC, C 679: 60; Barclay to Vincent, 17 June 1813, *SBD* 2: 246; Vincent to Prevost, NAC, C 679: 107; Procter to McDouall, 10 June 1813, NAC, C 679: 110.

9. Procter to McDouall, 10 June 1813, NAC, C 679: 110.

10. Prevost to Procter, 20 June 1813, NAC, C 679: 113; General Order 18 June 1813, *SBD* 2: 157; Prevost to Bathurst, 14 June 1813, *MPHC* 25: 468-69; Prevost to Warren, 26 Sept. 1813, *MPHC* 25: 530. Francis de Rottenberg (1757-1832) was born in Danzig, Poland. He served in the Polish and French armies before joining British service as a major in Hompesch's Hussars in 1795. Posted to Ireland during the rebellion of 1798 as lieutenant colonel of the 60th Regiment, he gained some prominence three years later for the preparation of a pamphlet entitled "Rules and Regulations for the Exercise of Riflemen and Light Cavalry," which the British army adopted as a standard text of instruction. After serving in the Low Countries, he came to Canada in the fall of 1810 as a major general, relieving Brock as commander of the Montreal District. *DCB* 6: 660-62.

11. Procter to Lt. Gen. Sherbrooke (Colonel of the 41st Regiment), 15 June 1813, NAC, C 679: 107.

12. Barclay, *BCM*, 301-02.

13. Procter to McDouall, 10 June 1813, NAC, C 679: 110; Augustus Porter to Governor Meigs, 28 July 1813, Knopf, *Document Transcripts* 2: 11.

14. Procter to McDouall, 29 June, 1813, NAC, C 679: 155; Van Horne, *Narrative*, 14.

15. Lt. Col. Thomas Clark to Lt. Col. Harvey, 11 July 1813, *SBD* 2: 176-79.

16. Rottenberg to Procter, 1 July 1813, NAC, C 679: 218.

17. Procter to Prevost, 4 July 1813, NAC, C 679: 181.

18. Procter to McDouall, 4 July 1813, NAC, C 679: 177.

19. Procter to Prevost, 4 July 1813, NAC, C 679: 181. Richard Mentor Johnson (1780-1850) was born in Kentucky, attended Transylvania University, practised law in 1802, and served as a member of the state legislature (1804-07) before becoming a congressman (1807-19). A prominent war hawk, Johnson raised a unit of mounted Kentuckians that he commanded during the War of 1812. *WAMB*, 202.

20. Barclay to Prevost, 6 July 1813, NAC, C 679: 197; Barclay to Prevost, 15 July 1813, NAC, C 680: 256; Barclay to Prevost, 16 July 1813, NAC, C 730: 33. Procter's assessments of the Erie defences were based on Barclay's reports of seven hundred soldiers (mainly raw Pennsylvania militiamen), two blockhouses, and a small redoubt. While these were hardly formidable, Procter would have had to employ his entire regular

force to deal with them, leaving his own positions defenceless, and subject to be overrun by Harrison. Without the regulars, the Natives would neither attack Erie nor defend Fort Amherstburg. Barclay to Vincent, 17 June 1813, *SBD* 2: 246.

21. Prevost to Procter 11 July 1813, NAC, C 679: 216.
22. *Ibid.*, 220.
23. Rottenberg to Prevost, 3 Aug. 1813, NAC, C 679: 301.
24. Prevost to Bathurst, 20 July 1813, *MPHC* 25: 501.
25. Barclay to Procter, 29 July 1813, NAC, C 730: 27.
26. Procter to Prevost, 13 July 1813, NAC, C 679: 224.
27. Hunt, *Memoirs*, 25.
28. Dickson to Freer, 23 June 1813, and Capt. Roberts to Freer, 23 and 25 June 1813, *MPHC* 15: 321-23; William T. Hagan, *The Sac and Fox Indians*, 55; Procter to Prevost, 13 July 1813, NAC, C 679: 220; Procter to Prevost, 9 Aug. 1813, NAC, C 679: 371; [Procter and Procter], "Campaigns," 426.
29. Richardson, *War of 1812*, 102-03.
30. Prevost to Procter, 12 July 1813, *SBD* 2: 255; Procter to Prevost, 13 July 1813, *SBD* 2: 256-57.
31. Rottenberg to Barclay, 18 July 1813, *NOW* 1: 229.
32. Chambers to Freer, Right Division Quartermaster Returns, 12 Aug. 1813, NAC, C 679: 418; Rottenberg to Baynes, 22 July 1813, NAC, C 679: 272.
33. Richardson, *War of 1812*, 177. Even Harrison was aware of the pivotal role of the Natives in allied decisions, spies reporting to him that they had "pressed Genl. Procter to make another attack upon Fort Meigs and ... much disatisfied [*sic*] with his putting them off." Harrison to Armstrong, *MLWHH* 2: 481.
34. Dickson to Freer, 23 June 1813; Capt. Roberts to Freer, 23 June 1813; Roberts to Freer, 25 June 1813, *MPHC* 15: 321-323; Prevost to Bathurst, 25 Aug. 1813, *DHCNF* 1813, Vol. 3: 63; [Procter and Procter], *Lucubrations*, 348-49.
35. Clay to Harrison, 20 June 1813, *The War*, 13 July 1813; Harrison to Armstrong, 4 Aug. 1813, *MLWHH* 2: 510-13; Clay to Harrison, 22 July 1813, *MLWHH* 2: 493-94; Cushing, *Diary*, 133-34.
36. Cushing, *Diary*, 135-36; Richardson, *War of 1812*, 178; Procter to Prevost, 9 Aug. 1813, *SBD* 2: 44. William Derenzy transferred to the 41st in 1794 from the 62nd Foot as a lieutenant and became captain in 1803. Two years later, he was mentioned at Amherstburg, serving as a member of a board of inquiry into the loss of the schooner, *Hope*. Sheaffe praised his role in the British victory at Queenston Heights. He joined the Right Division in early 1813 and was engaged in the actions

of Fort Stephenson and Moraviantown, where he was captured. In 1817, Derenzy transferred to the 72nd Foot. Lomax, *The 41st*, 65.

37. Richardson, *War of 1812*, 178; Procter to Prevost, 9 Aug. 1813, NAC, C 679: 371.

38. Harrison to Armstrong, 24 July and 4 Aug. 1813, *MLWHH* 2: 496; 512. George Croghan (1791-1849) was a Kentuckian who was thrust briefly into national prominence for his stuborn defence of Fort Stephenson. The following year, Croghan (pronounced Crawn) commanded the unsuccessful American attack on Fort Michilimackinac. *DAB* 2: 557.

39. Procter to Prevost, *SBD* 2: 45-47; Norton, *Journal*, 340-41.

40. Harrison to Armstrong, 4 Aug. 1813, *MLWHH* 2: 512-13; Croghan to Harrison, 5 Aug. 1813, *MLWHH* 2: 514-15. Accounts of this episode frequently confuse Robert Dickson, fur trader and member of the Indian Department, with Procter's engineer officer, Capt. Matthew Dixon.

41. Croghan to Harrison, 5 Aug. 1813, *MLWHH* 2: 515; Procter to Prevost, *SBD* 2: 45-47; Edmunds, *The Shawnee Prophet*, 210; C.H.J. Snider, *War Log of the Nancy*, xii; Procter to Prevost, 9 Aug. 1813, *SBD* 2: 44. William Evans joined the 41st in 1795 as an ensign. He became lieutenant that year, captain in 1805, and major in 1808. Appointed lieutenant colonel of the regiment on 13 August 1812, he accompanied the second battalion to Canada the next year. Many members of this battalion were young boys, retained at Montreal for garrison duty. Evans proceeded with 150 members to join Procter at the battle of Fort Stephenson and had charge of conducting the boats and impedimenta on the Thames retreat. Wounded and captured at the battle of Moraviantown, he was released the following summer and commanded the remnant of the 41st in Canada, Europe, and India until 1821. His subsequent life is unknown. Lomax, *The 41st*, 369-70.

42. Croghan to Harrison, 5 Aug. 1813, *MLWHH* 2: 514-15; Procter to Prevost, 9 Aug. 1813, *SBD* 2: 45.

43. William Charles Shortt (1767-1813) entered the 24th Regiment as an ensign in 1792 and served on the American frontier during the 1790s. He joined the 41st as a half-pay captain in 1803, became major in 1805 and brevet lieutenant colonel in 1812. While at Fort George, he married Jane Crooks, a woman of the Niagara area whose sister, Jean, was married to Henry Procter's brother, Capt. William Bruce Procter of the 104th Foot. Although General Procter complained that Shortt "brought his baggage to us and left provisions and baggage of the 41st Regiment to be destroyed or fall into the hands of the enemy," he eulogized Shortt's "intrepid bravery ... in this gallant though futile assault." Lomax, *The 41st*, 75-76; Procter to McDouall, 10 June 1813, *MPHC* 15: 314.

44. Procter to Prevost, 9 Aug. 1813, *MPHC* 15: 348-49; Richardson, *War of 1812*, 179-81.

45. Capt. Chambers, Sgt. White, *Bender CM*, 32, 120.

46. Capt. Chambers, Sgt. White, Ensign Fitzgerald, Sgt. Stagnell, *Bender CM*, 29, 32, 76, 111, 115-16, 120-23.

47. General Order of 3 Sept. 1813, Richardson, *War of 1812*, 183; *The War*, 13 Sept. 1813; Byfield, *Account*, 23; Pte. Noonan, *Bender CM*, 94; 111; Harrison to Armstrong, 4 Aug. 1813, *MLWHH* 2: 510-11; Croghan to Harrison, 5 Aug. 1813, *MLWHH* 2: 514-15; Procter to Prevost, 9 Aug. 1813, *MPHC* 15: 348.

48. Procter to Prevost, 9 Aug. 1813, *MPHC* 15: 348; Maj. Gen. Procter, *Bender CM*, 131; Richardson, *War of 1812*, 180.

49. Procter to Chambers, 27 Mar. 1813, NAUS, *MIC*, 71; Bender, *Bender CM*, 41-50, 56. Much of the internal activity of the 41st could have been explained by its regimental archives but these were lost during the summer of 1813, probably to fire. Procter wrote, "I am sorry to tell you that the 41st has lost all its books which were very complete and consequently every register, every document. An irretievable loss." Procter to Prevost, 4 July 1813, NAC, C 679: 181.

50. Harrison to Armstrong, 4 Aug. 1813, *MLWHH* 2: 513-14; Atherton, *Narrative*, 108-09; Hunt, *Memoirs*, 26.

51. Procter to Harrison, 7 Aug. 1813; Harrison to Procter, 10 Aug. 1813, *MLWHH* 2: 518, 521-22; Harrison to Armstrong, 4 Aug. 1813, *MLWHH* 2: 511-13; Chambers to Freer, 12 Aug. 1813, *MPHC* 15: 353; Perry to Secretary of the Navy, 4 Aug. 1813, *The War*, 17 Aug. 1813.

52. Procter to Prevost, 9 Aug. 1813, *SBD* 2: 45-46.

53. Richardson, *War of 1812*, 178; Anthony Shane, cited in Drake, *Harrison*, 186-87; Hunt, *Memoirs*, 63.

54. Harrison to Armstrong, 1 Aug. 1813, *MLWHH* 2: 506; John Johnson to Armstrong, *MLWHH* 2: 509; James Campbell, *Outlines of the Political History of Michigan*, 362; Jackson, *Black Hawk*, 68; Roberts to Freer, 28 Sept. 1813, *MPHC* 15: 393; Robert Dickson to John Lawe, 18 Aug. 1813, *WHC* 19: 346; Capt. Bullock to Freer, 28 Sept. 1813, *MPHC* 15: 393.

55. Calloway, *Crown and Calumet*, 196-232.

56. Procter to Prevost, 12 Aug. 1813, NAC, C 679: 371.

57. Barclay to Yeo, 19 July 1813, cited in Malcomson, "The Barclay Correspondence," 27. Robert A. Finnis came to the Canadas with Barclay in the spring of 1813. He commanded the *Moira* on Lake Ontario before Yeo ordered him to join Barclay on Lake Erie. Finnis commanded *Queen Charlotte* at the battle of Lake Erie. His unlucky death at the beginning of the action deprived Barclay of his principal officer for the duration of the engagement.

   Lt. Col. Francis Battersby (Glengarry Light Infantry) documented the most plausible explanation for Barclay's abandonment of the blockade.

He mentioned a report by Lt. OKeefe of the 41st (Barclay's acting marine officer) that Barclay left the blockade on account of bad weather. One would think, though, that this would have similarly hindered Perry's camelling operations. On the other hand, American accounts held that strong northerly winds reduced the clearance over the bar at Erie by several feet. Furthermore, by Robert Reynolds's narrative, "a gale drove Barclay away." The romantic version popularized by Amelia Harris, has "a pretty widow of an officer of some rank in Amherstburg" as detaining Barclay at Long Point. It is known that *Chippawa* delivered Lt. Col. Evans to Procter on the Sandusky River immediately before the battle of Fort Stephenson, where Shortt was killed. It is also true that Shortt's widow (the only "widow to an officer of some rank at Amherstburg") had family in the Niagara area. The difficulty with this explanation is the improbable timeframe. Shortt was killed on afternoon of 2 August and Barclay reappeared at Erie two days later, leaving too little time for the supposed events. A highly embellished version of this episode is presented in C.H.J. Snider's *The Story of the Nancy and Other Eighteen Twelvers*, 163-89. Battersby to Baynes, 31 July 1813, *MPHC* 15: 344; Reynolds narrative, cited in Coffin, *The War and its Moral*, 215; Memoirs of Amelia Harris, cited in Ryerson, *Loyalists*, 254-55; Snider, *The War Log of the Nancy*, xii.

58. Barclay, *BCM*, 302. Although Barclay's relaxation of the blockade attracted no scrutiny at his subsequent trial, one could argue that he might have left a schooner to weather the adverse winds. By leaving no vessel on watch and staying away, Barclay lost his best chance of engaging his enemy at advantage.

59. Procter to Baynes, 13 July 1813, NAC, C 679: 245; Malcomson and Malcomson, *HMS Detroit*, 41; Dillon, *We Have Met the Enemy*, 78. Kinzie and an accomplice, Chadrona (Jean Baptiste Chandonnai), actively incited the Natives against their allies. Procter arrested the pair and jailed them briefly at Amherstburg. Kinzie "was discovered by Tecumseh to be acting a treacherous part with the Indians. [Tecumseh] told General Procter that if he was not hung, the Indians would put him to death." Procter ordered Kinzie's arrest on three occasions, eventually sending him to Quebec. Chadrona hid on the upper River Rouge until the British retreat of 1813. Kinzie, *Wau Bun*, 195-99; *WHC* 19: 379n.; Hunt, *Memoirs*, 48; testimony of Capt. Nelson of the schooner, *Vermillion*, Fort Drummond Court of Inquiry, 15 Oct. 1815, *MPHC* 16, 333.

60. Lake Erie Squadron Return, 24 July 1813, *SBD* 2: 252; Malcomson and Malcomson, *HMS Detroit*, 62; Barclay to Hall, 14 Aug. 1813, Hall to Barclay, 14 Aug. 1813, *SBD* 2: 260-61; Freer to Procter, nd., *MPHC* 15: 362.

61. Gilmor to Couche, 6 Aug. 1813, 5 Oct. 1813, printed in *The Niles Register*, 4 Nov. 1813.
62. Prince Regent to Prevost, 10 Aug. 1813, NAC, C 679: 382; Bathurst to Prevost, 10 Aug. 1813, NAC, C 679: 395.
63. Prince Regent's General Order, 13 Aug. 1813, *DHCNF* 1813, Vol. 3: 19-20.
64. Harrison to Meigs, 6 Aug. 1813, *MLWHH* 2: 516-17; *The War*, 7 Sept. 1813.

12

DECISION AT PUT-IN-BAY

"I have the satisfaction to report to Your Lordship for the gracious consideration of His Royal Highness, the Prince Regent, that his majesty's flag waves on Lakes Erie, Ontario and Champlain, and with the blessing of the almighty, I hope soon to be enabled to add that it waves triumphantly the terror of its arrogant and unprincipled enemies." [1]

Prevost to Bathurst, 1 August 1813

HAVING IDENTIFIED his requirement for seamen to the colonial office and Admiral Warren, Prevost found that the response times would not meet the needs of the situation on Lake Erie. Therefore, he took action that was decisive but late and incomplete. On 1 August, he detained the crew of one of three troopships and forwarded them to Kingston for lake service. As he did not specifically earmark these for Lake Erie, Yeo promptly took the contingent aboard the Lake Ontario fleet. [2]

By the summer of 1813, the true situation of the Lake Erie squadron, one quite different from Prevost's glowing assessments, became common knowledge in the Canadas. The *Montreal Herald* summed it up: "On Lake Erie, it is said Commodore Perry has been reinforced with 300 seamen. He has about ten vessels, the largest about 20 guns. Our force is much inferior to that of the enemy." Withdrawing his vessels to the shelter of Amherstburg Harbour, Barclay awaited the arming and manning of *Detroit*, while Perry severed the British supply line on Lake Erie. [3]

At this critical period, Prevost personally rushed to Fort George. This was the furthest west he would ever go, reporting to the minister for war and colonies, "The great danger to which the Detroit Frontier was exposed in consequence of the naval superiority acquired by the enemy on Lake Erie, from my inability to obtain officers and seamen to man the vessels I had prepared on it, induced me to move forward to the centre division under Major General de Rottenberg to enable me from thence to second Major General Procter's undiminished ardour in maintaining an unequal contest."[4]

Despite these brave words, Prevost's presence produced no material result. His would-be diversion consisted of marching Vincent's troops before Fort George on 24 August in a "general demonstration" and marching back again "without a casualty." His tour convinced him of what Vincent already knew, that more troops, a naval bombardment, and a battering train were needed to retake that fort. Prevost then discovered that the Americans were concentrating at Sacket's Harbour and he hurried off to Kingston. That was the extent of his "seconding" of Procter's efforts. While acknowledging that the commander of the Right Division was contending with a "great superiority in numbers" and "extraordinary difficulties in providing provisions and supplies for his regular force and Indian warriors," Prevost predicted that the contest would soon "terminate gloriously for His Majesty's Arms."[5]

While Harrison was massing his thousands on the Ohio shore, Perry established a base in the nearby anchorage of Put-in-Bay, a natural harbour formed by a ring of islands. *Ottawa*, a small British tender, peeked into the bay, where its crew counted 12 vessels. *Scorpion* chased the spy vessel till nightfall, when the American schooner ran aground during a storm. Receiving intelligence of the naval concentration in Put-in-Bay, Procter wrote the commander-in-chief that he was "endeavouring" to dispose the warriors to meet an American landing. "I entreat your majesty to send me the means of continuing the contest," he pleaded. "Your excellency will find that we will do our duty but I heartily hope for more assistance from you. The immediate requirement was for seamen to man the squadron."[6]

Instead of assistance, Procter received a rebuke from Prevost for allowing "the clamour of the Indian warriors to induce you to commit a part of your valuable force in an unequal and hopeless combat [at Fort Stephenson]." The governor made it clear that Procter "ought not" count "too largely" upon his disposition to strengthen the Right Division, announcing, nonetheless, that he had ordered the 2nd

Battalion of the 41st to Amherstburg. (It would never arrive.) Eighteen naval gunners were also supposed to be on their way, along with an officer and 50 to 60 seamen from the troopship *Dover*. The governor growled that his movements to the Centre Division arose mainly from his anxiety for Procter's command. He expressed confidence in "the excellent description of your [Procter's] troops and seamen, valorous and well-disciplined." Prevost had words for Barclay, too. In his myopic view, the naval commander "has only to dare and the enemy is discomfited." He closed his letter, brimming with exhortation and invective by writing, "I conclude that M. Gen. de Rottenberg's requisition for the temporary aid of 4 or 500 Indians has been complied with."[7]

Procter could not let this taunting letter pass. He replied to Prevost, having lost neither his sense of humour nor his ability to play with words:

Your excellency speaks of seamen, valorous and well-disciplined. Except the 25 whom Capt. Barclay brought with him, there are none of that description on this lake, at least not on board His Majesty's vessels.... There are scarcely enough, and of a miserable description to work the vessels, some of which cannot be used for want of hands, such as we have. I have the highest opinion of Captain Barclay and have afforded him every aid I possibly could. We have but the one object in view, the good of his majesty's service, or preservation of the District. Captain Barclay has besides the Royal Newfoundland, one hundred and fifty of the 41st Regiment. Better soldiers there cannot be but they are only landsmen.... I will venture to offer that as long as Captain Barclay, without seamen can avoid the enemy, he should so do. All my ordnance is on board except the field.... Seamen should be pushed on even by dozens.... The enemy's fleet reconnoitred ours, laying off Hartley's Point, three miles below Amherstburg. They anchored off the [New] Settlement twenty miles below Amherstburg. Boats are collecting in numbers at the Islands.[8]

Procter and Barclay had done everything within their power to prepare the squadron. Convinced that all depended on the outcome of the impending naval engagement, Procter denuded the Fort Amherstburg ramparts of their assorted guns (these were of six classes and six calibres) to arm *Detroit*, placing a total of 250 foot soldiers on the vessels. Meanwhile, Barclay cannibalized sails, rigging, cables, and hardware for his flagship from *Queen Charlotte* and lesser vessels, drilling his mixed crews at the guns. Procter called out two companies of Essex militiamen to patrol the shoreline for signs of the impending invasion. He strengthened his shore defences by constructing a blockhouse and batteries at Bar Point (Hartley Point) and another blockhouse with two 24-pdr. guns on Bois Blanc Island. Perry sailed off Bar Point on 24 August and again on 1 September, challenging his opponent to fight. Until seamen arrived, Barclay could not comply.[9]

By this time, the Natives were extremely disgruntled, complaining about the lack of provisions and success. Observing the American fleet off shore, Tecumseh paddled his canoe to Amherstburg from Bois Blanc Island to determine why the British squadron did not meet the enemy. Browbeating Procter, he demanded, "You must and shall send out your fleet and fight them!" Not only were the warriors half fed but the unprecedented non-arrival of annual presents (ammunition, blankets, hatchets, knives, tobacco, decorative trinkets, and other merchandise) had a further dampening effect on their confidence. They viewed this latest disappointment as a symbolic abrogation of a traditional friendship. Procter had only recently acknowledged the long-awaited streamlining of the bureaucracy governing the distribution of presents. Now the Indian Department had no presents to dispense. The British commander purchased some goods locally with his limited funds but these were woefully inadequate. "If the Indian goods do not arrive here within a month, the most serious consequences may be apprehended," he warned, "I may appear importunate but I am not asking or urging more than a sense of duty dictates."[10]

Native disenchantment was so pervasive that even Harrison learned of "serious disputes" within the alliance. In late August, to instigate further dissension, he sent a deputation of pro-American chiefs to Brownstown where the Wyandot leaders notified Procter of the impending visit. Thus, the American delegation was disconcerted to find not the expected confidential council but a cool reception from Matthew Elliott, Thomas McKee, and Capt. Chambers. The delegates sat cross-legged in the council house to deliver a watered-down version of their message. In an attempt to demoralize the British allies, they reviewed Harrison's recent successes in Ohio and declared that the Northwest Army was poised to overrun the British positions. They extended Harrison's invitation to the pro-British chiefs to "come and talk with him." The Wyandot, Seneca, Delaware, and Shawnee representatives formally returned the proffered wampum, signifying a rejection of Harrison's proposals. Then the implacable Roundhead delivered a strong reply on behalf of the assembled allied chiefs: "We are happy that Your Father is coming out of his hole as he has been like a ground hog under the ground and will save us much trouble in travelling to meet him. We recommend you to remain at home and take no part in the war." [11]

Roundhead's rejection of Harrison's overture was unequivocal. The allied chiefs were so hostile that Chambers feared they would toma-hawk the American emissaries. "Nothing could be more noble than the behaviour of our Indians," he reported. To prevent the delegates from tampering with the British allies, Elliott took special precautions to keep their eight members under surveillance. Nonetheless, Walk-in-the-Water established clandestine contact with them and indicated his willingness to co-operate with the American advance by seizing the Huron Church at Sandwich. Roundhead's powerful speech was his last service to the alliance. In a few days, the 50-year-old chief, second in standing within the Native confederacy, died from natural causes. Lamenting his demise, Procter wrote, "The Indian cause and ours experienced a serious loss in the death of Roundhead." [12]

Barclay waited with growing impatience for the promised sailors. He sent a canoe to investigate the American activity in the islands, appre-hensive that a sailing vessel would be becalmed and captured. Barclay's predicament was difficult. Although his squadron was in no condition to meet the enemy, he knew that he must soon attempt to break the block-ade as provisions were running alarmingly low. "The quantity of beef and flour consumed here is tremendous. There are such hordes of Indians with their wives and children," he wrote to Yeo. "I am sure, Sir James, if you saw my Canadians, you would condemn every one (with perhaps two or three exception) as a poor devil not worth his salt." [13]

With the cumulative shortages threatening operational capabilities on both land and sea, Procter's letters and those of Barclay became more frequent and almost frantic. In a typical dispatch, the comman-der of the Right Division wrote:

I am at a loss to conceive why we are kept so destitute of money as Mr. Couche [Deputy Commissary-General] is no stranger to our necessities. The troops have been several months without pay, a circumstance which is productive of evil.... The civil artificers have ceased to work, from the want of payment which is much in arrear.

The want of money encreases [sic] the price of provisions as well as the difficulty of procuring them. We are under the necessity of taking articles of provisions of individuals on receipt, a mortifying circumstance, where our credit from bad payment is far from being good. The Indian Department suffer the greatest inconvenience from the mode in which they are paid, if they can be said to receive pay at all.[14]

At this eleventh hour, Prevost directed his staff to hastily repair some of the neglects of the Right Division. In response to Procter's lack of division staff, headquarters confirmed Lt. MacLean of the 41st as his aide-de-camp and designated Capt. John Hall (Canadian Fencible Regiment), brigade major. Neither of these measures would have been well received by the officers of the 41st. Procter had groomed MacLean for promotion by sending him as the bearer of good news after the battles of Frenchtown and Fort Meigs. MacLean's confirmation in the duties he performed for almost a year was hardly gratifying to himself or Procter. Furthermore, the appointment of Hall, a stranger to both the 41st and the Detroit frontier, served to distance Procter from his officers in the established command structure. Prevost announced that additional reinforcements were "intended." His military secretary, Noah Freer, wrote that with the seamen from the troopship, *Dover*, Barclay would "be able to make his appearance on the Lake to meet the enemy." Fifty seamen, one lieutenant, two midshipmen and two petty officers were said to be at York, with Thomas Talbot waiting at Burlington to rush them on by road. Furthermore, Yeo had transported twelve 24-pdr. carronades to Burlington for Barclay's squadron. Although these heavy guns would have been a welcome replacement for the light, mismatched armament of *Detroit*, the American naval ascendancy prevented their being mounted on Barclay's vessels. As overland transport of the guns to Amherstburg was out of the question because of the bad roads, these carronades would remain at Burlington, under tarpaulin, too little, too late. Oblivious to the Natives' mood and condition, Prevost again directed Procter to send "forthwith" six hundred warriors to the Centre Division.[15]

All depended on the arrival of sailors. In an update to Freer, Chambers wrote, "I am of the opinion that we shall be very shortly attacked here. If we had but a few sailors, the business would soon be settled." Barclay, however, could not wait indefinitely. On 6 August, Gilmor had warned of the ominous food situation. The untimely combination of lost supply line, mediocre harvest and the immense concentration of Natives produced an acute food shortage in the Detroit country. In the spring, Gilmor could feed the Natives only fish and bread, causing them to threaten his life. As the provisioning situation deteriorated over the summer, he fed them whitefish exclusively, broiled, boiled, stewed, and smoked. By September, Gilmor's situation was intolerable. The Natives "had been very clamorous for provisions," he wrote. "They had already killed working oxen, milk cows, hogs, sheep, and even dogs belonging to the inhabitants. They had waited upon me, threatening to take me to their camp and there keep me without provisions." Barclay was painfully aware of the food shortage: "There were above 14,000 Indians to victual, who had come from different countries, accustomed to every indulgence and prone to quarrel and turn their arms against their friends as well as foes if their wants were not supplied and liberally, too. To this number was to be added the whole population of that part of the country and the regular force attached to General Procter." [16]

Gilmor's desperation was complete. The small quantities of local produce being "hunted up" were woefully inadequate to satisfy demand, and he had no money with which to procure more. To compound this crisis, the main water mills on the Thames (McGregor's and Arnold's) had been damaged by the same heavy spring rains that prevented Procter's hotshot from igniting Fort Meigs. The windmills of the area were of little service at this time of year. Meat was also critically short as the warriors had wastefully killed most of the cattle to secure powder horns, leaving the carcasses to putrefy in the sun. Gilmor was forced to requisition the remaining milk cows from the unhappy residents of the area. Although his agents at Detroit, Sandwich, and Delaware scoured the countryside for flour, corn, and cattle, he realized that his was a losing battle. At the end of his wits, he felt obliged to declare to Procter that he would soon be in "absolute want," adding, "It gives me additional pain to be thus obliged to trouble you." Gilmor admitted, "I am completely worn out with fatigue." [17]

At about this time, entrepreneur Thomas Verchères de Boucherville managed to break through the blockade with a fleet of freight canoes. He eluded the American Navy by coasting along the north shore of Lake Erie to deliver a precious cargo of merchandise to Amherstburg. "I was so busy in the store that I scarcely had an opportunity to examine my invoices and place the goods on the shelves," he gloated. "By this time, they were in need of everything and no one wanted to miss a splendid chance.... The first day, I took in more than two thousand, four hundred dollars.... Everybody, townsmen, soldiers, sailors, [and] Indians had a supply of army bills bearing interest. The British government had no merchandise to give to the Indians and passed out this paper money as a substitute. I was master of the situation."[18]

Michilimackinac's need for foodstuffs was even more pressing than that of Amherstburg as the end of the navigation season was not far off. On 31 August, Procter sent the schooner, *Nancy*, loaded with flour, the last supply run that Michilimackinac would receive from its support base. Among the deck passengers were Capt. Richard Bullock of the 41st and his family; Bullock was to replace the ailing Roberts as post commander. The crewmen of *Nancy* were also on short allowances. "I received no part of the provisions due me from the Commissary since 18th July, 1813, except 2000 lbs. pork," observed her skipper, Capt. Alexander McIntosh. "The balance remains due. D.A.C.Gl. Gilmor at the time it was demanded, said it was not in store, consequently the rum, pease & bread are to be accounted for from the above date."[19]

From New York, Col. Thomas Barclay, the British commissioner-general for prisoners, warned Prevost's office by coded message that the Americans were preparing for a massive general offensive on all fronts. Procter's nightmare would soon be relegated to insignificance as British commanders to the east contended with the latest onslaught. The Right Division would become as isolated and neglected as Hull's army had been a year previously.[20]

Ironically, Procter's regular force of 1130 regulars (all ranks, counting those on Barclay's vessels) was larger than ever. He actually had the semblance of the regiment Brock had originally promised. His allies were also numerous, exceeding three thousand warriors. Unfortunately, the British general could neither use his combined force offensively nor sustain it. Clinging to Brock's cornerstones for defence, naval superiority and the Native alliance, Procter struggled to maintain his positions, writing Prevost, "I entreat Your Excellency to direct more sailors to be sent to this lake."[21]

It was the food situation that dictated British command decisions at Amherstburg. In prewar years, the Detroit country exported cultivated produce and imported livestock. In 1793 alone, local merchants shipped out four thousand bushels of corn and 95 tons of wheat. In 1813, though, adverse weather conditions and the combined effects of the war reduced agricultural output to little more than subsistence levels, leaving the Right Division dependent on external sources. By 5 September 1813, Gilmor found the situation "truly alarming," hunting up small quantities of food, for which he could not pay. Between 25 June and 24 September 1813, he accumulated a debt of £5131 to various local interests for goods and services. Required to issue almost four tons of flour per day, he had only 40 barrels on hand, substituting 14 cattle instead, rapidly depleting the herd. His remaining food stocks consisted of three hundred bushels of corn. On 5 September 1813, the day Gilmor reported these figures, Rottenberg wrote Prevost that flour and droves of cattle were en route to Amherstburg via the Thames to feed the division "hand to mouth." [22]

The famished Natives were now vociferous in their demands. With winter threatening military, Native, and civil communities alike, Procter thrust aside any attempt at niceties and predicted "ills of the greatest magnitude" if he were not resupplied. "The long awaited supplies cannot any longer be delayed without the most frightful consequences," he wrote. "The Indian and his family, suffering from cold will no longer be amused with promises.... Defection is the least of evils we can expect from him." The Natives were verging on hostility against their allies. [23]

Finally, on 6 September, Barclay received 36 sailors, two lieutenants, a master's mate, and two gunners. He met with Procter, who pointed out that an attempt must be made to reopen the water route. Barclay wrote Yeo, "I fully agree with the General." That same day, Prevost wrote a letter from Kingston that a further reinforcement of sailors from the troopship *Dover*, consisting of five officers, 40 seamen, and eight marines, had arrived there, destined for Amherstburg. On 8 September, Procter and Barclay agreed that the only hope lay in risking all on a naval engagement. Weighing anchor at 3 PM on Thursday, 9 September, the British naval commander sailed to meet the enemy. His last words to Procter were enigmatic: "You can speak to my having done my duty to the present hour." Barclay would state:

I should be obliged to sail with the squadron, deplorably manned as it was, to enable us to get stores and provisions of every description.... So perfectly destitute of provisions was the post, that there was not a days flour left in the store and the crews of the squadron were on half-allowances of many things and when that was done, there was no more. Such were the motives that induced Major General Procter to concur in the necessity of a battle being risqued [*sic*].... No intelligence of seamen having arrived, I sailed ... expecting to meet the enemy next morning. [24]

Lacking adequate officers and seamen, Barclay retired the tiny schooner, *Erie*. His remaining force consisted of: [25]

Vessel	Long Guns	Carronades
• *Detroit* (490 tons)	2 x 24-pdr.	1 x 24-pdr.
	1 x 18"	1 x 18"
	6 x 12"	
	8 x 9"	
• *Queen Charlotte* (400 tons)	3 x 12"	14 x 24"
• *Lady Prevost* (230 tons)	3 x 9"	10 x 12"
• *General Hunter* (180 tons)	2 x 6"	2 x 12"
	4 x 4"	
	2 x 2"	
• *Little Belt* (90 tons)	1 x 9"	
	1 or 2 x 6"	
• *Chippawa* (70 tons)	1 x 9"	

Detroit sails into Lake Erie, 9 September 1813. Stoutly built but lightly armed and undermanned, Barclay's flagship sets sail for her first and only battle. *Little Belt* and *Chippawa* are shown on the left, Amherstburg Harbour on the right.

Courtesy of artist Peter Rindlisbacher

The twelve 24-pdr. carronades at Burlington would have greatly augmented Barclay's broadside capability and general efficiency in action. Although stoutly built, the flagship, *Detroit*, was in poor condition for combat. In the heat of battle, the guns of diverse calibres would generate confusion and inefficiency in the delivery of ammunition from below, particularly among an inadequate and inexperienced crew. Each calibre had its own sponges, ladles, and ammunition. Second, most of *Detroit's* guns were long pieces. While useful at a distance, they were of small calibre and awkward, requiring more deck space and manhandling for muzzle-loading after each discharge than the shorter, lighter carronades. In a "warm action," with debris and rigging cluttering the decks, long guns would become even more unwieldy. Finally, the condition of the improvised armament was poor, matches and tubes being so defective that the guns had to be ignited by firing pistols into the touch holes.[26]

Barclay's vessels threw 196 pounds of broadside metal from long guns and 460 pounds from carronades. Much would depend on the performance of the two principal vessels, the combined weight to be thrown by the smaller vessels being substantially less. It is worthy of note that the largest vessel and flagship, *Detroit*, threw less metal than her consort, *Queen Charlotte*, whose battery of fourteen 24-pdr. carronades was the most formidable of the squadron, while *Chippawa's* pop-gun 9-pdr. "broadside" was virtually insignificant.

The British squadron was manned by 440-450 men. Of these, 250 were foot soldiers of the 41st under Lt. Arthur O'Keefe, and Newfoundlanders under Lt. James Garden. The crews included 53 seamen and naval officers, most of whom had arrived three days previously. The remainder were a farrago of voyageurs, colonial mariners, and two Native warriors.[27]

The American vessels consisted of the following:[28]

Vessel	Long Guns	Carronades
• *Lawrence* (480 tons)	2 x 12-pdr.	18 x 32-pdr.
• *Niagara* (480 tons)	2 x 12"	18 x 32"
• *Caledonia* (180 tons)	2 x 24"	1 x 32"
• *Ariel* (112 tons)	4 x 12"	
• *Somers* (94 tons)	1 x 24"	1 x 32"
• *Scorpion* (86 tons)	1 x 32"	1 x 32"
• *Porcupine* (83 tons)	1 x 32"	
• *Tigress* (96 tons)	1 x 32	
• *Trippe* (60 tons)	1 x 24"	

Perry's long guns were capable of throwing 288 pounds of broadside metal while his carronades threw 1248 pounds. He enjoyed a superiority at long range of three to two (288 versus 196 pounds) and at short range of better than two to one (1248 versus 460 pounds). Although the outcome of an engagement would depend on a host of diverse considerations, the American squadron was clearly superior in armament.[29]

Perry did not provide an exact strength return for his squadron, his prize list of 532 names probably including those men down with lake fever. Careful to omit figures for either side, his official report after the action merely says, "The exact number of the enemy's force has not been ascertained but I have good reason to believe that it exceeded ours by nearly one hundred men."[30]

At 5 AM on 10 September, Perry's lookouts sighted Barclay's vessels bearing down on the Bass Islands from the northwest, and the American squadron got under weigh. The sky was clear with a light westerly wind. As the two squadrons approached each other, the wind changed from southeast to southwest, giving Perry the weather gauge, the luxury of selecting his position in relation to Barclay's squadron. As a result, the British commander reduced sail and awaited the enemy approach from windward. Perry came on at a 25° angle to the enemy, his flotilla straggling in a two-mile line, with the van, consisting of two schooners and the flagship, *Lawrence*, shooting ahead under full sail.

At 11:45 AM, Barclay opened fire on *Lawrence*, with the long guns of *Detroit*, and the fateful battle was joined. With only two 12-pdr. long guns with which to reply, Perry's brig took the punishment and pressed forward to achieve carronade range. Only the lead American schooners were close enough to help *Lawrence*, playing their heavy long guns on the British vessels. *Niagara*, commanded by Lt. Elliott, remained out of range, holding her position behind the lumbering *Caledonia*. *Queen Charlotte*, unable to engage her designated adversary, the lagging *Niagara*, brought up her strong battery to assist *Detroit*. Thus, the opening phase of the battle consisted largely of a duel between the *Detroit* and *Queen Charlotte* against *Lawrence*, creating frightful carnage aboard the three vessels. Amid the smoke and din of battle, men struggled at their duties, choked by the acrid smoke of the guns and stumbling over debris that littered the decks. Below decks, wounded men uttered muted screams and literally bit the bullet as surgeons worked frantically to hack off their shattered limbs. Two warriors on *Detroit* volunteered to climb the masts as snipers, but the action was too warm and they scurried down. One American punster later had them attempting to "tree" themselves in the masts with Splitlog "killed by splinters" while his companion, Walk-in-the-Water, ended up "walking under the water to Put-in-Bay and immortality."

By 2:00 PM, *Lawrence* had been battered into an unmanageable hulk, her crew largely casualties, and all but one of her guns dismounted from their carriages. Incredibly, Perry, dressed as a common seaman, remained uninjured. The booming of cannon was heard from Detroit to Cleveland. Unlike the cautious manoeuvres played out on Lake Ontario, Perry and Barclay were clearly pushing for a decision.

At 2:30, as the two squadrons paralleled each other in a southwesterly direction, *Lawrence*, a perfect wreck, dropped from the line. *Niagara*, fresh and uninjured, then came up on her port or sheltered side. Perry abandoned the disabled *Lawrence* and transferred his flag (oddly enough, it read "Don't Give Up The Ship!") to *Niagara*. The crew of *Lawrence* then lowered her flag in surrender. Like Procter, Barclay had engaged his superior enemy piecemeal and done well. Though the British squadron was badly shot up with most of her officers dead or wounded, the enemy flagship was out of action. Thus far, Barclay's flotilla had showed better squadron discipline and seamanship, maintaining a tight defensive line while the American flotilla straggled in two irregular groups.

At this point, Barclay's luck changed. Two serious wounds obliged him to seek medical attention below. Meanwhile, his adversary took the deck of *Niagara* and prepared to resume the attack. Perceiving Perry's design, the crews of *Detroit* and *Queen Charlotte* tried to manoeuvre their vessels to bring their uninjured batteries to bear against this fresh and dangerous enemy. In the process, the two vessels collided and became entangled, the mishap immobilizing the main British vessels. Perry seized his chance and swept through the British line in Nelsonian fashion, releasing the destructive power of his 32-pdr. carronades at half-pistol range against his handicapped enemy. *Niagara*'s broadsides raked *Detroit*, *Queen Charlotte*, and *General Hunter* to starboard and *Lady Prevost* and *Little Belt* to port. Then, turning about, Perry repeated the manoeuvre. It was over. The British crews hauled down their colours at 2:50 PM on all vessels except *Chippawa* and *Little Belt*, which made sail for Amherstburg. *Scorpion* and *Trippe* overhauled these vessels, leaving no British vessel to report the disaster.[31]

The battered flotillas gathered in Put-in-Bay to conduct emergency repairs and bury the dead. *Detroit* and *Queen Charlotte* were so battered

Courtesy of artist Peter Rindlisbacher

Months of feverish preparation on both sides culminated in an intense three-hour struggle at the Battle of Lake Erie, 10 September 1813. With the battered *Detroit* and *Queen Charlotte* entangled, Perry cuts Barclay's line in *Niagara*. Within minutes, the battle was over.

that both lost their masts in a gale on 13 September while at anchor. These riddled ships remained out of commission for the duration of the war. British casualties totalled three officers and 38 men killed and nine officers and 85 men wounded. American losses were 27 men killed and 96 wounded (three fatally).[32]

Two days after the battle, Perry notified Harrison of the outcome of the struggle, writing his famous dispatch: "We have met the enemy and they are ours. Two ships, two brigs, one schooner and one sloop. Yours with great respect and esteem. O.H. Perry." Wasting no time, he patched up the damaged vessels and prepared to convey Harrison's army to Canada.[33]

It was on the day of the battle of Lake Erie that Rottenberg received word of the second division of *Dover* seamen and wrote:

I am happy to hear that the Dover seamen are on their way and as soon as they arrive at the Head of the Lake they will be forwarded with all expedition.

Major General Procter writes me word on the 6th instant that he cannot give sanction to our fleet seeking that of the enemy if seamen are not sent to him immediately. He further adds that if they are not here [he] must starve for want of provisions. He has sent Captain Chambers here for the purpose of hurrying on the seamen. In order to feed that army from hand to mouth until we get superiority on the lake, I have ordered Captain Chambers to Ancaster with a detachment of a sergeant and 12 dragoons, provided with a press warrant for the purpose of collecting all the wagons in Dundas Street, Oxford and the back settlements in order to convey flour by land to the point where the Thames becomes navigable.[34]

The British camp did not immediately know the results of the naval contest. Lt. Col. Warburton observed the action from an elevated position in the New Settlement, 16 miles from Amherstburg, and considered the British the victors. By 12 September, no news having arrived to the contrary, Procter concluded the worst. "With the deepest regret" he reported to Rottenberg the probable loss of the entire squadron, along with his fort ordnance, a third of his effective troops, and all hope of meaningful resupply. Procter proposed a prompt retreat via the Thames River, calling the naval defeat "calamitous," leaving him "at a loss" respecting the Native allies. He urged the occupation of Turkey Point to protect the Long Point facilities, now open to attack. The next day, Procter wrote much the same letter to Prevost. Days later, the British commander received Prevost's letter of 6 September and grimly learned of the second *Dover* contingent, five officers, forty seamen, and eight marines.[35]

On receiving Procter's notification of the naval disaster, Rottenberg directed Lt. Col. John Harvey to prepare a reply. In a cold, stiffly worded tone, Harvey demanded to know who had ordered Barclay's sailing to meet the enemy when the British squadron was so "incompetently manned," and seamen were known to be on the way. Rottenberg's sudden understanding of the condition of Barclay's vessels differed from his letter of nine days earlier in which he had written to Prevost that should Harrison advance, Procter was to "fall upon the American armament ... in co-operation with Barclay's squadron."[36]

Strangely, by 20 September, Procter's letter of 13 September concerning Barclay's defeat had not reached Prevost at Kingston. That day, Baynes wrote on Prevost's behalf that Procter was to "impress upon Captain Barclay ... that the squadron ... is to be devoted to their [the army's] preservation and if necessary, sacrificed to the last atom." While urging that the "large proportion" of *Dover*'s crew be allocated to Barclay, Prevost also pressured Yeo to take action on Lake Erie in his letter of 14 September: "I cannot hesitate in desiring that some bold attempt be made without delay by Captain Barclay to gain an ascendancy and open an outlet for the supplies now lying at Long Point for that division of the army." On 19 September, he repeated his demand to Yeo: "You are already acquainted with the decided line of conduct which I wish to be pursued on Lake Erie by Captain Barclay and you will not fail to impress upon that officer the absolute necessity of regaining naval superiority and to preserve uninterrupted the intercourse between Amherstburg and Long Point." [37]

On receiving news of Barclay's defeat, Prevost abruptly altered his position, complaining to Bathurst of the "protracted contest on Lake Ontario" and of Yeo "leaving Captain Barclay on Lake Erie to depend almost entirely on the exertions of soldiers belonging to the 41st Regiment and the Royal Newfoundland." While there was some truth to Prevost's complaints, colonial observers saw things differently and made direct observations on the commander-in-chief's management of the war. Rector John Strachan was particularly incensed at the neglect of the Lake Erie squadron over the last year, declaring, "Volunteers for a small praemium might have been found to serve on the Upper Lakes for three months and in that time, the question would have been decided. More than three hundred vessels (I presume) have visited Quebec this season and surely a little expense and address might have collected two hundred seamen from them, a number which would have enabled the brave Captain Barclay to have gained a complete victory." [38]

As the extent and consequences of the disaster sank in, Prevost struggled to reverse its effects. He acquainted Admiral John Warren at Halifax with Barclay's defeat, seeking urgent aid to regain control of Lake Erie and ensure the survival of the Right Division. In response to his appeal, six troop-ships containing two battalions of Royal Marines, two companies of marine artillery, and a rocket company immediately set sail. These substantial reinforcements would arrive at Montreal on 31 October, too late. [39]

Yeo's assessment of the defeat was just as devious as that of Prevost, generously laced with half-truths. The commodore admitted that Barclay's squadron was inadequately manned but asserted, "I am perfectly uninformed as to Captain Barclay's reasons for risking an action before his reinforcement of seamen arrived." Questioning Barclay's credibility, he wrote, "I am not competent to judge whether that very great scarcity [of food] did or did not exist." To further avert criticism from himself, Yeo whitewashed the affair by blaming Procter for forcing Barclay into "a hazardous and unequal contest." [40]

While Prevost, Rottenberg, and Yeo were seeking to avoid responsibility for the disaster, Barclay dictated his report. Dangerously wounded in the thigh, the bedridden officer could not write, as his right arm had been badly mangled in the recent battle (the other arm had previously been "devoted" to the service). He attributed his need to sail with a "fleet deplorably manned" to the critical shortage of foodstuffs at Amherstburg, "no intelligence of seamen having arrived." He noted that Procter "concurred" in his decision and concluded with, "The honour of His Majesty's flag has not been tarnished."[41]

Perry released the severely wounded commander on humanitarian grounds, but since he had lost an entire squadron, Barclay was required to stand trial to answer for the unprecedented British naval disaster. The tribunal assembled at Portsmouth, England, a year after the engagement. Barclay flatly denied any knowledge of the second division of the *Dover* seamen. Had they been on their way from Kingston, it would have taken weeks to march the six hundred miles. Barclay was angered by Yeo's "insinuations" of his rashness, that he had "everything to gain and nothing to lose," pointing out that the few sailors he received came not from his superior but from Prevost, through Procter. The court fully and honourably acquitted Barclay, finding his defeat attributable to the defective equipment at his disposal, his lack of seamen, the superior force of the enemy, and the fall of his officers early in the action. Barclay's efforts were publicly commended.[42]

Neither Yeo nor Prevost was ever called upon to explain his role in the disaster. Although Procter maintained a professional silence at the time, he later attributed Barclay's defeat to Prevost's lethargy: "The most fatal and palpable error of the commander-in-chief was his neglect to preserve the ascendancy on Lake Erie and Lake Ontario which was enjoyed by the British at the opening of the contest." Indeed, the British broadside capability in 1812 on the Great Lakes was 1191 pounds versus 1050 for the Americans. In 1813, the situation drastically altered, as the American broadside of 2875 pounds greatly outweighed the British figure of 2091. Had Brock swept the germinating American lake installations in 1812 as he hoped, British command on Lake Erie would have most certainly been retained.[43]

The *Quebec Gazette* reported the details of the battle of Lake Erie on 7 October 1813, based on American accounts. "We have been relieved of the anxiety regarding the fate of our fleet on Lake Erie," it read, "the result has been the total loss of our naval force ... but has left the enemy in such a shattered condition as to leave little probability of

his effectively co-operating this season with his land forces in the contemplated attack on the portion of Upper Canada joining Lake Erie."
The strategic consequences of Barclay's defeat were not lost on public
opinion in the Canadas. The *Montreal Gazette* concluded, "We have
lost all but 'our honour'.... What men could do under existing circumstances, Barclay and Procter have effected." Although none of the
colonial newspapers blamed local commanders, the *Quebec Gazette* designated Prevost as the culprit in all but name, highlighting strategic
mismanagement as the cause of Barclay's defeat. Its article was reprinted
in U.S. newspapers as "Groanings From the *Quebec Gazette*":

The contest, if it ought to have ever been so called between Great Britain and
the United States, on the water, has been indeed gratifying to Americans and
mortifying to British subjects beyond anything that could have been figured
by the utmost strength of the imagination. Vessels of an inferior class, very
badly manned, have been as it were, thrown in the way of the enemy's
vessels, fresh from port, fully prepared and manned with picked seamen,
so as to afford them, at least, a semblance of superiority over British officers
and seamen, beyond what was ever obtained by the most powerful and
brave of the numerous nations with whom they have contended.

How long this disgraceful state of things is to last we cannot tell; but
we are sure that if it is not quickly remedied, we are sure it will not only
prove ruinous to these provinces, but dangerous to the naval existence of
Great Britain.... We have been conquered on Lake Erie and so we shall on
every other lake if we take as little care to protect them. Their success is less
owing to their prowess than to our neglect.[44]

In contrast, American newspapers reported Perry's victory as one of
epic proportions, rivaling the classical feats of Marathon:

The victory was the most complete of any in naval annals.... It may be
affirmed without fear that there is nothing in naval history equal to the late
achievement on Lake Erie, where an American fleet, inferior in size, weight
and number, captured the whole of the British fleet it vanquished. What are
Lord Nelson's most splendid victories to this? Or what in his brilliant annals
can be compared with commodore Perry's leaving a disabled vessel and under
showers of bullets, making good his way on board another, with which he
dashed into the thick of his enemies and compelled them to strike their flag![45]

Although President Madison reported the Battle of Lake Erie
to Congress as "a sanguinary conflict ... against a superior force ... a

victory never surpassed in lustre, however it may be in magnitude," the American victory did not need to be magnified to establish its significance. The outcome immediately placed the Northwest Army on the offensive for the first time since Hull's invasion. A renewed enthusiasm swept throughout the republic, and the cry was once again, "On to Canada!"[46]

NOTES

1. Prevost to Bathurst, 1 Aug. 1813, *MPHC* 25: 506-07.
2. *Ibid.*, 508.
3. *Montreal Herald*, 28 Aug. 1813.
4. Prevost to Bathurst, 25 Aug. 1813, *MPHC* 25: 511.
5. *Ibid.*, 511.
6. Chambers to Freer, 22 Aug. 1813, *MPHC* 15: 356; Perry to Armstrong, 2 Sept. 1813, *DHCNF* 1813, Vol. 4: 12; *The War*, 7 Sept. 1813; Procter to Prevost, 18 Aug. 1813, NAC, C 679: 447.
7. Prevost to Procter, 22 Aug. 1813, NAC, C 257: 139.
8. Procter to Prevost, 26 Aug. 1813, NAC, C 679: 494.
9. Cochran, *Narrative*, PAC, MG 40, G4, File 2: 50; Barclay, *BCM*, 298-319; Anthony Shane narrative, cited in Drake, *Tecumseh*, 187. Procter placed a proportion of effectives from each company of the 41st on the vessels, to join the hundred men of the Royal Newfoundland Regiment. Procter to Prevost, 26 Aug. 1813, NAC, C 679: 494; Byfield, *Account*, 24.
10. Procter to Baynes, 19 Aug. 1813, *SBD* 2: 263; Procter to Prevost, 29 Aug. 1813, *SBD* 2: 266-67.
11. Matthew Elliott's Transcript of Council Proceedings, 23 Aug. 1813; Chambers to Freer, 26 Aug. 1813, *MPHC* 15: 358-59.
12. Harrison to Armstrong, 22 Aug., 8 Sept. 1813, *MLWHH* 2: 526, 537; Clarke, *Wyandotts*, 118; Procter to Rottenberg, 23 Oct. 1813, NAC, C 680: 273. Although one is tempted to perceive foul play in the timing of Roundhead's death, no evidence exists to support this notion. In a later account, Procter attributes Roundhead's death to natural causes. Writers maintain that the chief was killed scouting Harrison's army after it landed (Edmunds), or at the battle of Moraviantown (Eckert): neither assertion is substantiated. [Procter and Procter], *Lucubrations*, 335; Edmunds, *The Shawnee Prophet*, 140; Allan W. Eckert, *A Sorrow in our Heart: The Life of Tecumseh*, 813.
13. Barclay to Yeo, 1 Sept. 1813, *SBD* 2: 268.
14. Procter to Freer, 3 Sept. 1813, NAC, C 680: 7.
15. Freer to Procter, 25, 26 Aug. 1813, NAC, C 679: 490, 500.

16. Chambers to Freer, 26 Aug. 1813, NAC, C 679: 445, Gilmor to Deputy Commissary General Edward Couche, 5 Sept. 1813, NAC, CO 42: 152; Barclay, *BCM*, 304-05.

17. Gilmor to Couche, 5 Sept. 1813, NAC, CO 42: 152; Gilmor to Commissary General William Robinson, 3 Dec. 1813, NAC, WO 57: 14; Richardson, *War of 1812*, 190; Gilmor to Procter, 14 Aug. 1813, *DHCNF* 1813, Vol. 3: 21.

18. Boucherville, *Journal*, 134.

19. Snider, *War Log of the Nancy*, xii, xlii.

20. Col. Thomas Barclay to Baynes, 31 Aug. 1813, *DHCNF* 1813, Vol. 3: 91.

21. Return for the Right Division, in Prevost to Bathurst, 25 Nov. 1813, *MPHC* 25: 556; Procter to Prevost, 29 Aug. 1813, NAC, C 679: 364.

22. Gilmor to Couche, 5 Sept. 1813, *SBD* 2: 291-92; Gilmor to Commissary General Robinson, 3 Dec. 1813, NAC, WO 57: 14; Gilmor's Statement of Disbursements, 27 Dec. 1813, *MPHC* 15: 488; Rottenberg to Prevost, 5 Sept. 1813, NAC, C 680: 22.

23. Procter to Freer, 6 Sept. 1813, NAC, C 680: 26-28.

24. Barclay to Yeo, 6 Sept. 1813, *SBD* 2: 292-93; Barclay, *BCM*, 303-04; Prevost to Procter, 6 Sept. 1813, NAC, C 680: 360; Barclay to Yeo, 12 Sept. 1813, NAC, C 731: 116.

25. Malcomson and Malcomson, *HMS Detroit*, 87; Barclay, *BCM*, 315. Although the original identities of *Chippawa* and *Little Belt* are thought to be *Cuyahoga Packet* and *Friend's Goodwill*, other candidates exist. William Foster to S. Grovenor, 22 Sept. 1813, cited in *The War*, 5 Oct. 1813; Report from Erie, *DHCNF* 1813, Vol. 1: 82; *Saga of the Great Lakes*, 125-26; K. Jack Bauer, "U.S. Warships on the Great Lakes, 1796-1941," 60; George A. Cuthbertson, *Freshwater*, 144.

26. Stokoe, *BCM*, 313-17.

27. Adjutant General's Return for the Right Division, enclosed in Prevost to Bathurst, 25 Nov. 1813, *MPHC* 25: 556; Barclay, *BCM*, 306; Alfred Brunson, *Western Pioneer*, 130; Malcomson and Malcomson, *HMS Detroit*, 87. The most thorough review of the British crews is Robert Malcomson's, "The Crews of the British Squadrons at Put-in-Bay: A Composite Muster Role and its Insights."

Arthur O'Keefe became an ensign in the 41st in 1804 and lieutenant two years later. Serving in the Canadas prior to the war, he recruited members for the 41st in England in early 1813 and accompanied the second battalion to the colonies in the spring of that year, arriving at Amherstburg in time to command the contingent of the 41st on Barclay's vessels. Lomax, *The 41st*, 80.

John Garden was a lieutenant in the Royal Newfoundland Regiment. He had charge of a battery of guns at Fort Erie in March 1813 and commanded the marine contingent of his regiment on Barclay's squadron. He was killed in the first minutes of the naval engagement on Lake Erie by the same cannonball that felled Capt. Robert Finnis (RN).

28. Theodore Roosevelt, *The Naval War of 1812*, 242. Two of Perry's vessels did not participate in the engagement. He beached the unseaworthy *Amelia* at Erie and sent Daniel Dobbins in *Ohio* to Erie for supplies.

29. For an examination of the firepower of both sides, see Frederick C. Drake, "Artillery and its Influence on Naval Tactics: Reflections on the Battle of Lake Erie," in Jeffrey Welsh and David Skaggs, eds., *War on the Great Lakes: Essays Commemorating the 175th Anniversary of the Battle of Lake Erie*, 17-29. This issue contains a collection of recent writings related to the battle of Lake Erie as does John R. Claridge, ed., *175th Anniversary of the Battle of Lake Erie*.

30. Perry also begged for seamen, threatening to resign over the numbers given him. Taking on 130 Kentucky volunteers, as marines, he was "pleased to see anything in the shape of a man." One-quarter of Perry's crew were Black. Perry certainly had more seamen and a greater aggregate force than Barclay. An examination of his crews is contained in Gerald T. Altoff, "Deep Water Sailors — Shallow Water Soldiers." Perry's Report to Secretary of the Navy, 13 Sept. 1913, *DPCUS* 1813-14, Vol. 2: 2546-50; Roosevelt, *Naval War*, 240; Harrison to Armstrong, 15 Sept. 1813, *MLWHH* 2: 541.

31. The preceding narrative was based on Barclay to Yeo, 12 Sept. 1813, NAC, C 731: 116; Lt. George Inglis (RN) to Barclay, 10 Sept. 1813, *SBD* 2: 278; Logbook of the *Lawrence*, *DHCNF* 1813, Vol. 3: 116; Perry's Report to Secretary of the Navy, 13 Sept. 1813, James, *Naval Occurrences* 1, Appendix 58; James Fennimore Cooper, *Naval History of the United States to 1856* 2: 190-99; Roosevelt, *Naval War*, 243-54; *The War*, 5 Oct. 1813; Mahan, *Sea Power* 2: 80-97. An accurate recent work is *HMS Detroit* by Malcomson and Malcomson.

32. Perry to Secretary of the Navy, 13 Sept. 1813, James, *Naval Occurrences* 1, Appendix 58; *Vermont Mirror*, 6 Oct. 1813; British Casualty Report, *SBD* 3: 281; Roosevelt, *Naval War*, 249; Logbook of the *Lawrence*, 10 Sept. 1813, *DHCNF* 1813, Vol. 3: 116.

33. Perry to Harrison, 12 Sept. 1813, *MLWHH* 2: 540.

34. Rottenberg to Prevost, 10 Sept. 1813, NAC, C 680: 58.

35. Procter to Rottenberg, 12 Sept. 1813, NAC, C 680: 71; Anthony Shane, cited in Drake, *Tecumseh*, 187; Procter to Rottenberg, 12 Sept. 1813, NAC, C 680: 71; Procter to Prevost, 13 Sept. 1813, *MPHC* 25: 522-24; Prevost to Procter, 6 Sept. 1813, NAC, C 680: 30.

36. Harvey to Procter, 17 Sept. 1813, NAC, C 680: 75; Rottenberg to Prevost, 8 Sept. 1813, *MPHC* 15: 374.

37. Baynes to Procter, 20 Sept. 1813, NAC, C 680: 105; Prevost to Yeo, 14 Sept. 1813, *DHCNF* 1813, Vol. 3: 128; Prevost to Yeo, 19 Sept. 1813, *MLWHH* 2: 544.

38. Prevost to Bathurst, 22 Sept. 1813, *DHCNF* 1813, Vol. 3: 161; Strachan to John Richardson (NW Co.), 12 Oct. 1813, Spragge, *Strachan Letter Book*, 51.
39. Prevost to Bathurst, 31 Oct. 1813, *DHCNF* 1813, Vol. 4: 111.
40. Yeo to Warren, 10 Oct. 1813, NAC, C 731: 124.
41. Barclay to Yeo, 12 Sept. 1813, NAC, C 731: 116.
42. Barclay, *BCM*, 298-308; Sentence by deputy judge advocate, *BCM*, 318.
43. [Procter and Procter], "Campaigns," 414; R. Louis Gentilcore, *Historical Atlas of Canada* 2: plate 22.
44. *Quebec Gazette*, 7 Oct. 1813; *Montreal Gazette*, 5 Oct. 1813; *Niles Weekly Register*, 20 Nov. 1813.
45. *The War*, 5 Oct. 1813.
46. President Madison's speech to U.S. Congress, 7 Dec. 1813, *Annual Register for 1813*, 445; Edgar, *Ten Years*, 222.

13

CRISIS AT AMHERSTBURG

"What a sudden ... complete reverse! If poor Barclay and I had been attended to, our reverse would not have happened." [1]

Procter to Talbot, 23 September 1813

PROCTER REMAINED IN SUSPENSE of the outcome of the naval struggle for two days, hopeful that Lt. Col. Warburton's impressions of a British victory might prove true. Concluding the worst by 12 September, he sent an officer of the Indian Department and some Natives in a birch canoe to ascertain Barclay's fate. The spies returned that same day with news that confirmed his worst fears. They had found most of the vessels at the mouth of the Portage River, preparing to embark Harrison's troops. They also reported four large de-masted vessels anchored in Put-in-Bay, along with two schooners, one of which chased the canoe off. The British commander concluded that his positions were no longer tenable. For the first time in his 14 months at Amherstburg, he seriously contemplated a prompt retreat through a backwoods that he had never seen. In imminent danger of being cut off, Procter had no choice but to radically reshape his strategy amid nightmarish physical and moral constraints.[2]

On receiving Procter's letter of the naval disaster, Prevost directed a response through Adjutant-General Baynes, who urged Procter to call forth "the combined discipline and gallantry of the troops ... to cripple and repulse the enemy." Having pronounced this rousing exhortation, he hinted at the possible need for retreat, one that was to be conducted with "order and regularity." In particular, "no heavy or superfluous baggage" was to impede the march. By baggage, Baynes referred to the personal property of the regulars, not public stores, equipment, or the private property of civilians. Although Baynes did not forbid the movement of the soldiers' baggage, it was not to retard the withdrawal. He made no mention of the greatest impediment to a retreat from the Detroit frontier, Native opposition, although Brock had warned Prevost of just such a circumstance a year previously: "I should be unwilling in the event of retreat, to have three or four hundred of them hanging on my flanks.... If they could be brought to imagine that we should desert them, the consequences must be fatal."[3]

On 23 September, Prevost replied personally to Procter's notification of Barclay's naval disaster. This letter was understanding of the circumstances that prompted the engagement and was essentially positive in seeking the best course of action for the future. Prevost suggested displeasure, saying, "It would have been prudent to have awaited the arrival of the remainder of the Dover seamen." He gave qualified authority for Procter's withdrawal, saying, "The concentration of your force has become indispensable and your nearer connection with the Centre Division may be requisite" but slipped in the caveat that such an eventuality was subject to Rottenberg's decision. Having neatly absolved himself of responsibility for the outcome, Prevost announced that he was required to hasten back to Lower Canada as the enemy were making menacing demonstrations in that quarter. He enjoined the beleaguered Procter to meet the new distress with "fortitude."[4]

Rottenberg, who thus far provided no meaningful contributions to Procter's command, also wrote Procter. Through Lt. Col. John Harvey, he declared that he did "not clearly see the necessity or expediency of immediately retiring." He strictly forbade any "precipitate retrograde movement," surmising that a three-hour action would call for extensive repairs to Perry's fleet. Rottenberg directed Procter to consult with the allied chiefs and jointly adopt the best course of action. He was to impress upon them the fidelity of the British government to their interests, a daunting task given the record of British support in the last year. Rottenberg still didn't understand the effects of the severe shortages at Amherstburg. He was certainly aware of his inability to address Procter's supply problems, writing, "The whole commissariat, with the exception of Mr. Coffin is laid up with the fever and Mr. Couche is actually out of his senses."[5]

Procter's dilemma did not emanate solely from his superiors. Tecumseh, indignant that Brock's promises had not been fulfilled, spoke out with increasing vehemence against the inadequate British resources dedicated to secure the Native homeland. Procter certainly didn't need to be reminded; his dozens of letters had covered this subject most adequately. Nonetheless, the spokesman for the confederacy vented his frustrations on Procter as the representative of the Crown. To compound Native disappointment over waning allied fortunes, the tribesmen were unhappy with their ill-provisioned, sedentary lifestyle. As livestock and dogs in the area disappeared, the Natives hunted down deer, bear, porcupine, and raccoon, and augmented their meagre rations with sun-dried whitefish, parched corn, and maple sugar. When these gave out, they nibbled crab apples, wild grapes, chestnuts, and cranberries. During the summer of 1813, a mysterious epidemic (possibly whooping cough or typhoid) swept the region, proliferating in their squalid, unsanitary conditions, ravaging the malnourished Potawatomi and Wyandot of the Detroit country and the Ojibwa along the St. Clair River. It was under these conditions that Procter summoned their leaders to a grand council, knowing what he had to propose would be unwelcome.[6]

The simple fact remained that Procter's positions were no longer tenable and retreat was imperative. On the day of the battle of Lake Erie, Gilmor had sent a number of bateaux to Long Point for food. Three days later, his stock of flour was depleted. For four or five days, he had no flour or bread whatever, substituting wheat and potato issues to the voracious troops and Natives. At this point, William Jones, superintendent of issues for the Indian Department, estimated ten thousand Native adults in the area, a third of them warriors, plus an unknown number of children.[7]

Procter was aware that Harrison was massing for a major offensive drive. On 14 September, Governor Isaac Shelby joined the Northwest Army, leading a fresh contingent of four thousand mounted Kentucky men. "Greatly mortified" by the poor response to his latest call for volunteers, Shelby had been forced to resort to the unpopular draft. He had assured the Kentuckians of a limit of sixty days service and promised to personally lead them. The timely news of the battle of Fort Stephenson allowed Shelby to dispense with the draft as volunteers stepped forward for one last effort. In addition, Col. Richard Johnson's trained regiment of mounted Kentuckians arrived from Fort Meigs, augmenting the 2600 regulars and several thousand Ohio and

Pennsylvania militiamen already there. Armstrong's plan for a North-west Army of regular troops had not fully matured, and Harrison had little choice but to place continued reliance on volunteers. The Kentuckians' horses were corralled into an enormous enclosure formed by the Portage Peninsula, while the men boarded Perry's enlarged fleet.[8]

When certain elements of the Northwest Army refused to cross into Upper Canada, the Kentucky men related a celebrated anecdote to illustrate the lack of "constitutional scruples" of their patriotic state:

So fierce was the military spirit in Kentucky that even some of her four footed inhabitants seemed possessed with a desire to march against the British and one of them did so.... The Harrodsburg Company ... saw two pigs fighting in the street and delayed their march to watch the combat. When the march was resumed, the victorious pig followed the company ... plunged into the (Ohio) river ... joined them on the other side.... He would run through the camp, squealing at the top of his voice and take position at the head of the line, so as to have a good start next morning.... He was a great favorite with the whole army.... The men would not take him to Canada ... and the stout-hearted pig ... could not swim across Lake Erie.[9]

In the meantime, Rottenberg's letter of 17 September to Prevost showed little sense of immediacy. At the very time that Procter faced the challenge of convincing his allies to abandon their ancestral lands, Rottenberg complained to Prevost that "Major General Procter would not allow the Indians to proceed until the last batch of sailors had arrived." Yet, the very day that he had forbidden Procter from undertaking "precipitate retrograde movement," Rottenberg became so alarmed at news of Barclay's "terrible disaster" that he declared that if a "complete victory" did not occur on Lake Ontario, he would evacuate the Niagara Peninsula to Burlington Heights.[10]

While Rottenberg and Prevost contemplated the best method by which to avoid involvement in the retreat of the Right Division (and any consequential responsibility), Procter had to act. He declared martial law on 13 September to facilitate the requisitioning of foodstuffs, horses, and wagons, as well as to apprehend "traitorous or disaffected persons." Then he summoned the principal chiefs to Amherstburg, and met with the heads of the various departments at Sandwich, issuing co-ordinating instructions for the military evacuation of the Western District by way of the Thames River. In preparation for this movement, he placed Lt. Col. Evans in charge of removing eastward the noncombatants and impedimenta. By withdrawing inland to the "back route," Procter hoped to nullify the effects of American naval superiority while shortening and protecting his solitary communication with the Centre Division. Despite the urgency of the situation, the chiefs took three to four days to gather from their distant camps. Arriving there, they took exception to Procter's preparations, perceiving that Procter's decision to retreat had already been taken without their input. Procter had instructed Capt. Dixon to initiate "quietly" the dismantling of Fort Amherstburg; however, the workmen misunderstood their orders, tearing apart the fort without scruple. Nor were the warriors alone in feeling left out. Warburton also remained unacquainted with Procter's intentions for several days. While logistic arrangements called for early implementation, Procter's failure to advise his second in command of the broad plan was unusual. One can only infer that his "secret instructions" were aimed at containing Native apprehensions until the matter of retreat was formally addressed in council.[11]

While Procter considered a prompt retreat imperative, he was greatly hampered by a lack of information. His reconnaissances had been conducted in Michigan and Ohio for purposes of offense. As he had never seen the Thames country, he had only a vague idea of the terrain for defensive purposes or locations for his depots and troop accommodations. He received little help from Chambers and other officers of the division who, having passed down the river, asserted that "the Thames afforded no [suitable] position." Rummaging frantically through old files, Procter learned that Lieutenant-Governor Simcoe considered the Forks of the Thames a good defensive site, one that afforded reasonable depth of water for lake vessels. On the other hand, Thomas Talbot recommended the high ground of Moraviantown for a defensive position, one that possessed the added advantage of being closer to the Centre Division. Furthermore, this site could be provisioned from Long Point. Despite any advantages of these sites, neither was ideal, as American seaborne forays could cut them off.[12]

The location of a strong point for the Right Division depended on several imponderables. Would the Centre Division hold its ground to Procter's rear? How far from their lands would the Natives be prepared to go? Could the commissariat sustain his division? Where could the soldiers find shelter during the winter? Would the heretofore cautious Harrison pursue his fleeing army into the interior? Military considerations dictated Burlington as the objective, but Native opinion would certainly object to this measure.

Given the mass of uncertainties, Procter acted on three guiding assumptions. First, the alliance must be preserved. Second, retreat was essential for the survival of his command. Third, the Thames was the only practical route. Procter acted on these principles and prepared to make decisions as circumstances should dictate. The constraints greatly simplified his options, leaving no meaningful alternative.

On 15 September, at the Amherstburg council house, Procter addressed the assembled Native leaders through translators. "After a brief exposition of the defenseless state of the garrison, the almost utter impossibility of preventing the landing of the enemy and the alarming destitution into which the magazines of provisions had fallen," wrote witness John Richardson, "General Procter proposed that the forts of Detroit and Amherstburg, together with the various public buildings should be destroyed, and that the troops and Indians should retire on the Centre Division at Niagara." [13]

By Richardson's account, the chiefs were divided in their opinions, but Tecumseh, "whose gallant and impetuous spirit could not brook the idea of retiring before his enemies," delivered a strong and unequivocal argument to remain at Amherstburg and fight the Americans on the beach. In a speech powerful with pathos and irony, the war chief related the history of British-Native relations, reproaching his allies for decades of neglect and abandonment. Although Procter had declared Barclay's squadron lost, Tecumseh argued that his defeat was still uncertain. In his metaphoric language, he vented his rage on Procter, personally, accusing the general of planning to abandon the tribesmen to the "big knives." He compared Procter's conduct to that of "a fat animal that carries its tail upon its back, but when affrighted, it drops it between its legs and runs off." [14]

The British general must have winced at Tecumseh's reminder of Brock's pledge (one that he also had repeated): "When the war was declared, our father stood up and gave us the tomahawk and told us he was then ready to strike the Americans; that he wanted our assistance, and that he would certainly get us our lands back which the Americans had taken from us." Clearly, the Natives perceived the retreat proposal as an abrogation of the British commitment and an abandonment of their interest. Retreat "was not agreeable to the speeches that came from their father to them, which were that they should be supported," recalled William Caldwell. "We told them that it was owing to the loss of our fleet and the great scarcity of provisions. They said to me this is like the peace of 1783 ... and said this is the second [actually the third] time we have been deceived by our father." The Shawnee war chief concluded his oration by declaring that if Procter wanted to leave, he should leave the arms and ammunition so that the Native warriors might continue the struggle alone. This Procter was unwilling to do, as he later recalled: "All the officers of the Indian Department concur in saying that if I had retreated from the western parts of Upper Canada ... without the concurrence of the Indians, they would, in all probability, have laid waste the country and perhaps attacked the division under my command." [15]

At the conclusion of Tecumseh's "contumelious speech," the council erupted in anger. The chieftains, attired in wampum chokers, bears' teeth necklaces, belts of eagle feathers, and headpieces of wildcat and staghorn, "started up to a man, and brandishing their tomahawks in the most menacing manner, vociferated their approbation of his sentiments," continued John Richardson. "The council room was a large lofty building, the vaulted roof of which echoed back the wild yells of the Indians; while the threatening attitude and diversified costume of these latter formed a striking contrast with the calm demeanour and military garb of the officers grouped around the walls. The most prominent feature in the picture, however was Tecumseh.... It was evident that he could be terrible." Given the emotionally charged atmosphere, Procter could not hope to achieve a meaningful consensus, Tecumseh's criticisms of the British side having damaged relations within an already precarious alliance. Refusing to be moved by argument, insult, or threat, Procter promised an answer in a few days. In the meantime, he directed Elliott and the other officers of the Indian Department to defuse dissension by reasoning with the chiefs. [16]

Allied relations reached the breaking point when Procter returned to Amherstburg from Sandwich on the 18th of September. He found Elliott "alarmed beyond measure, having wholly failed in his endeavours to convince or persuade the chiefs." Elliott warned Procter to prepare himself for "consequences the most unpleasant." He went on to say if the British commander persisted in his plans for a retreat, "the Great Wampum Belt in the centre of which was the figure of a heart and at each end, that of a hand, would be produced in council and in our presence cut in two, figuratively representing our eternal separation." This situation was one Brock had hoped to avoid, writing, "In the event of a disaster, the love of plunder will prevail and they may act in a manner to be the most dreaded by the inhabitants of the country." Procter fully appreciated the potential consequences: "There was every reason to expect that the Indians would not confine their indignation to a mere dissolution of the alliance." William Caldwell, long-time associate of the tribes (having fought by their side in the Revolutionary War and at Fallen Timbers), became so alarmed that he removed his family to Lower Canada, fearing a blood bath. The most knowledgeable local persons on Native affairs asserted that in the event of a unilateral British retreat, the warriors "would have fallen on us and joined the enemy." Tecumseh was said to have again proposed to abandon the alliance, but the Ojibwa and Sioux leaders prevailed, arguing that he must honour his commitment as leading spokesman of the Native coalition.[17]

Faced with a heightened crisis, the British commander decided to avoid another scene of histrionics in the council house. Prior to the second meeting, he drew Tecumseh aside, and in the presence of Warburton, Evans, Elliott, and his headquarters staff, Procter drew out a map to explain in detail the need for a retreat. He pointed out that American naval control gave his enemy the means to cut off the Natives in Michigan and surround the exposed allied positions, that American "double balls" (chain shot) from their ships could facilitate an opposed landing. Procter succeeded in convincing Tecumseh that he would stand by the Natives and fight again, offering the compromise of a stand on the Lower Thames. Satisfied that retreat was both necessary and limited, the Shawnee chief spent two hours prior to the council convincing most of the other chiefs. As a result, the second council meeting was much more dignified than the first, and the majority of chiefs agreed to accompany the British retreat to the Thames. Despite Tecumseh's harsh words of the 15th, Procter respected his leading role, later writing, "It was one more example of his talents and influence, that, in spite of all their prejudices and natural affection for the seat of their habitations, he had determined a large portion of his nation to give their cooperation to the step which they had violently opposed."[18]

Although Procter had restored an allied consensus of sorts, observers at the deliberations with Tecumseh differed on the destination of a retreat. Capt. John Hall, Procter's brigade major, recalled his commander mentioning Dolsen's (also called Dover) as the place to make a stand. Warburton recalled Chatham (the Forks of the Thames) as the destination, that it was "to be occupied with the least possible delay." Capt. Billy Caldwell remembered Elliott's telling the warriors in council that they would find the Forks fortified. Procter denied any such promise, admitting only that "I told them that I should fortify the Forks." Ensign Cochran was also of the opinion that "Chatham should be fortified." Unfortunately, Elliott's translation of an intention in English became a promise in Shawnee, leading the chiefs to believe they would arrive at Chatham to find entrenchments and artillery batteries.[19]

The leaders certainly agreed to fall back on the Lower Thames. Even Harrison, upon landing in Canada, knew from informers that "General Procter ... at Dolsen's ... intended to fortify and wait to receive me." Procter's purpose of occupying the lower reaches of the river was not solely to boost the warriors' confidence, but also to maintain a naval facility at the Forks, the head of navigation on the Thames, shielding that site with a strong point below. He still had the decked gunboats, *Eliza* and *Myers*, plus the transports, *Mary*, *Ellen*, *Miamis*, and a number of smaller craft and bateaux. "If I could succeed in maintaining a position upon the Thames, I should be enabled to preserve the naval and military stores, and thereby facilitate the recovery of a naval ascendancy on Lake Erie," he later said. "As they could be conveyed in vessels and boats to a depot on the Thames, no time was lost and in the event of our being obliged to retreat farther, they might be destroyed." The Forks was the logical site for a marine facility, having produced the two gunboats for which timbers were floated downriver from the Longwoods Wilderness (also for *Lady Prevost* and probably for *Detroit*). Procter discussed the subject of throwing up works at the Forks with his engineer officer, Capt. Matthew Dixon. Although cannon and entrenching tools were sent off by boat, Dixon remained bedridden until 2 October, unable to supervise the project. For a time, the British commander even entertained hopes of establishing a post on the St. Clair River to prevent American vessels from passing up to Lake Huron.[20]

While the chiefs were no longer openly hostile to the idea of a retreat, Tecumseh's first council speech had damaged Native confidence. Of the estimated three thousand warriors in the vicinity, a mere third would accompany the retreat, and many of these were prepared to desert at the slightest setback. By Native custom, "The commander-in-chief governs only by advice and can neither reward nor punish. Every private may return home when he pleases without assigning any reason for it. Any number may leave the main body ... without being called to account for their conduct. Every individual regards himself free and independent and would never renounce the idea of liberty. Therefore injunctions, conveyed in the style of a positive command, would be disregarded and treated with contempt."[21]

The diverse objectives of Prevost's ill-defined strategy and Tecumseh's unchanged mission were now exposed and brought into sharp focus, appearing in stark contrast. Given the meager British presence on the Detroit frontier and the poor provisioning, Tecumseh had concrete reasons to doubt British sincerity. Just as the capture of Detroit had consolidated Native support, its abandonment jeopardized the alliance. It was left to Procter to rationalize the political contradiction as best he could. The ambiguity generated by a policy without substance heightened tensions and again forced Procter to compromise his military decisions as he struggled to appease Native opinion.

On 2 September, Rottenberg had announced the impending arrival of an abundant supply of Indian goods from Quebec, prompting Procter to make further empty promises. In an attempt to induce the Natives to cross over from Michigan, the British commander asserted that winter clothing and goods would be distributed at McKee's Point, south of Sandwich. Yet on 13 September, Procter complained to Prevost that the goods were nowhere to be seen. By 18 September, many of the Potawatomi, Ottawa, Miami, Sac, and Fox tribesmen under the influence of Main Pock and Five Medals repudiated their association by refusing to cross the Detroit River. Although many of these were totally disenchanted with false promises, others undoubtedly remained in Michigan because they refused to leave their ancestral lands. In a desperate attempt to humour them, Procter purchased a large number of deerskins at Detroit as a substitute for presents.[22]

Despite the adversities, Procter had to make the best of this unpromising situation and get on with the retreat. With Col. James Baby repairing the bridges between Sandwich and the Thames, Lt. Col. Evans removed the "women, children, sick and everything that might be an encumbrance to the regiment on its march." These advanced elements and the remaining prisoners departed on 22-23 September by boat. The commissariat established a small depot, slaughterhouse, and bake ovens at Dolsen's toward which place sheep from Baldoon were driven down. Clay ovens were also constructed at Sherman's. Procter asked Thomas Talbot to build two huts and cover for horses at "Fourteen Mile Tree" (Ward's) in the Longwoods Wilderness as a communications station, anticipating the principal depot for the Right Division to be located at Delaware. Talbot repaired the road between Moraviantown, Delaware, and Oxford and blazed another from Port Talbot to Munceytown, 28 miles upstream from Moraviantown, where he deposited supplies and flour.[23]

Luckily, Gilmor's five bateaux returned to Amherstburg on 23 September with 131 barrels of flour, which was converted to sufficient biscuit to sustain the retreat to the mouth of the Thames, where the newly constructed ovens at Dolsen's would bake more. The following day, Procter concentrated his main force at Sandwich, Warburton having torched Fort Amherstburg, the dockyard, and the public buildings the day before. Procter awaited the Natives, allowing time for the stores, baggage, convalescents, prisoners, dependents, and civilians to move up the Thames to safety. The civilian evacuation amounted to a small migration. Matthew Elliott sent off "only his plate and the most valuable part of his portable effect," worth £1500, in nine wagons hauled by 30 horses.[24]

Even with the loss of 250 effectives on Barclay's vessels, Procter's strength was still respectable on paper. He command 880 all ranks (including officers, surgeons, and drummers); however, they were not combat-ready troops. Of 763 rank and file, over a hundred were sick or recovering from wounds. Two hundred more either attended the sick, escorted prisoners, manned boats, drove cattle, or transported impedimenta. Procter did not call out the local militiamen en masse, as they had their own concerns. While many of the militia officers preceded the retreat with their families and effects, the rank and file generally remained on their farms, lacking conveyance for their possessions and loved ones. Enough militiamen eventually left to reform the 1st Essex and 1st Kent Regiments and Caldwell's (Western) Rangers.[25]

The letter of a dragoon officer to his parents in England bears testimony to allied relations during these tense days:

Detroit, 26 September 1813

Our fleet upon the lake has sailed about 20 days ago from our port into that of the Americans after a close action of 3 hours and a half, without one making their escape; the consequence of which is we have lost all hope of regaining command of the lake. Our army consisting of 550 regulars and 2500 wild Indians, are now upon the retreat to the Thames River, although contrary to the wishes of the Indians; who have declared they will not budge an inch further, and remind us of our general having promised to conquer or leave his bones with them. As we are now completely in the savages' power, we are obliged in a great measure to act as they think proper. The celebrated chief, Tecumseh, dined with me last Friday and assured me his Indians were determined to give battle the moment the Americans approach. Our General, should he act contrary to their wishes, may repent his rash opposition, however prudent he may conceive a retreat at such an awful crisis. These savages have no mercy. The tomahawk and scalping knife decides immediately the wretch who falls in their hands and many dread the war whoop may sound in our ears, if we act contrary to their ideas, which are as wild as themselves. We have spread a net which may catch us. I hate these savage barbarians. You cannot place sufficient confidence in them and without a force sufficient to keep them in check, they are more plague than profit.[26]

Procter left a small detachment of dragoons at Amherstburg to observe American movements. On 27 September, this scouting body notified Procter of Harrison's landing that day. At 5 PM the British commander ordered the Right Division onto the King's Road, while Capt. Muir torched Fort Detroit and crossed his 120-man garrison to join the main body that night. As he embarked in the boats, Chadrona, a pro-American warrior with a price on his head, approached boldly and offered defiant gestures to Muir. The 13-month British occupation of Michigan was ended.[27]

While Procter struggled with his problems, officials to the east attempted to help him with belated and desperate efforts. The commissariat rushed an emergency fund of £20,000 to pay off Gilmor's accumulated debts. The under-strength Second Battalion of the 41st was on the march from Kingston; it would never arrive. Rottenberg who had forbidden "precipitate retrograde movement," suddenly declared, "Had General Procter's army joined me, and the fact ascertained, I should not hesitate falling back on Kingston, but situated as that General is, I should not feel authorized in abandoning him, and if fall we must, we will fall together." The degree to which Rottenberg held to his intention to stand by Procter will be seen.[28]

The rapidly unfolding events left Prevost even more confused than Rottenberg. As late as 29 September, Baynes wrote Procter that "supplies of every description" were on their way to Amherstburg. Additionally (and incredibly), he sent Capt. Richard O'Conner (RN), acting commissioner of HM Naval Dockyard, Kingston, to Amherstburg to study the feasibility of building a single vessel there. By this time, Amherstburg was in American hands. In volleying the question of Procter's retreat between them, Prevost and Rottenberg neglected to provide Procter with even discretionary authority to retire. On 30 September, three days after Procter left Sandwich, Rottenberg wrote, not to Procter but to Prevost, announcing, "I think it is now high time he [Procter] should seriously endeavour to bring his force in connection with mine provided the Indians will permit him."[29]

The first news of Procter's retreat drew little surprise from British and colonial newspapers. The *London Examiner* of 21 November casually remarked that Procter's retreat was "a natural consequence of the victory on Lake Erie," while the *Quebec Gazette* summed up the situation:

The hope having vanished by the loss of the fleet, want of provisions may have probably induced that distinguished officer to retire from a country, the occupation of which was of so much importance, and in which with the Indians inhabiting the country, a few hundred British troops have furnished occupation to ten thousand of the enemy and captured more than four times their number.... This success opens the most favourable prospects to General Harrison and his capacity to command will be brought to the final test, after a year of moving vast bodies of militia through the intense cold of last winter, as well as in this summer, without any consequence resulting, except the extreme suffering of men and an enormous expense to the public.[30]

NOTES

1. Procter to Talbot, 23 Sept. 1813, *TP*, 193.
2. *Defence of Major General Procter*, 10; Procter to Prevost, 13 and 21 Sept. 1813, *MPHC* 25: 524, 528-29.
3. Baynes to Procter, 20 Sept. 1813, NAC, C 680: 105; Brock to Prevost, 3 July 1812, Brock to Prevost, 18 Sept. 1812, *SBD* 1: 348, 593.
4. Prevost to Procter, 23 Sept. 1813, NAC, C 680: 112.
5. Harvey to Procter, 17 Sept. 1813, *SBD* 2: 282-83; Rottenberg to Prevost, 28 Sept. 1813, *MPHC* 15: 395.
6. Tucker, *Tecumseh, Vision of Glory*, 296; Tanner, *Atlas of Great Lakes Indian History*, 173 .
7. Gilmor to Couche, 6 Aug. 1813, *DHCNF* 1813, Vol. 2: 317; Gilmor, William Jones (Indian Dept.), *PCM*, 182, 178.
8. Quisenberry, *Kentucky in the War*, 89; Hammack, *Kentucky*, 71.
9. Capt. Sympson Diary, cited in Quisenberry, *Kentucky in the War*, 100.
10. Rottenberg to Prevost, 17 Sept. 1813, NAC, C 680: 78.
11. Cochran, *Narrative*, NAC, MG 40 G4 File 1: 55-56; Col. William Caldwell, Dixon, Lebreton, Evans, Warburton, *PCM*, 176, 96, 168, 48, 8.
12. *Defence of Major General Procter*, 18.
13. *Ibid.*, 10; Richardson, *War of 1812*, 204.

14. *Ibid.*, 204.

15. *Ibid.*, 204; Col. William Caldwell, *PCM*, 175-76; *Defence of Major General Procter*, 31-32.

16. *Defence of Major General Procter*, 10; Richardson, *War of 1812*, 206-07. Although Tecumseh understood English, he spoke only Shawnee in official dealings, relying on interpreters to assure clarity of understanding. Hatch, *Chapter*, 116. Detroit resident, John Hunt, recalled accounts of the proceedings that largely agreed with Richardson's assertions: "Tecumseh got up in Counsel and told Genl. Procter that he reminded him of one of their Indian dogs. If he whiped [*sic*] a few long-knives on land he would strut about with his epaulettes on his shoulders like one of our fat dogs, (with his tail curled over his back) but when you loose [*sic*] a few canoes on the water, you remind me of one of our poor sneaking dogs, you put your tail between your legs and sneak off." Hunt, *Memoirs*, 40.

17. *Defence of Major General Procter*, 10-11; [Procter and Procter], *Lucubrations*, 355; Brock to Prevost, 9 Sept. 1812, Tupper, *Brock*, 303; Col. William Caldwell, William Jones (Indian Dept.) François Baby, Lebreton, Hall, *PCM*, 175-76, 180-81; 148, 169, 237; Drake, *Life of Tecumseh*, 191. Procter returned to Sandwich after the first council, asking Warburton to reason with the chiefs in his absence. The latter made no attempt to comply, asserting ignorance of earlier British promises and that he "didn't wish to interfere." Jones, *PCM*, 179.

18. *Defence of Major General Procter*, 11; Warburton, *PCM*, 8; [Procter and Procter], *Lucubrations*, 356. It is remarkable that Tecumseh's emotional but unsound arguments are better remembered than Procter's success at convincing him to adopt the opposite measure. Richardson ignored the second meeting as well as Procter's pivotal role in winning over Tecumseh after the Indian Department officers had failed to do so. Historians have held up Tecumseh's arguments for awaiting the American advance as an example of his oratory skill without examining the proposal itself, which was a desperate one. His argument assumed knowledge of the time and place of the American attack. Furthermore, as half the warriors remained in Michigan after Barclay's defeat, their willingness to fight was in question. Even if one assumed that the allies could drive the Americans into the lake, American naval superiority would have assured an allied withdrawal solely for provisioning reasons.

19. Capt. John Hall, Warburton, Capt. Billy Caldwell, *PCM*, 8, 138, 238; Cochran, *Narrative*, NAC, MG 40, G4, File 2: 56.

20. *Defence of Major General Procter*, 11-12, 18; Harrison to Armstrong, 9 Oct. 1813, *MLWHH* 2: 558; Procter to Rottenberg, 23 Oct. 1813, *MPHC* 15: 428; Capt. James Hill, *PCM*, 114; Recollections of Aura Stewart, *MPHC* 4: 325.

21. Trumbull, *Indian Wars*, 102.

22. Rottenberg to Procter, 2 Sept. 1813, NAUS, *MIC*, 261; Drake, *Life of Tecumseh*, 191; Procter to Prevost, 13 Sept. 1813, *MPHC* 25: 523; McAfee, *Late War*, 381; Col. William Caldwell, *PCM*, 159.

23. Evans, Gilmor, Dolsen, Crowther, Talbot, *PCM*, 48, 140, 283, 190, 186-87; [Procter and Procter], "Campaigns," 430; Procter to Talbot, 23 Sept. 1813, *TP*, 193.

24. Gilmor to Freer, 23 Sept. 1813, NAC, WO 57: 31-32; Evans, *PCM*, 49; Sarah Elliott Memorial, 29 Aug. 1814: *MPHC* 25: 595-97.

25. Return for the Right Division, enclosed in Prevost to Bathurst, 25 Nov. 1813, *MPHC* 25: 556; L. Homphray Irving, *Officers of the British Forces in Canada During the War of 1812-15*, 91-95.

26. Letter of a British dragoon, *The War*, 23 Nov. 1813. This letter allegedly fell into American hands during the Thames campaign but its anonymity makes it suspect. On the other hand, if one makes allowance for an error in dates, it lends indirect support to Boucherville's otherwise vague recollection that Tecumseh changed his mind about a retreat. According to Boucherville, Tecumseh argued for a stand at Sandwich on learning of the approach of the American fleet on the 27th. Boucherville, *Journal*, 140-43.

27. Evans, *PCM*, 48; Hunt, *Memoirs*, 48-49.

28. Thomas Ridout to Thomas Ridout, Sr., 21 Sept. 1813, Edgar, *Ten Years*, 227; Rottenberg to Prevost, 28 Sept. 1813, NAC, C 680: 119. British resources were stretched to the limit by the late summer of 1813. At the very time that Harrison was massing more than eight thousand men in Northern Ohio, another five thousand were gathering at Plattsburg, with yet another army of ten thousand at Sacket's Harbour. These concentrations were favoured by American naval superiority on Lake Ontario. With improved training and organization, the U.S. was preparing for a general offensive on all fronts.

29. Baynes to Procter, 29 Sept. 1813, NAC, C 680: 91; Rottenberg to Prevost, 30 Sept. 1813, NAC, C 680: 125.

30. *Quebec Gazette*, 14 Oct. 1813.

IV

THE INVASION OF CANADA

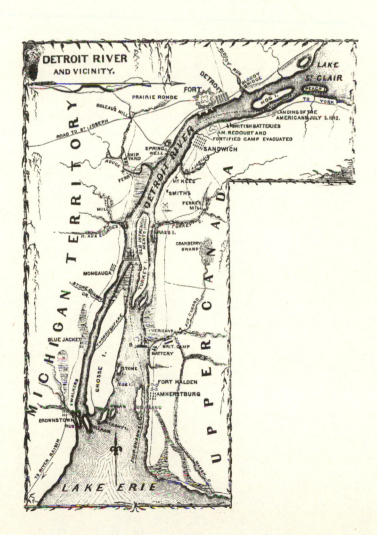

14

CHASE ON THE THAMES

"I feel the weight of my responsibility, I shall act to the best of my judgment and hope that I shall be fairly judged."[1]

Procter to Prevost, 21 September 1813

HARRISON HAD INDEED LANDED in Canada. Although half the garrisons of Fort Meigs and Fort Stephenson were down with bilious fever, huge contingents had arrived from Kentucky, Ohio, and Pennsylvania. The months of labourious preparations finally culminated in the concentration of the largest standing army ever seen west of the Appalachians, more than eight thousand men. By 15 September, Harrison assembled his force at the mouth of the Portage River and was busily embarking men and stores onto Perry's vessels. As Procter had anticipated, the American commander's aim was to occupy the Detroit country and capture Michilimackinac. Armstrong then expected Harrison to drive the Centre Division from the Niagara region and roll up Upper Canada from the west, as Hull had attempted. Whether Procter was pursued or cut off, he would have little time to establish himself on the Thames.[2]

On 22 September, the Northwest Army proceeded to Put-in-Bay Island and viewed the captured vessels. Adverse winds detained the force there for two days. On the 25th, the army landed on the staging area, tiny East Sister Island, three acres in size, seven miles from the New Settlement. Meanwhile, Harrison and Perry conducted a reconnaissance of Amherstburg on the 26th. From *Ariel,* they observed a burned-out blockhouse at Bar Point but formed the impression that the enemy still occupied the area. That night, high winds raised the lake level several feet and the troops on East Sister Island were almost inundated by the pounding surf. One observer reported that the violent waves dredged up and cast ashore a 32-pdr. round shot attached to the body of a man killed on the 10th. The next morning, 27 September, as the weather was fair, Harrison prepared detailed orders for the amphibious landing from 16 vessels and over a hundred boats. At 3 PM they landed unopposed at Bar Point, three miles below Amherstburg.[3]

By his estimate, the American general had with him "about 5000 [men] of which 2000 are regulars and the rest, Kentucky and Pennsylvania regiments." The troops advanced into Amherstburg by echelon movement to the tune of "Yankee Doodle." Harrison found the public buildings and a "considerable quantity of timber" burned and still smouldering near the fort. The abandoned water battery on Bois Blanc Island still mounted an 18-pdr. gun. The town was largely deserted with the remaining residents being predominantly *Canadiens*. Governor Shelby assured protection to a delegation of women while Perry's fleet anchored in Amherstburg harbour. As the main division of Americans occupied the east side of the Detroit River, another thousand men, the trained mounted regiment under Col. Richard Johnson, advanced up Hull's Road, unperceived by the British dragoons.[4]

"There is no possibility of overtaking the enemy," Harrison wrote, under the impression that Procter had "upwards of 1,000 horses," while he could find only one pony for the "venerable," 66-year-old Governor Shelby. Harrison's assumption was erroneous. The warriors had stolen many horses on both sides of the river, and Procter had difficulty finding mounts even for his dispatch riders. The residents were using draft horses to haul their possessions to the east, and any remaining animals had been commandeered to transport stores and baggage. With the exception of the recently arrived 40 provincial dragoons who had their own horses, most of Procter's men were on foot. In total, the Right Division mustered exactly 99 horses.[5]

On 28 September, the Americans drove off a party under Ensign Benjamin Holmes (Canadian Light Dragoons) as it was burning the Canards bridge. The Northwest Army encamped at Petite Côte for the night, arriving at Sandwich the following day, delayed by the need to repair the bridges over the unfordable waters of the Canards River and Turkey Creek. Harrison moved into the popular François Baby mansion while his troops occupied the ground Hull's troops had taken the previous summer. John Hunt of Detroit gave his impressions of the arrival of the American fleet at Detroit on the 29th: "I shall never forget the beautiful morning and to us most beautiful sight of our fleet of seventeen vessels and one hundred and fifty boats in the river with the Army upon the Canada shore as they turned the point of Sandwich with their flags flying and their martial music playing Yankee Doodle." Perry's vessels fired a few rounds to drive off the Natives hanging about the town. Col. Johnson's mounted men arrived at Detroit on the 30th and crossed to Sandwich.[6]

Deserters provided Harrison with information on Procter's strength and movements. They further reported that most of the Potawatomi, Ottawa, Ojibwa, Wyandot, Miami, Kickapoo, and Delaware had deserted. Nonetheless, Harrison suspected the 1200 warriors lurking in the woods behind Detroit of plotting unspecified "skullduggery" and left a strong garrison under Brig. Gen. McArthur in the town. The famished warriors remained peaceful enough, though, imploring McArthur for food, "Father, we are unarmed. We are at your mercy. Do with us as you think proper. Our squaws and children are perishing. If you take us by the hand, we are willing to take up the tomahawk against any power, either white or red, which you may direct." McArthur accepted their professions of friendship on condition that they wage war against their former allies.[7]

On the 29th, Harrison proclaimed the re-establishment of American authority in Michigan and garrisoned Amherstburg, Sandwich, and Detroit before calling a council of officers to determine his next move. The assembly concluded that the retreating enemy could be overtaken in three or four days. Despite Armstrong's observation that reliance on irregulars had resulted in "waste, peculation, disorder and defeat," the better part of the pursuing force of 3500 men consisted of Harrison's favourite fighters, Kentucky volunteers, including Johnson's mounted brigade. More than two hundred Wyandot, Shawnee, and Seneca warriors from Ohio also accompanied the pursuit under their chiefs, Colonel Lewis, Black Hoof, and Big Snake. A thousand regulars of Brig. Gen. Cass's brigade and the corps of Lt. Col. James Ball remained at Sandwich to follow as soon as their baggage arrived from the islands. Local residents reported Procter's main body with reasonable accuracy as consisting of "475 regulars of the 41st and Royal Newfoundland Regiments, 60 of the 10th Veteran Battalion, 45 dragoons, and from 600 to 1000 Indians." Harrison was aware that Procter intended to make a stand at Dolsen's and expected to engage him there. Since the bridges over the rivers that emptied into Lake St. Clair were left intact, Harrison concluded that Procter did not expect to be pursued.[8]

The first phase of the British retreat was slow, averaging five miles per day. Given the reports of the observation detachment of Ensign Holmes, Procter considered "no reason to apprehend a speedy attack of the enemy," as "this force was not one which ought to have excited very great alarm." Yet neither complacency nor the frequent rains held back the retreat; its progress was determined by the lagging Natives. On the first night, Procter halted the troops at La Vallée's, ten miles east of Sandwich. He spent the evening "between the enemy and the Division," in an effort to reassure the Natives and induce them to join the retreat.[9]

A noteworthy feature of the allied retreat was that its two principle elements were of divergent impulses. While Procter struggled to tempt the warriors forward, his regulars were anxious to make tracks eastward with all possible expedition. Those dejected tribesmen who still adhered to the allied cause trailed well behind the troops, further slowed by their families and possessions, while Tecumseh remained at Sandwich, desirous of fighting the Americans at any opportunity. On the other hand, Procter "observed an impatience to retire," among his officers, tired of their ordeal on the frontier and pessimistic of the Right Division's ability to maintain itself in the backwoods. According to Capt. Chambers, the troops could have made Moraviantown by 1 October had they not been held back.[10]

On the 28th, through a misunderstanding, Lt. Col. Warburton resumed the retreat from La Vallée's, producing "a mischievous effect on the minds of the Indians." Through Elliott, Procter sent a message to reassure Tecumseh that the army would await the Natives on the Thames. Since Procter had assigned dragoons to scout American movements, it is uncertain why Tecumseh remained at Sandwich until the 29th. His stay there produced no material result, whereas his accompanying the soldiers might have convinced by example more tribesmen to join the retreat before it was too late. Prevost would later attribute Procter's "easy marches" to the encumbrances of "forbidden" personal baggage. Yet, according to Warburton, "There was no baggage with the division when they were moving.... The waggons were all at the Moravian village."[11]

Aside from the Natives' impediment to unified movement, the Right Division faced tremendous physical obstacles. The 30 September diary entry of Thomas McCrae of Raleigh Township on the Thames reads, "This morning still raining and rained all day. The roads are most shocking bad. The people from Malden are all flocking up on their way, through the Americans having taken possession of Malden on Monday last." [12] The men

stumbled over rotting trees, protruding stumps, a bit of a half-submerged corduroy road for one short space, then a mile or two or more of black muck swamp ... possibly clay-logged and footsore and with much pain in the small of his back, find himself by sundown at the foot of a hemlock or cedar, with a fire at his feet, having done manfully about ten miles for his day's work. Apart from the fire and the blessed rest, practice deducts woefully from the poetry of bush life ... the soldier, with his musket and full supply of ammunition, a weight calculated ... to exceed sixty pounds. [13]

While the troops plodded eastward, the boats containing the heavy stores and ammunition wound their way up the Thames. Unknown to Procter, the entrenching tools in *Mary* and *Ellen* (destined for his intended works at the Forks) had to be unshipped to surmount the six-foot sandbar at the mouth of the river. The reloading was in reverse order and the tools were buried in the bottoms of the vessels. William Atherton, one of a party of 17 prisoners, observed that it took two days to unship and reload one vessel. [14]

The moody Native allies created another circumstance that contributed to future problems. The road from Sandwich to the Thames crossed over seven rivers and creeks that flowed into Lake St. Clair (Petite River, Pike's Creek, Rivière aux Puces, Belle River, Carp River, Ruscom River, and Indian Creek). These bridges, if destroyed, could somewhat impede a pursuing enemy. Capt. Chambers affirmed that the bridges were deliberately left intact because of the Natives who, according to Warburton, were "constantly straggling ... some in rear, some in front." Indian Department officials and others were unanimous in pointing out that had these bridges been destroyed, the trailing Native families would have been cut off and the warriors would certainly have fallen on their allies. Unaware of Procter's circumstance, Harrison viewed the nondestruction of bridges solely in military terms as a major blunder and concluded that Procter "had lost his senses." [15]

On 29 September, the British main body, consisting of four to five hundred soldiers, trudged over the spongy mud of the wetlands through a cold, driving rain to Louis Trudell's farm, three miles from the mouth of the Thames. Procter ordered the shivering troops to shelter there, to await his allies once more. Most of the remaining tribesmen did not join the army until the next evening. Others arrived the following day. François Baby overtook them at their encampment on the Ruscom River and advised Elliott and Tecumseh to hurry along as the Americans had occupied Sandwich.[16]

Although slow, the retreat was controlled, and Procter managed to reconcile a number of divergent priorities. Tecumseh and a respectable 1200 warriors had joined. The stores, military dependents, baggage, and vessels were well upriver, shielded by the main party. In keeping with his instructions, Procter had maintained the alliance, left no materiel to the enemy, and conducted an orderly retreat. His frequent references to Dover (Dolsen's) and his insistence on maintaining the vessels and naval stores indicate that his initial intention was to occupy the lower Thames in order to maintain his marine resources upriver at the Forks.

On 1 October, the incessant rain and miserable condition of the troops prompted Procter to remain at Trudell's. As the dragoon observation party produced no intelligence of an enemy advance, the British commander used the interlude to examine his line of retreat. In his words, Moraviantown "secured our line of communication for provisions; it served to protect our rear and our sick might have been in security there. In the event of our being dislodged from Dover we might have retreated to it." Procter set off, but an express from Warburton overtook his carriage, reporting enemy vessels on Lake St. Clair. The British general returned immediately to find the troops removed some miles upstream, crossing the river in scows at John Dolsen's. The allies were now on opposite sides of the river. Procter sent his brigade major, Capt. John Hall, to examine the enemy threat and destroy major bridges to the rear. Hall returned at 10 PM to report one large vessel on Lake St. Clair. He had destroyed one bridge with the help of three inhabitants and left an observation party under Ensign Holmes to destroy another.[17]

The following morning, 2 October, Procter rode back with Capt. Hall to the mouth of the Thames to examine the threat first hand. He observed one American vessel far out to sea and assumed she was hunting for *Nancy*, expected back from Michilimackinac. The British commander directed a boat to be sent down to assist any remaining Natives at the bridge destroyed by Holmes. Satisfied that there was no sign of a pursuit, Procter resumed his preparations. He directed Capt. Dixon, the engineer officer (sick since 24 September but now recovered), to inspect the Forks. On doing so, Dixon declared both Dolsen's and Chatham unsuitable strong points as the former was devoid of natural defences while the Forks lacked troop accommodations.[18]

As a result of Dixon's dismal assessment, Procter resolved to investigate the remaining possibility, Moraviantown. In the meantime, the commissariat ovens at Dolsen's were in place to feed the troops, and Dolsen's mill, tavern, trading store, distillery, blacksmith shop, and outbuildings provided shelter from the continuing rains. Lt. Col. Evans reported difficulties in clearing the military dependents (88 wives with 141 children) still stranded at Dolsen's because of the bad weather and poor roads. With no word of an American pursuit, Procter ordered the main body to stay put while he examined Moraviantown. Before leaving on the morning of 3 October, he sent Ensign Holmes to destroy another major bridge at Jeanette's Creek and appointed Lt. William Crowther assistant engineer, directing him to put Dolsen's in the best possible state of defence that "time and circumstances would admit." Then the British general set off, accompanied by Capt. Dixon and Lt. MacLean. Although Procter would maintain "I had determined to make a stand at Dover," his action of taking the engineer officer with him raised doubts among his men. Crowther undertook to cut loopholes in the buildings and throw up works but he learned that the entrenching tools were upriver at the Bowles farm. The assistant engineer sought to recover these, only to learn that they were buried in the bottoms of the vessels. Lacking boats or wagons with which to convey them down to Dolsen's, he returned to that place. Before he could do anything else, Warburton ordered a resumption of the retreat, receiving the first certain news of Harrison's advance. Within two hours of Procter's departure, the soldiers had their knapsacks on their backs.[19]

Harrison was close, indeed. On 31 September, the first day of the pursuit, his army covered 25 miles. Unencumbered by baggage and stores, it made good progress over the road hardened by a sudden frost, encamping that night on the Ruscom River. Perry had sent four vessels to Lake St. Clair to intercept the fleeing British vessels but these had slipped into the shelter of the Thames. On 2 October, *Scorpion, Porcupine,* and *Tigress* entered the river, accompanied by 50 small boats containing the troops' baggage. Harrison sent Johnson's regiment ahead on 3 October to secure any bridges in his path. This detachment came upon Ensign Holmes and 13 privates in the act of destroying the bridge over Jeanette's Creek and captured the lot. From them, Harrison

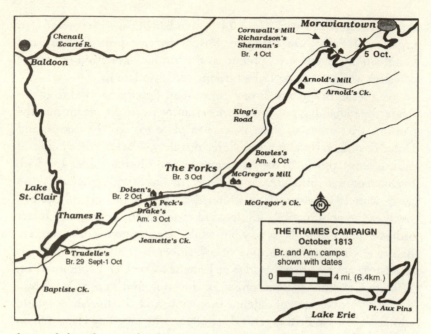

learned that the next bridge was already broken up but that Procter had no certain knowledge of the pursuit. By the evening of the 3rd, the army arrived at the farms of John Drake and John Peck opposite from Dolsen's, eight miles from the mouth of the Thames. The American vessels remained at Drake's with a guard of 150 men while the army sped forward.[20]

While Warburton withdrew the main body, Procter was riding towards Moraviantown, 26 miles distant, unaware of the sudden turn of events. This time, he arrived at his destination an hour before dusk. On examining the village, he agreed with Dixon that compared to Dover and Chatham, the features of the village were favourable for defence. According to the Moravian church diary for 3 October, Procter determined to build a kind of fortification at the elevated east end of the village. The diarist, Brother Christian Dencke, went on to reveal that the British commander "purchased" (more likely, requisitioned) the entire community, "houses, Indian corn, garden vegetables, furniture and everything we could spare." He added, "The Christian Indians for the duration of the war were to be assigned another piece of land ... also ... food and clothing from the King's Store." That night, 36 wounded and sick soldiers arrived at the Moraviantown church and school to join the 70 their attendants had already relocated from the nearby barn of Lemuel Sherman the previous day. Satisfied that he had a defensive site, Procter bedded down for the evening of the 3rd. In the early morning, he was roused from his slumber by Lt. Thomas Coleman (Canadian Light Dragoons) with another express from Warburton, reporting the evacuation of Dolsen's in the face of the oncoming enemy. Leaving at daylight, Procter hurried off to rejoin the troops.[21]

Given the third unauthorized withdrawal of the Right Division, Procter was somewhat justified in saying that many of his problems emanated from "a strong disposition of a large part of the officers to retire from the territory," resulting in "apathy" and "indifference" to the execution of specific orders. The previous withdrawals, while unauthorized, had not precluded the possibility of protecting the vessels at Chatham; however, the evacuation of Dolsen's dashed this prospect. Although Procter's selection of Moraviantown would have also forced their abandonment, the cargoes could have been saved. Now, in Procter's words, "It rendered absolutely necessary the destruction of the vessels and stores which had been brought up with much trouble and exertion from Amherstburg to prevent their falling into the hands of the enemy.... No alternative was left to me but to adopt those dispositions which so new and unexpected a situation called for." As a participant at the meeting with Tecumseh on 18 September, Warburton was fully conversant with the aim of making a stand on the Lower Thames. Left in command, he made no effort to work toward the plan. Upon hearing that the Americans were four or five miles distant, he abandoned the sparse defences afforded by Dolsen's buildings and fences, marched a mile and a half, halted, formed the troops, marched another two miles to the Forks, and bivouacked there for the night.[22]

Who initiated this latest withdrawal is unclear. Lt. Col. Evans supported Warburton's contention that it was done at the urging of Tecumseh who, believing that a fortified site awaited them at the Forks, did not favour the open terrain at Dolsen's. On the other hand, Capt. Hall considered the Natives averse to further retreat, wanting to fight at Dolsen's and demanding that Warburton bring the soldiers across to the south bank. He reported the abandonment of Dover "created a very unfavourable impression" upon them. Col. William Caldwell confirmed that the Natives wanted to fight at Dolsen's and said that six hundred warriors (half the total) deserted there, as their children and baggage could not outpace the rapid American advance. From this point, the Right Division ceased to respond meaningfully to the American threat, all its actions becoming reactive to immediacies.[23]

Years later, a story sprang up concerning loose gossip among the soldiers at Dolsen's. It's author, "an anonymous British officer," identified Lt. Benjamin Geale of the 41st as repeating talk among other officers to remove the general from command. Muir was alleged to say Procter should be "hanged" for being away and that Warburton ought also to be "hanged" for not assuming command. In a separate incident, on hearing that Procter had left for Moraviantown, the Prophet was said to have remarked that he had a mind to "tear the epaulets from Procter's shoulders," as he was not worthy of wearing them. While the sudden, certain knowledge of the American pursuit probably generated grumbling among both the warriors and the troops, it is unlikely that these constituted more than frustrated outbursts. Ensign Cochran's observations on the rumours are the only ones recorded by a participant. He called them "twaddle," adding, "Who would volunteer to 'bell the cat?' Geale and Muir were a brace of chattering geese." This story is even more suspect given that the anonymous officer turned out to be John Richardson who, to add credibility to his assertions, quoted his own anonymous writings.[24]

Nonetheless, Procter's actions cannot be said to have inspired confidence, if it could be inspired under the circumstances. By trying to save the alliance, he had held back the retreat with only a fraction of the warriors to show for it. He had no defences established anywhere and the rapid advance of the enemy threatened to catch his tired, outnumbered force in the open country. Procter searched for a strong point that could be not only defended but resupplied, one that offered shelter from the impending winter blast and was acceptable to his allies. Above all, he had to maintain, in fact to restore, Native confidence.

Ironically, Native confidence received another serious blow when the tribesmen arrived at the Forks and found the site unfortified. It will be recalled that through a subtle error in translation, Elliott had promised them a fortified position at the Forks. Although Procter had sent Lt. Crowther there a week earlier to initiate work, the vessels containing the entrenching tools, *Mary* and *Ellen*, were repeatedly delayed by mishaps and consequently, nothing had been done. The Native chiefs found only three or four cannon dumped on the ground, along with some arms in a nearby cabin. This lack of preparation revived their suspicions as their indignation once more brewed to the breaking point. Warburton wanted to resume the retreat, but the angry chiefs demanded that he join them on the south side of the river to resist the American advance. Elliott approached Warburton and Evans in tears, insisting that he would not be "sacrificed," that "he could not answer for the consequences." Warburton agreed to remain at the Forks on the evening of the 3rd.[25]

For reasons that are unclear, the chiefs changed their minds the next day, demanding that Warburton proceed to Moraviantown. According to Ensign Cochran, Indian Department officials managed to convince them to continue the retreat, perhaps in the hope that a better site awaited them upriver. A portion of the braves, led by Tecumseh and Ottawa chief Naiwash, covered the withdrawal of the Native families and tore up partially the planks of the McGregor's Creek bridge, its rain-soaked timbers resisting incendiary efforts.[26]

At this time, Walk-in-the-Water took advantage of the confusion to effect his planned defection with some 60 Wyandot followers. Warrior numbers had peaked in the summer when Dickson's contingent swelled the total to over 3500 active fighters. With many of Dickson's followers returning home after the second Maumee expedition, the overall number of warriors remained at 3500 in September (although not all of these were fighters, it seems). Of the 1200 at Dover, half fell away. Now, even that remnant diminished.[27]

Procter's plan, such as it was, fell apart completely. The vessels and stores laboriously hauled four miles upriver to the Bowles farm, the high point of navigation for the larger craft, were imperiled. On hearing of the latest withdrawal, Procter sent Warburton a message to join him there. When he arrived, Warburton found his commander directing the destruction of the vessels and their cargoes. Ammunition, entrenching tools, and other essential stores were loaded into flatbottom bateaux capable of going up the river. Procter ordered Capt. George Benson Hall (late of the Provincial Marine, not to be confused with Procter's brigade major) to "warp two vessels down" and sink them across the river to obstruct enemy gunboats. Lieutenants MacLean and Crowther ended up scuttling and setting afire *Mary* and *Ellen*, while Chambers destroyed the remaining materiel, mainly marine stores. Procter accelerated the march to Sherman's farm where the exhausted soldiers bedded down in the hay of his large, new barn, recently vacated by the division hospital. Lt. Bullock's grenadiers and Muir's company formed a rear guard a mile down river at Edward Richardson's tavern and pear orchard.[28]

Some of the militiamen's families also fell behind during the accelerated retreat. One participant recollected being overtaken by American horsemen:

We were taken prisoners a short distance above the village of Chatham while ascending the Thames. Father had been left behind at Chatham to destroy a vessel which was there, and only came up with our detachment a short time before we were taken. It was very late when he reached us. He at once went ashore to reconnoitre from a hill nearby, from where he saw the Kentucky rifle militia coming across the fields on horseback. We intended to reach an old empty house on the other side of the river and attempted to do so but before we succeeded, the bank was full of men who fired some shots at us because we did not come ashore fast enough when ordered and they shot a woman through the cheeks. When they got us ashore, they robbed us of everything they could carry away, even my mother's young baby clothes. They chopped up everything else, including a feather bed and our blankets they put on our shoulders. Father was furious. He told them if there had been only half a dozen of them, he would have defied them to touch anything and would have thrown them in the river. One of them named Knaggs, who knew us and who had formerly lived in Detroit, had to beg and pray of father to be quiet, fearing that they would shoot him. Soon after, the American regulars under General Harrison came up and my father was placed under a regular guard when he at once complained of the treatment we had received. He was advised to complain to the General so my mother went and spoke to him. Harrison was very kind to her and said "My good woman, I will do everything I can for you." But the militia only said "who cares for General Harrison? None of his business what we do." [29]

When Harrison arrived at the Forks of the Thames, he found both bridges across McGregor's Creek partially destroyed, and warriors on the east side disputing his passage. The rapid American advance was greatly facilitated by information obtained from local informers, notably an American immigrant, Matthew Dolsen, who had switched sides early in the war. Additionally, a woman, described as a "guardian angel," detailed the British positions of the previous day to Harrison. Concluding that the entire enemy force was arrayed before him, Harrison deployed his main force in battle order. A few rounds from two 6-pdr. guns drove off the warriors, both sides sustaining a handful of casualties in the skirmish. Repairing the bridges within two hours, the Americans doused the flames of torched buildings to recover some thousand muskets on the north side of McGregor's Creek along with several thousand bushels of wheat in John McGregor's Mill. Half a mile upstream, Harrison's men came upon a large two-masted vessel (probably *Miamis*) on fire, loaded with arms and ordnance stores. At the Bowles farm, they found *Mary* and *Ellen*, containing stores and ammunition, near a large distillery, all on fire. "Bombs were exploding every eight or ten minutes" on the British vessels. Two of Hull's carriage-mounted 24-pdr. artillery pieces were also retaken along with quantities of shot and shell. Encouraged by these visible signs of a disorderly retreat, the Americans pressed the pursuit.[30]

Procter spent the evening of the 4th with his family at Moraviantown. Given Warburton's mediocre performance to date, the British commander may have been justified in relieving his second-in-command; however, his other senior officer, Evans, was sick during much of the retreat. In any case, Procter would have been well advised to remain with the troops, especially with the Americans in hot pursuit. By leaving them for the night he gave the impression that his soldiers were of secondary importance. Despite his past record of energy and foresight, Procter was evidently worn down by his ordeal. Over the months, his optimistic and elegant letters clearly regressed into scrawls done in haste and anxiety. His decision to spend time with his family was partially driven by a desire to avoid heightened allied dissension. There was certainly unpleasantness to avoid. While at Sherman's, an angry Sac chief, who had had to abandon his children at Dolsen's, threatened to shoot Elliott, maintaining that the British troops had "run off."[31]

Far to Procter's rear, the Centre Division was also in serious straits. On 3 October, with both Right and Centre Divisions endangered by overwhelming force, Rottenberg received word of menacing demonstrations at Sacket's Harbour and decided that his leadership was required at Kingston. With the two best regiments, he rushed off, leaving Vincent to contend with a dismal circumstance, threatened in front and flank, with diminished strength, half his remaining troops too ill to move. Vincent had "no batteaux that will swim" and few wagons or serviceable horses. The Centre Division could offer Procter no help. Aside from the local efforts of Thomas Talbot on the Upper Thames, the British commander was totally on his own.[32]

It is doubtful that anyone in Procter's position could have negotiated this miserable situation to a satisfactory conclusion. There had been no clear answers to his myriad past problems, and now his slender options were drastically diminished. Torn between military judgment and the need to preserve the Native alliance, Procter had compromised both priorities. With the Native warriors greatly reduced in number and his main body unprotected by any sort of defensive works, he was nearly overtaken by a superior force. As the exhausted, fever-ridden, and demoralized men of the Right Division bedded down in their spartan accommodations, the command structure of the Right Division and its operational effectiveness were badly depleted. Procter could not have slept well, knowing that he may have to face an enemy under adverse tactical conditions. Having been inexorably drawn into the web of an incoherent strategy, Procter was now hopelessly ensnarled.[33]

NOTES

1. Procter to Prevost, 21 Sept. 1813, *MPHC* 25: 529.
2. Harrison to Armstrong, 15 Sept. 1813, Armstrong to Harrison, 22 Sept. 1813, *MLWHH* 2: 541, 544.
3. McAfee, *Late War*, 365; Capt. Sympson Diary, cited in Quisenberry, *Kentucky in the War*, 109; Brown, *Campaigns*, 6; Harrison's General Order, 27 Sept. 1813, *MLWHH* 2: 546-50.
4. Harrison to Armstrong, 27 Sept. 1813, *MLWHH* 2: 546-47; Brown, *Campaigns*, 58-63; Perry to Secretary of the Navy, 27 Sept. 1813, cited in the *Vermont Mirror*, 27 Oct. 1813.
5. Harrison to Armstrong, 27 Sept. 1813, *MLWHH* 2: 550-51; Weekly State of Right Division, 22 Sept. 1813, *PCM*, Appendix 29.
6. Hunt, *Memoirs*, 22.
7. Brown, *Campaigns*, 106; Harrison to Armstrong, 30 Sept. 1813, *MLWHH* 2: 554-56; *The War*, 2 Nov. 1813; McArthur to Armstrong, 6 Oct. 1813, cited in the *Vermont Mirror*, 27 Oct. 1813.
8. Harrison to Armstrong, 30 Sept. 1813, *MLWHH* 2: 555.
9. Procter to Rottenberg, 23 Oct. 1813, NAC, C 680: 273; *Defence of Major General Procter*, 15-16, 36; Ensign Holmes, William Jones (Indian Department), *PCM*, 135, 178.
10. Chambers, *PCM*, 87; Procter to Rottenberg, 23 Oct. 1813, NAC, C 680: 273; Richardson, *War of 1812*, 207; *Defence of Major General Procter*, 25. *Tecumseh's Last Stand*, by John Sugden, is to date the most detailed attempt to examine the Thames campaign produced. Sugden's work is partial to Tecumseh and echoes Richardson's simplistic conclusions in attributing the results of the campaign to Procter's incompetence.
11. *Defence of Major General Procter*, 25; Hall, François Baby, Warburton, *PCM*, 241, 146, 27.
12. McCrae Diary, *DHCNF* 1813, Vol. 3: 180.
13. Coffin, *The War and its Moral*, 219-20.
14. Atherton, *Narrative*, 111; Crowther, Dixon, *PCM*, 98, 190-91.
15. François Baby, Col. William Caldwell, William Jones, Chambers and Warburton, *PCM*, 148, 176, 93; Armstrong, *NOW* 1: 184. According

to Lt. Col. Evans, the question of destroying bridges was largely immaterial. Had these bridges (including the important ones at Ruscom and Trudell's) been destroyed, they could have been repaired in a matter of hours. Evans, *PCM*, 66.

16. McCrae Diary, *DHCNF* 1813, Vol. 3: 180; *Defence of Major General Procter*, 25; François Baby, *PCM*, 146.

17. *Defence of Major General Procter*, 18-20, 38; Wood, Hall, *PCM*, 206, 245.

18. Dixon, *PCM*, 100; *Defence of Major General Procter*, 18.

19. *Defence of Major General Procter*, 18; Evans, Dixon, Crowther, *PCM*, 59, 97, 119, 193-94, Appendix 9. William Crowther joined the 41st in 1806. Praised for his role in the battle of Queenston Heights, he arrived at Amherstburg on August 5, 1813. Procter made unsuccessful attempts to exchange him for Capt. William Bruce Procter (the general's brother, serving with the New Brunswick Fencibles). Captured at Moraviantown, Crowther left the army on half pay after his repatriation in 1814. Lomax, *The 41st*, 65, 72.

20. Cooper, *Naval History* 2: 199; Harrison to Armstrong, 9 Oct. 1813, *MLWHH* 2: 558-59.

21. Dixon, *PCM*, 98; Moravian Church Diary and Brother Schnall Diary, cited in Elma Gray, *Wilderness Christians*, 229-30; *Defence of Major General Procter*, 20.

22. *Defence of Major General Procter*, 19-25; Procter to Rottenberg, 23 Oct. 1813, NAC, C 680: 273.

23. Warburton, Evans, Hall, Col. William Caldwell, *PCM*, 11, 50, 249, 160-62; Lt. Bullock to Maj. Frend, 6 Dec. 1813, Lomax, *The 41st*, 109.

24. Diary of an anonymous British officer, cited in Richardson, *War of 1812*, 226; Cochran, *Notes*, PAC MG 40, G4, File 1, 134.

25. Lt. Bullock to Maj. Frend, 6 Dec. 1813, Lomax, *The 41st*, 109; Warburton, Billy Caldwell, Evans, *PCM*, 11, 50, 55, 138. After reloading the entrenching tools to get over the sandbar at the mouth of the Thames, the crews of *Mary* and *Ellen* were detained by head winds. Crowther, *PCM*, 191.

26. Procter to Rottenberg, 23 Oct. 1813, NAC, C 680: 273; Lt. Bullock to Maj. Frend, 6 Dec. 1813, Lomax, *The 41st*, 109; Cochran, *Narrative*, NAC, MG 40, G4, File 2: 61. Many straggling Native families were overtaken by the Americans during the retreat. One Wyandot chief, Adam Brown, lagged behind the main body with his daughters and grandchildren. He was taken to Detroit and tried by court martial for his alleged role in Frenchtown massacre of 23 January 1813. Testimony credited him with saving the life of a Kentucky militiaman at Dudley's defeat on 5 May 1813, and he was acquitted. Clarke, *Wyandotts*, 116.

27. Billy Caldwell, *PCM*, 160; Rottenberg to Prevost, 3 Oct. 1813, *DHCNF* 1813, Vol. 3: 192; *Defence of Major General Procter*, 10.

28. Warburton, Evans, Chambers, Crowther, *PCM*, 12, 60, 86, 196; *Defence of Major General Procter*, 21; Lt. Bullock to Maj. Frend, 6 Dec. 1813, Lomax, *The 41st*, 110.

29. Recollections of Andrew Kemp, cited in the *Amherstburg Echo*, 21 Jan. 1938.

30. Richardson, *War of 1812*, 242n. McAfee, *Late War*, 384; Harrison to Armstrong, 9 Oct. 1813, *MLWHH* 2: 559-60; Maj. Gen. Darroch to Prevost, 22 Oct. 1813, NAC, C 680: 129; Capt. Sympson Diary, cited in Quisenberry, *Kentucky in the War*, 103.

31. Sugden, *Tecumseh's Last Stand*, 91; Capt. Billy Caldwell, *PCM*, 164.

32. Rottenberg to Prevost, 3 Oct. 1813, NAC, C 680: 138; Thomas Ridout to Thomas Ridout, Sr., 14 Oct. 1813, Edgar, *Ten Years*, 238; Vincent to Rottenberg, 9 Oct. 1813, Col. Robert Young to Vincent, 9 Oct. 1813, *DHCNF* 1813, Vol. 3: 222-23; Maj. Gen. Duncan Darroch to Prevost, 2 Oct. 1813, NAC, C 680: 129.

33. Richardson's suspicions have been embraced and exaggerated in historical writings. One imaginative account has Procter abandoning his command for a full week! In fact, Procter was away from the troops for only a few hours on 1 October, during the day and evening of the 3rd, and during the evening of the 4th. Norman S. Gurd, *Tecumseh*, 166.

15

FINALE AT MORAVIANTOWN

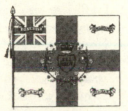

"The reasons which determined my mind were not confined to myself, but
were the plain dictates of prudence, sanctioned by all who had the best means
of judging, but who, like myself, could only judge from probabilities." [1]
Defence of Major General Procter

MORAVIANTOWN (OR FAIRFIELD) was the largest settlement on the
Thames. It consisted of a church, school, and some 60 modest log
dwellings on the north bank of the river. Founded by Moravian mis-
sionaries, the village was established for a group of Christian Delaware
Indians from the United States as a refuge from both White and Native
persecution. These people had been successively driven from the Chesa-
peake area, Ohio, and Michigan. In 1812, Brock had planned to establish an outpost at this prosperous community to halt Hull's raiders.
Since that time, the peaceful Moravians had been undisturbed by the
ravages of war.

On 3 October, after rejecting Dover and Chatham as defensive
sites, Procter had determined to establish his strong point at Moraviantown. The settlement was flanked by a ravine to the west and some
high ground to the east. With the planned food depot upstream at
Delaware, and the road blazed by Talbot from Long Point to Muncey-
town, Procter had reason to believe the Right Division might survive
the winter there. Having purchased the entire village, he planned to
billet his officers in the clergymen's homes and use the Native huts as
troop barracks. The factors of terrain, location, accommodation, and

provisioning combined to justify the selection of Moraviantown not only for a temporary stand but a permanent defensive post as well. That day, Dixon accompanied his commander to Bowles's where he recovered the entrenching tools from the bottoms of the vessels, and loaded them into boats. As these craft had not arrived, little if anything was done toward throwing up works by 5 October.[2]

Amid a complicated retreat, the commissariat had managed to feed the Right Division until the 3rd of October. Although Warburton had left five hundred loaves of bread in the ovens at Dolsen's that day, the main body of troops carried sufficient bread for the following day. On the night of the 4th, all companies were issued fresh bread except the rear guard at Richardson's farm, who fended for themselves. Procter had directed Robert Gilmor to prepare bread for the morning of the 5th, but the storekeeper in charge "disobeyed his orders," running off to look after his family. Consequently, bread was prepared late on the morning of the 5th. Just as it was ready to be served, Warburton suddenly ordered the men to arms. The Americans were advancing again. The beef on hand on the 4th and 5th went unprepared, "left on the ground," since the cooking utensils were at Moraviantown. Thus, after receiving nothing but bread on the 4th, the men were issued no rations but whiskey the next morning. Meanwhile, Gilmor undertook renewed feeding arrangements at Moraviantown, where he feverishly prepared the beef, bread, cabbage, and potatoes purchased there.[3]

Before the troops resumed the retreat, Warburton directed Lt. Felix Troughton, the artillery officer, to forward the remaining field train (one 6-pdr. gun, three 3-pdr. pieces, and one howitzer) to Moraviantown. Rejoining the troops, Procter detached one of these, a 6-pdr. gun, to accompany the march. The main body did not quite get to Moraviantown, though. Procter halted the Right Division a mile and a half short of the village. Although John Richardson postulated that the British commander selected the location for some "selfish motive ... to cover the departure of his family and personal effects," Moravian Church records prove otherwise. By Brother John Schnall's diary, Procter's family arrived at Moraviantown on 29 September, Elizabeth Procter, bristling with a sense of her importance, "demanding definitely Brother Denke's home for the time being." Schnall's diary goes on to show Procter's family (three of his children were aged 5 to 11) leaving the village by boat for Delaware early on the 5th, some ten hours before the battle.[4]

The presence of noncombatants at Moraviantown may have influenced Procter's selection of the battle site. Most of the Native residents of the village had fled six miles upstream the previous day, along with most of the sick and wounded soldiers, fleeing refugees of the Western District, and dependents. However, the Moravian clergymen and part of the division field hospital still remained. While humanitarian concerns may have influenced Procter's decision to halt before the village, the tactical considerations of the day likely prompted him to do so. The open layout of the village would have allowed the enemy to use their numerical strength to advantage on a wide front. Without entrenching tools, and with less than two days to fortify the site, it is unlikely that Capt. Dixon achieved much in the way of preparing entrenchments with the few able-bodied men on hand. In Procter's words, "The idea of occupying the village and the high grounds in the rear of us might be stated on paper, but ought not to appear elsewhere."[5]

Participants varied in their opinions to explain the selection of the battle site. According to Lt. LeBreton, the British force was adequate to occupy only a third of the village buildings. Capt. Dixon also believed that Moraviantown could not have been held long. Warburton, on the other hand, postulated: "The Division was halted by accident and the line ordered to be formed where they stood." Evans recalled that the proximity of the Americans compelled the British column to turn on the pursuers. François Baby saw the site on the road, as did Procter, offering the best natural defences in which the warriors, still his strongest arm, could be used to advantage. Billy Caldwell recalled that Tecumseh, ever eager to fight the Americans, adamantly refused to retreat any further. Lt. Bullock stated that the column was halted just about the time that refugees from the boats arrived to report the Americans just one mile away. The combined evidence strongly points to the proximity of the Americans forcing Procter to turn about and form on the most favourable terrain at hand. Thus, despite the overwhelming opinion (including Procter's) that Moraviantown was the preferred long-term site for the Right Division, the troops deployed across the road a short distance from the village.[6]

The Right Division was half-fed, exhausted, outnumbered, demoralized, and ill-equipped. It could neither outpace the American horsemen nor fight them to advantage. Brought to bay, Procter could either surrender ignominiously or risk all on a general engagement. Accompanied by Capt. Hall and Matthew Elliott, he rode forward to examine the threat, and at 1:00 PM, "came galloping back, desiring the troops to form line."[7]

During the forced march of the 4th, the main body had passed the boats containing the ammunition and entrenching tools. That evening, Chambers reported to Warburton at Sherman's that they were endangered. Warburton committed a crucial and incomprehensible error by taking no action. It was not until 8 AM of the 5th that Procter, returning from Moraviantown, sent an escort of dragoons to secure the imperiled craft. It was too late. Two hours later, fugitives brought the disheartening news that all the ammunition boats, along with 94 attendants, had been captured. Procter himself called the loss "disastrous." American horsemen also overtook the ammunition wagons struggling to bring up their charges over the muddy road. With no reserve, the soldiers had only 50 cartridges each in their pouches.[8]

To make up for the loss of his ammunition, Procter made a futile attempt to secure powder and ball from the Centre Division. Through Samuel Wood, clerk of ordnance stores, he sent Rottenberg an urgent request for an immediate supply of ammunition. Unaware that Rottenberg had left for Kingston two days previously, Procter expressed himself in superlatives: by "prompt and most serious attention to the utmost verge of possibility, pray use every effort to supply what is so essentially necessary." Later, he admitted some concern over the shortage of ammunition, but stated that he "awaited the results of the attack with full confidence."[9]

Procter drew up his regulars across a wedge-shaped clearing between the Thames River and Backmetack Marsh. By deploying his troops across this lightly-wooded 250-yard opening, the general secured his flanks and confined the enemy's frontal strength to that distance. This dry ground was interspersed with maple and white oak (beech); there was little undergrowth except in a small swamp in the middle. On the right, the warriors occupied the marsh that ran roughly parallel to the river for two miles, inclining toward the Thames to the east. This morass consisted of "moss hung trees and twisted trunks fallen and rotten, overgrown with a vegetation tangled and thick, smothered by too much moisture and too little air, knee-deep at the best and often deeper." Procter's left rested on the road which was about one hundred feet distant from the thickly forested 40-foot river bank. Lt. William Gardiner, who had served the artillery during the siege of Fort Meigs, commanded the single 6-pdr. gun situated on the road. Its effective range, according to Richardson, was limited by the intervening trees to a few hundred yards. In addition to the attending gunners, the piece was protected by four sharpshooters and ten dragoons, the remaining horsemen posted further back as a reserve. Harrison's description of the site agrees with British accounts: "The road passes through a beech forest without any clearing and for the first two miles near to the river bank. At from two to three hundred yards from the river, a swamp extends parallel to it, throughout the whole distance. Across this strip of land, its left appayed [*sic*] upon the river, supported by artillery placed in the wood, their right in the swamp covered by the whole of the Indian force, the British troops were drawn up."[10]

Procter initially formed the troops in a single continuous line. His plan called for a volley from the infantry line, accompanied by an artillery discharge of spherical shot to throw the Americans into confusion. On the signal of the artillery, the warriors were to fall on the American flank and drive the invaders back. Lt. Bullock observed that the men experienced some confusion deploying into line. The grenadiers found themselves in the centre, while the light company turned up on the right of the line. (Standard tactical formation for a battalion normally had the grenadiers on the right with the light company to the left. Their role was to deal with skirmishers and irregular troops, leaving the battalion companies to concentrate on delivering volleys to their front.)[11]

Suddenly, Procter altered his dispositions, ordering the grenadiers and number one company to form a reserve line. This second line under Muir's command was situated some two hundred yards to the rear of the first. Warburton, in charge of the first line, attributed the new disposition to Tecumseh's interference: "From some objection on the part of Tecumseh, rather more than a company was taken out of that line and formed as a reserve, the files of the first line being very open." Billy Caldwell confirmed that the new line had been formed at Tecumseh's insistence, though Capt. Hall agreed it was necessary, "that the men were too thickly posted, that they would be exposed to the enemy's riflemen and thrown away to no advantage."[12]

In any event, the British commander altered the standard British infantry line of shoulder-to-shoulder formation into two highly extended lines in open order. Ensign Cochran subsequently observed that the new disposition "was neither extended nor closed but somewhat irregularly between both ... losing the advantage of close order without benefit of the extended." In this formation, the average spacing between the soldiers of the first line was about three feet. Not only had the force of their firepower been diminished but the physical separation of the two lines exposed them to being overwhelmed separately.

Just as the retreat had been compromised by his allies, Procter's latest concession to Tecumseh now jeopardized the British tactical formation on the field of battle. Procter never blamed him, stating only that "the troops were disposed in extended order as used in woods in the last American war in which I commenced my service." The allies awaited the American attack for over three hours, unable to prepare abatis as there were no tools on hand.[13]

Adjacent to the first British line, the buckskin-clad Tecumseh led the warriors' left while the Ojibwa chief, Oshawahnah (John Naudee), headed the warriors in the forward fringes of Backmetack Marsh. Other noteworthy Natives present were Tecumseh's brother, Tenskwatawa; his 16-year-old son, Pachetha; his brother-in-law, Wasegaboah; his aides, Shabbona (an Ottawa chief of the Potawatomi) and Sauganash (Billy Caldwell); Winnebago chiefs, Naw Kaw and Four Legs; Ottawa chief, Naiwash; Potawatomi chief, Mad Sturgeon (brother-in-law to Main Pock); Roundhead's Wyandot brother, Splitlog; and possibly the Sac chief, Black Hawk.[14]

Warrior numbers, as usual, could only be estimated as they fluctuated constantly. Most of the remaining braves joined their allies on the battlefield shortly before the fighting started, having moved their families to safety beyond Moraviantown. Others returned too late to participate in the engagement. Warburton estimated their strength on site at a mere two hundred, as did Ensign Cochran. Lt. Bullock placed the number of warriors at a more respectable eight hundred. John Norton's estimate, based on statements by fugitives, was five hundred warriors, mainly Muncey, Wyandot, Ottawa, Ojibwa, and Sac. The braves were eager to fight the "yallar bellies."[15]

Although the number of British soldiers on the field varies widely by account, the morning state of the regimental adjutant, Lt. John Smith, is the most reliable indicator. His return of 5 October showed:[16]

358 other ranks
  22 officers
144 in boats [including one officer, most captured]
  28 regimental gunners [most at Moraviantown]
101 sick and wounded [at Delaware and Moraviantown]
  63 attending sick and baggage [at Delaware or Moraviantown]
  25 Royal artillery [most at Moraviantown]
  43 Colonial cavalry [Canadian Light Dragoons]
   1 Indian Department
———————————————————————————
784 Total

By deducting those soldiers who were either non-effective or absent, 451 all ranks (429 rank and file and 22 officers) remain, very close to Procter's own figure of 450 men. Earlier that morning, some soldiers had been sent to assist with the bateaux, which were nonetheless captured along with most of the soldiers in them. Only small contingents of the Royal Newfoundland Regiment and 10th Veteran Battalion remained with the Right Division and most of these had been taken in the boats that morning, leaving perhaps a dozen soldiers of these corps mingled into the ranks of the 41st. Very few militiamen were with the division. Colonels William Caldwell, Matthew Elliott, and François Baby were known to be present. Others accompanied the retreat, but most were well ahead with their families and effects.[17]

The American strength is more easily established. Harrison left Sandwich with 3500 men, which were reduced to "something above 3,000" by the 5th. This is an accurate estimate, since he had left 150 men at Dolsen's to guard Perry's gunboats, while casualties at the Forks and sickness further trimmed the numbers. His force on the day of battle consisted of five infantry regiments of Kentucky Volunteer Militia, Johnson's Regiment of Mounted Infantry, and 120 regulars of the 27th U.S. Infantry under Col. George Paull. Some two hundred warriors also accompanied his expedition. Most British estimates of the American numbers are grossly inflated, Evans, Warburton, and Lt. Bullock gave the American strength as six thousand, Capt. James Hill at 6300, and Ensign Cochran at five thousand. Procter's estimate agrees with Harrison's figure of three thousand Americans facing him on the battlefield. Although Harrison had several light pieces of artillery, he did not use them that day.[18]

All told, the Americans were led by no fewer than ten "generals," most of whom lacked military experience. Nonetheless, the Kentucky men were in good spirits, led by such charismatic figures as the legendary frontiersman, Elisha Whittlesey, the popular Governor Shelby, and Harrison, "the victor of Tippecanoe." The heroic Oliver Hazard Perry also accompanied the invasion as an aide to Harrison along with Brig. Gen. Cass, "the hero of Ta-ron-tee." The American force consisted predominantly of Kentuckians who were eager to avenge their fallen comrades, viewing the impending contest as the culmination of a long crusade. In gross numbers, the Northwest Army had a numerical superiority of at least three to one over the allied force. More important, the Americans were buoyed by recent successes and animated by a sense of mission.

In contrast, the British troops were tired and dispirited by the cumulative effects of their ordeal. The men of the 41st had been recruited with bounties and wonderful images of travel and romance with lavish provisions of beer. Most members had endured 13 years of extended hardships in the Canadian wastelands and given a good account of themselves in a year of frontier warfare. Few were accompanied by their wives. In the assessment of Lt. MacLean, hardships had worn down their *esprit de corps* and their confidence in Procter. According to Lt. Col. Evans, the troops had been subjected to "considerable privation" well before the retreat began, having gone unpaid for six and even nine months. They could buy nothing, "not even soap." Their uniforms "in rags," some of the soldiers went barefoot. They lacked greatcoats, tents, and blankets. Sickness and disease had also worn down their constitutions, and colic, smallpox, bilious (intermittent) fever, mumps, and whooping cough were common among the ranks. Medical treatments were haphazard at best, frequently more destructive than the ailments they were intended to cure. Bleeding, for example, was a prescription for fevers. The men were also physically run down from working "incessantly" on defences "without salt or spirits." The confused, reactive movements of the last few days had left them disoriented on the field of battle, their bulldog toughness much eroded. The men of the 41st had given their all for a system that demanded too much of them.[19]

When the British soldiers in their stiff leather neck stocks formed line, they barely knew their battalion commander, Warburton, who had arrived some months previously and was not of their regiment. Evans of the 41st, a newcomer to the Canadas, was also unknown to the men. All things considered, it is surprising that the men of the 41st had withstood their hardships as well as they had. A sister regiment, the 49th, arrived in Canada in 1803 and three years later, a number conspired to mutiny at Fort George. On the eve of the battle of Queenston, disgruntled elements of the 49th again threatened to shoot their officers. Despite their longer stay and their dispersed state in the remote posts of Upper Canada, the 41st Foot had not yet faltered. Ironically, the First Battalion was brought together only in the summer of 1813, just in time to endure the worst neglects arising from the failing logistics system. By 5 October, the discipline and moral fibre of Procter's steady veterans were badly depleted. In short, they were in no condition to fight.

Given their condition, the soldiers of the 41st lost faith, not in Procter personally, but in the commander who had tried and failed to look after their needs. The implicit contract between soldier and commander, ready obedience in return for regimental welfare, had been violated by the very system that both served. According to Capt. Dixon, some of the "much harassed" men muttered that they would be "cut to pieces." Although painfully aware of the condition of his command, Procter relied on his steady veterans "in the full confidence of victory." Ensign James Cochran was of a similar opinion: "The attack was silently awaited, each determined to do his duty, but few with any doubt as to the result."[20]

The braves, while unhappy about abandoning their lands, were eager to fight. Prior to the battle, Tecumseh expressed satisfaction with the final dispositions and reassured Procter, "Father, tell your young men to be firm and all will be well." The war chief passed along the British lines, pressing the hand of each officer and making some appropriate remark in Shawnee, accompanied by expressive signs of encouragement. He then returned to Backmetack Marsh to conduct his customary pre-battle "harangue" of the warriors. Although unhappy with the progress of the war and disappointed at the conduct of his allies, Tecumseh was pleased that he could finally fight his old foes.[21]

On the morning of the 5th, Harrison had pressed the pursuit with Johnson's horsemen. His efforts were rewarded near Christopher Arnold's mill in the overtaking of the burnt *Myers* and *Eliza*, and several bateaux loaded with ammunition, entrenching tools, and provisions, the very cargoes Procter had tried to save from the scuttled vessels. The Americans also took prisoner most of the British soldiers aboard these craft. According to Ensign Cochran, the boats fell into enemy hands as a consequence of the retreating warriors' failure to hold the Americans on the south side of the river. Harrison forded his army to the north side of the Thames at Arnold's mill. The foot soldiers crossed the waist-high water behind the horsemen, some in canoes and small boats, and some on foot. They soon passed Joshua Cornwall's mill set on fire by the enemy, and later came upon their vacated camp at Sherman's farm. Here the Americans helped themselves to the fresh bread found in the eight British ovens, a welcome change to their recent diet of jerked beef. Harrison pressed his advantage in an effort to force battle on his harried enemy. Johnson's horsemen sped ahead and overtook the British ammunition wagons that became mired in the road "so cut up as to be nearly impassable." One of the wagoners described British positions to Harrison, who ordered forward his main body.[22]

With his entire force brought up, Harrison prepared his attack. He initially planned an infantry assault, as Procter had anticipated. A division of three brigades of five hundred men each, commanded by Maj. Gen. William Henry, took up positions fronting the British lines. A second division under Maj. Gen. Joseph Desha faced the warriors in the marsh. Harrison's plan called for the first division to charge the British lines while the second refused the enemy left, that is, he left the warriors unengaged unless they emerged from the shelter of the marsh. Johnson's mounted regiment was to turn the left of the Native line, dividing the allied position.[23]

Learning of the open and extended order of the British lines, Harrison accepted Col. Johnson's proposal for a corresponding change in the attack. Instead of an infantry assault, Johnson was to charge the British lines with his mounted men, followed by the foot soldiers. As Johnson advanced to the point of attack, he found the ground too constricting and changed his plan. He led half his regiment through the small swamp against the warriors while his brother, Lt. Col. James Johnson, would attack the British lines with the remainder. James Johnson's men advanced in four columns of double files, picking their way through the trees. The infantry brigades followed about three quarters of a mile to the rear. The long-awaited contest between the Northwest Army and the Right Division was about to begin.[24]

Shortly before 4:00 PM, as the sound of bugles reverberated among the trees, the leading American skirmishers, termed "spies," opened fire on the British line. Their purpose was to screen the American arrangements and draw the fire of the enemy, preparatory to the main attack. The responding discharge from the British line was premature and straggling. It came without orders, producing little effect except to cause the horses in the front of the columns to recoil. Then the Kentucky mounted infantrymen, armed with "muskets, rifles, tomahawks, small hatchets, and butcher knives," got into motion with the cry, "Remember the Raisin!" In Harrison's words, they "broke through the enemy with irresistible force. In one minute the contest was over." According to Warburton, "I do not think a man of the first line loaded a second time. They immediately dispersed, some towards the second line, some into the wood. The officers were calling in all directions but it had no effect." After dispersing the first line, the horsemen sustained the momentum of their charge, breaking through the second one as well, effectively gaining the British rear. Although some of the British officers maintained that the second line held out for up to ten minutes, these were only the remnant on the right who sniped at the Americans from the woods.[25]

The relative consistency of the American accounts and the few casualties point to a very brief engagement indeed. Johnson's proposal to use the speed and momentum of his attack columns to dash through the weak lines proved highly effective. Horsemen were normally employed to rout the enemy that had been broken by the infantry. These mounted infantry were not equipped with swords in the manner of cavalry but with rifles. Their purpose was not to cut down the men of the British lines but rather to charge through them, dismount, and take the enemy lines in the rear. Individually British soldiers could shoot five rounds a minute from their "Brown Bess" muskets; in formation, they were capable of delivering three rounds. The sudden onslaught greatly limited the number of British volleys as Harrison reported a mere three Americans wounded during the charge for 12 British troops killed and 22 wounded. The weight of evidence strongly indicates that the Kentucky mounted infantrymen gained the rear of the British positions within three minutes.[26]

John Richardson, on the extreme right of the first line with the light company, was unable to see what happened, but stated simply that the British left and centre were initially overwhelmed. This impression is supported by Ensign Cochran: "A column of mounted riflemen charged and turned the left of the first line which, falling back on the second, threw it also into disorder and both gave way." Lt. Bullock, on the right of the second line observed the general movements toward the road through the intervening trees:

I heard a heavy firing of musketry and shortly after saw our dragoons retreating in confusion, followed closely by the enemy's cavalry, retreating behind the second line which stood fast and fired an irregular volley obliquing to the right and left which appeared to check the enemy. The line having commenced firing, my attention was directed to that part of the enemy moving directly to my front. Hearing the fire slacken, I turned towards the line and found myself remaining with 3 non-commissioned officers of the Grenadier company. The enemy's cavalry had advanced so close, before the reserve could commence firing, from the number of trees, that before a third round could be fired, they broke through the left, and the rest not being formed in a manner to repel cavalry, were compelled to retreat.[27]

Other observers provided more specific details. Capt. Hall was with Procter on the road at the time of the charge. In his letter of the day, he attributed the collapse of the first line to the cannon not firing: "One of the guns being deserted early in the action, the troops near it gave way." Procter held a similar view: "The gun which certainly should have produced the best effect if managed properly, was in the possession of the enemy immediately as the attack commenced, without having fired a shot. This circumstance operated so very unfavourably that the line commencing on the left gave way and notwithstanding the exertions of the officers in general, they could not be reformed or the men rallied." Despite John Richardson's assertions (decades later) that the piece was unloaded, Procter and others confirmed that the gun was loaded, "with spherical case shot, laid and the port fire light [lit]."[28]

Once the Kentuckians broke the first line on the road, they spurred on their mounts, driving off the British dragoons, along with Procter and his staff. American accounts consistently describe the Kentuckians as charging in "column." Thus they pierced both lines on the road, stampeding the enemy before them, and caused the British left and centre to buckle and fall back upon the woods. By this movement the Kentuckians encircled and flanked the remnant of both lines. Shocked by the sudden turn of events and unprepared for forming square to repel horsemen, the British either ran for the woods or threw down their muskets, their arms raised in surrender. An American observer said that they were "passive as sheep."[29]

A closer examination of the accounts leads to a more detailed reconstruction of the events. British participants agree that the first line broke initially on the left, on the road. Bullock wrote of a "heavy fire of musketry" there preceding the collapse. Since the British fire was "straggling" and the horsemen would not have fired a volley while charging in "close column," this musketry came from elsewhere. Prior to the engagement, Harrison had positioned a body of 120 regulars with a dozen friendly warriors under Col. Paull in the thickly wooded riverbank "for the purpose of seizing the enemy's artillery." Their sudden, concentrated fire was probably the cause for the artillery horses being "frighted." According to Muir, who was also near the cannon, these horses dragged their limber into woods, stampeding the dragoons and initiating the retreat of the entire line from the left. The gun itself remained on the road, unfired, and fell into enemy hands. Exploiting the breach, the American horsemen "charged down the road" still in

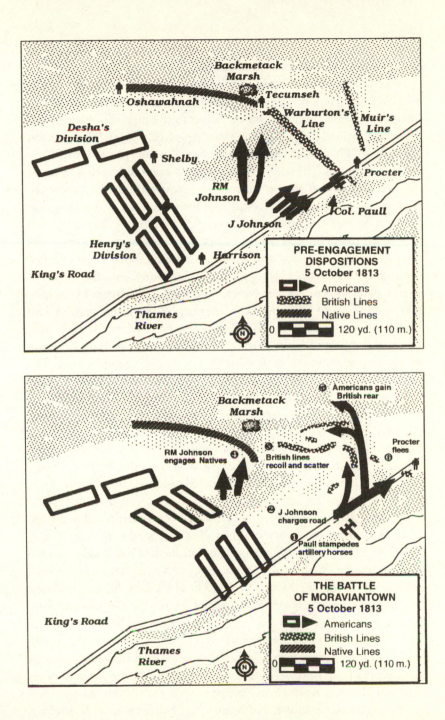

Backmetack Marsh

Oshawahnah

Tecumseh

Warburton's Line

Muir's Line

Desha's Division

Shelby

Procter

RM Johnson

J Johnson

Col. Paull

Henry's Division

Harrison

King's Road

Thames River

N

PRE-ENGAGEMENT DISPOSITIONS
5 October 1813

▶ Americans
British Lines
Native Lines

0   120 yd. (110 m.)

---

⑤ **Americans gain British rear**

Backmetack Marsh

RM Johnson engages Natives ④

③ British lines recoil and scatter

Procter flees

⑥

② J Johnson charges road

① Paull stampedes artillery horses

King's Road

Thames River

N

THE BATTLE OF MORAVIANTOWN
5 October 1813

▶ Americans
British Lines
Native Lines

0   120 yd. (110 m.)

attack column, driving the dragoons and Procter's party before them and encircling both lines simultaneously.[30]

Several officers saw Procter on horseback between the two British lines and near the first one when the action began. Shaken by the disintegration of his front line, he called out to the men in a manner variously represented as "For shame 41st Regiment!"; "41st! What are you about?"; or "Halt, 41st! For shame on you! Why do you not form?" By his own account, "although everything now seemed hopeless, I urged the first line, by all the sentiments of shame and duty to meet the enemy. It was unavailing." Procter had little time to do anything else. Situated on the road where the Americans pressed the attack, he was almost captured himself. As the horsemen separated him from the remaining troops toward the woods, his staff guided their stunned commander to safety. "Having in vain endeavoured to call the men to a sense of duty," Procter later wrote, "and having no chance by remaining, but of being captured, I reluctantly quitted the ground and narrowly escaped being taken by the enemy's cavalry." At this time, François Baby was thrown from his horse near a small bridge, and in an attempt to remount, he bowled over several dragoons' horses. The American pursuit was thus obstructed and the British general made good his inglorious escape, along with Hall, Coleman, Matthew Elliott, and the provincial dragoons. An American mounted detachment pursued them as far as Moraviantown.[31]

The opinion of several British officers was that the men did not act properly that day, that they discharged their weapons without orders, and either ran off or tamely surrendered. In his forthright manner, Private Shadrach Byfield presents a corroborating assessment: "After exchanging a few shots, our men gave way. I was in the act of retreating when one of our sergeants exclaimed, 'For God's sake, men stand and fight!' I stood by him and fired one shot but the line was broken and the men retreating. I then made my escape farther into the wood." Positioned among the thickets to the right of the line, John Richardson remained on the field longer than most of the troops, but in attempting to escape, he and a companion lost their direction and found themselves cut off by the enemy on the road, to whom they surrendered. By his distorted account, "3000 men, 1500 of them mounted riflemen ... dashed through the front line." This is certainly incorrect as no more than six hundred of Johnson's mounted regiment took part in the charge.[32]

Simultaneous to the action against the British line, Col. Richard Johnson led the attack against the warriors. After crossing the small

This is one of many fanciful depictions of the Battle of Moraviantown, 5 October 1813. Major General Harrison points the way in the foreground, while to the left, Colonel Johnson slays Tecumseh.

National Archives of Canada, Ottawa: C-41034

swamp with about four hundred of his mounted men, he charged the Natives' position in the marsh. Being well sheltered and concealed in the thickets, they put up a stubborn struggle, maintaining their ground for up to half an hour. Initially, Johnson attacked only the left of the warriors' position, leading 20 men styled the "forlorn hope" to draw the enemy fire. Fifteen men including Johnson were cut down by the concentrated fire that was delivered at ten to fifteen paces. The colonel personally killed a chief before himself losing consciousness from blood loss. That chief was believed to be Tecumseh, although the point was widely disputed afterward. The horsemen eventually dismounted to dislodge the warriors from their concealment. Those on the extreme right, led by Oshawahnah, actually advanced on Desha's division, temporarily driving it back. Governor Shelby saw the danger and brought up a regiment, which with Johnson's men, steadily drove the braves back. Procter later acknowledged his allies as having done their part in the battle "faithfully and courageously." Eventually the warriors yielded the field to superior numbers and melted into Backmetack Marsh.33

It is certain that Tecumseh was killed that day and likely that his body was carried away and buried in the bush by his followers. Two prisoners, Capt. Edward McCoy of the 41st and the mortally wounded interpreter, Andrew Clark, declared the chief killed. It was commonly believed that some of the Kentuckians cut strips of his skin for razor straps, but that point has been disputed. Simon Kenton, an experienced Indian fighter of Kentucky, one of the few Americans who could recognize Tecumseh's body, denied finding it on the field. He insisted that the warriors, with their reverence for the dead, would never abandon the remains of their foremost leader.34

Satisfied that the warriors were in retreat, Harrison detailed Maj. Devall Payne with a part-battalion of mounted infantry to capture Procter, whom they pursued some six miles beyond Moraviantown to Twenty-four Mile Creek. Here, their progress was impeded by snarled wagons in the muddy stream; Procter escaped by a side path into the woods. Although most of the Americans gave up the chase, eight American officers led three privates to continue the pursuit for some miles until the onset of darkness. The pursuing party returned with some 50 captives (including noncombatants) at 10 PM that evening. An American officer by the name of Sholes, would later write, "I had a very pleasant ride back to Detroit in Procter's beautiful carriage. I found in it a hat, a sword, and a trunk. The latter contained many letters in the handsomest writing I ever saw by Procter's wife to her dear Henry."35

Late that night, after an exhausting ride through the Longwoods Wilderness, Procter arrived at Delaware, some 40 miles upstream from Moraviantown. Decades later, John Richardson described Procter's escape as a base desertion of his troops, the crowning example of his "poltroonery." On reading Richardson's account, Cochran embellished that version of Procter's escape: "An indifferent horseman, he never rode faster in his life. For well he knew Kentuckian horsemen in pursuit had sworn to scalp him. Within 24 hours he rode 70 miles." About 50 other British soldiers made good their escape from the field of battle, including Lt. Bullock and Pte. Byfield.[36]

The sudden and definitive allied defeat threw the other elements of the retreat into considerable disorder. The much harassed Robert Gilmor described the ensuing pandemonium:

On the day of the action, I had about 170 head of cattle which I had sent six miles above the Moravian Village.... They were in charge of a captain of militia, who I had employed as an agent for purchases. He had then a sufficient number of herds and drivers under his orders. On hearing of the battle, he immediately put them in motion and had got them sufficiently advanced, had it not been for the universal panic which seems to have seized every person of our army who had escaped. I was then in the rear of most of those who had fled, and on coming up with the cattle found that two of the drivers only remained with them ... but an alarm of a party of enemy's cavalry being very near prevented me from getting any more assistance and frightened away the two men which had to that time remained faithful to their duty.

Gilmor's own wagon containing pay lists, receipts, accounts, and his personal baggage then overturned. On perceiving the accident, the warriors recessed from their retreat to plunder the contents.[37]

In a highly glamourized account of the culminating engagement of his campaign, Harrison estimated the number of warriors engaged as well over a thousand. He counted 33 dead braves on the field, although others were undoubtedly carried away by their retreating companions. He reported 601 British regulars captured, implying that these were taken in battle. In fact, this figure was the aggregate total for the entire campaign including those prisoners taken during the retreat and those stragglers, refugees and convalescents picked up after the engagement. Warburton, Evans, Muir, and Chambers were taken, along with most of the other officers of the division. Harrison reported light American casualties with seven killed and 22 wounded (five fatally).[38]

The Americans retrieved six cannon in the vicinity of Moravian-town, in addition to two 24-pdr. guns taken a few days previously. Three of the brass pieces had been originally captured by the Americans during the Revolutionary War and subsequently recaptured from Hull at Detroit. Although the colours of the 41st were not taken on the field, the Americans managed to capture one stand, Tecumseh's large battle flag, blue with a British ensign in the corner. Observing that Procter "escaped by the fleetness of his horse escorted by forty dragoons and a number of mounted Indians," Harrison added, "When it is recollected that they had chosen a position that effectually secured their flank which it was impossible for us to turn and that we could not present to them a line more extended than their own, it will not be considered arrogant of me to claim for my troops the palm of superior bravery."[39]

Harrison's carefully crafted report to Armstrong was written in grandiose terms. It prompted one naive Congressman from South Carolina to declare in the House of Representatives, "The victory of Harrison was such as it would have secured for a Roman General, in the best days of the Republic, the honors of a triumph." Some American newspapers were less impressed, contrasting the commander's hyperbolic references to "destructive fire" with his "trifling losses."[40]

The *Vermont Mirror* was direct in its criticism of the general's varnished account:

In pomp, parade and bombast, it outstrips any of the French bulletins. While reading it, the imagination is prepared for the dreadful encounter of ten times ten thousand in either host and the destruction of at least half their numbers. But at the close, we are relieved by the discovery that the General "has raised a tempest merely to drown a fly". Only 7 are killed and 22 wounded on the part of the Americans and but 12 killed and 22 wounded on the other side of the enemy besides some 20 or 30 Indians while the prisoners (comprising the whole of the enemy's army) amount to but about 600, including officers.[41]

The long awaited victory in the west created euphoria in the United States. Towns were illuminated and medals struck in honour of the Perry and Harrison. After a year of defeats and desultory warfare, American arms had not only recovered Michigan Territory (except Michilimackinac) but occupied what President Madison termed "Uppermost Canada."

Kentuckians had particular cause to celebrate. Harrison's successful campaign represented the apex of their frontier struggles dating back to the American Revolution. To them, Procter and Tecumseh represented the final obstacle to occupation of the old Northwest. This immense territory was opened up for settlement largely through the blood of the hardy Kentuckians.

The day after the battle, Prevost, hopelessly out of touch with the rapidly unfolding events, wrote Procter from Montreal, authorizing a retreat that began over a week earlier: "I entirely approve of your determination consequent upon the disastrous event [the battle of Lake Erie], of your making a stand upon the Thames and have the fullest reliance upon the zeal and ability you have hitherto manifest to control your retreat so as to afford the enemy no decided advantage over you."[42]

NOTES

1. Procter to Thomas Talbot, 23 Sept. 1813, *TP*, 193.
2. Brother Schnall Diary, 5 Oct. 1813, cited in Gray, *Wilderness Christians*, 230.
3. Evans, Muir, Hill, Fitzgerald, Quartermaster Bent, Gilmor, *PCM*, 56-57, 78, 116, 127, 132-34, 140-44, 195. While the feeding arrangements certainly failed, it would be most surprising if the soldiers had not devised imaginative methods of local procurement on the Richardson and Sherman farms. None of the officers at Procter's trial expressed undue concern over the feeding arrangements on the 4th and 5th. The assertion that the men had nothing to eat for two days is exaggerated, rooted in Richardson's writings. Richardson, *War of 1812*, 226.
4. Lt. Troughton, *PCM*, 108; Procter to Rottenberg, 16 Nov. 1813, *SBD* 2: 340; Indian Johnson's account, cited in O.K. Watson, "Moraviantown," 128; Richardson, *War of 1812*, 223; Brother Dencke Diary, 29 Sept. 1813, Brother Schnall Diary, 5 Oct. 1813, and Moravian Church Diary, cited in Gray, *Wilderness Christians*, 227-31. The location of the battlefield has been established by the numerous artifacts found in the vicinity of Lot 4 in the Gore of Zone, Kent County, near the village of Thamesville. Katherine Coutts, "Thamesville and the Battle of the Thames," 23.
5. Procter to Rottenberg, 23 Oct. 1813, NAC, C 680: 273; Schnall Diary, cited in Gray, *Wilderness Christians*, 231; *Defence of Major General Procter*, 23.
6. LeBreton, Dixon, Warburton, Evans, François Baby, *PCM*, 27, 51, 101, 153, 169; Bullock to Frend, 6 Dec. 1813, Lomax, *The 41st*, 110-11; William Hickling interview with Billy Caldwell, cited in Blanchard, *Northwest*, 320.

7. Warburton, *PCM*, 13.
8. Dixon, Sgt. Brooks, Hall, *PCM*, 107, 204, 252; Cochran, *Narrative*, NAC, MG 40, G4, File 2: 62.
9. Procter to Rottenberg, 5 Oct. 1813, NAC, C 680: 208; Rottenberg to Prevost, NAC, C 680: 138; Procter to Rottenberg, 23 Oct. 1813, NAC, C 680: 273; *Defence of Major General Procter*, 21.
10. Indian Johnson's account, cited in Watson, "Moraviantown," 128; MacLean narrative, cited in Coffin, *The War and Its Moral*, 227; Evans, *PCM*, 72; Harrison to Armstrong, *MLWHH* 2: 561; Bennett H. Young, *The Battle of the Thames*, 61; Richardson, *War of 1812*, 228; *Defence of Major General Procter*, 23; Harrison to Armstrong, 9 Oct. 1813, *MLWHH* 2: 561. While most accounts situate the road adjacent to the river bank, some say that the distance between them was another two hundred yards. The confusion probably stems from observers referring to the gun in the "centre" of the British position. In fact, it was on the far left on the road which most participants agree was immediately beside the river bank. MacLean narrative, cited in Coffin, *The War and its Moral*, 227.

   William Gardiner, of the 41st Foot came to Canada in 1811. Although the junior lieutenant of the regiment, in rank only since 1812, Procter praised "his science in artillery" as demonstrated in management of the siege guns at Fort Meigs on the first Maumee expedition. He had charge of the single British 6-pdr. at the engagement of Moraviantown. It appears he eluded capture as he provided input for Lt. Bullock's report to Maj. Frend. Gardiner was taken prisoner at Fort Erie in August 1814, and retired on half pay in 1821. Procter to Prevost, 14 May 1813, NAC, C 678: 261; Lomax, *The 41st*, 92.
11. Procter to Rottenberg, 16 Nov. 1813, *SBD* 2: 340; MacLean narrative, cited in Coffin, *The War and Its Moral*, 228. For an example of the scathing assessments of Procter's role on the Thames campaign, see Victor Lauriston's "Tecumseh." Lauriston subsequently reversed his position completely and became Procter's champion in "The Case For General Procter." Lauriston moved from calling Procter "the most pathetic mockery in Canadian military history" to acknowledging him as the most neglected of the British commanders. He reaffirmed this view in *Romantic Kent, The Story of a County, 1626-1952*. For a concise assessment of the conditions under which the British soldier of this period laboured, see Donald E. Graves, *The Battle of Lundy's Lane*, 41-55.
12. Lt. Bullock to Maj. Frend, 6 Dec. 1813, Lomax, *The 41st*, 111; Warburton, *PCM*, 13; William Hickling interview with Billy Caldwell, cited in Blanchard, *Northwest*, 320; Hall, *PCM*, 256.
13. *Defence of Major General Procter*, 23; Cochran, *Narrative*, 63; Hall, *PCM*, 281. Standard British battle formation called for deployment in two lines in close order of depth. According to military theorist

Duparcq, the front of a deployed battalion of a thousand men in three ranks should not exceed 170 yards. Although somewhat protected by trees, Procter's frontage was considerably longer with much fewer men. Ed. de la Barre Duparcq, *Elements of Military Art and History*, 66, 72.

14. Warburton, *PCM*, 14; Morning State of 41st Regiment, 5 Oct. 1813, Lomax, *The 41st*, 88; Cochran, *Narrative*, NAC, MG 40, G4, File 2: 63-64; Lt. Bullock to Maj. Frend, 6 Dec. 1813, Lomax, *The 41st*, 112; Sugden, *Tecumseh's Last Stand*, 108; Tucker, *Tecumseh*, 309. Although Black Hawk documented a credible account of the fall of Tecumseh, his own autobiographical narrative has him leaving the Right Division for the Upper Mississippi after the siege of Fort Stephenson with no mention of the Thames Campaign. Drake, *Tecumseh*, 202-03; Jackson, *Blackhawk*, 68.

Wasegaboah (Firm Elbows) was married to Tecumseh's sister, Tecumpeace. He was killed with Tecumseh on 5 Oct. 1813. Drake, *Life of Tecumseh*, 208.

Shabonna (Burly Shoulders) was an aide to Tecumseh. He was a Potawatomi chief who accompanied Tecumseh from the beginning of the war till the latter's death at Moraviantown. Drake, *Life of Tecumseh*, 200.

15. Warburton, Hall, *PCM*, 14, 154-55; Norton, *Journal*, 342.

16. Morning State of 41st Regiment, 5 Oct. 1813, Lomax, *The 41st*, 88.

17. Procter to Rottenberg, 5 Oct. 1813, NAC, C 680: 208; Sgt. Brooks, *PCM*, 203.

18. Harrison to Armstrong, 9 Oct. 1813, *MLWHH* 2: 559-61; Warburton, Evans, *PCM*, 14, 53, 59; Lt. Bullock to Maj. Frend, 6 Dec. 1813, Lomax, *The 41st*, 112; Hill Narrative, Lomax, *The 41st*, 87; Cochran, *Narrative*, NAC, MG 40, G4, File 2: 59; *Defence of Major General Procter*, 36.

19. Lt. MacLean's reminiscences, cited in Coffin, *The War and its Moral*, 229; Whitehorne, *Welch Regiment*, 64; Evans, *PCM*, 59. Procter later admitted the men were "discouraged by the retreat and by the privations to which they had been long exposed." [Procter and Procter], *Lucubrations*, 357-58.

20. Dixon, *PCM*, 103; Cochran, *Narrative*, NAC, MG 4, File 2, 63. To assess the relative strength of each side, one should also consider the famous maxim of the scholar of Napoleonic warfare, Carl von Clauzewitz, that "the moral is to the physical as three is to one."

21. [Procter and Procter], *Lucubrations*, 357; Richardson, *War of 1812*, 212.

22. Capt. James Sympson Diary, Quisenberry, *Kentucky in the War*, 104; Cochran, *Narrative*, 61-62; Brown, *Campaigns*, 68; Brunson, *Western Pioneer* 1: 137; Harrison to Armstrong, 9 Oct. 1813, *MLWHH* 2: 560.

23. *Ibid.*, 561-62.

24. *Ibid.*, 562; R.M. Johnson to Armstrong, 22 Dec. 1834, *NOW* 1: 233. James Johnson (1774-1826), elder brother of Richard Johnson, was

second in command of the mounted regiment of Kentucky Riflemen. After the war, he became a congressman, dying in office in his first term. *WAMB*, 202.

25. Warburton, *PCM*, 38; *Defence of Major General Procter*, 43; *NOW* 1: 232; Harrison to Armstrong, 9 Oct. 1813, *MLWHH* 2: 563; Evans, Muir, Chambers, *PCM*, 60, 77, 89.

26. Harrison to Armstrong, 9 Oct. 1813, *MLWHH* 2: 565.

27. Richardson, *War of 1812*, 223; Cochran, *Narrative*, 64; Lt. Bullock to Maj. Frend, 6 Dec. 1813, Lomax, *The 41st*, 111-12.

28. Capt. Hall to Col. Harvey, 5 Oct. 1813, NAC, C 680: 205; Richardson, *War of 1812*, 227; Bombardier Lambe, *PCM*, 235; Procter to Rottenberg, 23 Oct. 1813, NAC, C 680: 273.

29. Brown, *Campaigns*, 71.

30. Richardson, *War of 1812*, 228; Harrison to Armstrong, 9 Oct. 1813, *MLWHH* 2: 562; Muir, Fitzgerald, Lefevre, MacLean, *PCM*, 82, 128, 213, 225; Procter to Rottenberg, 16 Nov. 1813, NAC, C 681: 118. Although Harrison mentioned Paull's regulars in the pre-battle dispositions, he neglected mention of their actual role in the battle, perhaps to reserve full credit for the Kentuckians, especially Richard Johnson who, as a congressman, nominated Harrison for command of the Northwest Army.

31. Dixon, Coleman, Lefevre, and Fitzgerald, *PCM*, 104, 123-24, 128, 212, 261; *Defence of Major General Procter*, 28.

32. Warburton, Dixon *PCM*, 38, 103; Byfield, *Account*, 26; Richardson, *War of 1812*, 221-22.

33. Harrison to Armstrong, 9 Oct. 1813, *MLWHH* 2: 563; Procter to Rottenberg, 16 Nov. 1813, *SBD* 2: 338-41. The stories of Tecumseh's death contain a self-evident contradiction. If Johnson killed Tecumseh early in the action and the warriors retreated on his death, the action did not last 30 minutes. Conversely, if it lasted 30 minutes and Johnson was incapacitated at the outset, he did not kill Tecumseh.

34. Edna Kenton, *Simon Kenton*, 285; Cochran, *Notes*, NAC, MG 40, G4, File 2: 124. Perhaps the most credible statement relating to Tecumseh's death was that of Andrew Clark. Raised among the Shawnee but closely associated with the Wyandot, Clark was an aide to Tecumseh during the Thames campaign. During the battle, Clark was mortally wounded by 15 buckshot. The Americans found him hiding among the roots of a large tree and wrapped him in bandages "from the neck to the knees." Before dying, Clark told Harrison that he had witnessed the death of Tecumseh and seen his body carried off the field. Rumours surrounding the great chief's demise arose partly from Harrison's failure to mention anything about his death. Two decades later, in response to public accusations by some "knave and fool" that he suppressed knowledge of Tecumseh's death to avoid the subject of mutilation of the body,

Harrison stated that he simply wasn't certain at the time whether Tecumseh was killed. Alfred Brunson, *A Western Pioneer* 1: 140-41; Harrison to Tipton, 2 May 1834, *MLWHH* 2: 750-53. The various possibilities concerning Tecumseh's death and the disposition of the body are fully examined in Sugden, *Tecumseh's Last Stand*, 136-81.

35. Kingsford, *History of Canada* 8: 322; McAfee, *Late War*, 393; Edgar, *Ten Years*, 232.
36. Cochran, *Notes*, NAC, MG 40, G4: 122.
37. Robert Gilmor Statement, nd. NAC, WO 57: 4, 14.
38. Harrison to Armstrong, 9 Oct. 1813, *MLWHH* 2: 565.
39. *Ibid.*, 564-66. Tecumseh's flag survives as an exhibit in the Kentucky Military Museum, Frankfort, Kentucky.
40. Speech of Representative Cheeves of South Carolina, cited in Auchileck, *A History of the War*, 227.
41. *Vermont Mirror*, 3 Nov. 1813.
42. Prevost to Procter, 6 Oct. NAC, C 680: 149.

16

CONSEQUENCES

"No strength can protect entirely from a stroke in the dark." [1]
Defence of Major General Procter

HARRISON'S MEN spent the evening of the 5th on the battlefield. Initially, relations between the invaders and the Moravians were cordial. Brother John Schnall's wife, Margaret, opened her kitchen to the throngs of Kentuckians and fed them until her cupboard was literally bare. But relations cooled drastically when the invaders discovered several boxes of papers belonging to Procter in one of the homes. Accusing the clergymen of harbouring public property, the Americans ransacked all houses, and plundered the village indiscriminately. Although Perry protected the brothers from the unruly soldiers, Harrison was unsympathetic to their protests, asserting that he "had not time to listen." He ordered the brethren to Detroit, along with other fugitives who had been overtaken during the campaign. [2]

Harrison placed Capt. Robert McAfee in charge of a fatigue party charged with transporting the village booty down the Thames on 17 rafts. After stripping the settlement, McAfee burned Moraviantown to the ground on 7 October. Although Harrison's reason for destroying the village was probably to prevent its occupation as a British outpost, the act may have been partly motivated by revenge. Some of the young men of the village had participated in the operations of the Right Division, despite the restraining influence of the clergymen. Harrison refused the Moravians restitution for material losses, declaring Moraviantown "an English garrison town."[3]

For reasons that are not entirely clear, Harrison did not take advantage of his victory by attacking Vincent's exposed flank as Armstrong wished. He may have been reluctant to advance into the wilderness with limited provisions and winter approaching. He had few regulars with him and Shelby's 60-day enlisted men clamoured to return home to get on with their wheat flailing, corn husking, and "hawg-butcherin." Harrison returned to Sandwich on 10 October, in time to encounter a violent storm. The furious winds capsized a schooner and several boats coasting along the shore of Lake St. Clair, dumping much of the booty and equipment acquired on the Thames campaign. The same storm prompted Harrison and Perry to postpone any attempt on Michilimackinac for the year.[4]

The Northwest Army followed its commander to Sandwich, straggling over a five-mile stretch. One participant observed, "I am well assured that in the disorder of our march down the River Tranche, 100 Indians hanging on our rear might with safety have cut off double their number." At Sandwich, the troops were "finely quartered on the enemy ... all the rails were taken for firewood, the hay for tents ... hogs, cattle and sheep taken at will." Released from service to return home, the Kentucky volunteers stopped at the Raisin River to bury the "great numbers of human skulls and bones" of their fallen comrades. Then, after reclaiming their mounts in Ohio, Governor Shelby led his men on their long trek homeward. "It appears to me more like a beaten army retreating before the enemy than a victorious army retreating at ease with the trophies of success," observed Capt. James Sympson of the disorderly march. [5]

On 16 October, Harrison concluded a formal armistice with the Potawatomi, Miami, Ottawa, Ojibwa, Wea, and Wyandot in preparation for a general council with these nations. The tribesmen agreed to surrender all remaining prisoners in their possession and to provide hostages as a guarantee of good faith. Furthermore, they were to render up any of their number found to be committing depredations. The following day, 17 October, Harrison and Perry issued a proclamation keeping in force Procter's declaration of martial law within the Western District. Harrison installed Brig. Gen. Lewis Cass as military and civil governor of Michigan Territory and left a thousand regulars to garrison the Detroit frontier (troops of the 17th, 26th, 27th and 28th U.S. Infantry and a company of artillerymen). Then, on 23 October,

Harrison embarked with his remaining 1300 regulars for Buffalo to co-operate in offensive operations on the Niagara frontier.[6]

Meanwhile, just before daylight on the morning of the 6th, Procter arrived at Delaware after an exhausting 14-hour ride through the wilderness. From there, Capt. Hall scribbled a hasty note to Col. Harvey at Ancaster, the first official notification of the British defeat:

I am commanded by Maj. Gen'l. Procter to acquaint you for Gen'l. de Rottenberg's information with the result of an affair that took place with the enemy near Moravian Town this afternoon about 4 o'clock. One of the guns being deserted early the action, the troops near it gave way and the consequence was a complete route, notwithstanding the exertions of the General to rally them, so much so that I thought it impossible he could not escape being taken. We are just arrived here. The General is so fatigued by riding from the field of battle on the other side of Moravian Town, through the Wilderness that he cannot write and I am not much better.[7]

While Procter gathered the remnants of his shattered division, Prevost fortified him with a promise, that "a liberal allowance of [Indian] presents" was en route to the Thames. Prevost's tone suddenly became cold and confirmed his purpose of seeking blame for Barclay's defeat. "It would have been satisfactory to me to have received from you a more detailed account of the reasons which induced you to urge Captain Barclay to a meeting with the enemy before the arrival of seamen," he wrote, "Until I receive your report on the subject, I shall do you the justice to believe that in adopting the measure, you have acted with the best motives and upon grounds that will justify it. As any reinforcements would only serve to increase your embarrassments with regard to provisions, you need not expect any."[8]

Oblivious to his own role in repeatedly urging a naval engagement on Lake Erie, the commander-in-chief distanced himself from the disaster, writing to Bathurst, "I have required of Major General Procter his reasons for allowing Captain Barclay to wage an unequal contest with an enemy so superior to him, before the arrival of the remainder of the seamen belonging to *Dover* which were on their way to him, but I have no doubt the peculiar circumstances under which the Major General was placed and the distress which he was suffering, as well as apprehending the want of provisions, will fully justify him in this measure." Three days after the battle of Moraviantown, he reported optimistically to Bathurst, "On the 23rd ... Major General Procter was still at Sandwich, making arrangements for falling back on the Thames. Should the enemy succeed in penetrating the barrier of Indians opposed to their approach to Detroit, and where he is to make a stand and connect himself with the Centre Division, provided the Indians are faithful to their promises, otherwise he will be obliged to continue to retreat towards the Head of Lake Ontario."[9]

It gave Procter little satisfaction to know that Prevost "entirely approved" of a stand on the Thames in his letter penned a day after the battle of Moraviantown. Within a few days, however, news of Procter's defeat filtered eastward. Outposts of the Centre Division were the first to be panic-struck. Lt. Col. Robert Young (8th Foot) wrote frantically to Vincent from Burlington that Procter's division had been "completely annihilated," that "it is impossible to repel the force coming on." Lt. Col. Christopher Hamilton (100th Foot) had already begun his retreat from Turkey Point, abandoning the Long Point region to Harrison's anticipated advance. Alarmed at this threat to his flank, Vincent immediately raised his siege of Fort George and evacuated the entire Niagara frontier, leaving behind sick men, stores, and baggage.[10]

These hasty withdrawals originated with Warburton's battalion adjutant, Lt. John Reiffenstein. Although he had been in the army since 1795, he had resigned in 1811 after having been found guilty by court martial of "accounting irregularities." With the outbreak of war, he served in the militia of Lower Canada and became staff adjutant to Warburton, whom he accompanied to Amherstburg in April 1813. At the battle of Moraviantown, Reiffenstein, described caustically by John Richardson as "a little, red-faced, yellow-haired, obese, German," quit the field of battle and rode off, ahead of his commander, giving exaggerated reports of the defeat and its implications.[11]

Procter arrived at the Grand River, and on perceiving the air of panic, countermanded Hamilton's orders, directing him to return to Turkey Point as "I had not any expectation now, of the enemy advancing, soon at least thro' the wilderness." Even after his defeat, Procter stubbornly adhered to Native considerations in planning future movements, writing to Vincent, "The consequences of the enemy's advance and again cutting off the Indian families would be very serious." Procter estimated at least two hundred soldiers and four hundred warriors with him.[12]

Although somewhat reassured by Procter's short letter, Vincent was in a difficult situation. Rottenberg, it will be recalled, had left him in charge, having taken the two best battalions of the Centre Division with him to Kingston. An alarming number of Vincent's remaining 1097 troops were rendered *hors de combat* from the effects of ague and fever. The militiamen had almost totally deserted, and even the remaining regulars were deserting at the rate of six per day. Vincent had neither bateaux nor wagons with which to bear off his wounded and impedimenta. Like Procter, he was in no position to conduct a proper retreat. Nonetheless, he fell back on Burlington Heights. Although still vulnerable to attack, Vincent decided against sacrificing the depot there until the need to do so became apparent. He chose to consult with Procter in order to better assess the situation. As a precaution, he directed the road to York repaired to facilitate a speedy retreat, should one become necessary.[13]

Meanwhile, Reiffenstein tore off eastward to continue his work of inciting panic. He had been on the Grand River but disobeyed his orders to remain there, having written a note to Procter's brigade major, Capt. Hall, that his "delicate state of health" required him "to proceed a little further on the road in order to obtain medical assistance." That "little further" turned into a wild ride of several hundred miles to Ancaster, York, Kingston, and Montreal, as he spread magnified accounts of Harrison's advance. He regaled a large dinner party at York with his story and repeated it to Rottenberg's aide, whom he met on the road. He then falsified his identity, maintaining he was a relative of Rottenberg to gain an interview with Maj. Gen. Duncan Darroch, commander of the Left Division at Kingston. Darroch was not entirely duped, questioning Reiffenstein's credibility, dubious of his story, and demanding a written report. Reiffenstein hastily took his leave and rushed to Montreal, where he gave his distorted version of events to a more gullible Prevost.[14]

On hearing Reiffenstein's story, Rottenberg sent Vincent discretionary orders to fall back on Kingston. Vincent held firm, writing, "I should rather risk an action than leave General Procter and his scattered army behind, especially having great hopes that in two days I may have an opportunity to find out the number that can be collected." In fact, Procter was gathering his force on the Grand River, sending dragoons with Lt. Bullock to round up stragglers while Elliott did likewise with the warriors. Recovering from the sudden turn of events, Procter sent Lt. LeBreton under a flag of truce to Harrison seeking good treatment for the captured soldiers and civilians. Then on 16 October, he marched into Ancaster. In his first brief of the battle, he mentioned "with regret" that "the conduct of the troops was not on this unfortunate occasion such as I have on every other witnessed with pride and satisfaction."[15]

By 16 October, Rottenberg had calmed down, writing: "From the letters ... just received from Major General Vincent and Procter, affairs in that quarter are by no means so disastrous as has been most shamefully represented by Staff Adjutant Reiffenstein whose false reports and speculations upon the extent and consequences of Major General Proctor's [sic] defeat have been openly circulated by that officer and created the greatest alarm in all classes of people throughout the whole country." Nonetheless, he ordered Vincent to evacuate Burlington.[16]

On 17 October, the Right Division mustered at Ancaster 18 officers, 15 sergeants, nine drummers, and 204 rank and file for a total of 246 all ranks. Two days later, Vincent reported Procter's arrival at Burlington, affording him "every assistance as second in command." Rottenberg now minimized the extent of Procter's defeat, writing, "The affair of the 5th appears to have been a sudden irruption of an overwhelming force upon the 41st Regiment, which gave way and is rapidly recollecting. The enemy, satisfied with his slight success appears immediately to have fallen back upon Sandwich."[17]

The following day, Elliott arrived with 150 warriors, estimating another five hundred following with their families. These included fleeing Delaware and Muncey tribesmen from the Upper Thames. On 26 October, a detailed headcount produced 374 men and 688 women and children, exclusive of the Grand River Natives. The confederacy was shattered and demoralized. With Tecumseh and Roundhead dead and Main Pock, Splitlog, Five Medals, and Walk-in-the-Water subdued on American territory, the warriors lacked both numbers and leadership to assert their former influence. Although Naiwash and the Prophet remained in the British camp, the warriors' impact was reduced to a shadow of its former might.[18]

On 23 October, Procter wrote his first detailed report on the Thames campaign. Significantly, in his attempts to explain the complications that had led to his defeat, he included negative observations on his command again. He noted that the idea of a stand on the Lower Thames had been treated as "visionary" by his officers, who demonstrated an "impatience to retire" immediately after the loss of Barclay's squadron became known. He also complained of the "apathy" with which orders had been received, that Dover had been abandoned without his authority, and that the troops had not demonstrated their usual "confidence" in themselves during the battle. While these observations were undoubtedly true, Procter omitted to explain the condition of the men and the impact of the Natives upon the retreat, seemingly presuming that his previous letters had clarified these circumstances. His observations, while factual and later confirmed by his officers, looked too much like blame.[19]

With the Right and Centre divisions united, the British commanders reassessed their options. Embarrassed at his hasty order to abandon much of Upper Canada, Rottenberg wrote his superior that "the order ... was given by me in consequence of the information, false and scandalous as now appears which was given to me by Lt. Reiffenstein .... I hope some serious and public notice will be taken of ... [his] scandalous conduct." Meanwhile, Vincent reaffirmed his intention to remain at Burlington, writing to Rottenberg: "I see no reason to retire from this position.... I was not in the habit of seeing your private letters from the Commander of the Forces in the plan and defence of the country." Procter certainly did not favour a retreat and performed his last significant service to the Canadas at this time. As Vincent's second in command, he chaired a committee to study the matter of retreat. Procter's committee, consisting of the principal officers of the Centre Division (cols. Robert Young of the 8th Foot, Archibald Steward of the 1st, John Murray of the 100th, and Lt. Col. John Gordon of the 1st), recommended holding fast at Burlington. Vincent concurred and stood his ground.[20]

Although satisfied that Harrison was not advancing up the Thames, Prevost found alternate reasons to evacuate Upper Canada. He considered the combined American concentrations in the Niagara region and at Sacket's Harbour as insurmountable and continued to press for Vincent's withdrawal. Rottenberg readily repeated these instructions, writing his chief: "I have thought it right or rather to repeat my directions to Major General Vincent to hasten his arrangements for retiring to York by sending to that place as fast as he can all his stores, guns, provisions, sick, and in short, every encumbrance and to march with his whole division to that place." As late as 30 October, Rottenberg still complained that Vincent had not yet withdrawn, criticizing, on the other hand, the latter's "shameful" retreat to Burlington and its "unnecessary precipitation."[21]

Caught in the political dilemma of having to rationalize Prevost's fallback strategy with the demands of defending Upper Canada, Rottenberg proposed that "that the conduct of operations of the Centre Division may be safely confided to Major Gen'l. Vincent." The self-evident implication is that Prevost's strategy had been withheld from Vincent and certainly from Procter. By his letter of 5 November, Rottenberg again alluded to Prevost's direction for a retreat as having been conveyed to Vincent, who he wrongly assumed was preparing to evacuate Burlington.[22]

The senior commanders now descended on Procter. Rottenberg, who on 16 October had written Prevost, "I am ... satisfied with the firmness evinced under his difficulties by M. General Procter," adopted Prevost's unfriendly tone, calling Procter's report on the Thames campaign "very unsatisfactory" and "subject to further explanation." Prevost needed little encouragement, having already begun the process of blaming Procter for Barclay's defeat. Reiffenstein reported at his Montreal headquarters on 17 October, and without waiting for Procter's official report or any corroborating information, Prevost issued a general order the next day. Although this public notice acknowledged some of the difficulties under which the Right Division laboured, it contained significant material errors, estimating Harrison's force as "from ten to twelve thousand strong, including troops of every description" and that the warriors had retreated toward Georgian Bay. More important, the general order contained open criticisms of Procter's command ("A six pounder on the flank was by some unpardonable neglect, left destitute of ammunition"). In the meantime, Procter received "an intimation" of Prevost's intentions and objected to the unfairness of being prejudged on the basis of information provided by an junior officer of dubious credibility. He requested an investigation of Reiffenstein's conduct.[23]

By 1 November, the situation of the Centre Division was somewhat stabilized and Rottenberg gave Vincent discretionary authority to remain at Burlington. He now took credit for the retention of Upper Canada, congratulating himself that Prevost had approved his recommendation to remain at Burlington. He also announced that Prevost was to have taken the matter of the Indians under "serious consideration," that "they shall never be abandoned by us," and that "powerful reinforcements" would soon secure the Native homeland. At this late hour, Prevost reversed his views suddenly and completely, forwarding almost all the regulars in the lower province to Upper Canada.[24]

There was little good news for Procter. Recalling the treatment of Dr. McKeehan, Harrison detained the British emissary, Lt. LeBreton, finally releasing him via the Niagara frontier with a letter not to Procter but to Vincent. After providing assurances of the "justice and liberality" with which the British prisoners would be treated, Harrison went on to itemize and decry the barbarities of the "savage monsters" under Procter's command, implying that the British general permitted atrocities.[25]

Prevost now prepared to destroy Procter. Ignoring his proven record on the Detroit frontier and the strategic errors and logistical failures that had placed his division in such desperate straits, Prevost depicted Procter's report to London as "extremely confused, indistinct and unsatisfactory." His intentions were clear as he wrote, "I have desired Major General de Rottenberg to call upon him for a more clear, detailed and comprehensive statement of facts in order that the subject may be brought before His Majesty's Government for their decision upon the conduct to be observed towards Major-General Procter, should it appear that in this instance he has acted with negligence in the discharge of his duty towards his king and country."[26]

Following Prevost's wishes, Rottenberg directed Procter to produce a second report. In his account of 16 November, Procter expanded on details but once more attributed his defeat to the men's misconduct: "The Indians did turn the left of the enemy and executed their part faithfully and courageously. If the troops had acted as I had seen them and as I confidently expected, I am still of the opinion notwithstanding their numerical superiority the enemy would have been beaten. All ranks of officers exerted themselves to rally the men tho' ineffectual."[27]

Rottenberg expanded the blame-laying, demanding explanations for Vincent's headlong retreat to Burlington. Vincent was able to counter by implicating Rottenberg's own actions, effectively discouraging the witch hunt. "I shall commence from the first moment that you did me the honour of announcing your intention of leaving me in command of this army," he wrote with words heavy with meaning. "It will easily occur to your recollection that the necessity which suggested itself for the sudden removal of three corps from the Centre Division to reinforce Kingston deprived me of all further means of sending away any sick by water as every serviceable bateau was employed in that very important service." Rottenberg dropped the matter.[28]

Prevost issued a second general order on 24 November, one of unparalleled severity. He insisted that "the principal events that marked this disgraceful day [5 October]" as depicted in his first general order were confirmed. While the commander-in-chief acknowledged his error of having shown the Indians to be retreating towards Machedash, he now said the deceased Tecumseh and his braves had harassed the Americans on their retreat to Sandwich. Having established the bravery of the warriors, Prevost denounced all the Right Division but the soldiers on the vessels and those few who had been "rescued by an honourable death from passing under the American yoke." He maintained that the division had been "encumbered with an unmanageable load of ... forbidden baggage," while the ammunition and any attempt to impede Harrison's advance were "totally neglected." Prevost declared "with poignant grief and mortification" the division's previous "gallantry and steady discipline" as "tarnished and its conduct calling loudly for reproach and censure." American newspapers gleefully published this general order, willingly promulgating British dissension. On reading it, even Harrison condemned it as a "misrepresentation of falsehood in almost every line," declaring Procter's division "at least equal to ours."[29]

Maj. Richard Frend, acting commander of the newly arrived Second Battalion of the 41st Foot, became involved, seeking to secure the statements of officers engaged in the battle. Frend wrote to Lt. Bullock, the senior line officer of the 41st to escape the field, "You cannot be too particular in your statement, as I am sorry to say there are reports afloat disgraceful in the extreme to the regiment and every individual with it that day. I think it but proper to inform you that I saw Major General Procter's official report which highly censures the conduct of the regiment, and in which he says he never went into action more confident of success." While Bullock's report was factual, Frend's insinuations had their effect, as his concluding statement shows: "I beg leave to remark that from the well-known character of the Regiment, any observations emanating from those whose interest it is to cast a direct or indirect reflection upon its conduct, cannot be received with too much distrust."[30]

At this point, Procter had not been charged with any offenses despite the severity of Prevost's general orders and his hint to London that Procter's conduct should be examined. Prevost was clearly fearful of his government's reaction to the twin defeats in the west, particularly as London had committed itself to the Native interest and urged that more attention be devoted to the defence of Upper Canada. Indeed, the secretary for war and colonies expressed displeasure that two cornerstones of the defence strategy for the Canadas, "the maintenance of naval superiority on the Lakes and the uninterrupted communication with the Indians," had been compromised. Nonetheless, Bathurst was explicit that "His Royal Highness sees no reason to impute the failures which have occurred to any want of exertion on

your part or on the part of the officers or troops under your command." In short, Bathurst recognized the setbacks but chose not to
seek blame. He even acknowledged his own "omissions" in neglecting
the inland navy. Not only was Prevost spared, but he was not required
to produce a scapegoat. Bathurst defined as "the primary object" the
resumption of an "intercourse" with the western Indians by way of
Georgian Bay. By the time Prevost received this letter, he had already
initiated serious actions from which he could not backtrack. He had
condemned the 41st and publicly damaged Procter's reputation. Left
without options, Procter demanded that his actions be "speedily and
publickly" investigated.[31]

Back in the west, the captured soldiers of the Right Division were
taken to Ohio and billeted comfortably in private homes. Their treatment soon changed. At this time, Prevost had become involved in a
"tit-for-tat" retaliatory game with the American government concerning the treatment of prisoners. Among the Americans captured at the
battle of Queenston Heights a year previously, the British found a
number of British-born soldiers, who had been taken to England and
held in close confinement, to be tried as traitors. On learning of this,
the American government retaliated by ordering 23 British officers
(those captured at Moraviantown and on Lake Erie) into close confinement in Frankfort Penitentiary in Kentucky. They were imprisoned
in the company of three rapists, seven murderers, five forgers, and 25
thieves. Prevost reacted by ordering 46 American officers into close
confinement, prompting Washington to again reciprocate in kind.
Prevost then ordered all captured American officers into close confinement. These childish games inflicted severe suffering on all prisoners.[32]

One American officer, Samuel White, imprisoned at Halifax,
described his treatment:

A complaint was made to him [the turnkey or jailer] of the badness of the
beef served out to the prisoners, upon which he collected them together,
mounted the stair case and began a most passionate harangue, declaring that
the beef was good enough and a d—d deal better than they had in their
own country; and if they did not eat it, they should have none. He then
went on as follows: Hundreds of you d—d scoundrels have been to me
begging and pleading that I would interpose my influence that you might
be the first exchanged, to return to your families who were starving in your
absence, and now you have the impudence to tell me to my face that the
King's beef is not good enough for your dainty stomachs. Why, some of that

there beef is good enough for me to eat. You are a set of mean rascals, you beg of an enemy the favors which your own government won't grant you.

You complain of ill treatment when you never had better in your lives. Had you been in a French prison and fed on horse beef, you would have some grounds of complaint but here in His Britannic Majesty's Royal Prison you have everything that's right and proper for persons taken fighting against his crown and dignity. There is a surgeon here for you if you are sick and physic to take if you are sick, and a hospital to go to in the bargain. And if you die, there are boards enough (pointing to a pile of lumber in the yard) for to make your coffins and one hundred and fifty acres of land to bury you in. And if you are not satisfied with all this, you may die and be d—d![33]

Manacled in irons in a cold, damp dungeon, John Richardson described his guard as "a gaoler of the most ruffian-like character." Once the prisoner retaliations ceased, conditions for the British prisoners improved substantially as their captors billeted them in a hotel. Many of the Americans went out of their way to make the British officers comfortable. Maj. George Madison (captured at Frenchtown) arrived from detention at Quebec and provided guided tours for them in the vicinity of Frankfort. Lt. Robert Irvine of the Provincial Marine became particularly attached to Madison's daughter, presenting her with a finely crafted miniature of a fighting vessel. It was so well received that Midshipman Jonathan Nelson decided to emulate the gesture. Unfortunately, his model boasted a British flag, and when he placed his work in the hotel window to dry, it attracted less than admiring attention from the local citizenry. An angry throng stormed into his quarters, smashed his creation, and admonished poor Nelson and his companions with, "You British rascals, if you show your tarnation colours here again, we'll throw you after them!"[34]

In the spring of 1814, the belligerent powers concluded a general prisoner exchange, but only in late August were the men of the Right Division forwarded to Sandusky for repatriation. While encamped on a marshy plain, awaiting transport to Canada, most of the captives contracted malaria. Finally, a vessel arrived for them, but it was upset near Cleveland where the malnourished, exhausted, and disease-ridden men staggered ashore in a pitiable state. Finally on 4 October 1814 (a year less a day after the battle of Moraviantown), the men landed at Long Point. In Richardson's words, "Disease had worn away our persons and our minds were deeply tinged with that morbid melancholy which is a characteristic feature of the complaint. Existence itself had lost its value with its charms and, in our then tone, liberty or captivity were situations of indifference." Several of the men and one officer of the 41st, Lt. William Hall Jones, had died of malaria. Lt. Col. Evans, who had been released earlier, met the returning troops at Long Point and reported, "All the officers and almost all the men were ill when they arrived and I fear a great number will never recover."[35]

At Montreal, Prevost's harsh denunciations of the Right Division generated a public debate. Procter's long years in the Canadas and his success in holding the Northwest Army at bay for 14 months had earned him considerable popularity. Colonial newspapers reflected the general perception that Prevost's public strictures were arbitrary and unmerited. "We are happy to have it in our power to state from authority that the intelligence which has been received of the attack on General Procter's Division of the army was a gross exaggeration of the misfortune which has befallen that officer," declared the *Montreal Herald.* "We are truly rejoiced to find it has neither been so disastrous nor discreditable as was first represented." Likewise, the *Quebec Gazette* concluded, "The General Order relative to the affair of the 5th instant [this month] between Harrison's army and Gen. Procter is contradicted."[36]

Despite Procter's defeat, colonial newspapers pressed allied expansionism. The *Quebec Gazette* asserted, "These [Natives] are the people whom some persons would have us believe that England is about to abandon! We venture to assert that not one inch of the territory belonging to Great Britain or her allies in this war will ever be abandoned to the United States."[37]

American newspapers, flushed with the victories in the west, expressed the opposite sentiment: "The recent subjugation of the Northern Indians ... we should think, force conviction on the minds of our legislators of the necessity of a change in policy heretofore pursued towards these infatuated wretches, of courting with their amity and subsidizing their forbearance. We have warmed the adder in our bosom and he has stung us in return. Let all the savages ... be compelled to retire beyond some fixed boundary."[38]

The American press continued to relate British collusion to Native savagery. On 7 December 1813, "Barbarities of the Enemy," which had been featured in weekly installments, first mentioned Procter as responsible for cruelties. His name figured prominently in future issues. *The War* reported a new story by an anonymous correspondent, "It is a fact that a room in Maj. Muir's quarters ... was decorated with scalps which were strung and hung in festoons over the fireplace." In his congressional address, President Madison joined in the campaign of words, decrying the "indiscriminate massacre of defenseless inhabitants ... maltreatment of Indian prisoners" and "carnage without a parallel."[39]

NOTES

1. *Defence of Major General Procter,* 14.
2. Schnall Diary, cited in Gray, *Wilderness Christians,* 237-40.
3. McAfee Papers, cited in Gray, *Wilderness Christians,* 245; Brown, *Campaigns,* 74; Brother Denke to Secretary of the Society for the Furtherance of the Gospel, 10 June 1813 and Schnall Diary, cited in Gray, *Wilderness Christians,* 223, 240-43. Although the Moravian mission was, by policy, a peaceful one, some of its Delaware members took part in hostilities as individuals. In February 1814, the U.S. House of Representatives heard a petition from the Moravians requesting compensation for the the destruction of their village but turned it down. Norton, *Journal,* 314; *DPCUS* 1813-14, Vol. 2: 1578.
4. Harrison to Armstrong, 16 Oct. 1813, *MLWHH* 2: 579-80.
5. Captain James Sympson Diary, cited in Quisenberry, *Kentucky in the War,* 106-08.
6. Harrison's Proclamation, 16 Oct. 1813, *The War,* 23 Nov. 1813; *NOW,* 1: 174; Proclamation of 17 Oct. 1813, Russell, *The History of the War,* 274-75; Farmer, *History of Detroit,* 283.
7. Capt. Hall to Col. Harvey, 5 Oct. 1813, NAC, C 680: 205.
8. Prevost to Procter, 6 Oct. 1813, NAC, C 680: 149.
9. Prevost to Bathurst, 8 Oct. 1813, *DHCNF* 1813, Vol. 3: 205-08.
10. Prevost to Procter, 6 Oct. 1813, NAC, C 680: 149; Young to Vincent, 9 Oct. 1813, NAC, C 680: 184; Vincent to Rottenberg, 9 Oct. 1813, NAC, C 680: 186.
11. Reiffenstein to Capt. Hall, 5 Oct. 1813, NAC, C 680: 169; *DCB* 7: 743-44; John Richardson, *Westbrook, the Outlaw,* 9.
12. Reiffenstein to unaddressed, 5 Oct. 1813, NAC, C 680: 169; Procter to Vincent, 9 Oct. 1813, NAC, C 680: 210.
13. As of 1 Oct. 1813, Vincent's sick list totalled 1112 men. Vincent to Rottenberg, 15 Nov. 1813, *DHCNF* 1813, Vol. 4: 187; Vincent to Rottenberg, 11 Oct. 1813, NAC, C 680: 212.
14. Reiffenstein to Hall, nd., NAC, C 680: 292; Rottenberg to Prevost, 16 Oct. 1813, NAC, C 680: 216; Darroch to Freer, 12 Oct. 1813, NAC, C 680: 169.
15. Vincent to Rottenberg, 14 Oct. 1813, NAC, C 680: 235; Procter to Rottenberg, 16 Oct. 1813, NAC, C 680: 259.
16. Rottenberg to Prevost, 16 Oct. 1813, NAC, C 680: 216.

17. General Order, 24 Nov. 1813, cited in Robert Christie, *A History of the Late Province of Lower Canada* 2, 114; Vincent to Rottenberg, 19 Oct. 1813, NAC, C 680: 264; Rottenberg to Prevost, 19 Oct. 1813, NAC, C 680: 242.

18. Vincent to Rottenberg, 18 Oct. 1813, NAC, C 680: 261; Return of Western Indians by William Claus, 26 Oct. 1813, *DHCNF* 1813, Vol. 4: 97.

19. Procter to Rottenberg, 23 Oct. 1813, NAC, C 680: 273.

20. Rottenberg to Prevost, 18 Oct. 1813, NAC, C 680: 242; Vincent to Rottenberg, 18 Oct. 1813, *MPHC* 15: 420; Robert Nichol Memorial, 24 Sept. 1817, *MPHC* 25: 654.

21. Rottenberg to Prevost, 18 Oct. 1813, *MPHC* 15: 418; Rottenberg to Prevost, 30 Oct. 1813, *MPHC* 15: 430.

22. Rottenberg to Prevost, 16 Oct. 1813, NAC, C 680: 216; Rottenberg to Prevost, 5 Nov. 1813, NAC, C 681: 15.

23. Rottenberg to Prevost, 16 Oct. 1813, NAC, C 680: 216; Rottenberg to Prevost, 30 Oct. 1813, *MPHC* 15: 430; General Order, 18 Oct. 1813, *Quebec Gazette*, 21 Oct. 1813; Procter to Rottenberg, 3 Nov. 1813, NAC, C 680: 290.

24. Rottenberg to Vincent, 1 Nov. 1813, *DHCNF* 1813, Vol. 4: 117; Prevost to Bathurst, 30 Oct. 1813, *SBD* 2: 394.

25. Harrison to Vincent, 3 Nov. 1813, *MLWHH* 2: 590-94

26. Prevost to Bathurst, 4 Nov. 1813, *DHCNF* 1813, Vol. 4: 137.

27. Rottenberg to Procter, 8 Nov. 1813, NAC, C 680: 293; Procter to Rottenberg, 16 Nov. 1813, *SBD* 2: 338-41.

28. Vincent to Rottenberg, 15 Nov. 1813, *DHCNF* 1813, Vol. 4: 187. If Procter had immediately implicated the roles of Prevost and Rottenberg in the manner of Vincent, he may have similarly avoided embarrassment. Only in 1822 would he publicly declare Prevost's "imbecility in judgement and irresolution." [Procter and Procter], "Campaigns," 413, 427. Although John Richardson subsequently criticized Procter's role without reserve, he labelled Prevost's strictures "cruel and ungenerous" and incorporated Procter's words to describe Prevost's "marked imbecility and want of resolution." Richardson, *War of 1812*, 229.

29. General Order, 24 Nov. 1813, *MPHC* 25: 550-53; *The War*, 27 Dec. 1813.

30. Maj. Frend to Lt. Bullock, 30 Nov. 1813, Richardson, *War of 1812*, 229-30; Lt. Bullock to Maj. Frend, 6 Dec. 1813, cited in Lomax, *The 41st*, 108-12. Richard O'Farrel Frend joined the 41st as an ensign in 1793 and became major in December 1813. After Evans's capture, he became acting commander of the 2nd Battalion of the 41st. His name does not figure in major engagements. Frend retired from the army in 1822. Lomax, *The 41st*, 78.

31. Bathurst to Prevost, 3 Dec. 1813, *MPHC* 15: 448-49; Procter to Drummond, 14 Nov. 1813, *MPHC* 15: 452.

32. The escalating diplomatic broadsides over the treatment of prisoners are contained in *DPCUS* 1813-14, Vol. 2: 2095-238. Richardson also describes the episode, along with a first-hand account of his personal experiences in captivity. Richardson, *War of 1812*, 243-93.

33. White, *American Troops*, 69-70.

34. Richardson, *War of 1812*, 270-71.

35. Whitehorne, *Welch Regiment*, 107.

36. *Montreal Herald*, 23 Oct. 1813; *Quebec Gazette*, 28 Oct. 1813.

37. *Quebec Gazette*, 14 Oct. 1813.

38. *The War*, 7 Dec. 1813.

39. *The War*, 7, 14 Dec. 1813, 13 Jan. 1814.

17

AFTERMATH

"The safety of the Canadas depends less on the operations in the field than on the superiority on the lakes."

London Times, 18 November 1813

THE CONSEQUENCES FOR PROCTER did not come quickly. Although Prevost officially blasted his competence in general orders, he refused Procter's request of 3 November for a court martial, lacking the evidence to assure a conviction. Procter had no choice but to sit in a state of disgrace without having been heard.[1]

Procter found his situation extraordinary. He questioned the logic and fairness of Prevost's "public slander" that lacked adequate evidence to frame formal charges. Aware that Prevost had forwarded unfavourable reports to London, Procter resigned his command and asked for authority to proceed there himself, "to ask justice where it never was denied nor where any individual condemned unheard." He appealed to the commander-in-chief of the army, the Duke of York, complaining that he was condemned and punished "short of being cashiered," without having been heard. He argued that any errors and neglects of two or three days should not negate 32 years of service.[2]

By the time Procter's letter reached England, Prevost's negative assessments had already primed senior officials in London. Prevost then forwarded Procter's request to Bathurst, who recommended a speedy court martial to "strictly investigate" Procter's conduct. Bathurst wrote to the Duke of York, "The officer appears by the documents which are before His Majesty's Government to have occasioned in a great measure the misfortune which befell the body of troops retreating under his command ... by his want of military judgment and exertion." Further, Prevost led Bathurst to believe that Procter was also responsible for Barclay's disaster: "The destruction of His Majesty's naval force upon Lake Erie may be attributed to the order that Captain Barclay appears to have received from General Procter to sail with a force very inferior, altho' the Major General must have been aware that a reinforcement of seamen was to be expected." Prevost was less than gracious in his treatment of the officer of whom he had written just a few months previously, "Colonel Procter has been so fortunate as to have had frequent opportunities of evincing sound military judgment and a happy decision in all the various difficulties attendant on his situation in a remote and occasionally inaccessible district of this province."[3]

Prevost's engineered misrepresentations had their effect. The Prince Regent directed Prevost to assemble a court and left it to him to frame the charges. In effect, the biased accuser was left to dispense justice. Prevost sought supporting evidence from the returning members of the Right Division. Among the first of the emaciated officers to arrive in the spring was the redoubtable Chambers, who stormed ashore "determined to bring General Procter to a court martial."[4]

In May 1814, Prevost's adjutant-general, Edward Baynes, informed Procter that unspecified charges would be preferred against him. Procter sought a statement of charges in order to prepare his case and asked that the trial be held in Upper Canada rather than Montreal. Baynes replied that charges could not be framed as many of the Right Division officers were detained in the United States, and refused to hold the tribunal in the upper province. Procter continued to demand a statement of charges and a date for his trial, but Baynes replied that the tribunal would meet "whenever it becomes practicable to do so."[5]

By September 1814, Procter was still waiting for the charges. He again appealed to the Duke of York, itemizing the obstacles to a fair trial. He noted that Prevost refused to provide him with documentary evidence for the preparation of his case and that the convening of the court martial in Lower Canada prevented his calling of key witnesses. In addition, he observed that although two months had elapsed since the return of all Right Division prisoners, he had still not been served with charges. He asked for protection and redress, calling himself "a victim of prejudice." The Duke of York directed Prevost to afford Procter "every fair indulgence and especially that such public papers and witnesses as he may require should be furnished." Nonetheless, he left the management of Procter's case with Prevost.[6]

In addition to his professional woes, Procter experienced financial ones. Having lost much (if not all) of his personal property during the Thames campaign, his pay, like that of his men, was in arrears. He had not received his share of prize money for the capture of Detroit or the vessels, *Adams, Mary,* and *Salina*. Nor had he received any pay as a post commander at Fort George prior to the war or any remuneration as a division commander or as an officer on staff. Although Brock and Sheaffe had both recommended payment for Procter's "on staff" status over a year previously, Prevost found a loophole in the regulations, and replied with a ponderous, bureaucratic negative: "[It] does not apply to his situation at Detroit which cannot be considered as coming within the provision of the Secretary of War's letter of the 10th of January as it confines the allowance of 10 and 20 shillings per diem to cases of Regimental officers without regular staff appointments succeeding to the command of His Majesty's troops abroad by the death or absence of the commanding officer."[7]

Finally, a year after the battle of Moraviantown, Procter was served with five charges. His court martial convened some months later in Montreal on 21 December 1814 and sat until 28 January 1815. Its president (selected by Prevost) was none other than Maj. Gen. Rottenberg, an accessory to the events. The members of the court included three other major generals, six colonels, and six lieutenant colonels, most of them recent arrivals from the continent. The charges were extremely open ended, identifying errors in judgment and omissions associated with the Thames campaign, including those of Procter's subordinates. Clearly, the aim of the "scatter gun" nature of the allegations was to uncover fault in Procter's actions with a view to securing some sort of conviction.[8]

The charges and findings are summarized as follows:

1. That Procter did not immediately after the loss of the fleet on Lake Erie on the 10th of September, promptly make military arrangements "best calculated" for effecting the retreat and that he delayed it until the 27th.

   [Procter was found not guilty and wholly acquitted of this charge.]

2. That he failed to take "proper measures for conducting the retreat." Although he had reason to believe the enemy with superior num-

bers, would follow and endeavour to harass his march, he did not use due expedition, having encumbered the division with large quantities of useless baggage, having unnecessarily halted the troops for several whole days and having omitted to destroy the bridges, thereby affording the enemy an opportunity to come up with the division, "betraying professional incapacity."

[Procter was found guilty only in that "he did not take the proper means for the conduct of the retreat," but found not guilty and acquitted of the remainder of this charge.]

3. That he did not take the necessary measures for affording security to the boats, wagons, and carts laden with the ammunition, stores and provisions, allowing them to remain in the rear of the division on the 4th and 5th of October; consequently they fell into the enemy's hands or were destroyed to prevent capture and that the troops were left "without provisions" for a whole day previous to being attacked.

[Procter was found guilty of not having afforded adequate security to the boats but found not guilty and acquitted of the remainder of the charge.]

4. That he assured the Indian chiefs at Amherstburg that they should find the Forks of the Thames fortified, but that he neglected to fortify the same. That he neglected to occupy the heights above the Moravian village (although he had previously removed his ordnance, with the exception of one 6-pdr.), at which place he might have awaited the attack and engaged the enemy. He halted his division within two miles of the said village and formed it in a situation highly unfavourable for receiving an attack.

[Procter was found guilty of failing to occupy the heights above the Moravian village but found not guilty and acquitted of the remainder of the charge.]

5. That he did not make the military dispositions best adapted to meet or resist the attack, and that after the troops had given way, he did not make any effectual attempt in his own person or otherwise to rally or encourage them, or co-operate with the Indians, he having quitted the field soon after the action commenced, thereby "sacrificing" the division in his charge, such conduct betraying great professional incapacity and being disgraceful to his character as an officer.

[Procter was found guilty in failing to adopt the military dispositions best calculated to meet or resist the attack but found not guilty and acquitted of the remainder of the charge.]

The court concluded with 430 pages of testimony delivered by 34 witnesses, finding that, despite the "extraordinary circumstances of his situation," Procter had been "erroneous in judgment and deficient in energy" during the retreat. It recommended that he be "publickly reprimanded and suspended from rank and pay for the period of six calendar months."[9]

On 9 September 1815, almost two years after the Thames Campaign, the Prince Regent reviewed the findings of the court and criticized them as lenient on the one hand, while reducing the punishment on the other. He confirmed the findings on the first, third, fourth, and fifth charges but questioned how the court could deliver a finding of guilt on the second charge while acquitting Procter of the supporting specifications. He attributed the circumstance to a "mistaken lenity" based on Procter's "general good character and conduct." Rather than reconvene the court, the Prince Regent upheld only the public reprimand portion of the sentence, dispensing with the suspension of rank and pay. Nonetheless, he directed Prevost to convey "His Highness's high disapprobation of his conduct, together with His Royal Highness's regret that any officer of the length and service and of the exalted rank which he has attained, should be so extremely wanting in professional knowledge and so deficient in those active and energetic qualities, which must be required of every officer, but especially of one in the responsible situation in which the Major-General was placed." As was the custom for the trial of officers, the charges, findings, and sentence were read at the head of every regiment of the British Army, assuring the de facto end of Procter's military career.[10]

Warburton's conduct at the court martial was as mysterious as it had been during the Thames campaign. He asserted several times that Procter had given him no directions. Yet, he readily admitted ordering resumptions of the retreat without orders, asserting, on the other hand, that he was merely the "senior officer" when Procter was absent. While the other officers showed some understanding of the impact of the Native alliance, he maintained that he did not know why the division halted in the early phases of the march. The colonel's colourless testimony and his overall conduct during the campaign must have raised questions among court members, but then, Warburton was not on trial. In contrast, Evans, who only joined the Right Division two months before its retreat, showed more understanding of the events, having tried to work toward the broad plan, despite a serious illness at the time. His views on Procter's directions were what one would expect of a senior commander: "I consider the intimation of the General's intention as equivalent to an order." Moreover, his detailed description of the condition of the men served to explain their lacklustre performance during the battle.[11]

The charges were framed in terms such as "Did not make the dispositions best adapted to meet or to resist the said attack," prompting Procter to exclaim, "Perfection belongs not to humanity!" With the benefit of hindsight, the prosecution merely looked for signs of failure and concluded that better decisions might have produced better results. Procter could not contain his contempt for one of the charges. He turned it back upon prosecutor Ensign Andrew Cochran, demanding "What were the arrangements best calculated for promptly effecting the retreat which I omitted to make?"[12]

Representing himself, Procter presented a spirited defence. Yet he experienced difficulty in relating clearly the complex and rapidly unfolding circumstances that forced him to repeatedly alter his plans; the consequent ambiguity certainly attracted attention. Moreover, his emphasis on the Native impact seemed to make little impression on the members of the court who viewed matters solely from the standpoint of a commander's military responsibility. Significantly, the testimony reflected a rift between Procter and his regiment. Most of the witnesses called by the prosecution were officers of the 41st while the defence witnesses were a cross section of participants (41st, other corps, militia, Indian Department, and support departments). Aside from a comment that the men were "in no condition to fight," Procter made little mention of their deplorable condition to explain their performance on the battlefield. Since he was not allowed to introduce evidence from the time prior to the loss of Barclay's squadron, he could not identify the roles of Prevost and Rottenberg as contributing to the situation. His only attempt to indirectly relate the cause of his failure was, "If my recommendation respecting Presque Isle had been attended to, that [American] navy would have been destroyed." Nonetheless, cumulative testimony provided sufficient evidence to substantiate allegations that the retreat was disorganized and Procter's errors of judgement contributed to it.[13]

Although the Indian Department officers' testimonies attributed several of Procter's military decisions to the impact of the Native allies, the prosecutor stated in his closing argument that the Native commitment was Procter's fault, too: "No pledge has ever been made, unless it has been by some unauthorized act of Major General Proctor [*sic*] himself that the country in which the Right Division was placed would not be abandoned if even in a military point of view it became necessary.... Never was it ... a paramount consideration to all others." As the principal architects of the alliance (Brock, Tecumseh and Elliott) were dead, Procter was virtually alone in explaining the Native commitment. Furthermore, in an effort to hold him responsible either way, Cochran attributed Native dissatisfaction to Procter's "want of frankness and candour" in initiating retreat preparations prior to gaining the chiefs' approval. Ignoring the Native influence on Procter's initial proposal to retreat to Burlington, the prosecutor scoffed at his subsequent intention of occupying the Thames country, which was "destitute of resources ... surrounded by a wasteful host of 12,000 Indians."[14]

If the aim was to equate failure with guilt, Procter was certainly guilty. Nonetheless, his case was the only British example during the war in which failure was used as the measure of guilt. Brock was not charged posthumously for his failed assault at Queenston Heights. Sheaffe was not indicted for his unsuccessful defence of York. Rottenberg was never called upon to answer for his strategic blunder in misdirecting his operations in the summer of 1813 and disobeying directions to forward the 41st to Amherstburg. Yeo was never called upon to answer for his failure to properly man the Lake Erie squadron. Using the logic of the prosecution, none of these officers took the "best measures" conceivable. They all did their best and failed, as did Procter. In this context, Procter was not only neglected but disgracefully used. No other British officer of the war was subjected to his public degradation on such selective pretexts.

With the Right Division ejected from the Detroit country, about a thousand American soldiers garrisoned the posts of the area. Fort Covington, a new facility near the burned-out Fort Amherstburg, became "the strongest fort on the Northwest frontier," mounting 22 pieces of ordnance. Fort Shelby (formerly Fort Detroit) was strengthened with cannons mounted in the parapets and an abbatis built on the north side. The school at Sandwich became a barracks surrounded by a log palisade, large spikes embedded in the tops of the posts.[15]

Although Governor Lewis Cass faced no crucial military threats from the enemy after the battle of Moraviantown, he inherited Procter's logistics nightmare which in itself was formidable. The American garrisons suffered terribly from hunger and sickness during the winter of 1813-14. No fewer than seven hundred soldiers died in a mysterious epidemic (probably the same that had ravaged the Native communities in the summer). The soldiers were so short of provisions that they had to work the fields themselves. Despite the arrival of new levies, discipline broke down and one general order condemned the rampant "robberies, idleness, drunkenness, contempt and mutiny" of the Detroit garrison.[16]

The destitute Natives continued to linger around the settlements, begging for food. One observer noted, "I have seen women and children searching about the ground for bones and rinds of pork which were thrown away by the soldiers. Meat in a high state of putrefaction which had been thrown into the river was carefully picked up and devoured. The feet, heads and entrails of cattle slaughtered by the public butchers were collected and sent off to the neighbouring villages." Meager provisioning led to renewed Native unrest and Cass sent desperate appeals to Washington, seeking food and presents for the tribesmen to avert their defection or hostility.[17]

Given the shocking conditions in Michigan, U.S. authorities helped themselves to provisions on the Canadian side. The military governor of the Western District, Col. John Miller (17th U.S. Infantry, veteran of the siege of Fort Meigs), issued a proclamation detailing the delivery of all surplus grain produced between Point Pelée and the Lower Thames to depots at Amherstburg, Sandwich, and Dolsen's. With the boot on the other foot, Canadians were outraged by the heavy-handed requisitioning policy of the occupiers. One New Settlement resident, John Stockwell, left his farm, 14 miles east of Amherstburg, for the British lines and offered to guide soldiers to drive off the Americans. Despite the prewar rhetoric, the U.S. government made no attempt to annex the Western District.[18]

The new commander in Upper Canada, Lieut. Gen. Gordon Drummond, arrived in December 1813. Forty-one years of age, the Canada-born commander had served in North America, as well as Holland, Egypt, Jamaica, and Ireland. He purchased his commissions even faster than Brock, commanding the 8th Regiment of Foot at age 21! By all accounts, Drummond was an astute, energetic, and imaginative leader. Yet he considered the question of regaining the Western District subject to the same conditions as Procter had defined for its retention. He was not prepared to undertake another half-measure for the occupation of the west unless he had a force that was "completely effective, well appointed and which has not been harassed and disorganized." The British commander was pragmatic on the question of a Native homeland, placing little value on Native warriors. "I am convinced that Detroit and the whole of the Western District might be reoccupied by us without difficulty ... however ... troops alone are not sufficient for the purpose," he wrote. "The corps, however small, should be equipped with field train, engineer and artificers, commissariat, barrack and every other department. This measure appears to me to offer the only means of getting rid of the Western Indians, who when their presence here ceases to be useful, will be an intolerable burthen." Despite his difficulties with the allies, Drummond reaffirmed the Native commitment in the manner of his predecessors, writing, "It is highly satisfactory to know that the interests of the Indians will not be forgotten in any arrangement that may take place." [19]

Drummond had serious reservations about supporting a force in the devastated countryside. On conducting a tour of the Thames region, he reported the desolation to Prevost: "I was concerned to state to your Excellency that I seldom entered a house to the westward, where the claims of individuals for cattle and provisions furnished, taken and destroyed by the troops and the Indians in the retreat of [Right] division were not numerous." [20]

Nonetheless, the governor, at Bathurst's insistence, pressed for the recovery of lost territories and the rejuvenation of the Native alliance. On 29 November 1813, Yeo proposed that Erie could be taken by a strike force of six hundred men conveyed across Lake Erie in prefabricated, hide-covered boats. The larger American vessels were to be destroyed at their moorings while the smaller ones would convey the strike force to Put-in-Bay for the recapture of *Detroit* and *Queen Charlotte*. Prevost eagerly passed this scheme on to Drummond who expressed severe reservations about the weather conditions. [21]

Prevost persisted. By his calculations, the five vessels frozen in the ice at Put-in-Bay could be destroyed and Amherstburg and Sandwich recaptured by 25 February 1814. Having defined the objective, he wrote Drummond, "You must be sensible to my total inability of augmenting your present force." With the British reoccupation of the Niagara frontier in early 1814, Drummond planned a strike force of no less than 1760 effectives to descend on the Detroit frontier in two columns, one along the Thames, the other along the lake shore. The expedition was to sweep down by sleigh, averaging 30 miles per day, seize Amherstburg and Sandwich, then proceed over the ice to destroy the enemy vessels. An early thaw prevented execution of this ambitious scheme.[22]

As an alternative to the occupation of the Detroit country, Drummond suggested a diversion toward the mouth of the Thames to allow two hundred tribesmen to deliver powder and ball to their counterparts in Michigan territory. As the warriors refused to undertake this mission without a strong British escort, this scheme died. Nonetheless, the hungry Natives of Michigan Territory maintained contact with the British officials. Learning of Drummond's contemplated advance, 1200 braves under Main Pock assembled near Detroit, ready to take up the hatchet against the Americans.[23]

In late spring of 1814, Drummond deferred the planned construction of a naval base at Turkey Point for want of adequate defences and the problems associated with transporting naval stores. Since the retention and subsequent support of the Detroit country were entirely dependent upon the recovery of Lake Erie, Drummond scrapped all plans in the west until "we have superiority on Lake Ontario," putting the initiative back on Yeo. The eastern extremity of American influence extended along a line from the mouth of the Thames south to Point aux Pins. The Americans occupied an outpost at Raleigh on the Lower Thames while the British established a counterpoint upriver at Delaware.[24]

Sporadic raiding occurred in the buffer zone between the enemy outposts. In December 1813, a British militia patrol surprised 35 Americans (including 8 Canadian renegades) at Raleigh and captured the lot. Cass, enraged at the "infamous and unprecedented transaction," threatened harsh reprisals, including the destruction of the properties of all Canadian participants in the raid. Although the Americans never reconstituted the outpost, they dislodged their enemy from Delaware after defeating a British force at the battle of Longwoods on 5 March 1814. In the meantime, Canadian renegades Abraham Markle and Andrew Westbrook settled old scores by leading like-minded dissidents against loyal settlers in the Upper Thames and Long Point areas. The British fell back on a line drawn north from Long Point.[25]

The needless destruction of Newark (near Fort George) in December 1813, resulted in a deliberate retaliatory action in the razing of the American side of the Niagara River. Fort Niagara was captured and Lewiston, Black Rock, and Buffalo burned. The Americans responded with predatory incursions. Eight hundred raiders conducted a destructive sea-borne assault on Long Point from Erie in April 1814. They destroyed a total of 20 houses, three flour mills, three distilleries, 12 barns, and all livestock encountered. Although the American government disapproved of the destruction of private property, the commander of the raid received only a reproof.[26]

The most spectacular of the American raids occurred in November 1814, when Brig. Gen. Duncan McArthur, succeeding Harrison as commander of the Northwest Army, conducted a well-planned foray from Michigan. His mounted force of eight hundred Kentuckians secretly crossed the St. Clair River near Baldoon and advanced swiftly to Moraviantown before British officials were aware of its presence. His expedition methodically ravaged the Long Point country. An assortment of British, militia and Native detachments under Chambers, Muir, Splitlog, and Lt. Col. Henry Bostwick (Oxford Regiment) could only hold the marauders at the Grand River. While the destruction of private property was unpopular, McArthur achieved his military purpose. His freebooting foray virtually destroyed what remained of the region's economy. After this raid, not a single barrel of flour was to be had in the Long Point district, prompting Drummond to abandon all offensive plans in the west.[27]

Intent on preventing a British reoccupation of the Detroit country, some American officials favoured a "scorched earth policy" for Upper Canada. These ideas ranged from totally depopulating the Western District to "a little bloodletting" to halt communications between the residents and British officials. Governor Cass proposed to deny the wheat crops to the enemy by breaking up the farms on the Thames, using the Frenchtown experience as justification. Secretary of War Armstrong agreed. "The only efficient mode of quitting your frontier and breaking asunder the chain that holds the Indians and enemy together is to sweep the whole of the British settlements from Thames, Long Point etc.," he wrote McArthur. Although the Americans pursued a "slash and burn" policy, they stopped short of converting the countryside into an utter wasteland.[28]

Despite Drummond's complaints of "this infamous species of uncivilized warfare" characterized by "the incendiary system that appears to the Westward," the American strategy was militarily successful. By April 1814, Drummond reported that unless flour and provisions were shipped to the Right Division, it would not be able to hold its ground in the Long Point area, "even though the entire resources of the country should be at our command." He asked Yeo to dedicate the whole of the Lake Ontario squadron to transporting foodstuffs in November

1814. Apprehensive of bad weather and the lack of protective anchourages, Yeo protested that the tasking was "the height of imprudence and hazardous in the extreme." For the duration of the war, the Western District remained occupied territory, and areas west of the Grand River languished in the misery and anxiety of a lawless no-man's land.[29]

Through the capture of Amherstburg, Michilimackinac lost its support base. It will be recalled that Procter had sent *Nancy* to this outpost prior to the battle of Lake Erie. Its new commander, Capt. Richard Bullock, sent that vessel back to Amherstburg prior to receiving Procter's notification of the retreat. On the day of the battle of Moraviantown, Capt. McIntosh had tried to run *Nancy* down the St. Clair rapids, and learned of recent events from local inhabitants. Before he could return his schooner to the safety of Lake Huron, *Canadien* militiamen from Michigan commanded by one Lt. Col. Beaubien, summoned him to surrender. A short fight ensued with minor injuries as *Nancy* tacked her way against the strong river current to Lake Huron, which she reached two days later. After further adventures arising from the hazards of fall navigation, *Nancy* returned empty-handed to Fort Michilimackinac on 19 October 1813 to go into repairs. That post faced the winter with only 68 pounds of salt meat and one month's flour in the store.[30]

Desperate for provisions, Bullock sent two freight canoes and a bateau to Machedash for flour and pork. These had to turn back because of bad weather, leaving the men to subsist on half a pound of meat served four days weekly. They augmented their diet with fish and Indian corn. In the meantime, Drummond established a new supply route to the post from York to Georgian Bay via Yonge Street. This project proceeded vigorously with facilities constructed at Machedash, Penetanguishene, Holland Landing, and the mouth of the Nottawasaga River. Bullock's men survived the dismal winter, and in the spring of 1814, the newly promoted Lt. Col. Robert McDouall (having returned from England) relieved the post with provisions and a reinforcement of some 90 men of the Royal Newfoundland Regiment.[31]

The British defeat in the west had an adverse impact on British fur-trading interests. The North West Company was thoroughly alarmed by the American occupation of the Detroit frontier as it effectively ruptured the ancient commercial artery for their trade. The Americans having built Fort Gratiot in 1814, at the foot of Lake Huron, the merchants feared that Michilimackinac would also fall. Anticipating total

British defeat on the Upper Lakes, the company undertook contingency measures to maintain their trade links to Fort William on Lake Superior through the Arctic thoroughfare of its competitor, the Hudson's Bay Company.[32]

Despite apprehensions of a complete British collapse in the west, Fort Michilimackinac was retained to sustain British operations on the Upper Mississippi. Through this base, Dickson's western warriors continued to receive support, making possible, on 17 July 1814, the British capture of the principal American position on the Upper Mississippi at Prairie du Chien. With the aid of strong detachments of Winnebago, Sac, and Sioux warriors, the British beat off repeated efforts to recover that post. Although McDouall found the warriors "fickle as the wind," they were also instrumental in repulsing Lt. Col. George Croghan's seaborne attack of 4 August 1814 on Fort Michilimackinac. Nonetheless, the hero of Fort Stephenson managed to annihilate the puny British marine presence on the Upper Lakes. He destroyed one of the remaining British schooners, *Perseverance*, captured another, *Mink*, and forced the *Nancy*'s crew to blow her up to prevent her capture.[33]

Ironically, Croghan's expedition facilitated the re-establishment of a British naval force on Lake Huron. After his withdrawal to Detroit, he left two schooners, *Tigress* and *Scorpion*, to blockade the approaches to Fort Michilimackinac. The crew of *Nancy*, with part of the fort garrison, captured both schooners in early September 1814. These became *HMS Surprize* and *HMS Confiance*, providing uninterrupted support to allied operations in the west for the duration of the war.

Although not seriously challenged on the Upper Lakes, the American Navy substantially diminished after Perry's victory. *Ariel* and *Chippawa* broke up after being driven ashore off Buffalo in late 1813 and their hulks were burned during a British raid on 29 December of that year. The following day, the British also burned the ice-bound *Trippe* and *Little Belt*. On 12 August 1814, a British cutting-out party captured *Somers* and *Ohio* off Fort Erie; these were taken into British service as *HMS Sauk* and *HMS Huron*. Given the loss of *Tigress* and *Scorpion* and that *Detroit* and *Queen Charlotte* were out of commission, the American fleet was drastically reduced in size.

In the meantime, the Royal Navy undertook strenuous efforts to regain command on the Upper Lakes. In December 1814, artificers laid down the keel for a vessel of no less than 44 guns at Penetanguishene on Georgian Bay. Despite enormous expenditures incurred in her construction at this isolated location, she remained uncompleted at war's end. Likewise, two schooners of four guns each, *HMS Tecumseh* and *HMS Naiwash*, were built on the Niagara River but not launched till August 1815, too late to influence matters.[34]

Native resistance to American encroachment in the Detroit country virtually ceased after the battle of Moraviantown. Occasionally, small parties of warriors trekked from Michigan to join the British army on the Niagara. The majority, however, feared such collaboration since they were closely watched by the Americans. Starvation conditions compelled some of the chiefs, notably Blackbird and Splitlog, to repeatedly switch sides.[35]

Marauding by the natives did not entirely cease with the American occupation. One farmer in Michigan became utterly destitute when the warriors killed all his livestock and burned his home. Such incidents constituted little more than isolated acts of desperation with no military purpose. Indeed, most of the tribesmen within Michigan Territory had effectively given up the struggle. Cass reported 8890 warriors and 41,400 dependents under his superintendency in the fall of 1813. These included the better part of the Wyandot, Shawnee, Seneca, Ottawa, Ojibwa, Potawatomi, Menominee, Delaware, Winnebago, Miami, Piankashaw, and Sioux nations.[36]

The uprooted tribes were reduced to pitiful conditions. In early 1814, over a thousand famished Miami appeared before Fort Wayne; they had already eaten their horses, and their families faced starvation. The Potawatomi were in similar straits, their members dying daily. Although American agents issued them some rations and small amounts of ammunition for hunting, their numbers were decimated by the effects of exposure, malnutrition, and disease. The "Lake Indians" and Wabash nations would never again go on the warpath.[37]

On the Niagara frontier, the remnant of Tecumseh's confederacy mustered only a few hundred braves. Drummond considered them more trouble than they were worth, complaining about the "lavish expenditure of provisions" required to maintain them. At the raid on Lewiston, 14 December 1813, they became drunk and ran amok. The braves plundered houses, shot one soldier of the 41st, and tomahawked a Canadian militiaman. "I have never witnessed such a scene before and hope I shall not again," wrote Charles Askin.[38]

Prevost made repeated attempts to rejuvenate the Native confederacy with tokens and promises. In early 1814, he invited Tecumseh's son and sister to the Castle of St. Louis, Quebec for an audience. Also present were the principal Ojibwa, Ottawa, Sac, Fox, Kickapoo,

Meeting Governor-General Prevost for the first time at Quebec City in 1814, a deputation of Natives appealed for material aid and protection from encroaching Americans. One of the women in this contemporary painting is believed to be Tecumpeace, Tecumseh's sister.

National Archives of Canada, Ottawa: C-134461

National Archives of Canada, Ottawa: C-114384

Wearing British medallions, two Ottawa Chiefs from Michilimackinac sought recognition of their ancestral land rights. Despite Prevost's assurances, they were abandoned at war's end. One of these chiefs is probably Naiwash.

Delaware, Muncey, Mohawk, Winnebago, and Shawnee representatives. On 15 March, after entertaining them with martial music, refreshments and a calumet dance, the governor conferred with the delegates. Their views were voiced by the Sac chief, Metoss:

Father, we have heard of you from our young men, but we never saw you before.

Father, we are come now a long distance to smoke the Pipe of Peace with you.

Father, the Long Knives are our enemies as well as yours; but Father, when you made peace with them [1783] we buried the tomahawk in the ground....

Father when the Long Knives made war with you last year, they drove us from our hunting grounds because they knew we loved you and our great Father across the Salt Lake....

Father, we will not bury the tomahawk again until our great Father desires us. But Father, you must never make peace with the Long Knives until we have conquered back our hunting grounds, from which the Long Knives have now driven us.[39]

Metoss and Naiwash emphasized the impoverished condition of their people but expressed a desire to persevere, soliciting arms for the warriors and clothing for the women and children. They also reported that the Americans "are taking our lands from us every day; they have no hearts, Father. They have no pity for us, they want to drive us beyond the setting sun; but we hope, although we are few, and are here as it were upon a little island, our great and mighty Father who lives beyond the great lake, will not forsake us in our distress, but continue to remember his faithful red children." In response, Prevost reaffirmed the common cause, repeating that there would be no peace until their hunting grounds had been restored. The governor promised that more troops would arrive from England to recover "our lands." He exhorted the Natives to greater efforts and to conduct war in a humane fashion. Prevost expressed great sorrow at the loss of Tecumseh and the other warriors, showering Tecumpeace, sister of the great chief, with gifts of bereavement. The governor presented the other delegates with silver ornaments, wampum, and fashionable items of clothing. After several days of revelry in Quebec, the Natives packed up their presents and returned to their camps.[40]

Prevost's attempts to re-energize the Native alliance misfired miserably. Given the desperate condition of the tribesmen, the gifts collected at Quebec became an object of dispute back at camp. If Prevost had any hopes of designating Pachetha, the 17-year-old son of Tecumseh, to lead the Native confederacy, he was disappointed. Pachetha was too young to assert a leadership role, leaving the tribesmen without a strong unifying voice.[41]

In his quest to replace Tecumseh, Prevost was encouraged to hear that a grand council of the Natives had chosen Tenskwatawa as the "principal chief of the western nations." The governor presented him with a handsome sword and a brace of pistols. The gesture had little effect in restoring a dynamic Native alliance since the Prophet commanded little respect among the tribesmen. As a consequence, the displaced tribesmen, their traditional lifestyles in chaos, remained a minor military factor, loafing around Burlington and drinking and arguing among themselves.[42]

The second Treaty of Greenville (22 July 1814) administered another crushing blow to Native aspirations. By this agreement, the long struggle in the old Northwest was officially ended, as the Wyandot, Shawnee, Miami, Delaware, and Seneca tribes laid down the tomahawk for good, paving the way for wholesale land expropriations.

Between 1814 and 1832, Governor Cass extinguished Native land titles, superintending 19 negotiated settlements.[43]

Restoration of significant Native involvement in the allied cause remained dependent on a strong naval, military, and logistical British presence in the west. The prospects of such support were heightened in the summer of 1814 when Britain sent significant reinforcements to the Canadas. In early June 1814, Bathurst announced the impending arrival of 3177 regulars, the vanguard of an additional contingent of ten thousand seasoned troops. These were accompanied by £200,000 and ten thousand rations for six months. Bathurst was explicit that after the reduction of American naval bases, these powerful resources were to be used offensively, particularly with a view to the reoccupation of Michigan Territory.[44]

As the war progressed, Prevost's conduct attracted increasing scrutiny. His limp defence policy for Upper Canada drew vocal criticism from colonials, notably Rector Strachan and the principals of the Northwest Company. His readiness to abandon Upper Canada certainly did not bolster confidence in that province. Sneers of his leadership at Sacket's Harbour and Fort George mounted steadily among his colonels while relations with the naval establishment also became strained. Furthermore, the British mercantile élite within Lower Canada became increasingly resentful of Prevost's pandering to the French in that province.

It was Prevost's attempt at commanding the largest concentration of regulars ever assembled in British North America that drew the most serious criticisms. During the summer of 1814, Prevost's standing forces in Lower Canada were augmented by eleven thousand of Wellington's veterans, whom he formed into an enormous division under Rottenberg. Prevost personally led this force against New York via the Richilieu River in September 1814. After the defeat of the British flotilla on Lake Champlain, Prevost ordered a hasty withdrawal. His headlong but unpursued retreat before a vastly inferior enemy resulted in the abandonment of his wounded, along with vast quantities of foodstuffs, ordnance stores, and ammunition. The battle of Plattsburg cost Prevost the confidence of troops who were primed to meet the enemy. The soldiers considered themselves disgraced. Worse yet, this defeat dashed any hope of recovering Michigan Territory, and with it, the pledge of a Native homeland.[45]

Mounting dissatisfaction with Prevost's handling of the war erupted into open acrimonious debate. Newspapers exposed his alleged military and political blunders in a series of critical and anonymous but well-informed writings. In 1815, two series of articles appeared in the *Montreal Herald* and were subsequently published in pamphlet form as *The Letters of Veritas* and *Nerva*. With the assistance of Rottenberg, Prevost used his authority to ferret out the authors, and although the unfortunate Procter fell under suspicion for a time, the writers turned out to be a pair of disgruntled colonial Tories. These criticized Prevost's feeble efforts in the defence of Upper Canada as well as his personal ineffectiveness in the field. Prevost came to be reviled by English-speaking élites in the colonies as a "nincompoop." Wytsius Ryland, clerk of the executive council of Lower Canada reflected this growing contempt, writing, "There he sits, like an idiot in a skiff, admiring the rapidity of the current which is about to plunge him into the abyss!!!"[46]

Prevost's list of enemies grew. When he quibbled with the newly arrived veteran generals from Europe over dress regulations, they complained to London. "It is very obvious to me that you must remove Sir George Prevost," wrote the Duke of Wellington to Bathurst. "I see he has gone to war over trifles with the general officers I sent him, which are certainly the best of their rank in the army."[47]

Having alienated the army, Prevost drew direct criticism from the navy, as well. The court martial that investigated the causes of the naval defeat on Lake Champlain concluded that Prevost had urged the ill-prepared squadron into action prematurely and then, once engaged, failed to support it. Yeo pointedly attributed the naval disaster to Prevost's mismanagement. In a manner reminiscent of his own handling of Procter, Prevost complained to the Prince Regent of the prejudication of his conduct, adding haughtily that naval officers were not qualified to pass judgment on military matters.[48]

On 26 August 1815, Yeo framed charges and the Prince Regent ordered a court martial. Prevost was recalled to England to answer the allegations in a trial scheduled for 12 January 1816; however, his sudden death of dropsy halted proceedings. His widow, Lady Catherine Anne Prevost, and his brother, Col. William Augustus Prevost, bombarded the Prince Regent with dozens of letters, seeking recognition of the dead governor's contributions. Not wishing to offend a grieving widow, yet unwilling to declare Prevost "the saviour of Canada," the Prince Regent issued a statement reflecting credit on Prevost's performance of "arduous duties" and approved some minor additions to the armourial bearings of the Prevost family crest.[49]

Napoleon's abdication on 11 April 1814 raised hopes that the prolonged conflict in North America would end. The belligerents met in

the Belgian city of Ghent to negotiate a peace. The British commissioners' opening position featured the mandatory demand for a Native
homeland:

It was a *sine qua non* that the Indians should be included in the pacification
and as incident thereto that the boundaries of their territory should be
permanently established. Peace with the Indians is so simple as to require
no comment.

With respect to the boundary which was to divide their territory from
that of the United States, the object of the British Government was that the
Indians should remain as a permanent barrier between our western settlements
and the adjacent British provinces to prevent them from being conterminous
to each other and that neither the United States nor Great Britain should
ever hereafter have the right to purchase or acquire any part of the territory
thus recognized as belonging to the Indians. With regard to the extent of
the Indian Territory and the boundary line, the British government would
propose the lines of the Greenville Treaty [about midway between the Ohio
River and Lake Erie] as a proper basis.[50]

The American representatives, Henry Clay (who had modified his
hawkish rhetoric by this time) and John Q. Adams, responded to the
British demand unequivocally: "The United States cannot consent that
the Indians residing within their boundaries, as acknowledged by
Great Britain, shall be included in any manner which will recognize
them as independent nations."[51]

The British position was strengthened substantially after the burning of the American capitol in August 1814; however, when news of
Prevost's defeat at Plattsburg reached Europe, negotiations became
deadlocked. The Duke of Wellington recognized the dubious British
position at the peace talks: "You ... have not even cleared your own territory of the enemy on the point of attack. You cannot, then, on any
principle of equality in negotiations, claim a cession of territory ...
except in exchange for other advantages which you have in your
power." Finally, through article 9 of the peace treaty, the delegates
agreed to restore to the Natives "all the possessions, rights and privi-
leges which they may have enjoyed or been entitled to in 1811" (few
as these may have been). Britain had abandoned the Natives of the
Northwest who were now relegated to the status of an internal
American problem. The Treaty of Ghent was signed on Christmas Eve,
1814, and ratified by the two governments on 17 February 1815. It

was a peace of *status quo ante bellum,* one that neither addressed the alleged causes of the war nor included any territorial changes.[52]

On receiving news of the ratification of the peace treaty, Detroit erupted in jubilation. On 24 March 1815, the town was illuminated and a gala "Pacification Ball" was held at the Steamboat Hotel. Among the invited luminaries were British officers from the opposite side of the Detroit River. Peace had finally come to this war-weary region.[53]

The new amity did not entirely heal the scars of war. Before the conflict, like-minded residents had been separated only by the Detroit River. The war experience made them conscious of a much deeper difference separating them. They perceived the contrast between democratic egalitarianism and a structured hierarchy of power. With time, the memories of the bitter struggle faded. Deflected from expansion at the expense of the other side, British and Americans found other frontiers for growth, respectfully observing the 49th parallel to the Pacific Ocean. Although border disagreements remained, the two sides never again engaged in a general war. The war cry, "Remember the Raisin!" was replaced by "Remember the Alamo!" and "Remember the Maine!" as Americans found new avenues by which to realize Manifest Destiny.

More than any other theatre, the Detroit country was ravaged from the outset, suffering consistently until war's end. The drained countryside of Michigan was in a deplorable condition, as Washington provided no federal relief until May 1815. "The desolation of this territory is beyond conception," lamented the returned Judge Woodward. "No kind of flour or meal to be procured and nothing for the subsistence of cattle. No animals for slaughter and more than half the population destitute of any for domestic or agricultural purposes.... It is a literal fact ... that the inhabitants of the Raisin River have been obliged to resort to chopped hay boiled for subsistence."[54]

Conditions were worse on the Canadian side. A traveller visiting the Western District was "sensibly struck with the devastation. Beautiful farms, formerly in a high state of cultivation, now laid waste, houses entirely evacuated and forsaken, provisions of all kinds very scarce, and where once peace and plenty abounded, poverty and destruction now stalked the land."[55]

The confirmed border had an adverse effect on the development of Essex County. The local role of the Indian Department was greatly curtailed as British political and commercial interests were locked out of American lands. The Provincial Marine station removed to Penetanguishene, while the military garrison was reduced to a few

dozen men, removing the economic stimulation of government contracts. The communities of Sandwich and Amherstburg regressed,
denied the economic spurs that prompted their initial growth. The
New Settlement also fell into decay. A traveller described the eastern-
most reaches of the area two decades later: "In the townships of Tilbury
and Marsea [Mersea] some farms had been deserted, which had a most
barren aspect, being overrun with weeds and scarcely producing a
blade of grass." Ten years after the peace treaty, the inhabitants received
partial compensation for war losses.[56]

As late as 5 June 1814, Lt. Col. McDouall encouraged the chiefs on
the Upper Mississippi with Prevost's promise: "My Children! Should
the King, your great Father deign to listen to the proposal which the
enemy have made for peace, it will be on the express condition that
your interests shall be first considered, your just claims admitted and
no infringements of your rights permitted in future." A mortified
McDouall soon had to announce to the stunned warriors that the captured territory would revert to American control. "This peace is to last
forever," he told them. "You will bury deep in the earth all private quarrels and animosities that may have subsisted ... before the war.... Live
in peace and may the Great Spirit give you long life." Flabbergasted,
McDouall privately predicted, "There will not be an Indian left between
this and the Rocky Mountains to plague either party [American or
British]." Indeed, by 1817, the Natives in Ohio were restricted to two
small reserves; four years later, their brethren in Michigan, Indiana,
and Illinois shared a similar fate.[57]

Postwar British treatment of Native rights was scarcely better than
that of the United States. By the mid-nineteenth century, Native lands
appeared as mere specks on the peninsula of Upper Canada. In 1816,
the Indian Department virtually ceased provisioning the area tribesmen,
and in 1842, the long practice of bestowing presents was discontinued.
The government expropriated for development even the remnant of the
Huron Reserve near Amherstburg. By 1862, the dwindling Wyandot,
who had provided essential support to their wartime allies, were badly
dispersed, many having moved to a bleak reservation in Kansas.[58]

After his trial, Procter remained in Lower Canada for some
months. During July 1815, he performed his last public act, testifying
on behalf of Lt. Benoit Bender in Montreal. Shortly afterwards, Procter
returned to England; his name disappeared from the Army List in
1816. One of his former subalterns, Ensign James Cochran (brother to
the prosecutor at Procter's trial), declared of his former commander,

"This wretched man was of course never again employed.... He slunk away into obscurity and we never heard of him more."[59]

Procter's legacy became heavily tinged with the accusations of his court martial, which largely overshadowed his substantial positive contributions. Yet, with scant resources, he had facilitated the capture of Detroit and the destruction of two enemy offensives during his 14-month struggle. Like the Natives, he had served the strategic purpose of defending the Canadas until significant reinforcements arrived from England. Ironically, his desperate attempts to honour the Great Wampum brought about his own downfall and drew sneers at his trial, a tragic end that reflected that of the Natives. The subsequent writings of John Richardson assured his place in posterity.[60]

Procter lived for several years in quiet semi-retirement until he learned that the Prince Regent had honoured Prevost's services in Canada. This prompted him to break his public silence. In collaboration with his nephew, he prepared at least two anonymous accounts of his war experiences. In 1822, in the London *Quarterly Review* article, "Campaigns in the Canadas," he finally told his story and declared his opinion of Prevost: "The attempt by Sir George Prevost to affix a stigma upon a tried and zealous soldier was even less excusable than his desire of sacrificing the honour of another to avert the disgrace of failure from himself." A short time later, on 31 October 1822, Henry Procter died at Bath, leaving a widow and five or six offspring. He was 59 years old.[61]

Procter's second piece of writing appeared posthumously in a book entitled *Lucubrations of Humphrey Ravelin*, published anonymously by his nephew. This was an essay entitled "Indian Warfare," which described the struggle on the Detroit frontier. In it, Procter expressed a sense of loss that the "red children of the lake and the forest" had relinquished their "haunts" forever. Although there were no clear-cut winners in this war, the Natives were clearly the losers. Procter summed up their role and their tragic fate:

The devotion, courage and fortitude of their warlike tribes had been exerted in vain. Driven successively from every position by the superior knowledge and power of the merciless usurper, they had been chased to the remotest forests, systematically debased in character and thinned in numbers and physical strength by the insidious supply of liquors. They have dwindled to a miserable remnant.... They have been made the victims, not the pupils of civilization.

To the tribes at the head of Lake Erie, on the western shores of [Lake] Huron and from thence towards the Mississippi is the preservation of Upper Canada, in the first year of the war, mainly to be attributed.[62]

Amid the postwar Native dispersion, the wampum archives, that chronicle of their honoured past, became scattered. Among these was the Great Wampum, a lost artifact of a once grand idea.[63]

NOTES

1. Baynes to Drummond, 5 Jan. 1814, NAC, C 680: 301; Procter to Drummond, 14 Jan. 1814, *MPHC* 15: 470.
2. Procter to Drummond, 14 Jan. 1814, *MPHC* 15: 470; Procter to Duke of York, 14 Jan. 1814, *MPHC* 15: 470-71.
3. Prevost to Bathurst, 5 Jan. 1814, NAC, C 680: 301; Bathurst to Duke of York, 21 Feb. 1814, NAC, C 682: 132-33; Drummond to Prevost, 18 Dec. 1813, *MPHC* 15: 453; Prevost to Bathurst, 26 May 1813, *MPHC* 25: 454.
4. Duke of York to Prevost, 22 Feb. 1814, *MPHC* 15: 494; Col. William Claus to Lt. Daniel Claus, 1 May 1814, *DHCNF* 1813, Vol. 4: 168. While a prisoner in Kentucky, Chambers read Prevost's General Order of 24 Nov. 1813, and attributing its authorship to Procter's "representation," Chambers wrote, "He [Procter] never made any effort to rally his troops but was one of the first who fled." His letter formed the basis of the fifth charge against Procter and was introduced as evidence at the trial. When the time came for him to testify, Chambers altered his position. He asserted that he "could not positively say" whether Procter tried to rally the troops. Chambers, *PCM*, 95, Chambers to Myers, 5 Jan. 1814, *PCM*, Appendix 46.
5. Baynes to Procter, 21 May 1814, NAC, C 686: 40; Procter to Baynes, 25 May 1814, NAC, C 686: 41; Baynes to Procter, 1 June 1814, NAC, C 686: 42.
6. Procter to Baynes, 2 June 1814, Procter to Baynes, 7 July 1814, Baynes to Procter, 11 July 1814, Procter to Baynes, 16 July 1814, NAC, C 686: 43, 48, 49-50; Baynes to Procter, 20 July 1814, NAC, C 2774, Vol. 166: 114; Prince Regent to Prevost, 22 July 1814, Procter to Baynes, 29 July 1814, Procter to Baynes, 8 Aug. 1814, NAC, C 682: 137, 53, 56; Procter to Duke of York, 6 Sept. 1814, Prince Regent to Prevost, 20 Oct. 1814, NAC, C 686: 60, 39.
7. Byfield, *Account*, 29; Brock to Prevost, 9 Oct. 1812, *MPHC* 15: 163; Sheaffe to Prevost, 27 Oct. 1812, *SLB*, 296; Procter to Freer, 5 Nov. 1813, *MPHC* 15: 439; Prevost to Brock, 19 Oct. 1812, *MPHC* 15: 168.

8. Terms of Reference for Procter Court Martial, NAC, C 2774, Vol. 166: 24; Procter to Rottenberg, 3 Nov. 1813, *MPHC* 15: 435.

9. Charges and Findings of Procter Court Martial as confirmed by Prince Regent, 9 Sept. 1815, NAC, C 166: 184-87.

10. *Ibid.*, 187.

11. Warburton and Evans, *PCM*, 14, 24, 62.

12. Warburton and Evans, *PCM*, 14, 29, 41. Andrew William Cochran (1793-1849) was born in Nova Scotia where he met Prevost and followed him to Lower Canada. On 1 May 1813, Prevost appointed him assistant civil secretary and ensign in the Quebec militia. Prevost then made the young man deputy judge advocate in November 1814, his first big case being the Procter trial. After the war, Cochran continued in the civil service of Lower Canada and became a member of the provincial Legislative Council. *DCB* 7: 189-91.

13. *Defence of Major General Procter*, 9, 30.

14. Cochran's closing argument, *PCM*, 293-94, 299.

15. Cass to Armstrong, 30 Sept. 1814, McArthur to Armstrong, 10 Dec. 1814, *TPUS* 10: 497; Drummond to Prevost, 10 Jan. 1814, NAC, C 687: 21; Lt. George Jackson to Capt. Alexander Stewart, 12 Mar. 1814, *MPHC* 15: 514-15; Col. Thomas Talbot to Col. John Harvey, 7 Dec. 1814, NAC, C 686: 222.

16. General Order, 9 Jan. 1814, cited in Cushing, *Diary*, 77.

17. Cass to Armstrong, 4 Dec., 17 Dec. 1813, *MPHC* 40: 544, 551; Samuel Brown, *Views on Lake Erie*, 95.

18. Col. James Miller's Proclamation, 5 Nov. 1814, NAC, C 686: 250; John Askin to his children, *JAP* 2, 772; Lt. Col. Reginald James to Col. John Harvey, 11 Dec. 1814, *MPHC* 15: 681-82.

19. Drummond to Prevost, 22 Dec. 1813, NAC, C 681: 276; Drummond to Prevost, 2 Apr. 1813, *SBD* 3 Pt. 1: 42.

20. Drummond to Prevost, 5 Mar. 1814, NAC, C 680: 163.

21. Prevost to Drummond, 29 Jan. 1814, *MPHC* 25: 571.

22. Drummond to Prevost, 21 Jan. 1814, *MPHC* 15: 473-74; Drummond to Prevost, 19 Feb. 1814, NAC, C 682: 120.

23. Drummond to Prevost, 5 Mar. 1814, NAC, C 682: 163; Matthew Elliott to Col. Archibald Stewart, 4 Mar. 1814, NAC, C 682: 190; Report of Col. William Claus, 14 May 1814, NAC, C 683: 186.

24. Nichol to Drummond, 30 May 1814, *MPHC* 15: 570; Drummond to Prevost, 7 June 1813, NAC, C 683: 255.

25. Lt. Henry Medcalf to Lt. Col. Henry Bostwick, 25 Dec. 1813, NAC, C 682: 44; Col. Anthony Butler to Harrison, 7 Mar. 1813, Russell, *The History of the War*, 295; Cass to Armstrong, 17 Dec. 1813, *MPHC* 40: 553.

26. Richard Cartwright Deposition, 31 May 1814, NAC, C 683: 213.

27. Capt. John Bostwick to Lt. Col. Parry Jones Parry, 3 Nov. 1814, *MPHC* 15: 659; Capt. Chambers to Maj. Gen. A. Louis Charles de Wattville, 10 Nov. 1814, NAC, C 686: 187; Brig. Gen. McArthur to secretary of war, 18 Nov. 1814, Russell, *The History of the War*, 330-31; Drummond to Freer, 14 Nov. 1814, *MPHC* 15: 676.

28. Cass to Acting Secretary of War, 11 June 1814, Armstrong to McArthur, 8 Aug. 1814, *TPUS* 10: 462, 473.

29. Drummond to Prevost, 5 Mar. 1814, NAC, C 682: 157; Drummond to Prevost, 26 Apr. 1814, NAC, C 683: 52; Yeo to Drummond, 14 Nov. 1814, NAC, C 686: 173.

30. Capt. Bullock to Freer, 21 Oct. 1813, NAC, C 680: 251; Snider, *War Log of the Nancy*, xxi-xxxiii; McIntosh to Bullock, 16 Oct. 1813, NAC, C 680: 248. Procter had sent Capt. Francis Antone La Rocque of the Canadian Chasseurs to Michilimackinac in a canoe to notify Bullock of the evacuation of Amherstburg; however, La Rocque could not set off, unable to secure provisions. La Rocque, *PCM*, 208.

31. Capt. Bullock to Freer, 26 Feb. 1814, Capt. Bullock to Baynes, 21 Oct. 1813, Robert Dickson to Freer, 23 Oct. 1813, *MPHC* 15: 496, 421-24.

32. Simon McTavish, John McGuillivray, Thomas Thain, and Alexander Mackenzie (N.W. Co.) to Prevost, 8 Nov. 1813, *MPHC* 25: 543.

33. William McKay to McDouall, 27 July 1814, *MPHC* 15: 623-27; McDouall to Prevost, 14 Aug. 1814, *MPHC* 25: 593. Like Procter, McDouall held strong pro-Native views. He described the "indignation" of the warriors at the rough treatment of their people by Governor William Clarke of Missouri, whom he termed a "ruffian." He believed that co-operation with the Natives was necessary to prevent the "extermination" of the Misssissippi tribes and perhaps the loss of Upper Canada. McDouall identified their spokeman, Tête de Chien as "scarcely inferior to Tecumseh." After several councils, he agreed to send militia captain (designated lieutenant colonel) William McKay to the Upper Mississippi. With 120 *Canadiens* and officers of the Indian Department and 520 warriors, McKay attacked Prairie du Chien, driving off a "floating block house" of 14 guns and secured the surrender of the fort. McDouall to Drummond, 16 July 1813, McKay to McDouall 27 July 1813, *SBD* 3: 253-65.

34. K.R. Macpherson, "List of British Vessels," 176.

35. Drummond to Prevost, 13 May 1814, *MPHC* 15: 573.

36. John Meldrum to John Askin, 29 Mar. 1814, *JAP* 2: 778; Young, *The Life of General Lewis Cass*, 83-84.

37. *The War*, 14 Feb. 1814.

38. Drummond to Freer, 17 May 1814, NAC, C 257: 257; Charles Askin, "Charles Askin Journal," *JAP* 2: 775.

39. Drummond to Freer, 16 Feb. 1814, *MPHC* 15: 491-92; Drake, *Life of Tecumseh*, 62; Christie, *History of Lower Canada* 2: 179; "Speech of the

Indian Chief Me-tawth," WCHS, *Transactions* 4, (1903): 11-12. Metoss (Metawth) was a Sac chief, an active and loyal supporter of the alliance, having particularly distinguished himself at the first siege of Fort Meigs. Richardson relates a touching story on the death of his young son during the siege. Richardson, *War of 1812*, 155-58.

40. Christie, *History of Lower Canada* 2: 179-80; Prevost's speech to Native chiefs, cited in Sugden, *Tecumseh's Last Stand*, 196-97.
41. Matthew Elliott to Glegg, 31 Jan. 1814, *MPHC* 15: 485.
42. Drummond to Prevost, 19 Apr. 1814, *MPHC* 15: 534.
43. Tanner, *Atlas of Great Lakes Indian History*, 120. Cass's treaties are listed in Young, *The Life of General Lewis Cass*, 83.
44. Bathurst to Prevost, 3 June 1814, cited in Hitsman, *The Incredible War of 1812*, 249-51.
45. [Stephen Sewell], *Veritas*, 110-22; Christie, *History of Lower Canada* 2: 209-22; Kingsford, *The History of Canada* 9: 19.
46. Although authorship of *Veritas* was never definitely established, the evidence points to Stephen Sewell, Prevost's solicitor general. John Richardson, a principal merchant of Montreal and member of the executive council, also fell under suspicion. The writing of *Nerva* is attributed to Samuel Gale, another Tory activist. *DCB* 5: 697; *DCB* 6: 268-70, 643, 701.
47. Wellington to Bathurst, 30 Oct. 1814, cited in Gerald S. Graham, "Views of General Murray on the Defence of Upper Canada, 1815," 158n.
48. Christie, *History of Lower Canada* 2: 245-46. No scholarly assessment of Prevost's wartime service has been done. According to early Canadian historian Robert Christie, "The military character of Sir George Prevost sustained a shock [after his failed attack on Sacket's Harbour] from which it never recovered." Prevost's two subsequent attempts at commanding operations at Fort George and Plattsburg were also failures. He has a more favourable legacy in the civil sphere as a conciliatory governor of Lower Canada. *Ibid.*, 81.
49. Yeo to Secretary of the Admiralty John Croker, 5 Sept. 1815, *MPHC* 25: 635-36; Christie, *History of Lower Canada* 2: 220-47; *DCB* 6: 693-98; Kingsford, *History of Canada* 9: 19.
50. Note of British commissioners to their American counterparts, 19 Aug. 1814, *DPCUS* 1814-1815, Vol. 3: 1319.
51. Note of American plenipotentiaries to their British counterparts, 26 Sept. 1814, *DPCUS* 1814-1815, Vol. 3: 1349.
52. Wellington's supplementary dispatches, cited in J. Mackay Hitsman, "Sir George Prevost's Conduct of the Canadian War of 1812," 42; John Updyke, *The Diplomacy of the War of 1812*, 235-76; Article 9 to the Treaty of Ghent, Russell, *The History of the War*, 432-33; Sturtevant, *Handbook of North American Indians* 4: 156.

53. Woodford, *Woodward,* 123.

54. Woodward to Secretary of State, 5 Mar. 1815, cited in Farmer, *History of Detroit,* 287.

55. Tilly Buttrick, *Voyages, Travels and Discoveries,* cited in Fred Landon, *Western Ontario and the American Frontier,* 42.

56. Patrick Shirreff, *A Tour Through North America,* 207.

57. McDouall to Indian Council, 5 June 1814, *MLWHH* 2: 654; McDouall's Speech to the Native chiefs, nd. Mar. 1815, *MPHC* 25: 620-21; McDouall to Forster, 15 May 1815, NAC, C 688: 37; *DCB* 5: 799.

58. Clarke, *Wyandotts,* 124; Tanner, *Atlas of Great Lakes Indian History,* 121; Sturtevant, *Handbook of North American Indians* 15: 403.

59. Cochran, *Notes,* NAC, MG 40, G4, File 1: 9.

60. For a summary of the different views on Procter, see Ian C.B. Pemberton, "Historiography of the War of 1812: The Canadian View of the Battle of Lake Erie and its Aftermath," in Welsh and Skaggs, *War on the Great Lakes,* 78-86.

61. *DCB* 6: 616-18; [Procter and Procter], "Campaigns in the Canadas," 432. Although Procter was some 50 years old at the time of the war, he is frequently represented as half that age. This particular error is rooted in Morgan's *Sketches of Celebrated Canadians,* 187, in which the author confused Procter with one Henry Adolphus Proctor (1784-1859) who served on the Niagara frontier during the war as a major and later rose to lieutenant general rank. The result was a confused interweaving of the two biographies, perpetuating the false notion that Procter's career recovered after the cloud of the Thames campaign. Historians have been further confused by the incorrect spelling of Procter's name in official documents (Proctor rather than Procter), probably because of faulty spelling of the court martial transcripts. Procter's handwritten signature, as found in archival documents, clearly shows the latter form to be correct.

    Henry Procter, Jr., joined the 41st Foot as a gentleman volunteer on 1 July 1812, a few days before John Richardson, and is mentioned at the battles of Frenchtown, Fort Meigs, and Fort Stephenson. He became ensign in 1813 and lieutenant in the 8th Foot (John Richardson's new regiment) two years later. In 1816, he transferred to the 64th before retiring on half pay the following year.

    At least two brothers of the elder Procter served in Canada during the war, Capt. William Bruce Procter of the 104th and Capt. John Procter of the 43rd, appointed Maj. Gen. Procter's aide-de-camp on 26 September 1814.

    George Procter, the author, married Henry Procter's daughter, Sarah Anne, in 1819. Tupper asserts that the surnames were not coincidental, this Procter being the general's "nephew *and* son-in-law." He was, for a time, adjutant of the Royal Military College at Sandhurst and wrote several classical histories. George Procter also participated in the war, having come to Canada in 1814 with the 5th regiment. He later rose to lieutenant colonel but on 31 May 1842, he died from sunstroke off the coast of Aden at the age of 45, leaving a widow, five sons, and two daughters. *DCB* 6: 616-18; Tupper, *Brock*, 308; Klinck, "Some Anonymous Literature of the War of 1812," 49-60.

62. [Procter and Procter], *Lucubrations*, 324-25, 327, 359.

63. Clarke, *Wyandotts*, 124. What was long thought to be the Great Wampum is preserved at Fort Malden National Historic site, Amherstburg, Ontario. It has been recently identified by its construction and arrangement as dating from 1830 or later. The authentic wampum surfaced one last time at an allied council at Prairie du Chien in May 1815 at which time the peace terms were announced to the stunned Natives. Prior to presenting the belt to the western nations, Capt. T.G. Anderson of the British Indian Department ensured that it was "divested of its red colour and rendered blue." Its original significance denied, the great wampum was then sent off to the distant villages as the belt of peace and subsequently lost. Anderson testimony, Court of Inquiry at Michilimackinac, 6 and 10 Oct. 1915, *MPHC 16*: 194.

APPENDIX

POST-MORAVIANTOWN SKETCHES OF COMBATANTS

The 41st Regiment of Foot
The much enduring 41st survived defeat, imprisonment, and humiliation to fight again at Fort Niagara and Black Rock (December 1813), Lundy's Lane (July 1814), and Fort Erie (August 1814). By the end of the war, four officers and 129 other ranks of the 41st had been killed in combat. Its members sustained 339 serious wounds (all ranks). How many succumbed to exposure, malnutrition, imprisonment, exhaustion, and disease is not known. In 1815, the regiment's two battalions were consolidated into one (1251 all ranks) under Lt. Col. William Evans, and marched to Quebec City to board *Lord Cathcart*, arriving in Europe in July to participate in the occupation of Paris. The regiment then returned home after an absence of 16 years. Although disgraced by Prevost, the 41st earned more battle honours in the Canadas than any other regiment, its colours bearing "Detroit," "Queenstown," "Miami," and "Niagara." In the words of military historian C.P. Stacey, "This regiment saved Upper Canada, almost single-handedly [as far as White troops are concerned], in the decisive opening campaign in 1812.... Its victories are more memorable than its misfortunes." [1]

The Royal Newfoundland Regiment
The ranks of the amphibious Royal Newfoundland Regiment became so badly depleted by late 1813 that Prevost proposed to send the

survivors home as recruiters. Nonetheless, they remained in Upper Canada and in the spring of 1814, 90 of the regiment's hardy and versatile members accompanied the relief expedition to Fort Michilimackinac, facilitating the capture of *Scorpion* and *Tigress*. It was not until 21 July 1815 that these soldiers returned home from their post to (the somewhat less dreary) Newfoundland. Although generally dispersed during the war, the ranks of the RNR provided invaluable service as foot soldiers, seamen, marines, and extra gunners as they were needed. Studies of the battle of Lake Erie seldom take into account the maritime background of these men. Procter sought more of them for Barclay who considered them "his greatest reliance."[2]

The Western District Militiamen

Located at the seat of war, the men and families of the 1st Essex, 2nd Essex, and Kent Regiments sustained crushing material losses. The orchards, homes, livestock, and outbuildings of active Loyalists were particularly marked for destruction by the Americans. Although few could blame the Western District militiamen for withdrawing to attend to pressing domestic concerns, some maintained the struggle on the Upper Thames and Niagara frontiers until the end of the conflict. After the battle of Moraviantown, the Loyal Kent Volunteers (Kent Rangers) mustered 65 officers and men; the Loyal Essex Volunteers (Essex Rangers) had 20; while Caldwell's (Western) Rangers counted 18. The wartime casualty figures of these units show 23 dead (killed or died of disease) and 32 seriously wounded. Irregularly paid and equipped, the militiamen of the Western District performed essential service not only in the principal British victories at Detroit, Frenchtown, and Fort Meigs, but in their less glamourous but vital roles as boatmen, dispatch riders, artificers, guards, and mariners. While their visible contribution and sense of duty have been often marginalized, they gave as much as they could amid the harsh circumstances. For decades, the veterans spun the "militia myth," the notion that Loyalist Canadian militia soldiers single-handedly repelled the American hordes. This myth served to legitimize their privileged positions in the postwar oligarchy, the "family compact," a principal target of the Upper Canadian Rebellion of 1837.[3]

The Kentucky Volunteers

Of all the states, Kentucky was foremost in demanding and supporting aggressive operations in the Detroit country. Between four and five of every six Kentuckians of military age (totaling 25,000 men) bore arms during the war. Of the 1876 American soldiers killed during the conflict, 1200 were Kentuckians. Most of these died while serving in the ranks of the Northwest Army, of which Kentuckians formed the majority. The veterans of the battle of Moraviantown produced a vice-president, two governors, four lieutenant-governors, four senators, and 20 members for the House of Representatives, along with dozens of mayors, judges, and other civic leaders.[4]

ALLIED PERSONALITIES

Robert Heriot Barclay was released to British authorities after his naval defeat, because of his severe injuries. He wrote to his fiancée in London, Agness Cossar, describing his battered condition, discreetly offering her release from the engagement. She replied that if there was enough of him to contain his soul she would marry him, and she did so in 1814. That same year, Barclay was confirmed as commander and was honourably aquitted of charges stemming from the battle of Lake Erie. Nonetheless, his career remained marred by the unprecedented loss of an entire British squadron and he achieved full captain rank only in 1824, when he was assigned command of the bomb vessel, *Infernal.* Retiring to Edinburgh, Scotland, he died there in 1837.[5]

Shadrach Byfield was the only private of the Right Division to leave a record of his war experiences. He narrated his story in a straightforward vernacular, typifying that common soldier for whom the structured regimental life was everything. Obedient, reliable, and physically tough, he plodded from one misfortune to another without complaint. Byfield eluded capture at the battle of Moraviantown, escaped barefoot (his boots were worn out) to the Centre Division in the company of a group of warriors (with whom he felt extremely uncomfortable), and participated in actions on the Niagara frontier, in one of which his arm was shattered. With mulled wine as his sole anaesthetic, the surgeons amputated the limb and unceremoniously chucked it into a "dung heap." Indignant, Byfield retrieved the arm for proper burial in a tiny casket. Within three days, the stump healed sufficiently that he could "play a game of fives for a quart of rum." It is worth noting that his comrades (the Duke of Wellington called common soldiers "the scum of the earth") had sufficient generosity of spirit to collect several pounds, a considerable sum on private's pay, to alleviate Byfield's misfortune. He returned to England to be discharged from the army with a disability pension of nine pence per day with which to support his family. Gaining inspiration through a dream, Byfield asked a blacksmith to fabricate a primitive artificial limb with which he was able to practice his trade as a weaver for decades. Byfield was 24 years old at the battle of Moraviantown, having joined the militia at the age of 9. On hearing of his decision to enlist, his mother "was so affected that on the evening of the same day, she fell in a fit ... and expired the third day after."[6]

William Caldwell, Sr., led his tiny mounted unit, Caldwell's (Western) Rangers, throughout the war, notably at the battle of Longwoods in March 1814. That year, he succeeded Elliott in the Indian Department and secured positions in it for his sons, participating in the engagements of Lundy's Lane, Chippawa, and Fort Erie. Caldwell became involved in power disputes with his rival, John Norton, but was eventually superseded by his mixed-blood son, Billy Caldwell. After the war, he repaired his ravaged estate and became a magistrate and community leader in the Amherstburg area, dying on 20 February 1822.[7]

Peter Latouche Chambers continued his vendetta against Muir's brother-in-law, Lt. Bender, whose resulting court martial acquittal left Chambers somewhat embarrassed (as did his unsubstantiated allegations of Procter's cowardice). His aggressive temperament continued to hinder his advancement; he did not achieve major rank until 1821, still in the 41st. Impulsive as ever, "the fiery Chambers" received a severe spear wound in the face in 1824 while leading a charge upon a stockade in Kemmendine, Burma. Awarded the Cross of the Bath two years later, Chambers went on to attain his ambition of becoming lieutenant colonel of the 41st Foot, on 12 April 1827. He did not live long to enjoy the achievement, as both he and his wife died of cholera that year while visiting their children near Bangalore, India.[8]

Matthew Charles Dixon served out the war in Lower Canada, where he married a local woman. His role in the Thames campaign did not blemish his career and he rose to major general rank in 1854, dying four years later at Southampton, England.[9]

Matthew Elliott continued to co-ordinate the remnant of the Native confederacy in actions at Buffalo and Black Rock during the winter of 1813. Elliott lost most of his possessions during the Thames retreat and his extensive estate was broken up during the American occupation, leaving him struggling to support his family. The old bush ranger became ill and died on 7 May 1814, after a half century of frontier warfare.[10]

Robert McDouall maintained aggressive operations on the Upper Mississippi until the end of the war. When the terms of peace became known, he tried vainly to impede the evacuation of Fort Michilimackinac but accepted the Treaty of Ghent, complaining nonetheless, that "our negotiators as usual, have been egregiously duped." Retiring on half pay in 1816, McDouall was knighted a year later. He returned to active service, rising to major general in 1841 and died seven years later.[11]

Thomas McKee degenerated into an obnoxious drunk, staging wild orgies among the Natives on Burlington Beach. His "disgraceful conduct," combined with internal feuds within the Indian Department, prompted Superintendent William Claus to comment, "Indian affairs seem to be going wrong." McKee died in Lower Canada in 1815 from the effects of his drinking, leaving his wife destitute.[12]

Adam Charles Muir, the white-haired captain whom Procter called "a good old officer," participated in minor operations on the Grand River until the end of the war. The former sergeant-major returned to Europe with his regiment. In 1816, Muir sustained a serious hip injury from a riding accident in Dublin. Disabled for years, he resigned his commission from the army and received a modest pension. Settling in St. Andrée-Est, Lower Canada, he experienced acute financial hardship. Muir died in 1829, leaving his widow struggling to support ten children.[13]

John Richardson joined the 8th Foot as an ensign on repatriation, accompanying that corps to Europe in 1815. Three years later he retired because of poor health. In 1828, he published, anonymously, his first significant work, *Tecumseh; or The Warrior of the West: A Poem of Four Cantos with notes by an English Officer*, in which he glamourized Tecumseh's downfall as a romantic tragedy. In the 1830s, Richardson enlisted with the British Auxiliary Legion serving in Spain, where he became a major despite vicious, highly publicized disputes with his superiors. He then worked as a journalist for the *London Times*, returning to the Canadas to report on the post-1837 reforms. During this time, he wrote several accounts relating to the war, the best-known being *The War of 1812, First Series, Containing A Full And Detailed Narrative Of The Operations Of The Right Division, Of The Canadian Army* (later shortened to *Richardson's War of 1812*). His works met with an indifferent response from the public but earned him posthumous fame as Canada's first novelist. Finding it difficult to make ends meet, he moved to the U.S., but his literary efforts met with the same coolness there. Although twice married, he died alone and penniless in New York City in 1852, unable to support even his dog.[14]

Charles Frederick Rolette's ubiquitous naval career ended with the battle of Lake Erie. Early in that action, he took command of *Lady Prevost* after her captain was killed. He was seriously wounded and badly burned by exploding gunpowder before surrendering his battered, listing vessel. During the war, he was credited with taking no less than 18 prizes of all sizes. After a year as a prisoner of war, he returned to his native Quebec whose residents honoured him with a handsome sword and a land grant of 1200 acres. Rolette died from his extensive wounds in 1831 at the age of 46, leaving a widow and six children in poverty.[15]

Francis de Rottenberg resumed command in the Montreal District after being superseded by Drummond in December 1813. After the ill-fated Plattsburg offensive, he presided over Procter's court martial. Rottenberg escaped examination of his own conduct and was promoted to lieutenant general in 1819, dying at Portsmouth in 1832. His undistinguished wartime performance was eclipsed by the popularity of his young and engaging wife who earned unusual admiration among senior social circles in the Canadas.[16]

Thomas Bligh St. George recovered fully from the wounds he sustained at the battle of Frenchtown and became a Companion of the Order of the Bath, rising to major general in 1819. That year, he was also awarded a knighthood of the Royal Hanoverian Order. St. George died in England in 1836.[17]

Splitlog settled on the Huron reserve in 1815. Although Warrow had signed away much of that land in 1833, Splitlog championed the cause of the 150 remaining Wyandot in resisting government pressure to surrender more. Finally, in 1835, Lieutenant Governor Sir Francis Bond Head summoned the Wyandot chief to a coffee house at Amherstburg. Sporting a tattered military frock coat, cocked hat, and sword (presents from St. George or Procter), Splitlog listened in astonishment as the lieutenant governor personally dictated the terms of a forced expropriation. Of the remaining 23,630 acres, the British took all but 7700 acres. Embittered, Splitlog died in 1838. Five years later, most of the Canadian members of his nation moved to a reservation in Kansas. The remaining tribesmen gave up the trace of the Huron Reserve between 1853 and 1892, renouncing their very Native status in 1881.[18]

Thomas Talbot became a favourite target of renegade marauders after the battle of Moraviantown. They burned his home in 1814, and

Talbot himself barely eluded their grasp. He remained a die-hard expansionist. Decades later, the traveller-writer, Anna Jameson, visited him and wrote, "He took out a map and pointed out the foolish bargain [of giving away the Old Northwest]. The man covered his eyes with his clenched hands and burst into tears." Talbot died in 1853, aged 82, a wealthy, eccentric, reclusive bachelor.[19]

Tenskwatawa returned to the Amherstburg area after the war, Governor Cass frustrating his desire to settle at Tippecanoe or the Raisin River. British authorities considered the Prophet and his thousand fellow squatters as exiles and encouraged their return to the U.S. by reducing their rations. Two successive schooners bearing the diminished provisions foundered on Lake Erie in 1816 and 1817, creating acute hardship for his band of refugees. With Tecumseh's son, Pachetha, and 20 other Shawnee followers, Tenskwatawa withdrew to his secluded wartime camp on Cedar Creek near the New Settlement. In 1824, Cass allowed him to settle on an Ohio reserve, but four years later, Tenskwatawa moved to a reservation in Kansas accompanied by 250 of his tribesmen. He died in obscurity at Kansas City in 1836.[20]

Augustus Warburton was confirmed lieutenant colonel and transferred to the 41st Foot on 30 September 1813, just days before the battle of Moraviantown. He returned from captivity in Kentucky, serving with his new regiment on the Niagara frontier, but was placed on half pay with the amalgamation of the two battalions of the 41st. He returned to full pay status with the 85th Foot and became its lieutenant colonel in 1825, remaining with that regiment until his death in 1837.[21]

AMERICAN PERSONALITIES

Lewis Cass became Governor of Michigan Territory and Superintendent of Indian Affairs after the Thames campaign, positions he held till 1831. He was instrumental in conducting expropriations of Native lands, virtually ejecting the Natives from the Old Northwest. While secretary of war (1831-36), Cass suppressed the Black Hawk uprising. He was Minister to France (1836-42), a Michigan senator (1845-57), and secretary of state (1857-60), twice running unsuccessfully for president as a Democratic nominee. A fierce nationalist and expansionist, Cass adopted bellicose positions on the Oregon and Texas questions. He died at Detroit in 1866.[22]

William Henry Harrison's career waned after his victory on the Thames. Armstrong undermined his authority by giving direct orders to elements of his command, suggesting that Harrison might wish to take some leave. Fed up with the slights, Harrison quit the Northwest Army on 13 February 1814, resigning his commission from the U.S. Army some weeks later. Despondent over the "unmerited obloquy" to which he had been subjected, he compared his treatment to that of Procter: "I see my old opponent, Procter, has been severely reprimanded by the Prince Regent. My fate has been more hard than his." Nonetheless, unlike Procter, Harrison's fortunes improved as he became a congressman (1816-19), senator (1825-28), and presidential candidate (1836). Finally, in 1840, his reputation as a military hero and a "man of the people" gained him the presidency. After reading his four-hour inaugural address in a pouring rain without hat or coat, Harrison contracted pneumonia and died on 4 April 1841. His term in office was the shortest in American history.[23]

William Hull was released from British detention in late 1812 to receive a chilly reception in his country. Two years later, he was tried on charges of treason, cowardice, un-officer-like conduct, and neglect of duty. Having lost his official documents, he was denied access to government records with which to prepare his case. Although acquitted of the charge of treason, he was found guilty of the others and sentenced to be shot. The court recommended clemency to the elderly Revolutionary War hero, and President Madison duly commuted the sentence, but dismissed Hull from the army. Hull called his trial a "plot" based on "opinion ... and scandalous falsehood," adding, "My expedition was more prolific of promotions than any other unsuccessful enterprize I have ever heard of." In 1824, he published *Memoirs of the Campaign of the Northwest Army* and died the following year, a virtual pariah, aged 73. In 1848, his daughter, Maria Campbell, and his grandson, James Freeman Clarke, published works aimed at vindicating his tarnished name.[24]

Richard Mentor Johnson recovered from his wounds to serve in Congress until 1837. He was elected vice-president in the Van Buren administration, largely on the basis of his legendary combat with Tecumseh. After one term, he retired to Kentucky in 1841 and died there in 1850.[25]

Duncan McArthur succeeded Harrison as commander of the Northwest Army in 1814. After the war he became a congressman and later, governor of Ohio, dying in 1839 from injuries sustained in an accident.[26]

James Russel Miller was released from captivity in 1813 and became colonel of the 21st U.S. Infantry the following year, serving with distinction at the engagements of Chippawa, Lundy's Lane, and Fort Erie. During the war, Miller stood out among his peers as a quietly competent professional soldier. When asked if he could capture a British artillery battery at the battle of Lundy's Lane, his reply of "I'll try, sir!" came to be accepted as a well-known slogan in the U.S. Army. In 1819, he became governor of Arkansas Territory, and in 1825, collector of customs at Salem, Massachusetts. Miller died in 1851.[27]

Oliver Hazard Perry was promoted to post captain for his victory on Lake Erie and received the thanks of Congress, along with $12,000 as prize money. After the war, he remained in the U.S. Navy, commanding the 44-gun frigate, *Java*. Upon completing a diplomatic mission to Venezuela in 1819, he died at sea of yellow fever, aged 34.[28]

James Winchester remained prisoner at Quebec City for a year after his capture. On release, he commanded in the Mobile district till the end of the war. Resigning his commission in March 1815, he served on a federal commission to define the Tennessee-Mississippi boundary in 1819 and retired to his estate in Tennessee where he died six years later.[29]

Augustus Brevoort Woodward returned to Detroit in 1814 and assumed an active role in its post war reconstruction. Active in the intellectual development of Michigan, he published *A System of Universal Science* in 1816 and contributed substantially to the founding of "University Michigania." In 1826, Woodward became a Florida judge and died there the following year.[30]

NOTES

1. Charles P. Stacey, "Upper Canada at War, 1814: Captain Armstrong Reports," 39-40; Lomax, *The 41st*, 113.
2. Prevost to Bathurst, 4 Nov. 1813, *DHCNF* 1813, Vol. 4: 137; General Order, 21 June 1813, McDouall to Prevost, 14 Aug. 1814, McDouall to Maj. Gen. Robinson, 21 July 1815, *SBD* 3: 22, 273, 538; Procter to Prevost, 4 July 1813, NAC, C 679: 181; Robert Saunders, *Newfoundland's Role in the Historic Battle of Lake Erie*, 17.
3. A surprising number of surnames on the militia muster rolls continue to be reflected among modern-day residents of Essex and Kent counties. William Gray, *Soldiers of the King: The Upper Canadian Militia, 1812-15*, 249-84.

4. Hammack, *Kentucky and the Second American Revolution*, 109-11; Bennett Young, "Raisin River Memorial Dedication, 4 Oct. 1904," *MPHC* 35: 213.

5. *DCB* 7: 45-46; A. Blanche Burt, "Captain Robert Heriot Barclay, R.N.," 177.

6. Byfield, *Account*, 1, 27, 40-45.

7. *DCB* 6: 101-04.

8. Lomax, *The 41st*, 372

9. *DICSD*, 44n.

10. Horsman, *Matthew Elliott Indian Agent*, 216; *DCB* 5: 302-03.

11. *DCB* 7: 556-58.

12. Col. William Claus to Lt. William Claus, Jr., 11 May 1814, *DHCNF* 1813, Vol. 4: 168; *DCB* 5: 535-36.

13. *DCB* 6: 529-30.

14. Richardson's biographical sketches are contained in *DCB* 8: 743-47; David R. Beasley, *The Canadian Don Quixote*; and Alexander Clark Casselman's introduction to *Richardson's War of 1812*.

15. "Biographical Note on Frederick Rollette" in *DHCNF* 1812, Vol. 2: 59-61.

16. *DCB* 6: 660-62.

17. *DICSD*, 24n.

18. Clarke, *Wyandotts*, 124-28; Sturtevant, *Handbook of North American Indians* 15: 403; Gentilcore, *Historical Atlas of Canada* 2: plate 32; *DCB* 7: 821-22.

19. *DCB* 8: 857-61.

20. Edmunds, *The Shawnee Prophet*, 161-62; Tanner, *Atlas of Great Lakes Indian History*, 121; *DCB* 7: 849.

21. Lomax, *The 41st*, 84, 86; Cochran, *Notes*, NAC, MG 40, G4, File 1: 9.

22. *DAB* 2: 562.

23. *WAMB*, 167; Harrison to John McLean, 29 Dec. 1815, *MLWHH* 2: 712-13.

24. *WAMB*, 188; Hull, *Memoirs*, 154, 168. After the surrender of Detroit, Hull put his strength returns, diary, and other papers into a trunk conveyed by his daughter, Mrs. Hickman, on *Detroit I* to Fort Erie. All these records were lost when that vessel was destroyed. The charges, specifications, findings, and sentence of his court martial are contained in *DPCUS* 1813-14, Vol. 2: 2523-43. The entire trial transcript is found in *HCM*. Hull's most vicious accusers portrayed his actions as driven by "cowardice, mental imbecility and moral depravity or corrupt perfidy." Thompson, *Sketches of the Late War*, 24. Hull's principal defender was his grandson, James Freeman Clarke, in *History of the Campaign of 1812*, a work based largely on Hull's arguments in *Memoirs*. His daughter, Maria Campbell, attributed his disgrace to "political necessity" in *Revolutionary Services and Civil Life of General William Hull*.

25. *WAMB*, 202.
26. *DAB* 5: 549.
27. *WAMB*, 284; *DAB* 6: 628; John C. Fredricksen, *Officers of the War of 1812*, 89-90.
28. *WAMB*, 318.
29. *DAB* 10: 278; *WAMB*, 485.
30. *DAB* 10: 506-07.

BIBLIOGRAPHY

PRIMARY SOURCES

Archival Sources
National Archives of Canada (NAC)
Manuscript Group 11, Colonial Office 42 (Canada Originated Correspondence).
Manuscript Group 13, War Office 71 (Transcripts of the Procter Court Martial).
Manuscript Group 24, G46 (Col. Mahlon Burwell Journal).
Manuscript Group 40, G4, Files 1 and 2 (Cochran Notes and Cochran Narrative, Welch Regimental Museum, Cardiff, Wales, copied by National Archives of Canada).
Record Group 8, No. I, "C" Series (British Military and Naval Records), Volumes 166, 256, 257, 672, 673, 676, 678, 679, 680, 681, 682, 683, 687, 688A, 728, 730, 731, 909, and 2774.

Ontario Archives (OA)
MS-109, Microcopy No. T-836 (British Military Correspondence: Procter Papers).

National Archives of the United States (NAUS)
Microcopy 588, Roll 7 (Department of State, War of 1812 Papers: Miscellaneous Intercepted Correspondence (MIC) 16 Jul. 1812 to 10 Sept. 1813).

Published Documents

Annual Register or a View of the History, Politics and Literature for the Year 1812 and 1813. London: Otridge and Son et al., 1814.

Blume, William Wirt (ed.). *Transactions of the Supreme Court of the Territory of Michigan, 1805-1814.* Ann Arbor, MI: University of Michigan Press, 1935.

Carter, Clarence, E. (ed.). *The Territorial Papers of the United States* Vol. 10: *The Territory of Michigan, 1805-1820.* Washington, DC: Government Printing Office, 1942.

Coyne, James, H. (ed.). "The Talbot Papers." *Proceedings and Transactions of the Royal Society of Canada,* Third Series, Sect. 2, Part 1 (1907), 15-210.

Cruikshank, Ernest A. (ed.). *Documentary History of the Campaigns on the Niagara Frontier in 1812-1814.* 9 vols. Welland, ON: Tribune Press, 1896-1908.

———. *Documents Relating to the Invasion of Canada and the Surrender of Detroit.* Ottawa: Government Printing Bureau, 1912.

Defence of Major General Proctor [Procter] Tried at Montreal by a Court Martial upon Charges Affecting his Character as a Soldier. Montreal: John Lovell, 1842.

Esarey, Logan (ed.). *Messages and Letters of William Henry Harrison.* 2 vols. Indianapolis: Indiana Historical Commission, 1922.

Forbes, James G. (ed.). *Report of the Trial of Brig. General William Hull.* New York: Eastburn and Kirk, 1814.

Knopff, Richard C. (ed.). *Documentary Transcripts of the War of 1812 in the Northwest.* Vol. 2: *Return Jonathon Meigs Jr. and the War of 1812.* Columbus: Ohio Historical Society, 1957.

———. *Documentary Transcripts of the War of 1812 in the Northwest.* Vol. 3: *Thomas Worthington and the War of 1812.* Columbus: Ohio Historical Society, 1957.

Lajeunesse, Ernest J. (ed.) *The Windsor Border Region.* Toronto: Champlain Society, 1960.

Michigan Pioneer and Historical Collections. 40 vols. Lansing, MI: Thorpe and Godfrey, State Printers et al., 1877-1929.

Proceedings of a Court Martial Holden at Quebec for the Trial of Lieutenant Benoit Bender. Montreal: J. Lane, 1817.

Quaife, Milo (ed.). *The John Askin Papers.* Vol. 2 (1796-1820). Detroit: Detroit Library Commission, 1931.

Russell, John, Jr. (comp.). *The History of the War.* Hartford, CT: G. and J. Russell, 1815.

Severence, Frank H. (ed.). *General Sheaffe's Letter Book, in Publications of the Buffalo Historical Society.* Vol. 17. Buffalo: Buffalo Historical Society, 1913.

Snider, C.H.J. (ed.). *War Log of the Nancy.* Toronto: Rous and Mann, 1936.

Spragge, George W. (ed.). *The John Strachan Letter Book: 1812-34*. Toronto: Ontario Historical Society, 1946.

Thwaites, Reuben Gold (ed.). *Collections of the State Historical Society of Wisconsin*. Vol. 19. Madison: Wisconsin Historical Society, 1910.

Tupper, Ferdinand Brock. *Family Records Containing Memoirs of Major-General Sir Isaac Brock, K.B.* Guernsey, U.K.: Stephen Barbet, 1835.

————. *The Life and Correspondence of Sir Isaac Brock*. London: Simpkin, Marshall, 1845,1847.

U.S. Congress. *Mr. Monroe's Letter on the Rejected Treaty between the United States and Great Britain*. Portland, ME: Gazette Press, 1813.

————. *Report on the Spirit and Manner in which the War Has Been Waged by the Enemy*. Washington, DC: A. and G. Way, 1813.

————. *Barbarities of the Enemy*. Worcester, MA: Remark Dunnel, 1814.

————. *The Debates and Proceedings in the Congress of the United States, 1811-1814, Twelfth and Thirteenth Congress*. 3 vols. Washington, DC: Gales and Seaton, 1853-54.

U.S. House of Representatives. *An Address of the Members of the House of Representatives of the Congress of the United States to their Constituents on the Subject of the War with Great Britain*. New Haven, CT: Walter Steele, 1812.

Western Reserve Historical Society. *Northern Ohio During the War of 1812*. Tract 92, Part 2. Cleveland: Western Reserve Historical Society, 1913.

Wood, William (ed.). *Select British Documents of the War of 1812*. 3 vols. Toronto: Champlain Society, 1920.

————. (ed.). "Narrative of the Proceedings during the Command of Captain Barclay of His Majesty's Squadron on Lake Erie," in *Select British Documents of the War of 1812*, Vol. 2, 298-319.

Published Accounts by Participants

Aikins, Charles. "Journal of a Journey From Sandwich to York in the Summer of 1806," *Ontario History* 6 (1905), 15-20.

Armstrong, John. *Notices of the War of 1812*. 2 vols. New York: Wiley and Putnam, 1840.

Askin, Charles. "Charles Askin's Journal of the Detroit Campaign, July 24 to September 12, 1812." Ed. Milo Quaife, in *The John Askin Papers*. Vol. 2. 711-42.

Askin, John. "The John Askin Diary," in *Michigan Pioneer Historical Collections*. Vol. 32 (1903): 468-73.

Atherton, William. *Narrative of the Suffering and Defeat of the North-Western Army Under General Winchester*. Frankfort, KY: A.G. Hodges, 1842.

Black Hawk. *Black Hawk, an Autobiography*. Ed. Donald Jackson. Urbana: University of Illinois Press, 1964.

Boucherville, Thomas Verchères de. *The Journal of Thomas Verchères de Boucherville*. Ed. Milo Quaife, in *War on the Detroit*, 3-178.

Brenton, Edward B. *Some Account of the Public Life of ... Sir George Prevost.* London: T. Egerton, 1823.

Brown, Samuel R. *Views on Lake Erie Containing a Minute and Interesting Account of the Conflict on Lake Erie.* Troy, NY: P. Adancourt, 1814.

———. *Views of the Campaigns of the North-Western Army.* Philadelphia: William G. Murphy, 1815.

Brunson, Alfred. *A Western Pioneer.* Vol. 1. New York: Carlton and Lanahan, 1872.

Byfield, Shadrach. *A Common Soldier's Account.* Ed. John Gellner, in *Recollections of the War of 1812: Three Eyewitnesses' Accounts,* 1-45.

Casson, Dollier de, and Brehant de Gallinée. "Exploration of the Great Lakes, 1660-1670." Ed. James H. Coyne, *Ontario History* 4 (1903): 3-75.

Committee of Foreign Relations. *Report or Manifesto of the Causes and Reasons of War With Great Britain Presented to the House of Representatives.* Washington: A. and G. Way, 1812.

Craig, Gerald M. (ed.). *Early Travellers in the Canadas, 1791-1867.* Toronto: Macmillan, 1955.

Cushing, Daniel. *Orderly Book of Cushing's Company, 2nd U.S. Artillery April, 1813 to February, 1814.* Ed. Harlow Lindley, in *Fort Meigs and the War of 1812.*

———. *Personal Diary of Captain Daniel Cushing.* Ed. Harlow Lindley, in *Fort Meigs and the War of 1812.*

Darnell, Elias. *A Journal Containing an Accurate and Interesting Account of the Hardships, Suffering Battles, Defeat and Captivity of the Kentucky Volunteers and Regulars Commanded by General Winchester in the Years 1812-13.* Philadelphia: Lippincott and Grambo, 1854.

Davenport, John. "Narrative of John Davenport," in Elias Darnell, *Journal,* 91-98.

Douglas, John. *Medical Topography of Upper Canada.* London: Burgess and Hill, 1819.

Dunlop, William. *Recollections of the American War.* Toronto: Historical Publishing Company, 1908.

Edgar, Matilda. *Ten Years in Upper Canada in Peace and War, 1805-1815.* Toronto: William Briggs, 1890.

Fairchild, G.M., Jr., *Journal of an American Prisoner at Ft. Malden and Quebec in the War of 1812,* quoted in Francis Cleary, "Defence of Essex in the War of 1812," *Ontario Historical Society Papers and Records* 10 (1913): 72-78.

Finley, James B. *Life Among the Indians.* Cincinnati: Cranston and Curts, 1860.

[Foster, James.] *The Capitulation or A History of the Expedition Conducted by William Hull.* Ed. Milo Quaiffe, in *War on the Detroit,* 183-317.

Gellner, John (ed.). *Recollections of the War of 1812: Three Eyewitnesses' Accounts.* Toronto: Baxter, 1964.

Hall, Francis. *Travels in Canada and the United States, in 1816 and 1817.* London: Longman, Hurst, Rees, Orme and Brown, 1818.

Hatch, William Stanley. *A Chapter in the History of the War of 1812 in the Northwest.* Cincinnati: Miami Printing, 1872.

Howison, John. *Sketches of Upper Canada.* Edinborough: Oliver and Boyd, 1821.

Hull, William. *Memoirs of the Campaign of the Northwest Army of the United States, A.D. 1812.* Boston: True and Greene, 1824.

———. *Defence of Brigadier General W. Hull.* Boston: Wells and Lilly, 1814.

Hunt, John. *The John Hunt Memoirs.* Ed. Richard J. Wright. Maumee, OH: Maumee Valley Historical Association, 1977.

Indian Johnson. "Narrative of the Battle of the Thames," quoted in O.K. Watson, "Moraviantown," *Ontario Historical Society Papers and Records* 28 (1932): 125-31.

Jameson, Anna. *Winter Studies and Summer Rambles in Canada.* New York: Wiley and Putnam, 1862.

Kinzie, Mrs. John. *Wau Bun, the Early Day in the Northwest.* Philadelphia: J.B. Lippincott, 1873.

Knight, Dr. [John]. *A Narrative of a Late Expedition Against the Indians.* Philadelphia: Francis Bailey, 1783.

Lindley, Harlow (ed.). *Fort Meigs and the War of 1812.* Columbus: Ohio Historical Society, 1975 (1944).

Lucas, Robert. *The Robert Lucas Journal of the War of 1812.* Ed. John C. Parish. Iowa City: State Historical Society of Iowa, 1906.

McAffee, Robert Breckenbridge. *History of the Late War in the Western Country.* Lexington, KY: Worsley and Smith, 1816.

McCormick, William. *A Sketch of the Western District.* Windsor, ON: University of Windsor, 1980 (1824).

MacDonnell, Miles. "Captain Miles MacDonnell's Jaunt to Amherstburg in 1801." Ed. W.S. Wallace. *Canadian Historical Review* 25 (1944): 166-76.

McGregor, John. *British America.* Vol. 2. London: T. Cadell, 1833.

McKay, William. *The Journal of William McKay.* Ed. William Wood, in *Select British Documents.* Vol. 1. Toronto: Champlain Society, 1920.

Mallary, Timothy. "Narrative of Timothy Mallary," in Elias Darnell, *Journal,* 81-90.

Mann, James. *Medical Sketches of 1812, 1813, and 1814.* Dedham, MA: H. Mann, 1816.

Merritt, William. *The William Merritt Journal.* Ed. William Wood, in *Select British Documents.* Vol. 3, Part 2, 545-648.

Metawth [Metoss]. "Speech of Metawth." Women's Canadian Historical Society, Transaction No. 4 (1903): 11-12.

Norton, John. *The Journal of Major John Norton.* Eds. Carl F. Klinck and James J. Talman. Toronto: Champlain Society, 1970.

[Procter, Henry and George Procter.] "Campaigns in the Canadas,"
    Quarterly Review 27 (1822): 405-49.

[————.] *Lucubrations of Humphrey Ravelin.* London: G. and W.B.
    Whittaker, 1823.

[Richardson, John.] "A Canadian Campaign by a British Officer." *New
    Monthly Magazine and Literary Journal* 17 (1826): 541-48; 19 (1827):
    162-70, 248-54, 448-57, 538-51.

Richardson, John. *Eight Years in Canada.* Montreal: H.H. Cunningham,
    1847.

————. *Richardson's War of 1812.* Ed. Alexander Casselman. Toronto:
    Historical Publishing, 1902 (1842).

————. *Westbrook, The Outlaw or The Avenging Wolf, an American Border
    Tale.* Montreal: Grant Woolmer Books, 1973 (1851).

————. *Major General Isaac Brock and the 41st Regiment.* Ed. T.B.
    Higgison. Burks Falls, ON: Old Rectory Press, 1976 (1846).

[Sewell, Stephen.] *Letters of Veritas.* Montreal: W. Gray, 1815.

Shirreff, Patrick. *A Tour Through North America.* New York: Benjamin Blom,
    1971 (1835).

Smith, Michael. *A Geographic View of the Province of Upper Canada.*
    Hartford, CT: n.p., 1813.

Sympson, Capt. James. "Diary of Capt. Sympson." Ed. Anderson C.
    Quisenberry, in *Kentucky in the War of 1812.* Frankfort, KY: Kentucky
    Historical Society, 1915.

Talbot, Edward Allan. *Five Years' Residence in the Canadas.* 2 vols. London:
    Longman, Hurst, Rees, Orme, Brown and Green, 1824.

Thompson, David. *History of the War of the Late War Between Great Britain
    and the United States of America.* Niagara, ON: T. Sewell, 1832.

Van Horne, James. *A Narrative of the Captivity and Sufferings of James Van
    Horne.* Middlebury, VT: 1817.

Walker, Adam. *A Journal of Two Campaigns of the Fourth Regiment of U.S.
    Infantry.* Keene, NH: Sentinel Press, 1816.

Weld, Isaac. *Travels Through the States of North America and the Province of
    Upper Canada during the Years 1795, 1796, and 1797.* London:
    Stockdale, n.p., 1799.

White, Samuel. *History Of The American Troops During The Late War.*
    Baltimore: B. Edes, 1830.

Williams, Samuel. "Two Western Campaigns," in *Ohio Valley Historical
    Series Miscellanies.* Cincinnati: Robert Clarke, 1870.

Zeisberger, David, and Benjamin Mortimer. "From Fairfield to Schonbrun
    —1798." Ed. Leslie R. Gray. *Ontario History* 49 (1957): 63-96.

Newspapers

British / Colonial	American
Amherstburg Echo, Amherstburg, ON	*Buffalo Gazette*, Buffalo, NY
London Times, London, U.K.	*Chillicothe Journal*, Chillicothe, KY
Montreal Gazette, Montreal, QC	*Columbia Centinel*, Boston, MA
Morning Chronicle, London, U.K.	*New York Gazette*, New York, NY
Quebec Gazette, Quebec City, QC	*Niles Weekly Register*, Baltimore, MD
Quebec Mercury, Quebec City, QC	*Trump of Fame*, Toledo, OH
	Vermont Mirror, Middlebury, VT
	The War, New York, NY

SECONDARY SOURCES

Allen, Robert. *His Majesty's Indian Allies*. Toronto: Dundurn Press, 1992.

———. *The Battle of Moraviantown*. Canadian War Museum Pamphlet, no. 11. Toronto: Balmuir Book Publishing, 1994.

Allison, Archibald. *History of Europe, 1789-1815*. Vol. 4. New York: Harper and Brothers, 1844.

Altoff, Gerald. "Deep Water Sailors — Shallow Water Soldiers," *Inland Seas* 46, no. 1 (1990): 26-42.

Antal, S. "Myths and Facts on General Procter," *Ontario History* 79 (1987): 251-62.

———. "The Salina, a Stubborn Patriot," *Journal of Erie Studies* 20 (1991): 12-17.

Au, Dennis. *War on the Raisin*. Monroe, MI: Monroe County Historical Commission, 1981.

Auchinleck, Gilbert. *A History of the War Between Great Britain and the United States*. Toronto: Maclear, 1855.

Banta, R.E. *The Ohio*. London: William Hodge, 1951.

Bauer, K.J. "U.S. Warships on the Great Lakes," *Ontario History* 56 (1964): 58-64.

Beasley, David R. *The Canadian Don Quixote: The Life of Major John Richardson, Canada's First Novelist*. Erin, ON: Porcupine's Quill, 1977.

Beirne, Francis F. *The War of 1812*. New York: E.P. Dutton, 1949.

Berton, Pierre. *The Invasion of Canada, 1812-13*. Toronto: McClelland and Stewart, 1980.

———. *Flames Across the Border, 1813-1814*. Toronto: McClelland and Stewart, 1981.

Bird, Harrison. *War for the West, 1790-1813*. New York: Oxford, 1971.

Blanchard, Rufus. *The Discovery and Conquest of the Northwest*. Chicago: Cushing and Thomas, 1880.

Brackenbridge, H.M. *History of the Late War.* Philadelphia: James Kay, Jun
    and Brother, 1844.
Bradley, A.G. *The United Empire Loyalists.* London: Thornton Butterworth,
    1932.
Brant, Irving. *James Madison.* New York: Bobbs-Merrill, 1961.
Brereton, J.M. *A History of the Royal Regiment of Wales (24th/41st Foot) and
    its Predecessors, 1689-1989.* Cardiff, U.K.: The Regiment, 1989.
Brown, Roger H. *The Republic in Peril.* New York: Norton, 1964.
Buckie, Robert. "His Majesty's Flag Has Not Been Tarnished: The Role of
    Robert Heriot Barclay," *Journal of Erie Studies* 17, no. 2 (1988): 85-102.
Burt, A. Blanche. "Captain Robert Heriot Barclay, R.N.," *Ontario History*
    14 (1916): 169-78.
Burt, A.L. *The United States, Great Britain and British North America, 1783-
    1815.* New Haven, CT: Yale University Press, 1940.
Burton, Clarence M. *The City of Detroit, 1701-1922.* 2 vols. Detroit: S.J.
    Clarke, 1922.
Butterfield, Consul Willshire. *An Historical Account of the Expedition Against
    Sandusky Under Col. William Crawford in 1782.* Columbus, OH:
    Long's College Book, 1950 (1890).
———. *History of the Girtys.* Cincinnati: Robert Clarke, 1890.
Calloway, Colin. *Crown and Calumet.* Norman: University of Oklahoma
    Press, 1987.
Cambell, James V. *Outlines of the Political History of Michigan.* Detroit:
    Schober, 1870.
Campbell, Maria. *Revolutionary Services and Civil Life of General William
    Hull.* New York: D. Appleton, 1848.
Catlin, George B. *The Story of Detroit.* Detroit: Detroit News, 1923.
Christie, Robert. *A History of the Province of Lower Canada.* Vol 2. Quebec:
    T. Carey, 1848.
Claridge, John R. (ed.). *175th Anniversary of the Battle of Lake Erie, Journal
    of Erie Studies* 17, no. 2 (1988).
Clarke, James Freeman. *History of the Campaign of 1812 and Surrender of the
    Post of Detroit.* New York: D. Appleton, 1848.
Clarke, Peter Dooyentate. *Origin and Traditional History of the Wyandotts.*
    Toronto: Hunter, Rose, 1870.
Cleary, Francis. "Fort Malden or Amherstburg," *Ontario History* 9 (1910):
    5-19.
———. "Defence of Essex in the War of 1812," *Ontario History* 10 (1913):
    72-78.
———. "Notes on the Early History of the County of Essex," *Essex
    Historical Society Papers and Records* 1 (1913): 5-15.
Clift, G. Glenn. *Remember the Raisin!* Frankfort, KY: Kentucky Historical
    Society, 1961.

Coffin, William F. *1812: The War and its Moral: A Canadian Chronicle.* Montreal: J. Lovell, 1864.

Coles, Harry L. *The War of 1812.* Chicago: University of Chicago Press, 1965.

Cooley, Thomas McIntyre. *American Commonwealths: Michigan.* Boston: Houghton and Mifflin, 1897.

Cooper, James Fenimore. *Naval History of the United States to 1856.* Vol. 2. New York: G.P. Putnam, 1856.

Coutts, Katherine B. "Thamesville and the Battle of the Thames," *Ontario Historical Society Papers and Records* 9 (1908): 20-25.

Cowan, Hugh. *Canadian Achievement in the Province of Ontario: The Detroit River District.* Toronto: Algonquin Historical Society of Canada, 1929.

Creighton, Donald. *Empire of the St. Lawrence.* Toronto: Macmillan, 1956.

Cruikshank, Ernest A. "General Hull's Invasion of Canada in 1812," *Transactions of the Royal Society of Canada.* Series 3, Sect. 2, Vol. 1 (1907): 211-90.

———. "Harrison and Procter: The River Raisin," *Transactions of the Royal Society of Canada.* Series 3, Sect. 2, Vol. 4 (1910): 119-67.

Cuthbertson, George A. *Freshwater.* Toronto: Macmillan, 1931.

Dictionary of American Biography. 22 vols. New York: Scribner, 1958-64.

Dictionary of Canadian Biography. Vols. 4-8. Toronto: University of Toronto Press, 1976-88.

Dillon, Richard. *We Have Met the Enemy.* Toronto: McGraw-Hill, 1978.

Dobbins, William W. *History of the Battle of Lake Erie.* Erie, PA: Ashby Printing Co., 1913.

Douglas, W.A.B. *Gunfire on the Lakes.* Ottawa: National Museum of Man, 1977.

———. "The Anatomy of Naval Incompetence: The Provincial Marine in the Defence of Upper Canada before 1813," *Ontario History* 71 (1979): 3-25.

Drake, Benjamin. *Life of Tecumseh and of His Brother, the Prophet.* Cincinnati: H. and S. Applegate, 1852 (1841).

Drake, Frederick C. "A Loss of Mastery: The British Squadron on Lake Erie, May-September 1813," *Journal of Erie Studies* 17, no. 2 (1988): 47-75.

Drake, Samuel G. *The Book of the Indians of North America.* Boston: Josiah Drake, 1833.

Duparcq, Ed. de la Barre. *Elements of Military Art and History.* Trans. George W. Callum. New York: D. Van Nostrand, 1863.

Dutton, Charles J. *Oliver Hazard Perry.* New York: Longmans and Green, 1935.

Eckert, Allan W. *A Sorrow in Our Heart: The Life of Tecumseh.* Toronto: Bantam Books, 1992.

Edmunds, R. David. *The Potawatomis, Keepers of the Fire.* Norman: University of Oklahoma, 1978.

Edmunds, R. David. *Tecumseh and the Quest for Indian Leadership.* Glenview, IL: Scott, Foresman, 1984.

———. *The Shawnee Prophet.* Lincoln: University of Nebraska, 1983.

———. "The Thin Red Line, Tecumseh, the Prophet and Shawnee Resistance," *Timeline* 4, no. 6 (1988): 2-19.

Edwards, Dennis Carter. "The War along the Detroit Frontier: A Canadian Perspective," *Michigan Historical Review* 13 (1987): 25-50.

Emerson, George D. *The Perry's Victory Centenary.* Albany, NY: J.B. Lyons, 1916.

Ermatinger, C.O. *The Talbot Regime.* St. Thomas, ON: Municipal World, 1904.

———. "The Retreat of General Procter and Tecumseh," *Ontario Historical Society Papers and Records* 17 (1919): 11-21.

Farmer, Silas. *History of Detroit and Wayne County and Early Michigan.* Detroit: Gale Research, 1969 (1890).

Firth, Edith G. *The Town of York, 1793-1815.* Toronto: Champlain Society, 1962.

Fredriksen, John C. *Officers of the War of 1812 with Portraits and Anecdotes.* Lewiston, NY: Edwin Mellen, 1989.

Gentilcore, R. Louis (ed.). *Historical Atlas of Canada.* Vol 2. Toronto: University of Toronto Press, 1993.

Gilpin, Alec R. *The War of 1812 in the Old Northwest.* East Lansing: Michigan State University Press, 1958.

Goodrich, Calvin. *The First Michigan Frontier.* Ann Arbor: University of Michigan, 1940.

Goodrich, Charles A. *History of the United States of America.* Boston: Carter and Hendee, 1835.

Graham, Gerald S. "Views of General Murray on the Defence of Upper Canada, 1815," *Canadian Historical Review* 34, no. 2 (June, 1953): 158-65.

Graves, Donald E. *The Battle of Lundy's Lane.* Baltimore: Nautical and Aviation Publishing, 1993.

Gray, Elma E. *Wilderness Christians: The Moravian Mission to the Delaware Indians.* Toronto: Macmillan, 1956.

Guillet, Edwin C. *Early Life in Upper Canada.* Toronto: Ontario Publishing, 1933.

Gurd, Norman S. *The Story of Tecumseh.* Toronto: William Briggs, 1912.

Hagan, William T. *The Sac and Fox Indians.* Norman: University of Oklahoma Press, 1958.

Hamil, Fred C. *The Valley of the Lower Thames, 1640-1850.* Toronto: University of Toronto Press, 1951.

———. *Michigan in the War of 1812.* Lansing: Michigan Historical Commission, 1969.

Hammack, James Wallace, Jr. *Kentucky and the Second American Revolution.* Lexington: University of Kentucky Press, 1976.

Hannay, James. *The History of the War of 1812.* Toronto: Morang, 1905.

Headley, J.T. *The Second War With England.* 2 vols. New York: Scribner, 1853.

Hickey, Donald, R. *The War of 1812.* Chicago: University of Illinois Press, 1990.

Hitsman, J. MacKay. "Sir George Prevost's Conduct of the Canadian War of 1812," *Canadian Historical Association Report* (1962): 34-43.

———. *The Incredible War of 1812.* Toronto: University of Toronto Press, 1965.

Horsman, Reginald. *The Causes of the War of 1812.* New York: Barnes, 1962.

———. *Matthew Elliott, British Indian Agent.* Detroit: Wayne State University Press, 1964.

———. *The War of 1812.* London: Eyre and Spottiswoode, 1969.

Illustrated Historical Atlas of the Counties of Essex and Kent. Toronto: H. Belden, 1880.

Ingersoll, Charles, J. *Historical Sketch of the Second War between the United States of America and Great Britain.* Philadelphia: Lea and Blanchard, 1849.

Irving, L. Homfray. *Officers of the British Forces in Canada during the War of 1812-15.* Welland, ON: Canadian Military Institute, 1908.

James, William. *A Full and Correct Account of the Military Occurrences of the Late War Between Great Britain and the United States.* 2 vols. London: Author, 1818 (1816).

———. *Naval Occurrences of the Late War.* London: T. Egerton, 1817.

Jarvis, Russel. *A Biographical Notice of Commodore Jesse D. Elliott.* Philadelphia: Author,1835.

Josephy, Alvin. *The Patriot Chiefs.* New York: Viking Press, 1961.

Kenton, Edna. *Simon Kenton.* New York: Doubleday and Doran, 1930.

Kingsford, William. *The History of Canada.* Vols. 7-9. Toronto: Rowsell and Hutchison, 1894.

Klinck, Carl F. "Some Anonymous Literature of the War of 1812," *Ontario History* 49, no. 2 (1957): 49-62.

———. *Tecumseh, Fact and Fiction in Early Records.* Englewood Cliffs, NJ: Prentice-Hall, 1961.

Knapp, Horace S. *History of the Maumee Valley.* Toledo: n.p., 1877 (1872).

Landon, Fred. *Western Ontario and the American Frontier.* New York: Russel and Russel, 1970 (1941).

Lauriston, Victor. "Tecumseh," *Kent Historical Society Papers and Addresses* 3 (1917): 24-37.

———. "The Case for General Procter," *Kent Historical Society Papers and Addresses* 7 (1951): 7-17.

———. *Romantic Kent.* Chatham, ON: Shepherd Printing, 1952.

Lomax, David A.N. *A History of the Services of the 41st (the Welch) Regiment*. Devonport, U.K.: Hiorns and Miller, 1899.

Lossing, Benson J. *The Pictorial Field Book of the War of 1812*. New York: Harper and Brothers, 1868.

Lucas, Charles P. *The Canadian War of 1812*. Oxford: The Clarendon Press, 1906.

Lyman, Olin L. *Commodore Oliver Hazard Perry and the War on the Lakes*. New York: New Amsterdam Books, 1905.

M'Carty, William. *History of the American War of 1812*. Philadelphia: Author, 1816.

MacDonald, George. "The New Settlement On Lake Erie," *Essex Historical Society Bulletin* (1918).

MacDonnell, J.A. "Major-General Isaac Brock, K.B.," *Ontario History* 10 (1913): 5-32.

McHentry, Robert (ed.). *Webster's American Military Biographies*. New York: Dover, 1978.

McLeod, Malcolm. "Fortress Ontario or Forlorn Hope? Simcoe and the Defence of Upper Canada," *Canadian Historical Review* 53, no. 2 (1972): 149-78.

Macpherson, K.R. "Naval Service Vessels on the Great Lakes, 1775-1875," *Ontario History* 55 (1963): 173-79.

Mahan, Alfred T. *Sea Power in its Relation to the War of 1812*. Vol. 2. Boston: Little, Brown, 1905 (1903).

Mahan, Bruce E. *Old Fort Crawford and the Frontier*. Iowa City: State Historical Society of Iowa, 1926.

Mahon, John K. "British Command Decisions of the War of 1812," *Canadian Historical Review* 46, no. 3 (1965): 219-37.

————. *The War of 1812*. Gainesville: University of Florida Press, 1972 .

Malcomson, Robert. "The Barclay Correspondence: More from the Man Who Lost the Battle of Lake Erie," *Journal of Erie Studies* 20 (1991): 18-35.

————. "The Crews of the British Squadrons at Put-in-Bay: A Composite Muster Role and its Insights," *Inland Seas* Vol. 51 (1995), no. 2: 16-34 and no. 3: 43-56.

Malcomson, Thomas, and Robert Malcomson. *HMS Detroit, The Battle for Lake Erie*. St. Catharines, ON: Vanwell Press, 1990.

Mason, Philip P. (ed.). *After Tippecanoe: Some Aspects of the War of 1812*. Toronto: Ryerson, 1963.

Medert, Patricia Fife. *Raw Recruits and Bullish Prisoners*. Jackson, OH: Jackson Publishing, 1992.

Morgan, Henry J. *Sketches of Celebrated Canadians*. Quebec City: Hunter and Rose, 1862.

Nelson, Larry L. *Men of Partiotism Courage & Enterprise! Fort Meigs in the War of 1812*. Canton, OH: Daring Books, 1985.

O'Conner, Thomas. *History of the War*. New York: John Low, 1815.

Paré, George. *The Catholic Church in Detroit, 1701-1888*. Detroit: Gabriel Richard Press, 1951.

Parish, John C. *Robert Lucas*. Iowa City: State Historical Society of Iowa, 1907.

Perkins, Bradford. *The Causes of the War of 1812*. New York: Holt, Rhinehart and Winston, 1962.

Perkins, Samuel. *A History of the Political and Military Events of the Late War*. New Haven: S. Converse, 1825.

Pratt, Julius. *Expansionists of 1812*. New York: Macmillan, 1925.

Prentice, George D. *Henry Clay*. Hartford, CT: Samuel Hammer, Jr., 1831.

Quaife, Milo Milton (ed.). *War on the Detroit*. Chicago: Lakeside Press, 1940.

Quisenberry, Anderson C. *Kentucky in the War of 1812*. Frankfort: Kentucky Historical Association, 1915.

Read, D.B. *The Life and Times of Major General Isaac Brock, K.B.* Toronto: William Briggs, 1894.

Roosevelt, Theodore. *The Naval War of 1812*. New York: G.P. Putnam's Sons, 1882.

Rosenberg, Max. *The Building of Perry's Fleet, 1812-13*. Harrisburg: Pennsylvania Historical and Museum Commission, 1987.

Russell, Nelson Vance. *The British Regime in Michigan and the Old Northwest, 1760-1796*. Northfield, MN: Carleton College, 1939.

Ryerson, Egerton. *The Loyalists of America and Their Times*. Vol. 2. Montreal: William Briggs, 1880.

Saga of the Great Lakes. Toronto: Coles Publishing, 1980.

Saunders, Robert. *Newfoundland's Role in the Historic Battle of Lake Erie*. Poole, U.K.: J. Looker, 1954.

Shaler, N.S. *American Commonwealths: Kentucky*. Boston: Houghton and Mifflin, 1885.

Slocum, Charles Elihu. *The Ohio Country, 1783-1815*. New York: Knickerbocker, 1910.

Snider, C.H.J. *The Story of the Nancy and Other Eighteen-Twelvers*. Toronto: McClelland and Stewart, 1926.

Stacey, Charles P. "Upper Canada at War, 1814: Captain Armstrong Reports," *Ontario History* 48 (1956): 37-42.

———. "The War of 1812 in Canadian History," *Ontario History* 50 (1958): 153-59.

Stanley, George. "The Indians in the War of 1812," *Canadian Historical Review* 31, no. 2 (1950): 145-65.

———. *The War of 1812, Land Operations*. Toronto: Macmillan, 1983.

Sturtevant, William C. (ed.). *Handbook of North American Indians*. Vol. 15. Washington, DC: Smithsonian Institution, 1978.

Sugden, John. *Tecumseh's Last Stand.* Norman: University of Oklahoma Press, 1985.

Tanner, Helen H. (ed.). *Atlas of Great Lakes Indian History.* Norman: University of Oklahoma Press, 1987.

Thomson, John Lewis. *Historical Sketches of the Late War.* Philadelphia: John Bioren, 1816.

Todd, Charles S., and Benjamin Drake. *Sketches of the Civil and Military Services of William Henry Harrison.* Cincinnati: U.P. James, 1840.

Trumbull, Henry. *Indian Wars.* Boston: George Clark, 1831.

Tucker, Glenn. *Poltroons and Patriots.* 2 vols. New York: Bobbs-Merrill, 1954.

————. *Tecumseh, Vision of Glory.* New York: Bobbs-Merrill, 1956.

Updyke, Frank A. *The Diplomacy of the War of 1812.* Gloucester, MA: Peter Smith, 1965 (1915).

Walsh, G. Mark. "We Have Heard the Great Guns: British Indian Policy and the Battle of Lake Erie," *Journal of Erie Studies* 17, no. 2 (1988): 27-38.

Watson, O.K. "Moraviantown," *Ontario Historical Society Papers and Records* 28 (1932): 125-31.

Welsh, William J., and David C. Skaggs. *War on the Great Lakes: Essays Commemorating the 175th Anniversary of the Battle of Lake Erie.* Kent, OH: Kent State University Press, 1991.

Wendler, Marylin Van Voorhis. *The Foot of the Rapids.* Canton, OH: Daring Books, 1988.

White, Michael Gladstone. *War Drums Along the River.* Windsor, ON: Red Oak Press, 1991.

Whitehorne, A.C. *History of the Welch (41st) Regiment.* Cardiff: Western Mail and Echo, 1932.

Woodford, Frank B. *Mr. Jefferson's Disciple, A Life of Justice Woodward.* East Lansing: Michigan State College Press, 1953.

Young, Col. Bennett H. *The Battle of the Thames in which Kentuckians Defeated the British, French and Indians, October 5 1813.* Louisville, KY: Filson Book Club, 1903.

Young, William T. *Sketch of the Life and Public Services of General Lewis Cass.* Detroit: Markham and Elwood, 1852.

Zaslow, Morris (ed.). *The Defended Border: Upper Canada and the War of 1812.* Toronto: Macmillan, 1964.

ADDITIONS TO THE BIBLIOGRAPHY 2011

Bridges, Dianne. "In Defense of a Homeland: Indians at War Along the Detroit Frontier." Parks Canada Manuscript Report, 1986.

Couture, Paul Morgan. "War and Society on the Detroit Frontier, 1791 to 1815." Parks Canada Manuscript Report, 1986.

Gray, William. *Soldiers of the King: The Upper Canadian Militia, 1812–1815.* Erin, ON: Boston Mills Press, 1995.

Hitsman, J. MacKay. *The Incredible War of 1812.* Ed. Donald E. Graves. Toronto: Robin Brass Studio, 2002.

Sugden, John. *Tecumseh, A Life.* New York: Harry Holt and Co., 1997.

Willig, Timothy D. *Restoring the Chain of Friendship: British Policy and the Indians of the Great Lakes, 1783–1815.* Lincoln: University of Nebraska Press, 2008.

Winchester, James. *Historical Details Having Relation to the Campaign of the Northwest Army Under Generals Harrison and Winchester During the Winter of 1812–13.* Lexington, Ky.: Worsley and Smith, 1818.

Zuelke, Mark. *For Honour's Sake: The War of 1812 and the Brokering of an Uneasy Peace.* Toronto: Random House, 2007.

INDEX